Fire and Motor Insurance

Butterworths Insurance Library

First edition   1968
Second edition   1973
Third edition   1978
Fourth edition   1984

Fire and Motor Insurance

Fourth edition

E R Hardy Ivamy LLB, PhD, LLD
of the Middle Temple, Barrister,
Professor of Law in the University of London

London
Butterworths
1984

Butterworths Insurance Library

England	Butterworth & Co (Publishers) Ltd, 88 Kingsway, LONDON WC2B 6AB
Australia	Butterworth Pty Ltd, SYDNEY, MELBOURNE, BRISBANE, ADELAIDE and PERTH
Canada	Butterworth & Co (Canada) Ltd, TORONTO Butterworth & Co (Western Canada) Ltd, VANCOUVER
New Zealand	Butterworths of New Zealand Ltd, WELLINGTON
Singapore	Butterworth & Co (Asia) Pte Ltd, SINGAPORE
South Africa	Butterworth Publishers (Pty) Ltd, DURBAN
USA	Mason Publishing Co, ST PAUL, Minnesota Butterworth Legal Publishers, SEATTLE, Washington; BOSTON, Massachusetts; and AUSTIN, Texas D & S Publishers, CLEARWATER, Florida

Ivamy, E. R. Hardy
   Fire and motor insurance.—4th ed.
   1. Insurance, Fire—Great Britain
   2. Insurance, Automobile—Great Britain
   I. Title
   344.206.'86'1   KD1885

   ISBN 0 406 25253 X

Typeset by Colset Pte Ltd, Singapore

Printed by Billing & Sons Limited, Worcester

Preface

This book is the second volume in the Butterworths Insurance Library, the other volumes being *General Principles of Insurance Law*, *Marine Insurance* and *Personal Accident, Life and Other Insurances*. Although to a certain extent it is complete in itself, it should be read in conjunction with *General Principles of Insurance Law*, especially with regard to such matters as, for example, the making of the contract, the premium and the construction of the policy for these topics are common to all branches of the law of insurance.

The text and the footnotes have been completely reset to increase legibility.

In Part I, which concerns Fire Insurance, *Watkins & Davis Ltd v Legal and General Assurance Co Ltd* [1981] 1 Lloyd's Rep 674 and *S and M Carpets (London) Ltd v Cornhill Insurance Co Ltd* [1982] 1 Lloyd's Rep 674, CA, have been added to the earlier cases relating to the wilful act of the insured. *Woolcott v Excess Insurance Co Ltd (No 2)* [1979] 2 Lloyd's Rep 210 is an example of a material fact being deemed to be known by the insurers. *Spinney's (1948) Ltd v Royal Insurance Co Ltd* [1980] 1 Lloyd's Rep 406 is the latest authority on the meaning of 'civil war', 'civil commotion', 'usurped power', 'insurrection', 'hostilities' and the 'acts of terrorist organisations'. *Exchange Theatre Ltd v Iron Trader Mutual Insurance Co Ltd* [1983] 1 Lloyd's Rep 674 concerns a condition as to the use of a building. *Reynolds v Phoenix Assurance Co Ltd* [1978] 2 Lloyd's Rep 440, *Pleasurama Ltd v Sun Alliance and London Insurance Ltd* [1979] 1 Lloyd's Rep 389 and *Leppard v Excess Insurance Co Ltd* [1979] 2 All ER 668, CA, indicate the basis of calculation of loss in the case of property destroyed or damaged.

In Part II ('Motor Insurance'), the meaning of the term 'social, domestic and pleasure purposes' is illustrated by *Seddon v Binions (Zurich Insurance Co Ltd, Third Party)* [1978] 1 Lloyd's Rep 381, CA. *Cox v Orion Insurance Co Ltd* [1982] 1 RTR 1, CA, shows the importance of delivering particulars of loss within the required time. New cases on compulsory motor insurance include *Leathley v Tatton* [1980] RTR 21, DC, *Bennett v Richardson* [1980] RTR 358, DC, and *B (a Minor) v Knight* [1981] RTR 136, DC. The extent of the liability of the Motor Insurers' Bureau is explained in *Porter v Motor Insurers' Bureau* [1978] 2 Lloyd's Rep 463, *Elizabeth v Motor Insurers' Bureau* [1981] RTR 405 and *Cooper v Motor Insurers' Bureau* [1983] 1 All ER 353.

In the Appendices the statutes and the statutory instruments are all printed in their amended form.

The Agreements made between the Secretary of State for the Environment and the Motor Insurers' Bureau are reproduced by kind permission.

Specimen proposal forms and forms of policy are reprinted by the courtesy of the Sun Alliance & London Insurance Group, the Guardian Royal Exchange Assurance Group and Lloyd's Underwriters' Fire and Non-Marine Association.

I should like to thank the staff of Butterworths for undertaking the arduous job of preparing the Index and the Tables of Cases and Statutes and for seeing the book through the press.

University College London   E R HARDY IVAMY
January 1984

Contents

Table of Statutes

References in this Table to *"Statutes"* are to Halsbury's Statutes of England (Third Edition), showing the volume and page at which the annotated text of the Act will be found. Page references printed in bold type indicate where the Act is set out in part or in full.

Table of Cases

K

L

PAGE

M

PAGE

U

Y

Z

PART I

Fire insurance

CHAPTER 1

Introduction

This Part of this book deals exclusively with Fire Insurance. Although to a certain extent it is complete in itself, it should be read in conjunction with the first volume of this series,[1] especially with regard to such matters as eg the making of the contract, the premium, and the construction of the policy, for these topics are common to all branches of the law of insurance.

It is the purpose of this Part of this book to discuss in more detail those aspects which particularly concern fire insurance.

It is therefore necessary to consider what constitutes a contract of fire insurance,[2] and what its characteristics are.[3] As in other types of insurance it is essential for the insured to have an insurable interest in the subjectmatter.[4]

Some persons are under a duty to insure,[5] whilst others are entitled to insure.[6] But certain persons have no right to insure at all.[7]

The insured is required to answer certain questions in the proposal form,[8] and it is always necessary for him to describe the subject-matter to be insured.[9] He is under a duty to disclose to the insurers all material facts and not to make any misrepresentations.[10]

The form and contents of the policy will vary according as to whether the policy is issued by an insurance company or is a Lloyd's policy.[11] In either type of policy the perils insured against are expressly set out.[12] In some cases, however, the insured may desire to insure against a loss consequent on the destruction of or damage to the subject-matter since this type of loss is not covered by the ordinary type of policy.[13] It is the practice of insurers to insert 'exceptions' in the policy.[14] The insured is under a duty to observe the 'conditions' imposed by the policy.[15]

If a fire takes place, certain rights and duties arise in connection with the salving of the property.[16]

The insurers are only liable for a loss proximately caused by a peril insured against.[17] Any claim made by the insured must be in accordance with the procedure laid down by the terms of the policy.[18] The burden of proving a loss lies on the insured, whilst that of proving that the loss falls within an exception lies on the insurers.[19] Loss adjusters are employed to work out the damage

---

[1] Ivamy, *General Principles of Insurance Law* (4th edn, 1979, Supplement 1982).

[2] See Chapter 2, post.
[3] See Chapter 3, post.
[4] See Chapter 4, post.
[5] See Chapter 5, post.
[6] See Chapter 6, post.
[7] See Chapter 7, post.

[8] See Chapter 8, post.
[9] See Chapter 9, post.
[10] See Chapter 10, post.
[11] See Chapter 11, post.
[12] See Chapter 12, post.
[13] See Chapter 13, post.

[14] See Chapter 14, post.
[15] See Chapter 15, post.
[16] See Chapter 16, post.
[17] See Chapter 17, post.
[18] See Chapter 18, post.

[19] Ivamy, *General Principles of Insurance Law* (4th edn, 1979), pp 443–445. See further, Chapter 19, post.

suffered by the insured.[20] The amount to be paid by the insurers will then have to be calculated.[1]

Insurers who operate in London are under a duty to contribute to the expenses of the London Fire Brigade.[2]

---

[20] See Chapter 20, post.   [1] See Chapter 21, post.   [2] See Chapter 22, post.

CHAPTER 2

What constitutes a contract of fire insurance

A contract is not necessarily a contract of fire insurance because it imposes on one of the contracting parties the liability to make good at his own expense any loss or damage to the property specified in the contract sustained by the other party, which may be occasioned by fire.

This liability may, by express terms, be undertaken by one of the contracting parties in every species of contract in which there is a possibility of such loss or damage.

Thus, a tenant may contract to repair the premises demised to him, if they are damaged by fire, or a bailee to make good the loss by fire of the goods bailed to him. In neither case is the nature of the contract changed by the existence of the liability. It does not become a contract of fire insurance, but remains a contract of tenancy or bailment, as the case may be, with the advantage of containing an additional term for the protection of the landlord or bailor.[1]

Such a liability need not in every case be imposed by express terms. There are some contracts, eg the contract of carriage, in which, from the mere relation of the parties, a term imposing it is by law to be implied. In connection with such contracts, the party to whom the liability attaches is frequently called an insurer. This is, however, by way of defining the extent of his liability,[2] and distinguishing it from the narrower liability imposed in other contracts of an analogous nature. Such contracts cannot, therefore, be regarded as contracts of fire insurance any more than those in which the liability is added by express language.

To constitute a contract of insurance it is necessary that the insurers should, apart from the liability undertaken under the contract in question, have no interest or concern in the safety or destruction of the subject-matter of insurance.

They must derive no benefit from its safety except by virtue of their contract, and such benefit must be limited to the value of the consideration in exchange for which they have undertaken the liability.[3] Nor must they, if the subject-matter is destroyed, be under any liability wider or more extensive than that which the contract imposes.

---

[1] *North British and Mercantile Insurance Co v London Liverpool and Globe Insurance Co* (1877) 5 Ch D 569 at 584, C A, per Mellish L J: 'In my opinion it makes no difference that here the bailment, instead of being in the mere ordinary terms that the bailee should be liable to take due care in the case of loss by fire, is upon the terms that he should be absolutely liable in the case of loss by fire. That is not a contract of insurance so as to make the bailee himself an insurer'.

[2] *Joseph Travers & Sons Ltd v Cooper* [1915] 1 K B 73 at 101, C A (lighterman) per Phillimore L J.

[3] The benefit may, after loss, become greater by reason of the doctrine of subrogation. As to subrogation, see Ivamy, *General Principles of Insurance Law* (4th edn, 1979), pp 496–513.

The events giving rise to their liability must be those specified in the contract and no others; and the extent of the liability must be measured by the amount which, by their contract, they have agreed to pay, and not necessarily by the extent of the loss or damage sustained by the other contracting party.

Their relation to the subject-matter must depend solely on their contract, and must be created and regulated thereby. If they incur any liability beyond that imposed by the contract, or derive any benefit other than the agreed consideration, such liability or benefit is attributable to some right of property in the subject-matter, or to some other contract relating thereto which is more extensive in its operation, and the contract in question has in reality, therefore, no independent existence.[4]

Even though the contract under which the insurers incur liability in case of fire may be a contract of insurance, it is not solely for that reason a contract of fire insurance. Thus, a contract of marine insurance usually includes 'fire' amongst the perils insured against.[5] But it remains, in spite of the inclusion of fire, a contract of marine insurance.[6] A contract of insurance is not a contract of fire insurance unless its object is to insure against loss or damage occasioned by fire, and the peril insured against must be 'fire' and no other.[7]

---

[4] Cf *Admiralty Comrs v Ropner & Co Ltd* (1917) 117 L T 58 at 60 (charter-party) per Lord Reading C J.

[5] See the form of policy in the Marine Insurance Act 1906, Sch I, and Ivamy, *Marine Insurance* (3rd edn, 1979), pp 160–161. 'Fire' is not a 'peril of the sea': *Thames and Mersey Marine Insurance Co Ltd v Hamilton Fraser & Co* (1887) 12 App Cas 484 at 493 (marine insurance) per Lord Bramwell.

[6] But it is otherwise when the policy, though in the marine form, covers the risk of fire only: *Re United London and Scottish Insurance Co, Newport Navigation Co's Claim* [1915] 2 Ch 12, C A; *Imperial Marine Insurance Co v Fire Insurance Corpn Ltd* (1879) 4 C P D 166 at 171, per Lopes L J (reinsurance of fire risk on marine policy); or where any other risk insured against is negligible: *Re Argonaut Marine Insurance Co Ltd* [1932] 2 Ch 34.

[7] Sometimes combined policies are issued which include an insurance against other perils as well as fire, eg fire and public liability policies. Such policies are, however, to be considered, so far as insurance against fire is concerned, fire policies.

CHAPTER 3

The characteristics of the contract of fire insurance

The contract of fire insurance bears a general resemblance to all other contracts of insurance; it is, in fact, an offshoot from the contract of marine insurance.[1] The general principles of insurance law apply, with few exceptions, equally to all kinds of insurance,[2] and such differences as exist are to be attributed, as a rule, not to a difference in the principles to be applied, but rather to a difference in their mode of application.

The principal characteristics of a contract of fire insurance are that:

1 The utmost good faith must be shown in it by both parties.
2 It is a contract of indemnity.
3 It must be distinguished from a wager.
4 It must be distinguished from a guarantee.
5 The cause of the fire is generally immaterial.
6 It is a personal contract.
7 It is an entire contract.

1 The Duty of Good Faith

The contract of fire insurance, like other contracts of insurance, differs from an ordinary contract in that it requires, throughout its existence,[3] the utmost good faith (*uberrima fides*) to be observed on the part of both the insured and the insurers.

In addition to the ordinary obligation which exists in every contract that all representations made by the parties during the negotiations leading up to the contract shall be honestly made, the person seeking a contract of fire insurance must communicate to the insurers all matters within his knowledge which are, in fact, material to the question of the insurance, and not merely all those which he believes to be material.

A failure to comply with this requirement renders the contract voidable; for the insured, as being the person interested in the subject matter, has some acquaintance with its nature and surroundings, and must, therefore, be taken,

---

[1] Cf *Sadlers' Co v Badcock* (1743) 2 Atk 554.
[2] *Castellain v Preston* (1883) 11 QBD 380 at 386, CA per Brett LJ; *Thomson v Weems* (1884) 9 App Cas 671 (life insurance); *Leon v Casey* [1932] 2 KB 576 at 579, CA per Scrutton LJ (marine insurance).
[3] *Boulton v Houlder Bros & Co* [1904] 1 KB 784 at 791, CA (marine insurance) per Mathew LJ: 'It is an essential condition of a policy of assurance that the underwriters shall be treated with good faith, not merely in reference to the inception of the risk, but in the steps taken to carry out the contract'.

as against the insurers, to know what the matters are which ought to be communicated to them.

On the other hand, the insurers have, as a rule, no particular knowledge themselves relating to the subject-matter, and they place reliance on what they are told. Though it is open to them to make enquiries, they may, through ignorance of the circumstances, omit to make the enquiry which would have elicited the information which it is material for them to have. To guard themselves against the consequences of such an omission, they have therefore the right to a full disclosure of all material facts.

Similarly, it is the duty of the insurers to deal fairly with the insured.[4] They must place at his disposal any information which they may possess affecting the risk, and must not allow him, in ignorance of such information, to enter into a contract more unfavourable to himself than he would have otherwise made.

Statements in a prospectus or similar advertisement as to the nature or effect of an insurance must also be accurate, and the insured is entitled to call for a policy which conforms with the representations contained in such documents.[5]

Further, the contract which they make with him must be clearly expressed.[6] If the terms are ambiguous, they cannot rely upon a construction which would, in effect, make the contract misleading or unfair.[7]

2 A Contract of Indemnity

The contract of fire insurance resembles the contract of marine insurance, and differs from that of life insurance in that it is purely a contract of indemnity against losses actually sustained.[8]

Even where, by the terms of the contract, as is usually the case, the insurers expressly undertake, in the event of loss or damage by fire to the property insured, to pay or make good the loss or damage up to a specified sum, the contract is nevertheless one of indemnity,[9] and of indemnity only.[10]

---

4 *Carter v Boehm* (1766) 3 Burr 1905 at 1909 (marine insurance) per Lord Mansfield CJ; *Scottish Equitable Life Assurance Society v Buist* 1877 4 R (Ct of Sess) 1076 (life insurance).

5 *Sun Life Assurance Co of Canada v Jervis* [1943] 2 All E R 425, C A (life insurance), distinguishing *British Equitable Assurance Co Ltd v Baily* [1906] A C 35 (life insurance). See generally Ivamy, *General Principles of Insurance Law* (4th edn, 1979), p 174.

6 *Provincial Insurance Co Ltd v Morgan and Foxon* [1933] A C 240 at 255 (accident insurance) per Lord Wright, quoting Lord St Leonards in *Anderson v Fitzgerald* (1853) 4 H L Cas 484 at 510. See Ivamy, *General Principles of Insurance Law*, (4th edn, 1979), pp 386–392.

7 *Condogianis v Guardian Assurance Co Ltd* [1921] 2 A C 125, P C, approving *Joel v Law and Crown Insurance Co* [1908] 2 K B 863, C A (life insurance) and *Re Etherington and Lancashire and Yorkshire Accident Insurance Co* [1909] 1 K B 591, C A (personal accident insurance); *Re Bradley and Essex and Suffolk Accident Indemnity Society* [1912] 1 K B 415, C A (employer's liability insurance), considered in *T Dunn and W G Tarrant v Campbell* (1920) 4 Ll L Rep 36, C A (aviation insurance); cf *D and J Koskas v Standard Marine Insurance Co Ltd* (1927) 137 L T 165 (marine insurance), where reasonable notice of a condition was not given. See generally Ivamy, *General Principles of Insurance Law* (4th edn, 1979), pp 386–392.

8 *Dalby v India and London Life Assurance Co* (1854) 15 C B 365 at 387 (life insurance) per Parke B; *North British and Mercantile Insurance Co v London, Liverpool and Globe Insurance Co* (1877) 5 Ch D 569, C A, followed in *Darrell v Tibbitts* (1880) 5 Q B D 560, C A.; *Gould v Curtis* [1913] 3 K B 84 at 95,C A (life insurance) per Buckley L J. As to marine insurance being a contract of indemnity, see Ivamy, *Marine Insurance* (3rd edn, 1979), pp 5–7.

9 *Dane v Mortgage Insurance Corpn* [1894] 1 Q B 54 at 61, C A (insurance of securities) per Lord Esher M R.

10 *Dalby v India and London Life Assurance Co*, (supra), at 387, per Parke B: 'Policies of assurance

It is a fundamental principle of fire insurance that the insured, in case of a loss covered by the contract, shall, so far as the sum specified in the contract permits, be fully indemnified, but shall never be more than fully indemnified.[11]

To establish a right to an indemnity it is necessary for the insured to show that he has, in fact, sustained a loss by reason of his interest in the subject-matter of insurance.[12]

The extent of the insured's indemnity must, subject to the terms of the contract, be measured by the loss which he has actually sustained.

The insured is, therefore, not entitled to receive anything by way of indemnity, even though the property insured be destroyed by fire, if he has, in fact, suffered no loss.[13] Thus, if he has parted with the whole of his interest in the subject-matter of insurance before the happening of the fire which destroys it, he retains nothing to which the right of indemnity can attach.

Even where his interest remains at the time of the fire, he may in reality lose nothing, since his loss may have been made good to him by some third person who was under a legal obligation to do so. In neither case, therefore, is the insured entitled to recover anything from the insurers.[14] It further follows that if his loss has been in any way diminished, his right to an indemnity must be proportionately abated.

If the insured has once received from the insurers the full value of the subject-matter of insurance, he cannot retain for himself any benefit whatever arising out of his interest in such subject-matter, by reason of which he would be more than fully indemnified. He is bound, therefore, upon payment of his indemnity to account to the insurers for any compensation which he may receive from any third person legally responsible for the loss, and to hand over to them, if it is in his power to do so, whatever remains of the subject-matter of insurance together with all his rights, if any, against third persons arising out of the loss.

In working out the principle of indemnity, it frequently happens that the insured, either with the assistance of the insurers, or on their behalf, sues a person alleged to be responsible for the loss. Sometimes both parties may be insured in respect of the loss in question, and the action may not only be

---

against fire and against marine risks are both properly contracts of indemnity, the insurer engaging to make good, within certain limited amounts, the losses sustained by the assured in their buildings, ships, and effects'; *Castellain v Preston* (1883) 11 QBD 380 at 386, CA, per Brett LJ: 'The very foundation, in my opinion, of every rule which has been applied to insurance law is this, namely, that the contract of insurance contained in the marine or fire policy is a contract of indemnity, and of indemnity only'. See also *Darrell v Tibbitts* (1880) 5 QBD 560, CA; *Chapman v Pole* (1870) 22 LT 306; *West of England Fire Insurance Co v Isaacs* [1897] 1 QB 226, CA; *Britton v Royal Insurance Co* (1866) 4 F & F 905 at 908, per Willes J; *Mason v Sainsbury* (1782) 3 Doug KB 61 at 64, per Lord Mansfield; *London Assurance Co v Sainsbury* (1783) 3 Doug KB 245 at 253, per Lord Mansfield.

11 *Castellain v Preston,* (supra), at 386, per Brett, LJ. The statement of Lord Wright in *Maurice v Goldsborough Mort & Co Ltd* [1939] AC 452 at 466, PC, 'insurance does not necessarily give a perfect indemnity but gives sometimes more and sometimes less', should not, it is thought, be understood to contradict the principle stated. The policy in question in that case was a valued policy and the dispute was not as to the amount recoverable from the insurers, but as to the division of the proceeds between the owners of the goods and the brokers in whose hands they were at the time of the fire.

12 *Lucena v Craufurd* (1806) 2 Bos & P NR 269 at 307, HL (marine insurance) per Lawrence J.

13 *Garden v Ingram* (1852) 23 LJ Ch 478 at 479, per Lord St Leonards, LC.

14 *Castellain v Preston,* (supra), at 389, per Brett LJ.

brought but also defended on behalf of the respective insurers. In either case the contract of fire insurance is not offensive to the law against maintenance, since it is a contract of indemnity and is, therefore, not tainted with illegality.[15]

Where the insured has effected more than one contract of insurance in respect of the same subject-matter, he is nevertheless precluded from recovering more than a full indemnity. He may, in the absence of a condition in the contract limiting the insurers' liability in such a case, recover his indemnity against such of his insurers as he pleases, and the manner in which the loss is to be borne between the different insurers is left for them to adjust between themselves.[16] In such a case, if it appears that he has been paying a premium in excess of what is payable in respect of the indemnity to which he is actually entitled, a proportional return of premium may have to be made by the insurers, there being no consideration to justify the retention of the excess.[17]

The contract is, in theory, a contract of perfect indemnity, subject to the difficulty in practice of ascertaining what is a perfect indemnity, and subject also to a possible qualification in the case of valued policies.[18]

3 Distinction between Fire Insurance and a Wager

The fact that the contract is one of indemnity distinguishes the contract of fire insurance from a contract by way of gaming or wagering, in which no question of indemnity arises.[19]

The two contracts, in the classification of the law, may be grouped together as being both contracts to pay a sum of money upon the issue of an uncertain event.[20] But in the practical administration of the law they are dealt with differently.[1]

In order to ascertain the distinction between the two contracts, it is necessary to take into consideration the following matters:

    a The interest of the parties.

    b The issue of the event.

---

15 *British Cash and Parcel Conveyors Ltd v Lamson Store Service Co Ltd* [1908] 1 K B 1006 at 1014, C A (maintenance) per Fletcher Moulton L J, speaking of fire insurance; *Oram v Hutt* [1914] 1 Ch 98 at 106, C A (maintenance) per Lord Sumner. Maintenance is not punishable as a crime or actionable as a tort: Criminal Law Act 1967, ss 13 (1) and 14 (1). But the abolition of criminal and civil liability does not affect 'any such rule of law as to the cases in which a contract is to be treated as contrary to public policy or otherwise illegal': ibid s 14 (2).

16 Ivamy, *General Principles of Insurance Law* (4th edn, 1979), pp 521–542.

17 As to the return of the premium, see Ivamy, op cit, pp 212–222.

18 *Maurice v Goldsborough Mort & Co Ltd* [1939] A C 452, P C.

19 *Macaura v Northern Assurance Co* [1925] A C 619 at 632, per Lord Sumner; see also *Godsall v Boldero* (1807) 9 East 72 (life insurance), overruled, but not on this point, by *Dalby v India and London Assurance Co* (1854) 15 C B 365 (life insurance); *Rankin v Potter* (1873) L R 6 H L 83 at 119, (marine insurance) per Blackburn J, speaking generally of insurance. The principle of indemnity is not to be worked out by the application of the laws against wagering, which laws do not operate by way of qualifying contracts; they may render particular contracts void, but they cannot alter them: *Andrews v Patriotic Assurance Co (No 2)* (1886) 18 L R Ir 355 at 360, per Palles C B.

20 *Earl Ellesmere v Wallace* [1929] 2 Ch 1 at 26, C A (gaming) per Lord Hanworth M R, quoting *Anson on Contract* (15th edn), p 230.

1 *Wilson v Jones* (1867) L R 2 Exch 139 at 146, Ex Ch (marine insurance) per Willes J; *New York Life Insurance Co v Styles* (1889) 14 App Cas 381 at 391 (life insurance) per Lord Halsbury LC.

(a) The Interest of the Parties

In a wagering contract neither of the contracting parties has any other interest than the sum or stake which he will win or lose by the determination of the event.[2] In the event itself or in the subject-matter affected thereby he has no interest. If, therefore, he becomes entitled to be paid the sum fixed by the contract, his right to it depends solely upon the issue of the event, as previously agreed by the parties.[3] It is not paid to him by way of indemnity; for, in whatever way the event may be determined, or whatever may be the fate of the subject-matter, he can suffer no loss against which he may be indemnified.

In a contract of insurance, on the other hand, the insured has an interest in the subject-matter of insurance in respect of which he may suffer loss.[4] The uncertain event upon which the contract depends is, moreover, an event which is prima facie adverse to his interest, the insurance being to provide for the payment of a sum of money to meet a loss or detriment which will or may be suffered by such interest upon the happening of the event.[5]

(b) The Issue of the Event

It is an essential element of a wagering contract that either party to it may win or lose, the question whether either party will win or lose being dependent on the issue of the event, and therefore remaining uncertain until that issue is known.[6] If either of them may win, but cannot lose, or may lose, but cannot win, the contract is not a wagering contract.[7]

If this principle is applied to the contract of fire insurance, it will be seen that the insured cannot lose. He pays a premium, it is true, but this is in performance of the consideration for the contract, nor will he recover his premium, as he does his stake in gaming, if the event insured against occurs. The payment of the premium is not in any way dependent on the issue of the event; and the insured can never be called upon to pay anything more, whether a fire takes place or not. Further, the insurers cannot win, since they cannot receive more than their consideration.[8] If, however, a fire takes place, they are bound to lose, and the insured to win, since he thereupon becomes entitled to receive the sum agreed under the contract to be payable on the issue of the event.

Where a contract is in effect a wagering contract, it is immaterial that it purports to be a contract of insurance.[9]

---

2 *Carlill v Carbolic Smoke Ball Co* [1892] 2 Q B 484 at 491, (contract) per Hawkins J.
3 Accordingly, no action will lie to recover it: *London Assurance Co v Sainsbury* (1783) 3 Doug K B 245 at 249, per Buller J.
4 *Wilson v Jones,* (supra), at 150, per Blackburn J.
5 *Prudential Insurance Co v IRC* [1904] 2 K B 658 at 663, (life insurance) per Channell J, speaking, inter alia, of fire insurance.
6 *Thacker v Hardy* (1878) 4 Q B D 685 at 695, C A (contract) per Cotton L J, considered in *Richards v Starck* [1911] 1 K B 296 (contract); *Carlill v Carbolic Smoke Ball Co,* (supra), at 491, per Hawkins J; *A-G v Luncheon and Sports Club* [1929] A C 400 at 406 (gaming) per Lord Dunedin; *Earl Ellesmere v Wallace,* (supra), at 24, per Lord Hanworth M R.
7 *Carlill v Carbolic Smoke Ball Co,* (supra).
8 Cf *Paterson v Powell* (1832) 9 Bing 320 at 330 (bet on shares) per Tindal C J.
9 *Chapman v Pole* (1870) 22 L T 306; *Re London County Commercial Reinsurance Office Ltd* [1922] Ch 67 (peace insurance); cf *Brogden v Marriott* (1836) 3 Bing N C 88, where the wager was concealed under the form of a contract of sale of a horse.

4 Distinction between Fire Insurance and a Guarantee

Though the contract of fire insurance is a contract of indemnity, it is not a contract of guarantee,[10] nor are the insurers sureties.[11]

Under a guarantee, the loss for which the surety is responsible must be occasioned by the default of the person for whom the guarantee is given.

On the other hand, insurers do not undertake to answer for the default of another, but to make good a loss which may happen by reason of a certain event;[12] and it is therefore immaterial whether or not the event is brought about by the default of another or whether the loss is diminished or increased thereby,[13] unless the insurance itself is one to make good loss resulting from that default.[14] The effect of the principle of indemnity, however, is to give the insurers rights similar to those of sureties, in order to prevent the insured from recovering from them more than a full indemnity,[15] and also, where there are more insurances than one in respect of the same subject-matter, to enable the loss to be apportioned amongst the different insurers.

5 Immateriality of Cause of the Fire

The object of the contract is to provide for the payment of a sum of money, or for some corresponding benefit, to meet a loss or detriment which may be suffered by the insured on the happening of a fire.[16]

To carry the investigation, therefore, beyond the cause of the loss, and to cast on the insured the burden of establishing that the cause of the fire itself was covered by his contract, would largely defeat this object.

When it is once established that the loss is due to 'fire' within the meaning of the contract, the cause of the fire is, as a general rule, immaterial.

The fact that the fire was occasioned by negligence does not exempt the insurers from liability, for one of the objects of the contract of fire insurance is to provide against the consequence of negligence.[17] It is therefore immaterial

---

10 *Seaton v Heath* [1899] 1 QB 782 at 792, 793, (guarantee) per Romer LJ. This case was reversed in the House of Lords ([1900] AC 135), but without affecting this point; see *Re Denton's Estate, Licenses Insurance Corpn and Guarantee Fund Ltd v Denton* [1904] 2 Ch 178 at 188, CA (guarantee) per Vaughan Williams LJ. As to the distinction, see also *London General Omnibus Co Ltd v Holloway* [1912] 2 KB 72 at 86, CA (guarantee) per Kennedy LJ; *Re Law Guarantee Trust and Accident Society Ltd, Liverpool Mortgage Insurance Co's Case* [1914] 2 Ch 617, CA (insurance of debentures).

11 *Dane v Mortgage Insurance Corpn* [1894] 1 QB 54 at 60, CA (insurance of securities) per Lord Esher MR; *Parr's Bank v Albert Mines Syndicate* (1900) 5 Com Cas 116 at 119, (solvency insurance) per Mathew J.

12 *Scottish Amicable Heritable Securities Association Ltd v Northern Assurance Co* 1883 11 R (Ct of Sess) 287 at 303, per Lord Moncrieff; *Finlay v Mexican Investment Corpn* [1897] 1 QB 517 at 522 (insurance of securities) per Charles J; *Shaw v Royce Ltd* [1911] 1 Ch 138 at 147 (insurance of securities) per Warrington J.

13 *Castellain v Preston* (1883) 11 QBD 380 at 403, CA, per Bowen LJ.

14 In such cases it is a question of construction whether the contract is one of guarantee or of insurance: *Trade Indemnity Co Ltd v Workington Harbour and Dock Board* [1937] AC 1 at 17, per Lord Atkin.

15 *Castellain v Preston,* (supra), at p 387, per Brett LJ; cf *Darrell v Tibbitts* (1880) 5 QBD 560 at 563, CA, per Cotton LJ.

16 *Prudential Insurance Co v IRC* [1904] 2 KB 658 at 663 (life insurance) per Channell J, speaking, inter alia, of fire insurance.

17 *Shaw v Robberds* (1837) 6 Ad & El 75 at 84, per Lord Denman CJ; *Austin v Drewe* (1815) 4 Camp

whether a fire which causes a loss is lighted improperly, or, after being properly lighted, is negligently attended, since the insured is in both cases entitled to recover.[18]

It is equally immaterial whether the fire is caused by the negligence of employees or of strangers,[19] or even by the negligence of the insured himself.[20] Thus, Lord Denman C J, said:[1]

> 'There is no doubt that one of the objects of insurance against fire is to guard against the negligence of servants and others; and, therefore, the simple fact of negligence has never been held to constitute a defence: but it is argued that there is a distinction between the negligence of servants or strangers and that of the assured himself. We do not see any ground for such a distinction, and are of opinion that in the absence of all fraud the proximate cause of the loss only is to be looked to.'

It is to be noted, however, that the insured may, by his conduct after the outbreak of a fire, forfeit his rights under the contract, eg when he abstains from taking all reasonable steps to prevent the fire from spreading, or to remove the insured property to a place of safety, or when he wilfully prevents or interferes with other persons in their endeavours to do so. In these cases he not only becomes disentitled to recover in respect of the property which is lost in consequence of his conduct, but, in addition, forfeits all benefit under his contract.

The cause of the fire, however, becomes material in the following cases:

   a Where the fire is occasioned by the wilful act of the insured himself.

   b Where the fire is occasioned by a cause falling within an exception in the contract.

(a) Wilful Act of the Insured

Where the fire is occasioned not by negligence, but by the wilful act of the insured himself,[2] or of someone acting with his privity or consent, the cause of the fire becomes material.[3] In this case his conduct coupled with the making of a

---

360 at 362, per Gibbs C J; *A-G v Adelaide SS Co* [1923] A C 292 at 308 (charter-party) per Lord Wrenbury, speaking of fire insurance; *Jameson v Royal Insurance Co* (1873) I R 7 C L 126.

[18] *Dixon v Sadler* (1839) 5 M & W 405 at 414 (marine insurance) per Parke B, speaking of fire insurance; *Harris v Poland* [1941] 1 K B 462.

[19] *Shaw v Robberds,* (supra); *Dobson v Sotheby* (1827) Mood & M 90; cf *Busk v Royal Exchange Assurance Corpn* (1818) 2 B & Ald 73 (marine insurance); *Walker v Maitland* (1821) 5 B & Ald 171 (marine insurance), followed in *Bishop v Pentland* (1827) 7 B & C 219 (marine insurance).

[20] *Shaw v Robberds,* (supra); *Jameson v Royal Insurance Co,* (supra); *Trinder, Anderson & Co v Thames and Mersey Marine Insurance Co* [1898] 2 Q B 114 at 124, C A (marine insurance) per A L Smith L J, speaking of fire insurance.

[1] In *Shaw v Robberds* (1837) 6 L J K B 106 at 109. Other aspects of this case—(i) whether there was a misdescription of the premises insured; (ii) whether notice of an alteration in the business concerned had been given to the insurers; and (iii) whether there was a continuing warranty as to the use of the premises—are considered at pp 106, 114, and 115, post, respectively.

[2] *Upjohn v Hitchens* [1918] 2 K B 48 at 58, C A, per Scrutton L J; *City Tailors Ltd v Evans* (1921) 126 L T 439 at 443, C A, per Scrutton L J; *Moore v Wolsey* (1854) 4 E & B 243 at 254 (life insurance) per Lord Campbell C J; *Chisholm v Provincial Insurance Co* (1869) 20 C P 11.

[3] *Midland Insurance Co v Smith* (1881) 6 Q B D 561 at 568, per Watkin Williams J. But it is otherwise where property is deliberately burnt for the purpose of checking the progress of a fire. See p 148, post.

claim is a fraud on the insurers,[4] and he cannot enforce his claim against them.[5]

The policy may contain an express condition to the effect that if the fire was occasioned by the wilful act or procurement or with the connivance of the insured or any claimant thereunder, all benefits under it will be forfeited.[6]

On the other hand, where the act is committed without his privity, the insured, being guilty of no misconduct himself, does not commit a breach of good faith in making a claim in respect of his loss, and is therefore not precluded from recovery.[7]

If the act of the insured amounts to a crime, and the insurers resist payment on this ground, it is necessary for them to satisfy the jury that the crime imputed to the insured is as fully proved as would justify them in finding him guilty on a criminal charge for the same offence.[8]

(b) Cause Falling Within an Exception

Where the fire is occasioned by a cause falling within an exception in the contract, the cause of the fire becomes material.[9]

6 Personal Nature of Contract of Fire Insurance

The contract of fire insurance is a mere personal contract between the insurers and the insured for the payment of money.[10] Its purpose is not to insure the

---

[4] *Thompson v Hopper* (1858) E B & E 1038 at 1045, Ex Ch (marine insurance), per Bramwell B: 'There is nothing wrong in sending an unseaworthy ship to sea; though she is insured, there is nothing wrongful in burning her. The wrong is in making a claim founded on such an act . . . The act does not become wrongful where a claim is founded on it and its consequences, but the claim is'. See also *R v Robinson* [1915] 2 K B 342, C C A (criminal law), where it was held that the insured under a burglary policy, who had arranged a sham burglary with the object of defrauding the insurers, but who was arrested before he had made any communication to them, could not be convicted of an attempt to obtain money from them by false pretences; and cf *Jacobs v Schmaltz* (1890) 62 L T 121 (libel).

[5] *Shaw v Robberds* (1873) 6 Ad & El 75; *Britton v Royal Insurance Co* (1866) 4 F & F 905.

[6] See further, Ivamy, *General Principles of Insurance Law* (4th edn, 1979), p 293.

[7] *Logan v Hall* (1887) 4 C B 598 at 622, per Maule J; *Midland Insurance Co v Smith*, (supra), where a house was set on fire by the insured's wife. See also *Brewster v Blackmore* (1925) 21 Ll L Rep 258.

[8] *Thurtell v Beaumont* (1823) 1 Bing 339; *Prosser v Ocean Accident and Guarantee Corpn* (1910) 29 N Z L R 1157; *Watkins & Davis Ltd v Legal and General Assurance Co Ltd* [1981] 1 Lloyd's Rep 674, where the insurers were held to have established to the high degree of probability required that the fire had been deliberately started by the insured. (See the judgment of Neill J, ibid, at 680); *S & M Carpets (London) Ltd v Cornhill Insurance Co Ltd* [1982] 1 Lloyd's Rep 423, C A, where the insurers failed to prove that the fire had been deliberately started by the insured company's managing director. (See the judgment of Ormrod L J, ibid, at 426); *Exchange Theatre Ltd v Iron Trades Mutual Insurance Co Ltd* [1983] 1 Lloyd's Rep 674, where the insurers were held not to have proved that the insured was the fire-raiser. (See the judgment of Lawson J, ibid, at 687). But see *Hurst v Evans* [1917] 1 K B 352 at 357 (damage insurance) per Lush J, pointing out that the rules or evidence differ in criminal and civil cases, and that a civil court is not restricted to such evidence only as would warrant a conviction. As to the effect of a previous acquittal on the criminal charge, see *Gould v British America Assurance* (1868) 27 U C R 473 where a new trial was refused although there was strong evidence of arson.

[9] For the exceptions in the policy, see pp 80–90, post.

[10] *Rayner v Preston* (1881) 18 Ch D 1 at 11, C A, per Brett L J; *Phoenix Assurance Co Ltd v Spooner* [1905] 2 K B 753 at 756, per Bigham J; *Ocean Accident and Guarantee Corpn v Williams* (1915) 34 N Z L R 924. Hence, different persons may each have an insurable interest in the same property.

safety of any particular subject-matter, but to insure the insured against loss arising out of his connection with the subject-matter.[11]

It is not, therefore, a contract which, in the case of buildings insured against fire, runs with the land so as to pass the benefit of it to an assignee of the original owner,[12] or which is so connected with the subject-matter of the insurance[13] as to be transferred by a mere transfer of the subject-matter. As the effect of such transfer is to sever the insured's connection with the subject-matter, and to preclude him therefore from being injured by its subsequent destruction, the purpose for which the contract was made ceases to exist, and the contract itself is extinguished.

In order to transfer the contract it is necessary that there should be either a valid assignment of the contract itself, in which case its personal nature renders the consent of the insurers necessary, or a transfer of it by operation of law.[14]

It is nevertheless so far connected with the subject-matter that its transfer unaccompanied by a transfer of the subject-matter gives no rights, as a general rule, to the transferee, since he can suffer no loss in respect of which he may be indemnified.

7 Entire and Indivisible Contract

Where there are several subject-matters comprised in the same contract of insurance, as in the case of an insurance on a building and its contents, or on stock and machinery, the contract is, prima facie, an entire and indivisible contract.[15]

If the insured, in respect of one of the subject-matters covered by the insurance, fails to comply with a condition precedent, or is guilty of a breach of duty towards the insurers, which would be sufficient to have avoided the contract if it had related to that subject-matter alone, the contract as a whole is voidable.[16]

In the event of loss, therefore, the insured will not be entitled to recover anything from the insurers, and it is immaterial that there was not,[17] or even

---

11 *Sadlers' Co v Badcock* (1743) 2 Atk 554 at 556, per Lord Hardwicke LC.
12 *Rayner v Preston* (1881) 18 Ch D 1, CA; *Ocean Accident and Guarantee Corpn v Williams*, (supra).
13 *Mildmay v Folgham* (1797) 3 Ves 471 at 473, per Lord Loughborough LC.
14 *Rayner v Preston* (supra); *Phoenix Assurance Co Ltd v Spooner* [1905] 2 KB 753; *Forgie v Royal Insurance Co* (1871) 16 LCJ 34.
15 *Parkin v Dick* (1809) 11 East 502 (marine insurance); *Re Universal Non-Tariff Fire Insurance Co, Forbes & Co's Claim* (1875) LR 19 Eq 485, where the question was raised but not decided; cf *Keir v Andrade* (1816) 6 Taunt 498 (marine insurance), where the contract was held to be divisible; *Lewis Ltd v Norwich Union Fire Insurance Co* [1916] App D 509.
16 *Parkin v Dick* (1809) 11 East 502; *L'Union Fire Accident and General Insurance Co Ltd v Klinker Knitting Mills Property Ltd* (1938) 59 Can SCR 709, where the insured, after loss, failed to provide particulars of part of the property alleged to have been burnt.
17 *Ramsay Woollen Cloth Manufacturing Co v Mutual Fire Insurance Co* (1854) 11 UCR 516, where, in an insurance on buildings and stock, there was a double insurance on buildings; *Cushman v London and Liverpool Fire Insurance Co* (1862) 5 All ER 246, where there was a false swearing in respect of the stock, followed in *Gore District Mutual Fire Insurance Co v Samo* (1878) 2 SCR 411, where there was a non-disclosure as to the buildings; *Russ v Mutual Fire Insurance Co of Clinton* (1869) 29 UCR 73, where there was a breach of a condition against mortgaging the buildings; *Dunlop v Usborne and Hibbert Farmers' Mutual Fire Insurance Co* (1895) 22 AR 364, where, in an insurance on building and contents, there was a breach of condition as to the building.

that there could not be,[18] any breach of condition or duty affecting the subject-matter which is in fact destroyed.

The effect of the breach of condition or duty may, however, be restricted by the terms of the contract, and the insured will then be precluded from recovering in respect of the particular subject-matter.[19]

---

[18] *Sacks v Western Assurance Co* [1907] 5 T H 257, where, in an insurance upon stock, tools and fixtures, the condition broken could not apply to the fixtures. See also *Lewis Ltd v Norwich Union Fire Insurance Co* [1916] App D 509.

[19] *Daniel v Robinson* (1826) Batt 650; *King v Prince Edward County Mutual Insurance Co* (1868) 19 C P 134, where, on the construction of the condition, the insurers were held liable for not more than two-thirds of the value of each object insured.

CHAPTER 4

Insurable interest

To constitute an insurable interest[1] capable of supporting a contract of fire insurance,[2] three conditions must be fulfilled:

1 There must be a physical object capable of being destroyed by fire;[3]
2 Such physical object must be the subject-matter of insurance; and
3 The insured must stand in some relation thereto recognised by law,[4] in consequence of which relation he may benefit by its safety, or may be prejudiced by its loss.[5]

Where the insured is the owner of such object, possessing the whole legal property in it, he has undoubtedly an insurable interest in it;[6] and a part owner is in the same position.[7]

An insurable interest is not, however, confined to the interest arising from ownership. It includes every kind of interest that may subsist in or be dependent on an object exposed to danger from fire.[8] It need not, therefore, be a legal interest, an equitable or beneficial interest of any kind being equally insurable.[9]

It must, nevertheless, be more than a mere expectation, however probable.[10]

An expectation of acquiring a trust or charge respecting the object, without any present right, either absolute or contingent, in possession, reversion, or expectancy in the proper legal sense of the word, is not insurable;[11] for, notwithstanding that such object was not destroyed, the insured might never acquire his expected interest in it, and, therefore, even if it is destroyed by fire, the prejudice which he suffers cannot be referred with any degree of certainty to

---

[1] As to 'insurable interest', see further Ivamy, *General Principles of Insurance Law* (4th edn, 1979), pp 20–31.

[2] The definitions of insurable interest applicable in marine insurance apply also in fire insurance: *Castellain v Preston* (1883) 11 QBD 380 at 397, CA, per Bowen LJ. The question of insurable interest is a question of Mercantile Law: *Shaik Sahied Bin Abdullah Bajerai v Sockalingham Chettiar* [1933] AC 342 at 344, PC, per Lord Atkin.

[3] *Lucena v Craufurd* (1806) 2 Bos & PNR 269 at 301, HL (marine insurance) per Lawrence J.

[4] *Inglis v Stock* (1885) 10 App Cas 263 at 270 (marine insurance) per Lord Blackburn.

[5] *Lucena v Craufurd,* (supra), at 302, per Lawrence J. In *Macaura v Northern Assurance Co Ltd* [1925] AC 619 at 627, Lord Buckmaster pointed out the difficulty of defining a moral certainty so as to render it an essential part of a definite legal proposition.

[6] *Inglis v Stock,* (supra).

[7] See p 23, post.

[8] *Lucena v Craufurd,* (supra), at 303, 304 (marine insurance) per Lawrence J.

[9] *Castellain v Preston* (1883) 11 QBD 380 at 397, CA, per Bowen LJ.

[10] *Moran, Galloway & Co v Uzielli* [1905] 2 KB 555 (marine insurance).

[11] *Lucena v Craufurd,* (supra), at 299, per Chambre J; *Castellain v Preston,* (supra), at 397, per Bowen LJ.

the peril insured against so as to enable him to establish a claim to compensation on the ground that his loss has clearly been occasioned by such peril.[12]

The property in any object and the interest to be derived by the insured therefrom may be different.[13] An insurable interest is not, therefore, restricted to a proprietary right;[14] it may be founded on a right arising out of a contract,[15] under which the insured is to benefit, since by the destruction of the object he will be equally prejudiced.

Thus, the owner of a farm, who leases part of it on condition that the lessee does not remove the chaff, has an insurable interest in the chaff.[16]

Similarly, a buyer of goods has an insurable interest in them, though they have never been appropriated to the contract, or even ascertained. The contract, however, must be a valid[17] subsisting contract,[18] capable of being enforced between the parties to it. Where this is the case, it need not purport to give the insured any rights in or over the object itself; it is sufficient if it has reference thereto.[19] Where, therefore, the insured is not entitled under his contract to derive any direct benefit from the fact that the object remains unharmed, but is only subjected to a liability in case of its destruction by fire, he has nevertheless an insurable interest.[20]

Thus, whilst a covenant to insure certain buildings remains in force, as between the lessor and the lessee, after the expiration of the lessee's tenancy of such buildings, the lessee has, by virtue of his liability under the covenant, an insurable interest in the buildings.[1]

Similarly, an insurer who has entered into a contract of insurance to indemnify the insured against loss by fire in respect of a particular physical object, has himself an insurable interest in such object, and may protect himself by reinsurance against its loss and his consequent liability to the insured.[2]

Where a person is by statute required to insure against fire or empowered to do so, the existence of the statutory duty or power, as the case may be, constitutes an insurable interest, and an insurance effected in pursuance thereof will be valid.[3]

---

[12] *Lucena v Craufurd,* (supra), at 303, per Lawrence J. But the purchaser of an expectation is in a different position: *Cook v Field* (1850) 15 Q B 460 at 475 (covenant) per Lord Campbell C J.

[13] *Lucena v Craufurd,* (supra), at 302, per Lawrence J.

[14] Ibid.

[15] Ibid at 321, per Lord Eldon.

[16] *Steyn v Malmesbury Board of Executors and Trust and Assurance Co* [1921] C P D 96.

[17] If the sale is unlawful, as in the case of intoxicating liquor in a country where prohibition is in force, the buyer acquires no insurable interest: *Smith v National Guaranty Co* (1929) 64 O L R 240.

[18] *Hebdon v West* (1863) 3 B & S 579 (life insurance).

[19] *Colonial Insurance Co of New Zealand v Adelaide Marine Insurance Co* (1886) 12 App Cas 128 at 138, P C (marine insurance).

[20] See p 32, post.

[1] *Heckman v Isaac* (1862) 6 L T 383 at 385, per Crompton J; *Klein v Union Fire Insurance Co* (1883) 3 O R 234. But if the liability comes to an end, his insurable interest ceases: *Matthey v Curling* [1922] 2 A C 180 at 219, per Younger L J.

[2] *Forsikringsakt National (of Copenhagen) v A-G* [1925] A C 639 at 642, per Lord Cave L C.

[3] Persons so insuring have invariably an interest of some kind apart from the statute. The existence of the statutory interest may possibly affect, however, the amount recoverable under the insurance in case of loss. See p 179, post.

CHAPTER 5

Persons under a duty to insure

There appears to be no person who at Common Law is under any duty to insure against fire.[1] Any such duty must be created by the express terms of a statute or by virtue of some contract, express or implied.

WHERE THE DUTY IS IMPOSED BY STATUTE

The persons compelled to by a statute to insure are:

1 The Parsonages Board.
2 Tenants for life and others in a similar position who are only limited owners of property.
3 Owners of small holdings.

1 Parsonages Board

It is the duty of the Parsonages Board to insure all the parsonage houses in their diocese against all such risks as are included in the usual form of houseowner's policy relating to buildings.[2]

The words 'parsonage house' means a residence vested in the incumbent of a benefice (when the benefice is full) being his official residence except a residence held under a lease which makes the landlord wholly or mainly responsible for the repairs, and includes the buildings, gardens, orchards, paddock, walls, fences, and appurtenances necessary for the convenient occupation of the residence.[3] For the purposes of this definition the separate letting of a part of the residence is not to be deemed to exclude it from the residence unless it is excluded by a certificate of the bishop under the Parsonages Measure 1938, s 11.[4]

The insurance must be placed with the Ecclesiastical Insurance Office Ltd. or such other insurance office as may be selected by the Parsonages Board and approved by the Church Commissioners.[5]

---

[1] In the case of a captor, the existence of any duty has been expressly negatived: *The Sudmark (No 2)* [1918] AC 475 PC; *The New Sweden* [1922] 1 AC 229, PC where, therefore, property which might have been condemned is released, the premiums paid during the period of detention cannot be charged as part of the expenses of detention: *The Cairnsmore, The Gunda* [1921] 1 AC 439, PC, though it is otherwise where the property is detained only and cannot be condemned: *The United States* [1920] P 430.

[2] Repair of Benefice Buildings Measure 1972, s 12.

[3] Ibid s 31 (1).

[4] Ibid, s 31 (1).

[5] Ibid s 12.

If any question arises as to the risks to be covered, it must be conclusively determined by the Church Commissioners.[6]

It is the duty of the Board to cause an inspection to be made by a diocesan surveyor of all the buildings of each benefice in the diocese periodically at intervals not exceeding 5 years from the last inspection.[7]

On every inspection the diocesan surveyor must make a report to the Board including advice on the respective amounts for which the buildings of the benefice should be insured, and on the special risks to which they are liable.[8]

2 Tenants for Life and Other Limited Owners of Land

A tenant for life, or other limited owner of land, is required by various statutes to insure, and keep insured against fire, at his own expense, buildings which have been erected, improved or added to out of funds raised by means of charges on the settled land.

The statutes under which this duty is imposed are:

    a The Improvement of Land Act 1864.
    b The Limited Owners' Residences Act 1870.
    c The Settled Land Act 1925.

(a) Improvement of Land Act 1864

Farm houses, farm buildings, or works susceptible of damage by fire which have been erected, improved or added to under this Act must be kept insured by the person liable to make any periodical payments of the charge imposed by the Act, so long as any land continues subject to the charge.[9] The insurance must be for an amount equal at least to the principal amount originally charged on the land.[10] Once a year the person whose duty it is to insure must certify to the Minister of Agriculture, Fisheries and Food the fact of such insurance,[11] and the particulars thereof; he must also satisfy that the premium for the current year has been duly paid.[12]

In the case of his default either to insure, or keep insured, or to certify, as the case may be, the person entitled to the charge for the time being may, with the assent of the Minister, insure for an amount not exceeding the principal amount charged, either in the name of the person making default, or in the name of the landowner, and may continue the insurance so long as the charge remains.[13] Any monies paid by him for premiums or duty are to be repaid to him by the person in default on the day when the next payment on the charge

---

[6] Repair of Benefice Buildings Treasure 1972 s 12.
[7] Ibid s 3 (1).
[8] Ibid s 4 (1) (g). The Board must cause a copy of the report to be sent to the incumbent together with a notice stating his right to make representations and the date by which they must be made, which must not be less than one month from the date on which the notice is sent: ibid s 4 (4).
[9] Improvement of Land Act 1864, s 74.
[10] Ibid.
[11] Ibid.
[12] Ibid.
[13] Ibid.

becomes due, and, in default of repayment, may be recovered with interest at the rate of 5 per cent per annum from the date of payment.[14]

(b) Limited Owners' Residences Act 1870

Mansion houses or appurtenances erected, improved or added to under the provisions of this Act, must be insured in the same way and subject to the same conditions as the improvements above-mentioned.[15]

(c) The Settled Land Act 1925

Any building or work in its nature insurable against fire comprised in an improvement under this Act[16] must be insured, and kept insured at his own expense, by the tenant for life under the settlement[17] for such sum as the Minister of Agriculture, Fisheries and Food by certificate prescribes.[18]

The tenant for life must, if required by the Minister, on or without the suggestion of any person interested under the settlement, report to the Minister the fact and any particulars of any fire insurance.[19]

In case of any default by the tenant for life, any person interested has a right of action against him in respect thereof, and his estate is, after his death, liable to make good to the persons entitled under the settlement any damage occasioned by his default.[20]

3 Owners of Small Holdings

On the sale of a small holding by a County Council under the Small Holdings and Allotments Act 1926, any dwelling house or other building erected on the holding is to be kept in repair and insured against fire by the owner to the satisfaction of the Council.[1]

WHERE THE DUTY IS IMPOSED BY CONTRACT

Apart from the persons enumerated above, the obligation to insure can only arise by virtue of the terms of some contract, express or implied.[2]

---

14 Improvement of Land Act 1864, s 74.
15 Limited Owners' Residences Act 1870, s 8, applying Improvement of Land Act 1864, s 74.
16 For the list of improvements authorised by the Act, see ibid s 82, Sch III.
17 As to persons who are included in the term 'tenant for life', see ibid ss 19, 117 (1) (xxviii).
18 Ibid s 88 (1). The Minister may vary the certificate, but not so as to increase the liabilities of the tenant for life: ibid s 88 (4).
19 Ibid s 88 (3).
20 Ibid s 88 (5).
1 S 6 (1) (f). The receipts for the premium are to be produced when required by the Council: ibid. The obligation continues for 40 years from the date of the sale and thereafter so long as the holding remains charged with the terminable annuity representing the consideration for the sale: ibid s 6 (1).
2 *Martineau v Kitching* (1872) L R 7 Q B 436; *Armitage v Winterbottom* (1840) 1 Man & G 130, more fully reported 1 Scott N R 23.

The persons likely to be subjected to such an obligation are persons who are limited owners of property or who acquire by contract the possession of property belonging to others.

Where the obligation is imposed by express contract, eg where there is a covenant by the lessor[3], the lessee[4], or mortgagor, or an undertaking by an ordinary bailee, to insure, no difficulty arises; for the existence of the obligation is clear. Where there is no express contract, a contract to insure may be implied either from the custom of some particular business or locality, or from the practice of the particular person sought to be charged with the obligation.

A tenant for life, whether legal or equitable, of property, whether freehold or leasehold, may be expressly required by the will or settlement under which he claims to insure the property coming to him, or he may, on the construction of its terms, be obliged to do so, if he accepts the gift.[5]

---

[3] See eg *Gleniffer Finance Corpn Ltd v Bamar Wood & Products Ltd* [1978] 2 Lloyd's Rep 49, where the lessor covenanted to keep the premises insured and the lessee covenanted to pay the lessor a premium for insuring them for the 'full cost of reinstatement' against loss or damage by fire, and it was held that the words 'full cost of reinstatement' must have been intended by the parties to cover the cost which might properly be expected to cover the cost at the time when the reinstatement took place. (See the judgment of Forbes J, ibid, at 51–52). It was also held that the lessor in assessing the cost of reinstatement must exercise the power to insure the premises properly and charge a fair and reasonable premium: ibid, at 54.

[4] See eg *Argy Trading Development Co Ltd v Lapid Developments Ltd* [1977] 1 Lloyd's Rep 67, QBD.

[5] *Re Betty, Betty v A-G* [1899] 1 Ch 821, where the property was leasehold, the lease containing a covenant to insure, and it was held that the equitable tenant for life was bound to perform the covenant, though the liability for any breach would fall on the testator's estate, followed in *Re Gjers, Cooper v Gjers* [1899] 2 Ch 54; *Re Redding, Thompson v Redding* [1897] 1 Ch 876, where, on the construction of the will, it was held that the expense of insuring leasehold property was to be deducted from the income derivable therefrom, and the balance only was to be paid over to the beneficiary. The contrary view was taken in *Re Baring, Jeune v Baring* [1893] 1 Ch 61; *Re Tomlinson, Tomlinson v Andrew* [1898] 1 Ch 232; cf *Gregg v Coates* (1856) 23 Beav 33 at 38 (duty to keep in repair) per Romilly M R. See also *Re Skingley* (1851) 3 Mac & G 221 (duty to keep in repair); *Re Kingham, Kingham v Kingham* [1897] 1 I R 170.

CHAPTER 6

Persons entitled to insure

All persons are entitled to insure property who are either:

1   Owners of the property sought to be insured; or
2   otherwise so connected with it as to have an insurable interest in it.

OWNERS

To entitle a person to insure as owner[1] it is not necessary that he should have both the legal and the equitable ownership of the property to be insured; either form of ownership is sufficient to support an insurance.[2] Nor is it necessary that he should be in possession.[3]

The following persons may insure as owners of the property to be insured:

1   Absolute owners.
2   Trustees in bankruptcy and bankrupts.
3   Vendors and purchasers.
4   Trustees and *cestuis que trustent*.
5   Personal representatives and beneficiaries.
6   Mortgagors and mortgagees.
7   Limited owners.
8   Minors.
9   Persons of unsound mind.
10 Husband and wife.

1 Absolute Owners

The absolute owner of property is entitled to insure it against fire.[4] He need not be the sole owner; it is sufficient if he is a joint tenant or a tenant in common.[5] In particular, a partner has power to insure the property of the firm.[6]

---

[1] The fact of insuring is some evidence of ownership: *Harris v Truman* (1882) 9 QBD 264 at 267, CA (agent), per Lord Coleridge CJ; cf *Fragano v Long* (1825) 4 B & C 219 at 222 (negligence) per Bayley J.
[2] *Castellain v Preston* (1883) 11 QBD 380 at 397, CA, per Bowen LJ.
[3] *Ward v Carttar* (1865) LR 1 Eq 29 at 31, per Romilly MR.
[4] *Inglis v Stock* (1885) 10 App Cas 263 at 270 (marine insurance) per Lord Blackburn. It is immaterial that he has a contract of indemnity from a third person: *Hobbs v Hannam* (1811) 3 Camp 39 (marine insurance).
[5] *Page v Fry* (1800) 2 Bos & P 240 at 243 (marine insurance) per Heath J.
[6] For an instance of such an insurance, see *Reid v Hollinshead* (1825) 4 B & C 867.

2 Trustees in Bankruptcy and Bankrupts

On an adjudication in bankruptcy, the property of the bankrupt vests in the trustee in bankruptcy,[7] who is thereupon entitled to insure it as owner.

The bankrupt, however, does not, because of the adjudication, lose his right to insure such property as he retains in his possession as apparent owner;[8] and it is immaterial that he is fraudulently concealing it from his creditors.[9]

3 Vendors and Purchasers

A person who has contracted to sell property, whether land or goods, retains an insurable interest in it as owner till the completion of the conveyance, by reason of his legal estate.[10]

Thus, in *Collingridge v Royal Exchange Assurance Corpn*[11] the plaintiff insured his premises in Clerkenwell against fire for £1,600. Later they were required by the Metropolitan Board of Works under compulsory powers so that they might be pulled down for the improvement of a street. The amount of the purchase money was assessed at £2,926 by an arbitrator, and the Board accepted the plaintiff's title. But before he had executed a conveyance the premises were destroyed by fire.

When the insured claimed under the policy, the insurers contended that they were not liable to pay anything because he had no insurable interest, but that, if they were liable, the loss was incurred by the Board only and not by the insured.

The Queen's Bench Division[12] held that the insured had an insurable interest and was entitled to an indemnity.

Lush J, said:[13]

> 'The [insured] is in the position of a person who has entered into a contract to sell his property to another. The fact that the vendee is so important a corporation as the Board of Works can make no difference. The contract will no doubt be completed, but legally the buildings are still his property. The [insurers] by their policy undertook to make good any loss or damage to the property by fire. There is nothing to shew that any collateral dealings with the premises, such as those stated in the case, are to limit this liability. If the [insured] had actually conveyed them away before the fire, that would have been a defence to the action, for he would then have had no interest at the time of the loss. But in the present case he still has a right to the possession of his property, and the [insurers] are bound to pay him the insurance money, whether he is trustee of it for third persons or not.'

---

[7] Bankruptcy Act 1914, s 18 (1).

[8] *Marks v Hamilton* (1852) 7 Exch 323 at 334, per Pollock C B.

[9] *Goulstone v Royal Insurance Co* (1858) 1 F & F 276 at 278, 279, per Pollock C B; cf *Lambert v Anglo-Scottish General Commercial Insurance Co* (1929) 64 O L R 439, where the insured was held to have an insurable interest in his brother's property placed in his name to protect it from the brother's creditors.

[10] *Collingridge v Royal Exchange Assurance Corpn* (1877) 3 Q B D 173 at 177, per Lush J; *Castellain v Preston* (1883) 11 Q B D 380 at 385, per Brett L J; *North British and Mercantile Insurance Co v McLellan* (1892) 21 S C R 288.

[11] (1877) 3 Q B D 173.

[12] Mellor and Lush J J.

[13] (1877) 3 Q B D at 177. See also the judgment of Mellor J, ibid, at 177.

Similarly, in *Castellain v Preston*[14] where the vendor had contracted to sell the insured premises to the purchaser but they were burnt down before completion of the purchase, Bret LJ, said in the course of his judgment:[15]

> 'The [insured] were the owners of property consisting partly at all events of a house, and the [insured] had made a contract of sale of that property with third persons, which contract upon the giving of a certain notice as to the time of payment would oblige those third persons, if they fulfilled the contract, to pay the agreed price for the sale of that property, a part of which was a house, and according to the peculiarity of such a sale and purchase of land or real property the vendees would have to pay the purchase money, whether the house was, before the date of payment, burnt down or not. After the contract was made with the third persons, and before the day of payment, the house was burnt down. The vendors, the [insured], having insured the house in the ordinary form with the [insurance] company, it is not suggested that upon the house being burnt down the [insured] had not an insurable interest. They had an insurable interest, as it seems to me, first, because they were at all events the legal owners of the property; and, secondly, because the vendees or third persons might not carry out the contract, and if for any reason they should never carry out the contract, then the vendors, if the house was burnt down, would suffer the loss.'

After conveyance, his interest will continue, provided that his lien as unpaid vendor remains in force,[16] or he is responsible to the purchaser for the safety of the property;[17] but it will cease on the lien ceasing or being lost,[18] or upon his responsibility coming to an end.[19] On the other hand, a person who has purchased property acquires an insurable interest in it by virtue of the contract of purchase.[20] It is therefore immaterial that no conveyance of the property to him has yet been made;[1] or that he has not yet incurred any liability to pay for it;[2] or that the purchase is only on approval.[3]

Further, in the case of goods sold from bulk, it is not necessary that any specific goods should have been actually separated and appropriated to the contract.[4]

---

[14] (1883) 11 QBD 380, CA.

[15] Ibid, at 385.

[16] *Collingridge v Royal Exchange Assurance Corpn,* (supra); *Castellain v Preston,* (supra), at 401, per Bowen LJ. The value of his interest is the amount due at the date of the fire: *Weeks v Cumberland Farmers Mutual Insurance Co* (1930) 2 MPR 126.

[17] *North British and Mercantile Insurance Co v Moffatt* (1871) LR 7 CP 25.

[18] *Bank of New South Wales v North British Mercantile Insurance Co* (1881) 2 NSWLR 239, where the lien had been lost.

[19] *Martineau v Kitching* (1872) LR 7 QB 436.

[20] An option to purchase is sufficient: *Mutual Fire Insurance Co v Paquet Co* (1912) QR 21 KB 419.

[1] *Rayner v Preston* (1881) 18 Ch D 1 at 13, CA, per James LJ (who dissented from the rest of the Court on the main point of the case), cited with approval in *Ridout v Fowler* [1904] 1 Ch 658 at 661 (affd. [1904] 2 Ch 93, CA) per Farwell J; *Donaldson v Providence Mutual Fire Assurance Co* (1909) QR 36 SC 439.

[2] *Colonial Insurance Co of New Zealand v Adelaide Marine Insurance Co* (1886) 12 App Cas 128 at 138, PC (marine insurance): 'A man may have an insurable interest in goods for which he has neither paid nor become liable to pay'. Cf *Milligan v Equitable Insurance Co* (1858) 16 UCR 314 where the purchaser was in default with his payments; *Fensom v Bulman* (1907) 17 Man LR 309 where one instalment of purchase money had been paid.

[3] *Bevington and Morris v Dale & Co Ltd* (1902) 7 Com Cas 112 at 113 (sale of goods) per Kennedy J.

[4] *Inglis v Stock* (1885) 10 App Cas 263 at 274 (marine insurance) per Lord Blackburn; *Clark v Western Assurance Co* (1866) 25 UCR 209, where the purchaser was held entitled to recover on a policy covering 2,000 bushels of wheat in a store, although the 2,000 bushels had never been set aside; *Mathewson v Royal Insurance Co* (1871) 16 LCJ 45; *Wilson v Citizens Insurance Co* (1875) 19 LCJ 175; cf *Box v Provincial Insurance Co* (1868) 15 Gr 337; *Brij Coomaree v Salamander Fire Insurance Co* (1905) ILR 32 Calc 816.

4 Trustees and Cestuis Que Trustent

A trustee, by virtue of his legal ownership of his property, is entitled to insure it in his own name,[5] if and in so far as a contrary intention is not expressed in the instrument, if any, creating the trust.[6] He is not, however, under any obligation to do so,[7] unless such obligation is imposed by the terms of the instrument constituting the trust.[8]

A trustee is expressly empowered by statute[9] to insure against loss or damage by fire any building or other insurable property[10] comprised in the trust estate to an amount (including the amount of any insurance already on foot) not exceeding three-fourths of its full value, and to pay the premiums for such insurance out of the income of the trust estate or out of the income of any other property subject to the same trusts.[11] For this purpose it is not necessary to obtain the consent of any of the beneficiaries.[12]

A *cestui que trust* is by virtue of his equitable ownership entitled to insure the trust property equally with the trustee.[13]

5 Personal Representatives and Beneficiaries

Any personal representative, whether an executor,[14] including an executor trustee,[15] or an administrator, and, even it seems, an executor *de son tort*,[16] is entitled to insure the property which comes to him in that capacity as well as to renew any pre-existing contract of insurance by which it may be covered.[17]

He is, however, not under any obligation[18] to insure it if it was previously uninsured[19] or to keep alive any existing insurances upon it,[20] even though such

---

5   *Lucena v Craufurd* (1806) 2 Bos & P N R 269 at 324, H L (marine insurance) per Lord Eldon; *Ex p Houghton* (1810) 17 Ves 251 at 253; *Ex parte Yallop* (1808) 15 Ves 60 at 67; *Ebsworth v Alliance Marine Insurance Co* (1873) L R 8 C P 596 at 638 (marine insurance) per Brett J.

6   Trustee Act 1925, s 19 (1), (2).

7   *Dowson v Solomon* (1859) 1 Drew & Sm 1 at 14.

8   For an instance, see *Re Colyer, Millikin v Snelling* (1886) 55 L T 344.

9   Trustee Act 1925, s 19 (1). There is no statutory obligation on the trustee to insure and no statutory liability on the tenant for life to pay for the insurance: *Re McEacharn, Gambles v McEacharn* [1911] W N 23.

10   This includes chattels settled so as to devolve as heirlooms: *Re Egmont's (Earl) Trusts, Lefroy v Earl Egmont* [1908] 1 Ch 821; but not buildings or property which a trustee is bound forthwith to convey absolutely to any beneficiary upon being requested to do so: Trustee Act 1925, s 19 (2).

11   Trustee Act 1925, s 19 (1); cf Law of Property Act 1925, s 3 (1) (b) (i). The insurance is for the benefit of all persons interested: *Re Bladon, Dando v Porter* [1911] 2 Ch 350 at 354 (settled estate) (affd [1912] 1 Ch 45, C A) per Neville J.

12   Trustee Act 1925, s 19 (1).

13   *Ex p Yallop* (1808) 15 Ves 60, 67; *Ex p Houghton* (1810) 17 Ves 251, 253; *Pettigrew v Grand River Farmers' Mutual Insurance Co* (1877) 28 C P 70.

14   An executor may insure before probate: *Stirling v Vaughan* (1809) 11 East 619 at 629 (marine insurance) per Lord Ellenborough C J.

15   *Re Betty, Betty v A-G* [1899] 1 Ch 821 at 829; *Fry v Fry* (1859) 27 Beav 144.

16   *Lingley v Queen Insurance Co* (1868) 12 N B R (1 Han) 280, where it was held that a widow had an insurable interest as executrix *de son tort*.

17   *Parry v Ashley* (1829) 3 Sim 97 at 100, per Shadwell V-C: 'I shall not enter into the question whether she was bound to renew the policy of insurance or not. The fact is that she, being the executrix, did renew it, and therefore I must hold that prima facie she renewed it in the character in which she was entitled to renew it, namely, as executrix'.

18   See, however, *Re Betty, Betty v A-G*, (supra), at 829; *Re Kingham, Kingham v Kingham* [1897] 1 I R 170 at 175, per Chatterton. V C.

19   *Croft's (Lady) Executors v Lyndsey and Covil* (1676) 2 Freem Ch 1.

20   *Bailey v Gould* (1840) 4 Y & C Ex 221, where the fact that the policies lapsed a few days before the

insurances were effected under a covenant to insure running with the property in question.[1]

The beneficiary under a will is entitled to insure any property devised or bequeathed to him even before the executor has given his assent to the devise or request.[2] After the transfer of the property to him, he may, if absolute owner, insure it as such. Where the interest given to him is not absolute, he may, nevertheless, be compelled, by the terms of the will, to insure the property or be made responsible for its safety. In other cases he has the right of a limited owner to insure it.

6 Mortgagors and Mortgagees

Where the legal ownership and the equitable ownership of property are severed by the creation of a mortgage, two distinct insurable interests are created,[3] both the mortgagee, by virtue of the legal ownership given to him by the mortgage,[4] and the mortgagor, by virtue of the equitable ownership remaining in him,[5] being entitled to insure the mortgaged property.

Apart from the right arising from the legal ownership of the property, a mortgagee, where the mortgage is made by deed, is empowered by the Law of Property Act 1925, s 101 (1) (ii),[6] at any time after the date of the mortgage deed, to insure and keep insured against loss or damage by fire any building, or any effects or property of an insurable nature, whether affixed to the freehold or not, being or forming part of the mortgaged property, and to charge the premiums paid for any such insurance on the mortgaged property, in addition to the mortgage money, with the same priority, and with interest at the same

---

testator's death was held to be immaterial, and the Court laid down the general principle, followed in *Re McEacharn, Gambles v McEacharn* [1911] W N 23, where an application was made to increase the amount of the testator's insurances.

[1] *Fry v Fry*, (supra), where, though the will was not proved until after the fire, one of the executors was acting from the date of the testator's death, and it was held that the executors were entitled to charge against the estate moneys paid by them to the landlord as compensation for the breach of covenant, approved in *Re McEacharn, Gambles v McEacharn* [1911] W N 23.

[2] *Butler v Standard Fire Insurance Co* (1879) 26 Gr 341; affd 4 A R 391, where a married woman to whom a stock of goods had been bequeathed by her brother, insured them as her own property, although the executor of the will had not formally assented to the bequest.

[3] *Small v United Kingdom Marine Insurance Association* [1897] 2 Q B 311 at 313, C A (marine insurance) per Lord Esher M R 'The interests of the mortgagor and mortgagee are distinct interests; the mortgagee does not claim his interest through the mortgagor, but by virtue of the mortgage which has given him an interest distinct from that of the mortgagor'.

[4] *Dobson v Land* (1850) 8 Hare 216 at 220, per Wigram V-C; *Castellain v Preston* (1883) 11 Q B D 380 at 398, C A, per Bowen L J; *North British and Mercantile Insurance Co v London, Liverpool and Globe Insurance Co* (1877) 5 Ch D 569 at 583, C A, per Mellish L J; *Western Australian Bank v Royal Insurance Co* (1908) 5 C L R 533.

[5] *Provincial Insurance Co of Canada v Leduc* (1874) LR 6 P C 224 (marine insurance); cf *Kelly v Liverpool and London and Globe Insurance Co* (1870) 13 N B R 266; *Smith v Royal Insurance Co* (1867) 27 U C Q B 54; *Richards v Liverpool and London Fire and Life Insurance Co* (1866) 25 U C R 400 at 401, where it was said to be unnecessary to cite cases to establish the propositions stated in the text; *Barcha v Atlas Assurance Co* [1924] 2 W W R 467, where the owner of property which had been taken over by a municipality for unpaid taxes was allowed a specified period to redeem, and was held entitled to recover when the fire took place within the period; *Fordorchuk v Car and General Insurance Corpn Ltd* [1931] 2 W W R 586, where foreclosure proceedings had been taken.

[6] The section applies only if and as far as a contrary intention is not expressed in the mortgage deed, and is to have effect subject to the terms of the mortgage deed and to the provisions therein contained: Law of Property Act 1925, s 101 (4).

rate, as the mortgage money. The amount of the insurance must not exceed the amount specified in the mortgage deed, or, if no amount is therein specified, two-thirds of the amount which would be required, in case of total destruction, to restore the property insured.[7]

The power of insuring under the statute cannot be exercised by the mortgagee in the following cases:

a   where the mortgage deed contains a declaration that no insurance is required;

b   where an insurance is kept up by or on behalf of the mortgagor, in accordance with the mortgage deed; and

c   where the mortgage deed contains no stipulation respecting insurance, and an insurance is kept up by or on behalf of the mortgagor with the consent of the mortgagee to the amount in which the mortgagee is by the Act authorised to insure.[8]

A receiver appointed by the mortgagee, may, if so directed in writing by the mortgagee, insure to the extent, if any, to which the mortgagee might have insured and keep insured against loss or damage by fire any building, effects, or property of an insurable nature comprised in the mortgage, whether affixed to the freehold or not, and may pay the premiums out of the money received by him.[9]

7 Limited Owners

Where a person, who is a limited owner of property, is not obliged, by statute, or otherwise, to insure it, he is nevertheless entitled to do so.[10] Thus, a tenant in tail[11] or a tenant for life[12] whether legal or equitable, may insure the settled property.

8 Minors

Where the person entitled to insure is a minor, the trustees of the settlement,[13] or his guardian,[14] may insure on his behalf.[15]

9 Persons of Unsound Mind

Where the person entitled to insure is a person of unsound mind, the Court has

---

[7] Ibid s 108 (1).

[8] Ibid s 108 (2).

[9] Ibid s 109 (7). He may also pay the premiums on existing insurances: ibid s 109 (8) (iii). A receiver appointed by the Court is in the same position: *Re Graham, Graham v Noakes* [1895] 1 Ch 66.

[10] But he is not bound to do so, or to keep up existing insurances, since loss or damage by fire is due to *vis major: Re Kingham, Kingham v Kingham* (1897) 1 I R 170 at 175, per Chatterton V-C at 175.

[11] See *Warwicker v Bretnall* (1882) 23 Ch D 188; cf *Seymour v Vernon* (1852) 21 L J Ch 433.

[12] *Castellain v Preston* (1883) 11 Q B D 380 at 401, C A, per Bowen L J; *Gaussen v Whatman* (1905) 93 L T 101.

[13] Settle Land Act 1925, s 102 (2) (e). The insurance is for the benefit of the minor: *Re Bladon, Dando v Porter* [1911] 2 Ch 350 at 354 (settled estate) per Neville J. For an example of such an insurance, see *Re Quicke's Trusts, Poltimore v Quicke* [1918] 1 Ch 887.

[14] *Warwicker v Bretnall*, (supra).

[15] Presumably a minor, if absolute owner, can make a valid contract of insurance, being a contract for his benefit: *Clements v London and North-Western Rly Co* [1894] 2 QB 482, C A (accident insurance).

power to insure on his behalf by reason of the powers given to it by the Mental Health Act 1983.[16]

10 Husband and Wife

A wife may make a contract of insurance to cover her separate estate in the same way as if she were unmarried.[17] Her husband is also entitled to insure it,[18] at least while they are living together and sharing its use.[19]

PERSONS OTHERWISE INTERESTED

Any person who, by reason of some contract, express or implied, relating to property, is in danger of being prejudiced by the destruction of such property, may insure it. He may, by his contract, have a right to the possession of property from the safety or destruction of which he may receive benefit or prejudice, or merely a right to look to specific property for his pecuniary advantage.[20]

The right to insure in this case need not depend on the existence of any liability over to the owner of the property,[1] though it is competent to the parties to agree that any insurance effected shall only cover property for which the insured is so liable.[2] The persons whose right to insure depends upon the existence of a contract relating to the subject-matter of insurance may be classified as follows:

   a Bailees.
   b Tenants.
   c Equitable mortgagees.
   d Persons liable over.
   e Statutory bodies.

---

[16] Mental Health Act 1983, ss 93–101.

[17] Married Women's Property Act 1882, s 1 (2).

[18] *Littlejohn v Norwich Union Fire Insurance Society* [1905] 3 T H 374, where a husband was held entitled to insure a business belonging to his wife, on the profits of which they lived; *Patterson v Central Canada Insurance Co* (1910) 15 W L R 123, where the Court declined to go into the validity of the marriage; cf *Muldover v Norwich Union Fire Insurance Co* (1917) 40 O L R 536, where the property of various members of a family living together was held to be covered by an insurance in the name of one of them. But he should not describe himself as 'owner': *Lemieux v Compagnie Equitable d'Assurance contra feu* (1906) Q R 30 S C 490.

[19] *Goulstone v Royal Insurance Co* (1858) 1 F & F 276. Cf *Fell v Whittaker* (1871) L R 7 Q B 120, where a tenant was held entitled to sue for excessive distress levied on the wife's chattels in the matrimonial home.

[20] Thus, the occupier of a furnished house, who has no property in the contents, may insure: *Trotter v Watson* (1869) L R 4 C P 434 at 444, per Bovill C J.

[1] *Waters v Monarch Fire and Life Assurance Co* (1856) 5 E & B 870; *London and North-Western Rly Co v Glyn* (1859) 1 E & E 652, approved in *Martineau v Kitching* (1872) L R 7 Q B 436.

[2] *North British and Mercantile Insurance Co v Moffatt* (1871) L R 7 C P 25.

(a) Bailees

All bailees[3] have, irrespective of any liability to their bailors which of itself entitles them to insure, an insurable interest in the property entrusted to them in respect of the advantages which they are to derive from the bailment in the way of commission, lien or profit.[4] It is not necessary for a bailee insuring to disclose the nature of his interest, so long as the contract of insurance is effected solely on his own behalf.

The principal classes of bailees[5] are the following:

    i Carriers.[6]
    ii Factors,[7] warehousemen,[8] and wharfingers.[9]
    iii Pledgees[10] and pawnbrokers.
    iv Hirers.[11]
    v Innkeepers and livery stable keepers.

Thus, in *Waters v Monarch Fire and Life Assurance Co*[12] a warehouseman effected a fire insurance policy in respect of goods in his warehouse and 'on goods in trust or on commission therein'. A fire took place and all the goods in the warehouse were destroyed. The insurance company paid the value of the insured's own goods, and the amount of the lien on his customer's goods for the charges of storing them in the warehouse. But the company refused to pay the value of the customer's interest in the value of the goods beyond the lien.

In an action on the policy the Court of King's Bench[13] held that the insured had an insurable interest and could claim for the full value of all the goods destroyed.

Lord Campbell C J, said:[14]

'The last point that arises is, to what extent does the policy protect those goods. The [insurers] say that it was only the [insured's] personal interest. But the policies are in terms contracts to

---

[3] As to the difference between a bailment and a sale, see *South Australian Insurance Co v Randell* (1869) L R 3 P C 101, where the insured was held entitled to insure as owner.

[4] *Dalgleish v Buchanan* 1854 16 Dunl (Ct of Sess) 322, where a coach builder was held to have an insurable interest in carriages entrusted to him for repair.

[5] For a list of bailees entitled to insure, see *Castellain v Preston* (1883) 11 Q B D 380 at 398, C A, per Bowen L J.

[6] *Crowley v Cohen* (1832) 3 B & Ad 478 (insurance on goods in canal boats); *London and North Western Rly Co v Glyn,* (supra); *Joyce v Kennard* (1871) L R 7 Q B 78 (lighterman's insurance).

[7] *Dixon v Stansfield* (1850) 10 C B 398 at 417 (marine insurance) per Jervis C J, speaking of fire insurance.

[8] *Waters v Monarch Fire and Life Assurance Co* (1856) 5 E & B 870; *Martineau v Kitching* (1872) L R 7 Q B 436.

[9] *Sidaways v Todd* (1818) 2 Stark 400; *North British and Mercantile Insurance Co v London, Liverpool and Globe Insurance Co* (1877) 5 Ch D 569 at 398, C A, per Bowen L J. It is immaterial in this connection whether the insured is a factor, warehouseman, or wharfinger, the insurable interest of each in the goods entrusted to him depending on the same principles.

[10] *Sutherland v Pratt* (1843) 12 M & W 16 (marine insurance).

[11] A hirer under a hire-purchase agreement is not bound to insure the property, apart from a special contract: *Viviers v Juta & Co* (1902) 19 S C 222.

[12] (1856) 5 E & B 870.

[13] Lord Campbell C J, Wightman and Crompton J J.

[14] (1856) 5 E & B 870 at 881.

make good 'all such damage and loss as may happen by fire to the property hereinbefore mentioned.' That is a valid contract; and, as the property is wholly destroyed, the value of the whole must be made good, not merely the particular interest of the [insured]. They will be entitled to apply so much to cover their own interest, and will be trustees for the owners as to the rest.'

Crompton J, added:[15]

'The parties meant to insure those goods with which the [insured] were entrusted, and in every part of which they had an interest, both in respect of their lien and in respect of their responsibility to their bailors. What the surplus after satisfying their own claim might be, could only be ascertained after the loss, when the amount of their lien at that time was determined; but they were persons interested in every particle of the goods.'

(b) Tenants

Any tenant, including the lessee from year to year, although there may be no covenant or agreement to insure the property let to him, may do so by virtue of his beneficial enjoyment of the property of which he will be deprived in the event of its being destroyed.[16]

(c) Equitable Mortgagees

Although a creditor has no insurable interest in the property of his debtor by reason of his debt, nevertheless, if his debt is secured by an equitable mortgage upon specific property,[17] or if he has a lien[18] or charge,[19] or a similar equitable interest[20] upon specific property, he may insure such property,[1] but such property only.[2]

---

15 Ibid, at 882. See also the judgment of Wightman J, ibid, at 881.

16 *Simpson v Scottish Union Insurance Co* (1863) 1 Hem & M 618; *Castellain v Preston,* (supra), at 398, per Bowen L J; *Mutual Fire Insurance Co v Paquet Co* (1912) Q R 21 K B 419. Cf *Callaway v Ward* (1730) cited in 1 Ves at 318, where the lease had expired and the tenant had contracted for a new one.

17 *Westminster Fire Office v Glasgow Provident Investment Society* (1888) 13 App Cas 699; *Western Australian Bank v Royal Insurance Co* (1908) 5 C L R 533.

18 *Parker v Beasley* (1814) 2 M & S 423 at 426 (marine insurance) per Lord Ellenborough C J.

19 *General Accident, Fire and Life Assurance Corpn Ltd v Midland Bank Ltd* [1940] 2 K B 388, C A, where the bank held as security for an overdraft a floating charge on the property of the customer.

20 *Ebsworth v Alliance Marine Insurance Co* (1873) L R 8 C P 596 (marine insurance); *Hill v Secretan* (1798) 1 Bos & P 325 (marine insurance); *Clark v Scottish Imperial Fire Insurance Co* (1879) 4 S C R 192, where a person who had made advances to enable a ship to be built on the faith of a verbal promise that he was to have the selling of her, and was to repay himself out of the proceeds, was held to have an insurable interest in the ship during her construction; *Davies v Home Insurance Co* (1866) 3 E & A 269, where an accommodation indorser was held to have an insurable interest in goods the proceeds of which were to be applied in discharge of the notes indorsed by him.

1 *Westminster Fire Office v Glasgow Provident Investment Society,* (supra), at 708, 709, per Lord Halsbury L C; 'The error of law, I think, is in the suggestion that a creditor had not an insurable interest in the property of his debtor upon which property the debtor has given him a heritable security. I should have thought it was too well settled a proposition in insurance law to be susceptible of argument that a creditor under those circumstances is entitled to insure'.

2 *Milcher v Kingwilliamstown Fire and Marine Insurance Co* (1883) 3 Buchanan East Dist Ct (Cape) 271, where it was held that the holder of a general bond had no insurable interest in the property not affected by the bond.

A mere licence, however, to seize or retake property in a certain event does not, apparently, give an insurable interest to the licensee.[3]

(d) Persons Liable Over

A person is entitled to insure property when he has undertaken to its owner to be responsible for its loss.[4] Whether he is in possession of the property, as in the case of a carrier, or whether he is not, is immaterial, since his insurable interest in this connection depends not on any benefit which he is to derive from its safety, but on the prejudice which he will suffer on its loss.[5]

It is for this reason that an insurer has an insurable interest in the subject-matter of his insurance. He is, therefore, entitled to protect himself by reinsurance.

It is not, as a rule, necessary for the person insuring against a liability to arise under a contract, to indicate to his insurers the nature of his insurance, but he may, by an express term of the contract, be required to do so.

The right to insure need not be based on the existence of any contract relating to the subject-matter of insurance; it may be based upon possession. Any person who is in possession of property as its apparent owner is entitled to insure it.[6] Possession under a claim of ownership is not, however, necessary; possession of any kind,[7] if lawful,[8] is sufficient.[9] Thus, a person who finds property and takes it into his possesion may insure it.[10]

A person who may become liable to another by reason of the destruction of the latter's property, but whose liability is not based on any contract or on the possession of the property destroyed, may protect himself by insurance against such liability provided that he specifically insures against it.

---

[3] *Stainbank v Fenning* (1871) 11 C B 51 at 75 (marine insurance) per Jervis C J; *Stainbank v Shepard* (1853) 13 C B 418 at 443, Ex Ch (marine insurance) per Parke B.

[4] *Crowley v Cohen* (1832) 3 B & Ad 478 (insurance on canal boats); *Heckman v Isaac* (1862) 6 L T 383; *Joyce v Swann* (1864) 17 C B N S 84 at 104, (marine insurance) per Willes J, speaking of fire insurance.

[5] *Heckman v Issac*, (supra); *Klein v Union Fire Insurance Co* (1883) 3 O R 234, where property belonging to a firm was mortgaged, and it was held that a retired partner retained an insurable interest by reason of a covenant to insure contained in the mortgage deed, and also of his liability under the mortgage deed.

[6] *Marks v Hamilton* (1852) 7 Exch 323 at 324, per Pollock C B.

[7] A person, who merely permits the property of another to remain on his land, has no insurable interest in it: *Macaura v Northern Assurance Co* [1925] A C 619 at 628, per Lord Buckmaster.

[8] *Stirling v Vaughan* (1809) 11 East 619 (marine insurance).

[9] *Lucena v Craufurd* (1806) 2 Bos & P N R 269 at 323, H L (marine insurance) per Lord Eldon: 'The captors not only had the possession, but a possession coupled with the liability to pay costs and charges if they had taken possession improperly . . . I should be disposed to say that the King had an insurable interest as the person who had the *jus possessionis.* ' See also *Dixon v Whitworth* (1879) 4 C P D 371 at 375 (marine insurance) per Lindley J.

[10] *Marks v Hamilton,* as reported (1852) 21 L J Ex 109 at 110, per Pollock C B.

(e) Statutory Bodies

Certain statutory bodies, such as development boards set up under the Agricultural Marketing Act 1958, are authorised to insure commodities under their control.[11]

---

[11] Agricultural Marketing Act 1958, s 7 (1) (h).

CHAPTER 7

Persons not entitled to insure

A person who has no insurable interest in a particular object cannot insure it.[1]

Thus, a creditor for an ordinary debt, which is not in any way secured by a lien or charge of any kind on specific property, cannot insure his debtor's property,[2] since his right is against the debtor personally,[3] and not against his property.

Similarly, a shareholder in a company cannot insure the property of the company, since he has no insurable interest in any particular asset of the company, and it is immaterial that the company is a one-man company and that he is the sole shareholder in the company.[4]

Thus, in *Macaura v Northern Assurance Co Ltd*[5] a shareholder of almost all the shares in a company owning some timber was owed a large sum of money by the company, so on his own behalf he insured the timber against loss by fire. A fire occurred, and he claimed an indemnity from the insurance company, but liability was repudiated on the ground that he had no insurable interest in the timber.

The House of Lords[6] held that the claim failed because neither as a creditor nor as a shareholder had he an insurable interest. Lord Buckmaster in referring to the insured in his capacity of creditor said:[7]

> 'As a creditor his position appears to me quite incapable of supporting the claim. If his contention were right, it would follow that any person would be at liberty to insure the furniture of his debtor, and no such claim has ever been recognised by the Courts. It is true that since *Godsall v Boldero*,[8] where a creditor of Mr Pitt was held entitled to effect an insurance upon his life, this interest has always been recognised, but this depends, as was said by Lord Ellenborough, upon the means and probability of payment which the continuance of a debtor's life affords to his creditors and the probability of loss which would result from his death.'

---

[1] As to 'insurable interest', see Chapter 4 , ante, and Ivamy , *General Principles of Insurance Law* (4th Edn, 1979), pp 20–31.

[2] *Macaura v Northern Assurance Co Ltd* [1925] A C 619 at 626 per Lord Buckmaster, approving *Moran, Galloway & Co v Uzielli* [1905] 2 K B 555 at 562 (marine insurance) per Walton J; *Wolff v Horncastle* (1798) 1 Bos & P 316 at 323 (marine insurance) per Buller J.

[3] This is the reason why he has an insurable interest in his debtor's life to the amount of his debt: *Dalby v India and London Life Assurance Co* (1854) 15 C B 365 (life insurance); *Hebdon v West* (1863) 3 B & S 579 (life insurance).

[4] *Macaura v Northern Assurance Co Ltd,* (supra), discussing *Paterson v Harris* (1861) 1 B & S 336 (marine insurance) and *Wilson v Jones* (1867) L R 2 Exch 139 (marine insurance); *General Accident, Fire and Life Assurance Corp Ltd v Midland Bank Ltd* [1940] 2 K B 388 at 401, C A, per Greene M R.

[5] [1925] All E R Rep 51.

[6] Lord Buckmaster, Lord Atkinson, Lord Sumner, Lord Wrenbury and Lord Phillimore.

[7] [1925] All E R Rep 51 at 53.

[8] (1807) 9 East 72.

Further, in relation to the insured's capacity as a shareholder he remarked:[9]

'Turning now to his position as shareholder, this must be independent of the extent of his share interest. If he were entitled to insure because he held all the shares in the company, each shareholder would be equally entitled, if the shares were all in separate hands. Now, no shareholder has any right to any item of property owned by the company, for he has no legal or equitable interest therein. He is entitled to a share in the profits while the company continues to carry on business and a share in the distribution of the surplus assets when the company is wound-up. If he were at liberty to effect an insurance against loss by fire of any item of the company's property, the extent of his insurable interest could only be measured by determining the extent to which his share in the ultimate distribution would be diminished by the loss of the assets—a calculation almost impossible to make. There is no means by which such an interest can be definitely measured and no standard which can be fixed of the loss against which the contract of insurance could be regarded as an indemnity.'

That the insured had no insurable interest either as a creditor or as a share-holder was also stressed by Lord Sumner in his judgment:[10]

'It is clear that the [insured] had no insurable interest in the timber described. It was not his. It belonged to the Irish Canadian Sawmill Co Ltd of Skibbereen, Co Cork. He had no lien or security over it, and, though it lay on his land by his permission, he had no responsibility to its owner for its safety, nor was it there under any contract that enabled him to hold it for his debt. He owned almost all the shares in the company, and the company owed him a good deal of money, but, neither as creditor nor as shareholder, could he insure the company's assets. The debt was not exposed to fire nor were the shares, and the fact that he was virtually the company's only creditor, while the timber was its only asset, seems to me to make no difference. He stood in no "legal or equitable relation to" the timber at all. He had no "concern in" the subject insured. His relation was to the company, not to its goods, and after the fire he was directly prejudiced by the paucity of the company's assets, not by the fire.'

Whether an agricultural tenant who quitted his farm, still had an insurable interest in the hay and straw was considered in *Thomas v National Farmers Union Mutual Insurance Co Ltd*[11] In this case the insured was a tenant farmer, who insured hay and straw at a farm against loss by fire. A condition in the policy stated:

'The policy ceases to be in force as to any property hereby insured which shall pass from the Insured to any other person otherwise than by will or operation of law unless notice thereof shall be given to the Society and the continuance of the insurance in favour of such other person be declared by endorsement hereon and registered in the books of the Society and the expression—the Insured— shall include any person in whose favour the insurance is so declared to be or is otherwise continued and such person shall thereupon become a member of the Society.'

The insured quitted the farm on October 5, 1956. The insurers were re-quested to continue cover on the hay and straw there, and the policy was indorsed to that effect on 27 November. On 4 December the hay and straw were destroyed by fire. The insurers sought to avoid liability on the ground that under the Agricultural Holdings Act 1948, s 12 (1),[12] on the insured quitting the farm, his property in the hay and straw passed to his landlord and thereafter

---

9 [1925] All E R Rep 51 at 54.
10 Ibid, at 55.
11 [1961] 1 All E R 363, [1961] 1 WLR 386.
12 Section 12 (1) of the Act provides that: 'Where notice to terminate the tenancy of an agricultural holding is given either by the tenant or by the landlord, the tenant shall not, subject to any agreement in writing to the contrary, at any time after the date of the notice sell or remove from the holding any manure or compost or any hay or straw or roots grown in the last year of the tenancy unless before the sale or removal the landlord has consented thereto in writing.'

he had no insurable interest in the hay and straw. In its place, however, he was given the right to obtain compensation from the landlord under s 47 (1).[13]

Diplock J, held that this argument prevailed, and that the insured had no insurable interest. He observed:[14]

> 'It seems to me quite clear that at some point, either on or after the tenant quitting the holding, the property which he undoubtedly had before that date is divested from him and vested in the landlord. [Counsel] has argued that that does not occur until the amount of the compensation has been fixed by one method or other under the Act. I cannot accept that argument. It seems to me that once the tenant has quit the holding, or, in the words of s 47, 'on the termination of the tenancy, on quitting the holding', the tenant is divested of all rights in respect of the crops left on the holding pursuant to s 12 of the Act, and is granted, instead, the right to obtain compensation under the Act. He is not entitled to go on to the holding; he is not entitled to remove the hay and straw from the holding, and it seems to me that the clear scheme of the Act is that the property passes in the crops left pursuant to s 12 on the termination of the tenancy, on quitting the holding, as is stated in s 47; the property then passes to the landlord, and the tenant, instead, acquires the right to obtain compensation under the Act through the machinery which I have already dealt with.
>
> It follows, therefore, that I accept the contention of the Society that after he had quit the holding on 5 October, 1956, the claimant had no property in the hay or straw, the subject-matter of the insurance, nor had he any insurable interest therein.'

The insured argued that even if he had no insurable interest, the condition set out above had the result that his cover was not terminated by the passing of the property to the landlord as a result of the Act of 1948, for it had passed from the insured to another person by operation of law. Accordingly, it was contended, the condition had not the effect of divesting the insured of his right under the policy.

The learned Judge agreed with this argument, and held that the insured was entitled to claim under the policy and said:[15]

> 'I find great difficulty in seeing how it can be argued that that is not a passing of property by operation of law. It seems to me to be the result only of the statutory provisions to which I have referred. [Counsel] has argued that because s 12 of the Act entitles a landlord to consent in writing to the removal of hay or straw, it cannot be said that the passing of the property is by operation of law because the landlord and the tenant could have made an agreement to the contrary. I do not think that that is a sound argument and it does not seem to me to affect the meaning of the expression "operation of law". Where property passes automatically as the result of statutory provisions when certain circumstances arise, it seems to me that that is a passing of property by operation of law. It follows, therefore, that, under condition 3 (a) of the policy, it did not cease to be in force when the property passed to the claimant's landlord, his father.'

In accordance with the same principle, an agent or consignee, who has no lien on his principal's property for commission or otherwise, nor the possession or custody of it as a bailee, nor any liability to account for its loss by fire, cannot

---

[13] Section 47 (1) states that: 'The tenant shall, subject to the provisions of this Act, be entitled on the termination of the tenancy, on quitting the holding, to obtain from his landlord compensation for a new improvement carried out by the tenant and for any such matter as is specified in Part II of the Fourth Schedule to this Act. . .'.

[14] [1960] 2 Lloyd's Rep 444 at 448.

[15] Ibid, at 449. His Lordship went on to say (ibid, at 449) that, for the purposes of the dispute between the insured and the insurance company, it was unnecessary for him to express any view as to the capacity in which the insured would hold the insurance moneys when they were paid to him.

insure it on his own behalf.[16] Such an agent may, however, effect an insurance on his principal's behalf, where he has authority to do so,[17] provided that his principal has an insurable interest.

---

[16] *Seagrave v Union Marine Insurance Co* (1866) L R 1 C P 305 (marine insurance); *Ebsworth v Alliance Marine Insurance Co* (1873) L R 8 C P 596 at 643 (marine insurance) per Brett J.

[17] *French v Backhouse* (1771) 5 Burr 2727 (marine insurance). As to the effect of ratification by the principal, see Ivamy, *General Principles of Insurance Law* (4th edn, 1979), pp 569–577.

CHAPTER 8

The contents of the proposal form

The contents of the proposal form will vary from company to company. But in general they are substantially the same.[1]

Thus, the proposer has to state his name and addresses, and in the case of a firm, the name and addresses of all the partners, or, in the case of a limited company, the names and addresses of all the directors.

The business or profession must be given together with the situation of the property to be insured. The proposer has to describe the property to be insured, with the amount in respect of each item. He has to say how the building proposed to be insured is lighted, heated, and protected against fire.

He must disclose whether any manufacturing process or any hazardous trade is carried on in the building or near it.

If the property or any part of it is already covered by insurance against fire, the details of such insurance must be given.

There is always a question whether a previous proposal for fire insurance has ever been made by or on behalf of the proposer or ever been declined or accepted at an increased rate of premium.

Sometimes the proposer is asked whether a proposal in respect of any type of insurance policy has ever been declined and whether any insurance policy which has been effected by him has ever been cancelled or discontinued.

He is also required to state whether any property belonging to him has ever been destroyed by fire.

The proposer is also asked whether there are any other facts within his knowledge which are material to the insurance proposed. If so, he must give particulars of them.

The proposal form ends in a declaration, which has to be completed by the proposer. This states that he agrees that the answers to the questions are to be the basis of the contract,[2] and if any untrue statement has been made, the insurance policy will be null and void.

Proposal forms are used only occasionally in the negotiation of a Lloyd's policy.

---

[1] With the kind permission of the Sun Alliance & London Insurance Group, specimen proposal forms in current use issued by that company are reproduced in Appendix I.

[2] As to the 'basis clause', see Ivamy, *General Principles of Insurance Law* (4th edn, 1979), pp 181–183.

CHAPTER 9

The description of the subject-matter

It is the duty of the insured at the time of effecting the insurance to give to the insurers an adequate description of the property to be insured.[1]

The description required from the insured in fulfilment of his duty is not necessarily a description of the property alone. It may extend to a description of the locality in which the property is situated, or the purpose for which it is used, or any other material circumstances. In practice, the proposal form usually contains questions relating to the information which the insurers desire.[2]

DESCRIPTION OF THE PROPERTY ITSELF

The description of the subject-matter of insurance forms the basis of the contract, since the insurers are guided by it in accepting the insurance and in fixing the premium to be charged.[3] On its completeness and fairness, therefore, the validity of the contract depends.

Apart from this, a description of the subject-matter of insurance is an essential part of the contract, since, in the absence of any description, there is no contract.[4] For the purpose of identification this description must be an adequate description of the subject-matter.[5]

The subject-matter must be clearly identified with a particular object, because insurers do not, by their contract, undertake to indemnify the insured against loss by fire generally, but only against loss arising from the destruction of the specific object insured,[6] and the identity of any object destroyed with the subject-matter can only be established by reference to the description contained in the contract. Where, therefore, property belonging to the insured is destroyed by fire, and he seeks to recover under a contract of insurance, it is not sufficient for him to show that he intended to insure it. To entitle him to recover he must show:

---

[1] *Quin v National Assurance Co* (1839) Jo & Car 316, Ex Ch, where an unfurnished house in charge of a carpenter, who worked there daily, was held to be improperly described as a dwelling house occupied by a caretaker. Cf *A F Watkinson & Co Ltd v Hullett* (1938) 61 Ll L Rep 145 where, on a description of a business as 'paper boards', a stock of wastepaper was not covered.

[2] As to the contents of proposal forms, see p 38, ante.

[3] *Sillem v Thornton* (1854) 3 E & B 868 at 884 per Lord Campbell CJ, approved on this point in *Thompson v Hopper* (1858) E B & E 1038 at 1049, Ex Ch.

[4] *Griffiths v Bramley-Moore* (1878) 4 QBD 70 at 73, CA (marine insurance) per Brett LJ.

[5] *MacKenzie v Whitworth* (1875) 1 Ex D 36 at 40, CA, per Blackburn J (marine insurance); *Palmer v Pratt* (1824) 2 Bing 185 (marine insurance).

[6] *Collingridge v Royal Exchange Assurance Corpn* (1877) 3 QBD 173; and see the cases cited in the preceding note.

1   that it is, in fact, the property contemplated by the contract as the subject-matter of insurance; and
2   that it answers the description of the subject-matter contained in the contract under which he claims.

Unless he satisfies the Court on both these points, his action on the contract will fail.

1 Scope of the Description

It is not necessary that the description should so be framed as to specify a particular object. It may be expressed in general terms, and may specify a class of objects only.

Thus, it is sufficient to insure property under the description of 'goods' or 'stock-in-trade'.

Whether the description is specific or generic in its terms, it is intended to apply to a particular object.

The identity of the subject-matter, as described in the contract, with such object must, therefore, be established, and for this purpose parol evidence is, in case of need, admissible.[7]

If it is impossible to identify it with any particular object by reason of there being several objects all answering the description, and each of them equally likely to be the subject-matter of insurance, the contract is void for uncertainty.[8]

Similarly, if there is no object in existence to which the description is capable of being applied, the contract probably cannot be treated as insuring another object which does not answer the description; for the words will not be given a construction of which they are not fairly capable on a mere conjecture as to what the intention of the parties may have been.[9]

When property is insured under a description so specific as to be inapplicable to any other property, the contract relates to such property only, and not to any property of a similar kind which may be substituted for it.[10] This is so even where, from the nature of the property, its substitution by other property of a similar kind may be reasonably contemplated; for any such intention is inconsistent with the language which the parties have chosen to adopt.[11]

---

[7] See Ivamy, *General Principles of Insurance Law* (4th edn, 1979), p 243.

[8] Cf *Roberts v Anglo-Saxon Insurance Association Ltd* (1927) 96 LJ K B 590 at 594, C A, per Scrutton LJ. Where, however, there are, for instance, two buildings each of which corresponds with the description in the contract, and one of them is at the date of the contract already destroyed by fire to the knowledge of the insurers, the building undestroyed is clearly the subject-matter of the insurance.

[9] In *Joel v Harvey* (1857) 29 LTOS 75, where hops were held not to be covered under the description of 'stock-in-trade consisting of corn, seed, etc', Wightman J, was of the opinion that if there had been nothing on the premises but hops, the description might have been applicable, whilst Crompton J, was of the contrary opinion inasmuch as goods answering the description might have been brought upon the premises from time to time. The latter opinion appears to be correct.

[10] *Gorman v Hand-in-Hand Insurance Co* (1877) I R 11 C L 224; *Grant v Paxton* (1809) 1 Taunt 463 (marine insurance).

[11] *Gorman v Hand-in-Hand Insurance Co*, (supra), where the two ricks of hay in existence at the date of the policy were held to be specifically insured, and consequently the policy did not extend to cover the ricks which subsequently took their place.

Where, however, both parties contemplate that the property in existence at the date of the contract is from time to time to be consumed, or otherwise made use of, and that other property answering the description is to be substituted for it, they may, by using a description in sufficiently general terms, bring the substituted property within the terms of the contract,[12] notwithstanding that it was not in existence at the time when the contract was entered into.[13]

In such a case it may be said that the real subject-matter of insurance is the class designated by the description, and that, although the class must necessarily be represented by objects falling within the description, and, therefore, members of the class, a change in the identity of individual objects does not affect the identity of the class.

2 Adequacy of the Description

Where the description contained in the contract accurately describes the property intended to be insured, there is an adequate description of the subject-matter.[14] The insured is, therefore, entitled to recover on his contract in the event of such property being destroyed by fire. In this case parol evidence is admissible, if necessary, to establish the identity of the property destroyed with the subject-matter of insurance.

Thus, in *Doe d Pitt v Laming*[15] the lessee of Grigsby's Coffee House in the City of London was under a duty imposed on him by the terms of the lease to effect a policy of fire insurance in respect of the premises. His landlord claimed that the lease was forfeited because he had not taken out a sufficient policy, for it enumerated several trades which were considered as 'double hazardous', and declared that no insurance should be valid where any such trade was carried on unless a premium was paid in proportion. Among these trades was that of an innkeeper. The premium paid on the premises was the usual one. The landlord contended that the Coffee House was an inn, and, therefore, uninsured.

Lord Ellenborough CJ rejected this argument and held that an effective policy had been taken out, and that the claim for forfeiture failed. He observed:[16]

---

12 Ibid, at 235, per Palles CB; *Hill v Patten* (1807) 8 East 373 at 377 (marine insurance) per Ellenborough CJ; *Grant v Delacour* (1806), cited in 1 Taunt 465 (marine insurance); *Anstey v Ocean Marine Insurance Co Ltd* (1913) 109 LT 854 (marine insurance); *British American Insurance Co v Joseph* (1857) 9 LCR 448 (coal in store); *Clark v Western Assurance Co* (1866) 25 UCR 209 (wheat in warehouse). The renewal of an insurance may show an intention to use a term of description generically, and not as applicable to a specific object: *Merchants' Fire Insurance Co v Equity Fire Insurance Co* (1905) 9 OLR 241, where the insurance was on 120 sacks of coffee.

13 *Butler v Standard Fire Insurance Co* (1879) 4 OAR 391, where, under a policy on stock-in-trade, the insured was held entitled to recover under the policy, although the greater part of her stock at the time of effecting the insurance had been disposed of and other goods had been purchased. See also *Joel v Harvey* (1857) 5 WR 488 at 488, per Crompton J.

14 *Doe d Pitt v Laming* (1814) 4 Camp 73; *South Australian Insurance Co v Randell* (1869) LR 3 PC 101, where corn deposited with a miller by farmers on the terms that at any time an equivalent quantity of corn (but not necessarily the same corn) might be redelivered to the farmers was held to be adequately described as the sellers' own property, and not as 'goods in trust', which by the terms of the contract had to be specifically insured; *Malin v Union Assurance Co* (1910) 13 WLR 653, where a misdescription in the proposal was corrected in the policy.

15 (1814) 4 Camp 73 NP.

16 Ibid, at 77

'Grigsby's Coffee-house I happen to know is like any other coffee-house in the metropolis; and I think a coffee-house is not an inn within the meaning of the policy. Horses, waggons, and coaches come to an inn; there are stables and outhouses attached to it; people are going to these with lights at all hours; hence there is an increased danger of fire, and the trade of an innkeeper is considered double hazardous. But the trade of a coffee-house keeper is of a very different description.'

Where the description substantially describes the property intended to be insured, the description is adequate, notwithstanding that it might have been more complete.[17] Thus, an insurance on a 'lease' covers an agreement for a lease.[18]

Where the description is inappropriate to the property intended to be insured, there is not an adequate description of the subject-matter. The insured cannot, therefore, recover in the event of such property being destroyed by fire.

The description may be inappropriate where the property destroyed belongs to a species differing from that described in the contract. Thus, it is a misdescription to describe a building of 3 storeys as a building of 2 storeys,[19] or an unfinished house occupied by a carpenter for the purpose of working at his trade as a dwelling-house occupied by a caretaker,[20] or a document in the form of a bill of exchange, but payable only on a contingency, as a bill of exchange.[1] In this case parol evidence is not admissible to show that it was, in fact, intended to insure the property under such description.[2]

The description may also be inappropriate where the property destroyed falls literally within the description, but it may clearly appear from the language of the contract and the surrounding circumstances that it was never intended to include the particular property under the description.[3]

Thus, in *Watchorn v Langford*[4] a coach-plater and cow-keeper insured his stock-in-trade, household furniture, linen, wearing apparel and plate under a fire policy. A fire occurred at his premises and amongst other things destroyed was a large stock of linen drapery goods, which he had purchased a short time beforehand on speculation. He claimed an indemnity from the insurer on the ground that the goods fell within the description 'linen' in the policy.

---

[17] *Hall v Janson* (1855) 4 E & B 500 at 509 (marine insurance) per Lord Campbell C J.

[18] *Palmer v Pratt* (1824) 2 Bing 185 at 192 (marine insurance) per Burrough J.

[19] *Sillem v Thornton* (1854) 3 E & B 868, as explained in *Stokes v Cox* (1856) 1 H & N 533, Ex Ch.

[20] *Quin v National Assurance Co* (1839) Jo & Car 316; cf *Shanahan v Norwich Union Fire Insurance Society* (1914) 33 NZLR 833, where outside extensions were not covered unless mentioned in the policy; *Dia v County Fire Office Ltd* (1930) 37 Ll L Rep 24 (burglary insurance), where a residential flat, in which a doctor had installed an assistant, but in which he himself had never resided, was held not to fall within the description 'the assured's private dwelling'.

[1] *Palmer v Pratt*, (supra).

[2] *Hare v Barstow* (1844) 8 Jur 928; cf *Joel v Harvey* (1857) 5 W R 488; *Hutchinson v Niagara District Mutual Fire Insurance Co* (1876) 39 U C R 483, where paper bags were held not covered by an insurance on the 'tools' of a flour mill. Thus, a policy on a 'building and fixtures' does not include 'furniture', and parol evidence is not admissible to show that it was intended. See also *Platt v Young* (1843) 2 L T O S 17, 370, where an insurance on goods in a building was held not to cover goods in an open space around the building, and parol evidence to show the intention of the parties was rejected.

[3] *Scott v Globe Marine Insurance Co Ltd* (1896) 1 Com Cas 370 (marine insurance).

[4] (1813) 3 Camp 422, N P.

It was held that the action failed, Lord Ellenborough CJ, saying:[5]

'I am clearly of opinion that the word "linen" in the policy does not include articles of this description. Here we may apply *noscitur a sociis* . The preceding words are "household furniture", and the succeeding "wearing apparel". The "linen" must be "household linen or apparel".'

Where the description is expressed in clear and unequivocal language, the meaning of the description is a question for the Court, to be determined by the construction of the words which the parties have chosen to insert in the contract. For this purpose the ordinary rules governing the construction of a written contract apply. Words of description must, therefore, be understood in their plain ordinary meaning[6] as controlled by the context of the document containing them or by the surrounding circumstances.[7] Thus, the meaning of the term 'stock-in-trade' depends on the trade carried on by the insured,[8] but its application even as regards a particular trade may be narrowed by the language of the contract.[9] Parol evidence is not admissible to show that the words of description used in a particular contract were intended to apply to the property destroyed, if they do not adequately describe it, since the intention of the parties is to be gathered from the language of the contract only.[10]

Where the language of the description is ambiguous, eg where the street number is not correct,[11] or where it is contended that such language is not to be taken in its ordinary meaning, but is to be construed with reference to some usage or custom of trade restricting or extending the sense in which it was used,[12] parol evidence is admissible to show that the words of description, when understood in the meaning intended[13] to be attached to them by the parties, adequately describe the property destroyed.[14]

---

[5] Ibid, at 423.

[6] Thus, a stock of valuable furs is not 'general merchandise': *Herman v Phoenix Assurance Co Ltd* (1924) 18 Ll L Rep 371, CA; 'steel' is not 'iron': *Hart v Standard Marine Insurance Co* (1889) 22 QBD 499 at 502, CA (marine insurance) per Bowen LJ; 'goods' does not include wearing apparel: *Ross v Thwaite* (1776) 1 Park's Marine Insces 8th Edn, p 23 (marine insurance); or personal effects: *Brown v Stapyleton* (1827) 4 Bing 119 (marine insurance).

[7] *Bishop Fredericton v Union Assurance Co* (1911) 10 E L R 243, where a chime of bells was held to fall within the words 'all church furniture and fixtures', and not to be part of the fabric of the church.

[8] *Watchorn v Langford* (1813) 3 Camp 422; *Nicholson v Phoenix Insurance Co* (1880) 45 U C R 359, where it was held that a 'stock of groceries' included liquor.

[9] Thus, where there is an insurance on 'stock-in-trade consisting of corn, seed, hay, straw, fixtures, and utensils in business', other articles, such as 'hops and malting' are excluded, though they would have been covered if the insurance had been upon 'stock-in-trade' only: *Joel v Harvey* (1857) 5 W R 488.

[10] *Hare v Barstow* (1844) 8 Jur 928; *Watchorn v Langford,* (supra).

[11] *Hordern v Commerical Union Insurance Co* (1887) 56 LJPC 78; *Gélinas et Frères Ltee v Stanstead and Sherbrooke Montreal Fire Assurance Co* (1919) QR 57 SC 368. Cf *Liverpool and London and Globe Insurance Co v Wyld* (1877) 1 S C R 604.

[12] *Scott v Bourdillion* (1806) 2 Bos & P N R 213 (marine insurance).

[13] The amount of the premium may be evidence of the intention of the parties: *Shannon v Gore District Mutual Fire Insurance Co* (1878) 2 Tupper's R (N B) 396, where an insurance on a 'grist mill' was held to cover fixed and movable machinery.

[14] Cf *Hart v Standard Marine Insurance Co* (1889) 22 QBD 499 at 502, CA (marine insurance) per Bowen LJ, where the learned Judge pointed out that although 'steel' goods fall within a warranty against 'iron' goods so as to be excluded from the benefit of the insurance, they were not included under a description of the subject-matter as 'iron' goods.

DESCRIPTION OF THE LOCALITY OF THE PROPERTY

Since the danger of fire varies according to the place where the subject-matter of insurance happens to be, an insurance against fire is necessarily concerned with the locality in which the subject-matter is situated. A statement, therefore, as to the locality usually forms part of the description of the subject-matter required by the contract.

For the purpose of identifying the subject-matter, a statement as to its locality may be a necessary part of the description. Even when the statement is not necessary, it is, if included in the description, a material part of it. In either case, therefore, no property can be said to answer the description unless it is, in fact, situated in the stated locality.[15]

It is also necessary that the locality itself, as well as the subject-matter, should be adequately described.

Where the subject-matter of insurance is houses, buildings, or other immovable property, its locality forms, for the purposes of identification, an essential part of the description. If, therefore, the property destroyed is not situated in the locality described, it is incapable of being identified with the subject-matter of insurance, and is not covered by the contract.[16]

Where the subject-matter of insurance is goods or other movable property, the locality in which the subject-matter of insurance is situated may be an essential part of the description. This is clearly the case where, for instance, the goods insured are described generally as being in a particular place without being otherwise identified; for without such a statement, it would be practically impossible to identify the subject-matter, and the contract would be void for uncertainty.[17] It is, moreover, usual, even where it is not necessary, to include in the description a statement as to locality, and the locality is thereby made material for the purpose of identification.[18]

Wherever a statement as to locality is included in the description, the identity of the subject-matter depends on its locality. To entitle the insured to recover, in case of loss, it is necessary for him to have complied with the following rules:

a   The locality contemplated by the contract must be correctly described.
b   The place in which the property insured is situated must be the locality described in the contract.
c   The property insured must be in the locality described both at the time of effecting the policy and at the date of the loss.

---

[15] *Gorman v Hand-in-Hand Insurance Co* (1877) I R 11 C L 224 (fire insurance); *Grover & Grover Ltd v Mathews* (1910) 15 Com Cas 249 at 260 (fire insurance) per Hamilton J, at p 260.

[16] *Grover & Grover Ltd v Mathews,* (supra), (fire insurance). Cf *Renshaw v Phoenix Insurance Co* [1943] O R 223, where the insured had bodily removed a summer cottage from one location to another.

[17] Cf *Ionides v Pacific Insurance Co* (1871) L R 6 Q B 674 at 683 (marine insurance) per Blackburn J.

[18] *Gorman v Hand-in-Hand Insurance Co,* (supra) (fire insurance).

(a) Correct Description

It is very important that the locality should be correctly described.[19] A substantial misdescription of the location is fatal,[20] unless such description is the fault, not of the insured, but of the insurers.[1]

(b) Locality must be that Described in the Contract

It is vital that the place in which the property insured is situated is the same as the locality described in the contract.[2] As the locality forms part of the description, this is to be ascertained in accordance with the rules which regulate the adequacy of the description of the subject-matter.[3]

(c) Time at which the Property must be in the Locality

Where the property insured is not in the described locality both at the time of effecting the policy and at the date of the loss, it is not within the description.[4] Where the property insured is removed from the locality in which it is described as being, it ceases to be the subject-matter of insurance, inasmuch as it is no longer within the description.[5] If it is afterwards replaced in the described locality, it will again become the subject-matter of insurance, provided that

---

[19] *Newcastle Fire Insurance Co v Macmorran & Co* (1815) 3 Dow 225, H L; cf *Casey v Goldsmid* (1853) 4 L C R 107.

[20] *Grover & Grover Ltd v Mathews*, (supra).

[1] *Re Universal Non-Tariff Fire Insurance Co, Forbes & Co's Claim* (1875) L R 19 Eq 485, where the agent of the insurers wrongly described the material of which part of the premises was constructed; *Liverpool and London and Globe Insurance Co v Wyld* (1877) 1 S C R 604, where the insurers' agents omitted to include in the description the part of the building in which the goods actually were; *Somers v Athenaeum Fire Insurance Co* (1858) 9 L C R 61, where the insurers' agent wrongly copied and transmitted to the head office a diagram of the premises insured.

[2] *Australian Agricultural Co v Saunders* (1875) L R 10 C P 668; *Allom v Property Insurance Co* (1911) Times, Commercial Supplement, 10 February; *City Tailors Ltd v Evans* (1921) 126 L T 439 at 443, C A, per Scrutton LJ; *Holcombe v London Assurance* (1904) 4 S R (N S W) 198, where the goods insured in transit to a particular port were burned en route for a different port; cf *Fisher, Reeves & Co v Armour & Co* [1920] 3 K B 614 at 619, 622, C A (sale of goods) per Scrutton L J, distinguished in *Wulfson v Switzerland General Insurance Co Ltd* [1940] 3 All E R 221 ('all risks' insurance).

[3] Goods insured when in a 'garage' are not insured when in an enclosed but unroofed yard: *Barnett and Block v National Parcels Insurance Co Ltd* [1942] 2 All E R 55n, C A (burglary insurance). But a 'store' may include such a yard: *Wulfson v. Switzerland General Insurance Co Ltd*, (supra).

[4] *Gorman v Hand-in-Hand Insurance Co* (1877) I R 11 C L 224; *Ewing & Co v Sicklemore* (1918) 25 T L R 55, C A (war insurance); *Pennsylvania Co for Insurances on Lives and Granting Annuities v Mumford* [1920] 2 K B 537, C A (theft insurance); *Re Traders and General Insurance Association, ex p Continental and Overseas Trading Co Ltd* [1924] 2 Ch 187 (marine insurance); *Rolland v North British and Mercantile Insurance Co* (1869) 14 L C J 69; cf *Halhead v Young* (1856) 6 E & B 312 (marine insurance).

[5] *Pearson v Commercial Union Assurance Co* (1876) 1 App Cas 498; *Furber v Cobb* (1887) 18 Q B D 494 at 505 C A (bill of sale) per Hannen P; *Gorman v Hand-in-Hand Insurance Co*, (supra); *Arnold v British Colonial Fire Insurance Co* (1917) 45 N B R 285; cf *Smellie v British General Insurance Co* [1918] W C & Ins Rep 233 (liability insurance); *Roberts v Anglo-Saxon Insurance Association Ltd* (1927) 137 L T 243, C A (accident insurance). But removal of the engine from a motor lorry for the purpose of repairs did not take it out of the insurance in *Seaton v London General Insurance Co Ltd* (1932) 48 T L R 574. See p 229, post.

from its nature such removal and replacing were contemplated at the date of the contract.[6]

If, however, its removal and replacing were not so contemplated, the question whether the contract comes to an end or is merely suspended during the removal of the property depends on the effect of the description in the policy. If the description is merely one of identification or a statement of intention, and not a warranty or comprised in a condition that the property will not be removed, the contract revives on replacement.[7] Otherwise the consent of the insurers is necessary for revival.[8]

The parties may, by their contract, expressly provide for the substitution of a new locality to which the property insured is to be removed. In such a case the new locality becomes, and the old locality ceases to be, part of the description, so that property remaining in the old locality after the date of the substitution will no longer be the subject-matter of insurance,[9] unless the contract expressly so provides.

---

[6] *Pearson v Commercial Union Assurance Co* (1873) L R 8 C P 548 at 549, Ex Ch per Blackburn J; *Gorman v Hand-in-Hand Insurance Co* , (supra), where the insurance was on horses and agricultural machines, then being in a specified place, and it was held that although the policy ceased to attach when the horses or machines were removed from that place, nevertheless, on their being replaced there, it re-attached, since their frequent removal from the specified place was essential.

[7] *Provincial Insurance Co Ltd v Morgan and Foxon* [1933] A C 240, H L (accident insurance).

[8] *Kline Bros & Co v Dominion Fire Insurance Co* (1912) 47 S C R 252.

[9] *McClure v Lancashire Insurance Co* (1860) 6 Ir Jur 63, where, in the course of removal, a fire broke out and destroyed part of the property which was awaiting removal to the new locality.

CHAPTER 10

Non-disclosure and misrepresentation

As in the case of all other branches of the law of insurance the insured is under a duty to make a full disclosure of all material facts, and not to make a misrepresentation of material facts.

If there is no 'basis clause' in the proposal form or the policy, the insurer is entitled to avoid the policy only where the fact which has not been disclosed or which has been misrepresented is a material one.[1]

But where there is a 'basis clause',[2] the insurer can avoid the policy whether the fact which has not been disclosed or which has been misrepresented is material or not.[3]

This Chapter relates to:

1   Examples of material and immaterial facts.[4]
2   Waiver of non-disclosure.[5]
3   Continuing warranties as to the existence of facts.[6]

EXAMPLES OF MATERIAL AND IMMATERIAL FACTS

As in other branches of insurance, whether a particular circumstance is material or not is a question of fact in each case.

The decided cases on this topic can conveniently be classified into various groups in so far as they relate to:

1   The personal details of the proposer.
2   The locality and surrounding circumstances of the property proposed to be insured.
3   The value of the property proposed to be insured.
4   Previous losses by fire experienced by the proposer.
5   Other insurers.

1 Personal Details of Proposer

(a) Previous Trading under Other Names

In *Gallé Gowns Ltd v Licenses and General Insurance Co Ltd*[7] the stock of retail

---

[1] See Ivamy, *General Principles of Insurance Law* (4th edn, 1979), pp 183–184.
[2] See ibid, pp 181–183.
[3] See ibid, p 182.
[4] See pp 46–57, post.
[5] See pp 57–58, post.
[6] See p 58, post.
[7] (1933) 47 Ll L Rep 186, K B.

costumiers was insured against fire. A fire took place, and one of the grounds[8] on which the insurance company sought to avoid liability was that there had been misrepresentation and non-disclosure of material facts.

The proposal form was completed by a Mr Hershorn, who was the chairman of the insured company. In answer to a question in the form concerning his insurance record, he replied 'See previous records Hershorn.' In fact, he did not disclose that he had previously traded under other names[9] and that many of his previous concerns were financially unstable.[10]

The jury found that there had been misrepresentation and non-disclosure of these material facts,[11] and on their verdict Branson J, gave judgment for the insurers.

(b)   Tenancy at Will

In *Anderson v Commercial Union Assurance Co*[12] a tenant at will insured some machinery and trade fixtures. The Divisional Court of the Queen's Bench Division[13] held (obiter) that the fact that the insured was only a tenant at will was a material fact which ought to have been disclosed by him, as it might have made impossible the exercise by the insurance company of its option to reinstate the premises under a reinstatement clause in the policy.

(c)   Previous Conviction

In *Woolcott v Sun Alliance and London Insurance Ltd*[14] and *Woolcott v Excess Insurance Co Ltd*[15] the previous conviction of the insured for robbery was held material. But in *Reynolds v Phoenix Assurance Co Ltd*[16] the insurers failed to prove that the insured's previous conviction for receiving stolen property 12 years earlier was material.

2   Locality and Surrounding Circumstances

(a)   Fire in Adjoining Premises

In *Bufe v Turner*[17] the insured had a warehouse next to a boatbuilder's shop in

---

8   Another contention of the insurance company was that the claim put forward by the insured was a fraudulent one. As to this aspect of the case, see p 137, post.

9   The evidence on this point is set out in the Judge's summing up; (1933) 47 LlL Rep 186 at 191.

10   This matter is reviewed ibid, at 191–192.

11   Ibid, at 193.

12   (1885) 1 TLR 511, CA. The only issue actually decided in the case was whether the company had lost its right to reinstate under the terms of the policy. The decision of the Divisional Court was later affirmed on this point by the Court of Appeal: (1885) 55 LJQB 146, CA. But the issue as to whether there had been non-disclosure of a material fact did not come before the Court of Appeal. As to reinstatement by the insurer, see Ivamy, *General Principles of Insurance Law* (4th edn, 1979), pp 487–493.

13   Manisty and Wills JJ.

14   [1978] 1 All ER 1253, [1978] 1 WLR 493.

15   [1978] 1 Lloyd's Rep 633. But a new trial was ordered: [1979] 1 Lloyd's Rep 231, CA. At the new trial it was proved that the brokers, who were employed by the insurers, knew of the criminal record, and had failed to pass on this information to the insurers: *Woolcott v Excess Insurance Co Ltd (No 2)* [1979] 2 Lloyd's Rep 210. (See the judgment of Cantley J, ibid, at 216).

16   [1978] 2 Lloyd's Rep 440. (See the judgment of Forbes J, ibid, at 461).

17   (1815) 6 Taunt 338.

Heligoland. The shop caught fire, but the fire was extinguished in half an hour. On the same evening the insured instructed his agent to insure the warehouse. Two days later a fire again broke out in the shop and spread to the warehouse. In an action on the policy the jury found that the insured should have disclosed the circumstances of the first fire because this was a material fact.[18] Consequently the insurer could avoid the policy on the ground of non-disclosure.

(b) Previous Use of Building

In *Leen v Hall*[19] a castle in County Kerry in Ireland was insured against damage from riot, civil commotion, war, rebellion and fire. It was destroyed in May 1921 by members of the Irish Republican Army during the troubles of that year. When a claim was made under the policy, the underwriter pleaded that the insured had not disclosed that the castle had been occupied for short periods by Crown forces, and that it had been used by them for the detention of Sinn Fein prisoners.

In summing up to the jury Avory J, said:[20]

> 'The central question in the case was whether it was a material fact that the [insured] should communicate to the [underwriters] that Crown forces had occupied the castle.
>
> If it was a fact that ought to have been known by the underwriters, then it was not a material fact to be communicated by the [insured]. If it was, however, a fact that would have increased the risk in the mind of a reasonable underwriter, then it would be material. Underwriters had been effecting these insurances in this part of Ireland since about November 1920, and it was for the jury to judge whether the underwriters doing this business up to May 1921, must not have known that premises of this character might probably have been occupied for a short time by the Crown forces or used for the internment of Sinn Fein prisoners.'

The jury found that it was not material to communicate these facts, presumably because they considered that they were common knowledge.

(c) Material Ground by Mill

In *Pimm v Lewis*[1] the stock-in-trade of a water corn-mill was insured under a fire policy. Rice chaff, which was more inflammable than pollard, was used in the mill, but this fact was not disclosed to the insurance company. The company's agent resided in the neighbourhood, and knew the mill well and looked at the premises when the proposal was made. In an action on the policy the insurance company pleaded that there had been non-disclosure of a material fact.

In directing the jury Martin B, said:[2]

> 'The mill had been used for years for the grinding of rice-chaff, and used publicly and openly, and the company's officer resident in the neighbourhood well knew the mill. Did the [insured] then, *"omit"* to communicate the matter which he might well presume they knew?'' It all turns on that, for there is no pretence for imputing misrepresentation, as the [insured] made no representation at all. Was the matter, however, material to be known ''to the company''? Unless it was material, there could be no defence on any ground.'

---

18 The jury acquitted the insured of any fraud or dishonest design. See ibid, at 340.

19 (1923) 16 Ll L Rep 100, K B.

20 (1923) 16 Ll L Rep 103, K B. The jury also found that it was not material for the insured to communicate to the underwriter the facts as far as he knew them of the breaking and entering of the castle 3 nights before the castle was destroyed. See on this point: ibid, at 104.

1 (1862) 2 F & F 778.

2 Ibid, at 780.

The jury returned a verdict in favour of the insured.[3]

(d)   Fireworks on premises

In *Hales v Reliance Fire and Accident Insurance Corpn Ltd*[4] a retail shopkeeper took out a Compound Retail Shopkeepers' Policy under which his premises were insured against fire and explosion. The business consisted of grocery provisions, newspapers, tobacco and confectionery. For a period round about Guy Fawkes Day substantial quantities of fireworks were kept in a tin box and not in a place of safety as required by the Explosives Act 1875. A fire started in the tin box and the fireworks exploded, damaging the shop and trade property. The insured claimed for a loss under the policy, but the insurance company repudiated liability on the ground, inter alia, that there had been non-disclosure that the fireworks would be on the premises.

McNair J, gave judgment for the insurance company on the other issues[5] which arose in the case, and so found it necessary to decide expressly whether the fact which had not been disclosed was material or not, but he said (obiter):[6]

> 'I am not satisfied that there was any obligation upon the proposer of this insurance for this particular class of shop to disclose to the underwriters the fact that fireworks would be, or might be, on the premises at this short season because I think, on the evidence, that is a matter which the underwriters must be taken to have known.'

But his Lordship went on to add:[7]

> 'On the other hand, I am far from saying that I would not feel that it was a material fact to disclose that the fireworks were not kept as required by law in a secure place. I am quite clear in my mind that if it had been disclosed that fireworks were being stored in the shop under conditions not permitted by law (that would normally be a matter which would have to be disclosed), it clearly, I should have thought, would have resulted either in the insurance not being proceeded with, or, more probably, would have resulted in the fireworks being properly protected, in which event it is extremely unlikely that this fire would have occurred.'

3   Value of Property Proposed to be Insured

(a)   Average Value of Timber

In *Price Bros & Co Ltd v C E Heath*[8] the owners of some standing timber in Canada raised money by means of an issue of debentures to the value of £1,000,000. In order to provide additional security for the debenture holders, they effected a fire policy. The policy provided that the timber area should be divided into 15 blocks, and that the insured should bear the first £15,000 loss on each block. A fire occurred, and the underwriter contended that the policy was not enforceable because it had been procured by a representation that the timber limits comprising the 15 blocks were of the average value of £150 per square mile, and this was untrue.

---

3 (1862) 2 F & F, at 780.
4 [1960] 2 Lloyd's Rep 391, QB.
5 Ie as to whether (i) there was a continuing warranty as to the existence of a fact at the time of the proposal and during the currency of the risk (see p 58, post); and (ii) an untrue answer had been given by the insured to one of the questions in the proposal form (see p 109, post).
6 [1960] 2 Lloyd's Rep 391 at 397.
7 Ibid, at 397.
8 (1928) 32 Ll L Rep 166, CA.

The Court of Appeal,[9] after consideration of oral evidence and contemporary documents, held that there had been no misrepresentation by the insured. The insured had put forward the figure of £150 per square mile as the amount of security required for the debenture holders, and not as the average value per square mile of the timber limits.

Scrutton LJ, said:[10]

'Then [the underwriter] goes on: "After much discussion it was decided that for the purposes of this insurance £150 a square mile would be sufficient." What are the purposes of this insurance?—to protect the debenture holders. It was decided then that in order to protect the debenture holders it would be enough to insure for £150 per square mile. That is exactly what the assured is saying in this case. "In some cases it seemed that even that was not necessary"—necessary for what?—necessary to protect the debenture holders. That is because in some cases the value of a limit was less; it was not necessary to have £150 per square mile on that limit: £133 is the figure on some of them—"but that value having been arrived at"—we have got now to a stage where, to protect, in [the underwriter's] view, the interests of the debenture holders £150 per square mile would be enough to insure average— "the underwriters were not prepared to insure anything except a great disaster." That means, of course, they want the assured to take something himself; they only coming in for a very big fire—to insure a very big fire. "On the basis of the valuation therefore it was ultimately settled that no claim should attach unless about 100 square miles were destroyed by one fire and then"—this second stage—"that the loss should attach after deducting the 100 square miles at £150 a mile—or £15,000 in all. Even then Messrs Price, Forbes & Co. found it impossible to place the full amounts required. Therefore, although £150 was fixed as the value per square mile, the policy had to be "not subject to average" as the full mileage on this basis could not be insured." It seems to me that that letter exactly states the present assured's contention.'

(b) 'General Merchandise'

In *Herman v Phoenix Assurance Co Ltd*[11] a merchant wished to insure some furs under a fire policy whilst they were being stored in a building in Constantinople. A cover note describing the goods as 'general merchandise' was issued to him. A fire took place. When the insured claimed under the policy, the insurance company repudiated liability on the ground that there had been non-disclosure of a material fact in that he had not stated that most of the goods to be insured were valuable furs.

The Court of Appeal[12] decided in favour of the insurance company on another ground, viz that the insured's claim was a fraudulent one,[13] but Scrutton LJ, observed with regard to the contention that there had been non-disclosure of a material fact:[14]

'I think [the insured] would have failed on misrepresentation if he had not failed on fraud. Personally, I am extremely doubtful whether, if you insure general merchandise, and the nature of the greater part of it is valuable furs, you are not guilty of concealment in not stating what you know of the nature of the goods. I do not wish to be taken as agreeing with the view the Judge has taken that, if you go to insure general merchandise and know that two-thirds of the value insured are furs of a very valuable nature, you are not guilty of concealment if you say nothing to the underwriter except that it is general merchandise.'

---

[9] Scrutton, Greer and Sankey LJJ.

[10] (1928) 32 Ll L Rep 166 at 173. See also the judgment of Greer LJ, ibid, at 174, and that of Sankey LJ, ibid, at 175.

[11] (1924) 18 Ll L Rep 371, CA.

[12] Bankes, Warrington and Scrutton, LJJ.

[13] As to this aspect of the case, see p 135, post.

[14] (1924) 32 Ll L Rep 371 at 372. See also the judgment of Bankes LJ, ibid, at 371,

4 Previous Losses by Fire

In *Condogianis v Guardian Assurance Co Ltd*[15] a proposal form in respect of a fire policy relating to some laundry premises contained a question stating:

> 'Has proponent ever been a claimant on a fire insurance company in respect of the property now proposed, or any other property? If so, state when and name of company.'

The answer given was 'Yes. 1917. Ocean'. This answer was literally true since he had claimed against the Ocean Insurance Co Ltd in respect of the burning of a car. But he omitted to state that in 1912 he had made another claim against the Liverpool and London and Globe Co Ltd in respect of the burning of another car.

The Privy Council[16] considered that the answer, although literally true, was nevertheless false when taken in relation to other relevant facts which were not stated. Consequently the insurance company was entitled to avoid liability.

Lord Shaw of Dunfermline stated:[17]

> 'The argument of the [insured], however, was that it was sufficient to answer the question, "Has proponent ever been a claimant...? If so, state when and name of company"? by answering in the singular and giving one occasion and one occasion alone. Accordingly, if, say, several years ago a proponent had been a claimant under an insurance policy, it would be sufficient for him to mention that fact and to exclude from mention the further fact that every year since that occasion he had also been a claimant upon insurance companies for fire losses. It appears to their Lordships quite plain that this would be no good answer to the question, "has proponent ever been a claimant? If so, state when?" In short, when that question is reasonably construed, it points to the insurer getting the benefit of what has been the record of the insured with regard to insurance claims. This was distinctly its intention and in their Lordships' opinion is plainly its meaning. To exclude, however, from that record what might in the easily supposed case be all its most important items, however numerous these might be, and to answer the question in the singular, which again in the easily supposed case might be a colourless instance favourable to the claimant, would be to answer the question so as to misrepresent the true facts and situation and to be of the nature of a trap.'

In *Locker & Woolf Ltd v Western Australian Insurance Co Ltd*[18] a question in a proposal form in respect of fire insurance stated: 'Have you ever suffered loss by fire?' The insured was a company, and the reply was 'Yes, £5, Sea'. In fact, one of the directors of the company, when trading on his own account, had suffered a loss by fire in 1919. That loss, however, was a much more serious one.

The Court of Appeal[19] held that there had been non-disclosure of a material fact, and that the insurance company was entitled to avoid the policy.[20]

In giving judgment Slesser LJ, said:[1]

> 'Now, the proposal form contains the following questions: "How long have you conducted your business in these premises? Answer: Three weeks." There is no complaint made of that.

---

[15] [1921] 2 AC 125, PC.
[16] Viscount Haldane, Lord Buckmaster and Lord Shaw of Dunfermline.
[17] [1921] 2 AC 125 at 131.
[18] (1936) 54 Ll L Rep 211, CA.
[19] Slesser and Scott LJ, and Eve J.
[20] It was also held that the company could avoid liability because another insurer had declined to issue a motor insurance policy in respect of vehicles belonging to the insured, and this matter had not been disclosed to the company. As to this, see p 55, post. It was also decided that the company by its conduct had not waived its right to repudiate the contract. See p 57, post.
[1] (1936) 54 Ll L Rep 211 at 214.

Then: "2: Have you ever suffered loss by fire? Answer: Yes, £5, Sea." The word "Sea" there does not, as one might imagine, mean a loss by fire at sea, but refers to a loss by fire on land of £5 which was paid by the Sea Insurance Co. That statement, as we shall see when we come to examine the findings of the learned arbitrator, is either untrue or a considerable economy of the truth, because in reality one of these partners had suffered, at a date which is stated by the arbitrator in his award, a very serious loss by fire, a loss which involved not only a serious destruction of goods but actually caused the death of a person who was present in the warehouse. Now, as regards that matter, that loss was incurred by one only of the partners, and for that reason the learned arbitrator has found that in answer to the question, "Have you ever suffered loss by fire?" the answer "Yes, £5, Sea" was not an untrue answer, because 'you' collectively had not suffered that loss, but only one of the partners. Whether that is a right view or not it is not necessary for us to decide. It is very arguable, in my personal opinion, that even that use of the word "you" did not justify necessarily the answer to the question, but we need not determine it, because he has found, as I have indicated, in the alternative, that the non-disclosure of the fact that one of the partners had suffered a grievous loss by fire, though not possibly an untrue answer to this question, was a non-disclosure of a material fact.'

In *Golding v Royal London Auxiliary Insurance Co Ltd*[2] an insured under a fire policy relating to a shop in Tottenham was asked the following question in the proposal form:

'Have you ever had a fire in these premises or elsewhere?'

He answered 'No'. In fact, he had had a fire some years previously at a workshop occupied by him in Islington, and had obtained £67 from the Commercial Union Assurance Co Ltd in respect of it. He signed the proposal form without reading it through. The insurance agent employed by the company left him a duplicate form, and when he read the duplicate, he noticed the answer stating that he had never had a fire. A few days later the insured informed the agent about the previous fire, but the agent did not communicate this information to the company. A fire took place and the insured claimed under the policy, but the insurance company refused to indemnify him on the ground that he had made an untrue answer, and had warranted the truth of his answers, for the policy contained a 'basis' clause.[3]

Bailhache J, held that the company was liable. It was the duty of the agent to convey the answers to his employers, and when the mistake which had been made was corrected, it was his duty to inform them of the fact.[4]

In *Arterial Caravans Ltd v Yorkshire Insurance Co Ltd*[5] the plaintiff company, of which Sutherland was its sole director, was incorporated in 1955 with the purpose of selling caravans made by him. By 1957 it had become dormant. Sutherland (Tenulite) Ltd, of which Sutherland was also its sole director, was incorporated in 1956 with the object of manufacturing caravans. The company's premises were badly damaged by fire in 1965. It moved to another site until it suffered losses and was wound up in 1968. The plaintiff company was re-activated in that year and moved to the site which has been occupied by Sutherland (Tenulite) Ltd. Sutherland contacted the defendants with a view to insuring the premises, and they sent a representative to interview him. The representative was told nothing of the previous loss sustained by Sutherland (Tenulite) Ltd. The defendants' district manager also interviewed Sutherland,

[2] (1914) 30 TLR 350.
[3] As to the 'basis' clause, see Ivamy, *General Principles of Insurance Law* (4th edn, 1979), pp 181–183.
[4] As to the knowledge of the agent being imputed to the company, see Ivamy, op cit, pp 583–590.
[5] [1973] 1 Lloyd's Rep 169, QB.

who did not disclose the previous loss to him, although he was asked whether the business had had any experience of losses and claims in the past. No disclosure was made to a surveyor who was also sent by the defendants. No policy was issued but the plaintiffs were covered on a 'held covered basis' pending its issue. On 2 March 1970, the plaintiffs' premises were damaged by fire, and a claim was made against the defendants, who repudiated liability on the ground that the previous loss was material and had not been disclosed.

Chapman J, held that the claim failed,[6] for the business was all the same throughout its history, although at one stage it was run by an individual, then by one company, and then by another. It was highly material that the defendants should be told that substantially the same business, its predecessor in the company's history, had had a very serious and substantial fire three years before.

In *Marene Knitting Mills Ltd v Greater Pacific General Insurance Ltd*[7] the plaintiffs insured their premises at Melbourne with the defendant insurers who issued a cover note on 14 August 1973. The premises were damaged by fire the next day. The plaintiffs claimed under the cover note, but were met with the plea that the business had suffered fires in 1958, 1960, 1961 and 1965 which were material and had not been disclosed. The plaintiffs contended that the business was not the same since (i) there had been a change in the management of the company; (ii) the labour force was almost entirely different; (iii) the business had recently moved to Melbourne so that the fire had taken place in different premises from any of the previous fires.

The Privy Council[8] held that the claim failed. Lord Fraser of Tullybelton said[9] that although the changes in the business were important, the plaintiffs were carrying on the same business as had been carried on at the other premises. Once it was established that the businesses were the same, the occurrence of the fires in 1961 and 1965 at least were material.

5 Other Insurers

(a) Refusal to Transfer Policy

In *Golding v Royal London Auxiliary Insurance Co Ltd*[10] the insured was also asked the following question in the proposal form:

'Has any other office declined to accept or renew your insurance?'

He answered 'No'. In fact, he had previously bought another shop, and had asked the London and Lancashire Fire Insurance Co. to transfer to him a policy which they had issued to the vendor of the shop, but that company refused to make the transfer. A fire took place at the Tottenham shop, and the insured claimed under the policy. The insurance company denied liability on

---

6 The plaintiffs' contention that the defendants had waived any non-disclosure was also rejected. As to this aspect of the case, see p 58, post.

7 [1976] 2 Lloyd's Rep 631, PC.

8 Lord Diplock, Lord Hailsham of St Marylebone, Lord Salmon, Lord Edmund-Davies and Lord Fraser of Tullybelton.

9 [1976] 2 Lloyd's Rep at 641.

10 (1914) 30 TLR 350, KB. Another aspect of this case viz whether the insured had truthfully answered a question stating 'Are you or have you been insured in this or any other office?' is considered at p 56, post.

the ground that the answer given was untrue, and that the truth of the answers had been made the 'basis' of the policy.[11]

Bailhache J, held that the claim succeeded. The terms 'accept' and 'renew' were well understood, and meant something entirely different from a transfer, and so the answer was a perfectly true one in the circumstances.

(b) Previous Refusal of Proposal

In *Arthrude Press Ltd v Eagle Star and British Dominions Insurance Co Ltd.* [12] Arthur Surek carried on business as a string and paper merchant and printer. He telephoned an agent of the North British Insurance Co Ltd, and asked whether they would insure against fire the stock and premises of his business which he intended to reconstitute as the Arthrude Press Ltd. The insurance company declined to do so. The Arthrude Press Ltd was formed, and a proposal form was completed on its behalf by Arthur Surek, and sent to the Eagle Star & British Dominions Insurance Co Ltd. One of the questions in the proposal form stated: 'Has your insurance ever been declined by any office?' The answer 'No' was given. A fire took place and the insured claimed under the policy. But the insurance company refused to pay on the ground that the answer given was untrue.

The Court of Appeal[13] held in favour of the insurance company. Bankes LJ, said:[14]

> '... but in my opinion, reading this proposal and asking oneself what this means: "Has your insurance ever been declined by any office?", that is not referring to the individual who happens to put forward the policy. It is perfectly obvious the question was and ought to have been understood as meaning: "Has this risk ever been declined by any office?" '

In *Locker & Woolf Ltd v Western Australian Insurance Co Ltd*[15] Locker & Woolf Ltd insured their premises against fire. One of the questions in the proposal form stated: 'Has this or any other insurance of yours been declined by any other company?' The insured answered 'No'. In fact, Locker & Woolf, when trading in partnership two years before the policy was issued, had applied to the National Insurance Co of Great Britain Ltd. for a policy covering their motor vehicles, and that company had declined their proposal. A fire took place and the insurers repudiated liability under the fire policy on the ground that there had been non-disclosure of a material fact in that the insured had not mentioned the refusal of the other company to issue a motor insurance policy.

The Court of Appeal[16] held that the insurers were entitled to do so. Slesser L J, referred to the 'moral hazard'[17] ie to the fact that the insured by reason of

---

[11] As to the 'basis' clause, see Ivamy, *General Principles of Insurance Law* (4th edn, 1979), pp 181–183.

[12] (1924) 19 Ll L Rep 373, CA.

[13] Bankes, Scrutton and Sargant LJJ.

[14] (1924) 19 Ll L Rep, at 374.

[15] (1936) 54 Ll L Rep 211, CA. Another aspect of the case, ie whether the insurers had waived their rights to avoid the policy. See p 57, post. The Court of Appeal also had to consider whether an untrue answer had been given to a question referring to a previous loss by fire. As to this, see p 52, ante.

[16] Slesser and Scott LJJ, and Eve J.

[17] As to the 'moral hazard', see further Ivamy, *General Principles of Insurance Law* (4th edn, 1979), pp 145–147.

his previous experience in matters relevant to the insurance was not a person whose proposal could be accepted in the ordinary course of business and without special consideration.

In the words of the learned Lord Justice:[18]

> 'It is elementary that one of the matters which may be considered by an insurance company in entering into contractual relations with a proposed insurer is the question of his moral integrity—what has been called in the cases "moral hazard"— and I do not think it necessary to cite authority to the effect that once the conclusion arises that had certain knowledge been in the minds of the insurance company, they might have taken a different course in agreeing to or declining a particular proposal of insurance, and that it might have affected the conditions and the rates on which they would take it, this 'moral hazard' is one of the incidents which do become directly material.
>
> In my view, it is quite impossible in the present case to say that the non-disclosure of the fact that the person proposing to take out an insurance policy for fire has had a motor policy declined on the grounds of misrepresentation, untrue answers, and non-disclosure, is not one which is very material for the... insurance company to know. It is, in fact, a non-disclosure of the fact that the person who seeks to enter into the insurance has already been overtly discovered to be a person who tells untruths, conceals matters material, and is a person who at any rate the ... insurance company, whatever view they took, might reasonably have come to the conclusion was a highly undesirable person with whom to have any contractual relations whatever. It is unarguable, in my opinion, that such an answer was not a material matter, and was a non-disclosure of something which was essential.'

(c) Refusal to Renew Policy

The fact that another insurance company has refused to renew a policy is a material fact which must be disclosed when the proposer submits his proposal.[19]

(d) Previous Insurances Effected by the Insured

In *Golding v Royal London Auxiliary Insurance Co Ltd*[20] a question in a proposal form for a fire policy relating to a shop in Tottenham stated:

'Are you or have been insured in this or any other office?'

The insured answered 'No'. In fact, he had been and was still insured in respect of his dwelling house some miles away. He had also been insured at one time in respect of a workshop at Islington. A fire took place, and the insurance company repudiated liability on the ground that the answer he had given was untrue, and that the truth of the answers had been made the 'basis' of the policy.[1]

Bailhache J, held that the company was liable. The answer 'No' was true as far as the shop was concerned. He could not agree that the question included all property ever occupied. Other questions in the proposal form related to 'these premises', and if a company wanted information about other premises not the

---

[18] (1936) 54 Ll L Rep 211, at p 215.

[19] *Re an Arbitration between Yager and Guardian Assurance Co Ltd* (1912) 108 L T 38.

[20] (1914) 30 T L R 350, K B. Another aspect of this case viz whether the insured had truthfully answered a question stating: 'Has any other office declined to accept or renew your insurance?' is considered at p 54, ante.

[1] As to the 'basis' clause, see Ivamy, *General Principles of Insurance Law* (4th edn, 1979), pp 181–183.

subject-matter of the particular proposal, it should take care to make its meaning clear.

WAIVER OF NON-DISCLOSURE

In *Locker & Woolf Ltd v Western Australian Insurance Co Ltd*[2] after a fire on 11 April 1934, the insurance company instructed assessors to investigate the claim and the loss. The assessors took possession of the salvage which was sold by auctioneers at various times from July to December 1934. The insurance company did not receive any part of the salvage money, which remained in the hands of the assessors. The insurance company did not order the salvage sales, but knew that they were taking place, and the insured did not make any protest. In October 1934 the insurance company discovered that the insured had not disclosed a previous refusal on the part of another insurer to issue a motor insurance policy in respect of vehicles belonging to the insured,[3] and sought to avoid liability under the fire policy, and referred the matter to arbitration.

The insured contended that the insurers by their conduct had waived their right to avoid the policy on the ground of non-disclosure.

The Court of Appeal[4] held that the insurers had not waived their right. Slesser L J, said:[5]

> 'The [insurers], if they are to be said to have waived the conditions which justified them in repudiating the contract or elected to treat it as subsisting, are entitled to say that they did not know the full circumstances of the case; that whatever they knew, their information was not complete until they knew about the motor car; and that, therefore, the acts done by them with regard to allowing these goods which had been salved to be sold was not conclusive from any point of view before the time when they had full knowledge of the circumstances. There must be, in the first place, full knowledge of the circumstances, and, knowing the circumstances, the insurers must do some act which, apart from the policy, they are not entitled to do, and which can be justified only upon the footing that the policy is still in existence (*Yorkshire Insurance Co Ltd v Craine*[6]).'

After reviewing the sequence of events after the fire had taken place[7], the learned Lord Justice concluded:[8]

> 'That means, I think, that almost coincidently with the information derived for the first time of the serious material non-disclosure of the refusal of insurance in the motor car matter, the parties by agreement in writing agreed to refer the differences which were the differences arising out of the policy to the arbitrator, and in that short period of time I find no material on which we are justified in coming to the conclusion that the ... insurance company elected to treat the contract as subsisting or agreed to waive any conditions; indeed, quite the contrary.'

In *Arterial Caravans Ltd v Yorkshire Insurance Co Ltd*[9] the plaintiff company, which was covered against fire on a 'held covered' basis pending the issue of a

---

2 (1936) 54 Ll L Rep 211, C A.
3 As to this aspect of the case, see p 55, ante. The Court of Appeal also had to consider whether an untrue answer had been given to a question referring to a previous loss by fire. As to this, see p 52, ante.
4 Slesser and Scott L JJ, and Eve J.
5 (1936) 54 Ll L Rep 211 at 216. See also the judgment of Scott L J, ibid, at pp 219–220.
6 [1922] 2 A C 541.
7 See (1936) 54 Ll L Rep 211 at 217.
8 Ibid, at 217.
9 [1973] 1 Lloyd's Rep 169, Q B.

policy, contended that it had not been necessary to disclose a previous loss by fire[10] because the defendant insurers had waived any non-disclosure which there might have been since (i) their district manager had failed to ask the questions contained in a proposal form as to previous losses and to get the answers to them from the plaintiffs' sole director; (ii) after the receipt of the proposal form on which the questions were unanswered the defendants had accepted it; and (iii) they made no attempt to get an answer to those questions at any time.

Chapman J held that the plea of waiver had failed.[11] He said that the plaintiffs were seeking to put on the defendants the duty of asking questions when, in fact, the duty was the other way round. The duty was on the assured to disclose any material information which he had, and it was only if the insurers were put on enquiry about some particular matter that it could be said that they had waived the obligation as to disclosure. In the present case the defendants had been kept in total ignorance of there ever having been a fire in the history of the business. The fact that they did not ask questions did not amount to a waiver.

CONTINUING WARRANTIES AS TO EXISTENCE OF FACTS

In *Hales v Reliance Fire and Accident Insurance Corpn Ltd*[12] the insured, a retail shopkeeper, in answer to the question in the proposal form stating 'Are any inflammable oils or goods used or kept on the premises?', had said 'Lighter fuel'. A fire took place when some fireworks, which he stored on the premises 6 months after the acceptance of the proposal, exploded and damaged his shop and trade property. He claimed for a loss under the policy, but the insurance company repudiated liability on the ground, inter alia, that the question and answer in the proposal form were a warranty as to the existence of the fact at the time of the proposal and during the currency of the risk.[13]

McNair J, held that this contention succeeded.

---

[10] As to this aspect of the case see p 53, ante.

[11] [1973] 1 Lloyd's Rep at 180.

[12] [1960] 2 Ll L Rep 391, Q B.

[13] Other issues in the case arose as to whether (i) there had been non-disclosure of a material fact ie the existence of fireworks on the premises (see p 50, ante); and (ii) an untrue answer had been given by the insured to one of the questions in the proposal form (see p 109, post).

CHAPTER 11

The form and contents of the policy

A policy of fire insurance is in practice drawn up in common form. Different insurers may vary somewhat in the language and phrasing employed. But the framework and general effect of all policies are much the same.[1]

The contents, however, vary according to whether the policy is:

A   A fire insurance company's policy.

B   A Lloyd's policy.

A THE CONTENTS OF A FIRE INSURANCE COMPANY'S POLICY

The contents of the policy issued by a fire insurance company are usually as follows:[2]

1. Recitals.
2. The heading.
3. The name of the insured.
4. The description of the subject-matter.
5. The amount of the insurance.
6. The contract of the insurers to indemnify the insured.
7. The conditions.
8. The perils insured against.
9. The duration of the policy.
10. The extent of the insurers' liability.
11. The amount of the premium.
12. The signature of the insurers.
13. The schedule.
14. Special terms.
15. The outside cover.

1 Recitals

These state that a proposal has been made or that a premium has been paid.

---

[1] As to the forms and contents of policies in general, see Ivamy, *General Principles of Insurance Law* (4th edn, 1979), pp 230–236.

[2] Specimen fire insurance policies are set out in Appendix II, pp 375–388, post.

2 Heading

The heading states the name of the insurers,[3] and the number of the policy. Sometimes it includes a statement of the sum insured, the amount of the premium and the period of insurance.[4]

3 Name of the Insured

Where houses, buildings, or similar property are insured, the policy may, perhaps, be invalid unless the name of the person interested in such property, or for whose use, account, or benefit the policy is made, is inserted.[5]

In the case of a policy upon goods, the question of the name to be inserted is of less importance, since the person interested can as a rule claim the benefit of the policy, whether his name appears on the foot of the policy or not, provided that the policy was in fact intended to cover his interest.

4 Description of the Subject-Matter

The subject-matter must be adequately described for the purpose not only of identification, but also of defining the risk. The interest, however, of the insured in the subject-matter need not, as a rule, be described, unless expressly required.

5 Amount of the Insurance

Since the insertion of an amount in the policy does not make it a valued policy,[6] the parties must, if they intend it to be a valued policy, make their intention clear.

Where several subject-matters are included in the same policy, a separate sum is usually required by the terms of the policy to be specified for each.[7]

6 Contract of the Insurers

The insurers agree that, subject to the conditions contained in the policy, they will pay to the insured the value of the property at the time of the happening of its destruction or the amount of such damage or at their option reinstate or replace such property or any part thereof.

---

[3] If the insurers are a limited company, the word 'limited' or an abbreviation (*Stacey & Co Ltd v Wallis* (1912) 106 L T 544) must appear: Companies Act 1948, s 108 (1) (c).

[4] For the purpose of ascertaining the period for which a policy is in force, the operative words must be looked at and not the heading: *Isaacs v Royal Insurance Co Ltd* (1870) L R 5 Exch 296 at 301, per Cleasby, B.

[5] Life Assurance Act 1774, s 2. As to the application of this Act to fire policies, see pp 180–185, post.

[6] See p 164, post.

[7] The policy is then a policy on each item taken separately for the sum specified, and not a policy on the whole amount of the property: *Curtis & Sons v Mathews* (1918) 119 L T 78 at 81.

7 Conditions

The contract incorporates the conditions upon the fulfilment of which the validity of the contract or the liability of the insurers may depend. Such conditions are usually printed on the back of the policy,[8] but may be contained in other documents, if incorporated by express reference.[9]

8 Perils Insured Against

In practice, insurers invariably insert in the policy exceptions negativing their liability in certain specified events. The general words of the policy must, therefore, be considered in connection with the exceptions.

9 Duration of the Policy

The policy states its duration and includes provisions for renewal and in some cases days of grace.[10]

10 Extent of the Insurers' Liability

The policy states that the liability of the insurers shall in no case exceed in respect of each item the sum expressed in the schedule to be insured thereon or in the whole the total sum insured thereby, or such other sum or sums as may be substituted therefor, by memorandum thereon or attached thereto, filed by or on behalf of the insurers.

11 Amount of the Premium and Renewal Premium

The premium to be charged for insuring any property of an ordinary kind is determined by reference to tables or rates of premium. But special rates are charged where the insured seeks a protection wider than that which the insurers usually agree to give in respect of property similar to that sought to be insured.[11]

12 Signature of the Insurers

Where a policy issued under the seal of an insurance company purports to be duly executed by the proper officers of the company, the insured need not inquire whether all the formalities prescribed by the company's regulations have been properly observed, or whether the officers purporting to act on the company's behalf were in fact duly appointed.[12]

---

8 Sometimes express warranties are placed on the face of the policy, eg 'warranted no pipe stove except as stated'.
9 As to the incorporation of other documents, see Ivamy, *General Principles of Insurance Law* (4th edn, 1979), pp 238–239.
10 See Ivamy, op cit, pp 269–271.
11 See Ivamy, op cit, p 198.
12 The position is different where the validity of the policy is called in question in proceedings against third persons: *Phipps v Parker* (1808) 1 Camp 412, where the defendant had accused the

Where the policy is under hand, it may be signed by an agent on behalf of the insurers, provided that his authority extends thus far.

13 Schedule

The details of the particular insurance may be written into spaces left in the body of the contract for this purpose. In view of the possibility that these spaces may be left blank or incorrectly filled in, it is the practice to include all these details in a schedule, which is printed under the contract. The actual contract is then expressed in general terms, referring to the schedule for the details. All the matters requiring to be set out in detail are then brought together, and the danger of omission or mistake is obviated.

Schedules are also used where the subject-matters are numerous.

14 Special Terms

Where special terms are agreed, they are often printed on a slip of paper which is gummed to the policy. A slip on the face of the policy forms part of it, but, if on the back, it is not so unless expressly incorporated, or it is the intention of the parties that it should form part of the contract.[13]

15 The Outside Cover

A policy, when folded, exhibits an outside cover upon which is usually printed a docket or summary of the contents of the policy. Sometimes notices or warnings to the insured are added. These do not form part of the policy,[14] unless the clause of incorporation is wide enough to include them.[15]

B   THE CONTENTS OF A LLOYD'S POLICY

Lloyd's fire policy consists of:[16]

1   Recitals.
2   The perils insured against.
3   Exceptions.
4   Conditions.

---

plaintiff of wilfully setting fire to his house with intent to defraud the Sun Fire Office, and an action for slander failed, as the plaintiff was unable to prove that the policy had been properly executed.

[13] Cf *Bensaude v Thames and Mersey Marine Insurance Co* [1897] A C 609 (marine insurance).

[14] Cf *Hawke v Niagara District Mutual Fire Insurance Co* (1876) 23 Gr 139: *Stoness v Anglo-American Insurance Co* (1912) 21 O W R 405.

[15] *Mardorf v Accident Insurance Co* [1903] 1 K B 584 (accident insurance); *Scott v Scottish Accident Insurance Co* 1889 16 R (Ct of Sess) 630 (accident insurance); cf *Rowe v London and Lancashire Fire Insurance Co* (1866) 12 Gr 311.

[16] As to the Lloyd's form of fire policy, see Appendix III, p 389–402, post.

1 Recitals

The policy states that the premium has been paid to the insurers who undertake to insure the property from loss or damage by fire and/or lightning. The period from which the policy is to start is stated, as also is the time at which it will expire. It also provides for an extension for such further period or periods as may be mutually agreed upon by the parties.

2 The Perils Insured Against

As well as providing insurance cover in respect of loss or damage by fire and/or lightning, the policy also covers loss and/or damage to the property insured caused by:

    a Fire consequent upon explosion wherever the explosion occurs;
    b Explosion consequent upon fire on the premises insured;
    c Explosion of domestic boilers and/or of gas used for domestic purposes or for heating and/or lighting.

3 Exceptions

The policy does not cover loss or damage directly or indirectly occasioned by, happening through or in consequence of war, invasion, acts of foreign enemies, hostilities (whether war be declared or not), civil war, rebellion, revolution, insurrection, military or usurped power, riots, civil commotions or confiscation or nationalisation or requisition or destruction of or damage to property by or under the order of any government or public or local authority.

It does not cover destruction of or damage to any dynamo, transformer, motor, wiring, main or other electrical appliance which is directly caused by short-circuiting, overrunning, excessive pressure or leakage of electricity.

This cause, however, is not deemed to exclude loss or damage to any dynamo, transformer, motor, wiring, main or other electrical appliance caused by fire resulting from short-circuiting, overrunning, excessive pressure or leakage of electricity originating outside the dynamo, transformer, motor, wiring, main or other electrical appliance which is so destroyed or damaged by fire.

4 Conditions

One condition in the policy states that if the insured shall make any claim knowing the same to be false or fraudulent, as regards amount or otherwise, the policy is to become void, and all claim thereunder shall be forfeited.

Another condition states that the policy is subject to the 'Condition of Average', ie if the property covered by the insurance shall at the time of any loss be of greater value than the sum insured thereby, the insured shall only be entitled to recover such proportion of the loss as the sum insured by the policy bears to the total value of the property.

Other conditions may be added by the insurers to suit the circumstances of the particular property to be insured.

CHAPTER 12

The perils insured against by a fire policy

A THE SCOPE OF THE POLICY

In a contract of fire insurance in the strictest sense of the word, the peril against which protection is sought is fire, and fire only.[1] In practice, however, the scope of the contract is usually extended so as to protect the insured against certain other perils, which are analogous to fire, though they cannot, for the purposes of the contract, be treated as falling within the definition of the word. Thus, lightning and certain kinds of explosion are usually covered by the contract.[2]

Exception Clauses

It is at the same time the practice of insurers to narrow the scope of the contract by the introduction of exceptions which exclude their liability in certain cases of loss, notwithstanding the fact that such loss was caused by fire.[3]

Combined Policies

An insurance against fire may be combined in one contract with insurances against other perils, which are in no way analogous to fire, but which are equally likely to affect adversely the interest of the assured in the subject-matter of insurance. Thus, an insurance against loss by fire may be combined with an insurance against loss by theft, or against liability for accident, or against death by accident, or any other event likely to prove adverse to the interest of the insured.[4]

Fire as the Remote Cause

The doctrine of proximate cause is applied, not only for the purpose of ascertaining whether the subject-matter of insurance was destroyed by fire, but also for the purpose of determining how far the loss which the insured sustains in consequence of its destruction can be regarded as a loss by fire within the meaning of the policy.

---

[1] See pp 68–71, post.
[2] See pp 71–74, post.
[3] See pp 80–90, post.
[4] See eg *American Surety Co of New York v Wrightson* (1910) 103 L T 663 (fidelity insurance), where the policy covered loss by dishonesty of employees, loss by their negligence, and loss by the dishonesty of persons who were not employees, as well as loss by fire.

A loss of which fire is not the proximate cause, but only the remote cause, is not recoverable under an ordinary policy of fire insurance.[5]

The object of the policy is to indemnify the insured against the loss of the subject-matter of insurance.[6] A loss which is merely consequential on the loss of the subject-matter is not within its scope.[7]

Although the loss is one which, but for the fire, would not, or might not, have happened, it is not directly caused by the fire. It is not the natural, but only the accidental consequence of the fire, since it flows from the destruction of the subject-matter, and depends, as well for its existence as for its extent, on the circumstances attending the subject-matter.[8]

The different kinds of loss which are to be regarded as being only remotely caused by fire and which are, therefore, excluded from the scope of an ordinary policy, may be classified under the following heads:

1 Anticipated profit.
2 Continuing expenditure.
3 Increased expenditure.
4 Depreciation.
5 Liability to third persons.

1 Anticipated Profit

Where the fire destroys property, from the use of which the insured expects to earn a profit in the ordinary course of business, he does not merely lose his property. He loses, in addition, the chance of earning the profit which he might have earned if the property had not been destroyed.

The loss of anticipated profit is, however, regarded as too remote, and is not recoverable under an insurance on the property in question.[9] Accordingly, an insurance on an inn[10] or a factory[11] covers only the fabric of the inn or factory, and does not entitle the insured to be indemnified against loss of business.

---

[5] *Jones v Schmoll* (1785) 1 Term Rep 130n at 130n (marine insurance) per Lord Mansfield CJ.

[6] Cf *Moore v Evans* [1918] AC 185 (jewellery insurance), where the insured was indefinitely prevented from obtaining possession of jewellery through its detention in an enemy country, but there was no evidence that the jewels themselves were not intact.

[7] *Re Wright and Pole* (1834) 1 Ad & El 621, where an innkeeper, who had insured his inn, unsuccessfully claimed for loss of custom and for the cost of hiring other premises whilst the inn was under repair.

[8] *Theobald v Railway Passengers Assurance Co* (1854) 10 Exch 45 at 58 (accident insurance) per Pollock CB. Cf *Liesbosch (Dredger) v SS Edison (Owners)* [1933] AC 449 (collision), where it was held that the increased effect of the loss due to the shipowners' financial inability to purchase a replacement for the special work involved was either too remote a consequence or an independent cause.

[9] *Shelbourne & Co v Law Investment and Insurance Corpn* [1898] 2 QB 626 (marine insurance), where an insurance on barges against loss or damage by collision was held not to cover loss arising from the detention of the barges during repairs after a collision; *Lucena v Craufurd* (1806) 2 Bos & PNR 269 at 315, HL. (marine insurance); *Inman SS Co v Bischoff* (1882) 7 App Cas 670 (marine insurance), where the freight was lost owing to the operation of a cancellation clause. Cf *Maurice v Goldsbrough Mort & Co Ltd* [1939] AC 452, PC, where brokers, who had insured wool entrusted to them for sale which was destroyed by fire, were held not entitled to retain out of the policy moneys commission which they would have earned if the wool had not been destroyed.

[10] *Re Wright and Pole*, (supra).

[11] *Menzies v North British Insurance Co* 1847 9 Dunl (Ct of Sess) 694.

Thus, in *Re Wright and Pole*[12] the insured effected a fire insurance policy on the Ship Inn at Dover with the Sun Fire Office Co. A fire took place, and the insured included in his claim the sum which he had had to pay to his landlord by way of rent, the cost of hiring other accommodation whilst the insured premises were being repaired, and the loss which he had sustained through his customers not going there during the period of repair.

The Court of King's Bench[13] held that none of the above items were recoverable.

Lord Denman C J said:[14]

> 'The interest in question might have been the subject of insurance, but an arbitrator[15] cannot take into consideration the possible profits of an inn under the shape of an interest in buildings.'

Taunton J observed:[16]

> 'If a party would recover such profits as these, he must insure them *qua* profits. I have never heard of a recovery of profits of a business as an incidental part of the loss under an insurance upon a house or ship.'

Littledale and Williams J J concurred.

Anticipated profit, which is only a possibility at the date of the fire, must be distinguished from profit which has been ascertained or realised at that date. Ascertained profit is a factor which has to be taken into account in estimating the value of the subject-matter and in fixing the amount recoverable in respect of its loss.

2 Continuing Expenditure

The expenditure to which the insured is committed in consequence of his connection with the property insured does not necessarily cease when the property is destroyed, and the effect of the fire is, therefore, to prevent him from deriving any benefit from the payments which he is nevertheless compelled to continue.

Thus, in the case of a tenancy, unless the tenancy agreement provides otherwise, rent continues to be payable, notwithstanding the destruction of the demised premises, and it is immaterial that the premises are unfit for occupation, and that, until they are rebuilt, the payment of rent imposes a burden upon the tenant without any commensurate advantage.

In the same way, the insured, if an employer of labour, may have entered into contracts of employment, which are not dissolved by reason of the fire. He may continue liable to pay wages to his employees, or he may deem it wise to keep them in his employment, although he can derive no benefit from their services whilst the premises are derelict.

Nevertheless, the loss so incurred is only a remote consequence of the fire, and the insured is not entitled, under an insurance upon the building or

---

[12] (1834) 1 Ad & El 621.
[13] Lord Denman C J, Taunton, Littledale and Williams J J.
[14] (1834) 1 Ad & El 621 at 623.
[15] From whose award the appeal in the present case had been brought.
[16] (1834) 1 Ad & El 621 at 623.

factory, to recover anything in respect of expenditure thrown away upon rent[17] or wages.[18]

3 Increased Expenditure

The effect of the fire may be to involve the insured in additional expenditure which he would not have incurred but for the fire.

Thus, for the purpose of keeping his business going, he may be compelled to hire other premises whilst his own premises are being rebuilt or repaired. He is at least a loser by the difference between the rent paid for the hired premises and his original rent; whilst, if his liability for the original rent continues, his loss is represented by the whole of the rent paid for the hired premises.

Such loss, however, is regarded as too remote, and an insurance on buildings does not cover the cost of hiring other buildings to take their place during the period of reinstatement.[19]

Similarly, the cost of removal of goods from damaged property and their storage whilst repairs are being effected would not be recoverable.

4 Depreciation

Where part only of the property is destroyed, the effect of the fire may be to depreciate the value of the remainder.

Thus, in the case of goods, the value of the part which has not been burned may be diminished by prejudice or suspicion, although there is no damage, in fact.

A loss due to depreciation of this kind is regarded as too remote, and is not recoverable under an insurance on the goods.[20]

The position is different where the destruction of part affects the character and value of the whole. Thus, where different parts are combined to form a whole, the value of which depends on that combination, the loss of part breaks the combination and affects the value of the whole. If, therefore, the property is insured as a whole, the depreciation which the property suffers by the loss of part is recoverable, since it represents the diminution in value caused by the fire itself.[1]

---

17 *Re Wright and Pole* (1834) 1 Ad & El 621, followed in *Menzies v North British Insurance Co* 1847 9 Dunl (Ct of Sess) 694; *Westminster Fire Office v Glasgow Provident Investment Society* (1888) 13 App Cas 699.

18 *Menzies v North British Insurance Co,* (supra).

19 *Re Wright and Pole,* (supra); *Menzies v North British Insurance Co,* (supra); cf *Rogers & Co v British Shipowners' Mutual Protection Association Ltd* (1896) 1 Com Cas 414 (marine insurance), where an insurance covering costs and charges in respect of any illness was held not to extend to the cost of engaging substitutes for a crew disabled by sickness.

20 *Cator v Great Western Insurance Co of New York* (1873) L R 8 C P 552 (marine insurance); *J Lysaght Ltd v Coleman* [1895] 1 Q B 49, C A (marine insurance); cf *Brown Bros v Fleming* (1902) 7 Com Cas 245 (marine insurance), where damage to labels was held to be damage to the subject-matter.

1 Eg where two houses are covered by one insurance and one only of the houses is actually burned (*Westminster Fire Office v Glasgow Provident Investment Society* (1888) 13 App Cas 699 at 704, per Lord Watson), or where the site on which a building stands has a special value due to the presence of the building (ibid, at 704, 711 per Lord Selborne), or where part of a machine is destroyed (*Cator v Great Western Insurance Co of New York* (1873) L R 8 C P 552 at 559 (marine insurance) per Bovill C J).

5 Liability to Third Persons

The circumstances in which the destruction of the insured property takes place may involve the insured in liability to third persons for personal injuries, or for damage to property other than the property which is the subject-matter of the insurance. The loss, which the insured sustains in consequence of this liability being enforced, is not proximately caused by the fire, and therefore an insurance on the property does not cover payments made to third persons in respect of personal injuries[2] or of damage to their property.[3]

B   FIRE

The contract of fire insurance is a contract to indemnify the insured against loss by fire. The word 'fire' is used in its popular meaning. It does not extend to chemical actions which, though they may correspond in their effects to fire, do not result in an actual ignition. Thus, lightning may be a form of fire, but loss occasioned by lightning without ignition is not, in the ordinary meaning of the words, a loss by fire, although the contract as usually framed covers such loss.[4] Where, however, lightning results in ignition, a loss occasioned by such ignition is a loss by fire.[5]

In order to constitute a loss there must be an actual fire or ignition.[6] Hence, a mere heating or fermentation will not be sufficient to render the insurers liable for loss occasioned thereby.[7]

Again, where damage is caused by atmospheric concussion, the insurers will not be liable.

Thus, in *Everett v London Assurance*[8] a house was insured under a fire policy. A quantity of gunpowder in a gunpowder factory more than half a mile away ignited and exploded. The house was not set on fire by the explosion, but the windows and window frames were shattered, and the structure was damaged generally by the atmospheric pressure caused by the explosion.

The Court of Common Pleas[9] held that the loss was not caused by 'fire' within the meaning of the policy, for the house itself had not been burnt.

Erle C J observed:[10]

---

2   *Taylor v Dewar* (1864) 5 B & S 58 (marine insurance), where an insurance against loss by collision was held not to cover liability for loss of life; *Nourse v Liverpool Sailing Ship Owners Mutual Protection and Indemnity Association* [1896] 2 QB 16 (marine insurance); *Burger v Indemnity Mutual Marine Assurance Co* [1900] 2 QB 348, C A (marine insurance).

3   *De Vaux v Salvador* (1836) 4 Ad & El 420 (marine insurance).

4   *Roth v South Easthope Farmers Mutual Fire Insurance Co* (1917) 41 O L R 52.

5   *Gordon v Rimmington* (1807) 1 Camp 123 at 123, 124 (marine insurance) per Lord Ellenborough C J.

6   *Everett v London Assurance* (1865) 19 C B N S 126 at 133 per Byles J: ' "Loss or damage occasioned by fire" means "loss or damage either by ignition of the article consumed, or by ignition of part of the premises where the article is"; in the one case there is a loss, in the other a damage, occasioned by fire'; *Tempus Shipping Co Ltd v Louis Dreyfus & Co Ltd* [1930] 1 K B 699 at 708 (rvsd without affecting this point: [1931] 1 K B 195, C A) (marine insurance) per Wright J: 'Mere heating which has not arrived at the stage of incandescence or ignition, is not within the specific word "fire" '; *Fleming v Hislop* (1886) 11 App Cas 686 at 692, *per* Lord Selborne: ' "Ignition" and "burning" are synonymous'.

7   Loss of this kind is usually excepted by the terms of the policy. See p 81, post.

8   (1865) 34 L J C P 299.

9   Erle C J, Willes and Byles J J.

10   (1865) 34 L J C P 299 at 301.

'The contract by the [insurers] is to pay the amount of such loss or damage as should be occasioned by fire to the property of the [insured] thereby insured. The damage occasioned by an explosion of gunpowder at a distance does not, I think, come within those words; I, therefore, think such words do not apply to the damage sought to be recovered in this action. There is a stipulation as to lightning and gunpowder; but this, which is a damage from the explosion of gunpowder off the premises, is not expressed in the policy.'

Willes J was of the same opinion, and said:[11]

'In insurance cases we are bound to look to the immediate and not the remote cause of the loss. No one would say that the damage sustained by the [insured] in this case was occasioned by fire, but by a concussion of air, which was caused by an explosion of gunpowder, which was caused by fire. That is going to the causa causans, which cannot properly be done.'

Byles J agreed:[12]

'The contract is to pay for loss occasioned by fire, which means either ignition of the article itself, or of part of the premises where it is; in the one case the article might be lost and in the other damaged by fire. Otherwise it would offend the rule of law given by Lord Bacon: "*In jure non remota causa sed proxima spectatur.*"—*Bac Max Reg* 1. An eruption of Vesuvius might injure a ship sailing near it, and that might be said to be a damage by fire. Indeed, if the rule were broken into, there is no absurdity at which to stop; the heat of the sun might be too great, and a damage resulting from that might even be said to be a damage by fire. What the Court has to do, however, is to give only the ordinary construction to the words of the contract, and according to such a construction the policy does not cover this loss.'

Any loss attributable to the fire whether by actual burning or by cracking or scorching, or by smoke,[13] or otherwise,[14] will have to be borne by the insurers.

Where the cause of the loss is a fire lighted for the ordinary purposes for which a fire is used, eg for cooking, warming or manufacturing, and property adjacent to the fire is merely damaged by scorching or cracking, the loss is not covered whilst the fire is burning in the grate or furnace, for it is fulfilling the purpose for which it was lighted. Although the element of accident may be present, there is no ignition of the property, and nothing is on fire which ought not to be on fire.[15] If, however, the fire breaks its bounds and, by throwing out

---

11 (1865) 34 LJ CP at 299, 301.

12 Ibid, at 301.

13 *The Diamond* [1906] P 282 (marine insurance).

14 Hence, the melting of ice in a storehouse may be a loss by fire: *North British and Mercantile Insurance Co v McLellan* (1892) 21 SCR 288. Similarly, if, in the course of a fire, waterpipes are melted, damage done to goods by the escaping of water will be a loss by fire.

15 *Austin v Drew* (1816) 2 Marsh 130, where from negligence of an employee in not opening a register, smoke and heat from the fire used for the purpose damaged sugars which were in the course of being refined; SC (1815) 4 Camp 360 at 361, per Gibbs CJ: 'I am of opinion that this action is not maintainable. There was no more fire than always exists when the manufacture is going on. Nothing was consumed by fire. The [insured's] loss arose from the negligent mis-management of their machinery. The sugars were chiefly damaged by the heat; and what produced that heat? Not any fire against which the company insures, but the fire for heating the pans, which continued all the time to burn without any excess'; and at 362, referring to a remark by a juryman that if his employee by negligence set his house on fire, and it was burnt down, he would expect to be paid by the insurance company, 'and so you would, Sir; but then there would be a fire, whereas here there has been none. If there is a fire, it is no answer that it was occasioned by the negligence or misconduct of servants; but in this case there was no fire except in the stove and the flue, as there ought to have been, and the loss was occasioned by the confinement of heat. Had the fire been brought out of the flue, and anything had been burnt, the company would have been liable. But can this be when the fire never was at all excessive and was always confined within its proper limits? This is not a "fire" within the meaning of the policy, nor a loss for which the company undertake. They might as well be sued for damage done to a drawing-room by a smoky chimney'. Cf *R v Russell* (1842) Car & M 247.

sparks or otherwise, causes ignition to take place outside the grate or furnace, there is at once a loss by fire within the meaning of the contract.[16]

The converse case is where property is accidentally burned in an ordinary fire, such as a domestic fire. The fire never breaks its bounds, but something which was never intended to be burned falls or is thrown by accident into the grate and is burned. In this case, equally with the case where the fire breaks its bounds, there is an accident, and something is burned which ought not to have been burned. The only distinction between them is that in the one case it is the fire which escapes out of its proper place and comes into contact with the property destroyed, whereas in the other case it is the property which gets out of its proper place and comes into contact with the fire. This distinction does not make any difference to the result. The object of the contract is to indemnify the insured against accidental loss by fire, and so long as the property is accidentally burned, the precise nature of the accident is immaterial. The loss in both cases falls equally within the contract.[17]

Thus, in *Harris v Poland*[18] banknotes and jewellery were placed for safety in an unlighted grate. The fire was lighted by mistake and the property was damaged. The underwriter repudiated liability, contending that the loss was not covered since it did not fall within the terms of the policy, which only applied to 'loss or damage caused by fire' because the damage had been done to the insured property by fire in a place where it was intended to be, ie in the grate.

Atkinson J held that the underwriter was liable. He said that the risks insured against included the risk of the insured property coming unintentionally in contact with fire and being thereby destroyed or damaged. It made no difference whether the fire came to the insured property or the insured property came to the fire.

He observed:[19]

> 'I have no doubt that the ordinary man, when he insures against loss by fire believes that he is insuring against every kind of loss which he may suffer from the more or less compulsory use of fire by himself or his neighbour. If he were told that the words in a Lloyd's policy meant only loss from contact with fire where no fire ought to be, many questions would spring to his mind—as they spring to mine. Am I not covered, he would ask, if the wind blows something—say a valuable manuscript or a sheet of foreign stamps—into the fire in the grate? Or if a careless servant drops something into the grate? Or if my wife stumbles and causes her lace scarf or silver fox tie to be caught by a flame in the fire grate? To all these questions [Counsel] answers "No". But what if part of the scarf is consumed in the grate, and the rest of it outside the grate on the hearth-rug? Do I get compensation for the part burnt outside the grate, though not for the part burnt in the grate? And what if the burning scarf burns a hole in the carpet? That is not the fault of the fire in the grate; that fire has not broken bounds. Am I covered for that? And what is the position if the lace catches fire by coming in contact with a lighted candle on the dinner table? The flame of the candle is in the exact place where it is intended to be. Is it on a par with the fire in the grate? And what if the wind blows a curtain against a lighted gas jet and the curtain catches fire?
>
> I imagine that the ordinary man would say: "Your policy is no use to me. I should never know where I was. I want an underwriter who knows what he means and says what he means".'

---

[16] *Upjohn v Hitchens* [1918] 2 K B 48 at 51, C A per Scrutton L J; cf *Musgrove v Pandelis* [1912] 2 K B 43 at 50, C A (negligence), per Warrington L J.

[17] *Harris v Poland* (1941) 69 Ll L Rep 35, K B

[18] (1941) 69 Ll L Rep 35, K B.

[19] Ibid, at 37.

He considered that he could not read into the contract a limitation which was not there, eg some such words as 'unless the insured property is burned by coming in contact with fire in a place where fire is intended to be'. He then concluded.[20]

> 'Why should I? What justification can there be for so doing? To what absurdities would it lead? A red hot cinder jumps from the fire and sets some paper of value on fire—admittedly there is liability. A draught from the window blows the same paper into the same fire. Is that any less an accidental loss by fire? Are the words in the policy any less applicable to the latter than the former? A draught blows the flame of a candle against a curtain—admittedly there is liability. But what if the curtain is blown against the flame of the candle? Surely the result must be the same? If it is not the same, the result is an absurdity. If it is the same, why should the result be different if one substitutes a fire in a grate for the lighted candle in a candlestick?'

C EXPLOSION

In considering the question how far a loss by explosion is covered by a contract of insurance against fire, two kinds of explosions must be distinguished:

1 Explosions caused by an explosive substance, eg gunpowder or gas coming into contact with fire; and
2 Explosions caused by the application of fire to a substance not of itself explosive, eg a boiler.

1 Explosions of Gunpowder or Gas

An explosion caused by an explosive substance such as gunpowder or gas, coming into contact with fire is a fire of inconceivable rapidity, though it can hardly be considered a 'fire' in the popular sense of the word. Whether a loss by explosion is a loss by fire may, in individual cases, give rise to questions of great difficulty.

It is, therefore, the universal practice of insurers to deal specifically in their contracts with losses by explosions so as to express with precision the extent of their liability.

Where, however, the extent of their liability is not expressly defined, and the explosion has no connection with any fire within the meaning of the contract, the loss occasioned by the explosion, being attributable solely to concussion, is not a loss by fire.[1] But where property is actually burned in the course of the incident in which the explosion occurred, the loss is covered and it is unnecessary to inquire into the connection between the explosion and the fire. There is clearly a loss by fire whether the fire preceded and caused the explosion, or the explosion, however caused, results in fire.[2] This is also the case where the concussion created by an explosion causes an existing fire to spread more strongly.[3]

---

[20] (1941) 69 Ll L Rep at 38, K B.

[1] *Re Hooley Hill Rubber and Chemical Co Ltd and Royal Insurance Co Ltd* [1920] 1 K B 257 at 274, C A, per Duke L J: 'An explosion independent of fire would not be within the policy of all'.

[2] *Stanley v Western Insurance Co* (1868) L R 3 Exch 71 at 74, per Kelly C B; *Everett v London Assurance* (1865) 19 C B N S 126 at 133, per Byles J.

[3] *Stanley v Western Insurance Co*, (supra), at 75 per Martin B: 'With respect to the extent of the

Where the explosion is preceded by a fire within the meaning of the contract, and is caused thereby, and the subject-matter is situated in the same premises as the fire, the loss, though occasioned by concussion, is a loss by fire,[4] since the explosion is the direct consequence of the fire.

But where the subject-matter is situated in different premises from the fire, the loss, if caused by concussion, and concussion only, is not a loss by fire. The chain of causation is broken and, though the explosion is caused by fire, the fire is not the proximate cause of the loss.[5]

Where there is an explosion on other premises which causes a fire which in turn spreads to the insured premises, the insured is covered. Though the explosion is the origin of the loss, the intervention of the fire breaks the chain of causation. The proximate cause of the loss is fire and the effect of the explosion too remote.[6]

2 Explosions of Boilers

Where an explosion is caused by the application of fire in the ordinary course to a substance not of itself explosive, eg a boiler used for generating steam, any loss occasioned by the explosion is not a loss by fire.[7]

The insurers may, however, by the express terms of their contract accept liability for such a loss.[8]

Whether the loss, in fact, is covered by the terms of the policy is in each case a question of fact.

Thus, in *Willesden Corpn v Municipal Mutual Insurance Ltd*[9] a local authority had effected a fire policy in respect to Electric House, Willesden, which contained a showroom, a demonstration room, a model kitchen and a storeroom. In the basement was a low-pressure hot water system used solely for the purpose of heating the building. The policy provided for an indemnity:

---

damage, I should say that, even if the consequence of the explosion was to create a concussion that caused the existing fire to burn more strongly than before, that would be a loss by fire within the policy, and not within the exception, but as to what was caused by an explosion, the defendants are not liable'. See also *Beacon Life and Fire Assurance Co v Gibb* (1862) 1 Moo P C C N S 73 at 98.

4 Cf *Re Hooley Hill Rubber and Chemical Co Ltd and Royal Insurance Co Ltd* [1920] 1 K B 257 at 271, 272, C A, per Scrutton, L J; *Curtis & Harvey (Canada) Ltd v North British and Mercantile Insurance Co*, [1921] 1 A C 303, P C, approving *Hobbs v Northern Assurance Co* (1886) 12 S C R 631.

5 *Taunton v Royal Insurance Co* (1864) 2 Hem & M 135, where the insurers made a voluntary payment in respect of such a loss; *Everett v London Assurance* (1865) 19 C B N S 126, followed in *Tootal, Broadhurst, Lee Co v London and Lancashire Fire Insurance Co* (1908) Times, 21 May.

6 In *Walker v London and Provincial Insurance Co* (1888) 22 L R Ir 572, where there was an exception against fire caused by incendiarism, the insured was held not to be entitled to recover for loss due to an incendiary fire started in adjoining premises which spread to his own, but this decision was on the wording of the exception, and, in any event, there was no intervening factor to break the chain of causation.

7 *Thames and Mersey Marine Insurance Co Ltd v Hamilton, Fraser & Co* (1887) 12 App Cas 484 (marine insurance), disapproving *West India Telegraph Co v Home and Colonial Insurance Co* (1880) 6 Q B D 51, C A (marine insurance).

8 See eg *Spinney's (1948) Ltd v Royal Insurance Co Ltd* [1980] 1 Lloyd's Rep. 406, where the policy covered 'loss of or damage to the property insured by fire or otherwise directly caused by explosion, but excluding loss of or damage to boilers, economisers, or other vessels, machinery or apparatus in which pressure is used or their contents resulting from their explosion.'

9 (1945) 78 Ll L Rep 256, C A.

'If the property or any item or any part thereof . . . shall be destroyed or damaged by (inter alia) explosion . . . of boilers used for domestic purposes only.'

An explosion occurred in a large storage cylinder causing damage to the property, and the authority claimed to be indemnified under the policy. The insurance company denied liability, contending that the cylinder was not part of the boiler within the meaning of the policy nor was the apparatus used 'for domestic purposes only', which was the exclusive purpose covered by the policy.

The Court of Appeal[10] held that the loss fell within the policy, and that, therefore, the company was liable.

Mackinnon LJ, said:[11]

'First of all, it was said that that which exploded, the container, was not a boiler used for domestic purposes only. I am not sure that it is open to [Counsel] to argue that this was not a boiler, because the arbitrator has found as a fact that the container was part of the boiler, but assuming that [Counsel] is right in saying he can argue as a matter of law as to the meaning of the word 'boiler,' the facts not being in dispute as to the nature of the apparatus which heated the water, I think his argument that the container was not a "boiler" within the meaning of this clause is quite hopeless. [Counsel] rather took the credit for the reticence of the company in not taking the point, but, strictly speaking, I suppose it might be argued that a boiler was an apparatus for generating steam, but quite clearly nobody ever intended to generate steam in this low-pressure system. It was an apparatus for heating water, but though it is said that the insurance company ought to be given credit for not taking that point, it would have been as hopeless as I think the other points are, because quite obviously in common parlance we all talk of a boiler, using it in the sense of an apparatus for heating water, and never intend it, and indeed carefully prevent it, from being an apparatus for generating steam. I need not say any more about that first point. I think it is perfectly obvious that this container was part of the boiler.'

In considering whether the boiler was used 'for domestic purposes only' he added:[12]

'The second point is this. It is said that if the container was a boiler, it was not a boiler used for domestic purposes only. Now, the building had a great number of rooms in it which were used for various purposes. There was a general office, a clerk's office, an engineer's office, and a showroom, but there was one room in which some electrical goods were stored and in which store room it was an advantage to have a radiator to keep the things warm, and the things were stored there, I suppose, until they were wanted to put out in the showroom or perhaps to be sold to customers of the Borough. It is argued by [Counsel] that because there was that room used for storing, that prevented this boiler being used for domestic purposes only. I do not think it necessary to discuss that question at very great length; I think it is as unsound as the other argument about the meaning of the word "boiler".'

He said that the Court had been referred to a wearisome number of cases arising on similar words in the provisions about water companies and the supply of water for domestic purposes.[13] There were two dicta of Judges of inferior courts which had been expressly approved in the House of Lords.[14] One was the dictum of Buckley LJ, who said that the test was not whether the water was consumed or used in the course of trade, but whether the user of the

---

[10] Lord Goddard LCJ, Mackinnon and Du Parcq LJJ.

[11] (1945) 78 Ll L Rep 256 at 258.

[12] Ibid, at 259.

[13] But he said that for the construction of the present policy cases about similar words in Acts of Parliament about water companies and their supply of water had very little value: ibid, at 259.

[14] In *Metropolitan Water Board v Avery* [1914] AC 118, HL.

water was in its nature domestic.[15] Applying that test in the present case, the use of the hot water to heat radiators in the building was clearly in its nature domestic. The other dictum was that of Bray J, who said that:[16]

'If the water is used for a purpose which is common to all ordinary domestic establishments, it is none the less used for domestic purposes because it is ancillary to a trade, manufacture or business.'

Mackinnon LJ then went on to say:[17]

'On that test also it is quite clear that this heated water was used for a purpose which was common to all domestic establishments. It is not necessary in this case to go on and say: "It is none the less used for domestic purposes because it is ancillary to a trade, manufacture, or business." It was not in this case in any sense ancillary to a trade or business. All that can be suggested is that because one room heated by this apparatus was used for a purpose which might be said to be in the nature of a business, that it made the use of the apparatus, the boiler, not one for domestic purposes only. I think even upon those authorities which [Counsel] has produced to us that his argument is shown to be unsound. I am quite satisfied, and it is almost beyond argument, that the heating of this water and the use of the heated water was for a purpose in its nature domestic, and I am quite satisfied that it cannot be said to have ceased to be for domestic purposes only because incidentally in one room there is some activity carried on which possibly might not be carried on in the ordinary domestic use of such water.'

But if the explosion is caused by a fire within the meaning of the contract, the loss of the boiler is clearly a loss by fire.[18] Thus, if in the course of a fire, a boiler is caused to burst, the loss of the boiler is a loss by fire.

Any other loss occasioned by the explosion, at any rate in the premises in which the fire is, seems equally to be covered.

---

[15] In *Metropolitan Water Board v Avery* [1914] 1 K B 221 at 239, C A.
[16] In *Metropolitan Water Board v Avery* [1913] 2 K B 257 at 265, D C.
[17] (1945) 78 Ll L Rep 256 at 259.
[18] As to the meaning of 'fire', see pp 68–71, ante.

CHAPTER 13

The perils insured against by a consequential loss policy

Any loss which is excluded from the scope of an ordinary fire policy as being too remote may be specifically insured against.[1]

The practice of insuring against loss of profit has long been recognised in marine insurance;[2] and, although the practice of insuring against consequential loss in connection with fire insurance is a much later introduction, it is now well established.

A consequential loss insurance is intended to supplement the protection given by an ordinary fire policy. The policy usually contains conditions providing that the premises or property of the insured shall be kept insured against fire, and that no payment shall be made under the policy until the insurers under the ordinary policy have paid or admitted liability.

To give rise to a claim, the premises of the insured or his property[3] must have been destroyed or damaged[4] by fire,[5] and the business of the insured must in consequence have been interrupted or interferred with.[6]

A consequential loss policy, in the ordinary use of the phrase, deals with one or more of the following kinds of consequential loss:[7]

1 Loss of profit.
2 Standing charges.
3 Increased cost of working.
4 Increased cost of reinstatement.

---

[1] *Re Wright and Pole* (1834) 1 Ad & El 621 at 623, per Taunton J.

[2] *Barclay v Cousins* (1802) 2 East 544 (marine insurance).

[3] There are cases in which the consequential loss may be due to a fire on the premises belonging to other persons, eg a power station supplying power to the insured's factory.

[4] This is usually referred to as 'material loss or damage'.

[5] *Waterkeyn v Eagle Star and British Dominions Insurance Co* (1920) 5 Ll L Rep 42, where the insured, who had deposited money with a bank at Petrograd, effected an insurance against loss arising from the bankruptcy or insolvency of the bank directly due to damage or destruction of the premises and contents of the bank through riot, civil commotion, etc, and it was held that the policy contemplated an insolvency due to damage or destruction of the premises and contents, and did not apply to a loss due to the confiscations of the deposit by the Bolsheviks, and the consequent inability of the bank to continue business.

[6] The period of indemnity varies in accordance with the terms of the policy, and is based on the time which the insured considers will elapse before the business will become normal.

[7] Amongst other insurances which may be effected in practice may be mentioned insurances to cover architect's fees during rebuilding and the cost of collecting over again information about customers contained in books that have been burnt.

1 Loss of Profit[8]

The insurance is usually on net profit, ie upon the trade profit of the insured after making proper allowance for fixed and other charges, or capital receipts and accretions and outlay properly chargeable to capital, and for depreciation.[9]

The policy contains special provisions relating to the assessment of the amount of the loss. As a rule, a comparison is made with reference to a particular standard between the period affected by the fire and the corresponding period before the fire. The principal standards of comparison adopted are turnover or output,[10] and the basis of payment is frequently limited to an ascertained percentage of the sum by which the turnover or output of the period affected by the fire falls short of the similar sum for the basic period.[11]

A mere comparison is not sufficient. If the standard adopted shows a reduction in profit, the insured is not entitled, as a matter of course, to recover the whole amount of the reduction. He can only recover for loss of profit caused by the fire;[12] and it is accordingly necessary to ascertain what part of the reduction is attributable to the fire. All relevant factors, eg changes in trade conditions, must be taken into account and allowed for, since, in the particular case, they may tend to show that, even apart from the fire, the profit would have been reduced.[13]

The policy, in practice, contains a special condition dealing with this point, and stating that account is to be taken of any variations in the insured's business, and that allowance is to be made for any additions or deductions in respect of turnover, output, or other standards adopted which, having regard to any extraordinary circumstances, ought to be made.[14] Other conditions may provide for adjustment of the loss by reason of reduction of standing charges.[15]

---

[8] The fact that the insured is trading at a loss at the date of effecting the insurance may be a material fact which ought to have been disclosed: *Stavers v Mountain* (1912) Times, 27 July, C A, where it was held that the question of materiality ought to have been submitted to the jury.

[9] The policy moneys are thus liable to income tax: *R v British Columbia Fir and Cedar Lumber Co Ltd* [1932] A C 441, P C a case on the British Columbia Taxation Act 1924, but the judgment proceeds on more general grounds, following *J Gliksten & Son Ltd v Green* [1929] A C 381, which decided that when the insurance moneys on stock-in-trade exceeded their book value, the whole must be brought in as a trading receipt.

[10] Ie, tons, gallons, barrels, vats, or as the case may be. Other standards that may be adopted are .spindles or looms in use, consumption of raw material, productive wages, etc.

[11] The 'ascertained percentage' is defined as the percentage which the sum insured bears to the turnover or output in the comparable period, but not exceeding the percentage which the profits for the last financial year bear to the turnover. A single example will show how the sum payable is calculated. Turnover in basic year £100,000; sum insured £10,000; profits for the basic year £12,000; turnover for year following fire £20,000. Ascertained percentage is, therefore, 10 per cent, and this percentage of the difference between the turnover of the two periods is £8,000. See *Polikoff Ltd v North British and Mercantile Insurance Co* (1936) 55 Ll L Rep 279; *Plummer Hat Co Ltd v British Trading Insurance Co* [1932] N Z L R 576.

[12] *Recher & Co v North British and Mercantile Co* [1915] 3 K B 277; *Waterkeyn v Eagle Star and British Dominions Insurance Co* (1920) 5 Ll L Rep 42.

[13] Thus, an intensive advertising campaign in the basic year may bring about an increased turnover not likely to be repeated: *Polikoff Ltd v North British and Mercantile Insurance Co Ltd*, (supra).

[14] In *Plummer Hat Co Ltd v British Trading Insurance Co Ltd* [1932] N Z L R 576 it was held that, in the absence of any special conditions, the maximum provided by the calculation was the true measure of agreed indemnity, and not a mere arbitrary limit of the sum which might be paid.

[15] *City Tailors Ltd v Evans* (1921) 126 L T 439, C A; *Brunton v Marshall* (1922) 10 Ll L Rep 689; *Polikoff Ltd v North British and Mercantile Insurance Co Ltd* (1936) 55 Ll L Rep 279, where it was held

The policy may provide that the amount of the loss is to be assessed and certified by an accountant appointed by one or both of the parties. The accountant's assessment, in the absence of fraud, is conclusive as to the amount recoverable under the policy, unless it can be shown that he has misdirected himself on a point of law, or has omitted to take into consideration some material factor.[16]

Occasionally a valued policy is used, the loss of profit being valued at an agreed sum.[17]

Another form of policy provides for payment of a percentage of the sum insured, based on the ratio between the amount paid under the fire policy and the sum insured under it. Such a policy may be a valued policy.[18]

If, however, the policy contains further provisions for assessing the loss, effect must be given to them, and the policy will not be a valued policy; the percentage will be construed as limiting the amount payable for loss of profit, and the insured will only recover the actual loss up to the amount shown by taking the percentage.[19]

2 Standing Charges

The insurance under this head covers such items of expenditure as continue to be payable notwithstanding the fire and the consequent interruption of business,[20] including rent, rates and taxes, insurance premiums,[1] salaries[2] and directors' fees, interest on loans and debentures, and it may include such items as general expenses[3] or depreciation of any part of the insured property which is not actually destroyed by the fire.[4]

As the object of the policy is to cover losses attributable to interruption of business, the policy contemplates that the earnings of the business will

---

that this reduction was to be deducted from the sum found according to the ascertained percentage formula. Nor does it matter whether the reduction is directly due to the fire or to some other cause, eg the voluntary act of the insured in repaying a mortgage.

[16] *Recher & Co v North British and Mercantile Insurance Co* [1915] 3 K B 277, where it was held that, if the accountant was called as a witness in any proceedings upon the policy, he might be cross-examined, and evidence might be called to show that he had omitted to take into consideration the fact that the reduction in profit was due wholly or in part to causes other than the fire, but not to show that the conclusions of fact were incorrect.

[17] *City Tailors Ltd v Evans* (1921) 126 L T 439, C A, where it was held that profits made whilst carrying on the business in temporary premises after the fire could not be taken into account. But the decision might have been different if the condition requiring the insured to minimise the interruption of business had been more stringently worded, eg by requiring him to take other premises, etc. to continue the business, if practicable.

[18] *Beauchamp v Faber* (1898) 3 Com Cas 308 at 311, per Bigham J.

[19] *Brunton v Marshall*, (supra).

[20] The business must be treated as a continuing business before, during and after the suspension, and the calculations must not be as for a business which begins and ends with the period of suspension: *Mount Royal Assurance Co v Cameron Lumber Co Ltd* [1934] A C 313, P C.

[1] This does not include contributions under the National Health Insurance Acts: *Polikoff Ltd v North British and Mercantile Insurance Co Ltd* (1936) 55 Ll L Rep 279 at 288.

[2] Weekly wage earners are not in receipt of salaries: *Polikoff Ltd v North British and Mercantile Insurance Co Ltd* (1936) 55 Ll L Rep 279 at 285. As to the meaning of 'skilled employees' whose wages are sometimes included, see ibid, at 287.

[3] The test is whether such expenses are so shown in the books of the insured, or whether separate accounts are kept: *Polikoff Ltd v North British and Mercantile Insurance Co Ltd*, (supra), at 288.

[4] Any reduction in depreciation because there is no depreciation in the part destroyed must be taken into account: *Polikoff Ltd v North British and Mercantile Insurance Co Ltd*, (supra), at 289.

constitute the fund out of which the standing charges will be paid, and hence no claim is payable unless the effect of the fire is to diminish the fund in question. If the business is already carried on at a loss, the standing charges do not fall within the policy, except in so far as they are, in fact, paid out of earnings.[5]

In practice, the policy contains a condition dealing with this point, and stating that, in the event of the earnings of the business for the financial year preceding the fire being insufficient to meet fully the standing charges of the year in question, the insurance is only to apply to the extent to which the standing charges have been met by such earnings.

An ordinary policy of insurance on buildings frequently contains a rent clause, under which the insured is protected against the loss which he sustains, either as tenant, where the liability to pay rent continues, or as landlord, where the tenancy agreement suspends the payment of rent during the period of reinstatement. The rent clause usually provides that the insurers are liable only where the insured premises become untenantable, and for the payment of such proportion of the amount insured on rent[6] as the period of untenantableness (which is not to exceed the period necessary for reinstatement) bears to the term of rent insured. If, therefore, the loss of rent does not continue to be incurred during the whole of the period for which the policy is in force, but only for a portion of such period, the insured is not entitled to recover the whole of the loss, not exceeding the sum specified in the policy, but only such proportion of that sum as the period of untenantableness bears to the whole period of insurance.[7]

3 Increased Cost of Working

The insurance under this head is intended to cover the additional expenditure incurred in keeping the business going during the period of reinstatement.

Such expenditure includes the rent of temporary premises and the extra cost of labour or materials[8] required for the purposes of the business.[9] Sometimes provision is also made specifically for indemnity against damages awarded against the insured in respect of late delivery or inability to complete orders as a result of fire damage to premises, plant or goods.

---

[5] *Plummer Hat Co Ltd v British Trading Insurance Co Ltd* [1932] N Z L R 576, where there was no special condition. In *Mount Royal Assurance Co v Cameron Lumber Co Ltd* [1934] A C 313, P C, it was suggested that all revenue charges must have been earned before allocating receipts to profits.
[6] Or the rental, whichever may be the less.
[7] *Buchanan v Liverpool and London and Globe Insurance Co* 1884 11 R (Ct of Sess) 1032, where the insurance was for £500 to cover the rent of the premises for 12 months, and it was unsuccessfully contended by the insured, the total rent for that period being £2,345, that the amount payable was a sum bearing the same proportion to £2,345 as the period of untenantableness bore to 12 months, the amount not to exceed £500.
[8] Including partly manufactured goods, if bought for the purpose of keeping the business going: *Henry Booth & Sons v Commercial Union Assurance Co Ltd* (1922) 14 Ll L Rep 114.
[9] Where the policy covers net profits and standing charges as well as increased cost of working, provision is usually made for the amount payable in respect of increased cost of working to be proportionately reduced in the event of the sum insured being less than the amount of the net profit and all standing charges for the preceding financial year.

4 Increased Cost of Reinstatement

A special form of consequential loss insurance has been introduced to protect
the insured against what may be called the increased cost of reinstatement.

In consequence of abnormal trade conditions, the amount received under
the insured's ordinary fire policy, though fairly representing the value of the
subject-matter at the date of the fire, may prove insufficient for reinstatement,
as the cost of reinstatement may have largely increased by a rise in the price of
materials or the cost of labour after the date of the fire. A further difficulty
sometimes arises out of the fact that it may not be lawful to rebuild in the same
style or plan owing to the requirement of Building Acts or municipal bye-laws,
eg in the case of a theatre or other public building, which must be rebuilt in
accordance with modern standards of safety and comfort. Such increased cost
may also be the subject of insurance. Under this kind of insurance the insured is
entitled to be indemnified against the increased cost of reinstatement, and to
receive the difference between such cost and the cost of reinstatement estimated
as at the date of the fire.

Another form of reinstatement insurance, which deals with buildings and
machinery, is not confined to the increased cost of reinstatement; the
reinstatement is on the basis of reinstating the property in a new condition.
This form avoids the difficulty that may arise under an ordinary policy as to
whether any allowance should be made in respect of 'new for old'.

CHAPTER 14

The exceptions in the policy

The general undertaking of the insurers to indemnify the insured against loss by fire is, in practice, qualified by the introduction into the contract of exceptions, which expressly provide that the insurers are not to be liable for a loss occasioned by certain specified causes.

A THE SCOPE OF EXCEPTION CLAUSES

As a general rule an exception is a mere qualification: it excludes losses which fall within the scope of the contract of fire insurance, and which, therefore, would be covered, if they had not been excepted.

Thus, Duke LJ, said in one case:[1]

> 'I take it to be elementary that an exception such as this is an exception of something which would be in the policy if it had not been excepted. The intention then is to exclude loss by explosion which, but for the explosion, would or might have involved the insurers in liability . . . An explosion dependent on fire would not be within the policy at all.'

An exception may, however, have a wider scope and extend to losses which do not, or may not, fall within the category of losses by fire. In this case, the exception is inserted *ex abundanti cautela* to place it beyond question that the insurers do not accept liability.[2]

B SOME USUAL EXCEPTIONS

The causes of loss which are dealt with by the exceptions in ordinary use[3] are the following:

1 Spontaneous combustion.
2 Subjection to a heating process.
3 Explosion.

---

[1] *Re Hooley Hill Rubber and Chemical Co Ltd and Royal Insurance Co Ltd* [1920] 1 K B 257 at 273, C A; *Cory v Burr* (1883) 8 App Cas 393 at 397 (marine insurance) per Lord Selborne L C; *Robinson Gold Mining Co v Alliance Insurance Co* [1902] 2 K B 489 at 502, C A (insurance of gold) per Mathew L J. See also *Curtis & Harvey (Canada) Ltd v North British and Mercantile Insurance Co* [1921] 1 A C 303, P C.

[2] *Burger v Indemnity Mutual Marine Assurance Co* [1900] 2 Q B 348 at 352, C A (marine insurance), per Vaughan Williams L J.

[3] It is, of course, competent to the parties to arrange to cover the causes of loss thus excepted. In practice, the list of exceptions varies according to the locality of the risk, and the relative probability of a loss caused by the excepted perils.

4 Fires caused by human agency in the course of warfare or disturbance of the peace.

5 Fires caused by some convulsion of nature or other calamity.

1 Spontaneous Combustion

In practice, this exception is limited to the loss of the property actually affected, the insurers accepting liability in respect of any other property that may be set on fire. Apart from any exception, the insurers are free from liability where property is destroyed by its own peculiar vice or infirmity.[4]

2 Subjection to a Heating Process

This means any process in or by which the application of fire heat is necessary. Apart from any exception, a loss of this kind would not fall within the scope of the policy unless there is actual ignition.[5]

3 Explosion

An exception against explosion is not intended to except loss by explosion, where there is no fire, since such a loss is prima facie not within the contract.[6] The exception assumes the existence of a fire and a causal connection between the fire and the explosion. In the absence of any such connection, the exception has no application.

Where the explosion precedes the fire, it is important to consider whether the explosion is the cause of the fire or not. If the explosion is the cause of the fire, the loss occasioned by the fire falls within the exception, and the insured is not entitled to recover.[7] If, on the other hand, the fire was not caused by the explosion, but had an independent origin, the exception has no application.[8]

Where the fire precedes the explosion, the explosion is usually caused by the fire. The cause of the explosion is, however, immaterial, since the exception covers all explosions which occur in the course of a fire.[9] Any loss which is the direct consequence of the explosion falls within the exception;[10] and hence the

---

[4] *Boyd v Dubois* (1811) 3 Camp 133 at 133 (marine insurance) per Lord Ellenborough CJ: 'If the hemp was put on board in a state liable to effervesce, and it did effervesce and generate the fire that consumed it, upon the common principles of insurance law, the assured cannot recover for a loss which he himself has occasioned'. See also *Koebel v Saunders* (1864) 17 CB NS 71 at 77 (marine insurance) per Willes J; *Wilson v Jones* (1867) LR 2 Exch 139 at 148, Ex Ch (marine insurance) per Willes J; *Blower v Great Western Rly Co* (1872) LR 7 CP 655 at 663 (carrier) per Willes J, speaking of insurance; *The Knight of St Michael* [1898] P 30 at 33 (marine insurance) per Barnes J.

[5] See p 68, ante.

[6] *Re Hooley Hill Rubber and Chemical Co Ltd and Royal Insurance Co Ltd* [1920] 1 KB 257 at 273, CA, per Scrutton LJ.

[7] Ibid; *Curtis & Harvey (Canada) Ltd v North British and Mercantile Insurance Co* [1921] 1 AC 303, PC.

[8] The exception by terms may throw upon the insured the onus of proving that the fire was not caused by the explosion. See p 159, post.

[9] *Re Hooley Hill Rubber and Chemical Co Ltd and Royal Insurance Co Ltd*, (supra), at 274, per Duke LJ.

[10] See p 149, post.

exception is not limited to loss by concussion.[11] The explosion may itself be the cause of further fires, and any loss which is occasioned by such fires falls within the exception.[12] On the other hand, the original fire, to which the exception has, of course, no application, may continue to be in operation; and the insurers, therefore, remain liable for all the consequences of the fire, unconnected with the explosion,[13] so far as they can be distinguished.[14] Further, the exception has no application to the case where, in the course of a fire, property is intentionally destroyed by explosion for the purpose of checking the progress of the fire.[15]

In practice, the application of these principles is considerably modified by the special terms of the contract. In the ordinary course insurers accept full liability for loss occasioned by the explosion of boilers used for domestic purposes only,[16] or by the explosion, in a building not being part of any gas works, of gas used for domestic purposes or used for lighting or heating the building; and accordingly, in these two cases, loss by concussion is covered.

The word 'gas' in the exception means illuminating gas.

In *Stanley v Western Insurance Co*[17] an exception in a fire policy stated:

> 'Neither will the company be responsible for loss or damage by explosion, except for such loss or damage as shall arise from explosion by gas.'

The insured carried on business of extracting oil from shoddy.[18] Whilst this was being done, an inflammable vapour evolved from the shoddy and set fire to

---

[11] *Stanley v Western Insurance Co* (1868) L R 3 Exch 71, approved in *Re Hooley Hill Rubber and Chemical Co Ltd and Royal Insurance Co Ltd,* (supra), and in *Curtis & Harvey (Canada) Ltd v North British and Mercantile Insurance Co* (supra). The rule is applied differently in personal accident insurance, where an exception against a specified disease, such as hernia or pneumonia, does not exclude liability where the disease is a mere sequel of the accident: *Fitton v Accidental Death Insurance Co* (1864) 17 C B N S 122 (accident insurance); *Re Etherington and Lancashire and Yorkshire Accident Insurance Co* [1909] 1 K B 591, C A (accident insurance).

[12] *Stanley v Western Insurance Co,* (supra); *Curtis & Harvey (Canada) Ltd v North British and Mercantile Insurance Co,* (supra).

[13] *Stanley v Western Insurance Co,* (supra), at p. 74, per Kelly C B. In the cases cited above, liability for such loss was admitted.

[14] An inquiry as to the cause of the damage was directed in *Stanley v Western Insurance Co,* (supra), and in *Curtis & Harvey (Canada) Ltd v North British and Mercantile Insurance Co,* (supra). The onus of distinguishing may, by the terms of the exception, be thrown upon the insured: *Re Hooley Hill Rubber and Chemical Co Ltd and Royal Insurance Co Ltd,* (supra), at 269, per Bankes L J. Apart from this, the insured must fail unless he can show what part of the loss is not attributable to the explosion: *Stanley v Western Insurance Co,* (supra), at 75, per Martin B.

[15] *Stanley v Western Insurance Co,* (supra), at 74, per Kelly C B; *Re Etherington and Lancashire and Yorkshire Accident Insurance Co,* (supra), at 599, (accident insurance) per Vaughan Williams, L J, speaking of fire insurance; *Re Hooley Hill Rubber and Chemical Co Ltd and Royal Insurance Co Ltd,* (supra), at 271, per Bankes L J.

[16] Whether the explosion occurs in the boiler or in some other part of the heating system is a question of fact: 'Domestic purposes' refers to the user of the water and not to the user of the building: *Willesden Corpn v Municipal Mutual Insurance Ltd* [1945] 1 All E R 444n, C A. '[The] cases establish beyond all question what the test is. It is that the use or purpose to which the water is put, the heating of the building, is clearly a domestic use, and it does not cease to be a domestic use merely because a business is carried on on the premises' (per Atkinson J, in the Court below: (1944) 78 Ll L Rep 20 at 25).

[17] (1868) L R 3 Exch 71.

[18] Woollen yarn obtained by tearing to shreds woollen rags which, with the addition of new wool, is made into a kind of cloth.

the premises. The insured claimed under the policy on the ground that the loss was not excepted under the clause set out above.

It was held by the Court of Exchequer[19] that the claim failed because the word 'gas' meant ordinary illuminating coal gas. In giving judgment Kelly C B, said:[20]

> 'The words of the policy are to be construed not according to their strictly philosophical or scientific meaning, but in their ordinary and popular sense. Now in the ordinary language, not only of men of business, and the owners of property (the subject of insurance), but even of scientific men themselves, the explosion in the present case would not be said to have been caused by *gas*. It was not, therefore, within the saving to the exception, which, indeed, was obviously intended by the parties only to refer to gas in the more limited sense of ordinary illuminating gas.'

Except in the two cases mentioned above, viz the explosion of boilers used for domestic purposes and the explosion of gas used for domestic purposes or used for lighting or heating of buildings, the effect of the contract is to relieve the insurers from any liability for loss by concussion, even though the explosion is caused by fire, but to impose liability upon them if the subject-matter is set on fire, whether the explosion itself is caused by fire or not. Loss by concussion may, however, be covered by a special contract, and the special contract may be extended to apply, with or without qualification, to all kinds of explosion.

4 Fires in the Course of Warfare or Disturbance of the Peace[1]

The principal words used to indicate the scope of the exception are the following:[2]

    a Foreign enemy.
    b Riot.
    c Civil commotion.
    d Military or usurped power.
    e Insurrection.
    f Hostilities.

(a) Foreign Enemy

This phrase implies the existence of a war between the State of which the insured is a member and a foreign State. Whether a particular state of hostilities amounts to 'war' is a question of fact in each case.[3]

---

[19] Kelly C B, Martin and Channell B B.

[20] (1868) L R 3 Exch at 73. See further the judgment of Martin B, ibid at 75 and that of Channell B, ibid, at 75.

[1] Incendiarism is sometimes excepted in express terms: *Walker v London and Provincial Insurance Co* (1888) 22 L R Ir 572; *American Tobacco Co v Guardian Assurance Co Ltd* (1925) 69 Sol Jo 621, C A, where a policy effected in respect of tobacco warehoused in the town of Smyrna provided that the insurance did not cover loss or damage from hostilities, warlike operations or 'incendiarism directly connected therewith', and it was held that the losses fell within the exceptions clause.

[2] The actual words used vary according to the practice of different insurers. In the usual policy, the phrase is 'riot, civil commotion, war, invasion, act of foreign enemy, hostilities (whether war be declared or not), civil war, rebellion, revolution, insurrection, or military or usurped power'.

[3] See Ivamy, *General Principles of Insurance Law* (4th edn, 1979), p 277.

(b) Riot

This word is to be construed in its ordinary legal meaning. It involves a tumultuous disturbance of the peace by three persons or more. Mere malicious injury to property done by three or more persons does not constitute a riot.[4]

(c) Civil War

In *Spinney's (1948) Ltd v Royal Insurance Co Ltd*[5], the stock-in-trade of a number of shops and a business at Beirut were insured against fire under a policy which contained an exception of 'civil war'. During the disturbances in Lebanon in 1976, the stock-in-trade was destroyed and the insured claimed an indemnity under the policy. The insurers repudiated liability on the ground that the loss fell within the exception.

Mustill J, said[6] that he did not propose to attempt any general definition of 'civil' war but a decision on whether such a war existed would involve a consideration of the 3 following questions:- (1) Could it be said that the conflict was between two opposing 'sides'?; (2) what were the objectives of the 'sides', and how did they set about pursuing them?; and (3) what was the scale of the conflict and its effect on public order and on the life of the inhabitants?

The learned Judge held, that on the evidence, he could not find that matters had advanced between massive civil strife and virtual anarchy to the stage of a civil war.[7]

(d) Civil Commotion

This phrase is used to indicate a stage between a riot and a civil war. It has been defined to mean an insurrection of the people though not amounting to a rebellion. But it is probably not capable of any very precise definition. The element of turbulence or tumult is essential. An organised conspiracy to commit criminal acts, where there is no tumult or disturbance until after the acts, does not amount to civil commotion. It is not, however, necessary to show the existence of any outside organisation at whose instigation the acts were done.[8]

In *Spinney's (1948) Ltd v Royal Insurance Co Ltd*[9], there was an exception of 'civil commotion assuming the proportions of or amounting to a popular rising'. Mustill J said[10] that there was nothing in the reported cases compelling the Court to hold that a civil commotion must involve a revolt against the government, although the disturbances must have sufficient cohesion to prevent them from being the work of a mindless mob. Confused and fragmentary as the violence in Lebanon might appear, that requirement was satisfied and there was a state of civil commotion prevalent there. The words 'assuming the proportions of or amounting to a popular rising' had no recognised technical

---

[4] See Ivamy, *General Principles of Insurance Law* (4th edn, 1979), at 277–278.
[5] [1980] 1 Lloyd's Rep 406.
[6] Ibid, at 429–430.
[7] Ibid, at 432.
[8] Ibid, at 278–279.
[9] Supra.
[10] [1980] 1 Lloyd's Rep at 438.

meaning. Often they must mean the same as 'insurrection'.[11] Where there was a distinction, it probably lay in the greater spontaneity and looser organisation of a popular rising. But he would still be inclined to consider that there must be some unanimity of purpose among those participating, and also that the purpose must involve the displacement of the government. He doubted whether a violent attack by one section of the population on the other on grounds, eg of religion or race, would be described as a 'rising'. Adopting that interpretation, he would not say that the disturbances in Lebanon amounted to a 'popular rising'. But the disturbances 'assumed the proportions' of 'such a rising'. The word 'proportions' signified 'dimensions'. So one must identify the dimensions of a popular rising. That could not be done precisely. All one could say was that it must involve a really substantial proportion of the populace, although obviously not all the population need participate, and that there should be tumult and violence on a large scale. The events in Lebanon satisfied that test, and the exception, therefore, applied.

(e) Military or Usurped Power

This phrase includes not only the acts of foreign enemies engaged in warfare within the realm or of subjects of the Crown engaged in external rebellion, but also the acts committed by the forces of the Crown in repelling the enemy or suppressing the rebellion. The phrase clearly applies to an armed and organised rebellion, which has got to such a head as to be under authority and to assume the power of government by making laws and punishing disobedience to them.[12] The phrase, however, is probably not capable of being precisely defined. There must be something which is more in the nature of war or civil war than of riot or civil commotion, and the persons taking part must be guilty of high treason.[13]

Thus, in *Drinkwater v London Assurance Corpn*[14] a malting office at Norwich was insured under a fire policy which contained an exception stating that the company

> 'shall not be liable in case the same shall be burnt by any invasion of foreign enemies, or any military or usurped power whatsoever.'

A mob arose an account of the high price of provisions and spoiled and destroyed a quantity of flour. A proclamation was read and the mob dispersed. But later another mob arose and burnt down the insured premises.

The insurance company refused to indemnify the insured on the ground that the loss fell within the exception since the goods had been destroyed by 'usurped power'. The Court of King's Bench rejected this defence, and held by a majority of three Judges to one[15] that the company was liable.

Bathurst J was of the opinion[16] that the words 'usurped power' could only mean the invasion of the kingdom by foreign enemies to give laws and usurp

---

[11] See p 87, post.
[12] See Ivamy, *General Principles of Insurance Law* (4th edn, 1979) pp 279–280.
[13] Ibid, at 279–280.
[14] (1767) 2 Wils 363.
[15] Wilmot CJ, Bathurst and Clive JJ; Gould J, dissenting.
[16] (1767) 2 Wils at 363.

the Government, or an internal armed force in rebellion by making laws and punishing those who did not obey them.

Clive J considered[17] that the words 'usurped power' meant an usurped power as amounted to high treason. The offence of the mob in the present case was a felonious riot, for which the individuals suffered, but it could not be said to be an 'usurped power'.

Wilmot C J said:[18]

> 'My idea of the words "burnt by usurped power", from the context, is, that they mean burnt, or set on fire by occasion of an invasion from abroad, or of an internal rebellion, when armies are employed to support it. When the laws are dormant and silent, and firing of towns is unavoidable, these are the outlines of the picture drawn by the idea which these words convey to my mind. . . . Rebellious mobs may be also meant to be guarded against by the proviso, because this corporation commenced soon after the Riot Act; and if common mobs had been in their minds, they would have made use of the word mob. The words "usurped power" may have a great variety of meanings, according to the subject-matter where they are used, and it would be pedantic to define the words in all their various meanings; but in the present case they cannot mean the power used by a common mob. It has not been said, that if one or fifty persons had wickedly set this house on fire, that it would be within the meaning of the words "usurped power". It hath been objected, that here was an usurped power to reduce the price of victuals, and that this is part of the power of the Crown, and therefore it was an usurped power; but the King has no power to reduce the price of victuals. The difference between a rebellious mob and a common mob is, that the first is high treason, the latter a riot or a felony. Whether was this a. common mob or a rebellious mob? The first time the mob rises the magistrates read the proclamation, and the mob disperse; they hear the law, and immediately obey it: the next day another mob rises upon the same account, and damages the houses of two bakers; thirty people in fifteen minutes put this army to flight, and they were dispersed and heard of no more. Where are the species belli which Lord Hale describes? This mob wants a universality of purpose to destroy, to make it a rebellious mob, or high treason. . . . Here they fell upon two bakers and a miller, and the mob chastized these particular persons to abate the price of provisions in a particular place; this does not amount to a rebellious mob.'

Further, there must be probably be some kind of organisation.[19]

Thus, in *Curtis & Sons v Mathews*[20] which concerned premises destroyed by fire in the Easter Rising in Dublin in 1916,[1] Bankes L J, said (obiter)[2] that he did not propose to give a definition of what constituted 'usurped power', but added:

> ' "Usurped power" seems to mean something more than the action of an unorganised rabble. How much more I am not prepared to define. There must probably be action by some more or less organised body with more or less authoritative leaders.'

The words 'military power' include a *foreign* military power.

Thus, in *Rogers v Whittaker*[3] a bomb from an enemy Zeppelin during an air raid damaged a building which was insured under a fire policy excluding damage resulting from 'insurrection, riot, civil commotion or military or usurped power'. Sankey J, held that the words 'military power' included a

---

[17] (1767) 2 Wils 364.

[18] Ibid, at 364.

[19] See Ivamy, op cit, pp 279–280.

[20] [1919] 1 K B 425.

[1] For the facts of the case see p 89, post.

[2] [1919] 1 K B 425 at 429. He said that it was unnecessary to discuss the meaning of the phrase because the trial Judge (Roche J) had found that the damage was directly caused by 'bombardment', which was one of the perils insured against under the policy.

[3] [1917] 1 K B 942.

foreign military power. Consequently the insurer was not liable. The learned Judge observed:[4]

> 'Nor can it be properly contended that the words "military power" do not refer to military power of a Government lawfully exercised. The disjunctive "or" is used between and contrasts the words "military" and "usurped." The words are not "usurped military power." Without using words of rigorous accuracy, military and usurped power suggest something more in the nature of war and civil war than riot and tumult. To sum up, in my view this clause is not merely a riot clause from beginning to end, but it is a riot clause and a war clause combined. In the result the event is within the exception, is not one which is covered by the policy, and as a consequence the claim fails.'

In *Spinney's (1948) Ltd v Royal Insurance Co Ltd*[5], another exception exempted the insurers from liability for loss 'occasioned by . . . usurped power'. Mustill J said[6] that one must ask whether those participating in the events which had occurred had a sufficiently warlike posture, organisation and universality of purpose to constitute them an 'usurped power'. So far as concerned casual looters, armed men settling personal scores, young people firing off guns for the sake of it, the answer was 'No'. But for the trained militia and those armed civilians who were temporarily fighting at their side the answer was 'Yes'. The objectives were not identical; but the words of exception did not require this. By side-stepping the government and proceeding to direct action, the citizen groups arrogated to themselves the proper function of the State and thereby exercised or constituted an 'usurped power' within the meaning of the exception.

(f) Insurrection

This word means a rising of the people in open resistance against established authority with the object of supplanting it.[7]

In *Spinney's (1948) Ltd v Royal Insurance Co Ltd*[8], an exception of 'insurrection and rebellion' was held not to apply. Mustill J said[9] that as regards 'rebellion' he adopted the definition in the Oxford English Dictionary (Murray) ie 'organised resistance to the ruler or government of one's country; insurrection, revolt'. He said that he would add that the purpose of the resistance must be to supplant the existing rulers or at least to deprive them of authority over part of their country. The Dictionary defined 'insurrections' in a similar manner, but also suggested the notion of an incipient or limited rebellion. He believed that that reflected the distinction between two exceptions as they were used in the present clause, subject to the rider that a lesser degree of organisation might also mark off an insurrection from a rebellion. But with each exception, there must be action against the government with a view to supplanting it. In the present case, none of the factions had the intent at the time concerned to force a change of government by acts of violence.

---

4 [1917] 1 K B 944.
5 Supra.
6 [1980] 1 Lloyd's Rep at 435–436.
7 See Ivamy, op cit, p 280.
8 Supra.
9 [1980] 1 Lloyd's Rep at 436.

(g) Hostilities

This word does not refer to the mere existence of a state of war. There must be acts or operations of hostility committed by persons acting as agents of an enemy government or of an organised rebellion and not by private individuals acting entirely on their own initiative.[10]

In *Spinney's (1948) Ltd v Royal Insurance Co Ltd*[11], where there was an exception of 'hostilities', it was held that it did not apply because there was no state of war or rebellion in Lebanon at the relevant time nor were acts such as the capture of Damour and the clearing of Qarantina and Maslakh sufficiently close to whatever civil war might ultimately have come into existence in Lebanon to form part of a series of acts of belligerency.[12]

(h) Acts of Terrorist Organisations

In *Spinney's (1948) Ltd v Royal Insurance Co Ltd*[13], an exception stated that the insurers' liability was excluded if the loss was occasioned by 'any act of any person acting on behalf of or in connection with any organisation with activities directed towards the overthrow by force of the government *de jure* or *de facto* or to the influencing of it by terrorism or violence'. Mustill J held[14] that the exception related only to the terrorist acts of members of terrorist organisations and not to the acts of members of such organisations in furtherance of the organisations' aims.

5 Fires Caused by Convulsion of Nature or Other Calamity

These include earthquake,[15] subterranean fire, hurricane, volcanic action, or forest fire.[16]

C SPECIAL POLICIES COVERING RISKS USUALLY EXCEPTED

Losses due to the causes specified are, according to the practice of insurers, excluded from the risks ordinarily undertaken by them. But a special contract may be made to cover the whole or any part of such losses. Thus, the whole may be included under a war risk insurance;[17] or a special insurance may be effected to cover loss by riot or civil commotion[18], or loss by riot, strikes or malicious damage.[19]

---

10 See Ivamy, op cit, p 280–281.
11 Supra.
12 See the judgment of Mustill J: [1980] 1 Lloyd's Rep at 437.
13 Supra.
14 [1980] 1 Lloyd's Rep at 439.
15 *Tootal, Broadhurst, Lee Co Ltd v London and Lancashire Fire Insurance Co* (1908) Times, 21 May (a case arising out of the Jamaica earthquake of 1907). See Appendix IV, p 403, post.
16 *Commercial Union Assurance Co v Canada Iron Mining and Manufacturing Co* (1873) 18 L C J 80.
17 Eg *Curtis & Sons v Mathews* [1919] 1 K B 425, C A.
18 Eg *London and Manchester Plate Glass Co Ltd v Heath* [1913] 3 K B 411, C A.
19 See eg *Spinney's (1948) Ltd v Royal Insurance Co Ltd* [1980] 1 Lloyd's Rep 406.

In *Curtis & Sons v Mathews*[20] premises in Dublin were insured under a fire policy, which covered:

> 'The risk of loss and/or of damage to the property hereby insured directly caused by war, bombardment, military or usurped power, or by aerial craft (hostile or otherwise) including bombs, shells, and/or missiles dropped or thrown therefrom, or discharged thereat, and fire and/or explosion directly caused by any of the foregoing whether originating on the premises insured or elsewhere.'

The premises were within 100 yards of the General Post Office in Sackville Street. On Easter Monday, 24 April 1916, a Provisional Government proclaimed an Irish Republic and occupied with armed forces, estimated at some 2,000 men, various public and other buildings in Dublin and amongst them the General Post Office. The military forces of the Crown took action and after house and street fighting lasting until Saturday, 29 April, the Provisional Government and its followers surrendered. In the course of the week the General Post Office was bombarded by the Crown forces using 18-pounder field guns. On 28 April the shelling started a fire, which by 29 April reached and virtually destroyed the insured premises. The insurers refused to indemnify the insured on the ground that the loss was caused merely by a riot or civil commotion, and therefore not covered by the policy. It was further contended that the words 'war, bombardment, military or usurped power' referred to foreign enemies, and not to an internal commotion, and that the insurers were not liable.

The Court of Appeal[1] rejected both these arguments, and held that the action brought by the insured on the policy succeeded.

In holding that the loss was caused by 'war' Bankes LJ, said:[2]

> 'In this policy which we have to construe the words are "war, bombardment, military or usurped power." It does not seem to me to be very material to consider what in this clause "usurped power" means in view of the finding of fact by the learned Judge[3] that the damage was directly caused by the bombardment. But assuming that it is material to consider the meaning of "usurped power" I will merely say this: Usurped power seems to me to mean something more than the action of an unorganised rabble. How much more I am not prepared to define. There must probably be action by some more or less organised body with more or less authoritative leaders. Beyond that it is not, in my view, necessary to express any opinion, because the learned Judge said:[4] "I am satisfied that Easter week in Dublin was a week not of mere riot but of civil strife amounting to warfare waged between military and usurped powers and involving bombardment." In that conclusion, upon the facts before him, I entirely agree.'

As to his conclusion that the words of the clause referred to foreign enemies only he observed:[5]

> 'The second point was that the words in the clause referred to damage done by some hostile act of a foreign enemy, and this contention is founded on the words which immediately follow the part of the clause which deals with bombardment and military or usurped power—

---

[20] [1919] 1 K B 425, C A. The policy also contained an exception excluding the liability of the insurer if the loss was caused by 'destruction by the Government of the country in which the property is situated'. As to this aspect of the case, see p 90, post.

[1] Bankes, Warrington and Scrutton LJJ.

[2] *Curtis & Sons v Mathews* [1919] 1 K B 425 at 429.

[3] Roche J, in the Court below: [1918] 2 K B 825.

[4] [1918] 2 K B 825, at 829.

[5] [1919] 1 K B 425, at 429.

namely, ''aerial craft (hostile or otherwise).'' It is said that the fact that damage by aerial craft belonging to this country is expressly mentioned in that part of the clause indicates that damage by the forces of this country was not intended to be included in the earlier part of the clause. The learned Judge dealt with that contention in this way:[6] ''I cannot regard the insertion of words *ex abundanti cautela* in this later connection as altering or affecting the plain and natural construction of the words in the earlier part of the clause.'' I cannot express my view more concisely or more clearly, and I adopt his language as expressing my view on this contention.'

D   EXCEPTIONS IN SPECIAL POLICIES

The types of exceptions which are inserted in special policies covering the risks normally excepted will vary in accordance with the circumstances of the case.

In *Curtis & Sons v Mathews*[7] a war and bombardment policy in respect of some premises in Dublin contained an exception which stated:

'No claim to attach hereto for . . . confiscation or destruction by the Government of the country in which the property is situated.'

During the Easter Rising in April 1916, the General Post Office in Dublin was occupied by armed forces of the Provisional Government which had proclaimed an Irish Republic. The building was shelled by armed forces of the Crown, and a fire broke out and spread to the insured premises which were destroyed.[8]

The insurers repudiated liability on the ground that the loss fell within the exception set out above.[9] They pleaded that destruction by the Government was all that was necessary to bring the exception into operation.

The Court of Appeal[10] held that the insurers were liable because the exception applied only to deliberate destruction.

Bankes LJ, said:[11]

'It is next said that the case comes within the exception, ''no claim to attach for . . . destruction by the Government of the country in which the property is situated,'' because, on the findings of the learned Judge,[12] the case was one of destruction by the Government of the country in which the property was situated. It was pointed out by the learned Judge that, if that contention were correct, it would be in sharp contradiction to that part of the clause which immediately precedes it in reference to damage caused by aerial craft belonging to the forces of this country, because it might well be that a bomb dropped from one of our aeroplanes might fall on the premises insured and destroy them. The learned Judge was of opinion that this provision had reference to deliberate destruction, that is to say, deliberate in the same sense as confiscation, the word immediately preceding it, would be deliberate. In that conclusion I entirely agree.'

---

[6] [1918] 2 K B 825, at 830.

[7] [1919] 1 K B 425. Other aspects of the case (ie as to whether the premises had been destroyed as a result of war, and not merely as a result of a civil commotion; and whether the words 'war, bombardment, military or usurped power' referred only to *foreign* enemies, and not to an internal commotion) are considered at p 85, ante.

[8] The facts of the case are set out at greater length at p 89, ante.

[9] The other grounds on which the insurers repudiated liability are considered at p 89, ante.

[10] Bankes, Warrington and Scrutton LJJ.

[11] [1919] 1 K B 425 at 430.

[12] Roche J in the Court below: [1918] 2 K B 825.

CHAPTER 15

The conditions of the policy

Whether a particular stipulation in a fire policy is a condition or not is a question of construction in each case.[1]

If the stipulation is construed as a condition and it is not fulfilled, either the policy is not valid or the insurers never become liable under it.[2]

Sometimes literal performance of the condition is necessary, whereas in other cases substantial performance is sufficient.[3]

The burden of proving that a condition has been broken rests on the insurers.[4]

The usual conditions in a fire policy[5] are the following:

a Conditions as to proper description.
b Conditions as to alteration of risk.
c Conditions as to 'other insurance'.
d Conditions as to procedure in case of loss.
e Conditions as to the effect of a fraudulent claim.
f Conditions as to arbitration.

CONDITIONS AS TO PROPER DESCRIPTION

In so far as the description given by the insured during the negotiations[6] is not inserted in the policy, or incorporated into it by express reference, the effect of its inaccuracy depends on whether, in the circumstances of the particular case, the insured is to be regarded as guilty of non-disclosure or misrepresentation.[7]

Where, however, it is inserted in the policy, as must necessarily be the case to some extent at least, or where it is incorporated into the policy, different considerations apply. The description then becomes an integral part of the policy. Any inaccuracy, therefore, in the description amounts to a misdescription of the subject-matter, and constitutes a breach of contract on the part of the insured.

The policy is not, however, avoided unless the misdescription in question goes to the root of the contract, or unless the contract is subject to a condition,

---

[1] See Ivamy, *General Principles of Insurance Law* (4th edn, 1979), pp 294–302.
[2] Ibid pp 308–310.
[3] Ibid pp 303–306.
[4] Ibid p 308.
[5] For various forms of policies in current use, see Appendix II (forms of policies issued by an insurance company) and Appendix III (form of Lloyd's form of policy), post.
[6] As to the description given by the insured during the negotiations, see pp 39–45, ante.
[7] As to non-disclosure and misrepresentation, see pp 47–57, ante. See further, Ivamy, *General Principles of Insurances Law* (4th edn, 1979), pp 110–176.

express or implied, that the description shall be accurate. In this latter case the effect of an inaccurate description depends on the scope of the particular condition applicable.

Description of the Property to be Insured

A description of the subject-matter of insurance itself necessarily appears on the face of every policy. The description is to be regarded, as a general rule, as proceeding from the insured,[8] and it is therefore, in the absence of any ambiguity, conclusive against him,[9] though the onus of proving that it is inaccurate rests on the insurers.[10] The insured may, however, show that the description in the policy did not proceed from him, but was, in fact, inserted by the insurers themselves in reliance on the information given to them by their own agents.[11]

The question whether the subject-matter must be specifically described, or whether a description in general terms is sufficiently accurate, depends partly on the materiality of a specific description in the particular case, and partly on the terms of the policy.[12]

A policy usually contains a condition providing for a specific description of the following classes of property:

1   Goods held in trust or on commission.
2   Money,[13] securities, stamps, documents, manuscripts, business books, patterns, models, moulds, plans, designs and explosives.[14]

---

[8] *Birrell v Dryer* (1884) 9 App Cas 345 at 352 (marine insurance) per Lord Blackburn.

[9] *Hare v Barstow* (1844) 8 Jur 928 at 929, per Lord Denman CJ.

[10] *Baxendale v Harvey* (1859) 4 H & N 445 at 541, per Pollock CB.

[11] *Re Universal Non-Tariff Fire Insurance Co v Forbes & Co's Claim* (1875) LR 19 Eq 485 at 495, per Malins V-C, following *Parsons v Bignold* (1846) 15 LJ Ch 379 (life insurance), where it was 'assumed throughout that if the misrepresentation had been the fault of the agent of the insurance company, the policy would have been valid'; cf *Newcastle Fire Insurance Co v Macmorran & Co* (1815) 3 Dow 255 at 263, HL, per Lord Eldon LC. See further, *City of London Fire Insurance Co v Smith* (1888) 15 SCR 69, where the word 'boards' in the agent's handwriting was misread by the insurers as 'brick'; *Malin v Union Assurance Co* (1910) 13 WLR 653, where a misdescription in the proposal was corrected in pencil at the head office, and the property was accurately described in the policy; *Drysdale v Union Fire Insurance Co* (1890) 8 SC 63, where the proposal, which was filled up by the company's agent after full inspection of the premises, stated that the walls of the insured premises were of brick and iron, whereas some were of wood, brick and iron, and there were two partitions of canvas. For cases where inaccurate plans of the buildings insured were prepared by agents of the insurers, who were accordingly held bound by them, see *Guardian Insurance Co v Connely* (1892) 20 SCR 208; *Quinlan v Union Fire Insurance Co* (1883) 8 AR 376, following *Hastings Mutual Fire Insurance Co v Shannon* (1878) 2 SCR 394; *Somers v Athenaeum Fire Insurance Co* (1858) 9 LCR 61, where the agent made and transmitted to the head office a diagram of the buildings insured, describing them as detached instead of as connected with other buildings. See also *W Malcolm Mackay Co v British American Assurance Co* [1923] SCR 335, where the insurers' agent had inspected the property before the insurance and had, by mistake, reported that it complied with the warranty to be inserted in the policy.

[12] *Gorman v Hand-in-Hand Insurance Co* (1877) IR 11 CLR 224, where two specific risks were insured; *Grover & Grover Ltd v Mathews* [1910] 2 KB 401, where a factory was described as located at A, whereas it was at B; cf *Rogerson v Scottish Automobile and General Insurance Co Ltd* (1931) 146 LT 26, HL (motor insurance), where the policy was held not to apply to a new car though similar. See p 244, post.

[13] In the absence of an exception, money would be included under the description of 'goods': *Da Costa v Firth* (1766) 4 Burr 1966 (marine insurance).

[14] Cf *King v Travellers' Insurance Association Ltd* (1931) 48 TLR 53 (burglary insurance), where a fur

If, therefore, any such property is not specifically described as such in accordance with the condition, the insured cannot recover in the event of its loss.

Description of the Locality of the Property

A knowledge of the locality in which the subject-matter of insurance is situated may be, and usually is, material to the insurers as affecting the risk.[15] It is therefore, as a rule, the duty of the insured to give them an accurate description of such locality. This duty is based on the doctrine of disclosure.

In practice, the insured is called upon to answer specific questions as to the information required by the insurers on this point. The answers to these questions are usually incorporated into the policy, and thus become part of the description.

If a description of locality is inserted in the policy or incorporated into it, its accuracy is governed by the same principles, and the consequences are the same as in the case of a description of the subject-matter itself.[16]

Where the subject-matter of insurance is a building, a statement as to its locality forms part of its description.[17]

A description of locality necessarily includes a statement as to the district in which the building insured is situated, and it may further comprise full particulars as to the relation of the building to its surroundings. An inaccuracy in the description of the situation of the building, therefore, avoids the policy, not only because the building can no longer be identified, but also because the condition as to accuracy of description has not been fulfilled.[18]

On the other hand, a statement as to the relation of the building insured to its surroundings is not necessary for the purpose of its identification, and, therefore, an inaccuracy in this respect will not prevent the subject-matter of insurance from being identified, if its description is otherwise clear. If, however, such a statement is included in the description, it becomes part of the description and must therefore be accurate.

In the case of goods, a statement as to the place in which they are is not a necessary part of the description except where required for the purpose of

---

coat was held not to be a specially valuable article which was excepted from the policy unless declared.

15 *Grover & Grover Ltd v Mathews* (1910), as reported in 15 Com Cas 249 at 260, where instead of the locality of the building to be insured being inserted in the 'slip', the address of the person effecting the insurance was given, and Hamilton J said: 'For no purpose that I am aware of has an underwriter at Lloyd's any interest at all in knowing the postal address of the assured . . . on the other hand, an insurance against fire on a building . . . I should have thought involved as one of the most essential factors some knowledge on the part of the underwriter as to where it was situated, considering that the risk of the loss being partial or total, and very often the risk of there being a loss at all is largely affected by the locality'. See also *Pearson v Commercial Union Assurance Co* (1876) 1 App Cas 498 at 505, per Lord Chelmsford.

16 Thus, in *Dawsons Ltd v Bonnin* [1922] 2 A C 413 a misdescription of the place where a motor lorry was garaged, though held not to be material, nevertheless avoided the policy by reason of a condition requiring accuracy.

17 *Grover & Grover Ltd v Mathews* [1910] 2 K B 401.

18 *Grover & Grover Ltd v Mathews,* (supra), where the postal address of the person effecting the insurance, ie Bank House, Newington Green, N, was inserted in the policy, whereas the building insured was situated at New Southgate, and it was held that this was a misdescription avoiding the policy; *Renshaw v Phoenix Insurance Co* [1943] O R 223, where the insured moved a summer cottage bodily from an island to the mainland.

identification. Such a statement is, however, usually made part of the description,[19] and, where this is the case, it must be accurate[20] whether it relates to the building,[1] or to that part of the building[2] in which the goods may be.

The description may further include a statement as to adjacent or contiguous buildings and the like, or, if the goods are not in any building, it may deal with the nature and surroundings of the place in which they are.[3]

In these cases also, the statement forms part of the description and must, therefore, be accurate.

Description of Other Circumstances

The description contained in the policy may further contain a statement referring to the user of the subject-matter of insurance, or any other circumstances which the insured may have chosen to mention, or the insurers to require.[4]

This part of the description, though it is not, as a rule, necessary for the purpose of identifying the subject-matter, is important in that it serves to define the limits of the risk which the insurers have undertaken.[5] It must, therefore, be accurate equally with any other part of the description, and its accuracy is to be determined in the same way.[6] An inaccuracy in this respect may constitute a misdescription, and its effect on the validity of the policy will then depend partly on its materiality,[7] and partly on the language of the particular condition applicable.[8]

The circumstances, which may be stated in the policy as part of the description, are usually the following:

---

[19] *Pim v Reid* (1843) 6 Man & G 1; *Barrett v Jermy* (1849) 3 Exch 535; *Baxendale v Harvey* (1859) 4 H & N 445; *Merrick v Provincial Insurance Co* (1857) 14 U C R 439.

[20] A misdescription in the proposal may be corrected by reference to a plan on the back of the proposal: *Guardian Insurance Co v Connely* (1892) 20 S C R 208.

[1] *Barnett and Block v National Parcels Insurance Co Ltd* [1942] 1 All E R 221 (burglary insurance), where a van parked in an enclosed but unroofed yard was held not to be in a 'garage'; cf *Wulfson v Switzerland General Insurance Co Ltd* [1940] 3 All E R 221 (accident insurance), where an insurance on 'goods in store' covered them when they were in vans standing in an uncovered yard. See also *Gordon v Transatlantic Fire Insurance Co* [1905] 3 T H 146, where the building in which the goods insured were was described as a brick building, whereas in truth 3 rooms were not built of brick; *Rolland v North British and Mercantile Insurance Co* (1869) 14 L C J 69, where it was held that an insurance on goods described as being in Nos 317, 319, St Paul Street did not cover goods in No 315 adjoining. Such a statement relates to the construction of the building, not to the insured's interest in it: *Friedlander v London Assurance Corpn* (1832) 1 Mood & R 171.

[2] *Liverpool and London and Globe Insurance Co v Wyld* (1877) 1 S C R 604, where some of the goods insured were in a part of the building not included in the description.

[3] *Palatine Insurance Co v Gregory* [1926] A C 90, P C.

[4] These facts need not be stated, unless required in the clearest and plainest language: *Baxendale v Harvey* (1859) 4 H & N 445, following *Stokes v Cox* (1856) 1 H & N 533, Ex Ch; *London and Northwestern Rly Co v Glyn* (1859) 1 E & E 652.

[5] See Ivamy, *General Principles of Insurance Law* (4th edn, 1979), pp 18–19.

[6] See pp 95–96, post.

[7] *Re Universal Non-Tariff Fire Insurance Co, Forbes & Co's Claim* (1875) L R 19 Eq 485 cf; *Friedlander v London Assurance Co* (1832) 1 Mood & R 171; *Perrins v Marine and General Travellers' Insurance Society* (1859) 2 E & E 317 (accident insurance); *Holdsworth v Lancashire and Yorkshire Insurance Co* (1907) 23 T L R 521 (employers' liability insurance).

[8] *Bancroft v Heath* (1901) 6 Com Cas 137, C A.

a The user of the building insured or containing the property insured.

b The fact that the insurance is intended to cover goods held by the insured in trust or on commission.

c The interest of the insured in the property insured.

(a) The User of the Building

A statement as to user[9] may include one or other of the following matters:

i The user of the building itself.[10] In this connection the name given to the building in the policy may be a sufficient statement as to its user.[11]

ii The user of some specified object or objects in[12] or near[13] the building.

iii The presence in, or absence from the building, of some specified object or objects.[14]

---

[9] A condition requiring a description of the building does not imply a description of user: *Baxendale v Harvey* (1859) 4 H & N 445. A statement as to user is important when taken in connection with a condition as to subsequent alteration.

[10] *Whitehead v Price* (1835) 2 Cr M & R 447, where the description of a mill as 'worked by day only' was held to be accurate notwithstanding that a steam engine in the mill was worked by day, the mill itself not being worked except by day, approved in *Mayall v Mitford* (1837) 6 Ad & El 670; *Shaw v Robberds* (1837) 6 Ad & El 75, where the building was described as a kiln for drying corn in use; *Dia v County Fire Office Ltd* (1930) 37 Ll L Rep 24 (burglary insurance), where a policy on the 'assured's private dwelling' did not cover a flat in which he had installed an assistant, but had never himself resided; *Laurentian Insurance Co v Davidson* [1932] SCR 491, where a statutory condition that, if the premises were unoccupied for 30 days, the insurers should not be liable, did not apply where the tenant left the premises for good, but a fire occurred within the 30 days; *Metcalfe v General Accident Assurance Co* (1930) 64 OLR 643, where premises described as a dwelling were held to be covered during a temporary vacancy; *Lambert v Anglo-Scottish General Commercial Insurance Co* (1929) 64 OLR 439, where a similar description was held not to apply where the insured was not living in the building, although he had left some furniture and clothing in it.

[11] *Quin v National Assurance Co* (1839) Jo & Car 316, Ex Ch, where an unfinished house in charge of a carpenter, who worked there daily, was held to be improperly described as a dwelling-house occupied by a caretaker; *Richards v Guardian Assurance Co* [1907] TH 24, where premises were described as a dwelling-house though used as a brothel.

[12] *Stokes v Cox* (1856) 1 H & N 533, where the description stated that no steam engine was employed on the premises; *Beauchamp v National Mutual Indemnity Insurance Co Ltd* [1937] 3 All ER 19, where the description stated that no explosives would be used; *Lyon v Stadacona Fire Insurance Co* (1879) 44 UCR 472, where there was a stove which was not used.

[13] Thus, in insurances on timber, no sawmill must be within a specified distance: *Palatine Insurance Co v Gregory* [1926] AC 90, PC, where the condition was inoperative under a Canadian statute; cf F *Gliksten & Son Ltd v State Assurance Co* (1922) 10 Ll L Rep 604, where the insurers had notice that a scheme of rearrangement of a number of policies had not yet been completed, and accordingly the provisional cover which had been effected still remained good; *Guimond v Fidelity-Phoenix Fire Insurance Co of New York* (1912) 47 SCR 216 (no railway passing through, or within 200 feet from, the property insured); *St Paul Lumber Co v British Crown Assurance Corpn Ltd* [1923] SCR 515 (property should be entirely surrounded by ploughed lands to prevent the risk of prairie fires); *W Malcolm MacKay Co v British America Assurance Co* [1923] SCR 335 (no standing wood, brush or forest within a specified distance); *Fidelity Phoenix Fire Insurance Co of New York v McPherson* [1924] SCR 666 (no scrub, brush or railway within specified distance).

[14] Thus, there may be a provision, general or qualified, prohibiting stoves: *Daniel v Robinson* (1826) Batt 650; *O'Neill v Ottawa Agricultural Insurance Co* (1879) 30 CP 151; gunpowder: *Beacon Life and Fire Assurance Co v Gibb* (1862) 1 Moo PCCNS 73; or other hazardous goods; see further pp 107–110, post.

    iv   The trade or business carried on in the building.[15]
    v   The occupancy of the building.[16]

Whatever form the statement as to user may take, it relates only to the user subsisting at the date of effecting the insurance, and does not necessarily imply an undertaking on the part of the insured that no change in such user shall take place during the currency of the policy.[17]

(b) Goods Held in Trust or On Commission

The policy almost invariably contains a condition excepting from its protection goods held in trust or on commission unless specifically described in the policy as such.

    The expression 'goods held in trust' is not limited to goods held in trust in the strict technical sense of the phrase, but extends to goods with which the insured is entrusted.[18] It, therefore, includes all goods which are in the possession of the insured as bailee, whatever the nature of the contract by which they come into his possession.[19]

    The insured must be in possession of the goods as bailee only, and the property must be in someone else.[20] If the effect of the transaction by which the goods come into his possession is to pass to him the property in them, the goods are his own, and not goods held in trust. They need not, therefore, be specifically described as such.[1]

    The condition applies to cases in which the insured seeks to cover the interest of the bailor in the goods as well as in his own. If, therefore his intention is to cover nothing more than his own interest in the goods as bailee, it has been

---

[15] *Shaw v Robberds* (1837) 6 Ad & El 75; *Pim v Reid* (1843) 6 Man & G 1; *Peck v Phoenix Mutual Insurance Co* (1881) 45 U C R 620, where the buildings were insured as occupied as a grocery store and dwelling-house.

[16] *Quin v National Assurance Co* (1839) Jo & Car 316, Ex Ch; *Hordern v Commercial Union Insurance Co* (1887) 56 L J P C 78, where the insured omitted to state that he was joint-occupant only; *Harding v Victoria Insurance Co* [1924] N Z L R 267, where the insured, the owner, described the premises as occupied by a tenant, although he regarded the occupant as a trespasser; cf *Gendron v Provident Assurance Co* (1930) 66 O L R 147, where the occupancy was not, in fact, described in the policy.

[17] As to the effect of a change of user, see Ivamy, *General Principles of Insurance Law* (4th edn, 1979), pp 320–324.

[18] *Waters v Monarch Fire and Life Assurance Co* (1856) 5 E & B 870 at 882, per Crompton J, approved in *Maurice v Goldsbrough Mort & Co Ltd* [1939] A C 452, P C; *South Australian Insurance Co v Randell* (1869) L R 3 P C 101, 107; cf *Lake v Simmons* [1927] A C 487 (jewellery insurance). The condition does not apply where the trust does not arise until after the date of the insurance: *Bank of New South Wales v North British and Mercantile Insurance Co* (1881) 2 N S W L R 239.

[19] Such as, eg warehousemen (*Waters v Monarch Fire and Life Insurance Co* (1856) 5 E & B 870); carriers (*London and Northwestern Rly Co v Glyn* (1859) 1 E & E 652); coachbuilders (*Dalgleish v Buchanan* 1854 16 Dunl (Ct of Sess) 332); millers (*Cochran & Son v Leckie's Trustee* 1906 8 F (Ct of Sess) 975).

[20] The condition may extend to the goods, whilst they are in the custody of the insured, or of any person to whom the insured may have entrusted them: *Genn v Winkel* (1912) 107 L T 434, C A (sale of goods), where it was held that a policy insuring jewellery against loss did not cover goods delivered on 'sale or return', if the property had passed to the buyer.

[1] *South Australian Insurance Co v Randell* (1869) L R 3 P C 101; *North British and Mercantile Insurance Co v McLellan* (1892) 21 S C R 288, where the insured was to manufacture and keep the goods until the buyer sent a ship for them, and the goods were destroyed whilst still in the insured's possession.

suggested that it is unnecessary for him to describe them specifically as goods held in trust, since he is sufficiently protected by an insurance in general terms.[2] But under the form of condition at present in general use it would appear that he must declare them in any event since they are held in trust by him, whatever may be the division of responsibility between the insured, the insurers, and the owner.

Where goods held in trust are specifically described as such, the insured is entitled in the event of their loss to recover their full value.[3] It is immaterial, unless the condition expressly provides to the contrary,[4] that he himself is not responsible[5] to the bailor for their safety.[6]

The expression 'goods held on commission' is used in a narrower sense, and means that the goods are in the hands of the bailee for the purpose of sale.[7]

(c) The Interest of the Insured in the Property Insured

It is not, as a general rule, necessary for the insured to describe the nature or extent of his interest in the property insured.[8]

Hence, if he describes himself as its owner, the validity of the policy is not affected, provided that this description, though not strictly accurate, substantially defines his relation to the property.[9]

Thus, during the period between the date of the contract for the purchase of the property insured and the date of completion, both the vendor[10] and the purchaser[11] may describe themselves as owner.

---

[2] *London and Northwestern Rly Co v Glyn* (1859) 1 E &. E 652 at 664, per Crompton J; *Crowley v Cohen* (1832) 3 B & Ad 478 (insurance on canal boats). The fact that the goods are not so described is evidence of his intention: *Gillett v Mawman* (1808) 1 Taunt 137.

[3] *Waters v Monarch Fire and Life Assurance Co* (1856) 5 E & B 870. But he must account to the owner for the whole sum recovered, less charges accrued due, and cannot deduct prospective profits arising from the future disposal of the goods: *Maurice v Goldsbrough Mort & Co Ltd* [1939] A C 452, P C.

[4] *North British and Mercantile Insurance Co v Moffatt* (1871) L R 7 C P 25.

[5] This means 'legally responsible': *Engel v Lancashire and General Assurance Co* (1925) 41 T L R 408 (burglary insurance).

[6] *Waters v Monarch Fire and Life Assurance Co* (1856) 5 E & B 870, where the insured was under no liability.

[7] *Waters v Monarch Fire and Life Assurance Co* (supra) per Lord Campbell C J, at 879; *North British and Mercantile Insurance Co v Moffatt*, (supra).

[8] As to when it is material to state the insured's interest, see Ivamy, *General Principles of Insurance Law* (4th edn, 1979), pp 26–28.

[9] *Gilbert v National Insurance Co* (1848) 12 Ir L R 143, where it was held that a statement in a policy that the premises insured were the property of the insured did not amount to a warranty; *Friedlander v London Assurance Co* (1832) 1 Mood & R 171. A husband must not describe himself as owner of property belonging to his wife: *Lemieux v Compagnie Equitable d'Assurance Contra feu* (1906) Q R 30 S C 490. But husband and wife may describe themselves as owners where part of the property belongs to the husband and the rest to the husband and wife jointly: *Harrison v Western Assurance Co* (1903) 1 Can Com L R (Can) 490, reversed without affecting this point (1903) 33 S C R 473.

[10] *Gill v Canada Fire and Marine Insurance Co* (1882) 1 O R 341; *Chatillon v Canadian Mutual Fire Insurance Co* (1877) 27 C P 450.

[11] *Brogan v Manufacturers' and Merchants' Mutual Fire Insurance Co* (1878) 29 C P 414; *O'Neill v Ottawa Agricultural Insurance Co* (1879) 30 C P 151; *Donaldson v Providence Mutual Fire Assurance Co* (1909) Q R 36 S C 439; contra, *Ouellette v La Jacques Cartier* (1907) Q R 31 S C 29.

On the other hand, a person whose interest is only that of a lessee,[12] or bailee,[13] should not describe himself as owner; and it is immaterial that under his contract he has an option to purchase, which has not been exercised.

The policy may, however, contain a condition requiring a particular description of his interest, in which case the description must be accurate.[14] Thus, if the existence of incumbrances on the property insured is required to be specified, a description of the property as 'unencumbered' will avoid the policy,[15] but not otherwise.[16] Any such condition will, however, be strictly construed.[17]

Effect of a Misdescription

Where the policy contains an express condition relating to the accuracy of the description, the effect of a misdescription depends on the language of the particular condition.

The condition may provide that the policy is to be avoided in the event of misdescription in any material particular. Under a condition in this, the usual, form, a misdescription, to avoid the policy, must be material;[18] an immaterial description is disregarded.[19]

---

[12] *Walroth v St Lawrence County Mutual Insurance Co* (1853) 10 U C R 525; *Shaw v St Lawrence County Mutual Insurance Co* (1853) 11 U C R 73; *Crockford v London and Liverpool Fire Insurance Co* (1851) 10 N B R (5 Allen) 152. But all the information in the possession of insurers must be taken into account: *Mutual Fire Insurance Co v Paquet Co* (1912) Q R 21 K B 419.

[13] *Bacon v Provident Washington Insurance Co* (1914) Q R 47 S C 71, where the owner of furniture sold it and hired it from the purchaser with a right of redemption at the expiry of the hiring; cf *Toronto Type Foundry Co v Alliance Assurance Co* (1918) Q R 55 S C 483 where there was insufficient description. In *Banton v Home and Colonial Insurance Co* (1921) Times, 27 April, Bailhache J, held that the description of 'owner' was inaccurate, when applied to a purchaser under a hire-purchase agreement; but his decision was reversed in the Court of Appeal on 6 July 1921 (not reported). See also *Arlet v Lancashire and General Insurance Co Ltd* (1927) 27 Ll L Rep 454, where the description was held sufficient, there being no specific question in the proposal.

[14] *James v Royal Insurance Co* (1908) 10 N Z Gaz L R 244; *Norwich Union Fire Insurance Co v Le Bell* (1899) 29 S C R 470; cf *Condogianis v Guardian Assurance Co* [1921] 2 A C 125, at 128, P C.

[15] *Phillips v Grand River Farmers' Mutual Insurance Co* (1881) 46 U C R 334, where the insured described the house as 'held in fee and unencumbered', the house being, in fact, movable and held by its own weight on blocks of wood on land of which the insured was joint-owner and on which there was a mortgage, and the Court held that the house formed part of the realty and was not a chattel, and that, therefore, it was wrongly described; *Mason v Agricultural Mutual Assurance Association of Canada* (1868) 18 C P 19, where the incumbrance was personal to the insured, whereas the property was held by him jointly with his wife; cf *Foster v Standard Insurance Co of New Zealand* [1924] N Z L R 1093, where the insured, who had been debited with the price of a car in his account with the seller, and had subsequently given a bill of sale over it to him, was held, in the absence of a specific question as to incumbrance, to be entitled to describe the car as paid for.

[16] *Chatham (Roman Catholic Bishop) v Western Assurance Co* (1882) 22 N B R 242.

[17] *Ashford v Victoria Mutual Assurance Co* (1870) 20 C P 434, where a condition requiring incumbrances to be specified was held to apply to the goods insured, and not to the building in which they were; *Western Assurance Co v Temple* (1901) 31 S C R 373; *Sinclair v Canadian Mutual Fire Insurance Co* (1876) 40 U C R 206, where the insured failed to answer a question as to incumbrances when, in fact, there was a small incumbrance which was about to be removed.

[18] *Dawsons Bank Ltd v Vulcan Insurance Co Ltd* (1934) 50 Ll L Rep 129, P C, where the description 'brick walls' was held to be a material misdescription when one of the walls was wholly and two partly of timber; *Dodge v Western Canada Fire Insurance Co* (1912) 20 W L R 558, where a description of a house 'as in course of construction' was held to imply that the house was in process of construction, and was accordingly held to be inaccurate and misleading, as work had been abandoned before the proposal and was not resumed.

[19] *Re Universal Non-Tariff Fire Insurance, Forbes & Co's Claim* (1875) L R 19 Eq 485, where buildings

The policy may be so framed as to make the accuracy of the description a condition precedent to the validity of the policy.[20] In this case the description, as stated on the face of the policy, must be strictly accurate in every particular, even though it may consist in part of unnecessary and immaterial statements. Any misdescription, therefore, whether intentionally made or not, will avoid the policy,[1] and no question of materiality can arise.[2]

Where the policy contains no express condition relating to the accuracy of the description, it is an implied term of the contract that the description of the subject-matter shall substantially be accurate; and the policy is not avoided unless the description is material.[3]

Except in the cases in which the subject-matter is required to be described with literal accuracy, a description which is substantially accurate for the purpose of identification is not to be regarded as a misdescription avoiding the policy merely because the insured might have described the subject-matter with greater accuracy.[4]

The question is purely one of degree. If the insurers by the description which is, in fact, given are fairly informed of the nature of the subject-matter and the circumstances attending the risk, the insured has sufficiently performed his duty notwithstanding the inaccuracies of detail.[5]

Where, however, the inaccuracies, though not so great as to confuse the identity of the subject-matter, are material, in that the insurers might have refused the risk or charged a higher premium if the subject-matter had been more correctly described, the misdescription is material and the policy is avoided.[6]

Where the description on the face of the policy, though accurate so far as it goes, is incomplete by reason of the omission of particulars which might have been included, the omission may not be sufficient to affect the identification of the subject-matter; but even in the absence of fraud, the policy will be avoided if the effect of the omission is to render the description a misdescription in any

---

were described as built of brick and slate, whereas, in fact, one of the buildings was not roofed with slate, but with tarred felt, and this was held to be an immaterial misdescription; cf *Friedlander v London Assurance Co* (1832) 1 Mood & R 171, where a description of goods as being in the dwelling-house of the insured, though the insured had only one room as a lodger, was held not to be a misdescription.

[20] *Newcastle Fire Insurance Co v Macmorran & Co* (1815) 3 Dow 255, H L, where a mill was warranted to be of a specified class; *Dawsons Ltd v Bonnin* [1922] 2 A C 413.

[1] Unless the misdescription is the fault of the insurers or their agent. See Ivamy, *General Principles of Insurance Law* (4th edn, 1979), p 583.

[2] *Dawsons Ltd v Bonnin* (supra). See also *Bancroft v Heath* (1900) 5 Com Cas 110 at 114, per Mathew J; affd (1901) 6 Com Cas 137, C A.

[3] *Dobson v Sotheby* (1827) Mood & M 90 at 92, per Lord Tenterden C J: 'The word "barn" is not the most correct description of the premises; but it would give the company substantial information of their nature; there would be no difference in the risk, and the insurance would have been at the same rate whether the word "barn" or a more correct phase had been used. I think, therefore, that they were substantially well described'; *Konowsky v Pacific Marine Insurance Co* [1924] 2 D L R 1029.

[4] *Dobson v Sotheby* (supra); *Re Universal Non-Tariff Fire Insurance Co, Forbes & Co's Claim* (1875) L R 19 Eq 485 at 496, per Malins V-C, citing Smith's *Mercantile Law* (8th edn), p 405, which is evidently based on *Dobson v Sotheby*, (supra).

[5] *Dobson v Sotheby*, (supra).

[6] *Quin v National Assurance Co* (1839) Jo & Car 316 at 331, per Joy C B. See also *Yorkshire Insurance Co Ltd v Campbell* [1917] A C 218, P C (marine insurance).

material particular. The omission to state a fact which is not fairly required by the condition,[7] or, where specific questions are asked, does not fall within the scope of the questions,[8] does not avoid the policy.

If the description is so inaccurate as to be wholly inapplicable to the object intended to be insured, the contract is void both on the ground that the subject-matter of the contract is incapable of being identified,[9] and also because the description is false, and therefore the condition as to the accuracy of description is not fulfilled.[10]

Examples

In the light of the above principles considered in the preceding pages, one can turn to examples of cases concerning conditions as to proper description. These relate to:

   a The 'class' of a mill.
   b The nature of the walls of a building.
   c The roofing material of a factory.
   d The stock of a waste paper merchant.
   e The fact that the insured was only a lodger in the insured premises.
   f The fact that a steam engine had been adapted for additional work in the insured premises.
   g The description of the use of a kiln.

(a) 'Class' of Mill

In *Newcastle Fire Insurance Co v Macmorran & Co*[11] a cotton mill was insured under a fire policy. The insured warranted that it was of the 'first class' for the purpose of a proposal form, which was incorporated into the policy. The proposal form stated that for the purpose of calculating the premium payable, cotton mills were divided into two classes. A lower rate of premium was payable in the case of mills of the first class.

Class 1 comprehended:

> 'Buildings of brick or stone, and covered with slate, tile, or metal, having stoves fixed in arches of brick or stone on the lower floors, with upright metal pipes carried to the whole height of the building through brick flues or chimneys, or having common grates, or close or open metal stoves or coakles, standing at a distance of not more than one foot from the wall, on brick or stone hearths, surrounded with fixed fenders, and not having more than two feet of pipe leading therefrom into the chimney, and in which, or in any building adjoining thereto, although not communicating therewith, no drying stove or singeing frame shall be placed.'

---

[7] *Baxendale v Harvey* (1859) 4 H & N 445, where an omission to mention certain machinery did not avoid the policy; *Mathys v Strathcona Fire Insurance Co* (1918) QR 58 SC 199, where a house only occupied as a summer residence was held to be sufficiently described as a private residence.

[8] *Laidlaw v Liverpool, London, and Globe Insurance Co* (1867) 13 Gr 377, where the fact that the building was unfinished, and that it was lathed on the outside, was not included in the description.

[9] See p 42, ante.

[10] *Sillem v Thornton* (1854) 3 E & B 868, where the building was described as of two storeys, whereas at the date of the policy, which was retrospective, a third storey had been added; *Doherty v Canada National Insurance Co Ltd* [1918] 1 WWR 366.

[11] (1815) 3 Dow 255, HL.

Class 2 comprehended:

'Buildings of brick or stone, and covered with slate, tile, or metal, which contain any singeing frame, or any stove or stoves having metal pipes or flues, more than two feet in length, and in which, or in any building adjoining thereto, although not communicating therewith, no drying stove shall be placed.'

A fire occurred and the insurance company refused to indemnify the insured on the ground that the mill, though warranted to be of the first class, was of the second class in fact.

The House of Lords held that the warranty had been broken, and that the insurance company was not liable.

Lord Eldon L C, said:[12]

'It is a first principle in the law of insurance, on all occasions, that where a representation is material, it must be complied with—if immaterial, that immateriality may be inquired into and shown; but that if there is a warranty, it is part of the contract that the matter is such as it is represented to be. Therefore the materiality or immateriality signifies nothing. The only question is as to the mere fact. It is proposed then that the matter should stand over for a day or two in order to examine the case again for the purpose of further inquiry as to that fact; but my present impression is that the mill was not such as it was warranted to be.'

After further consideration of the case, the learned Lord Chancellor said two days later:[13]

'Since I had the honour of addressing your Lordships the other day on this case, I have looked again at all the papers. . . . Another ground was that this summons proceeded on a policy, dated 16 April 1805, and that it contained a warranty that the building belonged to the first class, described as having the stoves not more than one foot from the wall, with pipes or flues not more than two feet in length. I stated the doctrine of warranty, and on the best consideration I have been able to give the case, I do not think that the warranty was made good.'

(b) Walls

In *Dawsons Bank Ltd v Vulcan Insurance Co Ltd*[14] the risk under a fire policy in respect of some buildings in Moulmeingyun (in Burma) was described as:

'Three buildings, the property of the insured, situated at the corner of Strand Road and Ferry, Moulmeingyun, Myaungmya District. Said buildings are constructed of brick walls and cement flooring in the ground storey, timber walls and flooring in the upper storey with shingled roof. Used as retail shop for hazardous and non-hazardous goods in the ground floor and above dwellings.'

The premises were totally destroyed by fire. When the insured claimed under the policy, the insurance company resisted the claim on the footing that there had been a material misdescription of the property.

It was proved in evidence that the back wall of the premises was undoubtedly built of brick, and that the front wall was undoubtedly built of timber. It consisted of folding doors which were open during business hours, but which, when closed, formed a wooden wall. The side walls were partly of brick and partly of timber. They were partly of brick up to one-third of their length from the rear to the front, or of that part of the premises which consisted of the back

---

[12] (1815) 3 Dow 255, at 262, H L.
[13] Ibid, at 265.
[14] (1934) 50 Ll L Rep 129, P C.

wall and one-third of the side wall. The latrines were built wholly of brick, and the kitchens of the various shops had a brick side wall and a brick back wall. But the rest of the side walls were of timber.

The Privy Council[15] held that there had been a material misdescription, and that the insurance company was not liable.

Lord Atkin said:[16]

> 'Two witnesses were called on behalf of the [insurance company], gentlemen of experience; one of them of very large experience, and the other being a gentleman who had some experience in insurance business, and not being connected with this particular company, who said that in their opinion this misdescription was a material misdescription, because in their view if the premises consisted of one wall being brick at the back and the other three walls being timber, it was a building which they would have classed under Class III[17] of the tariff, and they would, therefore, have charged a higher premium on it than if it had been put in Class II.
>
> It appears to their Lordships, as it appeared to the Court of Appeal, that that evidence must apply in commonsense to a case where as to the remaining three walls, one was of timber and both the lateral walls were as to two-thirds of their length timber. In such a case it would appear that the danger would be substantially greater if the building caught fire, because the two-thirds of the timber falling down would bring down the superstructure above it, and there would be a most material question as to the danger of fire in the first place, and the amount of damage caused by the fire in the second place.
>
> It appears to their Lordships, on the footing that those two outside lateral walls were as to one-third of their length brick and as to two-thirds timber, quite impossible to resist the inference that that would be a material departure from the actual description, which was that all the ground floor walls were brick. There seems to be some controversy as to what the lateral divisions were which divided up the building. Whether they were of brick, as this witness stated, right through from back to front, in two cases, and made of corrugated iron in respect of the other two, it still leaves the description of the building inaccurate, and it is, as appears to their Lordships, inaccurately described in a matter which was material for insurance purposes.'

(c) Roofing Material

In *Re Universal Non-Tariff Fire Insurance Co*[18] the insured effected a fire insurance policy in respect of a factory. One of the conditions of the policy stated:

> 'Any material misdescription of any of the property proposed to be hereby insured or of any building or place in which the property to be so insured is contained, and any mis-statement of, or omission to state, any fact material to be known for estimating the risk, renders the policy void as to the property affected by such misdescription, mis-statement or omission respectively.'

The factory was described in the policy as being built of brick and slate, but when the fire took place, it was discovered that portions of the roof consisted of tarred felt. The insurance company went into voluntary liquidation, and the liquidator refused to pay the claim of the insured on the ground that there had been a material misdescription of the property, and that, therefore, there had been a breach of the condition set out above.

Malins V-C, held that the claim succeeded because the misdescription was not a material one. He observed:[19]

---

15 Lord Atkin, Lord Alness and Sir Shadi Lal.

16 (1934) 50 Ll L Rep 129 at 131.

17 These classes refer to the four classes adopted in the tariff of Burma fire companies as a method of classifying buildings. See (1934) 50 Ll L Rep 129 at 130.

18 (1875) 44 LJ Ch 761.

19 Ibid, at 763.

'It is suggested on the part of the company, that they would have refused the risk if they had known of the felt roof; but I am satisfied they would not have done so, and that a higher premium would not have been required; and I do not, therefore, consider that it was a "material misdescription" within the meaning of the first condition of the policy, and I am satisfied that no such defence would have been set up if it had not been for the poverty and insolvency of this company, to which I have already referred.'

(d) Stock of Waste Paper Merchant

In *A F Watkinson & Co Ltd v Hullett*,[20] the insured, who carried on business as waste paper merchants, filled in a proposal form in respect of fire insurance and stated in it that they were 'paper-board manufacturers'. The policy related to 'stock situated at Leigh's Nurseries, Causeway Road, Ponders End'. In fact, the stock consisted of between 400 and 500 tons of waste paper, and the whole of it was destroyed. The insured claimed under the policy, but the underwriter denied liability on the ground that the risk which had been underwritten was the stock of a paper board manufacturer, and not of a waste paper merchant.

Goddard J held that the claim by the insured failed, and said:[1]

'Mr Huxtable[2] was intending to underwrite, or did underwrite, the risk of a stock belonging to a waste-paper merchant, which everybody agrees is an exceedingly hazardous risk.

That is enough for me to decide this case upon. The stock which Mr Hullett intended to underwrite, and did underwrite, was the stock of a paper board manufacturer and not a waste paper business at all. That is how they are described in the policy and that was all that was told him. "Contents situate in or about premises at Leigh's Nurseries, Ponders End" meant, as far as the underwriters were concerned, that they were underwriting the stock of a paper board manufacturer; they were not underwriting the stock of a waste paper merchant at all.'

(e) Insured only a Lodger

In *Friedlander v London Assurance Co*[3] the insured had only one room in a dwelling house in which he lived as a lodger. He insured his goods and described them as 'goods in a dwelling house'. The policy contained a condition stating that 'the houses, buildings or other places where goods are deposited and kept shall be truly and accurately described'. The insurance company repudiated liability for a loss by fire on the ground that there had been a breach of the condition in that the house had not been properly described because the insured had failed to state that he was only a lodger in it. Lord Tenterden CJ, held that there had been no breach of condition, for the condition related to the construction of the house, eg whether it was of brick, slated, tiled or thatched, and not to the interest of the parties in it.

(f) Steam Engine Adapted for Additional Work

In *Baxendale v Harvey*[4] a fire policy in respect of a warehouse effected with the Norwich Union Fire Insurance Society contained a condition (No 3) which stated:

---

[20] (1938) 61 Ll L Rep 145, K B.
[1] Ibid, at 148, K B.
[2] One of the deputies of the underwriter who was sued. For Mr Huxtable's evidence, see (1938) 61 Ll L Rep at 147.
[3] (1832) 1 Mood & R 171 (Guildhall).
[4] (1859) 4 H & N 445.

'Every policy issued by this Society will be void unless the nature and material structure of the buildings and property insured, and of all buildings which contain any part of the property insured be fully and accurately described in such policy, and unless the trades carried on in all such buildings be correctly shown; and unless it is stated in such policy whether any hazardous goods are deposited in any such buildings; and whether there be any stove or apparatus for producing heat (other than common fire places in private houses) used or employed in such buildings, or in any building, yard or other place adjoining or near to the property insured, and belonging to or occupied by the party insured . . .'

The insured were carriers. In 1843 they erected a steam engine on the premises which they used for working cranes in hoisting goods up to the warehouse. The Society was given notice of this and of the purpose for which it was used, and the premium was increased. In 1844 the insured applied the engine to grinding provender for their horses. They attached it to a horizontal shaft, which was carried through the floor to an upper room, where they erected winnowing and grinding machines. The policy was renewed in 1857. The Society was not notified of the erection of the additional machinery or that the steam engine was used for grinding. The premises were destroyed by fire, and the Society refused to indemnify the insured on the ground that there had been a misdescription of the property insured.

The Court of Exchequer[5] held that there had been no misdescription and that the Society was liable, for the machinery was not part of the building insured.

Martin B, said:[6]

'The question is whether such a use of the steam engine vitiates the policy. By the third condition, "Every policy issued by this Society will be void, unless the nature and material structure of the buildings and property insured be fully and accurately described in such policy." In my opinion the machinery attached to this steam engine was not a part of the nature and material structure of the building and property insured. The condition also says, "and of all buildings which contain any part of the property insured." This is not the case of a building; it is an operation carried on in a building, by which the [insured] provide food for their horses. The condition also says, "and if there be any building of a hazardous nature or structure, or in which hazardous trades are carried on, or hazardous goods deposited, the same must also be specified in the policy." It was a question for the jury whether the operation which the [insured] carried on, and which was necessary for their trade as carriers, so increased the risk as to be of a hazardous nature, and they have found it did not. Therefore, the case not being within the third condition, it was not necessary under the fourth condition[7] for the [insured] to give notice that they had applied the steam engine to the purposes of grinding. *Stokes v Cox*[8] is an authority that, if the insurers wish to make it a condition precedent to the validity of the policy that there shall be no alteration in the circumstances, whether the risk is increased or not, they must do so in distinct terms.'

---

[5] Pollock C B, Martin, Bramwell and Channell BB.

[6] (1859) 4 H & N 445 at 449.

[7] The fourth condition of the policy stated: 'If any alteration or addition be made in, or to any building insured or in which any insured property is contained, or in or to any building adjoining or near to the property insured belonging to or occupied by the party insured by which the risk of fire to which the building or property insured, or the building containing such property is or may be exposed, be increased; or if such risk be increased either by any of the means adverted to in the third condition, or in any other manner; or if any property insured be removed into other premises, such alteration or addition, increase of risk, or removal, must be immediately notified to the Society in order to its being allowed by indorsement on the policy, such indorsement being signed by one of the Society's secretaries or agents, otherwise the policy will be void'.

[8] (1856) 1 H & N 533. This case is considered at 112, post.

Bramwell B, observed:[9]

'The third condition requires the nature and material structure of the buildings and property insured to be fully and accurately described in the policy. Then the question is whether there has been any want of a full and accurate description of them. The buildings had in them a steam engine which was described in the policy. This steam engine was formerly used for hoisting, but afterwards some machinery was added to it and it was used for grinding food for horses. Then, does that circumstance render the description, which would otherwise be accurate, one that is not so. In my opinion it does not. The "nature and material structure of the buildings" whether they are built of stone, brick or wood; or whether they are tiled, slated or thatched. The term manifestly refers to what may be called the essence of the building and not to its incidents. There is no condition making it obligatory on the insured to describe every alteration in the buildings.'

Channell B, was of the same opinion and said:[10]

'The question is whether, under the third condition, this machinery is a part of "the nature and material structure of the buildings insured." In my opinion it is not. What is meant is, whatever be the nature and structure of the buildings, whether built of stone, brick or wood, or covered with slate or tiles, they must be accurately described. I do not think this machinery can be considered as part of the nature or structure of the buildings. That being the construction of the third condition, the fourth does not carry the argument any further.'

Pollock C B, agreed, but placed his judgment on a different ground, saying:[11]

'In this case the Society had notice that the steam engine was on the premises, and that it was employed for a particular purpose; but their objection is that it was afterwards employed for another purpose, which they did not know of or anticipate, and which increased the danger. The answer is, that the Society allowed the erection of the steam engine without any qualification whatever as to its purpose; and if they meant it to be confined to the one use, they should have stipulated that it should be used for the purpose of hoisting only. The jury found that there was no increase of risk by using the steam engine for grinding, and the Society having had notice of the nature of the risk were not entitled to any notice by reason of the increase of danger. A person who insures may light as many candles as he please in his house, though each additional candle increases the danger of setting the house on fire.'

(g) Description of Use of Kiln

In *Shaw v Robberds*[12] a fire insurance policy had been effected with the Norwich Union Fire Insurance Society in respect of a granary and a kiln 'used for drying corn'.

A condition (No 3) of the policy stated:

'Persons insuring will forfeit their right to the sums insured by the policies unless the buildings insured or containing the goods insured be accurately described, the trades carried on therein specified, and the nature of the property correctly stated, so that it may be placed under separate classes, and charged at the appropriate rates of premium.'

The kiln had been used for drying corn until 1832 when a lighter laden with bark sank in a river near the insured premises. The insured allowed the owner of the bark to dry it in the kiln. A fire resulted, and the whole of the insured's property was destroyed.

[9] (1859) 4 H & N 445 at 450.
[10] Ibid, at 451.
[11] Ibid, at 451.
[12] (1837) 6 LJ K B 106.

The insurers[13] refused to indemnify the insured on the ground that the condition as to the proper description of the premises had been broken.

The Court of King's Bench[14] held that they were liable, for there had been no breach.[15]

Lord Denman C J, delivering the judgment of the Court said:[16]

'The third condition points to the description of the premises given at the time of insuring, and that description was in this instance perfectly correct. Nothing which occurred afterwards, not even a change of business, could bring the case within that condition which was fully performed when the risk first attached.'

CONDITIONS AS TO ALTERATION OF RISK

The alterations of the risk which are usually dealt with by express conditions[17] may be classified as follows:

1   Structural additions and alterations.
2   Fallen buildings.
3   Introduction of prohibited articles.
4   Use of prohibited articles.
5   Use of building.
6   Change of occupancy.

1 Structural Additions and Alterations

The making of additions to or alterations of the buildings insured, or containing the property insured, may be provided for by an express condition, under which the policy is avoided if the addition or alteration made violates the condition.[18] The condition does not usually prevent ordinary renewals or minor alterations.[19] Adjacent buildings are sometimes brought within its scope.[20]

---

13 The action was brought against the directors of the insurance company.
14 Lord Denman C J, and Patteson J.
15 Other aspects of this case (i) Whether notice of an alteration in the business concerned had been given to the insurers; (ii) whether there was a continuing warranty as to the use of the premises; and (iii) whether negligence on the part of the insured constituted a defence to the claim—are considered at pp 114, 115, and 13, ante respectively.
16 (1837) 6 L J K B 106 at 109.
17 It is impossible to enumerate the various forms of conditions that may be used, or to discuss their application in detail, since much depends on the circumstances of the particular case. See *Thompson v Equity Fire Insurance Co* [1910] A C 592 at 596, P C.
18 See *Kuntz v Niagara District Fire Insurance Co* (1866) 16 C P 573, where the condition provided that any alteration or addition to the building insured, if not notified, should avoid the policy, and it was held that an addition to the hotel insured and an alteration in the outbuildings, which were included in the insurance, avoided the whole policy, though otherwise divisible.
19 The distinction between minor and major alterations is sometimes drawn by the number of days upon which workmen may be on the premises, often 30, without the work falling within the condition.
20 Cf *Littlejohn v Norwich Union Fire Insurance Society* [1905] 3 T H 374, where the condition provided that the policy should be void if the insured failed to give notice of a change in the nature of the occupation of the premises insured or of the adjacent premises.

2 Fallen Buildings

Where the whole, or part,[1] of the building insured, or containing the property insured, falls either from weakness or other cause not proceeding from and without the agency of fire, there may be a condition providing for the immediate cesser of the policy. In these case the insurers are discharged from their obligations under the policy by the fall either of the building as a structure or of such a substantial and important part of it as would impair its usefulness as such, and leave the remaining part of the building subject to an increased risk of fire.[2]

Apart from such a condition, if the whole building insured falls, it ceases to exist as a building, and, therefore, the description of the subject-matter in the policy is wholly inapplicable. In this case, therefore, the policy apparently becomes void, and does not cover a subsequent destruction by fire of the ruins.

The clause may, however, provide that if only a portion of the building falls, the portion is still applicable to the remainder.[3]

In the case of goods specifically insured as contained in a building, the fall of the building, if complete, equally appears to invalidate the policy, the statement as to the building being an integral part of the description.[4]

If, however, goods are simply insured under the general description of 'goods', a fall of the building in which they happen to be can have no effect on the validity of the policy.

3 Introduction of Prohibited Articles

The policy may contain a condition relating to the introduction of certain specified articles[5] into the building insured or containing the property insured.[6]

The condition may be framed in terms so stringent as absolutely to prohibit the introduction of the specified article, in which case its mere presence in the building is a breach of the condition and avoids the policy.[7]

---

[1] Where the condition only refers to the fall of a building, and does not use the words 'or any part' of it, the condition does not apply unless the whole building falls.

[2] The condition is commonly called the 'fallen buildings clause'. See *Tootal, Broadhurst, Lee Co v London and Lancashire Fire Insurance Co* (1908) Times, 21 May, where the building containing a portion of the goods insured collapsed in the Jamaica earthquake. This case is set out in Appendix IV, pp 403–406, post.

[3] *Wairoa Farmers' Co-operation Meat Co Ltd and Bank of New Zealand v New Zealand Insurance Co Ltd* (1931) 7 N Z L J 267.

[4] See p 44, ante.

[5] The fact that the policy is framed in terms wide enough to cover such articles does not exclude the operation of the condition: *McEwan v Guthridge* (1860) 13 Moo P C C 304, where the condition prohibited the presence on the premises of more than 56 lbs of gunpowder, unless specially provided for, and it was held that the fact that the insurance purported to cover hazardous goods, which were defined in the policy to include gunpowder, did not amount to a special provision and did not exclude the condition.

[6] Their introduction into another building not comprised in the insurance is not a breach of the condition: *Guardian Insurance Co v Connely* (1892) 20 S C R 208.

[7] *Daniel v Robinson* (1826) Batt 650; see also *Dobson v Sotheby* (1827) 1 Mood & M 90 at 92, per Lord Tenterden C J. A general prohibition against the introduction of dangerous articles is broken although the dangerous character of the article was unknown to both parties: *Hillerman v National Insurance Co* (1870) 1 V L R 155 where gasoline, a then comparatively unknown substance, was introduced.

Whether or not the prohibition is an absolute one is a matter of construction in each case.

On the other hand, a condition may not prohibit the introduction of a specified article absolutely, but may limit the quantity of it which may be introduced.[8] In this case the policy is only avoided by its presence in excess of the quantity so limited.[9]

In either case, where the presence of the prohibited article amounts to a breach of the condition, it is immaterial whether the fire was or was not occasioned thereby.[10]

A form of this condition provides that certain articles shall not be 'kept' or 'stored or kept' in the building insured or containing the property insured. Such articles usually belong to the class of goods called hazardous.[11] This form of the condition is less stringent in its application. The prohibition does not extend to the occasional or casual introduction for a specific purpose of an article specified in the condition,[12] or to its presence in small quantities for domestic or other similar use.[13] In neither case, therefore, is the policy avoided, even though the prohibited article is in fact the cause of the fire.[14]

Thus, in *Dobson v Sotheby*[15] 'a barn, situate in an open field, timber built and tile' was insured under a fire policy, which contained a clause stating that no fire was to be kept on the premises or hazardous goods deposited. It also stated that 'if buildings of any description insured with the company shall, at any time after such insurance, be made use of to stow or warehouse any hazardous goods' without the permission of the company, the policy would be forfeited. The premises required tarring. A fire was lighted, and a tar barrel was brought into the building for this purpose. The tar boiled over, and the premises were burnt down. The insurance company refused to indemnify the insured on the ground that there had been a breach of condition.

Lord Tenterden C J, held that the company was liable, and said:[16]

---

[8] *Beacon Life and Fire Assurance Co v Gibb* (1862) 1 Moo P C C N S 73, where the condition provided that if more than 20 lbs. of gunpowder should be on the premises at the time when any loss happened, such loss would not be made good; *Calf v Jarvis* (1850) 1 Searle's R (Cape) Sup Ct 1, where only sufficient spirits were to be kept in stock for the purpose of preparing wine.

[9] *McEwan v Guthridge* (1860) 13 Moo P C C 304; *Queen Insurance Co v Parsons* (1881) 7 App Cas 96, P C; *Thompson v Equity Fire Insurance Co* [1910] A C 592, P C.

[10] *Beacon Life and Fire Assurance Co v Gibb,* (supra), at 99.

[11] Such goods include gunpowder and other explosives, petrol, benzine, and other highly inflammable substances.

[12] *Dobson v Sotheby* (1827) Mood & M 90.

[13] *Thompson v Equity Fire Insurance Co* [1910] A C 592, P C, where the condition excluded liability for loss occurring whilst gasoline 'is stored or kept in any building insured', and it was held that the condition was not broken by the presence of a small quantity of gasoline in a stove; *Merrick v Provincial Insurance Co* (1857) 14 U C R 439, where the use of sulphur in a stove for bleaching bonnets was held not to be a breach of a condition prohibiting the keeping of, inter alia, sulphur, on the ground that the word 'keeping' meant keeping in stock; *Mitchell v City of London Assurance Co* (1888) 15 A R 262, where the keeping of a gallon of lubricating oil for the purpose of lubricating an engine was held not to be a 'storing or keeping' of oil within the meaning of the condition; *Patterson v Central Canada Insurance Co* (1910) 15 W L R 123; *Evangeline Fruit Co v Provincial Fire Insurance Co of Canada* (1915) 51 S C R 474, where a supply of gasoline was kept for the use of an oil engine known by the insurers to be on the premises; *Hall v Connecticut Fire Insurance Co* [1931] 2 W W R 200.

[14] *Thompson v Equity Fire Insurance Co* [1910] A C 592, P C.

[15] (1827) Mood and M 90.

[16] Ibid, at 92.

'If the company intended to stipulate, not merely that no fire should habitually be kept on the premises, but that none should ever be introduced upon them, they might have expressed themselves to that effect; and the same remark applies to the case of hazardous goods also. In the absence of any such stipulation, I think that the condition must be understood as forbidding only the habitual use of fire, or the ordinary deposit of hazardous goods, not their occasional introduction, as in this case, for a temporary purpose connected with the occupation of the premises.'

The words 'storing and keeping' mean habitual keeping[17] in considerable quantities,[18] and apply to the introduction of the prohibited articles for such purposes as warehousing or as keeping for stock for trade.[19]

Whether fireworks were 'inflammable oils or goods' was considered in *Hales v Reliance Fire and Accident Insurance Corpn Ltd.*[20] The insured, a retail shopkeeper, was asked the following question in a proposal form for a Compound Retail Shopkeeper's policy by which his premises were to be insured against fire and explosion, 'Are any inflammable oils or goods used or kept on the premises?' He replied 'lighter fuel'. In fact, after the policy was issued, he stored some fireworks on the premises. A fire started in the box in which they were kept, and an explosion followed, as a result of which the premises and trade property were damaged. When the insured claimed for a loss under the policy, the insurance company repudiated liability on the ground[1] that he had given an inaccurate answer to the above question, the truth of the answer being made the 'basis' of the policy.[2] The company maintained that the fireworks fell within the expression 'inflammable oils or goods used or kept on the premises'.

McNair J, agreed with this contention, and held that the company was not liable, and said:[3]

'There has been no expert evidence as to the meaning of the word "inflammable". Although the [insured] himself admitted that fireworks such as he kept were clearly inflammable, I do not attach very much importance to that. I attach some importance to the fact that fireworks are quite clearly "explosive" within the meaning of the Explosives Act 1875, and that there

---

17 *Dobson v Sotheby* (1827) Mood & M 90.
18 *Thompson v Equity Fire Insurance Co* [1910] AC 592 at 596, PC, per Lord MacNaghten: 'What is the meaning of the words "stored or kept" in collocation and in the connection in which they are found? They are common English words with no very precise or exact signification. They have a somewhat kindred meaning, and cover very much the same ground. The expression, as used in the statutory conditions, seems to point to the presence of a quantity not inconsiderable, or at any rate not trifling in amount, and to import a notion of warehousing or depositing for safe custody or keeping in stock for trading purposes. It is difficult, if not impossible, to give an accurate definition of the meaning, but if one takes a concrete case, it is not very difficult to say whether a particular thing is "stored or kept" within the meaning of the condition. No one probably would say that a person who had a reasonable quantity of tea in his house for domestic use was "storing or keeping" tea there, or (to take the instance of benzine, which is one of the prescribed articles) no one would say that a person who had a small bottle of benzine for removing grease spots or cleansing purposes of that sort was "storing or keeping" benzine'. See also *Benge and Pratt v Guardian Assurance Co Ltd* (1915) 34 NZLR 81, where 'stored' was held to mean brought into the store, whether for sale or not.
19 *Thompson v Equity Fire Insurance Co*, (supra).
20 [1960] 2 Lloyd's Rep 391, QB.
1 Other issues in the case arose as to whether (i) there had been non-disclosure of a material fact, ie the existence of fireworks on the premises (see p 50, ante); and (ii) there was a continuing warranty as to the existence of a fact at the time of the proposal and during the currency of the risk (see p 58, ante).
2 As to the 'basis clause', see Ivamy, *General Principles of Insurance Law* (4th edn, 1979), pp 181–183.
3 [1960] 2 Lloyd's Rep 391 at 396.

are statutory provisions which regulate the keeping of fireworks in small quantities when they are kept for sale in a shop like this, and which require that they shall be kept in some place of security and not exposed, as these fireworks were, and unprotected, to any chance contact with flame or match or anything of that kind.

It seems to me that, reading this question in its context, this policy on the trading goods, which includes probably the most important item, the fire risk, the term "inflammable" means something which increases the fire risk by reason of the fact that the goods have an inherent quality of being easily set on fire. I do not believe that anybody, if asked the simple question "Are fireworks inflammable?", would have the slightest doubt in answering the question "Yes", although he may have the recollection that sometimes on a wet November evening, when having a firework party, it is difficult to set them alight, but as a matter of ordinary common sense it seems to me quite plain that in the ordinary sense of the word fireworks are inflammable.'

4 Use of Prohibited Articles

There may be a condition relating to the use of specified or indicated articles in the building insured, or containing the property insured.

Some conditions are so stringently framed that they prohibit absolutely the use of the article therein named. A single act of user, therefore, is a breach of this condition, and avoids the policy, however short the period, and whatever the purpose for which the article is used.[4] It is nonetheless a breach, although it is wholly unconnected with a subsequent fire and was, in fact, committed long before.[5]

Thus, in *Glen v Lewis*[6] a cabinet-maker insured his stock-in-trade under a fire policy with the West of England Fire and Life Insurance Company.

One of the conditions (No 1) of the policy stated:

'If in the building insured or containing any property insured shall be used any steam engine, stove, etc., or any description of fire-heat other than common fire places, or any process of fire-heat be carried on therein, the same must be noticed and allowed on the policy; and if any omission or misrepresentation take place, the policy is void. In case of any circumstances happening after an insurance has been effected whereby the risk shall in any way be increased, the insured is required to give notice thereof of the Company, and the same must be allowed by endorsement on the policy, otherwise the policy is void.'

Another condition (No 4) stated that:

'In case of any alteration being made in a building insured, or containing any property insured, or of any steam, steam engine, stove, etc, or any description of fire-heat being introduced, or of any trade, business, process or operation being carried on . . . not comprised in the original insurance or allowed by endorsement thereon . . . notice thereof must be given, and every such alteration must be allowed by indorsement on the policy . . . and unless such notice be given . . . no benefit will arise to the insured in case of loss.'

The insured erected a brick furnace on his premises. To this he attached a small steam engine in order to see whether it was worth his while buying it. A fire was lit and the engine was set to work. But it proved wholly unfit for the purpose for which the insured required it. A few days afterwards a fire broke out on the premises, and the stock was destroyed. No notice of the use of the steam engine had been given to the company, which repudiated liability on the ground that there had been a breach of the condition set out above.

---

[4] *Glen v Lewis* (1853) 8 Exch 607.
[5] Ibid, at 617 per Parke B; cf *Barrett v Jermy* (1849) 3 Exch 535.
[6] (1853) 8 Exch 607.

The Court of Exchequer[7] held that the claim failed. The mere introduction of the steam engine without fire-heat being applied to it would not have been a breach of the condition. But it was a different matter where fire-heat had been applied, as in the present case. It was immaterial that the steam engine was being tried out. The length of the trial was also of no consequence.

Parke B, delivering the judgment of the Court, said:[8]

'Now the clause in question implies, that the simple introduction of a steam engine, without having fire applied to it, will not affect the policy; but if used with fire-heat, it will; and nothing being said about the intention of the parties as to the particular use of it, and as, if it be used, the danger is precisely the same, with whatever object it is used, it seems to us that it makes no difference, whether it is used upon trial with the intent of ascertaining whether it will succeed or not, or as an approved means of carrying on the [insured's] business, nor does it make any difference that it is used for a longer or a shorter time. The terms of the conditions apply to the introduction of a steam engine in a heated state at any time, without notice to the Company, so as to afford an opportunity to them to ascertain whether it will increase the risk or not.'

He then went on to observe:[9]

'There is not a word to confine the introduction of the steam engine to its intended use as an instrument or auxiliary in carrying on the business in the premises insured. If a construction had already been put on a clause precisely similar in any decided case, we should defer to that authority. But in truth there is none. All the cases upon this subject depend upon the construction of different instruments, and there is none precisely like this. Indeed, it seems not improbable that the terms of this policy have been adopted, as suggested by Sir F Thesiger, to prevent the effect of previous decisions; the provision "that no description of fire-heat shall be introduced," in consequence of the ruling of Lord Tenterden in *Dobson v Sotheby*;[10] and the addition of "process or operation" to trade or business, to prevent the application of that of *Shaw v Robberds*.[11] The latter case is the only one which approaches the present. One cannot help feeling that the construction of the policy in that case may have been somewhat influenced by the apparent hardship of avoiding it, by reason of the accidental and charitable use of the kiln, the subject of the insurance. The Court considered the conditions in that case to refer to alterations either in the building or the business, and to those only. Here, the introduction of a steam engine, or any other description of fire-heat, is specifically pointed out, and expressly provided for. If, in that case, the condition had been (inter alia), that no bark should be dried in the kiln without notice to the company, which would have resembled this case, we are far from thinking that the Court could have held that the drying which took place did not avoid the policy, by reason of its being an extraordinary occurrence and an act of charity.'

Some conditions, however, point to something in the nature of an habitual or permanent user. In this case the occasional or experimental use of the article will not avoid the policy.[12]

What acts amount to a user within the meaning of the condition depend on the particular words of the policy,[13] and on the nature of the articles specified or indicated.[14]

---

7 Pollock C B, Clarke, Platt and Martin BB.
8 (1853) 8 Exch 607 at 618.
9 Ibid, at 619.
10 (1827) Mood & M 90. This case is considered at p 108, ante.
11 (1837) 6 Ad & El 75. This case is considered at p 105, ante.
12 *Glen v Lewis*, (supra), at 617 per Parke B, cf *Barrett v Jermy*, (supra).
13 *Stokes v Cox* (1856), 1 H & N 533, Exch; *Whitehead v Price* (1835) 2 Cr M & R 447; *Mayall v Mitford* (1837) 6 Ad & El 670.
14 *Whitehead v Price*, (supra); *Mayall v Mitford*, (supra).

Thus, in *Stokes v Cox*[15] a fire insurance policy in respect of some buildings stated that part of the lower storey was used as a stable, coach house and boiler house, and

> 'No steam engine employed on the premises: The steam from said boiler being used for heating water and warming the shops. N B The process of melting tallow by steam in said boiler house, and also the use of two pipe stoves in said building are hereby allowed.'

One of the conditions (No 7) of the policy stated:

> 'If after the assurance shall have been effected, the risk shall be increased by any alteration of circumstances and the particulars of the same shall not be endorsed on the policy by the secretary or some other agent of the Company, and a proportionately higher premium paid, if required, such insurance shall be of no force.'

After the policy had been effected the insured erected in the stable the machinery of a steam engine, which was supplied with steam by the boiler mentioned in the policy. No notice of the erection or use of the steam engine was given to the insurance company. The premises were destroyed by a fire, which was not attributable to the erection or use of the steam engine. The jury found that the risk of fire was not increased by the erection or use of the steam engine, or by the alterations in the insured premises.

The Court of Exchequer Chamber[16] held that there had been no breach of the condition set out above, and that the insurance company was liable to indemnify the insured.

Cockburn C J, said:[17]

> 'It is unnecessary for us to express any opinion as to implied warranty in a policy not containing such a clause as the 7th condition in this policy. In our judgment the effect of the 7th condition is restrictive. All that an insured is called upon to do is, in the event of an increase of the risk,—and in that event only, to give notice to the insurance company of the alteration of circumstances. Here it is found as a fact that there was no increase of risk; therefore there was no necessity to give notice.'

Again, in *Whitehead v Price*[18] a cotton mill and a steam engine in an engine house were insured against fire. The policy stated that:

> 'The buildings are brick-built and slated; warmed exclusively by steam; light by gas, etc, worked by the steam engine above mentioned; in the tenure of one firm only, standing apart from all other mills and "worked by day only".'

The steam engine was kept going at night to convey power to other mills. A fire took place and the mill was destroyed. The insured claimed under the policy, but the insurer refused to pay on the ground that there had been a breach of the condition.

The Court of Exchequer[19] held that the action succeeded, and that the insurer was liable. Parke B, said that the words 'worked by day only' applied to the mill and not to the steam engine. Consequently there had been no breach of the condition. In the words of the learned Baron:[20]

---

[15] (1856) 1 H & N 533.
[16] Cockburn C J, Wightman, Williams, Crompton, Crowder and Willes J J.
[17] (1856) 1 H & N 533 at 540.
[18] (1835) 2 Cr M & R 447.
[19] Lord Abinger C B, Parke, Bolland and Alderson B B.
[20] (1835) 2 Cr M & R 447 at 454.

'Now, first, we may assume that the steam engine and part of the gear have been worked without the leave and consent of the [insurer], or of the directors of the company, by night and not by day only; and the question is, does that avoid the policy; and that depends entirely upon the construction to be given to the words "worked by day only". In the policy itself the language is somewhat obscure; but I think the words "worked by day only" cannot be applied to the steam engine, or any part of the gear, but apply to something else. I think that is a fair construction of all the terms that are used in this part of the policy. The insurance is on the larger end, and another end of a mill called the Union Mill, upon the building of the engine house and steam engine, and the building of the warehouse used for the blowing and scutching of cotton. The policy recites, "that the aforesaid buildings were brick buildings, and slated, lighted by gas," that applies to all the buildings; "and worked by the steam engine above mentioned." Now, all the buildings cannot be worked by the steam engine above mentioned. We must put a limited construction upon these expressions. I take it to mean, "all the buildings above mentioned which are capable of being worked by the steam engine"; and, therefore, I read this part of the insurance, that the cotton mill should be worked by the steam engine and worked by day only; and it appears to me that the meaning of this insurance is that it insures the cotton mill, which is worked by steam engine, and by day only.'

This decision was followed in a case two years later where the facts were substantially the same.[1] But it must be noted that a mere introduction of the specified article into the building in question is not a breach of this condition. It is the use and the use only that is prohibited.[2]

In *Farnham v Royal Insurance Co Ltd*[3] where a fire policy contained a warranty[4] stating

'. . . no artificial heat . . . or unenclosed artificial light to be used, no petrol or other motor spirit (except that which may be in the containers of motor vehicles) be stored, and cellulose paint, cellulose varnishes or cellulose thinnings be used or stored in said buildings.'

Ackner J, held that the insurers failed in their allegation that the warranty had been broken by a calor gas radiant heater being used there, for this was not established by the evidence.[5]

Sometimes the condition does not absolutely prohibit use of the article, but only limits the time, manner, or purpose of its use. The principles of construction indicated above apply equally to such a condition.[6]

---

1 *Mayall v Mitford* (1837) 6 Ad & El 670.
2 *Barrett v Jermy* (1849) 3 Exch 535 at 543, per Parke B: 'Mere alterations, in the case of the removing of a firegrate or furnace, never increased the risk; it is only the use, and the ordinary use of a fireplace so put up that increases the risk; as, for instance, a man might alter his house so as to cause in every room the beams which support the roof to come into the chimney or fireplace; or he might put up a fireplace in the centre of his drawing room. But the mere alteration would not increase the risk, but the use and employment added to the ordinary use would, and that seems to have escaped the observation of the Judge and jury.' See also *Glen v Lewis* (1853) 8 Exch 607 at 608, per Parke B. Cf *Stokes v Cox* (1856) 1 H & N 533, Exch, per Bramwell B, in the Court below, at 336.
3 [1976] 2 Lloyd's Rep 437, QB.
4 A condition of the policy stated: 'Every Warranty to which the property insured or item thereof is, or may be, made subject, shall from the time the Warranty attaches apply and continue to be in force during the whole currency of this Policy, and non-compliance with any such warranty, whether it increases the risk or not, shall be a bar to any claim in respect of such property or item . . .'
5 [1976] 2 Lloyd's Rep at 443. But the insured failed in the claim under the policy for it was proved that a condition stating that any alteration whereby the risk of destruction or damage was increased had been broken. As to this aspect of the case, see p 115, post.
6 *Whitehead v Price* (1835) 2 Cr M & R 447, where the condition was that the mill insured should be worked by day only, approved in *Mayall v Mitford* (1837) 6 Ad & El 670; *Calf v Jarvis* (1850) 1 Searle's R (Cape) Sup Ct 1, where the condition permitted the introduction of spirits only for preparing wine, and spirits were subsequently brought in and kept for sale.

5 Use of Buildings

The policy may contain a condition as to alteration in the use for which the building insured, or containing the property insured, may be occupied, or in the trade or business which is carried on therein.[7]

It must be noted that a description in the policy of the user,[8] or of the trade or business carried on,[9] does not necessarily import a condition that such user or trade or business, as the case may be, shall not be altered.[10]

Thus, in *Shaw v Robberds*[11] a policy was effected with the Norwich Union Fire Insurance Society in respect of a granary and a kiln. The kiln was used for drying corn. A lighter laden with bark was sunk near the insured premises. The insured gratuitously allowed the owner of the bark to dry it in the kiln. A fire took place and the insured premises were destroyed. The insurers repudiated liability on the ground that there was an implied warranty that nothing except corn should ever be dried in the kiln.

The Court of King's Bench[12] held that this defence failed for, as Lord Campbell C J, said in giving judgment:[13]

> 'There are no facts or rule of legal construction from which an implied warranty can be raised.'

The condition may prohibit or restrict any such alteration in the same way as in the case of any other alteration. The question as to what acts amount to a breach of this condition so as to avoid the policy is determined by reference to the same principles.

A condition against alteration of trade or business clearly contemplates an alteration of a permanent character,[14] and is not broken by the insured engag-

---

[7] Such conditions are usually directed against an increase of risk by reason of the introduction of processes of manufacture, or of changes of trade or business to another of a more hazardous nature. See eg *Marzouca v Atlantic and British Commercial Insurance Co Ltd* [1971] 1 Lloyd's Rep 449, P C, where a condition of the policy stated that the insurance was to cease 'if the trade or manufacture carried on be altered, or if the nature of the occupation of or other circumstances affecting the building insured or containing the insured property be changed in such a way as to increase the risk of loss or damage by fire'. As to the facts and decision in this case, see p 118, post.

[8] *Shaw v Robberds* (1837) 6 Ad & El 75, where the property insured was described as a 'kiln for drying corn in use'. See p 105, ante.

[9] *Pim v Reid* (1843) 6 Man & G 1; cf *Peck v Phoenix Mutual Insurance Co* (1881) 45 U C R 620, where a policy on a grocer's shop was held not to be avoided by the shop being subsequently used for dealing in furniture and a small room behind it for carpentering.

[10] A condition against alteration of the property does not prohibit alteration of user: *Baxendale v Harvey* (1859) 4 H & N 445.

[11] (1837) 6 L J K B 106. Other aspects of this case, viz. whether (i) there was a breach of a condition as to the description of the insured premises; (ii) a condition concerning the increase of risk had been broken; and (iii) the insurers were liable where the fire had been caused by the negligence of the insured—are considered at pp 105, 115, and 13, of this book respectively.

[12] Lord Campbell C J, and Patteson J.

[13] (1837) 6 L J K B 106 at 109.

[14] *Merrick v Provincial Insurance Co* (1857) 14 U C R 439, where a policy on a dry goods store was avoided by the assured introducing into the premises the business of hat-bleaching which was a hazard within the meaning of the condition; *Sovereign Fire Insurance Co v Moir* (1887) 14 S C R 612, where the business introduced, though less hazardous than the business described in the policy, was held to avoid the policy; cf *Chapman v Lancashire Insurance Co* (1875) 2 Stevens Digest 407, P C, where the sub-letting of part of the insured premises, described in the policy as being occupied by the insured as a bonded warehouse and by other tenants as offices, to a common

ing in an isolated transaction outside the business specified in the policy.[15]

In *Shaw v Robberds*[16] the facts of which have been mentioned above,[17] a condition (No 6) of the policy stated:

'If any alteration or addition be made in or to the building or covering of any premises insured, or in which any insured property is contained, or the risk of fire to such building is exposed, be by any means increased . . . such alteration, addition, increase of risk . . . must be immediately notified, and allowed by endorsement on the policy, the endorsement being duly made and signed by one of the Society's partners or agents, otherwise the insurance as to such buildings or goods will be void.'

The insured gratuitously allowed the owner of the bark to dry it in the kiln. No notice of this was given to the insurers. The kiln caught fire and the whole of the insured property was destroyed. The insurers refused to indemnify the insured on the ground that the condition set out above had been broken. The jury found that the drying of bark was more dangerous than the drying of corn.

The Court of King's Bench[18] held that the condition had not been broken, for the use of the kiln by the owner of the bark was not such an alteration of the business and increase of the risk as required to be notified to the insurers. Accordingly, they were liable for the loss suffered.

Lord Denman C J, said:[19]

'The sixth condition points at an alteration of business as something permanent and habitual; and if the [insured] had either dropped his business of corn drying and taken up that of bark drying, or added the latter to the former, no doubt the case would have been within that condition. Perhaps if he had made any charge for drying this bark, it might have been a question for the jury whether he had done so as a matter of business, and whether he had not thereby, although it was the first instance of bark drying, made an alteration in his business within the meaning of that condition, but according to the evidence, we are clearly of opinion that no such question arose for the consideration of the jury, and that this single act of kindness was no breach of the sixth condition. The case of *Dobson v Sotheby*[20] was decided by Lord Tenterden upon the same principle, and is an authority nearly in point upon this part of the case.'

In *Farnham v Royal Insurance Co Ltd*[1] the plaintiff insured a barn under a fire policy issued by the defendants. The policy contained a condition which stated:

'This policy shall be avoided with respect to any item thereof in regard to which there may be any alteration after the commencement of this insurance . . . whereby the risk of destruction or damage is increased . . . unless such alteration be admitted by memorandum signed by or on behalf of the insurers.'

---

warehouseman for the storage of goods, was held to avoid the policy. In *Prairie City Oil Co v Standard Mutual Fire Insurance Co* (1910) 44 S C R 40, a policy on 'stock consisting chiefly of illuminating and lubricating oils and all other goods kept for sale' was held to cover gasoline.

15 *Shaw v Robberds* (1837) 6 Ad & El 75.

16 (1837) 6 L J K B 106. Other aspects of this case, viz whether (i) there was a breach of a condition as to the description of the insured premises; (ii) there was an implied warranty that nothing but corn should ever be dried in the kiln; and (iii) the insurers were liable where the fire had been caused by the negligence of the insured—are considered at pp 105, 114, and 13, ante respectively.

17 Supra.

18 Lord Denman C J and Patteson J.

19 (1837) 6 L J K B 106 at 109.

20 (1827) Mood & M 90. This case is considered at p 108, ante.

 1 [1976] 2 Lloyd's Rep 437, Q B.

The insured made an agreement with a third party for the storage of metal cargo containers on the land, and allowed repairs to them to be carried out in the barn. The repairs involved the use of oxy-acetylene cutting and electric arc-welding apparatus. The barn caught fire and the insured claimed under the policy. The defendants repudiated liability on the ground that there had been a breach of the condition set out above. Ackner J, held that the condition had been broken for the risk of damage had been increased.[2]

In *Exchange Theatre Ltd v Iron Trades Mutual Insurance Co Ltd*[3] the following items were insured under a fire policy relating to a bingo hall: (i) item 1, the building; (ii) item 2, machinery, plant, trade and office furniture, fixtures, fittings and utensils; and (iii) an external sign. The policy contained a condition which stated

> 'This policy shall be avoided with respect to any item thereof in regard to which there be any alteration . . . whereby the risk of destructional damage is increased.'

The insured brought into the hall a petrol generator and a quantity of petrol. Subsequently, the premises were destroyed by fire and explosion. When a claim was made under the policy, the insurers repudiated liability on the ground that the insured had broken the condition set out above.

Lawson J gave judgment for the insured for the introduction of the generator and the petrol was an alteration to item 2 ie the contents of the building, so that the increased risk thereby involved entitled the insurers to avoid liability in respect of that item. But they were not entitled to avoid liability in respect of item 1 ie the building, because there was no alteration with regard to that item.[4]

As a rule, the user to which the condition is intended to apply is not a casual or temporary user, but a real change in the purpose for which the building in question is used.

Thus, the calling in of a carpenter to do casual repairs or work of a similar occasional nature is not a breach of the condition ordinarily employed.[5] But there is plainly an alteration within the meaning of the condition, if, after the date of the policy, he begins to work habitually at his trade in the building.[6] A single act of user may, however, if the condition is sufficiently stringent, avoid the policy.[7]

---

[2] [1976] 2 Lloyd's Rep 437 at 443, QB. An allegation that there had been a breach of a warranty as to the introduction of artificial heat by the use of a calor gas radiant heater was held not to have been established. As to this aspect of the case, see p 113, ante.

[3] [1983] 1 Lloyd's Rep 674.

[4] Ibid, at 688. His Lordship pointed out (ibid at 688) that in *Farnham v Royal Insurance Co Ltd* [1976] 2 Lloyd's Rep 437 the alteration was an alteration to the very item which covered both the building and its use. The alteration was an alteration of the use of the item which was part of what was in the specification of the policy, ie on a similarly worded condition, the insurers were held entitled to avoid in respect of the building, but it was an alteration of the item which not only described the building itself but also the use of the building.

[5] *Ottawa and Rideau Forwarding Co v Liverpool and London and Globe Insurance Co* (1869) 28 U C R 518, where the temporary introduction of painters and carpenters was held not to be a breach of the condition, there being a finding that the risk was not increased; cf *Shaw v Robberds*, (supra).

[6] Cf *Quin v National Assurance Co* (1839) Jo & Car 316 at 330, Ex Ch.

[7] *Shaw v Robberds*, (supra), where it was suggested that, if there had been an actual change of business, the first instance of user might be sufficient.

6 Change of Occupancy

The policy may contain a condition providing that the policy is to be avoided in the event of any change in the occupancy or tenancy of the building insured or containing the property insured.[8] Any such change is not an alteration in the use for which a building may be occupied; nor is it of itself an increase of risk. It does not, therefore, avoid the policy in the absence of an express condition to that effect.[9]

Leaving a building unoccupied is not a breach of a condition against change of occupancy;[10] nor, except in special circumstances, is it a breach of a condition against increasing the risk.[11]

To avoid the policy in such an event a special condition is necessary.[12] To constitute a breach of such a condition, the building must cease to be occupied.[13] A mere temporary absence from the building is not sufficient.[14] It is usual, however, where any such condition is inserted in the policy, to specify a limited number of days during which it may be so left.[15]

---

8 *Anderson v Norwich Fire Insurance Society* (1918) Q R 53 S C 409.

9 *Irving v Sun Insurance Office* [1906] O R C 24.

10 *Gould v British America Assurance Co* (1868) 27 U C R 473; cf *London and Lancashire Insurance Co v Honey* (1876) 2 V L R 7, where the fact that premises, described as a farmhouse, the column in the application form for the name of the occupant being left blank, were occupied at the date of the policy, and remained so up to the time of the loss, was held not to be a breach; and cf *Cooper v Toronto Casualty Insurance Co* (1928) 62 O L R 311, where the premises were insured only while occupied as a private dwelling.

11 *Foy v Aetna Insurance Co* (1854) 8 N B R (3 All.) 29, where it was held that leaving premises unoccupied was not a breach of a condition against increasing the risk, unless it was shown that, in the circumstances and situation of the building, its destruction by fire was more probable than when occupied; *Canada Landed Credit Co v Canada Agricultural Insurance Co* (1870) 17 Gr 418.

12 *Abrahams v Agricultural Mutual Assurance Association* (1876) 40 U C R 175, where it was held to be immaterial that the insured did not know that the tenant had left; *Williams v Canada Farmers' Mutual Fire Insurance Co* (1876) 27 C P 119. The condition may be so framed as merely to suspend the insurance, whilst the building is unoccupied: *Ross v Scottish Union and National Insurance Co* (1918) 58 S C R 169.

13 *Spahr v North Waterloo Farmers' Mutual Insurance Co* (1899) 31 O R 525, where the house was left for several weeks, and it was held that the condition was broken, although the house was visited from time to time, and although the insured's husband slept there twice; *Masson v Liverpool and London and Globe Insurance Co* (1909) 35 Q R 5 S C 455, where, in the case of a factory, the condition was held to be broken when the work ceased.

14 *Simmonds v Cockell* [1920] 1 K B 843 (burglary insurance), where there was a warranty stating that 'the said premises are always occupied', and it was held that the warranty had not been broken because on the day the burglary took place the premises were left unattended between 2.30 pm and 11.30 pm except that the insured returned there to change his clothes at 7 pm. The Court held that the warranty did not mean that the premises were never to be left unattended, but that they were to be used continuously and without interruption for occupation as a residence; *Nicholson v Colonial Mutual Insurance Co* (1887) 13 V L R 58, where it was held that a condition requiring a caretaker to be kept in charge during the currency of the policy did not necessarily mean that he must never be absent or that he must always be there; *Metcalfe v General Accident Insurance Co* (1930) 64 O L R 643; cf. *Winicofsky v Army and Navy General Assurance Association Ltd* (1919) 35 T L R 283 (burglary insurance), where it was held that temporary absence from the premises during an air raid was not a breach of a condition requiring the insured to take all due and proper precautions for the safety of the property insured.

15 *Abrahams v Agricultural Mutual Assurance Association*, (supra); *Laurentian Insurance Co v Davidson* [1932] S C R 491, where it was held that, when there was a condition against leaving the premises unoccupied for 30 days and the insured left the premises for good, but a fire occurred within the 30 days, there was no breach of condition.

A building 'becomes unoccupied' if there is no actual as distinct from constructive occupation of it, and there is no regular daily presence of someone in it.

Thus, in *Marzouca v Atlantic and British Commercial Insurance Co Ltd*,[16] a fire policy had been effected in respect of a hotel at Montego Bay, Jamaica. Condition 8 (b) stated:

> 'Under any of the following circumstances the insurance ceases to attach as regards the property affected unless the Insured, before the occurrence of any loss or damage, obtains the sanction of the Company signified by endorsement on the policy by or on behalf of the Company—
> (b) If the Building insured or containing the insured property become unoccupied and so remain for a period of more than 30 days.'

The hotel was used as a nurses' home until 30 September 1963, when the nurses moved out. The insured intended to convert the building into residential flats. The building was empty until 20 November when the work of conversion began. The insured employed a police constable to act as night watchman, but he never entered the building. During the period of conversion a night watchman occupied a hut in a building, which commanded only a partial view of the hotel. The police continued to keep an eye on the hotel, but had no access to the interior. The hotel was burnt down on the night of 19/20 May 1964. The insurers refused to indemnify the insured on the ground (inter alia)[17] that there had been a breach of condition. The Privy Council[18] held that they were entitled to do so. The condition had been broken for, on the evidence, the hotel became unoccupied and so remained for a period of more than 30 days, ie from 30 September to 20 November. Lord Hodson observed:[19]

> 'However, on the admitted facts in this case their Lordships are of the opinion in agreement with Eccleston J, and Luckhoo J,[20] that the [insured] was by 31 October 1963, already in breach of condition 8 (b). It is, as Luckhoo J, put it, the building and its contents which are insured, not the premises as such, and the words "become unoccupied" must relate to the absence of physical presence in the building as distinct from physical presence outside the building. This does not mean that mere temporary absence necessarily involves a cesser of occupation. In the nature of things one does not spend 24 hours under the same roof for 365 days in the year . . . The occupation to be effectual must, however, be actual not constructive. It must at least involve the regular daily presence of someone in the building. If there is no one present for a continuous period of more than 30 days, there is a breach of condition 8 (b),[1] and the insurance of the building and its contents comes to an end. In the instant case it had come to an end some three weeks before the contractors' men came into the building.'

---

16 [1971] 1 Lloyd's Rep 449, PC.

17 Another ground was that there had also been a breach of a condition stating that the insurance was to cease 'if the trade or manufacture carried on be altered, or if the nature of the occupation of or other circumstances affecting the Building insured or containing the insured property be changed in such a way as to increase the risk of loss or damage by fire', but the Privy Council did not base its decision on this ground, and stated that the trial Judge had mistaken the relevance of the evidence in relation to this condition to show that the fire risk had been increased, and had deprived himself of the assistance of the testimony of expert evidence on what was the decisive issue on this condition. See the judgment of Lord Hodson, [1971] 1 Lloyd's Rep at 454.

18 Lord Hodson, Lord Donovan and Lord Diplock.

19 [1971] 1 Lloyd's Rep 449 at 453.

20 In the Court of Appeal of Jamaica against whose decision the present appeal was brought.

1 Supra.

CONDITIONS AS TO 'OTHER INSURANCE'

A condition often states that if the property is insured under another insurance policy, the insurers under the policy in question will not be liable unless notice of the other policy is given to them.

The decided cases on this topic relate to:

1 The other insurance policy being ineffective.
2 Whether there had been a double insurance in fact.
3 Whether notice of the termination of the other policy had been given.
4 Whether there had been a substitution of the other policy.
5 The amount of existing insurance on a building.
6 Whether the highest rate of premium had been paid.
7 Whether the other insurance was at the same rate.

1 Other Insurance Policy Ineffective

In *Equitable Fire and Accident Office Ltd v Ching Wo Hong*[2] stock-in-trade and other goods in a shop in Shanghai were insured under a fire policy. One of the conditions in the policy was as follows:

'On effecting any insurance or insurances during the currency of this policy elsewhere on the property hereby insured . . . the insured must . . . give notice to the company thereof so that the particulars thereof may be endorsed on the policy, and unless such notice be given, the insured will not be entitled to any benefit under this policy . . . The giving of such [notice] shall be a condition precedent to the recovery of any claim under this policy.'

The property was destroyed by fire on 5 December 1904. Prior to this date a policy covering the same goods had been effected by the insured with the Western Assurance Co, but the premium on it was never paid. The 11th condition of that policy stated:

'This insurance will not be in force until, nor will the company be liable in respect of any loss or damage happening before the premium, or a deposit on account thereof, is actually paid . . .'

When a claim was made on their policy, the Equitable Fire and Accident Office Ltd refused to indemnify the insured, alleging that he was guilty of a breach of the condition requiring him to notify them of any additional insurance which he had effected.

The Privy Council[3] held that the claim succeeded because there had been no breach of condition, since the additional insurance never became effective by reason of the premium not having been paid.

The judgment of their Lordships was delivered by Lord Davey, who said:[4]

'Their Lordships think that in any case the parties should not be held in equity to be estopped as between themselves from showing that the consideration had not, in fact, been paid. But in the present case they think that the condition read with the operative part of the instrument negatives any such estoppel; for the only meaning which can be given to the words is that the consideration must be not only expressed to be paid, but actually paid. Their Lordships

---

[2] [1907] AC 96, PC.
[3] Lords MacNaghten, Davey, Robertson and Atkinson.
[4] [1907] AC 96 at 100.

cannot treat the fact of the executed policy having been handed to the [insured] as a waiver of the condition or attach any importance to the circumstances. What was handed to the [insured] was the instrument with this clause in it, and that was notice to them, and made it part of the contract that there would be no liability until the premium was paid. It is not a question of conditional execution, but of the construction of what was executed.'

2 Double Insurance

In *Australian Agricultural Co v Saunders*[5] the insured effected a policy with the defendant (as chairman of a fire insurance company)[6] for '£3,000 on wool in bales . . . in all or any shed or store or station, or in transit to Sydney by land only or in any shed or store, or any wharf in Sydney until placed on ship'.

The policy contained a condition which stated:

'No claim shall be recoverable if the property insured be previously or subsequently insured elsewhere, unless the particulars of such insurance be notified to the company in writing.'

Subsequently the insured took out another policy with the Indemnity Mutual Marine Insurance Co in respect of wool to the amount of £16,500. The risk was described as being:

'At and from the River Hunter to Sydney per ships and steamers, and thence per ship or ships to London including the risk of craft from the time that the wools are first waterborne and of transhipment or landing and reshipment at Sydney.'

The fact that this policy had been effected was not communicated to the defendant. While in the warehouse of the stevedores, who were going to load the vessel on which the wool was to be carried, the wool was destroyed by fire. The insured claimed an indemnity from the defendant. But he repudiated liability on the ground that the lack of notice constituted a breach of the condition set out above.

The Court of Exchequer Chamber[7] held that the claim succeeded. The marine insurance policy did not cover the wool whilst it was in the stevedores' warehouse, so no notification that the marine insurance policy had been effected was necessary.

Bramwell B, said:[8]

'I think no action could have been maintained against the underwriters on the marine policy in respect of the loss. It seems to me clear that the words of that policy did not cover any loss by fire during the time when the goods were stored on land, as described in the case. The time when they were so on land formed no part of any act of transhipment or landing and reshipment. The suggestion is that there was a virtual reshipment when they were delivered to the stevedore. But in point of fact, they were not on board ship, and we must deal with words, in the absence of any usage, according to their natural ordinary signification. In point of fact, these goods were not in the course of landing and reshipment. Inasmuch as the loss would not have been recoverable from the underwriters of the marine policy, I think the plaintiffs are not brought within the words of the 5th clause of the fire policy. It is true that there was a subsequent insurance of the goods, but the words must be read with some limitation, or the result would be absurd. The insurance elsewhere must, to be within the clause, be an insurance as to a portion of the risks covered by the policy sued on. If that is so, it

---

[5] (1875) L R 10 C P 668, Ex Ch.

[6] Viz the Liverpool and London and Globe Insurance Co Ltd.

[7] Bramwell, Pollock and Amphlett, BB, Blackburn, Lush and Quain JJ.

[8] (1875) L R 10 C P at 674. See further, the judgment of Blackburn J, ibid, at 675; of Lush J, ibid, at 676; and of Quain J, ibid, at p 677.

seems to me this is not a case of double insurance such as was intended, inasmuch as the plaintiffs could not have recovered this loss on the marine policy. It was argued on the defendant's behalf that a possibility that the same risk might be covered by both the policies was sufficient under clause 5 to defeat the fire policy. I doubt very much whether that is so. I doubt whether a mere possibility that some portion of the risk covered by both policies might accidentally coincide constitutes such a double insurance as was meant.'

He concluded that, whether that were so or not, there seemed to be no evidence of any overlapping of the two policies, ie the possibility of any case in which both policies would have covered the same loss.[9]

3 Notice of Termination of Other Policy

In *Sulphite Pulp Co Ltd v Faber*[10] some mills and machinery were insured against fire with Lloyd's underwriters. The policy contained the following clause:

'This policy is subject to the same premium, terms and conditions as a policy . . . of the North British and Mercantile Company . . . on identical interest.'

This policy was dated 28 September 1893. The insured had effected a policy with the North British and Mercantile Co on 29 February 1892. That policy contained the following condition (Article 5 (d)):

'The insured shall notify the Company . . . if any insurance previously effected ceases'.

It also included a condition (Article 6) which stated:

'The insurance shall cease to attach and remain void until [the above stipulation] shall have been complied with, and it shall be optional for the Company, whenever such notification be made, to cancel the policy.'

The North British and Mercantile Co declined to renew the policy on 19 February 1894, but the insured gave no notice of this fact to Lloyd's underwriters.

A fire occurred on 1 July 1894. When a claim was made on the policy, Lloyd's underwriters refused to indemnify the insured on the ground that there had been a breach of the condition in that the lack of notice of the cesser of the North British and Mercantile Co's policy relieved them from liability.

Lord Russell of Killowen CJ, agreed with this contention, and held that the claim failed, saying:[11]

'In my judgment it is clear that on the failure by the insured to comply with the above requirement the liability of the insurers came to an end. The [insured] put their argument in this way. Article 4 (e)[12] deals with the notification by the assured of existing insurances, and Article 5 (d)[13] only deals with insurances notification of which is required under Article 4 (e); and as by the terms of the [insurers'] policy the [insured] are relieved from giving notice of existing policies, so they are relieved from notifying the cessation of existing policies. I cannot accept that view. In the first place, Articles 4 (e) and 5 (d) are addressed to different subject-matters. Article 4 (e) relates to existing policies, while Article 5 (d) deals not merely with

---

9 (1875) L R 10 C P at 674. See further the judgment of Pollock B, ibid, at 678; and of Amphlett B, ibid, at 678.
10 (1895) 1 Com Cas 146.
11 Ibid, at 152.
12 Article 4 (e) stated: 'When taking out an insurance the insured must state and have specified on the policy if the insured property is already covered by insurance'.
13 Article 5 (d) stated: 'So long as the insurance remains in force the insured shall notify to the company and have specified on the policy if some other insurance is taken out, or any insurance previously effected ceases'.

existing insurances but with policies to be thereafter taken out. Further, underwriters may well be content to dispense with notice of the existence of all previous policies, except that particular policy specifically referred to, under the wing of which they mean to shelter themselves; but it is an entirely different question whether they may not reasonably desire to know whether a previously effected insurance has gone off. If an insurer goes off the risk, it is likely that he has done so because he thinks the risk open to special danger; and Article 6 gives the second insurers under such circumstances an opportunity of considering their position and saying whether they will or will not continue the insurance. On Article 5 (d) I am clearly of opinion that on the failure of the [insured] to notify the cessation of the "previously effected" policy of the North British and Mercantile Co the liability of the [insurers] came to an end, there having been a breach of a condition which went to the root and substance of the contract.'

4 Substitution of Other Policies

In *National Protector Fire Insurance Co Ltd v Nivert*[14] a skating rink at Smyrna and its contents were insured under two policies in French, each for £600, with the National Protector Fire Insurance Co Ltd. Condition No 3 of these policies stated that if the property should be insured elsewhere, either before or after the two policies were effected, the insured was

> 'Tenu de le declarer, par écrit et de faire mentionner soit dans la police même, soit par un endos inscrit par la compagnie sur la dite police.'

At the time of effecting the policies the insured had concurrent insurances on the building with the General (United Counties) Co for £300, and with the Law Guarantee Co for £300. He had also a policy in respect of the contents with the British Crown Co for £600. All these facts were communicated to the National Protector Fire Insurance Co Ltd and endorsed on their two policies.

Subsequently the two policies on the building for £300 with the General (United Counties) Co and for £300 with the Law Guarantee Co were replaced by two policies issued by the Property Insurance Co, the first for £350 and the second for £350 (of which £300 only was on the building). The increase in these insurances from £600 to £650 on the building was to cover some extra decoration. Similarly, the policy on the contents with the British Crown Co for £600 was replaced by a policy issued by the Property Insurance Co for £600. Another policy with this company was effected for £350, which also covered £50 on some extra articles put into the building. These substituted insurances were not communicated to the National Protector Fire Insurance Co Ltd. A fire occurred, and the company repudiated liability on the ground that the insured had broken Condition No 3.

The Privy Council[15] held that there had been no breach of condition, and that the company was liable. The condition meant only that the fact that the property was further insured should be declared, and this had been done.

Lord Atkinson said:[16]

> 'The main question for decision is, therefore, whether this omission deprives the [insured], under Condition 3, of all right to recover on the policies sued upon. It was contended on behalf of the [insured] that the policies effected with the Property Insurance Co for £650 on the building merely replaced those previously effected with the United Counties Co and the

---

[14] [1913] A C 507, PC.
[15] Lords Atkinson, Shaw of Dunfermline and Moulton.
[16] [1913] A C 507 at 512.

Law Guarantee Co respectively for £300 each, and that the policies effected with the Property Insurance Co for £650 on the contents replaced the policy previously effected with the British Crown Insurance Co for £600, the extra £50 being intended in each case to cover some new decoration of the building and some additional furniture put into it. The dates at which the several policies were effected with the Property Insurance Co would of themselves suggest that some such replacement or substitution was designed to be effected. If it, in fact, took place, then, as the increases by the sum of £50 are to be disregarded, the amount covered by the policies of insurance remained the same, nothing was altered but the identity of the insurers, which is one of the very things Condition 3 did not require to be disclosed.'

He then continued:[17]

'It is clear from the course of the trial and the judgment of the learned Judge that it was not suggested that the policies, memoranda of which were indorsed on the policies sued on, were still in existence. They must, therefore, have either been surrendered or allowed to lapse, or the risk they covered must have been taken over by the Property Insurance Co through the machinery of the new policies, which last is what would appear to have been intended to be described by the word "transferred" used in the evidence. It is not suggested that they were allowed to lapse or were surrendered. And if the third course was that which was, in fact, taken, then that particular condition of things of which the third condition required the [insurer] to be informed, namely, the fact that premises were insured by others, remained practically unaltered, save to this extent, that the identity of the insurers was not the same.'

5 Amount of Existing Insurance on Building

In *Bancroft v Heath*[18] the insured effected a fire policy on his stock-in-trade. The policy contained a clause which stated:

'Warranted same gross rate, terms, and conditions as, and to follow, the British Law which company has £1,750 on the block of brick buildings in which the risk is a portion of the same.'

In fact, the buildings were not insured with the British Law Co for £1,750, but for £1,350 only. Some of the goods were destroyed by fire, but, when a claim was made by the insured, the underwriter refused to pay on the ground that the statement set out above as to the amount for which the buildings were insured was a condition, and that this condition had been broken.

The Court of Appeal[19] held that the underwriter was justified in his refusal to pay.

Sir A L Smith M R, observed:[20]

'Now, what is the meaning of that clause? In my judgment it means that the underwriters at Lloyd's before they write a fire risk wish to know whether any well-known fire insurance office has taken a risk on the same buildings. The clause is in my opinion a warranty that the British Law Company had insured the buildings for £1,750, and that is a condition precedent to the liability of the underwriters. As a matter of fact, at the time the policy was underwritten the company had not £1,750 on the buildings; but considerably less, namely £1,350. I agree, therefore, with the judgment of my brother Mathew[1] that, the condition precedent not having been performed, the underwriters have a good defence to the action.'

Vaughan Williams LJ, agreed that it was a condition, but said that he had some doubt. He said that the ordinary rule for ascertaining whether a statement was a condition or a representation was to ascertain whether or not the

[17] [1913] A C 507 at 513.
[18] (1901) 6 Com Cas 137, C A.
[19] Sir A L Smith M R, Vaughan Williams and Romer LJJ.
[20] (1901) 6 Com Cas 137 at 139.
[1] (1900) 5 Com Cas 110.

statement was material to the contract about to be entered into. On first looking at the language of the clause, it was not easy to see what the materiality of the statement was, because the policy with the company was not a policy on the same subject-matter as the insured's policy, but on the buildings, and, therefore, as the subject-matters were different, it was not quite clear how the risk was increased by the mis-statement. However, he concluded:[2]

> 'That has, however, been explained, because it is said that the underwriters at Lloyd's are not so familiar with fire insurance as with marine insurance, and have not the same facilities for making inquiries, and, therefore, a clause such as this is put in the policy for their protection. It is said that the underwriters would never have accepted this risk had it not been for the fact that the goods were in a building which had already been insured in a respectable office for £1,750. Mathew J arrived at the conclusion that that is a true statement of the way in which the business of fire insurance is done at Lloyd's, and, if that is so, I suppose that, the clause must be read as a condition precedent, and not as a mere representation.'

6 'Warranted Highest Rate'

In *Walker & Sons v Uzielli*[3] buildings and their contents were insured for £20,000 at a premium of 2/6d per cent. A clause in the policy stated:

> 'Warranted same premium and conditions as the Union Assurance Society with £1,500 and to follow their settlements in case of loss. Warranted highest rate.'

The same subject-matter had already been insured with the Westminster Fire Office at a premium of 7/6d. per cent. The buildings and contents were damaged by fire. In an action on the policy Mathew J, held that the insurer was not liable because the warranty had been broken, and observed:[4]

> 'But there was also a policy of the Westminster Fire Office, in which the same two subject-matters of insurance were protected for a premium of 7s 6d applicable to both. It is clear that the [insurer] has not had the "highest rate" at which the assured was protected elsewhere. It is argued that the lump sum of 7s 6d may have been arrived at by allowing more for "works" than 7s 6d and less for buildings and contents than 2s 6d. But I can enter upon no such speculation. I must act on the terms contained in the policies, and it seems to me the warranty has been broken.'

7 'Warranted to be on Same Rate'

In *Barnard v Faber*[5] the insured took out a fire policy on furniture and other effects at Barnard's Palace of Varieties and the Bell Tavern, Portsmouth. The amount insured was £1,000 and the rate of premium 25/- per cent. The policy covered the whole of the furniture and effects as one interest. One of the clauses in it stated:

> 'Warranted to be on same rate, terms and identical interest as Union Insurance Co £800, and Glasgow and London £700, and to follow their settlements.'

The property was destroyed by fire, but the underwriter repudiated liability on the ground that there had been a breach of the condition because the'

---

2 (1901) 6 Com Cas 137 at 140.
3 (1896) 1 Com Cas 452.
4 Ibid, at 455.
5 [1893] 1 QB 340, CA.

premium in the Union Insurance Co's policy was 31/6d. instead of 25/-, and the 'interest' was different because the sum insured by that policy was split into separate sums on separate 'interests', ie upon separate sets of chattels. Further, the wording of the policies was also different.

The Court of Appeal[6] held that the claim failed because there had been a breach of condition. Lindley L J, said:[7]

'It appears to me that the clause can have only one object, and that is this: "We will insure provided we are satisfied that the Union and the Glasgow have insured at the same rate, the same terms and the same interest." I do not profess to understand what the word "terms" means: I suppose it means terms as to risk; it cannot mean terms which are immaterial for the purpose of the contract. It seems to me that what was contemplated was the risk. What, I apprehend, the underwriters mean is this: "Satisfy us that these two offices have insured the same risk, the same interest, at the same rate, and we will effect this insurance." I cannot myself think that the term "warranted" is important; for I should construe this policy in precisely the same way whether the word was in or not. I do not think the policy is made plainer by the introduction of that word. I look upon part of the clause as a condition precedent.'

Bowen L J, was of the same opinion:[8]

'A term as regards the risk must be a condition. Then let us look at what the particular words are—the "same rate and identical interest". The "same rate and identical interest" are, obviously, words so material to the transaction that we can only construe them as creating a condition precedent. With regard to the word "terms," it is not necessary for us to decide, or to explain exactly what it means. I do not myself doubt that there is a limitation which can be put upon it—a limitation to be derived from the character of the document, from the nature of the transaction, and from the nature of the stipulation itself, which reduces within defined and reasonable limits that which otherwise might be vague, impracticable, and illimitable. But when you regard the words which alone we have to look at for the purposes of this appeal, the "same rate and identical interest" as the insurance companies, I do not doubt for a moment that it is a condition without which the contract is not to be binding.'

CONDITIONS AS TO PROCEDURE IN CASE OF LOSS

A condition usually refers to the procedure which must be followed in case of a loss.

The decided cases relate to:

1   The time limit within which particulars of the loss must be given.
2   The sufficiency of the particulars of loss.
3   The absence of a proper certificate in corroboration of the claim.
4   Non-compliance with the correct procedure caused by the insurers' agent.

1 Time Limit

In *Roper v Lendon*[9] a condition of a fire policy issued by the Kent Fire Insurance Co stated:

---

6 Lindley, Bowen and A L Smith LJJ.
7 [1893] 1 Q B 340 at 342.
8 Ibid, at 344. See also the judgment of A L Smith L J, ibid, at 344–345.
9 (1859) 28 L J Q B 260. The case also concerned an arbitration clause. As to this point, see p 140, post.

'All persons insured by this Company sustaining any loss or damage by fire, shall forthwith give notice thereof to the directors or secretary of this Company at their office in Maidstone, and within 15 days after such fire, deliver in as particular an account of their loss or damage as the nature of the case will admit of, and shall also make proof of the amount of such loss or damage, by his, her or their solemn declaration or affirmation, by their books or accounts, and by such other proper vouchers as shall be reasonably required.'

A fire occurred, but the insured failed to deliver to the insurers the required particulars. The Court of Queen's Bench[10] held that the delivery of particulars within the required period was a condition precedent to the right to sue.

Lord Campbell C J, said:[11]

'[Counsel] very properly admitted that the delivery of particulars is a conditon precedent to the [insured's] right to recover; and that being so, the whole of the condition as expressed in the policy must be precedent to the [insured's] right to recover. The delivery must be within fifteen days after the fire, and it is very reasonable that it should be so; it being of the utmost importance to the company to know, as soon after the loss as possible, the exact amount for which the [insured] claims compensation.'

In *Mason v Harvey*[12] a condition in a fire policy effected with the Norwich Union Insurance Society stated:

'Whenever any fire shall happen, the party insured shall give immediate notice thereof to one of the secretaries or agents of the society, and within 3 calendar months deliver to such secretary or agent, under his or her hand, accounts exhibiting the full particulars and amount of the loss sustained, estimated with reference to the state in which the property destroyed or damaged was immediately before the fire happened.'

The insured delivered no such particulars of loss within the prescribed period, and the insurers repudiated liability.

The Court of Exchequer[13] held that they were entitled to do so because the condition had been broken. Pollock C B, observed:[14]

'By the contract of the parties, the delivery of the particulars of loss is made a condition precedent to the right of the assured to recover. It has been argued that such a construction would be most unjust, since the [assured] might be prevented from recovering at all by the accidental omission of some article. But the condition is not to be construed with such strictness. Its meaning is that the assured will, within a convenient time after the loss, produce to the company something which will enable them to form a judgment as to whether or not he has sustained a loss. Such a condition is, in substance, most reasonable; otherwise a party might lie by for 4 or 5 years after the loss, and then send in a claim when the company perhaps had no means of investigating it.'

In *Northern Suburban Property and Real Estates Co Ltd v British Law Fire Insurance Co Ltd*.[15] a condition in a fire policy stated:

'On the happening of any loss or damage, the insured shall forthwith give notice thereof in writing to the company, and shall within 30 days or such further time as the Company may allow, deliver to the Company a claim in writing containing as particular an account as may be reasonably practicable of the several items of property and articles destroyed or damaged and of the account of the loss or damage thereto respectively, and shall give to the Company such further particular proofs and information as may be reasonably required, and if such claim be not delivered and such requirements be not complied with, the Company shall not be liable for any loss or damage.'

---

10 Lord Campbell C J, and Hill J.
11 (1859) 28 L J Q B 260, at 262.
12 (1853) 8 Exch 819.
13 Pollock C B, Alderson, Platt and Martin BB.
14 (1853) 8 Exch 819 at 821.
15 (1919) 1 Ll L Rep 403, K B (Commercial Court).

The property was damaged by fire, and within 30 days a claim was put forward by the insured giving details of the repairs which were necessary. Later on, after the 30 days had expired, another estimate was put forward from another contractor, who quoted a price more than twice the original estimate. The insurance company refused to accept the second estimate. The matter was referred to arbitration, and the umpire refused to consider the second estimate.

Bailhache J said that it was not a new claim, and that it must be considered by the umpire.

His Lordship said:[16]

> 'The first claim is one that was formed and sent in within 30 days, and it does not seem to me, by that Condition 2, that the assured are precluded from putting forward as their claim a view which has been taken at a later date about the same damage, about the same fire, and about the same place, and taken on a more favourable basis, and at a figure which would afford more compensation than the original claim. There is no prejudice or difficulty in the matter. The damage done remains to be seen, and is precisely the same.
>
> I do not think, myself, the clause applies in such a case as this. It is not a new claim in the sense that it is a new matter entirely, sprung upon the insurance company. It is a new claim only in the sense that it differs from the first claim, and includes some items and excludes others, but relates to the same subject-matter, and, in my judgment, the umpire was perfectly entitled to consider it. In my judgment, the figure which the company must pay the assured in this case is the figure which the umpire has arrived at based on the new claim, or what he calls the new claim—the second claim—and not upon the first claim.'

2 Sufficiency of Particulars of Loss

In *Hiddle v National Fire and Marine Insurance Co of New Zealand*[17] the stock-in-trade of some general store keepers was insured under a fire insurance policy, one of the conditions of which stated:

> 'The insured sustaining any loss or damage by fire shall forthwith give notice to the company in Dunedin . . . and shall within 15 days after such fire deliver to the same an account in detail of such loss or damage as the nature and circumstances of the case will admit.'

A fire took place on 10 January 1894 when the whole stock of the insured, with a trifling exception, was destroyed. Some of the books including the cash-book and the customers' ledger were in a safe, and were saved from the fire. The stock-book, however, and the stock-sheets of the end of 1893 were destroyed.

On 24 January 1894, the insured in assumed compliance with the condition set out above forwarded to the insurance company a statutory declaration that they had sustained a loss amounting to £2,250 as per a detailed statement in the form shown on p 128.

The insurance company declined to accept this statement as sufficient compliance with the condition or to accept any liability. When an action was brought by the insured against the company, the Supreme Court of New South Wales directed that the insured should be non-suited. This order was confirmed by the Privy Council,[18] because the evidence given by the insured showed that they could have complied with the condition much more fully and completely than they had done.

---

[16] (1919 1 Ll L Rep 403.
[17] [1896] A C 372, P C.
[18] Lords Watson, Hobhouse, Davey and Sir Richard Couch.

Particulars of Items burnt.	Value at time of fire.	Present value.	Amount claimed.	Remarks.
	£		£	
Drapery and clothing . .	1600		600	
Boots	200		100	
Fancy goods, crockery and stationery . .	150		100	
Ironmongery . .	150		100	
Grocery . . .	150		100	
	£2250		£1000	

Lord Davey observed:[19]

> 'It was contended on behalf of the [insured] that they were only bound to give such an account as the nature and circumstances of the case would admit of, or (in other words) the best account they could, and that whether they had done so was a question of fact which ought to have been submitted to the jury. Their Lordships, however, accept the rule laid down by Willes J, in the case of *Ryder v Wombwell*,[20] and they think that the non-suit was proper, although there may have been some evidence to go to the jury, if the proof was such that the jury could not reasonably give a verdict for the [insured]. In the present case their Lordships doubt whether the statement forwarded by the [insured] was an account at all within the meaning of the sixth condition, and they consider it proved by the evidence of the [insured] themselves that at the time of forwarding their statement they had in their possession materials which enabled them to give a much fuller, more detailed, and better account for the purpose of enabling the insurance company to test the reality and extent of the loss.'

In *Welch v Royal Exchange Assurance*[1] a fire policy contained a condition which stated:

> 'The insured shall also give to the Corporation all such proofs and information with respect to the claim as may reasonably be required . . . No claim under this policy shall be payable unless the terms of this condition have been complied with.'

A fire occurred, and the insured claimed an indemnity under the policy. The insurance company requested information as to the bank accounts used and controlled by the insured for the purpose of his business. The insured operated and controlled banking accounts in the name of his mother, and did not disclose the accounts as requested, but eventually did so when the claim was referred to arbitration.

The insurance company contended that the condition set out above had been broken, and that it was under no liability to the insured.

---

[19] [1896] AC 372 at 375.
[20] (1868) LR 4 Exch 32, where Willes J said, at 39; 'It was formerly considered necessary in all cases to leave the question to the jury if there was any evidence, even a *scintilla*, in support of the case; but it is now settled that the question for the Judge . . . is . . . not whether there is literally no evidence, but whether there is none that ought reasonably to satisfy the jury that the fact sought to be proved is established'.
[1] (1938) 62 Ll L Rep 83, CA.

The Court of Appeal[2] agreed with this contention, and held that the claim failed.

MacKinnon and Finlay LJJ held that th econdition was a condition precedent. In the course of his judgment MacKinnon LJ said:[3]

'It was then argued that in the last sentence of condition 4, "unless" should be construed as meaning "until". I do not think this is sound. I think Branson J was right in saying that the last 10 words of that sentence mean no more and no less than "if the terms of this condition have not been complied with." But in truth the more formidable argument for the [insurers] does not depend on the last sentence of condition 4. They say that the promise in the body of the policy is "subject to the conditions, which, so far as the nature of them permits, shall be deemed to be conditions precedent to the right of the insured to recover." In condition 4 there is the provision that "the insured shall give all such information as may reasonably be required." The nature of this does permit compliance with it to be a condition precedent to the right of the insured to recover. It is found by the arbitrator that it has not been complied with. There has, therefore, been a breach of a condition precedent to the right of recovery.'

The learned Lord Justice then went on to say:[4]

'I have said that I arrive at that conclusion with some regret. The insurance company failed to establish any of their numerous charges of fraud. The arbitrator has found that the assured ought to have produced these accounts, but that, when produced, they contained, in fact, nothing which justified, or tended to justify, a refusal to pay his claim. This means that the [assured] had an honest claim for a large amount, but by reason of his stupid obstinacy over an immaterial matter he has enabled the [insurers] to refuse to pay anything. To lose any sum, however large, may be the proper penalty of dishonesty. To lose some £20,000 as the result of stupidity does seem excessive, even if it be true that the claimant has only himself to blame for that result.'

Slesser LJ, preferred to leave open the question whether the condition was a condition precedent, but based his judgment on the fact that the insured had failed to give the necessary information before the claim was made by him. He said that:[5]

'In these circumstances, even if the requirement of information in condition 4 be not a condition precedent, but merely a condition that the insurance company need not pay until the information required in condition 4 is provided, the [insured] fails because he cannot say that such information was, in fact, given before the claim was made, and, therefore, it becomes to my mind unnecessary in this case to determine whether the failure to comply with condition 4 as to information was a failure to satisfy a condition precedent. For myself, I would wish to keep open that question. Had the phrase at the end of condition 4 been, "No claim under this policy shall be payable *until* the terms of this condition have been complied with," instead of the word "unless," the case would have resembled that of *Weir v Northern Counties of England Insurance Co*,[6] where it was held that such words did not constitute a condition precedent but only a requirement to be satisfied before a liability to pay arose, but it may well be said that here the word "unless" has no such temporal limitation.'

---

2 Slesser, MacKinnon and Finlay LJJ.
3 (1938) 62 Ll L Rep 83 at 90. Finlay LJ said, ibid, at 91: 'In *Worsley v Wood* ((1796) 6 Term Rep 710) it was held by the Court of King's Bench that the condition in the policy in question was a condition precedent. If the terms of that policy are compared with the terms of the policy now in question, I think that some support is obtained for the construction which has been put upon the present policy by MacKinnon LJ.'
4 (1938) 62 Ll L Rep 83 at 91.
5 Ibid at 88.
6 (1879) 4 L R Ir 689.

3 Absence of Proper Certificate

In *Oldman, Assignees of Ingram (a Bankrupt) v Bewicke*[7] a condition in a fire policy issued to the insured by the Sun Fire Office stated:

> 'Persons sustaining any loss or damage by fire, are forthwith to give notice thereof at the office, and as soon as possible afterwards, to deliver in as particular an account of their loss and damage as the nature of the case will admit of, and make proof of the same by their oath or affirmation, (according to the form practised in the said office,) and by their books of account, and such other proper vouchers, as shall be reasonably required, and procure a certificate under the hands of the minister and churchwardens, together with some other reputable inhabitants of the parish not concerned in such loss, importing that they were well acquainted with the character and circumstances of the person or persons insured, and do know or verily believe that he, she or they really and by misfortune, without any fraud or evil practice, have sustained by such fire the loss and damage as his, her or their loss, to the value therein mentioned, but till such affidavit and certificate of such insured's loss shall be made and produced, the loss money shall not be payable; and if there appears any fraud or false swearing, such sufferers shall be excluded from all benefit by their policies, etc.'

A fire took place, and the insured produced a certificate as to the loss signed by some reputable inhabitants, but it was not signed by the churchwardens or by a minister. The insured said that the minister resided a long distance from the parish, and was wholly unacquainted with his character, and, therefore, wholly unable to complete the certificate.

When an action was brought on the policy, the insurance company[8] pleaded that the condition had not been complied with, and that consequently it was not liable to pay the sum claimed.

The Court of Common Pleas[9] agreed with this contention, and gave judgment for the insurance company.

Gould J said:[10]

> 'Till the affidavit is made, and the certificate procured, the money is not to be payable: the time of payment therefore is not yet come. Though a person were a bona fide sufferer, still he is not entitled without a certificate. The stipulation is a condition precedent, that there shall be a certificate that there is no kind of fraud. Nothing is said about the churchwardens: and the excuse of the minister living at a distance is frivolous.'

This decision was followed in *Worsley v Wood*.[11] In this case the insured had effected a fire policy with the Phoenix Insurance Co. One of its clauses stated:

> 'Persons insured shall give notice of the loss forthwith, deliver in an account and procure a certificate of the minister, churchwardens and some reputable householders of the parish importing that they knew the character, etc of the assured, and believe that he really sustained the loss and without fraud.'

The insured forwarded to the company a certificate signed by 4 reputable householders of the parish, but the minister and churchwardens refused to sign it.

The Court of Common Pleas[12] held that the delivery of the certificate in the correct form was a condition precedent to the liability of the company. The fact that the minister and churchwardens had refused to sign it was material.

---

7 (1786) 2 Hy Bl 577n.
8 The action was, in fact, brought against the directors of the company.
9 Lord Loughborough, Gould and Nares JJ.
10 (1786) 2 Hy Bl at 577n.
11 (1796) 6 Term Rep 710.
12 Lord Kenyon CJ, Ashurst, Grose and Lawrence JJ.

Lord Kenyon CJ said:[13]

'In this case however it is said that, though the minister and churchwardens did not certify, some of the inhabitants did certify, and that that was sufficient, it being a performance of the condition cy près. But I confess I do not see how the terms cy près are applicable to this subject; the arguments for the [insured] below go to show that if none of the inhabitants of this parish certified, a certificate by the inhabitants of the next or of any other parish would have answered the purpose. But the assured cannot substitute one thing for another. So here it was competent to the insurance office to make the stipulations stated in their printed proposals; they had a right to say to individuals who were desirous of being insured, "Knowing how liable we are to be imposed upon, we will, among other things, require that the minister, churchwardens and some of the reputable inhabitants of your parish shall certify that they believe that the loss happened by misfortune and without fraud, otherwise we will not contract with you at all." If the assured say that the minister and churchwardens may obstinately refuse to certify, the insurers answer "We will not stipulate with you on any other terms." Such are the terms on which I understand this insurance to have been effected.'

Ashurst J added:[14]

'The question is whether the certificate required be or be not a condition precedent; if it be, the [insured] below cannot maintain their action. It is perfectly immaterial whether they have entered into an improvident contract; if they choose to take the burden upon themselves, they cannot call on the insurance office until they have complied with the condition. I think that it is a condition precedent, and that the assured engaged at all events to procure the certificate before they applied to the office for an indemnity. Nor is there anything unreasonable in these terms. It is well known that great frauds are sometimes practised on the insurance offices, and, therefore, it behoves them to take all care to prevent frauds. In order to guard more effectually to protect the Phoenix Co, they insist on having a certificate from the minister and churchwardens, from persons who are not likely, from their situations in life, to assist in such frauds. But as the [insured] below have not procured that certificate, they cannot maintain this action.'

4 Non-Compliance Caused by Company's Agent

In *Hadwin v Lovelace*[15] the agent of the Phoenix Insurance Co in Gibraltar had refused to pay the insured the value of property insured under a fire policy on the ground that the loss had not been ascertained in the mode prescribed by the company. The Privy Council held that the company was liable, for, although the damage had not been calculated according to the method provided by the policy, it had been fairly ascertained. The agent had been the cause of the failure to follow the prescribed manner.

Sir William Grant said:[16]

'Here the [insurer] alone seems to blame. After the fire he is required to attend a survey to investigate the loss. This he refuses, without assigning any reason, but signifying his intention to protest against any claim that might afterwards be made against the company. After some time the [insured] brings his action in the civil court; the [insurer] pleads he is not prepared, and is sentenced to pay the amount of the loss sustained. From this he appealed to the Superior Court,[17] stating, for the first time, the reason of his objecting to the demand, namely, that the demand had not been substantiated by the [insured] agreeably to the proposals of the company for effecting the insurance and ascertaining any loss that might be sustained in order to entitle them to repayment. This could not fairly be attributable to the

---

13 (1796) 6 Term Rep 710 at 719.

14 Ibid, at 720.

15 (1809) 1 Act 126.

16 (1809) 1 Act 126 at 127.

17 Of Gibraltar.

[insured], since the [insurer] had absolutely refused to assist in ascertaining the damages sustained. Notwithstanding the [insured] had not exactly complied with the printed requisitions of the Company for ascertaining the property lost, the two inferior Courts had been of opinion he had fairly accounted to them for the claim instituted, by his own affidavit, and the certificate of several merchants who had attended the survey.'

CONDITIONS AS TO EFFECT OF FRAUDULENT CLAIMS

A condition usually states that if the insured makes a fraudulent claim, all benefit under the policy will be forfeited.[18]

Whether the claim is a fraudulent one is in each case a matter of fact.

Examples of Fraudulent Claims

In *Levy v Baillie*[19] an upholsterer insured his stock-in-trade for £1,000. The policy contained a clause which stated:

'If there appear fraud in the claim made, or false swearing or affirming in support thereof, the claimant shall forfeit all business under such policy.'

A fire took place and the insured swore an affidavit to the effect that he had sustained a loss of £1,085 in respect of his stock-in-trade, viz £85 for goods which were damaged in the process of removal, and £1,000 for goods which had been abstracted by a crowd that had assembled at the scene of the fire. The goods alleged to have been lost consisted of four-poster beds, mahogany tables, couches, chairs, stools and carpets. The insurer contended that the claim was fraudulent, and called witnesses to show that it was impossible for so many bulky goods to have been carried off undiscovered. These witnesses stated that policemen were on the spot as soon as the fire was discovered, that a cordon was established round the premises almost immediately, that the fire was out in about two hours, and that no article of any size could have been removed. The jury gave a verdict in favour of the insured for £500.

The insurer applied to the Court of Common Pleas for an order for a new trial on the ground that the verdict of the jury amounted to an affirmation of fraud in making a claim for the larger amount. The Court granted the application because it felt that the case ought in all the circumstances to be submitted to a second investigation, on payment of costs by the insurer.

In *Britton v Royal Insurance Co*[20] a clothier insured his furniture, trade fixtures and stock-in-trade for £550 under a fire policy. The property was destroyed by fire, and he claimed the full sum insured. The insurance company refused to indemnify him on the ground that the claim was a fraudulent one. Their witnesses gave evidence that the stock could not be anything like as large as had been represented, and that its real value was £120, though the insured had placed it at £490.

In directing the jury Willes J said:[1]

---

[18] As to fraudulent claims, see generally Ivamy, *General Principles of Insurance Law* (4th edn, 1979), pp 433–438.

[19] (1831) 7 Bing 349.

[20] (1866) 4 F & F 905 (Maidstone Civil Court, Kent Summer Assizes).

[1] Ibid, at 908.

'But it is not less clear that, even supposing it were not wilful, yet as it is a contract of indemnity only, that is, a contract to recoup the insured the value of the property destroyed by fire; if the claim is fraudulent, it is defeated altogether. That is, suppose the insured made a claim for twice the amount insured and lost, thus seeking to put the office off its guard, and in the result to recover more than he is entitled to, that would be a wilful fraud, and the consequence is that he could not recover anything. This is a defence quite different from that of wilful arson. It gives the go-bye to the origin of the fire, and it amounts to this—that the assured took advantage of the fire to make a fraudulent claim. The law upon such a case is in accordance with justice, and also with sound policy. The law is that a person, who has made such a fraudulent claim, could not be permitted to recover at all. The contract of insurance is one of perfect good faith on both sides, and it is most important that such good faith should be maintained. It is the common practice to insert in fire policies conditions that they shall be void in the event of a fraudulent claim; and there was such a condition in the present case. Such a condition is only in accordance with legal principle and sound policy. It would be most dangerous to permit parties to practise such frauds, and then, notwithstanding their false-hood and fraud, to recover the real value of the goods consumed. And if there is wilful falsehood and fraud in the claim, the insured forfeits all claim whatever upon the policy.'

The jury brought in a verdict for the insurance company.

In *Chapman v Pole*[2] the insured had insured his household goods with the Sun Fire Co under a fire policy. A fire took place, and he claimed £418. The company[3] refused to pay on the ground that the claim was grossly exaggerated. It appeared from an inspector's report that there could not have been that quantity of goods in the building at the time. In one of the rooms, which was not burnt, the contents valued at £30 were not worth £3. In the bedrooms the remains of cheap iron bedsteads worth a few shillings were found in the place of mahogany ones stated as worth £30. The debris of crockery, which was found, represented only a few shillings instead of £33, which was stated as its value. Strong evidence was given on the part of the insurance company to show that the furniture was of the poorest description, and was not worth more than £50, that a great part of it had been removed before the fire took place, and that the remainder was not worth more than £30.

In summing up to the jury Cockburn C J said:[4]

'It is not certainly a question of mere accuracy or inaccuracy. A man may make a mistake in his claim and it may be quite honestly. If, for instance, a man either fails to recollect the precise quantity of goods he has on his premises at the time of the fire, or mistakes the value of those of which he was in possession, and thus he presses a claim according to what he believes honestly to be true, but which may, in the end, turn out to be mistaken, the only consequence which ensues is, that inasmuch as the contract of insurance is simply a contract of indemnity, he can only recover to the extent of the real value of the goods he has actually lost. . . . Therefore, in all the cases the only question—supposing the claim to be honest—is, what was the real and actual value of the goods destroyed? But beyond that—although the insured has not caused the fire—yet, if he has made a fraudulent claim, then, on such a condition as is contained in this policy, he must fall by the fraud he has thus attempted to perpetrate, and is not entitled to recover at all. Such being the legal principles on which the question to be determined arises, it is for you to determine upon the evidence. If you believe the evidence for the defence, it is clearly established, and it is a gross and scandalous case of fraud. According to that evidence the claim was grossly excessive, not only in point of value, but as to the quantity and character of the furniture insured; and it is not easy to conceive of such gross exaggeration being honest. A man may be somewhat mistaken as to the exact value or the precise number of the articles of furniture he possesses, but he can scarcely be so grossly ignorant of the furniture of the rooms in which he lives and sleeps as honestly to represent

---

[2] (1870) 22 L T 306 (Kingston Civil Court, Surrey Spring Assizes).
[3] The action was brought against the 'public officer' of the company.
[4] (1870) 22 L T 306 at 307.

articles worth a few shillings or pounds as worth large sums of money. If, then, you believe the evidence for the defence, it is your duty to find for the [insurer], as in that view a more scandalous fraud never was attempted.'

The jury returned a verdict for the insurance company.

In *Norton v Royal Fire and Life Assurance Co*[5] a grocer's stock-in-trade and furniture were insured to the value of £450 against fire. A fire occurred, and the company entered into possession of the premises. The insured made a claim for £274 including fixtures, fittings, etc. of which £196 was claimed for stock-in-trade. The insurance company resisted the claim, alleging that it was excessive. Negotiations ensued, and the insured reduced his claim to £187 ie £87 for the goods and £100 for damages for the retention of possession. The company still resisted his claim, and the insured brought an action on the policy for £150 as due under the policy and £100 as damages. At the trial of the action he admitted that the stock burnt was only worth from £80 to £100, but said: 'My friends told me that I should never get what I claimed, and so I put a little on to everything, and I thought the claim first sent for the stock was right'.

In directing the jury, the Judge said:[6]

'Men often estimate their property much beyond what it is really worth, and they do it sometimes to get what the company are ultimately willing to pay. They may hope, on the one hand, to get as much as they can, and at all events to secure the real value, and the company, on the other hand, are anxious to cut down as much as they can, and I suppose the claims are usually cut down. I daresay there is hardly a case of a small insurance in which a larger value is not put on the property than it is worth and than it is known to be worth. No doubt it is wrong, very wrong, and in this case no one can say it was right to "put it on" in order that it might be taken off and that the party might ultimately get what he had really lost. That is not right, but whether it is fraudulent in the sense of intending to defraud may appear to you to deserve consideration. It is one thing to do it with intent to get all out of the company; no doubt it is wrong to put forward an exaggerated claim; but it is a question whether it is a fraudulent claim in the sense of endeavouring to get and knowingly getting far beyond the value. That would be a distinct fraud. No doubt it is very wrong, and in a certain sense it is a fraudulent thing; but you must look at all the circumstances and come to a conclusion one way or the other. I desire to take your opinion on that point, whether the first claim was fraudulent. I have already said that it was not a false claim if all the articles were there merely because too high a value was placed upon them; but you must look at the whole conduct of the [insured], and say whether it was a fraudulent claim. You would hardly say that it was a fraud if immediately after the fire he made out a claim to the best of his memory, stating the values too highly, and if upon careful inquiry he found that he had put them too highly and then sent in an amended claim. No doubt he sent in an exaggerated claim, but you must look to his whole conduct to see if it were fraudulent.'

The jury found for the insured and awarded him £187, ie £87 for the goods and £100 as damages for the retention of possession.

The insurance company applied to the Queen's Bench Division[7] for a new trial, but this was refused.

Lord Coleridge said[8] that no doubt the insured had first put forward an exaggerated claim, but it had been reduced before action to the amount recovered. In the circumstances he could not say that there had been any misdirection. The trial Judge had said that what the insured had done was no

---

[5] (1885) 1 T L R 460, Q B.
[6] Ibid, at 460.
[7] Coleridge L C J, and Cave J.
[8] (1885) 1 T L R 460 at 461. See also the judgment of Cave J, ibid, at 461.

doubt morally wrong in putting forward a claim which he knew to be exaggerated. But he had left it to the jury to say whether it was fraudulent in the sense of an intention to deceive and defraud the company by getting out of them money which he knew he had no right to, and that must depend upon all the circumstances. He himself could not see that the jury's verdict could be disturbed either as being against the weight of the evidence or on the ground of misdirection.

In *Beauchamp v Faber*[9] stock-in-trade of a grocery and provision business was insured with the Sun Insurance Office against fire. A loss occurred and a claim of £11,600 was made by the insured. The claim was not admitted, and the matter was referred to arbitration. The umpire found that the true value of the stock at the time was only £4,656. He held that the claim was a fraudulent one, and that the insurer was not liable on it.[10]

In *Albion Mills Co v H Babington Hill*[11] the insured claimed £30,000 under a fire policy on stock destroyed by fire at a wharf. The underwriter repudiated liability on the ground that the claim was fraudulent. The policy contained a clause stating:[12]

'If the insured shall make any claim knowing the same to be false or fraudulent as regards amount or otherwise, this policy shall become void and all claims thereunder shall be forfeited.'

Sir Edward Pollock (the Official Referee) held that there had been falsification of the stock books[13] on which the insured relied, and that the claim failed.

In *Herman v Phoenix Assurance Co Ltd*[14] the insured claimed for a loss of some furs under a fire policy. He contended that they were stored in a building at Constantinople at the time of the fire. The insurance company repudiated liability on the ground that the claim was a fraudulent one because the furs were never on the premises at all.

The Court of Appeal[15] gave judgment for the insurance company.[16] In reviewing the evidence Bankes LJ said:[17]

'But the second point, on which the Judge[18] ultimately rested his judgment, was this. He came to the conclusion that this large quantity of furs was never on the premises at all at the time of the fire. [The insurers] rested their case on that point on the evidence of several gentlemen who had very considerable experience in reference to the effect of fierce fire on furs, and who said that in their opinion it was quite impossible that this quantity of furs could have been on these premises, otherwise they would have seen some traces of them either by the crinkled skin or by the ash, or by discovering here and there a paw, a bone, a claw, or

---

9 (1898) 3 Com Cas 308.
10 The case also concerned the effect of another policy taken out by the insured with Lloyd's underwriters who had agreed to pay the same percentage on their policy as might be 'settled' by the Sun Insurance Office on the first policy. As to this aspect of the case, see p 139, post.
11 (1922) 12 Ll L Rep 96 (Official Referee's Court).
12 As to an express condition usually inserted in policies to the effect that if the claim is in any respect fraudulent, all benefit under it is to be forfeited, see Ivamy, *General Principles of Insurance Law* (4th edn, 1979), p 434.
13 The evidence is set out in (1922) 12 Ll L Rep at 97–98.
14 (1924) 18 Ll L Rep 371, CA.
15 Bankes, Warrington and Scrutton LJJ.
16 The Court of Appeal also held obiter that there had been non-disclosure of a material fact. As to this aspect of the case, see p 51, ante.
17 (1924) 18 Ll L Rep 371 at 371.
18 Bailhache J: (1923) 17 Ll L Rep 224.

something that was hard and difficult to destroy. I quite agree that it is difficult to prove a case of that kind, particularly where as here the roof had fallen in, and the whole of the floor where the goods were said to have been was apparently covered with tiles, and the gentlemen do not appear to have moved these tiles to any large extent. I quite appreciate the difficulty of proving a case founded on evidence such as that. But we are dealing with the decision of a Judge of great experience who heard the witnesses, and is evidently not biased against the [insured], and in substance says he is ''driven to the conclusion that the furs could not have been there.'' It seems to me quite impossible for this Court, which has not seen the witnesses, to upset the decision of the Judge; and speaking for myself I feel it quite impossible to arrive at a different conclusion from that arrived at by the Judge.'

Scrutton LJ added:[19]

'There is a fire in a warehouse and the roof has fallen in. There is said to have been in that warehouse a very mixed and valuable assortment of furs. Two classes of witnesses are called—people who did not see this fire but have seen very large fur fires in London. They say one would always find traces of the furs. Sometimes it is skin; sometimes it is the tails and bones or the head and other pieces which one knows very well are kept on the fur for appearance's sake. Then there are called two assessors and a third gentleman, who went into this particular place and found no trace whatever of fur. The Judge, having heard that, has accepted the evidence to this extent, that in his view there cannot have been in that warehouse anything like the large and valuable assortment which [the insured] says was there. Any such conclusion leads irresistibly to the conclusion that a fraudulent claim is being made; and the Judge dismissed the claim.'

In *Harris v Evans*[20] the insured, who was carrying on business as a shoe manufacturer, claimed under a fire policy, alleging that some of the stock had been damaged in a fire. The claim was for £4,701. The underwriter refused to pay on the ground that the claim was exaggerated to such an extent that the insured must have known that it was false, and that the putting it forward in that exaggerated form was an attempted fraud, and brought into operation a condition of the policy which stated:[1]

'If the assured makes any claim knowing the same to be false or fraudulent as regards amount or otherwise, then the policy shall become void and all claims thereunder shall be forfeited.'

Branson J held that the claim was fraudulent, and that the underwriter was not liable. The insured knew that the claim was fraudulent when put forward, but hoped to support it by a stock sheet.

After reviewing the evidence,[2] his Lordship said:[3]

'I think, viewing the case as a whole, I am driven to the conclusion there was nothing like the amount of stock there is alleged to have been. I think one can reach that conclusion independently along a number of avenues. If the receiver's evidence is in the least correct, and if the value that Mr Morris Harris gave for the business was anything like the right value, the stock could not have been worth more than £1,000. Is it to be believed that between 17 August, when Morris Harris became the purchaser, and September when he handed it over to his sons, he had spent £2,500 in stock? Therefore, I am convinced that that stocktaking in August 1922, does not represent the truth. . . .

Another avenue is this, that if you take the amount of purchases which the books show the [insured] made between September 1921, and the end of December 1922, you cannot make

---

[19] (1924) 18 Ll L Rep 371 at 372.

[20] (1924) 19 Ll L Rep 303 at 346, K B.

[1] As to an express condition usually inserted in policies to the effect that if the claim is in any respect fraudulent, all benefit under it is to be forfeited, see Ivamy, *General Principles of Insurance Law* (4th edn, 1979), p 434.

[2] For the details of the evidence, see (1924) 19 Ll L Rep 346 at 347–348.

[3] Ibid, at 348.

the stock £5,300 which they represent in this stock sheet, even assuming they had £3,500 worth from their father. This stocktaking is something upon which I cannot place any reliance.
    The result is that I come to the conclusion that this is a fraudulent claim. I accept the evidence given for the defence as to the probable amount of stock on the premises.'

In *Herbert v Poland*[4] a bungalow and its contents were insured under a fire policy. Seven months after the issue of the policy both were destroyed by fire. When a claim was made by the insured, the insurer refused to pay on the ground that the fire was not accidental, and that the setting light to the premises was done at the instigation of the insured.

Swift J, after reviewing the evidence,[5] said that the insurer was not liable. It had been proved beyond any reasonable doubt that the bungalow had been destroyed in consequence of previous arrangements entered into between the insured and her nephew.

In *Gallé Gowns Ltd v Licenses and General Insurance Co Ltd*[6] the insured were retail costumiers, who had effected a fire policy in relation to their stock. A fire occurred, and the insurance company refused to indemnify the insured on the ground that the claim was fraudulent in that every item in it was exaggerated.[7]

In directing the jury, Branson J said that the word 'fraudulent' meant that what the insurance company set out to prove was that the insured had made a claim which they knew to be an exaggerated claim, ie knowing that the goods were not of the value they put on them, they still put that value on them in the hope of making an illicit profit out of the company.

His Lordship continued:[8]

'It was said by [the insured] that valuers and claims assessors, who gave evidence in the person of Mr. Beecroft, were employed by the [insured] to inspect the goods and ascertain their value. It was also said that that process was watched and checked by the [insurers'] representatives. It would appear from the evidence that the schedules that were prepared were known to represent the cost price of the goods. The only ground for the assertion that the goods had been overvalued was a suggestion that as the goods had ceased to be fashionable, some discount should have been allowed before the claim was put forward. If the jury were satisfied that nobody was really deceived into thinking that the figures were other than the cost price of the goods, the first defence put up by the insurance company fell to the ground, because, in order that there should be fraudulent exaggeration of the claim, the jury would have to be satisfied that the figures were put forward with the knowledge of the [insured] that the figures were untrue and represented a larger claim than was justified by the value of the goods.'

The jury found that the insured were not guilty of fraudulent exaggeration in making their claim.[9]

In *Central Bank of India v Guardian Assurance Co and J Rustomji*[10] the insured sued the insurance company on a policy of fire insurance relating to a stock of

---

4 (1932) 44 Ll L Rep 139, K B.
5 The evidence is reviewed ibid, at 142–145.
6 (1933) 47 Ll L Rep 186, K B.
7 It was also contended on behalf of the insurance company that there had been misrepresentation and non-disclosure of material facts. As to this aspect of the case, see p 47, ante.
8 (1933) 47 Ll L Rep 186 at 190.
9 See ibid, at 192.
10 (1936) 54 Ll L Rep 247, P C.

wheat, wheat products and gunny bags stored in godowns. The Privy Council[11] held that the claim was a fraudulent one,[12] and that the action failed.

In *Ewer v National Employers' Mutual General Insurance Association Ltd*[13] the insured claimed a declaration, concerning an insurance against fire by the insurance company of a garage and its contents, that the policy was valid and of full force and effect. The insured was asked to complete a claim form in respect of the loss of contents. The great majority were parts that he had removed from lorries when they were broken up or a carburettor removed from a lorry because it was working badly and another substituted, and one removed put aside to be repaired. He used them in his business as spares. It would be very difficult for him to make a list of them because he had no stock book. It was not possible to produce any invoices for them, as he was requested to do because he never had bought stuff separately except some of the things such as sparking plugs and wires which he bought new. He could not, therefore, fill up the claim form completely, for it required such information as 'cost price of articles destroyed', 'date of purchase' and 'value of salvage'. So he filled up a claim with only one column of figures, and sought to recover £900. The company repudiated liability on the ground that the claim was fraudulent.

MacKinnon J granted the declaration claimed, and held that the policy was valid. The insured had put down the cost price of new things. But he was not doing that as in any way a fraudulent claim, but as a possible figure to start off with as a bargaining figure.

His Lordship observed:[14]

> 'We have been told that the [insurers] wanted to see invoices. The invoices, of course, would show what the articles cost. As the [insured] could not produce the invoices showing what the articles cost, I think he did the best he could in substitution for it. He put down that which would have been on an invoice, namely, the cost price of the article. In short, I think the truth of putting forward these figures is that the [insured] was furnishing a document of the nature spoken to by [Counsel] in his very able argument which he addressed to me. [Counsel] rightly dwelling upon the extravagance of these figures, said, "If it were only a case of a man asking for more than he could get and putting forward a bargaining figure, of course, I could not say it was fraud in that case." I think that is what this figure amounts to. It was putting forward a bargaining figure. The [insured] knew the claim would be discussed and probably drastically criticised by the assessors; he had been asked for invoices, and he started the bargaining with them by putting down the cost price of these articles as if they were new.'

The insurance company also maintained that the sum claimed in respect of the repairs to the building was also exaggerated and fraudulent. But the learned Judge rejected this contention, and said:[15]

> 'In regard to that, [the insured] consulted a man named Sullivan, who is a builder. Mr Suilivan gave him an estimate of £220 for his own building work and added to it an estimate from an electrician of £60 for doing the electrical work, the total being £280. That was submitted to the assessors of the [insurers]. They said, "This is excessive. We can get all that work done for £230." [The insured] told Mr Sullivan and Mr Sullivan said, "Well, I will do it for £230," and the result was that that figure of £230 was put by [the insured] in his claim in regard to the building. It is certainly a matter of some astonishment to me that the [insurers], until, I am afraid, I poured derision upon it, took the point that there was fraud in

---

[11] Lord Atkin, Lord Alness and Lord Maugham.
[12] The evidence is reviewed by Lord Maugham in (1936) 54 Ll L Rep at 250–259.
[13] (1937) 57 Ll L Rep 172, K B.
[14] Ibid at 182.
[15] Ibid at 181.

putting forward a claim for £280, when on their representation it was reduced to £230. They relied upon the suggested fact that Mr Sullivan's estimate was not true, that it was altogether a bogus thing and written out in the [insured's] office. I am satisfied that this was a genuine estimate on Mr Sullivan's part, the facts being that he is a builder of considerable experience, who had done a lot of work, and somebody said, "Your writing is bad; get it typewritten." He accordingly went to a typewriting clerk in Mr Smart's office, not the [insured's] office, although it happens to be in the same building in Mare Street, and asked her to type it out for him, which she did. That is the whole burden of that matter. To suggest that there was fraud because they originally put forward a figure of £280 and then reduced it to £230, seems to me fantastic.'

In *London Assurance v Clare*[16] fires took place at the premises of the insured[17] in 1931 and in 1933. The insurance company paid £25,000 in respect of the first fire, but refused to pay anything in respect of the 1933 fire, and alleged that the claim was grossly exaggerated. The company also sought to recover the £25,000 on the ground that the claim in that case too had been exaggerated.

Goddard J reviewed the evidence as far as the 1931 fire was concerned, and said that the claim made amounted to £80,000, though it was undoubtedly true that a figure of £20,000 had earlier been put forward on the insured's behalf, when the stock was offered for sale. He directed the jury that:[18]

'Mere exaggeration was not conclusive evidence of fraud, for a man might honestly have an exaggerated idea of the value of the stock or suggest a higher figure as a bargaining price.'

His Lordship referred to the absence of documents after the respective fires, and said that after the fire in 1931 invoices were available, but the insurance company's assessors were unable to see trading accounts or balance sheets. After the 1933 fire there were trading accounts, balance sheets and stock sheets, but no invoices. There were 'crude' alterations in the stock sheets. The question was whether the stock concerned was genuine stock or was 'junk' which had accumulated over a long period of years.

The jury[19] found that fraudulent claims had been made in respect of both fires. Accordingly, his Lordship directed that the insurance company was entitled to recover the £25,000 which it had paid in respect of the 1931 fire, and to repudiate liability in respect of the 1933 fire.

Effect of Fraudulent Claim under Another Policy

In *Beauchamp v Faber*[20] the stock-in-trade of a grocery and provision business was insured for £11,600 under a fire policy with the Sun Insurance Office. The insured also took out another policy with Lloyd's underwriters against loss of profits and goodwill in the event of fire. This policy contained the following clause:

'In the event of fire to pay the same percentage on this policy as may be settled by the Sun on their policy or policies for £12,000 at 5s per cent insuring the contents.'

---

16 (1937) 57 Ll L Rep 254, K B.
17 Mr Willie Clarkson, one of the best known theatrical costumiers of his generation. See (1937) 57 Ll L Rep at 254.
18 (1937) 57 Ll L Rep 254 at 268.
19 In summing up Goddard J said that it must be a cause of great satisfaction to the parties that the case had been tried before a City of London special jury, who were well acquainted with business and accounts and balance sheets: ibid, at 267.
20 (1898) 3 Com Cas 308.

A fire occurred, and the Sun Insurance Office refused to pay under their policy on the ground that the claim was a fraudulent one. The matter was referred to arbitration. The umpire agreed with this contention, and held that the company was not liable.[1] When the insured claimed against Lloyd's underwriters under the loss of profits policy, they repudiated liability on the ground that the claim had not been 'settled' within the meaning of the clause set out above.

Bigham J held that their refusal to pay was justified, and that the action failed. He observed.[2]

> 'The meaning of that clause, in my opinion, is, that, when the company have agreed the amount of the loss and have accepted liability for it, and nothing more remains to be done except to pay the sum in question, then the underwriters on the Lloyd's policy will pay such a sum as bears to the total sum underwritten by them the same percentage as the sum agreed by the company bears to the total amount insured with the company. Now, there never was in this case a settlement of the claim against the company. The company were prevented from settling by reason of the fraudulent claim which was put forward, and therefore, the [insured] is not entitled to recover on the Lloyd's policy. I base my decision on the fact that it was a condition precedent to the [insured's] right to recover on the Lloyd's policy that there should have been a settlement of the claim by the company, and that condition precedent has not been performed.'

CONDITIONS AS TO ARBITRATION

A condition usually states that any dispute arising out of the policy shall be settled by arbitration, and that arbitration is to be a condition precedent to the liability of the insurers. But whether the condition is or is not to be regarded as a condition precedent to liability is a matter of construction, and will depend on the precise wording of the condition in question.

Thus, in *Roper v Lendon*[3] a clause in a fire policy issued by the Kent Fire Insurance Co stated:

> 'In case any difference or dispute shall arise between the insured and the company, touching any loss or damage or otherwise, in respect of any insurance, such difference shall be submitted to the judgment and determination of two indifferent persons as arbitrators, of whom one shall be chosen by this company and the other by the insured . . . and if any fraud or false swearing shall appear on the part of the insured, . . . the party insured shall forfeit all claim under the policy.'

The Court of Queen's Bench[4] held that the reference to arbitration of the amount of the loss was not a condition precedent to the right to sue on the policy.

Lord Campbell C J said:[5]

> 'I think the sixth plea is bad, it not being a condition precedent to the [insured's] right to maintain this action that he should have offered to refer the amount of his claim to arbitration. The agreement to refer does not oust the jurisdiction of the Court. In *Scott v Avery*[6] the contract

---

[1] As to this aspect of the case, see p 135, ante.
[2] (1898) 3 Com Cas 308 at 311.
[3] (1859) 28 L J Q B 260. The case also concerned a condition relating to the delivery of particulars of loss. As to this point, see p 125, ante.
[4] Lord Campbell C J, and Hill, J.
[5] (1859) 28 L J Q B 260 at 262.
[6] (1856) 5 H L Cas 811.

of insurance stipulated, in the most express terms, that until the arbitrators had determined, no action should be brought. We decided that such contract did not oust the Courts of their jurisdiction. The House of Lords, in giving judgment, took care to distinguish between that case and a case in which the contract between the parties simply contains a clause or covenant to refer to arbitration; then an action may be brought in spite of that clause, although there has been no arbitration: and that is the case now before us. Such contract does not oust this Court of its jurisdiction.'

Hill J, was of the same opinion, and observed:[7]

'The 15th condition does not enable the [insurer] to dispute his liability because the amount has not been determined by arbitration, and to say that the assured is to lose all the benefit on his contract. The engagement to refer to arbitration is merely collateral, and not a condition precedent to the [insured's] right to recover. A breach of such collateral condition cannot be set up in answer to this action.'

On the other hand, in *Elliott v Royal Exchange Assurance Co*[8] a clause in a fire policy stated:

'In case any difference shall arise touching any loss or damage, such difference shall be submitted to the judgment and determination of arbitrators indifferently chosen, whose award in writing shall be conclusive and binding on all parties; but if there shall appear any fraud or false swearing, the claimant shall forfeit all benefit of claim.'

The Court of Exchequer[9] held that the submission to arbitration of a dispute arising under the policy was a condition precedent to the right of the insured to recover under the policy.

Kelly C B said:[10]

'Collecting the meaning of the parties from the language used by them in this sentence, and putting on it the ordinary and usual construction, the effect is not that the [insured] is, in the event of loss, entitled immediately to recover the amount of his loss; but what he is entitled to recover is the amount of the loss after it has been adjusted, which means, adjusted between the parties in the manner pointed out by the subsequent article. It appears to me that to decide to the contrary would be to disregard entirely the obvious intentions of the parties, expressed in words which state emphatically that before the loss is paid its amount shall be adjusted.

We were pressed with the weight of authority, and it was ably argued that it was impossible to decide in favour of the [insurers] consistently with prior decisions, and with the well recognised principle that no contract shall oust the jurisdiction of the Courts of law; and it was urged that the contract was neither more nor less than a contract on the part of the company to make good the loss, with a separate and collateral stipulation that the amount should be referred to arbitration. It is, no doubt, difficult to reconcile and give effect to two propositions so nearly in direct opposition as that no contract of the parties shall oust the jurisdiction of the Courts, and that, on any difference arising between two parties, it shall be referred to arbitration. But the fair result of the authorities is, that if the contract is in such terms that a reference to a third person, or to a board of directors, is a condition precedent to the right of the party to maintain an action, then he is not entitled to maintain it until that condition is complied with; but if, on the other hand, the contract is to pay for the loss (or other matter in question), with a subsequent contract to refer the question to arbitration, contained in a distinct clause collateral to the other, then that contract for reference shall not oust the jurisdiction of the Courts, or deprive the party of his action. Now it seems to me impossible, without directly overruling or disregarding the decision of the House of Lords in *Scott v Avery*,[11] to say that the stipulation here is not a condition precedent.'

---

7 (1859) 28 L J Q B 260 at 263.
8 (1867) L R 2 Exch 237.
9 Kelly C B, Martin and Pigott BB; Bramwell B dissenting.
10 (1867) L R 2 Exch 237 at p 242. See also the judgment of Martin B, ibid, at 244, and that of Pigott B, ibid, at 247.
11 (1856) 5 H L Cas 811.

In alluding to *Roper v Lendon*,[12] where it had been held that the agreement referred to was only a collateral stipulation, the learned Chief Baron[13] said that he did not enter into the question whether the true construction was put on the policy in that case. The point seemed to have been given up early in the argument, and the matter was hardly discussed.

Again, in *Viney v Bignold*[14] a clause in a fire policy effected with the Norwich Union Fire Insurance Society stated that:

> 'If any difference shall arise in the adjustment of a loss, the amount (if any) to be paid by the Society shall, whether the right to recover on the policy be disputed or not . . . be submitted to . . . arbitration . . . The party insured shall not be entitled to commence or maintain any act . . . upon his policy until the amount of the loss shall have been referred and determined as hereinbefore provided . . .'

No submission of the dispute to arbitration was made, but the insured brought an action in respect of the loss which he had suffered.

The Queen's Bench Division[15] held that he was not entitled to do so, and that the action failed because the clause set out above was a condition precedent to the liability of the Society.

Wills J observed:[16]

> 'The question to be decided is: what is the meaning of this provision? I am of opinion that it means that in case of difference the amount to be paid shall be determined by arbitration, and until this is done, no liability shall arise; in short, the condition means what it says; the only contract on the part of the [insurers] which is applicable where, as in the present case, a difference has arisen, is that they will pay such amount as shall be awarded by arbitrators or their umpire. Where, therefore, no arbitration has taken place, no covenant of the [insurers] has been broken. This appears to be the reasonable construction of the policy.'

---

[12] (1859) 28 L J Q B 260. See p 140, ante.
[13] (1867) L R 2 Exch 237 at 244.
[14] (1887) 20 Q B D 172.
[15] Wills and Grantham JJ.
[16] (1887) 20 Q B D 172 at 174. See also the judgment of Grantham J, ibid, at 176.

CHAPTER 16

The salving of the property

When a fire breaks out, certain rights and duties of the parties relating to salving the property arise.

THE RIGHTS AND DUTIES OF THE INSURED

On the outbreak of a fire, as at any other period during the currency of a policy, it is the duty of the insured to observe good faith towards the insurers.

Since it is not the happening of a fire, but the suffering of a loss which entitles him to enforce the policy, he must do his best to avert or minimise the loss.

For this purpose he must take such measures as are reasonable to extinguish the fire or to prevent it from spreading.[1] In the discharge of this duty he is required, at the same time, not to interfere with the fire brigade or other persons in their endeavour to do so.[2]

Further, he must, if it is practicable, remove the property insured to a place of safety,[3] and must not wilfully obstruct other persons who are endeavouring to do so.[4]

In both cases the performance of the duty is sometimes made an express condition of the policy.[5]

By failing to perform either duty the insured may aggravate the loss, and increase the burden cast upon the insurers. If, therefore, his failure is wilful, he is precluded not merely from recovering the value of the property lost in consequence of his failure, but also from receiving any indemnity under the policy.[6]

Where, in the performance of his duties, the insured sustains a loss, he may be entitled to have it made good by the insurers as being a loss by 'fire' within the meaning of the policy.

Thus, any loss or damage which the insured property may itself sustain, whether in consequence of the measures taken to extinguish the fire,[7] or during

---

1 *City Tailors Ltd v Evans* (1921) 126 LT 439 at 443, CA, per Scrutton LJ.

2 *Devlin v Queen Insurance Co* (1882) 46 UCR 611, at 621.

3 *McPherson v Guardian Insurance Co* (1893) 7 Nfld LR 768, where it was held that the insured had done all that a prudent man could do, and that the property was only abandoned after all hope to save it was given up; cf *Currie & Co v Bombay Native Insurance Co* (1869) LR 3 PC 72 (marine insurance), where the captain of a stranded vessel failed to take reasonable steps to save the cargo.

4 *Devlin v Queen Insurance Co*, (supra), where the jury found that the plaintiff wilfully neglected to save and prevented others from saving the insured property.

5 *McPherson v Guardian Insurance Co*, (supra); *Parent v Provident Mutual Association* (1909) QR 36 SC 377.

6 *Devlin v Queen Insurance Co*, (supra).

7 See p 148, post.

removal,[8] is to be treated as a loss or damage by 'fire' within the meaning of the policy, and is, therefore, recoverable from the insurers as such.

It is doubtful whether, any expenses incurred by the insured in extinguishing the fire or in removing the property insured, are recoverable by him as a loss under the policy. The amount of such expenses, when added to the amount recoverable in respect of the loss of the property itself, must not, however, exceed the sum specified in the policy. The insured cannot recover any sum in respect of such expenses where the effect of so doing would be to make the total sum payable on account of the fire greater than the amount specified in the policy, and thus to extend the liability of the insurers beyond that which they have undertaken,[9] unless, as is sometimes the case, the policy contains a stipulation to that effect.[10]

THE RIGHTS AND DUTIES OF THE INSURERS

The insurers, on the outbreak of a fire, appear at Common Law to have powers correlative to the duties imposed upon the insured, ie to take all reasonable measures to extinguish the fire and to salve the property insured.[11]

In the exercise of these powers they are entitled to enter the premises on which the fire takes place and to remain there for a reasonable time,[12] though probably not to the exclusion of the insured.[13] They are also entitled to take possession of the salved property and keep it for a reasonable time.[14]

It is of importance to insurers to be able to minimise the damage and thus reduce the amount payable to the insured,[15] and it is also important to them that they should be able to check the claim put forward by the insured.

These, however, are not the only purposes for which powers to deal with the salvage are required. All claims are not honest, and it is of the greatest impor-

---

[8] See p 148, post.

[9] A fire policy does not, as a rule, contain a 'suing and labouring' clause, which entitles the insured to recover such expenses although he had been paid for a total loss; Marine Insurance Act 1906, s 78(1). See generally Ivamy, *Marine Insurance* (3rd edn, 1979), pp 480–489.

[10] *Thompson v Montreal Insurance Co* (1850) 6 U C R 319; but see *McLaren v Commercial Union Assurance Co* (1885) 12 A R 279, where the Court differed as to the construction of the stipulation.

[11] It was formerly the practice of insurance offices to maintain their own fire brigade in London for the protection of property insured with them. See an extract from the original proposal form issued by the Sun Fire Office in 1710, printed in *The Early Days Of the Sun Fire Office* by Edward Baumer. For the London Salvage Corps, see p 187, post.

[12] *Oldfield v Price* (1860) 2 F & F 80, where the insurers admitted liability by a payment into Court for remaining in possession for an unreasonable time; *Norton v Royal Fire and Life Assurance Co* (1885) Times, 12 August, C A, affg in this respect, S C (1885) 1 T L R 460, where the insurance company remained in possession for over 2 months, which the jury found to be an unreasonable time, and the Court refused to disturb this finding.

[13] *Oldfield v Price (Secretary of General Fire Assurance Co)*, (supra) (reporter's note).

[14] *Alexander v Southey* (1821) 5 B & Ald 247, where it was held that an action for conversion did not lie against an employee of the insurers for refusing to give up the goods to the insured without an order from the insurers. This right is recognized by the Metropolitan Fire Brigade Act 1865, s 29. See p 186, post. In *Scott v Mercantile Accident and Guarantee Co Ltd* (1892) 66 L T 811 (burglary insurance) it was suggested by Cave J, that if the insurers on a fire policy resisted liability on the ground of a fraudulently excessive claim, the Court would not make an order under R S C Ord 50 r 3, directing the salvage to be taken from the insured and kept until trial. This Order is now replaced by R S C Ord 29 r 2.

[15] *Ahmedbhoy Habbibhoy v Bombay Fire and Marine Insurance Co* (1912) 107 L T 668 at 670, P C.

tance, not only to the insurers themselves, but also to the public, that the insurers should be placed in a position to make a thorough investigation both into the details of the claim and into the circumstances of the fire, and this involves taking and keeping possession of the salvage and the premises on which the salvage is until the investigation is complete.

The Common Law powers in these respects are inadequate, and it is there-fore the practice to insert in the policy an express condition extending and amplifying the powers of the insurers.

Under the condition the insurers are empowered to enter, take and keep possession of the building or premises in which the loss or damage has hap-pened, to take possession of, or require to be delivered to them, any of the property insured by the policy, and to deal with such property for all reasonable purposes, and in any reasonable manner.[16]

It is in such a case made a further term of the policy that if the insurers are hindered or obstructed in the exercise of their rights under the condition by the insured or any person acting on his behalf, or if their requirements are not complied with, all benefit under the policy is to be forfeited.

If by the form of the condition the powers conferred on the insurers are expressly made exercisable so long as the claim is not settled, their exercise by the insurers presupposes that a valid claim has been made and that all that remains to be done is to settle the amount. Consequently, the insurers, by taking and keeping possession after the receipt of a claim, may be estopped from contending that the claim is invalid through non-compliance with some condition of the policy, eg a failure to deliver detailed particulars within the prescribed time.[17]

In many cases, however, it is impossible for the insurers to decide whether to contest the validity of the claim until all the circumstances attending the loss have been investigated. It frequently happens that decisive evidence showing eg that the claim is fraudulent does not emerge until the close of a prolonged and searching examination of the salvage. In order to preclude any question of estoppel, the present condition in use provides in effect that the exercise of the powers which it confers shall not impose any liability on the insurers or diminish their right to rely upon any condition of the policy.

The insurers are liable in damages as trespassers if they remain in possession beyond a reasonable time, unless the condition specifies the period during which they are to retain possession.[18]

They will also be responsible, if whilst in possession they have failed to take steps to minimise it, for any further deterioration which the property may sustain in consequence.[19]

Thus, in *Ahmedbhoy Habbibhoy v Bombay Fire and Marine Insurance Co*[20] an insurance company acting under the powers contained in a fire policy took

---

16 In *Locker & Woolf Ltd v Western Australian Insurance Co Ltd* [1936] 1 K B 408, C A (reported on this point in 154 L T 667) the question whether 'deal with' included the power of sale was not decided, though referred to: Scott LJ, ibid at 672, inclined to the view that it did. But even an express power of sale cannot extend to the property of third parties in the hands of the insured, without the consent of the owners: *Inglis v Richardson & Sons Ltd* (1913) 29 O L R 229.

17 *Yorkshire Insurance Co Ltd v Craine* [1922] 2 A C 541, P C.

18 *Oldfield v Price (Secretary of General Fire Assurance Co)* (1860) 2 F & F 80; *Norton v Royal Fire and Life Assurance Co* (1885) Times, 12 August, C A.

19 *Ahmedbhoy Habbibhoy v Bombay Fire and Marine Insurance Co* (1912) 107 L T 668, B C.

20 (1912) 107 L T 668 P C (on appeal from the High Court of Judicature at Bombay).

possession of a building insured against fire in order to minimise the damage by salvage operations. The fire was extinguished by water, but the damage to the property was seriously increased by the length of time the water had been allowed to remain on it.

The Privy Council[1] held that the insurance company was liable for the whole of the damage caused, for the subsequent demage was the natural and direct consequence of the fire. The loss fell to be determined at the time when the company gave up possession of the premises, and not at the moment when the fire was extinguished.

Lord Moulton said:[2]

'It raises, therefore, the plain and simple issue whether the loss due to fire and water under such a policy is to be determined at the moment when the fire is extinguished, or when the companies give up possession of the premises to the owner after exercising the powers given to them by the policy for the purpose of enabling them to minimise the damage. It is, however, scarcely necessary that their Lordships should formally negative the contention of the companies in this respect, for it is so obviously unreasonable that the eminent Counsel, who appeared for them on the appeal, did not attempt to support it.'

He then went on to observe:[3]

'The fundamental error in the contention of the [insurers] seems to their Lordships to have arisen from a misapprehension of the position of an insurance company taking and holding possession of property damaged by a fire under the provisions of the policy in that behalf. The provisions in virtue of which it does so are for the purpose of enabling it to minimise the damage. Inasmuch as it has to bear the loss, there is no one so directly interested in doing everything that is wise for the purpose of making the best of the situation. It does so in its own interest, not because it is under a duty to the assured. Its powers are of the nature of a privilege to do that which is most for its own benefit under the circumstances so as to reduce the loss. In the present case, therefore, there is no question of tort on the part of the companies. They may have thought that it was not worth while to expend money in drying the machinery. In this view they may have been right or wrong, but they unquestionably had full power to take the course which in fact they did take. But when they have thus taken possession of the premises and done what in their opinion was wisest to minimise the damage, they cannot say that the actual damage is not the natural and direct consequences of the fire.'

---

[1] Lord Macnaghten Lord Moulton, Sir John Edge and Mr Ameer Ali.
[2] (1912) 107 L T 668 at 669.
[3] Ibid, at 669.

CHAPTER 17

The doctrine of proximate cause

When a loss takes place two questions arise:

   a Was the loss caused by a peril insured against?
   b Was the loss caused by an excepted cause?

In answering both these questions, the doctrine of 'proximate cause' is applied.[1]

A WAS THE LOSS CAUSED BY A PERIL INSURED AGAINST?

A loss which is not occasioned by the direct action of fire on the subject-matter of insurance is not a loss by 'fire' within the meaning of the policy, unless it is proximately caused by fire.[2]

Where the loss is the necessary consequence of the fire, or in other words, where, apart from the fire, the loss could not have happened, the fire is, for the purposes of the policy, the cause of the loss. Thus, the loss may be actually attributable to smoke arising from the fire, or to explosions occasioned during the progress of the fire by the application of intense heat to substances not in themselves explosive. Nevertheless, the connection between the fire and the loss is so close that the relation of cause and effect is clearly established. In accordance with the same principle, any loss occasioned by the fall of the walls or other parts of the building in which the fire takes place in consequence of the structural weakness resulting from the fire, is to be considered a loss by "fire".[3]

---

[1] For the meaning of 'proximate cause', see Ivamy, *General Principles of Insurance Law* (4th edn, 1979), pp 404–419.

[2] The application of the doctrine of proximate cause does not depend, as a general rule, on the particular words used in the policy, but on the intention of the parties; see *Marsden v City and County Assurance Co* (1865) L R 1 C P 232 (plate glass insurance), where the words were loss or damage 'originating from' any cause whatsoever, following *Ionides v Universal Marine Insurance Co* (1863) 14 C B N S 259 (marine insurance), where the words were 'consequences of' hostilities'; *Walker v London and Provincial Insurance Co* (1888) 22 L R Ir 572, where the words were 'occasioned by or in consequence of' incendiarism; *Tootal, Broadhurst, Lee Co v London and Lancashire Fire Insurance Co* (1908) Times 21 May, where the words were 'occasioned by or through' and 'in consequence of' earthquake; *Cooper v General Accident, Fire and Life Assurance Corpn Ltd* (1923) 128 L T 481 at 485, H L, per Lord Dunedin, where the words were 'occasioned through riot or civil commotion'; *Ocean SS Co Ltd v Liverpool and London War Risks Insurance Association Ltd* [1946] K B 561, C A, where the words were 'in consequence of warlike operation'.

[3] *Johnston v West of Scotland Insurance Co* 1828 7 Sh (Ct of Sess) 52; *Re Hooley Hill Rubber and Chemical Co Ltd and Royal Insurance Co Ltd* [1920] 1 K B 257 at 271, C A per Scrutton L J; *Roth v South Easthope Farmers Mutual Fire Insurance Co* (1918) 44 O L R 186, where lightning damaged the roof of a barn which was shortly afterwards further damaged by a high wind, and it was held that the whole of the damage was caused by lightning.

It is immaterial in this connection that the loss arises in an adjacent building which does not itself catch fire,[4] or that the fall does not take place until after the fire is extinguished, provided that it takes place within a reasonable time after the fire.[5]

Where the loss is the reasonable and probable consequence directly and naturally resulting in the ordinary course of events from the happening of a fire, the fire may be regarded as the cause of the loss. Thus, losses incurred by the insured in attempting to check the progress of a fire or to save property may be attributed to the fire, provided that the steps taken are reasonable, bona fide, and apparently necessary.[6] Property may actually be destroyed or damaged by water, which is being employed for the purpose of extinguishing the flames;[7] or houses may be blown up by the fire brigade in the hope of preventing the fire from spreading.[8] In both cases, however, though the property concerned is not burned or in any way damaged by the direct action of the fire, the connection between the loss and the existence of the fire is so close that the fire must be regarded as the efficient cause of the loss.[9]

Similarly, where the insured removes the property from the building in which the fire is raging, either with the view of depriving the fire of material upon which to feed,[10] or with the intention of placing the property in safety so as to minimise the loss,[11] any loss occasioned to such property by reason of such

---

[4] *Johnston v West of Scotland Insurance Co*, (supra). Cf *Westminster Fire Office v Glasgow Provident Investment Society* (1888) 13 App Cas 699 at 704, per Lord Watson.

[5] *Johnston v West of Scotland Insurance Co*, (supra), where the fall took place 2 days after the fire, and the insured was held entitled to recover; *Roth v South Easthope Farmers Mutual Fire Insurance Co*, (supra), where a building after being damaged by lightning was further damaged by a wind following almost immediately, and it was held that lightning was the proximate cause of all the damage.

[6] *Stanley v Western Insurance Co* (1868) L R 3 Exch 71 at 74, per Kelly C B, approved in *Symington & Co v Union Insurance Society of Canton Ltd* (1928) 139 L T 386 at 391, C A (marine insurance). There must, however, be a real danger: *The Knight of St. Michael* [1898] P 30 (marine insurance); it is not sufficient that danger was believed to exist: *Kacianoff v China Traders Insurance Co* [1914] 3 K B 1121, C A (marine insurance); *Joseph Watson & Son v Firemen's Fund Insurance Co of San Francisco Ltd* [1922] 2 K B 355 (marine insurance); cf *Watts, Watts & Co Ltd v Mitsui & Co Ltd* [1917] A C 227 at 230 (marine insurance) per Lord Dunedin; *Becker, Gray & Co v London Assurance Corpn* [1918] A C 101 at 114, (marine insurance) per Lord Sumner.

[7] *Ahmedbhoy Habbibhoy v Bombay Fire and Marine Insurance Co* (1912) 107 L T 668, P C; *Thompson v Montreal Insurance Co* (1850) 6 U C R 319; *McPherson v Guardian Insurance Co* (1893) 7 Nfld L R 768; *The Diamond* [1906] P 282 (marine insurance).

[8] *Stanley v Western Insurance Co*, (supra), at 74, per Kelly C B, holding that an exception against explosion would not apply to such a case; *Symington & Co v Union Insurance Society of Canton Ltd*, (supra), where port authorities destroyed or damaged cork lying on a jetty, in order to prevent a fire raging nearby from spreading.

[9] *Stanley v Western Insurance Co*, (supra) at 74, per Kelly C B; *Re Etherington and Lancashire and Yorkshire Accident Assurance Co* [1909] 1 K B 591 at 599, C A (accident insurance) per Vaughan Williams L J, speaking of fire insurance; *Drumbolus v Home Insurance Co* (1916) 37 O L R 465, where the damage was caused by the freezing of pipes in consequence of the heat being cut off to prevent the fire from spreading.

[10] *Stanley v Western Insurance Co*, (supra).

[11] *Marsden v City and County Assurance Co* (1865) L R 1 C P 232 (plate glass insurance), where it was suggested that an exception against removal would have no application; *McLaren v Commercial Union Assurance Co* (1885) 12 A R 279, where it was held that the insured was entitled to recover under his policy in respect of damage resulting from bona fide efforts to save the insured property by removal; *Thompson v Montreal Insurance Co*, (supra); cf *Levy v Baillie* (1831) 7 Bing 349, where a portion of the claim related to goods damaged or stolen during the process of removal, and no objection was taken to the claim on this ground.

removal, may, if the removal be justified, be considered to be a loss by 'fire', although the property may be, in fact, damaged by rain in the street,[12] or may be damaged by being thrown from a window.[13]

Even where the removal is from a building in which there is no fire at the time, but which is adjacent to the building in which the fire is, the removal may be justified so as to make a loss occasioned thereby a loss by 'fire'. In both cases the question whether the removal is justified or not, depends on the circumstances in which it takes place, the principal factors to be considered being the imminence of the fire and the reasonableness of the measures taken. It is doubtful whether the expenses of a justifiable removal are chargeable to the insurers as being the direct consequence of the fire.[14]

In accordance with the same principle a loss by theft, when, owing to the confusion consequent on the happening of a fire, the property stolen is withdrawn from the effective control of the insured, is to be considered a loss by 'fire', whether the theft takes place on the premises where the fire is, or during their removal, or from the premises to which the goods are removed for safe custody.[15]

B WAS THE LOSS CAUSED BY AN EXCEPTED CAUSE?

The object of an exception is to relieve the insurers from liability where the loss is caused by an excepted peril. The doctrine of proximate cause applies equally to exceptions, and precludes the insured from recovering in respect of a loss which is proximately caused by an excepted peril.[16]

Where the subject-matter of insurance is not burned, but is destroyed by an excepted peril, the insured cannot recover, and it is immaterial that the excepted peril was preceded and brought into operation by fire.[17] Thus, where there is an explosion in the course of a fire, the concussion damage (in adjacent property) caused by the explosion falls within an exception against explosion, even though the explosion is merely incidental to the fire. But such damage caused in the building where the fire is raging is regarded as so intimately connected with the fire as to be part of the damage caused by the fire.[18]

Where the subject-matter of insurance is burned, but the fire which burned it was preceded and brought into operation by an excepted peril, the position of

---

12 *McPherson v Guardian Insurance Co*, (supra).

13 *Stanley v Western Insurance Co*, (supra).

14 See p 144, ante.

15 *McGibbon v Queen Insurance Co* (1866) 10 L C J 227, where it was held that the insurers were liable for losses occasioned to the insured by theft of the goods at the fire; *Harris v London and Lancashire Fire Insurance Co* (1866) 10 L C J 268, where a loss by theft during a fire was treated as equivalent to a loss by fire (both cases cited with approval in *The Knight of St Michael* [1898] P 30 at 36, per Gorell Barnes J); *Thompson v Montreal Insurance Co*, (supra); *MacPherson v Guardian Insurance Co*, (supra); cf *Levy v Baillie*, (supra), where a claim for goods so stolen was not objected to on this ground.

16 *Leyland Shipping Co Ltd v Norwich Union Fire Insurance Society Ltd* [1918] A C 350 at 365 (marine insurance) per Lord Atkinson, approving *Ionides v Universal Marine Insurance Co* (1863) 14 C B N S 259 at 286, (marine insurance) per Willes J.

17 *Tatham v Hodgson* (1796) 6 Term Rep 656 (marine insurance); *Livie v Janson* (1810) 12 East 648 at 653 (marine insurance) per Lord Ellenborough C J. Cf *Fooks v Smith* [1924] 2 K B 508 at 515 (marine insurance) per Bailhache J.

18 See pp 81–82 ante.

the insured depends on whether the excepted peril is to be regarded as the proximate cause of the loss or only as its remote cause. If the fire is the natural consequence of the excepted peril, the excepted peril is the proximate cause of the loss resulting from the fire, and the insured cannot recover.[19]

Thus, where an incendiary bomb, dropped from an enemy Zeppelin, set fire to a warehouse, the loss, though caused by fire, is proximately caused by enemy action, and was therefore within an exception against 'military or usurped power'.[20]

On the other hand, if the fire is only the accidental consequence of the excepted peril, the excepted peril is the remote cause of the loss. The insured is, therefore, entitled to recover, since the loss is a loss by 'fire' and the exception has no application.

The effect of the rule may be conveniently illustrated by reference to the manner in which the doctrine of proximate cause is applied to spreading fires. Where the fire spreads in the natural and ordinary course of events from an excepted fire, eg owing to a shift in the wind, the exception applies to the spreading fire no less than to the original fire.[1] Nothing has intervened to divest the fire of its original character, and its identity remains unchanged. So also, where a fire is originated by an incendiary and spreads by the operation of natural causes from the premises in which it originated to other premises, the latter fire is, equally with the original fire, a fire originated by an incendiary for the purposes of an exception against 'incendiary fires'.[2] Similarly, where premises are burned by a fire which has spread without the intervention of other than natural causes from a burning forest, the fire in such premises is a 'forest fire', and the insurer will not be liable where 'forest fires' are excepted by the terms of the policy.[3]

Where the fire which destroys the property insured, though ultimately deriving its existence from the excepted fire, in the sense that the latter fire is its original source, spreads from it, not in the ordinary and natural course of events, but by reason of the intervention of some unexpected and unlikely cause,[4] the exception does not apply, since the fire which actually causes the

---

[19] *Stanley v Western Insurance Co* (1868) L R 3 Exch 71; *Holder v Phoenix Assurance Co of London* (1912) 31 N Z L R 257, where a car was destroyed by fire in consequence of an accident in which it overturned and caused an escape of benzine, the vapour of which was set on fire by the lighted lamps of the car, and it was held that the proximate cause of the loss was the lamps on the car, and hence the loss fell within an exception against loss caused by a 'fire originating in the car itself'.

[20] *Rogers v Whittaker* [1917] 1 K B 942. Cf *Wadsworth v Canadian Railway Accident Insurance Co* (1913) 28 O L R 537 (accident insurance), where an exception excluding injuries resulting from fits was held to apply where the insured knocked over a lamp in the course of a fit and was burned.

[1] *Tootal, Broadhurst, Lee Co Ltd v London and Lancashire Fire Insurance Co* (1908) Times, 21 May (earthquake fire). See Appendix IV, p 403, post.

[2] *Walker v London and Provincial Insurance Co* (1888) 22 L R Ir 572.

[3] *Commercial Union Assurance Co v Canada Iron Mining and Manufacturing Co* (1873) 18 L C J 80, where the fire spread from a burning forest to trees by the side of a street, and then to a lumber yard, and finally to the insured's property, and it was held that the insured's loss was a loss by 'forest fire' within the meaning of an exception in the policy.

[4] *Marsden v City and County Assurance Co* (1865) L R 1 C P 232 (plate glass insurance), where the breaking of a plate glass window by a mob, brought together for the purpose of plunder by a fire next door, was held to be proximately caused by the lawless act of the mob and only remotely caused by the fire, so that an exception against 'fire' did not apply.

loss is a new fire,[5] and cannot be regarded as a direct or probable consequence of the original fire. Thus, where in the course of removing goods from a house which has been set on fire by incendiarism, a person accidentally throws some burning material on or near to adjacent premises so as to communicate the fire to them, such fire cannot be regarded as a mere spreading of the original fire so as to bring loss occasioned by it within an exception against 'incendiary fire', provided that it is shown that the accidental act could not reasonably have been anticipated as a result of the existence of the original fire.[6]

Where the fire and the excepted peril are concurrent causes, and are both in operation at the time of the loss, the existence of the excepted peril does not prevent the insured from recovering for the loss which is caused by the fire.[7] The insured must, however, be able to distinguish the consequences of the fire from the consequences of the excepted peril; otherwise he must fail, seeing that the cause of loss is as much the excepted peril as the fire.[8] Thus, where a fire causes an explosion, which in its turn causes a second fire, the insured is, of course, entitled to recover for the loss caused by the first fire as being unconnected with the explosion, but the exception may preclude him from recovering for the loss caused by the second fire.[9]

In *Stanley v Western Insurance Co*[10] business premises were insured under a fire policy which contained an exception stating:

> 'Neither will the company be responsible for loss or damage by explosion, except for such loss or damage as shall arise from explosion by gas.'[11]

The insured carried on the business of extracting oil from shoddy. An inflammable and explosive vapour evolved in the course of the process. It caught fire and set fire to other things. It afterwards exploded and caused a further fire. Damage was caused to the premises both by the explosion and the second fire.

The Court of Exchequer[12] held that the insurance company was liable in respect of the damage caused by the original fire, but not that caused by the explosion or the second fire.

Martin B said:[13]

> 'With respect to the extent of the damage I should say that, even if the consequence of the explosion was to create a concussion that caused the existing fire to burn more strongly than before, that would be a loss by 'fire' within the policy and not within the exception, but that as to what was caused by the explosion, the [insurers] are not liable. But if the [insured] cannot distinguish the one from the other, that misfortune must fall on him and not on the [insurers].'

---

5 *Stanley v Western Insurance Co* (1868), as reported 17 L T 513; *Tootal, Broadhurst, Lee Co Ltd v London and Lancashire Fire Insurance Co*, (supra).
6 *Walker v London and Provincial Insurance Co* (1888) 22 L R Ir 572 at 577, per Palles C B.
7 *Stanley v Western Insurance Co* (1868) L R 3 Exch 71; *Pawsey & Co v Scottish Union and National Insurance Co* (1908) Times, 17 October, P C, where there were two independent fires, one of which was found by the jury not to be within the exception.
8 Cf *Leyland Shipping Co Ltd v Norwich Union Fire Insurance Society Ltd* [1918] A C 350 (marine insurance).
9 Under the usual form of policy the loss by the second fire is covered.
10 (1868) L R 3 Exch 71.
11 As to the meaning of 'gas' in this context, see p 82, ante.
12 Kelly C B, Martin and Channell B B.
13 (1868) L R 3 Exch 71 at 75.

Kelly C B observed:[14]

> 'Counsel has ingeniously argued that . . . the real meaning is this; that the company are not to be responsible for any loss arising from explosion, provided the explosion is not occasioned by a fire already in existence upon the premises; but, on the other hand, if there be already a fire upon the premises so that the explosion is incidental to and is occasioned by that fire, and then lends itself to further the fire and so to increase the loss, the whole of the damage caused is within the insurance of the policy. But to give the instrument this construction would be, in fact, to introduce into it words not found there; while the natural construction of the words gives a probable and easily intelligible sense. In consequence of the wide-spread and highly mischievous effects of explosions, the policy excludes liability for any of their consequences. If there be a fire, in the course of which an explosion occurs, for the result of the fire, unconnected with the explosion, the [insurers] make themselves liable, but not for any of the consequences of that explosion. But [Counsel] further contends that the opposite construction should be given to the policy, on the ground that where a fire arises, and in the course of the exertions made to extinguish it property is destroyed or injured, this loss is covered by the insurance against fire. I agree that any loss resulting from an apparently necessary and bona fide effort to put out a fire, whether it be by spoiling the goods by water, or throwing the articles of furniture out of the window, or even the destroying of a neighbouring house by an explosion for the purposes of checking the progress of the flames, in a word, every loss that clearly and proximately results, whether directly or indirectly, from the fire, is within the policy. But that an explosion under those particular circumstances would not be within the exception, affords no ground for excluding from it this explosion, which arises in a totally different mode, and to exclude which would almost amount to expunging the clause altogether from the policy.'

In *Re Hooley Hill Rubber and Chemical Co Ltd and Royal Insurance Co Ltd*[15] manufacturers of explosives insured their factory at Ashton-under-Lyne and its contents under a fire policy, which contained an exception stating:

> 'This policy does not cover . . . loss or damage by explosion of illuminating gas elsewhere than on premises in which gas is manufactured or stored.'

There was also a typewritten memorandum endorsed on the policy. This stated:

> 'The policy does not cover loss or damage by explosion nor loss or damage by fire following an explosion unless it be proved that such a fire was not caused, directly or indirectly thereby, or was not the result thereof.'

A fire broke out at the factory, and a quantity of TNT exposed to the heat of the fire exploded and destroyed the building and its contents.

The Court of Appeal[16] held that the insurance company was not liable for damage caused by the explosion, although the explosion occurred in the course of the fire.

Scrutton LJ said that the case fell within the decision in *Stanley v Western Insurance Co*[17], which he would follow:[18]

---

[14] (1868) L R 3 Exch 71 at 73.

[15] [1920] 1 K B 257 at 264.

[16] Bankes, Scrutton and Duke LJJ.

[17] (1868) L R 3 Exch 71. This case is considered at p 151, ante.

[18] [1920] 1 K B 257 at 272. He said that he was not impressed by the fact that a different view had been taken by American Courts on American policies. Those Courts frequently differed from ours on the construction of mercantile documents by the light of English decisions: ibid, at 272. In the course of his judgment Duke LJ alluded to this point, and said that with regard to the American cases great respect was due to the opinion of every Judge who applied his mind to a system of law analogous to our own and in many cases identical with it. But on some questions of

'Fifty years ago it was submitted, as a possible construction of a similar clause excepting loss or damage arising from explosion, that it only shut out explosions where there was no antecedent fire. That was [Counsel's] argument in *Stanley v Western Insurance Co.*[19] The Court of Exchequer decided against it. The result is that for fifty years there has been authority in England for construing condition 3 of this policy as excluding loss or damage from an explosion although it is the consequence of an antecedent fire. I feel bound to read the words of the condition in the light of existing English decisions. It would take a very strong case to induce me to give to the words a meaning different from that given to them by an English decision unquestioned for fifty years.'

He went on to say that the matter did not stop at the printed exceptions, for the effect of the memorandum had still to be considered. On this point he observed:[20]

'I agree that the memorandum contemplates four cases of fire with or without an explosion; first, fire without explosion. Clearly the memorandum has nothing to do with that. Secondly, explosion without fire. It seems clear that this (unless it were a gas explosion) would not be within the policy. Thirdly, explosion followed by fire; as to that the memorandum says that the policy does not cover loss caused by the fire unless it be proved that the fire was not caused directly or indirectly by the explosion, or was not the result thereof. The effect of this is that, where damage is done by an explosion and fire following it, the assured cannot recover unless he can prove that the fire was not caused by the explosion. This case is specifically dealt with by the last part of the memorandum. Fourthly, fire followed by explosion. This case is not within the latter part of the memorandum. It is dealt with separately in the earlier part of these words: "This policy does not cover loss or damage by explosion." I do not think those words were inserted to except loss from explosion where there was no fire, which prima facie would not be within the policy at all and would need no exception. In my view the intention was to except loss from an explosion following and caused by a fire and to repeat the decision in *Stanley v Western Insurance Co.*[1]'

Duke LJ agreed and said:[2]

'The intention then is to exclude loss by explosion which but for the exclusion would or might have involved the insurers in liability. Now, there are two classes of explosion which occur to the mind at once: (1) those mentioned in condition 3, that is to say, explosions which occur in the course of a fire, and (2) explosions which cause a fire. The exception deals with something more than explosions which cause a fire. It deals in its first words with loss or damage caused by explosion in the most general terms, and that must be such loss or damage caused by explosion as but for the exception would have been within the effective words of the policy. It must therefore be loss or damage caused by an explosion occurring in connection with fire. An explosion independent of fire would not be within the policy at all. The two classes of explosion are separately dealt with. In the present case there was an explosion in the course of a fire, and it seems to me that the parties have agreed in express and comprehensive terms that damage caused by such an explosion shall not be within the terms of the policy. In this investigation I am glad to have the guidance of *Stanley v Western Insurance Co.*[3] The arguments which prevail with me are those which prevailed with the Court of Exchequer in that case. In my view it was rightly decided.'

---

mercantile law, English and American decisions had diverged. One could not say, and it was unnecessary to inquire, how the construction of the policy under consideration would be treated by the Supreme Court of the United States: ibid, at 274.

[19] (1868) LR 3 Exch 71.
[20] [1920] 1 KB 257 at 272.
[1] (1868) LR 3 Exch 71. Scrutton LJ said that he appreciated the point that a policy against fire in a factory where high explosives were manufactured was not of much use if it did not cover loss or damage by explosion. That, however, was a matter between the insured and the insurers. It ought not of itself to outweigh the other considerations which he had mentioned: [1920] 1 KB 257 at 273.
[2] Ibid, at 274. See also the judgment of Bankes LJ, ibid, at 270–271.
[3] (1868) LR 3 Exch 71.

If the loss can be apportioned between the two fires, the insured is entitled to recover for such part of the loss as is attributable to the first fire,[4] but if the loss cannot be apportioned, he cannot recover at all.[5]

Where the exception is so framed as to preclude the insured from recovering in respect of any loss attributable, whether directly or indirectly, proximately or remotely, to the excepted peril, the proximate cause of the loss may be disregarded, provided that its remote cause is covered by the exception.[6] This principle applies where the excepted peril, from its nature, cannot be the proximate cause of fire, but only its remote cause.[7]

---

[4] *Stanley v Western Insurance Co* (1868) L R 3 Exch 71, where the case was remitted to the arbitrator to ascertain how much of the loss after the explosion was attributable to the first fire; *Re Hooley Hill Rubber and Chemical Co Ltd and Royal Insurance Co Ltd* [1920] 1 K B 257, C A, where liability for the fire loss was admitted; *Curtis and Harvey (Canada) Ltd v North British and Mercantile Insurance Co* [1921] 1 A C 303, P C, where there was a similar admission.

[5] *Stanley v Western Insurance Co*, (supra), at 75, per Martin B.

[6] *Coxe v Employers' Liability Assurance Corpn Ltd* [1916] 2 K B 629 (accident insurance), where the exception excluded death directly or indirectly caused by or traceable to war.

[7] Such as eg earthquake: *Tootal, Broadhurst, Lee Co v London and Lancashire Fire Insurance Co* (1908) Times, 21 May; *Kingston General Comrs v Sun Insurance Office* (1907) Times, 20 June. Both these cases are set out in Appendix IV, pp 403–406, 411–412, post.

CHAPTER 18

The making of a claim

The policy usually contains special stipulations relating to the making of a claim on the insurers by the insured, and imposing on him the duty of notifying the insurers of the happening of a fire, and also the duty of furnishing them with full particulars of his loss.

NOTICE OF LOSS

It is the duty of the insured to give notice to the insurers of the happening of any loss for which he may intend to claim in order that they may be placed in a position to take such measures as they may deem advisable to estimate its cause or extent.

In the absence of an express condition to the contrary the notice of loss need not be given by the insured himself.[1]

In the absence of an express condition to the contrary the notice of loss need not be in writing.[2]

The notice need not, as a general rule, be given to the insurers personally.[3]

The notice should be given within the prescribed time, or, where there is no prescribed time, within a reasonable time since, if it is delayed beyond a reasonable time, the insurers may well be prejudiced by the disappearance of the traces of the fire, and by the greater difficulty of ascertaining the true facts relating to the loss.[4]

In some cases the insurers may be deemed to have waived the requirement of the policy as to notice.[5]

PARTICULARS OF LOSS

A condition usually states that the insured must at his own expense furnish particulars of the several articles or items of property destroyed or damaged, together with the estimated value of each of them respectively having regard to their value at the time of the fire, and, unless he does so, no claim under the policy is to be payable.[6]

---

[1] See Ivamy, *General Principles of Insurance Law* (4th edn, 1979), pp 421–422.
[2] See Ivamy, ibid, p 421.
[3] See Ivamy, ibid, pp 422–423.
[4] See Ivamy, ibid, p 423.
[5] See Ivamy, ibid, p 425.
[6] See pp 127–129, ante.

Usually the insurers supply a claim form, which the insured is required to fill up.[7] The details of information asked for by the insurers vary according to the nature of the insurance, but the insured is, as a rule, required to deal with the following matters:

1   The cause and circumstances of the fire,[8] and whether there is any suspicion of arson.
2   The occupancy of the premises as a whole, and not merely of the part occupied by himself.[9]
3   The capacity in which he claims, whether eg as owner, mortgagee, lessee, or otherwise.
4   The persons, if any, other than himself who are interested in the property destroyed or damaged.
5   Any other insurances in force on such property.
6   The details of such property, setting out each item separately, with a statement of its value at the time of the fire,[10] and the value of the salvage, if any, and of the amount claimed.

The particulars required must be given with such details as may be reasonably practicable.[11]

The question whether the details actually given are sufficient to satisfy the condition is one of degree depending on the materials at the insured's disposal, and the time within which the particulars have to be furnished.[12]

Where the insured's books and papers have been destroyed in the fire,[13] his statement must in all probability be made up largely from recollection. It cannot, therefore, be regarded as more than a rough estimate of the amount of his loss. This is clearly the case where it is impossible for him within the time allowed to procure further information from outside sources, eg in the case of goods, from manufacturers or other persons who supplied them. He must, therefore, be regarded as having discharged his duty when he has furnished the

---

[7] The sending of a claim form is not waiver of a breach of condition: *James v Royal Insurance Co* (1908) 10 NZ Gaz LR 244.

[8] *Guimond v Fidelity-Phoenix Insurance Co of New York* (1912) 2 DLR 654 (affd without dealing with this point: 9 DLR 463), where a reply stating that the origin of the fire was unknown was held insufficient to satisfy a requirement to state knowledge and belief as to the origin of the fire. Cf *Smith v Queen Insurance Co* (1868) 12 NBR (1 Han) 311, where it was held, on a claim in respect of a house which had been left unoccupied, that the insured ought to state the circumstances of his leaving the house, the fact that it was locked up, and where he was at the time of the fire.

[9] *Mason v Western Assurance Co* (1859) 17 UCR 190, where there was an express condition requiring this.

[10] It is not sufficient to state its value at the time of purchase: *Cameron v Canada Fire and Marine Insurance Co* (1884) 6 OR 392.

[11] See Ivamy, op. cit, pp 426–430. See further, *Mason v Harvey* (1853) 8 Exch 819 at 820, per Pollock CB; *Penney v Goode* (1854) 2 WR 49, where there was a secret trade process, and the failure to give particulars was apparently not insisted on; *Strong v Crown Fire Insurance Co* (1914) 29 OLR 33, where the whole stock was destroyed, and it was held that particulars of the last stock-taking were sufficient. If the value of the property wholly destroyed is greatly in excess of the sum insured, it is unnecessary to give details as to property partly destroyed: *Williamson v Hand-in-Hand Mutual Fire Insurance Co* (1876) 26 CP 266.

[12] *JR Mooney & Co v Pearl Assurance Co* [1942] 4 DLR 13 (fidelity insurance).

[13] Sometimes the policy contains a condition requiring books of accounts to be kept in a fire-proof safe: *Sacks v Western Assurance Co* [1907] 5 TH 257; *Lewis Ltd v Norwich Union Fire Insurance Co* [1916] App D 509; *Papas v General Accident, Fire and Life Assurance Corpn Ltd* [1916] CPD 619.

best particulars which, in the circumstances, he is able to furnish, however imperfect they may be, in fact.[14]

Where it is shown that from the information in his possession, power, or control, the insured could have furnished within the time allowed particulars fuller and more complete than those in fact furnished by him, he has not discharged his duty, and the particulars do not satisfy the condition.[15] Hence, where different classes of goods are comprised in the same policy, particulars must be given of each class.[16]

Where the insurers take possession of the salvage, and thus prevent him from furnishing the required particulars,[17] or where they repudiate their liability under the policy before the particulars are due, the insured is wholly discharged from any obligation to comply with the condition.

The particulars required must be furnished within the prescribed time, which is usually a period of thirty days after the fire.[18] The insured must, when required, verify the particulars by such documentary or other proofs as may be reasonably demanded by the insurers in accordance with the terms of the policy, and if he fails to do so, from whatever cause, he cannot recover.[19]

The facts, however, may show that the insurers have waived their right to demand proofs in accordance with the condition.[20]

---

[14] *Hiddle v National Fire and Marine Insurance Co of New Zealand* [1896] A C 372 at 375, P C; *Mulvey v Gore District Mutual Fire Assurance Co* (1866) 25 U C R 424.

[15] *Hiddle v National Fire and Marine Insurance Co of New Zealand*, (supra), at 375. See also *Mulvey v Gore District Mutual Fire Assurance Co*, (supra), where it was held that the insured must supply at least some details, although an account of every article in a country store, or of the precise quantity of any named article could not be reasonably expected; *Carnossky v New Zealand Insurance Co* (1893) 14 N S W L R 102, where the insured delivered an account without giving details; *Stevens v London Assurance Corpn* (1899) 20 N S W L R 153, where it subsequently appeared that the insured was possessed of detailed information which he had not furnished within the prescribed time.

[16] *Hiddle v National Fire and Insurance Co of New Zealand*, (supra).

[17] *Smith v Commercial Union Insurance Co* (1872) 33 U C R 69.

[18] See Ivamy, *General Principles of Insurance Law* (4th edn, 1979), pp 428–430.

[19] See pp 130–131 ante. See further, Ivamy, op cit, pp 430–433.

[20] See Ivamy, op cit, pp 432–433.

CHAPTER 19

The burden of proof

In considering the question on whom the burden of proof lies, one must distinguish:

    a Proof of loss; and
    b Proof that the loss falls within an exception,

for the burden varies accordingly.

PROOF OF LOSS

The burden of proving that the loss was caused by fire lies on the insured; and unless he discharges the burden, the claim must fail.[1]

He need not, however, conclusively prove the cause of the loss; it is sufficient if he establishes a prima facie case of loss by fire. Once he has done this, the burden of proof is discharged, and he is not, as a general rule, bound to go further and prove that the loss is not covered by an exception.[2]

When the insured has proved a prima facie case of loss within the policy, the burden of proof shifts to the insurers,[3] who must then prove that the loss falls within an exception.[4] They must produce affirmative evidence of facts supporting their contention, and such evidence must be sufficient to be submitted to the jury.[5]

If they fail to produce such evidence, they have not discharged the burden of proof, and the insured accordingly succeeds in his claim.[6]

If, however, the insurers discharge the burden of proof laid upon them, the burden shifts back to the insured and he must prove either that his claim falls within an exception to that exception,[7] or that, in the circumstances, the exception has no application, eg by reason of waiver,[8] or that, if it does apply, it does not apply to the whole of the loss.[9]

---

[1] See Ivamy, *General Principles of Insurance Law* (4th edn, 1979), pp 439–443.

[2] See Ivamy, ibid, p 439.

[3] See Ivamy, ibid, p 443.

[4] *Gorman v Hand-in-Hand Insurance Co* (1877) I R 11 C L R 224; *Motor Union Insurance Co Ltd v Boggan* (1923) 130 L T 588 at 590, per Lord Birkenhead, *Luciani v British America Assurance Co* (1931) 65 O L R 687.

[5] *Stormont v Waterloo Life and Casualty Assurance Co* (1858) 1 F & F 22 (life insurance).

[6] *Law Union and Rock Insurance Co v De Wet* [1918] App D 663, where liability was denied on the ground that the fire was caused by an explosion. See further, Ivamy, op cit, p 445.

[7] *Rowett, Leaky & Co Ltd v Scottish Provident Institution* [1927] 1 Ch 55 at 69, C A (life insurance) per Warrington L J.

[8] *Re Hooley Hill Rubber and Chemical Co Ltd and Royal Insurance Co Ltd* [1920] 1 K B 257, C A, where the point was not persisted in.

[9] *Stanley v Western Insurance Co* (1868) L R 3 Exch 71 at 75, per Martin B.

In the latter case, the insured must prove what part of the loss was not caused by the excepted peril; and if he fails to discharge the burden of proof in this respect, the whole of the loss will be regarded as falling within the exception.

In many cases direct evidence as to the cause of the fire is not available and the success or failure of the claim depends upon whether the burden of proof, upon the materials before the Court, has been discharged.[10]

PROOF THAT THE LOSS FALLS WITHIN AN EXCEPTION

Unless the contract otherwise provides, it is for the insurers to prove, in the event of the subject-matter of insurance being destroyed by fire, that they are relieved from liability under their contract by the operation of an exception.[11]

The more important exceptions are directed, on the one hand, against fires occasioned by earthquakes or some other convulsion of nature, and, on the other hand, against fires arising out of foreign invasion, riot, and the like causes.

In both cases the circumstances in which the fire takes place are likely to produce terror and confusion in the minds of all persons present, and it may therefore be difficult, in the case of any particular loss or damage, to prove whether the fire, which caused it, fell within the exception or originated from an independent source.[12]

Further, in most cases of fire, the subject-matter is under the management and control of the insured, and he is probably in a better position than anyone else to know the cause of the fire.

Consequently, it is the practice of insurers, for their protection, to introduce into the contract special terms shifting the burden of proof, and requiring the insured to show that the fire which occasioned the loss was not attributable to an excepted cause.

The exact extent to which the burden of proof is shifted depends upon the language of the particular contract.[13]

Sometimes the policy contains a condition by the terms of which the insured is required to prove to the satisfaction of the insurers that the loss was not caused by an excepted peril.[14]

Sometimes, however, the policy expressly shifts the burden of proof in any proceedings that may be taken to enforce the claim by imposing upon the insured the obligation of proving that the loss was not caused by an excepted peril.[15]

---

10 See Ivamy, *General Principles of Insurance Law* (4th edn, 1979), pp 441–443.

11 See Ivamy, ibid, pp 443–446.

12 Cf *Pawsey & Co v Scottish Union and National Insurance Co* (1908) Times, 17 October with *Tootal, Broadhurst, Lee Co v London and Lancashire Fire Insurance Co* (1908) Times, 21 May in which case a Jamaican jury and an English jury arrived at contrary conclusions, though the evidence in both cases was substantially the same. Both these cases are set out in Appendix IV, pp 403–412, post.

13 See Ivamy, op cit, pp 444–445.

14 See Ivamy, op cit, p 444. See eg *Spinney's (1948) Ltd v Royal Insurance Co Ltd* [1980] 1 Lloyd's Rep 406, where a condition stated: 'In any action, suit or other proceeding, where the Company alleges that by reason of the provisions of this Condition any loss or damage is not covered by this insurance, the burden of proving that such loss or damage is covered shall be upon the Insured.'

15 See Ivamy, op cit, p 444.

In some cases the policy contains a condition providing that if a fire takes place at a time when an excepted peril, eg earthquake or civil commotion, is in operation, the insurers are not to be liable for any loss occasioned by the fire, unless the insured proves that the fire arose independently.[16]

---

[16] See Ivamy, op cit, p 445.

CHAPTER 20

Adjustment of the loss

The first step which is taken by the insurers is to have the loss adjusted, or, as it is sometimes called, 'settled'.[1]

It is the practice of insurers to call in the assistance of skilled persons, who are known as loss adjusters[2], for the purpose of examining into the facts, and advising them as to whether the claim is a genuine one, and in that case, as to what is the amount of the loss.[3]

The adjusters take into consideration the particulars submitted by the insured, including the books and papers which, on their advice, the insurers may require to be produced. They inspect the premises on which the fire took place, and make all necessary investigations into the cause and effect of the fire. In addition, they interview the insured and any person who, in their opinion, is able to afford them useful information.

When the investigations have been completed, they report to the insurers upon the claim, stating whether in their opinion a fire has occurred within the meaning of the policy, whether the property in respect of which the claim is made was, in fact, destroyed or damaged by fire, whether the sum claimed fairly represents its value, and whether the claim as a whole is an honest one.

They then advise the insurers as to their liability under the policy.

If, after investigating a claim, the adjusters advise the insurers to accept liability, and the insurers decide to act on their advice, it is the practice for the adjusters, in their capacity as agents for the insurers,[4] to write to the insured, offering on behalf of the insurers to pay him the sum specified on the letter, in full discharge of his claim under the policy.

If the insured agrees to accept the sum specified, he is usually required to sign a printed form of agreement to that effect, and the terms of agreement are further embodied in the printed form of receipt which he is required to sign on receiving the actual payment for the loss.

---

1 *Beauchamp v Faber* (1898) 3 Com Cas 308.

2 The professional body is the Chartered Institute of Loss Adjusters.

3 In complicated cases it has also become customary for the insured to appoint assessors to guard his interests and negotiate with the insurers. As to the authority of the general manager of an insured to appoint assessors, see *Harris & Co v A E G Electric Co Ltd* (1931) 40 Ll L Rep 61.

4 The adjusters are only agents with a limited authority. Thus, they have no general authority to waive proof of loss or to extend the time for delivery: *Atlas Assurance Co v Brownell* (1899) 29 S C R 537. But the insurers may themselves waive the conditions of the policy as to proof of loss by concurring in the appointment of an adjuster to adjust the loss in a manner differing from that prescribed by the policy: *Toronto Rly Co v National British and Irish Millers' Insurance Co* (1914) 111 L T 555 C A; cf *Western Assurance Co v Pharand* (1902) Q R 11 K B 144; *Kirk v Northern Assurance Co* (1898) 31 N S R 325. The agents warrant their authority to settle the claim by making the offer and if they have no authority, are liable in damages: *Meek v Wendt* (1888) 21 Q B D 126 (marine insurance).

By the acceptance of the sum offered he is bound, and he cannot afterwards, on discovering that he has bona fide omitted to include in his claim the whole of the loss covered by the policy, claim a further sum, since the rights of the parties must be conclusively and finally ascertained at some time or other, and there must, therefore, always be the chance of some loss being suffered by ignorance or carelessness.[5]

On the completion of such an agreement the insurers become liable to pay to the insured the amount fixed by the adjustment,[6] and they can only resist liability on the ground that the insured has been guilty of fraud or breach of duty in connection with the policy[7] or the claim.[8]

If, however, the insurers have made a payment in accordance with the adjustment, and with a full knowledge of the facts, they cannot afterwards claim repayment[9] without proof of fraud.[10]

Where the insured is unwilling to accept the sum offered to him by the insurers, or where the insurers refuse to take any steps to have the loss adjusted,[11] or otherwise repudiate liability under the policy, the insured is entitled to have the question of liability determined, and the amount of the loss ascertained, by an action on the policy or by arbitration.

---

[5] *Elliott v Royal Exchange Assurance Co* (1867) L R 2 Exch 237 at 247, per Pigott B; *Adams v Saundars* (1829) 4 C & P 25 (marine insurance). But in order to obtain a stay of any subsequent proceedings by the insured, the insurers must show that the settlement was of all claims and that by reason of the agreement there was accord and satisfaction: *Lovell v Williams* (1939) 62 Ll L Rep 249.

[6] *Beauchamp v Faber* (1898) 3 Com Cas 308 at 311, per Bigham J; *Chandler v Poland* (1933) 44 Ll L Rep 349 (burglary insurance); *O'Connor v Norwich Union Life and Fire Insurance Society* [1894] 2 I R 723 at 728, per Holmes J. The adjustment may, however, be conditional in its terms: *Gammon v Beverley* (1817) 8 Taunt 119 (marine insurance).

[7] *Herbert v Champion* (1807) 1 Camp 134 (marine insurance), where there had been a non-disclosure of a material fact and Lord Ellenborough C J said at 136, 137: 'The cases are clearly distinguishable where, upon a dispute, the money is paid and where there is only a promise to pay. If the money has been paid, it cannot be recovered back without proof of fraud; but a promise to pay will not, in general, be binding unless founded upon a previous liability. What is an adjustment? An admission on the supposition of certain facts stated that the insured are entitled to recover on the policy . . . An underwriter must make a strong case after admitting his liability; but until he has paid the money he is at liberty to avail himself of any defence which the facts or law of the case will furnish.' See also *Christian v Coombe* (1796) 2 Esp 487 (marine insurance); *Shepherd v Chewter* (1808) 1 Camp 274 (marine insurance), where there had been a deviation. But the insurers may, by adjusting the loss on the footing that there are other insurances, waive the breach of a condition as to such insurances: *Mutchmor v Waterloo Mutual Fire Insurance Co* (1902) 4 O L R 606.

[8] *Queen Insurance Co v Devinney* (1878) 25 Gr 394. The fact that the agent of the insurers accepted the adjustment by mistake, owing to a wrongly translated telegram, is no defence: *Provincial Assurance Co v Roy* (1879) 2 Stephens' Quebec Digest 400.

[9] *Herbert v Champion* (1807) 1 Camp 134 (marine insurance); *Queen Insurance Co v Devinney*, (supra).

[10] *Herbert v Champion*, (supra), at 136, per Lord Ellenborough C J; *Da Costa v Firth* (1766) 4 Burr 1966 (marine insurance), applied in *Holmes v Payne* [1930] 2 K B 301 (jewellery insurance); *Queen Insurance Co v Devinney*, (supra), where the insured's claim was compromised and the insurers, on discovering several months after payment that the insured had himself feloniously caused the fire, were held entitled to recover the sum paid by them under the compromise; *Grunther Industrial Developments Ltd and G I D Ltd v Federated Employers Insurance Association Ltd* [1976] 2 Lloyd's Rep 259, C A, where a claim in respect of stock which was damaged by fire was settled for £31,000, and the insurers failed in their claim for repayment of this sum because their allegations that the claim was fraudulent and the documents supporting it had been forged were held not to have been made out.

[11] *Strong v Harvey* (1825) 3 Bing 304 (marine insurance).

In this case the insurers are not bound by any figures which may have been put forward on their behalf by the adjusters,[12] nor are they precluded by anything which may have been done by the adjusters from repudiating liability altogether.[13]

---

12 But the figures arrived at by the adjusters will be, as against the insured, evidence, though not conclusive evidence, of the amount of the loss: *Thomson v Liverpool and London and Globe Insurance Co* (1871) 2 Hannay (N B) 259, where an agent of the company had promised the insured that the amount of his claim would be paid within sixty days; *Bowes v National Insurance Co* (1880) 4 P & B (N B) 437, where in the course of adjusting the loss the company's agents made declarations as to its amount; cf *Shepherd v Chewter* (1808) 1 Camp 274 (marine insurance).

13 Cf *Luckie v Bushby* (1853) 13 C B 864 at 870 (marine insurance) per Cresswell J: 'It is an admission of the amount of the loss, but not of the underwriters' liability to pay.'

CHAPTER 21

The amount payable by the insurer

The amount of the loss which the insurers are under a liability to pay will depend on whether the policy is a valued or an unvalued one.[1] There is usually a condition inserted in the policy which limits the amount recoverable.[2] There are various rules for calculating the value of the subject-matter where the policy is an unvalued one.[3] Sometimes the insured's interest in the subject-matter is limited in value.[4] In such an event whether he can recover the full value of his interest will depend upon the circumstances.

VALUED AND UNVALUED POLICIES

The manner in which the amount of liability of the insurers in any particular case is to be calculated depends on whether the policy is a valued policy or an unvalued policy.

1 Valued Policies

Where the policy under which the claim of the insured arises is a valued policy, the valuation placed on the subject-matter in the policy, except in the case of fraud or mistake, conclusively establishes the sum required for the purpose of a full indemnity, in the case of a total loss.[5]

The insured is, therefore, dispensed from the necessity of dealing with questions of amount, and is entitled, on proving the fact of his loss, to recover the full amount insured on the subject-matter of insurance.[6]

In the case of a partial loss, where the subject-matter is not destroyed, but damaged, the insured, being entitled to an indemnity only, cannot recover more than the amount of the damage sustained. It is immaterial that the policy is a valued policy since what is valued is the subject-matter of insurance and not the amount of the loss.[7]

---

[1] As to valued and unvalued policies, see Ivamy, *General Principles of Insurance Law* (4th edn, 1979), pp 228–229 and pp 164–166, post.

[2] See Ivamy, ibid pp 227–228, and pp 166–167, post.

[3] See pp 167–176, post.

[4] See pp 177–185, post.

[5] But the valuation is only conclusive between the insured and the insurers issuing the policy, and not as regards other policies: *Bousfield v Barnes* (1815) 4 Camp 228.

[6] Even though the practical result may be to give the insured more than a true indemnity: *Maurice v Goldsborough Mort & Co Ltd* [1939] A C 452, P C.

[7] *City Tailors Ltd v Evans* (1921) 126 L T 439 at 444, C A, per Atkin LJ. Cf *Theobald v Railway Passengers Assurance Co* (1854) 10 Exch 45 (accident insurance), where the same principle was involved in a policy which was valued in the case of death, but the insured only suffered injury.

Where a partial loss occurs and the property is not reinstated, the valuation must be taken into consideration.

In *Elcock v Thomson*[8] a mansion was insured under a Lloyd's policy against loss or damage by fire. The agreed value was £106,850. A fire took place and the premises were partially destroyed. The value of the mansion before the fire was £18,000 and its value after the fire was £12,600, ie a depreciation of 30 per cent. The property was not reinstated. The insured made a claim under the policy, and a question arose as to how much was due under it.

Morris J held that the agreement as to value applied in the event of partial destruction as well as in the event of total destruction. He observed:[9]

'In my judgment, on the facts of the present case, the assured are entitled to be indemnified in respect of the depreciation which was caused by the fire, and, in quantifying such depreciation, the insurable value of the mansion as agreed by the parties cannot be set aside and disregarded. I observe that, at the end of the schedule to the policy, in the words by which such agreement as to value is expressed, it is stipulated that in the event of loss the property would be assumed to be of the value recorded and would be assessed accordingly. In the body of the policy the words used are ''to insure from loss or damage''. I have considered whether any significance is to be attached to the fact of the use only of the word ''loss'' at the end of the schedule, and whether it could be argued that the agreement as to value was only to apply in the event of the destruction or loss of an item as opposed to damage occurring to it. No such point was, however, taken or argued, and I cannot imagine that any significance attaches to the use only of the word ''loss''. It would be strange and unnatural if an agreed value were to apply only in the event of complete destruction and not in the event of partial destruction. The respective words ''loss'' and ''damage,'' as used in the policy, seem to be synonymous. It would not seem to be the case that the word ''loss'' is only referable to complete destruction. Apart from this, however, the opening words of the provision, viz, the words ''The sum set opposite each item in this specification has been accepted by the underwriters and the assured as being the true value of the property insured,'' appear to contain agreement as to value irrespective of the meaning of the word ''loss'' which is later used.'

He went on to say that depreciation could not properly be determined by having regard merely to the proportion to the whole structure of the part burnt out, ie 21 per cent of the whole.

The sum due to the insured should be arrived at by applying to the agreed value of £106,850 the percentage of actual depreciation arising from the fire, ie, 30 per cent. Accordingly the insurers were liable for 30 per cent of £106,850, ie £32,055.

In the words of his Lordship:[10]

'The result is that, in my judgment, the percentage of actual depreciation resulting from the fire should be applied to the agreed values as set out in the policy so as to arrive at the amount recoverable. On my findings, the mansion was worth £18,000 before the fire and £12,600 after the fire. There was, therefore, a depreciation of £5,400 in £18,000, or a depreciation of 3 in 10. By ''the mansion'' I mean the entirety described in items 1 to 5 of the schedule, which together had an agreed value of £106,850. The loss or damage which occurred to the [insured] was, therefore, 3/10ths of such figure, namely £32,055.'

It is to be noticed that the mansion was not in fact repaired. But the learned Judge said, obiter,[11] that if repairs were actually done, and done in a reasonable way it might be that the insurers were liable to pay the cost of them—in this case

---

8 [1949] 2 K B 755; [1949] 2 All E R 381, K B.
9 Ibid, at 763–4 and 387 of the respective reports.
10 Ibid, at 765 and 388 of the respective reports.
11 [1949] 2 All E R 381 at 387.

£43,252—up to the extent of this liability under the policy. Further, it might be that if repairs were not done, but could be done at a figure representing less than the insurer's liability on the basis of depreciation—in the present case £32,500—then they could limit this liability to the lower figure. But his Lordship particularly pointed out:[12]

> 'As the questions which I have posed do not call for present determination, I express no final opinion in regard to them, but I have considered it desirable to have them in mind when examining and testing the submissions made to me. It may well be that, if £43,252 had, in fact, been expended in repairing the damage done, underwriters would have been liable to pay this amount, subject only to the application of the fraction prescribed by the policy. It is not, however, necessary to express any concluded view in regard to this.'

2 Unvalued Policies

Where the policy is not a valued policy, the amount of insurance specified in the policy does not necessarily represent the measure of indemnity.[13]

LIMITATION OF THE AMOUNT RECOVERABLE

The liability of the insurers to pay the full amount of the loss may be, and usually is, limited by various conditions of the policy.

The limitation may depend on the existence of other insurances applying to the whole or part of the same subject-matter, or on the extent of the loss, the insured being required, in certain cases, to bear a portion of the loss himself.

Or again, the conditions may provide that in the event of the loss of any one object falling within the scope of the policy and not being separately insured, the liability of the insurers is not to exceed a specified sum. Such a condition is frequently employed in the case of insurances on pictures or items of jewellery. The effect of the condition is that if the actual amount of the loss exceeds the limits stated in the policy, such limit must, for all purposes connected with the policy, be treated as being the amount of the loss.

By another form of this condition the liability of the insurers is in all cases limited either to a specified sum or to a certain proportion of the actual value of the property insured at the time of its loss,[14] and in some cases specially valuable items may be excluded unless declared.[15]

It is to be noted, however, that in the absence of an express condition to that effect, the insured is not called upon to bear any part of the loss, however much the subject-matter of the insurance may be under-insured.[16] In this respect the

---

[12] [1949] 2 All E R 381 at 387.

[13] *Vance v Forster* (1841) Ir Cir Rep 47 at 50, per Pennefather B. The insured must prove the extent and value of his loss, and the amount recoverable will be calculated accordingly.

[14] *Williamson v Gore District Mutual Fire Insurance Co* (1868) 26 U C R 145, where the condition provided that, in case of loss, the insurers should only be liable as if they had insured two-thirds of the actual cash value. Where the limitation applies to individual items of the property insured, the effect is to constitute a separate insurance on each item: *Curtis & Sons v Mathews* (1918) 119 L T 78 at 81; *King v Prince Edward County Mutual Insurance Co* (1868) 19 C P 134; *McCulloch v Gore District Mutual Insurance Co* (1872) 32 U C R 610.

[15] *King v Travellers' Insurance Association Ltd* (1931) 48 T L R 53 (baggage insurance).

[16] *Sillem v Thornton* (1854) 3 E & B 868 at 888, per Lord Campbell C J, cf *Anglo-Californian Bank Ltd v London and Provincial Marine and General Insurance Co Ltd* (1904) 10 Com Cas 1 at 9 et seq (solvency insurance) per Walton J.

contract of fire insurance differs[17] from that of marine insurance in which a partial loss is subject to average.[18] The insured is, therefore, entitled to recover the full sum insured by his policy if his loss is equal to or exceeds the amount of insurance.[19]

RULES FOR CALCULATING THE VALUE

The value of the subject-matter is its value at the time of the loss,[20] and the policy may contain an express provision to this effect. The value of the subject-matter at any other time is immaterial. In particular, its value at the commencement of the risk,[1] or its prime cost[2] need not be taken into consideration. The rule thus differs from that applying in marine insurance where the amount recoverable is based, in the case of a ship, on her value at the commencement of the risk, and, in the case of goods, on their prime cost, with additions for shipping expenses and insurance charges.[3]

Further, the value of the subject-matter is its value at the place of the fire.[4]

---

[17] The distinction is well expressed in the argument in *Joyce v Kennard* (1871) L R 7 Q B 78 (carrier's insurance), at 81, as follows: 'There is a distinction between a contract of marine and fire insurance. In a fire insurance if goods valued at £20,000 be insured for £1,000, and a loss to the extent of £1,000 occurs, the insurer is liable for that amount; but with regard to a marine insurance, if goods to the value of £20,000 are insured for £1,000, it is necessary to ascertain what proportion the goods lost bear to the whole value, for the owner of the goods is his own insurer for £19,000'.

[18] Marine Insurance Act 1906, ss 69–71. See Ivamy, *Marine Insurance* (3rd edn, 1979), p 439.

[19] *Newman v Maxwell* (1899) 80 L T 681; *Thompson v Montreal Insurance Co* (1850) 6 U C R 319; *Peddie v Quebec Fire Assurance Co* (1824) Stu K B 174.

[20] *Chapman v Pole* (1870) 22 L T 306 at 309, per Cockburn L J; *Westminster Fire Office v Glasgow Provident Investment Society* (1888) 13 App Cas 699 at 711 per Lord Selborne; *Phoenix Assurance Co Ltd v Spooner* [1905] 2 K B 753 at 756 per Bigham J; *Re Wilson and Scottish Insurance Corpn* [1920] 2 Ch 28; *Hercules Insurance Co v Hunter* 1836 14 Sh (Ct of Sess) 1137; *Glasgow Provident Investment Society v Westminster Fire Office* 1887 14 R (Ct of Sess) 947 at 989 per Lord Young; *Vance v Forster* (1841) Ir Cir Rep 47; *Butler v Standard Fire Insurance Co* (1879) 26 Gr 341, where the insured was held entitled to recover the value of the stock-in-trade insured as at the date of the fire, though, in fact, greater than at the time of insuring; *Equitable Fire Insurance Co v Quinn* (1861) 11 L C R 170, where the insured was held entitled to recover the market value of his stock-in-trade as at the date of the loss; *Harrison v Western Assurance Co* (1903) 1 Can Com R 490 (revsd on other grounds, sub nom. *Western Assurance Co Ltd v Harrison* (1903) 33 S C R 473); *Cameron v Canada Fire Marine Insurance Co* (1884), 6 O R 392; cf *Re Routledge, & F Bateman* (1856) 8 De G M & G 263; *Goulstone v Royal Insurance Co* (1858) 1 F *ex p* 276.

[1] *Re Wilson and Scottish Insurance Corpn*, (supra), where the policy provided for making good the loss up to the full value, and the only question was whether the whole of the increase in value had accrued since the commencement of the risk.

[2] *Williams v Atlantic Assurance Co Ltd* [1933] 1 K B 81 at 92, C A (marine insurance) per Scrutton L J, speaking of the value of pictures; *Equitable Fire Insurance Co v Quinn*, (supra); *Cameron v Canada Fire and Marine Insurance Co*, (supra), where a statement giving the costs of the property a year before fire was held to be a breach of a condition of the policy requiring that the affidavit of loss should state the actual cash value of the property; *Harrison v Western Assurance Co Ltd*, (supra), where it was held that the arbitrators in a reference to ascertain the amount of the loss were wrong in attempting to fix the value of the property as at the time when the policy was effected. But, in practice, the invoice price is frequently taken where there is no fraud, if the purchase is recent.

[3] Marine Insurance Act 1906, s 16. The marine rule is an artificial one: *Usher v Noble* (1810) 12 East 639 at 645 (marine insurance) per Lord Ellenborough C J. See Ivamy, *Marine Insurance* (3rd edn, 1979), pp 101–102.

[4] *Rice v Baxendale* (1861) 7 H & N 96 at 101 (carrier) per Bramwell B, speaking of fire insurance; *Liverpool, London and Globe Insurance Co v Valentine* (1898) Q R 7 Q B 400; *Vance v Forster* (1841) Ir Cir Rep 47 at 50, per Pennefather B.

The value of the subject-matter is its real or intrinsic value[5] to the insured;[6] and no addition is to be made for merely sentimental value or *pretium affectionis*.[7]

In estimating the value of the subject-matter no allowance is to be made for loss of prospective profit or other consequential loss.

Basis of Calculation

The application of the above rules gives rise to questions of considerable difficulty.[8] The principal difficulty is to determine the basis on which the value of the subject-matter is to be calculated.[9] The contract of fire insurance is a contract of indemnity; and the insured is not adequately indemnified against the loss of his property, unless, so far as money can do so, he is restored to the position which he occupied at the time of the loss. No hard and fast rule can be laid down. That basis must be adopted which is best calculated in the particular case to carry out the intention of the parties.[10]

If he can be restored to his original position, as is usually the case, by the purchase of an equivalent or by reinstatement of the property destroyed, the amount of the indemnity must be sufficient for the purpose. Prima facie, therefore, the basis of calculation is either the market value of the property destroyed or the cost of reinstatement. It must be borne in mind throughout that what the insured is entitled to recover is the value of the property destroyed. Whichever basis is adopted, it is only as a basis for calculating the real value of the property, and the insured does not recover the market value or the cost of reinstatement as such.[11]

In many cases the market value of the property destroyed represents its real value. Payment of the market value is an adequate indemnity, since the insured, by going into the market and purchasing similar property, can be completely restored to his original position.[12] The amount recoverable under the policy is, therefore, calculated upon the basis of market value.[13]

---

[5] *Hercules Insurance Co v Hunter* 1836 14 Sh (Ct of Sess) 1137 at 1142, per Lord Moncrieff.

[6] *Canadian National Fire Insurance Co v Colonsay Hotel Co* [1923] S C R 688, where the value of a hotel was affected by the introduction of prohibition of intoxicating liquor. Cf *The Harmonides* [1903] P 1 at 6 (shipping) per Gorell Barnes, J: 'The test when there is no market, is what is the value to the owners as a going concern.'

[7] *Re Earl Egmont's Trust, Lefroy v Earl Egmont* [1908] 1 Ch 821 at 826 per Warrington J.

[8] In order to avoid this there is sometimes an agreed basis in the policy.

[9] This is a question which has been very infrequently before the Courts, and little guidance is to be obtained from such decisions as there are. The decisions make it clear that what the insured is entitled to recover is the value of the property at the time of the loss; but they do not, as a rule, except in very general terms, indicate in what manner this value is to be arrived at. The text, in so far as no assistance is to be obtained from the decisions, attempts to suggest the principles which appear best calculated to give the true measure of indemnity.

[10] *Liesbosch (Dredger) v Edison (Owners)* [1933] A C 449 at 463 (shipping) per Lord Wright, speaking of damages: 'The dominant rule is the principle of *restitutio in integrum*, and subsidiary rules can only be justified if they give effect to that rule'.

[11] See *Canadian National Fire Insurance Co v Colonsay Hotel Co* [1923] S C R 688; *Jackson v Canada Accident and Fire Assurance Co* (1924) 52 N B R 33; *Matergio v Canada Accident and Fire Assurance Co* (1926) 58 N S R 415.

[12] In many cases the market value is the selling value, eg as in the case of stock-in-trade; but in others there may be a wide difference between the selling and the purchase price, eg a sale by the insured of used furniture may only bring in the dealer's price, whereas he will have to pay a much greater price if he goes to the dealer to purchase similar articles. In case of difference, the insured is entitled to recover the latter price.

[13] *Equitable Fire Insurance Co v Quinn* (1861) 11 L C R 170; *Liverpool, London amd Globe Insurance Co v*

Where the property is enhanced in value before the fire, and its market value is accordingly increased, the objection may be raised that the enhancement of value represents profit, and cannot, therefore, be recovered, unless specifically insured. In a sense, no doubt, the enhancement of value is profit, and in marine insurance it must be insured as profit.[14] In fire insurance, however, the rule that profit must be specifically insured applies only to prospective profit, the chance of earning which is taken away by the fire. The property is valued as at the time of the fire, and not, as in marine insurance, at an earlier date. Consequently, any enhancement of value which has already taken place is not prospective profit, but accrued profit: it forms part of the value of the property at the time of the loss,[15] and is an element of its then market value.[16] The objection, therefore, is untenable, and the amount recoverable under an ordinary policy includes any enhancement of value which has taken place before the loss.[17]

Theoretically, the market value and the cost of reinstatement ought to be the same. In practice, however, there is frequently a difference between them. Further, property does not always possess a market value, and even where there is a market value, it does not necessarily represent the real value of the property.[18] Hence, the view which has sometimes been expressed that in all cases the basis of calculation is the market value of the property[19] is, it is submitted, unsound. There are cases in which the loss cannot be made good except by reinstatement; the insured is not restored to his original position if he is unable to reinstate the property out of the proceeds of the insurance,[20] either

---

Valentine (1898) QR 7 QB 400. Cf *Maurice v Goldsborough Mort & Co Ltd* [1939] AC 452, PC, where the value was taken as 'the gross selling price realisable by auction at the date of the fire'.

14 Marine Insurance Act 1906, ss 16, 67–71; *Lucena v Craufurd* (1806) 2 Bos & P N R 269 at 315, HL (marine insurance). See Ivamy, *Marine Insurance* (3rd edn, 1979), p 115.

15 Thus, in *Curtis & Sons v Mathews* (as reported (1918) 119 LT 78 at 81) the fact that the value of buildings was rising was taken into account. See also *J Gliksten & Son Ltd v Green* [1929] AC 381, followed in *R v British Columbia Fir and Cedar Lumber Co Ltd* [1932] AC 441, PC.

16 Cf *O'Hanlan v Great Western Rly Co* (1865) 34 LJ QB 154 at 158 (carrier) per Blackburn J; *British Columbia Saw-Mill Co v Nettleship* (1868) LR 3 CP 499 (carrier); *Toronto City Corpn v Toronto Railway Corpn* [1925] AC 177 at 191, PC (compulsory purchase) per Viscount Cave.

17 *Re Wilson and Scottish Insurance Corpn* [1920] 2 Ch 28, where it was held, in an insurance on a car, that the increase in value was recoverable if it had accrued since the last renewal; *Butler v Standard Fire Insurance Co* (1879) 26 Gr 341; affd (1879) 4 OAR 391; *Equitable Fire Insurance Co v Quinn* (1861) 11 LCR 170, where it was held that the insurers were liable to pay the market value at the time of the fire, which exceeded the cost price although the insured had not insured his profit. But different considerations may apply in a declaration policy: *Carreras v Cunard SS Co* [1918] 1 KB 118.

18 *McCuaig v Quaker City Insurance Co* (1859) 18 UCR 130, where, on a policy on a steamboat against fire, the insurers were held liable to pay the real value of the steamboat, and were not entitled to have taken into account a depression in the value of steamers generally, caused by circumstances which might be temporary only; *Grant v Aetna Insurance Co* (1862) 15 Moo PCC 516 at 518, 519, where the Judge at the trial directed the jury that the actual cash value of the steamer was not to be established by proof of what she was sold for, this point not being dealt with on appeal; *Green v Manitoba Assurance Co* (1901) 13 Man LR 395, where the insured was not precluded from showing the real value of the property by the fact that, in particular circumstances, he had offered to sell it for a smaller sum; cf *The Harmonides* [1903] p 1 at 6 (shipping) per Gorell Barnes J.

19 *Hercules Insurance Co v Hunter* 1836 14 Sh (Ct of Sess) 1137; *Glasgow Provident Investment Society v Westminster Fire Office* 1887 14 R (Ct of Sess) 947 at 989, per Lord Young.

20 It is assumed, throughout, that the insurance is sufficient to cover the amount recoverable,

by repairing it, if damaged, or by replacing it, if wholly destroyed, by its equivalent. Payment of the market value, therefore, does not give the insured an adequate indemnity, since he cannot reinstate the property for the sum representing its market value, but is necessarily compelled to incur further expenditure before he can be restored to his original position.[1] He is not adequately indemnified unless he receives the amount necessary and sufficient for reinstatement. Consequently, a basis of calculation must be adopted which gives him an adequate indemnity; and this basis is the cost of reinstatement.[2]

In the case of a partial loss, the cost of reinstatement is in many instances the only available measure of indemnity;[3] and the basis of market value has no application.[4] By repairing the damage,[5] the property can be put into the condition in which it was before the fire; and the insured, therefore, is adequately indemnified if he receives the amount required to pay for the repairs.[6]

---

whatever the basis of calculation adopted, and also, except where otherwise stated, that the insured is owner in possession, and entitled to recover the full value of the property. Different considerations apply where the owner is not in possession but is a reversioner only, and where the insurance is not intended to cover the whole interest in the property; cf *Moss v Christchurch RDC* [1925] 2 K B 750 (nuisance), where, in a subrogated action arising out of the burning of a cottage let to a tenant who was protected by the Rent Restriction Acts (a point emphasised by the Court), the Court held that the measure of damages recoverable by the landlord was not the cost of reinstatement, but the difference between the value of her reversionary interest before and after the fire. The Court also held, in the case of the tenant, that damages for the loss of his furniture were not to be measured by the cost of reinstatement. The decision, on the latter point particularly, cannot be regarded as satisfactory. The judgment is very short and neither from the report nor from the shorthand note does the question appear to have been fully discussed. Further, the Court in the result approved the decision of the Official Referee, who had awarded damages for the loss of the furniture on the basis of the cost of reinstatement.

[1] A useful test may be, what would a prudent person do, if uninsured. Cf *Le Blanche v London and North-Western Rly Co* (1876) 1 C P D 286 at 313, C A (contract) per Mellish L J.

[2] *Westminster Fire Office v Glasgow Provident Investment Society* (1888) 13 App Cas 699 at 713, per Lord Selborne: 'As between themselves and the prior encumbrancers, it was the right of the other insurance companies to satisfy their contracts of indemnity by reinstating the premises, which the fire had destroyed, or (which amount to the same thing) to pay those prior encumbrancers the amount necessary and sufficient for that purpose'; *Andrews v Patriotic Assurance Co (No 2)* (1886) L R Ir 355 at 366, per Palles C B: 'If a tenant in England wished fully to indemnify himself, he should insure in an amount sufficient to reinstate the premises'. See also *Vance v Forster* (1841) Ir Cir Rep 47; and cf *Hepenstall v Wicklow County Council* [1931] 2 I R 165, C A (malicious damage); *Reynolds v Phoenix Assurance Co Ltd* [1978] 2 Lloyd's Rep 440 (old maltings); *Pleasurama Ltd v Sun Alliance and London Insurance Ltd* [1979] 1 Lloyd's Rep 389 (bingo hall); *Leppard v Excess Insurance Co Ltd* [1979] 2 All E R 668, [1979] 2 Lloyd's Rep 91, C A. (cottage); *Exchange Theatre Ltd v Iron Trades Mutual Insurance Co Ltd* [1983] 1 Lloyd's Rep 674 (bingo hall). In *J Gliksten & Son, Ltd v Green* [1929] A C 381 it is stated that after the fire which gave rise to the case of *F Gliksten & Son v State Assurance Co* (1922) 10 Ll L Rep 604, the insurers paid on the basis of the cost of replacement £477,838 in respect of timber valued in the books of the insured at £160,824; but as at the time of the fire there was a boom in timber, it may be regarded as a case of enhanced market value.

[3] In the case of stock-in-trade, which can be sold in a damaged condition, the measure of indemnity is the market value, the amount recoverable being the difference between the market price and the actual selling price.

[4] There is no such thing in fire insurance as a 'constructive total loss'. Hence, the relation between the cost of the repairs and the repaired value is immaterial. As to 'constructive total loss' in marine insurance, see Ivamy, *Marine Insurance* (3rd edn 1979), pp 394–409.

[5] As to the meaning of the words 'repair' and 'renewal', see *Lurcott v Wakely and Wheeler* [1911] 1 K B 905 at 923, C A (covenant) per Buckley L J.

[6] *Scottish Amicable Heritable Securities Association v Northern Assurance Co* 1883 11 R (Ct of Sess) 287 at 295, per Lord Craighill; *Glasgow Provident Investment Society v Westminster Fire Office* 1887 14

Where the cost of reinstatement is taken as the basis of calculation, the reinstatement contemplated is a reinstatement sufficient to restore the property insured to the condition in which it was at the time of the loss.[7] Restoration in many cases necessarily means that the property destroyed will have to be replaced by new property, and by the replacement the insured may be put into a better position than before the fire.

Thus, if old machinery is destroyed, and replaced by new machinery, the new machinery will have a longer life. If, therefore, the insured is paid an amount representing the cost of reinstatement, he will in such cases be more than fully indemnified.

Consequently, some allowance will have to be made for the difference in value between the property destroyed and the new property of a similar description by which it is replaced.[8]

There is not, in fire insurance, as there is in marine insurance,[9] any certain standard by which the relative values of old and new property are to be measured,[10] and each case must depend on its own circumstances.[11] It may well be,

---

R (Ct of Sess) 947 at 989, per Lord Young. If the insured is able to get the repairs done more cheaply because of other repairs not covered by the policy, he receives the advantage and the insurers must pay the proper cost of the repairs: *Marine Insurance Co v China Transpacific SS Co* (1886) 11 App Cas 573 (marine insurance).

[7] Therefore the amount of the indemnity will not include increased cost of reinstatement due to the fact that local bye-laws or Buildings Acts prevent the property being rebuilt in the same style or without improved means of exit or safety precautions, eg in the case of a theatre, unless such increase is specifically insured.

[8] *Ewer v National Employers' Mutual General Insurance Association Ltd* [1937] 2 All ER 193 at 203 (where the insured claimed the price of new tools) per MacKinnon J: 'These things were not new; they were second-hand, but according to [the insured] they were efficient and he could use them in his business. If the law were otherwise, that might be very reasonable, but all he can recover is the reasonable value of the second-hand goods that have been destroyed'; *Vance v Forster* [1841] Ir Cir Rep 47 at 50, per Pennefather B: 'They [the jury] are to take into account the state of the machinery at the time the fire happened. They are to endeavour to ascertain that state by the examination of witnesses; by a consideration of the first cost and by the state of repair in which the machinery was kept and was immediately before the fire. It is said, on the one hand, that it is not unfair to go pretty near to the actual cost of new machinery, and, on the other side, it is contended that a certain rateable deduction ought to be made from the price of new machinery . . . These are not, to my mind, the tests by which the [insured's] loss should be estimated. It is impossible to lay down a general rule that one-third or one-fourth or one-half should be deducted from the original price or from the price of new machinery, because that would be excluding from the consideration of the jury the actual state or serviceable order of the machinery at the time of the fire; but the jury are to say what state of repair the machinery was in—what it would cost to replace that machinery by new machinery, taking into account the entire expense of replacing such new machinery and how much better (if at all) the mill would be with the new machinery than it was at the time of the fire, and the difference is to be deducted from the entire expense of placing there new machinery . . . I think the [insured] must be borne harmless from his actual loss, and therefore allowance should be made for transporting the machinery—for putting it up and replacing it in statu quo'.

[9] As a general rule, the insured can only recover, after a vessel's first voyage, the cost of repairs less one-third new for old: Marine Insurance Act 1906, s 69 (1), referring to the customary deductions. See Ivamy, *Marine Insurance* (3rd edn, 1979), pp 453–455.

[10] *Vance v Forster* (1841) Ir Cir Rep 47. An allowance of 'new for old' appears to have been made in *Curtis & Sons v Mathews*, as reported (1918), 119 LT 78, 81 (not reported on this point on appeal, except that it is stated in the report that the Court of Appeal reduced the amount awarded: [1919] 1 K B 425, C A). In *Reynolds v Phoenix Assurance Co Ltd* [1978] 2 Lloyd's Rep 440, where old maltings were insured, a deduction of £10,000 was made in respect of 'betterment'. (See the judgment of Forbes J, ibid at 452).

[11] See eg *Reynolds v Phoenix Assurance Co Ltd*, supra, where Forbes J, said (ibid at 453): 'Now the

in a particular case, that no allowance will have to be made because the position of the insured is in no way improved by the reinstatement.[12]

Further, there are cases in which the cost of reinstatement does not provide an adequate indemnity. Property is sometimes valuable through its antiquity, and though reinstatement in a sense is physically possible, the property, if reinstated, cannot fairly be regarded as equivalent to what was destroyed. If an ancient abbey or an Elizabethan manor house is destroyed by fire, the house, no doubt, can be rebuilt, but the building is essentially different, and it would therefore be idle to suggest that the cost of reinstatement represents the value of the original building. In such cases something over and above the cost of reinstatement must be added. Where the property had a market value before the fire, this may represent the true measure of indemnity.[13]

Certain special cases cannot be dealt with on the basis either of reinstatement or of market value, because reinstatement is impossible and market value does not exist. The case of family portraits may be taken as an example. A particular portrait, because of the artist by whom it was painted or the person whom it represents, may have something in the nature of a market value, and payment of this will be an adequate indemnity. In many instances, however, the portrait is of a different kind. Though it may have been the expensive production of a painter fashionable in his day, it remains an unattractive portrait of no one in particular and makes no appeal to any possible buyer. It may even have lost its appeal to the owner and be stowed away in a lumber room. The real value of such a portrait cannot be great. It may be nothing more than the value of the canvas and the frame.

On the other hand, the property may have no market value, except perhaps as scrap, and whilst it may be capable of physical reinstatement, it may not be commercially practicable to do this. In such a case the test is the real value to the insured at the time of the loss. This may be considerable in, eg the case of a going concern.[14] The value must be a matter of estimation after taking into account all the factors applicable to the particular case.

Application of the Rules

The application of the rules stated above may be conveniently considered in detail under the following heads:

---

principle of betterment is too well established in the law of insurance to be departed from at this stage even though it may sometimes work hardship on the assured. It is simply that an allowance must be made because the assured is getting something new for something old. But in this class of insurance there is no automatic or accepted percentage deduction. In some of the calculations put before me an attempt was made to establish a figure of 13.3 per cent as the appropriate reduction for betterment. This figure has no validity. It happens to be, mathematically, the result of stating as a percentage the figure agreed as a deduction for betterment between assessors and adjusters at the meeting of 5 June. But this deduction itself was clearly not the result of applying a percentage and particularly not one as unlikely as 13.3 per cent.'

12 This will happen, eg where the house destroyed, though not new, is substantially built and kept in good repair so that the insured is no better off because of the reinstatement. Cf. the case of an historic mansion such as Blenheim Palace, which cannot be sold.

13 *Williams v Atlantic Assurance Co Ltd* [1933] 1 K B 81 at 92, C A (marine insurance) per Scrutton L J, speaking of fixtures.

14 *Grainger v Martin* (1862) 31 L J Q B 186 (marine insurance); *The Harmonides* [1903] P 1 at 6 (shipping) per Gorell Barnes J.

a Buildings.
b Articles in use.
c Stock-in-trade.
d Goods still on the manufacturer's premises.

(a) Buildings[15]

Where a building has no market value, the only basis of calculation available is the cost of reinstatement.

Thus, if a church is destroyed by fire, a new church must be built to take its place. In the case of a mansion house or cottages on a country estate, the owner is not adequately indemnified, in the event of their destruction, if the measure of his indemnity is to be based on their selling or letting value, inasmuch as, for the purposes of the estate, rebuilding is practically a necessity.

In cases such as these, the real value of the subject-matter cannot be measured by a commercial standard, and the only satisfactory measure of indemnity is based on the cost of reinstatement.[16]

Even where the building, such as a house or a factory, has a market value, it does not necessarily follow that its market value is an adequate measure of indemnity.[17] The insured's loss is not limited to the market value; there are other factors which have to be taken into consideration. This is clearly the case where the insured is under a legal obligation to reinstate the building. Unless the amount recoverable under the policy is sufficient for the purpose, he is not fully indemnified.

In any event, and apart from any legal obligation to reinstate, he is deprived by the fire of his building, and is left only with a site from which he can derive no beneficial enjoyment so long as it remains vacant. He is not restored to his original position until the building is reinstated on the same site; and hence his indemnity is not complete if he receives less than the cost of reinstatement.[18]

Further, it is to be observed that certain persons interested in the building destroyed have a statutory right to insist on its reinstatement out of the proceeds of the insured's policy;[19] and, by the terms of the policy, an option to reinstate is usually reserved to the insurers.[20] The existence of the right and the reservation of the option both support the conclusion that the true measure of

---

[15] It may be pointed out that in the case of buildings, the loss, as a rule, is only partial.

[16] *Duke of Newcastle v Broxtowe Hundred* (1832) 4 B & Ad 273 (riot damage), where Nottingham Castle was demolished by rioters, and it was held that the measure of damages was the sum necessary to repair the damage and replace the building in the situation and state in which it was at the time of the outrage as nearly as practicable, the contention that the premises should be assessed on the rental being rejected. Cf *Herring v Janson* (1895) 1 Com Cas 177 at 177 (marine insurance) per Mathew J: 'The assured was not bound to value the yacht at what she would sell for. He was entitled to take into account what it would have cost him for necessary repairs and outfit of the vessel and further what he would have had to pay to replace her'.

[17] *Castellain v Preston* (1883) 11 Q B D 380 at 400, 401, C A, per Bowen L J.

[18] There may be cases in which the cost of reinstatement is less than the amount of the loss: *Westminster Fire Office v Glasgow Provident Investment Society* (1888) 13 App Cas 699 at 713, per Lord Selborne.

[19] See Ivamy, *General Principles of Insurance Law* (4th edn, 1979), p 492.

[20] Ibid, pp 486–488.

indemnity is the cost of reinstatement.[1] If this is not so, the option which the insurers think fit to reserve to themselves is futile and misleading, whilst the statutory right will either be unavailable for its intended purpose or result in working injustice to the insured by compelling him to accept an incompletely reinstated building, or, if, as the statute permits, he carries out the reinstatement himself, by requiring him to do so with insufficient funds.

(b) Articles in Use

This head includes machinery, furniture, and all kinds of personal property other than stock-in-trade. Such articles are provided by the insured for use and enjoyment or convenience in connection with his business or private life. They form part of his establishment, each article having its special function to perform in promoting his advantage or comfort. They are, therefore, to be regarded as something more than mere pieces of merchandise. They are the instruments by means of which the insured is enabled to conduct his business or his private concerns.

Consequently, the market value of the particular article destroyed or the price for which it could have been sold at the time of the loss, is not necessarily the true measure of indemnity.[2] To be restored to his original position, the insured must replace what he has lost, and he is not fully indemnified unless the amount recoverable under his policy is sufficient for the purpose.[3] It may, therefore, be concluded that the rule in this case is the same as in the case of buildings, and that the true measure of indemnity is based on the cost of reinstatement and not the market value of the property destroyed.[4]

(c) Stock-in-trade

When the insured is a merchant, the value of his stock-in-trade for the purpose of measuring his indemnity is its market value at the place and time of the loss.[5]

If, however, there is no available market, the value of the goods destroyed is a question of fact, which has to be determined on a consideration of all the circumstances. The value of goods at a place where there is no market is, for

---

[1] See *Westminster Fire Office v Glasgow Provident Investment Society*, (supra), at 713 per Lord Selborne; *Andrews v Patriotic Assurance Co (No 2)* (1886) 18 L R Ir 355 at 366, per Palles C B.

[2] *Vance v Forster* (1841) Ir Cir Rep 47, which was a case of machinery; *McCuaig v Quaker City Insurance Co* (1859) 18 U C R 130; *Grant v Aetna Insurance Co* (1862) 15 Moo P C C 516; cf *Herring v Janson* (1895) 1 Com Cas 177 (marine insurance).

[3] See *Grant v Aetna Insurance Co*, (supra), where importance was attached to the reinstatement clause. An outstanding example is the difference between the dealer's price at which second-hand goods can be sold and the price of purchasing similar second-hand goods from a shop.

[4] The contrary view was taken in *Hercules Insurance Co v Hunter* 1836 14 Sh (Ct of Sess) 1137, which was also a case of machinery. See *Ewer v National Employers' Mutual General Insurance Association Ltd* [1937] 2 All E R 193, as reported in 157 L T 16, per MacKinnon J at 21: 'Many an assured who has had an armchair burned to pieces has put forward the proposition: "Well I want an armchair to sit upon. This one is destroyed and I can only get one to sit upon by buying a new one." In some circumstances, if the law were otherwise, that might be very reasonable, but very often it is not recognised, and he realises to his chagrin that all he can recover is not his armchair to sit upon, but the reasonable value of the second-hand armchair that has been destroyed'.

[5] *Equitable Fire Insurance Co v Quinn* (1861) 11 L C R 170; *Liverpool, London and Globe Insurance Co v Valentine* (1898) Q R 7 Q B 400.

ordinary purposes, ascertained by taking the price at the place of manufacture, together with the cost of carriage to the particular place, and adding thereto a reasonable allowance for the importer's profit.[6]

There does not appear to be any valid reason why, in the case of fire insurance, the value of the goods destroyed should be ascertained in a different manner. But the allowance for profit creates some difficulty. It is open to argument that the insured is adequately indemnified if he receives sufficient under his policy to enable him to buy similar goods from the manufacturer and to pay for their carriage to the place of the fire,[7] and that the allowance for profit represents a consequential loss which ought to have been separately covered.

This argument appears to be unsound, since it disregards the fact that the question is the value of the goods at the place of the fire.[8] Where there is a market, the market price clearly includes the importer's profit, otherwise the goods would not be imported.[9] If, therefore, the importer's profit is an element in market value, it must equally be taken into account in fixing the value where there is no market.[10] The insured does not merely lose the money which he has expended in buying the goods and in getting them to the place of the fire; he loses the value of the goods at that place. The excess is a profit which has accrued, and is no more prospective profit than the profit which is included in the market value on the day of the fire, and to which the insured is undoubtedly entitled.

(d) Goods Still on Manufacturer's Premises

Where goods are destroyed whilst they are still on the manufacturer's premises, and whilst they are still the property of the manufacturer, a similar question arises as to the basis on which they are to be valued.

It has been suggested that in this case, as the insured is the manufacturer, he can manufacture other goods to take the place of the goods destroyed, and that the measure of indemnity is, therefore, the cost of production, and not the price at which the goods can be sold, or their market value.

The real question in this case, as in every case, is what has the insured lost by the fire? The effect of the fire is not that he has merely lost the labour and materials used to produce the goods; what he has lost is something more than these, it is the product of the labour and materials. The value of this product even in the manufacturer's hands is not measured by the cost of production; for the product is not merely the sum of its component parts. On the contrary, it is an independent marketable commodity, with a distinct value of its own, depending not on the cost of production, but on supply and demand.[11] The cost

---

[6] *O'Hanlan v Great Western Rly Co* (1865) 34 L J Q B 154 (carrier); *Horne v Midland Rly Co* (1873) L R 8 C P 131 (carrier).

[7] *Rice v Baxendale* (1861) 7 H & N 96 at 102, (carrier), per Bramwell B.

[8] *O'Hanlan v Great Western Rly Co*, (supra), contrasting *Rice v Baxendale*, (supra), at 102 per Bramwell B.

[9] *O'Hanlan v Great Western Rly Co*, (supra), at 158, per Blackburn J.

[10] Ibid.

[11] *Richard Holden Ltd v Bostock & Co Ltd* (1902) 18 T L R 317, C A (sale of goods); *Clay v Yates* (1856) 1 H & N 73 at 79 (work and labour) per Martin B, pointing out that a printer would be entitled to be paid for his labour and materials, although the book, when printed, might not be worth half the value of the paper used.

of production is, at most, only one, and not necessarily the most important of the elements which go to create the value of the product.[12]

What, therefore, the manufacturer requires to be indemnified against is not the loss of the component parts, which are not, in fact, insured by the policy, but the loss of the product, which is specifically insured. If he receives only the cost of the labour and materials necessary to replace the goods destroyed, he is being indemnified only against the loss of the component parts. His indemnity, therefore, is only partial, since he has lost more, ie the excess beyond the cost of production which makes up the value of the goods in the same way as the difference between cost price and market value in the case of merchants' stock-in-trade.[13] This is made clear where the insured, in fact, manufactures other goods and uses them to replace the goods destroyed. But for the fire, he would have had two sets of goods, each with its market value, whereas he has only one set, and, however the case is looked at, he has lost the market value of the other.[14]

Further, if the cost of production is the correct basis, a contract under which payment of the amount of the loss and replacement by the insurers are regarded as equivalent, entitles the insurers, in the case of a manufacturer, to say that the replacement, if at all, must be done by him, and that, in any event, their liability is to be measured by the cost of the labour and materials which he would use for the purpose. The insurers thus receive without payment and the manufacturer loses without compensation the benefit of the advantages and facilities which enable him to produce the goods, and which form an element in the value of the goods when produced.

Consequently, it is submitted that in the case of the manufacturer, equally as in the case of the merchant, the measure of indemnity is the market value of the goods destroyed, since on any other basis he cannot be adequately indemnified.[15]

---

12 Cf *Banco de Portugal v Waterlow & Sons Ltd* [1932] A C 452 (contract), where the damage was held to be the face value of the bank notes supplied in breach of contract and not merely the cost of production.

13 If goods are destroyed whilst in course of manufacture, an allowance must be made, in addition to the cost of labour and materials, to represent the increase in value of the finished product; cf *Reid v Fairbanks* (1853) 13 C B 692 (conversion), where the method approved by the Court of estimating the value of an unfinished ship at a particular date allowed more than the actual cost of construction up to that date.

14 Cf *Re Vic Mill Ltd* [1913] 1 Ch 465 at 473, C A (sale of goods) per Hamilton L J.

15 It does not follow, as a matter of course, that the insured is entitled to have the goods paid for at the current market value. What he is entitled to be paid for is the value of the goods, and of that value the market price is only evidence, though most cogent evidence. The question being one of fact, any circumstance relating to the real or intrinsic value of the goods is relevant for the purpose of showing that the current market price does not represent their value. The insurers would clearly be entitled to show that the market price included the expenses of marketing the goods which the insured would not have incurred, and probably also that the market price was only a nominal figure, or that the goods in question had little or no market value in that they could not have been sold for the market price. On the other hand, the insured might be able to show that he had actually sold the goods, owing to special circumstances, at a price above the current market price, and that owing to the fire he had been unable to produce or procure other goods in substitution in order to fulfil his contract.

WHERE THE INSURED'S INTEREST IS LIMITED IN VALUE

The insured is, as a general rule, precluded from recovering more than the value of his interest in the subject-matter,[16] since the measure of his loss is the interest in respect of which he has been prejudiced, and if he was permitted to recover a greater sum, he would be receiving more than was requisite for a full indemnity. The value of his interest is not necessarily the value of the subject-matter; it may be only a portion of such value, varying in extent according to the amount of interest possessed by the insured. If different interests in the same subject-matter belonging to different persons are separately insured, each insured is entitled to recover the amount representing his own loss, without regard to what may be recovered by the others. Hence it may happen that the aggregate amount recovered in respect of the different interests may exceed the value of the subject-matter.[17]

Where the insured is the owner of the subject-matter, the value of his interest is measured by the value of the subject-matter which has been destroyed. The amount recoverable under the policy is, therefore, the value of the subject-matter, since no other sum would sufficiently indemnify him against the loss which he has sustained.[18] It is immaterial whether he is the legal or the equitable owner. Thus, a mortgagor may, notwithstanding the existence of a mortgage, recover the full value of the property destroyed.[19]

Where the insured is not the absolute owner of the subject-matter, the value of his interest may, nevertheless, be the value of the subject-matter. His right of indemnity cannot always be measured by the market value of his proprietary interest in the subject-matter;[20] for the purpose of giving him a full indemnity, the value of his interest, and consequently the amount recoverable may have to be determined by the extent of the loss, without taking into consideration what the value would have been if the fire had never taken place.[1]

Thus, a tenant for life is entitled as a general rule, subject to the limits of his insurance, to recover the full value of the property insured.[2]

Similarly, in the case of leasehold property, a tenant, who by his lease is under covenant to repair in case of fire, cannot be fairly indemnified in the event of the property being destroyed by fire unless he receives from his

---

[16] *Castellain v Preston* (1883) 11 QBD 380 at 397, CA, per Bowen LJ; *Andrews v Patriotic Assurance Co (No 2)* (1886) 18 LR Ir 355 at 360, 361, per Palles CB; cf *North British and Mercantile Insurance Co v London, Liverpool and Globe Insurance Co* (1877), 5 Ch D 569 at 583, CA, per Mellish LJ; *Matthewson v Western Assurance Co* (1859) 10 LCR 8 at 12.

[17] *Westminster Fire Office v Glasgow Provident Investment Society* (1888) 13 App Cas 699, where the insured recovered the amount of his loss, though the reinstatement value of the premises had already been recovered by other parties. See *Scottish Amicable Heritable Securities Association v Northern Assurance Co* 1883 11 R (Ct of Sess) 287.

[18] Future expenses, which he might have incurred if the property had not been destroyed, are not to be taken into consideration: *Maurice v Goldsborough, Mort & Co Ltd* [1939] AC 452, PC.

[19] *North British and Mercantile Insurance Co v London, Liverpool and Globe Insurance Co*, (supra), at 583, per Mellish LJ; *Provincial Insurance Co of Canada v Leduc* (1874) LR 6 PC 224 (marine insurance); *North British and Mercantile Insurance Co v McLellan* (1892) 21 SCR 288.

[20] *Castellain v Preston* (1883) 11 QBD 380 at 401, CA, per Bowen LJ.

[1] Cf *Westminster Fire Office v Glasgow Provident Investment Society* (1888) 13 App Cas 699 at 704, per Lord Selborne.

[2] *Caldwell v Stadacona and Fire and Life Insurance Co* (1883) 11 SCR 212.

insurers its full value, although the market value of his interest as tenant is, in fact, diminished by the existence of the covenant.[3] Even a tenant, who is under no such covenant, is entitled to recover more than the market value of his tenancy,[4] seeing that such a sum will, in most cases, fall far short of an indemnity. By the loss of the property he is deprived of the beneficial enjoyment of the house in which he is living, as well as of its pecuniary value.[5] On the other hand, the insured is never entitled to more than an indemnity, and, therefore, circumstances which show that in the particular case his loss does not amount to, and cannot fairly be measured by, the value of the subject-matter, may be taken into consideration.[6]

The fact that the value of the insured's interest, after taking all the circumstances of the case into consideration, falls short of the value of the subject-matter, does not necessarily preclude him from recovering more than the value of such interest. In certain circumstances he may be entitled to recover the full value of the subject-matter. Since, however, the contract is a contract of indemnity, he cannot in such a case retain for his own benefit the whole amount recovered, but must, after appropriating as much of it as may be required to indemnify himself in respect of his personal loss, hold the balance in trust for the persons actually entitled to it.

In order to enable the insured, whose interest is limited in value, to recover the full value of the subject-matter, the following conditions must be fulfilled:

1   The form of the policy must be such as to enable the insured to recover the full value.

2   The insured must, at the time of insuring, intend to insure the whole value of the subject-matter for the purpose of covering not merely his own limited interest, but the interest of all other persons who are interested in the subject-matter.

3   There must be no statute prohibiting the insured from recovering the full amount of his insurance.

1 Form of the Policy

The form of the policy must be such as to enable the insured to recover the full value.[7] According to the ordinary form of policy, except in the case of goods held in trust or on commission, the insurance is effected by the insured on his own behalf, and does not purport to be effected on behalf of any other persons interested.

---

[3] In this case, however, his insurable interest depends not merely upon his possessory right as tenant, but also, and principally, upon his liability to the lessor, which is plainly to be measured by the value of the demised premises.

[4] *Castellain v Preston*, (supra), at 400, per Bowen, LJ; *Andrews v Patriotic Assurance Co (No 2)* (1886) 18 LR Ir 355 at 366, per Palles CB.

[5] *Castellain v Preston*, (supra), at 400, per Bowen LJ, explaining *Simpson v Scottish Union Insurance Co* (1863) 1 Hem & M 618.

[6] *Castellain v Preston*, (supra), at 401, per Bowen LJ: 'A man cannot be compensated simply by paying him for the marketable value of his interest. But it does not follow from that that he gets or can keep more than he has lost. I very much doubt whether, if a life tenant, having intended to insure only his life interest, dies within a week after the loss by fire, the Court would award his executors the whole value of the house'.

[7] *Castellain v Preston*, (supra), at 398, per Bowen, LJ.

The insured, may, however, so limit himself by the way in which he insures as not really to insure the whole value of the subject-matter, but only the value of his own interest therein.[8]

2 Intention to Cover Interests of Other Persons

The insured must intend to insure the interest of all other persons who are interested in the subject-matter.[9]

The question of his intention in insuring is a question of fact in each case, and he cannot recover more than the value of his own interest, unless it is shown that he intended at the time to cover more interests than his own.[10]

Thus, a carrier or wharfinger or other bailee, may, if he has effected an insurance on the goods entrusted to him[11] for their full value, for the purpose of covering not merely his own interest in them, but the interest of the owner also, recover the full value from the insurers. His right to do so is not affected by the fact that in the circumstances he is himself under no liability to the owner for their safety, the only question being whether it was his intention to protect the owner's interest as well as his own.[12]

Similarly, a mortgagee or an unpaid vendor, or a tenant for life, or years, may, if the amount of the insurance specified in the policy permits, recover the full value of the subject-matter, notwithstanding the fact that his own interest therein is limited, provided that the policy was effected for the purpose of covering not only his own interest, but also the interest of the mortgagor, purchaser, remainderman, or landlord, as the case may be.[13]

3 No Statutory Prohibition

There must be no statute prohibiting the insured from recovering the full amount of his insurance.[14] In the case of an insurance upon goods, no statutory prohibition exists. Where, however, the insurance is upon houses, buildings, or similar property, a question arises as to how far the provisions of the Life Assurance Act 1774 apply.[15]

4 Life Assurance Act 1774

(a) Provisions of the Act

The provisions of the Life Assurance Act 1774, by which the right of an insured with a limited interest to recover the full value of the subject-matter may be restricted, are the following:

---

8 *Castellain v Preston* (1883) 11 QBD 380 at 398, CA, per Bowen LJ.
9 *Castellain v Preston*, (supra).
10 See Ivamy, *General Principles of Insurance Law* (4th edn, 1979), pp 572–574.
11 As to the necessity of describing them as 'goods in trust or on commission'. see pp 96–97, ante.
12 See Ivamy, op cit, pp 572–574.
13 See Ivamy, op cit, p 573.
14 *Waters v Monarch Fire and Life Assurance Co* (1856) 5 E & B 870 at 882, per Wightman J.
15 Section 4 expressly exempts goods from its operation.

    i No policy is to be made without inserting the name or names of the person or persons interested, or for whose use, benefit, or on whose account the policy[16] is made.[17]

    ii No greater sum is to be recovered from the insurers than the amount or value of the interest[18] of the insured in the event.[19]

(b) Effect of the Act

Though the language of the statute is sufficiently wide to apply to policies of fire insurance since it includes within its ambit not only policies on lives, but also generally on other events,[20] the question whether its provisions affect the right of an insured with a limited interest to recover more than the value of his interest appears to be still undecided.

These provisions seem to be inconsistent with each other in that the first requires the names of the other persons whose interests are intended to be covered to be inserted in the policy, whilst at the same time the second provides that nothing more can be recovered than the value of the interest of the insured, so that, apparently, in spite of the insertion of the names of the other persons interested, the value of their interests cannot be recovered under the policy.

The first provision is imperative in its terms, requiring the names of all persons interested to appear in the policy.[1] It seems, therefore, to be necessary for a lessee or a tenant for life, who intends by his insurance to cover the interest of the lessor or remainderman[2] as well as his own, to insert the name of the lessor or remainderman in the policy, if the latter's interest is to be adequately protected.

In practice, however, the insured may insure in his own name without the name of the other person interested appearing on the face of the policy.[3] If this practice does not contravene the statute, it must be on the ground that the insertion of the other names in cases such as these is unnecessary. It is possible that the statute is intended to meet the case where the policy is effected on behalf of other persons for the purpose of covering their interests, and of enabling them to enforce the policy in case of need themselves, as being insured under it,[4] or, in other words, where the nominal insured is in effect their agent.

---

[16] This implies a written document: *Carlill v Carbolic Smoke Ball Co* [1892] 2 QB 484 at 493, (contract) per Hawkins J.

[17] Life Assurance Act 1774, s 2.

[18] This means pecuniary interest: *Halford v Kymer* (1830) 10 B & C 724 at 728 (life insurance) per Lord Tenterden CJ.

[19] Life Assurance Act 1774, s 3.

[20] Cf *Paterson v Powell* (1832) 9 Bing 320 at 327 et seq (bets on shares) per Tindal CJ.

[1] *Hodson v Observer Life Assurance Society* (1857) 8 E & B 40 at 42, (life insurance) per Erle J; *Evans v Bignold* (1869) L R 4 Q B 622 at 636, (life insurance) per Lush J.

[2] The provisions under consideration can have no application in the cases where an express power of insuring beyond the value of their interest is conferred by statute on mortgagees and others.

[3] Many policies, however, contain a statement that no other person is interested.

[4] See *Collett v Morrison* (1851) 9 Hare 162 (life insurance), where the policy was effected by a trustee, but the names of both parties appeared on its face; *Shilling v Accidental Death Insurance Co* (1857) 2 H & N 42 (accident insurance); *Dowker and Armour v Canada Life Assurance Co* (1865) 24 U C R 591 (life insurance), where it was held that the policy was void under the statute on the ground that the names of the persons interested were not inserted, and that a separate declaration of trust could not be incorporated into the policy.

Where, therefore, his intention is only to protect their interests in addition to his own, and to give them a share in the proceeds of the policy after his own loss is fully made good, it may be suggested that there is no need to specify their names, since they do not in reality become persons interested until after the proceeds have been received, and are, therefore, never, in fact, interested during the currency of the policy.

This explanation cannot be regarded as satisfactory, and is inconsistent with the language of the statute, since the policy is certainly effected for their benefit, if not for their account. It is also possible to defend the practice on the ground that, since the insured is himself interested, the insertion of his name is a sufficient compliance with the statute.[5]

This explanation is, however, equally inconsistent with the language of the statute, which is perfectly general in its terms, and requires the insertion of the name or names of the person or persons interested. It is, therefore, difficult to resist the conclusion that the practice in question cannot be justified if the statute is to be considered as applying to policies of fire insurance.

The second provision raises difficulties which are well-nigh insuperable, inasmuch as it restricts the amount recoverable to the amount or value of the interest of the insured. In the case of life insurance, to which this statute primarily applies, the restriction precludes the insured from recovering more than the amount or value of his interest at the time of effecting the policy, and nothing further can be recovered,[6] though at the same time he is permitted to recover that amount in spite of the fact that he has no insurable interest at the time when his claim arises under the policy.[7]

In applying this provision to policies of fire insurance, it is therefore necessary to consider its effect upon the amount or value of the interest of the insured. It has never been suggested, in the case of life insurance, that a creditor might insure the life of his debtor for a sum exceeding the amount of his debt, with the intention of covering other debts due to other creditors, and that he could upon the death of the debtor recover the full sum insured. The language of the statute is clear, and it seems impossible to hold, in the case of a policy of fire insurance, that the statute allows a person with a limited interest to recover more than the value of his own interest.[8]

Where the names of the other persons interested are, in fact, inserted in the policy, it may be said that such persons are in a sense the insured under the policy, and that the value of the amount of their interests is recoverable as being 'the amount or value of the interest of the insured' within the meaning of the statute.

---

[5] It may be pointed out that in the life insurance cases cited above, the nominal insured appears to have had no interest in his own right, and that consequently the policies would be invalid by reason of the lack of insurable interest, if the names of the real beneficiaries were not inserted. In the case under discussion, however, the insured has himself a sufficient insurable interest to support the validity of the policy, and, therefore, the policy is not invalid on the face of it where the names of the other persons interested are omitted.

[6] *Hebdon v West* (1863) 3 B & S 579 (life insurance); *Barnes v London, Edinburgh and Glasgow Insurance Co* [1892] 1 Q B 864 at 865, (life insurance) per Lord Coleridge C J; *Griffiths v Fleming* [1909] 1 K B 805 at 814, C A (life insurance) per Vaughan Williams L J.

[7] *Dalby v India and London Assurance Co* (1854) 15 C B 365 (life insurance).

[8] Cf *Hebdon v West*, (supra), at 591, per Wightman J.

Where, however, as may be the case, their names are not so inserted, this cannot apply, and it becomes necessary to consider whether the value of the insured's interest can by any possibility be taken to include the value of their interests. For this purpose it must be argued that in the circumstances of the particular case the value of the insured's interest is to be taken as the full value of the subject-matter.

This may possibly be established by showing that the insured may be regarded as in a sense interested in the whole subject-matter, inasmuch as in certain cases he may wish to reinstate it. This he cannot do unless he receives a sum adequate for the purpose, and hence he may be entitled to recover its full value. He recovers the full value, however, on the strength of his own interest in the reinstatement, and need not, therefore, show that he intended to benefit any other person than himself. Where, however, the value of his interest is, taken by itself, less than the full value of the subject-matter, he will be more than fully indemnified if he receives and retains anything beyond the actual value of his own interest.[9] To justify the recovery and retention of a larger amount, it is necessary for him, as in the case of insurances upon goods, to have recourse to the interests of other persons, and to show that he intended to include their interests in his policy.

This amount does not represent the value of his interest only, but covers the value of other interests belonging to persons who are not in any sense the insured under the policy. Even if it is admitted by the insurers in an action upon the policy, after it has been made apparent that the insured is not fully interested, that his intention was to cover the interests of other persons as well as his own, such interests are nevertheless not his own, and their value cannot, therefore, be recovered as being included in the amount or value of his interest. It therefore appears impossible to explain on this ground the right of the insured to recover the value of other interests than his own.

Further, it may be shown that the insured may be regarded as interested in the whole subject-matter, inasmuch as by intending to insure other interests than his own, and by effecting a policy in accordance with such intention, he is to be considered as a trustee of the proceeds of the policy on their behalf. He is certainly a trustee of the proceeds when once they have come into his hands; and it is but a slight extension to hold that he is in a sense a trustee from the inception of the insurance, and that his interest as insured is partly his own beneficial interest in the subject-matter, and partly his interest as a trustee. If this is so, there may be no contravention of the statute in allowing him to recover the full value, since it may possibly be said in such a case that he does not recover a greater sum than the value of his interest as insured. This explanation is equally unsatisfactory, and the language of the statute cannot fairly be interpreted as allowing the insurances under discussion. It therefore appears necessary to conclude either that such insurances contravene the statute, and are unlawful, or that the statute was never intended to apply, and does not in fact apply to policies of fire insurance.

It is more probable that the right of an insured, who has a limited interest only in houses or buildings, to cover the interests of other persons as well as his own, is not in any way affected by the provisions of the Life Assurance Act 1774 on the grounds that the statute does not apply to fire insurance at all.

---

[9] *Castellain v Preston* (1883) 11 QBD 380 at 401, CA, per Bowen LJ.

In support of this view the following points may be suggested for consideration:

   i The statute has never in practice been treated as applicable to fire insurance.

   ii The mischief which the statute was intended to remedy, did not, at the time of its passing, exist in connection with fire insurance.

   iii According to the construction placed on the statute in its application to life insurance, the amount recoverable by the insured is the value of his interest at the time of effecting the policy, and the fact that at the date of the loss his interest had ceased to exist does not prevent him from recovering this amount.

(i) Statute Never Treated as Applicable

Fire policies are frequently effected to cover other interests, and though, as a rule, the names of the other persons interested are inserted, this is not always done.

The question whether a fire policy may lawfully be effected to cover the interests of other persons has been discussed by the Courts on many occasions. This question has been treated as exclusively depending on the intention of the insured.[10] The provision requiring the names of the other persons interested to be inserted in the policy has never been referred to, and it has never been suggested that the omission of their names affected the position. On the contrary, the name inserted in the policy has been regarded as a matter of indifference.[11]

Nor has it ever been suggested that the provision of the statute as to the amount recoverable by the insured might limit his right to enforce the policy for the benefit of all the interests which he intended to cover. Indeed, no reference appears to have been made to this provision at all. Further, the provision requiring the insured to have an insurable interest, and invalidating the policy in its absence, has not been mentioned in any of the fire insurance cases dealing with the question of insurable interest.

Having regard to the fact that it is the duty of the Court to take the objection of illegality under the statute, if sound,[12] the judicial silence is significant.[13]

---

10 See eg *Rayner v Preston* (1881) 18 Ch D 1, CA, where Brett LJ at 10, points out that the defendants did not insure on behalf of any undisclosed principal, or on behalf of any person interested other than themselves.

11 *Nichols & Co v Scottish Union and National Insurance Co* (1885) 2 TLR 190, where Cave J at 191, says, on a question arising as to whether a policy on mills effected by a mortgagee, covered the mortgagor's interest, that whether the name of the mortgagor or mortgagee was given in a policy was immaterial to the mortgagee; *Matthey v Curling* [1922] 2 AC 180 where Atkin LJ at 199, regarded the question whether an insurance in the name of the tenant covered the lessor's interest as one of intention. See also ibid, at 241, per Lord Atkinson.

12 *Griffiths v Fleming* [1909] 1 KB 805 at 820, CA (life insurance) per Farwell LJ.

13 See particularly *Castellain v Preston* (1883) 11 QBD 380, CA, where Bowen LJ at 398 et seq, exhaustively discusses the legality of insurance to cover other interests and never mentions the statute. The only judicial reference to the statute appears to be *Hordern v Federal Mutual Insurance Co of Australia* (1924) 24 SR NSW 267, where the Court declined to 'determine the debateable question' whether the statute applied to fire policies, but held that, if it did, a policy effected by an insured, who was described in it as mortgagee of B, complied with the statute and covered B's

(ii) Non-existence of Mischief

It may be argued that the mischief which the statute was intended to remedy did not, at the time of its passing, exist in connection with fire insurance.[14]

The statute made a change in the Common Law, and was intended to invalidate policies of life insurance, where the insured had no insurable interest, in the same manner as policies of marine insurance without interest had previously been invalidated by the Marine Insurance Act 1745, both kinds of policies having, before the respective statutes, been valid at Common Law in spite of the absence of an interest in the insured.[15] In the case of fire insurance, however, it was, even before the date of either statute, necessary for the insured to prove an insurable interest,[16] and therefore in this branch of the law no change was required.[17]

(iii) Amount Recoverable by Insured

In the case of life insurance the amount recoverable by the insured is the value of his interest at the time of effecting the policy, even though at the date of the loss his interest had ceased to exist.[18]

In the case of a policy of fire insurance, however, the insured cannot recover more than an indemnity, which is to be measured by the value of his interest at the date of the loss, and, moreover, if, at that date, he has no interest, he cannot recover at all.

If, therefore, the statute applies to fire insurance, the same construction must apparently be placed on it in the case of fire insurance as in the case of life

---

interest. The statute has been referred to in the following reported cases— *Waters v Monarch Fire and Life Assurance Co* (1856) 5 E & B 870, where Counsel (afterwards Mellish L J) stated that the statute did not apply to fire insurance, if the insurance was not by way of gaming and wagering, but was a bona fide insurance for the benefit of the persons interested; *London and North-Western Rly Co v Glyn* (1859), as reported 28 L J Q B 188; *Grover & Grover Ltd v Mathews* (1910), as reported in 15 Com Cas 249; *Re Bladon, Dando v Porter* [1911] 2 Ch 350 (settlement).

[14] It may be pointed out that in *Griffiths v Fleming* [1909] 1 K B 805, C A (life insurance) the Court held that, even in the case of life insurance, insurances by husband or wife on the life of the other were not within the mischief of the statute, and hence, notwithstanding the statute, it was unnecessary in such insurances to prove the existence or amount of a pecuniary interest.

[15] *Dalby v India and London Life Assurance Co* (1854) 15 C B 365 at 387, (life insurance) per Parke B: 'Policies of assurance against fire and against marine risks, are both properly contracts of indemnity—the insurer engaging to make good, within certain limited amounts, the losses sustained by the assured in their buildings, ships and effects. Policies on maritime risks were afterwards used improperly and made mere wagers on the happening of those perils. This practice was limited by the 19 Geo 2, c 37, and put an end to in all except a few cases. But, at Common Law, before this statute with respect to maritime risks, and the 14 Geo 3, c 48, as to insurances on lives, it is perfectly clear that all contracts for wager policies, and wagers which were not contrary to the policy of the law, were legal contracts'. See also *Ramloll Thackoorseydass v Soojanmull Dhoondumull* (1848) 6 Moo P C 300 at 312 (wager).

[16] *Sadlers' Co v Badcock* (1743) 2 Atk 554 at 556, per Lord Hardwicke: 'These insurances from fire have been introduced in later times, and, therefore, differ from insurance of ships, because there *interest or no interest* is almost constantly inserted, and, if not inserted, you cannot recover unless you prove a property'. See also *Lynch v Dalzell* (1729) 4 Bro Parl Cas 431.

[17] It is to be noted that in *Dalby v India and London Assurance Co* (supra), Parke B, after referring to a policy of fire insurance, makes no further reference to it, and confines his discussion entirely to marine and life policies.

[18] *Dalby v India and London Life Assurance Co*, (supra).

insurance, and accordingly it will be necessary to draw the conclusion that a contract of fire insurance, when relating to houses, buildings or similar structures, is not a contract of indemnity at all, and the insured has a statutory right to recover the value of his interest at the inception of insurance, notwithstanding the fact that it no longer exists.[19]

If this construction is to be rejected as inconsistent with the authorities, as it certainly is, it becomes necessary to hold that the same words of the same section of the statute are to be construed in a different, and indeed in a conflicting sense, according as the policy relates to life insurance or to fire insurance. Either construction presents difficulties, and it may, therefore, be concluded that the statute does not, in fact, apply to fire insurance.

---

[19] The converse position arises in some types of insurance, eg that of a builder's risk in building a house, and in reinsurance under treaty, where there is no insurable interest or very small interest at the time when the policy is effected.

CHAPTER 22

Contribution to expenses of London Fire Brigade

Every insurance company which insures from fire any property in Greater London[1] must pay annually to the Greater London Council by way of contribution to the expenses of the London Fire Brigade a sum after the rate of £35 in £1,000,000 on the gross amounts insured by it, except by way of reinsurance in respect of property in Greater London.[2]

All contributions due from an insurance company to the Greater London Council are specialty debts and are recoverable accordingly.[3]

For the purpose of ascertaining the amount to be contributed, every such insurance company, on every 1 June, or on such other dates as the Greater London Council may appoint, must make a return to the Council in such form as they may require on the gross amount insured by it in respect of property in Greater London.[4]

There must be annexed to the return a declaration made by the secretary or other officer performing the duties of secretary of the company that he has examined the return with the books of the company, and that to the best of his knowledge, information and belief, it contains a true and faithful account of the gross amount of the sums insured by the company in respect of property in Greater London.[5]

The return made in the June of one year does not come into effect till 1 January of the succeeding year, and is the basis of the contribution for that year.[6]

If a company makes default in making such returns, it renders itself liable to a penalty not exceeding £5 for every day during which it is in default.[7]

The secretary or other officer having the custody of the books and papers of any insurance company that is required to pay a contribution, must allow any officer appointed by the Greater London Council to inspect, during the hours of business, any books and papers which will enable him to ascertain the amount of property insured by the company in Greater London, and the amount for which it is insured, and to make extracts from such books or papers.[8]

---

[1] Metropolitan Fire Brigade Act 1865, s 13, as amended by London Government Act 1963, s 48 (3). As to the definition of 'Greater London', see ibid., s 2 (2).

[2] Metropolitan Fire Brigade Act 1865, s 13.

[3] Ibid, s 14. An action on a specialty debt is barred after 12 years: Limitation Act 1980, s 8 (1).

[4] Metropolitan Fire Brigade Act 1865, s 15.

[5] Ibid, s 15.

[6] Ibid, s 15.

[7] Ibid, s 16. As to recovery of penalties, see ibid., s 24.

[8] Ibid, s 17.

Any secretary or other such officer of a company, who fails to comply with the above requirements in respect of such inspections and extracts, is liable on summary conviction to a penalty not exceeding £5 for each offence.[9]

If the companies insuring property within Greater London, or any such number as may in the opinion of the Greater London Council be sufficient, establish a force of men charged with the duty of attending at fires and saving insured property, it is the duty of the fire brigade, with the sanction of the Council and subject to any regulations that may be made by the Council, to afford the necessary assistance to that force in the performance of their duties.[10]

Further, upon the application of any officer of that force, the fire brigade must hand over to their custody property that may be saved from fire. No charge must be made by the Council for the services thus rendered by the fire brigade.[11]

The London Fire Brigade must, on the morning of each day with the exception of Sundays, send information by post or otherwise to all insurance companies, which contribute, of all fires which have taken place within Greater London since the preceding return, in such form as may be agreed upon by the Council and the companies.[12]

---

[9] Metropolitan Fire Brigade Act 1865, s 17. As to the recovery of penalties, see ibid, s 24. It is not thought that this penalty is affected by either the Criminal Law Act 1977, s 31 (6) or the Criminal Justice Act 1982, s 38 (1) since under the Metropolitan Fire Brigade Act 1865, s 24 penalties are payable to the Greater London Council and not to the Crown.

[10] Metropolitan Fire Brigade Act 1865, s 29.

[11] Ibid, s 29. This force has been established and is known as the London Salvage Corps.

[12] Ibid, s 31.

PART II
Motor insurance

CHAPTER 23

Introduction

This Part of this book deals exclusively with Motor Insurance. Although to a certain extent it is complete in itself, it should be read in conjunction with the first volume in this series,[1] especially with regard to such matters as, eg the making of the contract, the premium, and the construction of the policy, for these topics are common to all branches of the law of insurance.

It is the purpose of this Part of this book to discuss in more detail those aspects which particularly concern Motor Insurance.

The insured is required to answer certain questions in the proposal form.[2] He is under a duty to disclose to the insurers all material facts and not to make any misrepresentations.[3]

Various matters are set out in the body of the policy, whilst others are mentioned in the Schedule to the policy.[4] The policy may cover injury to the insured,[5] and loss of or damage to the insured vehicle.[6] It may also cover a person driving with the consent of the insured, or the insured himself whilst he is driving cars other than the insured vehicle.[7] It is the practice of the insurers to insert "exceptions" in the policy.[8] The insured is under a duty to observe the "conditions" imposed by the policy.[9]

Any claim made by the insured must be in accordance with the procedure laid down by the terms of the policy.[10]

Insurance against liability in respect of the death of or personal injury to third parties is generally compulsory.[11]

In certain circumstances a third party has a direct right to claim against the insurers in respect of injuries which he has suffered by reason of the negligent driving of the insured or of a person driving with the insured's consent.[12]

---

[1] Ivamy, *General Principles of Insurance Law* (4th edn, 1979), Supplement 1982.
[2] See Chapter 24, post.
[3] See Chapter 25, post.
[4] See Chapter 26, post.
[5] See Chapter 27, post.
[6] See Chapter 28, post.
[7] See Chapter 29, post.
[8] See Chapter 30, post.
[9] See Chapter 31, post.
[10] See Chapter 32, post.
[11] See Chapter 33, post.
[12] See Chapter 34, post.

The contents of the proposal form

The contents of the proposal form will vary from company to company.[1] But, in general, the contents are substantially the same.

Thus, the proposer will have to give his name and address and occupation in full and the class of insurance required eg (i) comprehensive (ii) third party, fire and theft; (iii) third party

The particulars of the car to be insured, eg the make and model, the registration, number the seating capacity, the year, the make, the value, and whether the proposer is the owner of any other vehicle must be stated.

The proposer must state whether the car is used solely for private purposes, and whether he will be the sole driver. His age must be given, and any details of any physical defects from which he suffers.

The insurance company will want to know whether he has ever been involved in an accident in the car to be insured, and whether he has ever made any claims in connection with any other car.

The proposer may be asked whether he has ever been convicted in respect of any offence in relation to the driving of cars eg in the last 3 years, or had his licence endorsed. Sometimes this question is extended in its scope so that the proposer has to give the details of any previous conviction of those persons whom he expects will drive the vehicle.

He is also asked whether any insurance company has declined his proposal or required an increased premium or imposed special conditions or cancelled or refused to renew his policy.

He then has to sign a declaration stating that the answers he has given are true, and that he agrees that the declaration shall be the 'basis' of the contact.

---

[1] For a specimen proposal form, see Appendix V, pp 413–415, post.

CHAPTER 25

Non-disclosure and misrepresentation

As in the case of all other branches of the law of insurance the insured is under a duty to make a full disclosure of all material facts, and not to make any misrepresentation of material facts.[1]

If there is no 'basis clause' in the proposal form or the policy, the insurer is entitled to avoid the policy only where the fact which has not been disclosed or which has been misrepresented is a material one.[2]

But where there is a 'basis clause', the insurer can avoid the policy whether the fact, which has not been disclosed or which has been misrepresented, is material or not.[3]

This chapter relates to:

1 Examples of material and immaterial facts.
2 The time at which the answer given by the insured must be correct.
3 Waiver of non-disclosure.
4 The burden of proving that a mis-statement has been made by the insured.
5 Continuing warranties.

EXAMPLES OF MATERIAL AND IMMATERIAL FACTS

As in other branches of insurance, whether a particular circumstance is material or not is a question of fact in each case.[4]

The decided cases on this topic in motor insurance can conveniently be classified into various groups in so far as they relate to:

1 The personal details of the proposer.
2 Driving experience.
3 Previous accidents.
4 Previous convictions.
5 Details of car proposed to be insured.
6 Previous losses and accidents to cars owned by proposer.
7 Other insurers.

---

[1] See Ivamy, *General Principles of Insurance Law* (4th edn, 1979), pp 132–196.
[2] See ibid, pp 183–184.
[3] See ibid, pp 181–183.
[4] See generally, ibid, p 141.

1 Personal Details of Proposer

(a) Age of Proposer

The age of the proposer may be a material fact.

Thus, in *Broad v Waland*[5] the proposer stated in the proposal form that his age last birthday was 21, whereas, in fact, he was just over 19½ years old. The proposal form was declared to be the 'basis' of the contract, and was subject to the express condition that the cover note and certificate of insurance were only issued by the underwriters and must only be accepted by the proposer on the distinct understanding that they did not apply if he was under 21. An accident occurred, and the underwriters claimed that they were entitled to avoid liability on the policy.

Atkinson J held that they could do so. It was a perfectly clear case of a cover note being obtained by non-disclosure or by a misrepresentation of a fact which was false in a material particular, and false to the knowledge of the person making it.

(b) Occupation of Insured

The occupation of the proposer may be a material fact which it is his duty to disclose.

Thus, in *Holmes v Cornhill Insurance Co Ltd*[6] a bookmaker wished to effect an insurance policy in respect of a car, and in the proposal form stated that he was a dealer. The form contained a 'basis' clause. When a claim was made under the policy, the insurance company repudiated liability on the ground that his statement that he was a dealer was untrue, and that he had failed to disclose that he was a bookmaker. The arbitrator, before whom the case first came, held that the company was entitled to do so because the statement was false, and that the fact that he was a bookmaker was material. Further, the proposer knew of its materiality because he had been told by the company's branch manager that it would not insure bookmakers. The arbitrator's decision was upheld by Morris J, on appeal to the King's Bench Division.

Again, in *McNealy v Pennine Insurance Co Ltd*[7], in answer to a question asking what his occupation was, the proposer replied 'Property repairer'. He was also a part-time musician. But his brokers knew from a leaflet issued by the insurance company that part-time musicians were among those persons whom the company were unwilling to insure. Nevertheless, the brokers effected a policy with the company. The proposer was involved in an accident resulting in damage to his car and personal injuries to his passenger. When he claimed an indemnity under the policy, the company repudiated liability on the ground that he had failed to disclose a material fact ie that he was a part-time musician. The Court of Appeal[8] gave judgment for the company. Lord Denning MR, in giving judgment, said that if the company had known this fact, they would not have given him any cover at all.[9]

---

[5] (1942) 73 Ll L Rep 263, K B.
[6] (1949) 82 Ll L Rep 575, K B.
[7] [1978] 2 Lloyd's Rep 18, C A.
[8] Lord Denning M R, Shaw and Waller L JJ.
[9] [1978] 2 Lloyd's Rep at 20.

(c) Physical Condition of Insured

The physical condition of the insured is material and the proposal form often contains a question relating to this matter.

In *James v British General Insurance Co Ltd*[10] the insurance company sought to avoid liability on the ground that the insured had made a false statement in the proposal form as to his physical condition. Roche J, reviewed the evidence,[11] and held that the allegation had not been made out, and that the insured was entitled to an indemnity in respect of the damages which he had had to pay to a third party injured in a motor accident.

His Lordship said:[12]

> 'The next point is that it is said that the plaintiff made untrue answers to a question in the proposal when he said that he was free from physical defects and infirmities, a statement which he made in January 1924, when this policy was first effected. The answer to that again is an answer of fact. I find upon the evidence that the plaintiff was at that date free from any physical defect or infirmity. He had at an earlier stage when he was in the Air Force, by reason of the service, a slight hernia, and he had some giddiness and some functional heart trouble, not amounting to a physical or permanent defect. His war record has been put in, and some time before this declaration was made all disability had ceased: all pension or other results had ceased, and the plaintiff had never claimed any more, because there was nothing to claim in respect of. He was cured and he was free at the material time, which is the time of the declaration, from any physical defect or infirmity.'

(d) Use of Maiden Instead of Married Name

The fact that the proposer uses her maiden name in signing the proposal form when she is, in fact, married, has been held to be a breach of warranty that all the statements which she has made in the form are true.[13]

In *Dunn v Ocean Accident and Guarantee Corpn Ltd*[14] the proposer signed a proposal form warranting the truth of the statements in it. She signed in her maiden name, viz Miss Dorothy Mary Treece—but for over four years had been secretly married to a Mr Hunt.[15] Avory J, held that there had been a breach of warranty, and that the insurance company was entitled to avoid liability on the policy. He said:[16]

> 'In view of the fact that the plaintiff was here entering into a contract which involved her in liability to pay premiums, and involved the defendant company in the risk, I have come to the conclusion that to state her name which was her maiden name was not a complete and correct statement of her name at that time.

---

[10] (1927) 27 Ll L Rep 328, KB. The case is considered on other points, viz (i) whether the insured had falsely stated that he was the owner of the car; and (ii) whether the insurance was void as being against public policy, at p 206, post, and Ivamy, *General Principles of Insurance Law* (4th edn, 1979), p 283, respectively.

[11] The evidence is set out at (1927) 27 Ll L Rep 328, at 329 and 331.

[12] Ibid, at 331.

[13] *Dunn v Ocean Accident and Guarantee Corpn Ltd* (1933) 45 Ll L Rep 276, KB.

[14] (1933), 45 Ll L Rep 276, KB.

[15] The manager of the motor car branch of the defendant company's business stated in evidence that the past history of the husband of a woman proposing to take out a motor car policy was most material for an insurance company. Had the company been told that the plaintiff was a married woman, the defendants would have asked for another proposal form from the husband showing what his own experience was.

[16] Ibid, at 280.

> This is not a case, as learned Counsel suggested, of a person who has acquired some particular reputation in her maiden name, and has continued to enjoy that reputation, in some particular vocation, after her marriage. The fact is—I do not want to say anything harsh unnecessarily, but the fact is that the plaintiff and her husband, Hunt, were concurring in using her maiden name for the purpose of deceiving her parents and his parents and her friends. It is not in any sense a case, in my opinion, where she was entitled in a business transaction, entering into a contract, to say that her maiden name was her name by reputation; and in the circumstances I think, therefore, that that statement was not a complete and correct statement of her name.'

When the case went to the Court of Appeal,[17] the insurance company did not press the point,[18] and the case was decided on other grounds.[19]

2 Driving Experience

(a) Previous Driving Experience of Insured

Questions are frequently asked in proposal forms as to the previous driving experience of the proposer.

In *Corcos v De Rougemont*[20] in answer to a question in a proposal form which said: 'Please state how long you have driven a motor car,' the proposer replied on 9 October, 1923: 'Several years'. She had driven cars from 1907 to 1912, and in 1916, and from October 1923. The insurance company repudiated liability on the ground that she had given a false answer, for her answer meant that she had been driving for several years immediately before the proposal was signed.

McCardie J held that the answer was a true one, and was not a ground for avoiding the policy. The words were ambiguous, and must be read against the insurance company.[1] He observed:[2]

> 'Do those years, "several years," refer to a period immediately preceding the signing of the proposal or must these words be taken in the answer to the question: "How long have you driven a motor car?" as referring to a time at some period before but not immediately preceding the issue of the proposal.
>
> It is plain that if the words are taken to mean a period just preceding the issue of the policy, many curious results would follow. It might well be that a man or woman had driven a car up to within a year of the time of the signing of the proposal form, and then by going abroad or for some other reason had not been able to drive a car. A further illustration is that of a chauffeur who might have driven a car for ten years up to within two years of the proposal and then have changed his business for a time and not have been driving a car in the interval.
>
> Now how are these words to be interpreted? With regard to a policy of insurance the general rule is, I think, that if the words of a policy are ambiguous, in most cases they are to be read against the insurance company issuing the insurance . . . Here I think the question is ambiguous. I think anybody reading that question as put is entitled to assume that the driving referred to need not be during the driving period immediately preceding the issue of the policy. To hold otherwise would involve many curious anomalies, including the two illustrations I gave a few minutes ago.'

---

[17] (1933) 47 Ll L Rep 129, C A.

[18] See the judgment of Lord Hanworth M R, ibid, at 131.

[19] Ie that she had failed to disclose the material fact that her husband had been involved in accidents. See on this point, p 200, post.

[20] (1925) 23 Ll L Rep 164, K B. Another aspect of this case, viz, the proposer's omission to take out a driving licence is considered p 198, post.

[1] See generally as to the *contra proferentem* rule, Ivamy, *General Principles of Insurance Law* (4th edn, 1979), pp 386–392.

[2] (1925) 23 Ll L Rep 164 at 166.

The learned Judge also remarked that he was bound to say that if insurance companies desired to secure knowledge of the driving experience of proposers in the period just preceding the proposal, the question ought to be framed in a different fashion.

(b) Time for which Licence Held

In *Babatsikos v Car Owners Mutual Insurance Co Ltd*[3] the proposer was asked 'How long have you held a driver's licence?' and answered '3 years and 4 months'. This was clearly a misrepresentation, for he had only held a licence for 3 years. Pape J, however, giving judgment in the Supreme Court of Victoria, held[4] that, on the evidence, the misrepresentation was not material, for it had not been established that the length of time of which the proposer had held a licence was a matter by which a prudent insurer would have been influenced in deciding whether to accept the risk or what premium he would ask had he accepted the risk.

(c) 'Driving Regularly and Continuously'

In *Zurich General Accident and Liability Insurance Co Ltd v Morrison*[5] one of the questions in the proposal form said: 'Have you driven cars regularly and continuously in the United Kingdom during the past twelve months?' The proposer answered 'Yes'. The insurance company repudiated liability on the ground that the insured had for just under 8 months driven regularly and continuously on the highway as well as at the Ebbw Vale Works, and for the last 4 months at the Works on private ground. The Court of Appeal[6] held that the answer he had given was not untrue, and that the company was liable.

MacKinnon LJ, said[7] that the question was one of extreme vagueness. No one could say what was meant by 'driving regularly and continuously', and the experts could not elucidate it. The insured had driven for 12 months, but for part of the time only in the big Works in which he was employed. The question did not say 'on the highway', and he himself could see no reason why it should be implied.

Lord Greene MR said[8] that the question was hopelessly vague, and he was quite unable to give any precise meaning to it. It was most unfortunate that questions framed in such a slovenly way should be put to a person making a proposal for insurance who might afterwards find himself accused of having given a false answer according to the construction which the insurer might, in his particular case, choose to put on the question. The practice was particularly vicious when, as in the present case, the proposer was required to warrant the truth of his answer.[9] Questions of this kind were—he did not say

---

3 [1970] 2 Lloyd's Rep 314.
4 Ibid, at 326–327.
5 (1942) 72 Ll L Rep 167, CA.
6 Lord Greene MR, MacKinnon and Goddard LJJ.
7 (1942) 72 Ll L Rep 167, CA, at 173.
8 Ibid, at 171.
9 As to the 'basis' clause whereby the proposer warrants the truth of the answers which he gives, see Ivamy, *General Principles of Insurance Law* (4th edn, 1979), pp 181–183.

designedly—mere traps, and insurance companies must not be surprised if they were construed strictly against them.[10]

Goddard L J said:[11]

'It is a most embarrassing question, and, if taken literally, no one could answer it otherwise than in the negative. The plaintiffs' witnesses themselves do not seem to know precisely what is meant by it. Mr Boston said it meant, ''at any rate several times a week,'' but when asked a few questions by the learned Judge he soon went away from that. Mr Jackson, the plaintiffs' underwriter, in answer to the learned Judge, agreed that the point was to make sure that the assured was keeping his hand in, and that is what I should myself think was the correct view. In view of the experience of driving that the assured in this case had, I see no ground for holding that this answer was untrue.'

(d) Proposer's Omission to take out Driving Licence

The non-disclosure of the fact that the proposer had failed to take out a driving licence for the period in which she had informed the insurers that she had had driving experience was held not to be material in *Corcos v De Rougemont*.[12]

In this case the proposer had driven a car from 1907 to 1912 and for part of 1916, but held no driving licence during this period, yet had informed the insurers that she had been driving for several years. McCardie J held that her failure to tell them that she had no licence was not material.

He observed:[13]

'Is the fact material? Learned Counsel on both sides, with hearty enthusiasm, each submitted that this point was clear. [Counsel] for the plaintiff said that it had nothing to do with the question, and [Counsel for the defendant] said that it was obvious to all that this was a serious omission. I myself think the point is one of some substance, but in considering the question of materiality one must look at the consequences. If there is a duty on the part of one to disclose that, when driving, one had no licence, it would lead to curious results. [Counsel for the defendant] put it on the footing that where people had been guilty of any breach of law, it should be revealed to the insurance companies so that they might ascertain the character of the person proposing. But the result of that would be that not only must you reveal to the insurance companies the omission to take out a driving licence but any breach of law with regard to anything; and I cannot myself see where the result would end if a person's character is to be weighed in connection with the insurance of a car; and [defending Counsel's] argument comes to this, that he would say it was the duty of a person to reveal to the insurance companies every irregularity in his past life. In my view that is not so; and I am not satisfied that by the omission here this lady is responsible. I would point out one further illustration. If a person had a licence expiring in October, and had not taken out a licence for 3 weeks, and had applied for an insurance and omitted to mention that fact, the insurance companies would be entitled to declare the insurance void.'

His Lordship said that if insurance companies desired information as to the period for which the proposer had held a driving licence, they must frame the question in the proposal form accordingly.

(e) Failure to Pass Driving Test

The mere fact that the insured has failed to pass a driving test has been held not material to underwriters who were issuing an inexperienced driver's policy.[14]

---

[10] As to the *contra proferentem* rule, see Ivamy, op cit, pp 386–392.

[11] (1942) 72 Ll L Rep at 175.

[12] (1925) 23 Ll L Rep 164, K B. Another aspect of this case, viz the previous driving experience of the insured is considered, p 196, ante.

[13] (1925) 23 Ll L Rep 164 at 167.

[14] *Zurich General Accident and Liability Insurance Co Ltd v Morrison* (1942) 72 Ll L Rep 167, C A.

In *Zurich General Accident and Liability Insurance Co Ltd v Morrison*[15] the proposer completed a proposal form for a motor policy. He did not disclose to the insurance company that he had failed his driving test. The Court of Appeal[16] held that this was not a material fact, and that the company could not avoid liability on the ground of non-disclosure.

Goddard L J said:[17]

> 'I cannot believe that if they are willing to insure inexperienced drivers, one, for instance, who has never driven a car in his life, they would refuse to insure one who had received instruction but had not got through his test the first time. It is common knowledge that many would-be drivers have failed several times. One result would be, if this were held material, that if a learner took out a policy admittedly as a learner with the £5 excess clause in it, and had failed to pass a test before he applied for a renewal, he would have to disclose that fact, although all he was seeking was a renewal of the inexperienced driver class of policy. I do not think it would ever occur to anyone in such circumstances to do so; yet if it is material, he has got only a voidable policy. I am well aware that if a fact is material and so ought to be disclosed, it is no answer to say that the assured did not think it was material. Nor is it of itself a good answer to say, 'If it was material, why did you not ask?' Underwriters cannot frame their questions so as to include everything that may affect any particular proposer, and the fact which ought to be disclosed may well be something peculiar to an individual case. But whether or not a person has failed in his test must, I should think, affect a very large number of proposers. The underwriter exhibits to them a long catechism in which he puts questions on matters which may affect any proposer, such as whether the car is to be used for hire, whether the person who will drive has any infirmity, or whether he has been convicted of any motoring offence, and I cannot help thinking that if it is material for the underwriter to know whether or not the proposer has failed in a test, he would ask the question.'

3 Previous Accidents

(a) Previous Accidents of Insured Himself

The fact that a proposer has been involved in a previous accident is usually material.

In *Dent v Blackmore*[18] a proposer in answer to a question in a proposal form stating: 'What accidents have occurred in connection with your motor cars during the past 2 years including cost?' had replied 'Damaged wings'. In the previous year he had had 7 accidents, in each of which the wings of the car had been damaged and in one he had knocked down a woman, and he subsequently received a claim for compensation in respect of her injuries. McCardie J held that the answer given was untrue, and since the truth of statements in the proposal form was declared to be the 'basis' of the contract, the underwriters were entitled to avoid liability.[19] He also said that in any case there had been a non-disclosure of a material fact, and on this ground too the underwriters were not liable.[20]

He said that the answer 'Damaged wings' conveyed to his mind the clear impression that the insured had suffered during the 2 years mentioned one

---

[15] (1942) 72 Ll L Rep 167, C A.
[16] Lord Greene M R, MacKinnon and Goddard L JJ.
[17] (1942) 72 Ll L Rep 167 at 175.
[18] (1927) 29 Ll L Rep 9, K B.
[19] Ibid, at 11.
[20] Ibid, at 12.

accident, and one accident only, of a trivial character—an accident that could rightly be described as one which had resulted only in the unimportant injury of damaged wings. His Lordship then observed:[1]

> 'Prior to the insurance with the defendants, that is, for the year preceding the plaintiff's insurance with the defendants, he had been insured with the Sun Insurance Company under a policy which was substantially similar, and while that insurance policy was running and during the period, January 1924 to January 1925, the plaintiff had had no less than 7 accidents to his motor car. It is an extraordinary number of accidents for such a period, and not only that but in my view it is quite plain that the results of those accidents were not confined to damaged wings at all. It is quite true that in each of the accidents there appears to have been damage to the wings of the plaintiff's car, but in one of them, that of 12 April, 1924, substantial injury was caused to a lady by the plaintiff's motor car. A writ was issued against the plaintiff and he handed it on to the Sun Insurance Company, and the result of that accident was a cost to the Sun Insurance Company of no less than £20 and 10 guineas costs in settlement. And, moreover, in the last of the accidents during this period, that in January 1925, in addition to injuries to both wings there was a strained steering, which is not without significance. The total cost of those 7 claims was well over £100.
>
> In view of those circumstances, to my mind, the answer of the plaintiff was wholly untrue.'

(b) Accident Record of Husband

The accident record of her husband who, to the proposer's knowledge will drive the vehicle, has been held to be a material fact.[2]

In *Dunn v Ocean Accident and Guarantee Corpn Ltd*[3] the insured knew that her husband, who was going to drive the car regularly, had been involved in accidents. She did not disclose them to the insurance company. The Court of Appeal held that this was a ground on which the company was entitled to avoid liability.

Lord Hanworth M R said:[4]

> '[The insured] knew her husband was a dangerous driver and had had a number of accidents.[5] Could anybody suppose that that was not a material fact to know? Any person, any business person, with sufficient knowledge and common sense must know that there is a greater risk in insuring a person who is likely to have an accident because of the way he drives a car. It appears to me that if we have to measure it by any standard, this lady failed to disclose material facts.'

4 Previous Convictions

(a) Previous Convictions of Insured

The previous convictions of the insured have been held to be material facts which the insured should have disclosed.

---

[1] (1927) 29 Ll L Rep 9, K B at 11.

[2] *Dunn v Ocean Accident and Guarantee Corpn Ltd* (1933) 47 Ll L Rep 129, C A.

[3] (1933) 47 Ll L Rep 129, C A.

[4] Lord Hanworth M R, Slesser and Romer L JJ.

[5] In cross-examination the insured agreed that in different letters to her, her husband had written: 'Everything has been going wrong with me lately. First, I had the flu and then I had another crash—this time a friend's car . . . A great tragedy has occurred. I have had another crash. I know it is getting almost monotonous'. For this evidence see (1933) 45 Ll L Rep 276 at 277 in the Court below.

Thus, in *Jester-Barnes v Licenses and General Insurance Co Ltd*[6] the insured had been convicted in 1924 of being drunk in charge of a car and driving in a manner dangerous to the public, and between April 1931 and August 1932 he was convicted once for using an unlicensed car and twice for having no Road Fund licence. Such convictions were held to be material, and since the insured had not disclosed them to the insurance company, the company was entitled to repudiate liability on the policy. The insured had warranted the truth of the statements in the proposal form, and had declared that he had not withheld any material information. MacKinnon J held that on this ground also the company could avoid liability, for the facts stated by the insured were untrue.[7]

But in *Mackay v London General Insurance Co Ltd*[8] Swift J held that the non-disclosure by the insured, who had effected a motor insurance policy, of a previous conviction many months before in respect of a motor cycle because a nut had become loose and he was fined 10/- for driving without efficient brakes, was not material. But his Lordship held that the company was not liable on the policy because it contained a 'basis' clause, and the insured had given an inaccurate answer to the question asked in the proposal form, ie 'Have you or your driver ever been convicted . . .?'

The question may relate to convictions for motoring offences only, but the insured may be under a duty to disclose his convictions in respect of other offences as well.

Thus, in *Cleland v London General Insurance Co Ltd*[9] the insured had anwered 'No' to the question 'Have you or your driver ever been convicted or had a motor licence endorsed?' He had, however, been convicted in January 1922 of breaking and entering a garage and stealing a motor cycle and sidecar. In July 1922 he was convicted of forging a cheque, and in September 1922 of breach of recognisances, and in July 1926 of breaking and entering a shop, and stealing furs and jewellery. The Court of Appeal[10] held that the question in the proposal form related to motoring offences only, but that he should have disclosed the other convictions because he had expressly warranted in the proposal form that he had not withheld any information whatever which might tend in any way to increase the risk of the insurance company or influence the acceptance of the proposal, etc. Consequently the company was entitled to repudiate liability.

Again, in *Taylor v Eagle Star Insurance Co Ltd*[11] MacNaghten J held that the company could avoid liability on the policy because the insured had failed to disclose that he had been previously convicted of drinking offences in no way connected with the driving of a motor vehicle, for such convictions were material.[12]

A question in a proposal form which stated 'Have you or your driver been convicted of any offence in connection with the driving of any motor vehicle?'

---

6 (1934) 49 Ll L Rep 231 K B. The insured also failed to disclose the previous convictions of his chauffeur. See p 203, post.
7 (1934) 49 Ll L Rep 231 at 237.
8 (1935) 51 Ll L Rep 201, K B.
9 (1935) 51 Ll L Rep 156, C A.
10 Greer, Slesser and Roche L JJ.
11 (1940) 67 Ll L Rep 136, K B.
12 Evidence to this effect was given on behalf of the company by the manager of its motor department and by two independent witnesses, who had considerable experience of underwriting and issuing motor insurance policies: see ibid, at 137, 140.

has been held to indicate that it was directed to some offence committed in the act of driving the car, and not merely to an offence under the Road Traffic Acts.[13]

Thus, in *Taylor v Eagle Star Insurance Co Ltd*[14] the insured had replied 'No' to a question in the above form. He had, however, been convicted in 1931 of permitting a car to be used without a policy of insurance, and in 1933 of driving a car with no Road Fund licence in force.[15] MacNaghten J held that the answer which had been given was a true one, and said that he would follow *Revell v London General Insurance Co Ltd*[16] where MacKinnon J had given judgment to similar effect. MacNaghten J said:[17]

> 'It may be said that it would be possible for other people to take a different view of the meaning of the question, but a person who answered the question in the sense in which (MacKinnon J) would have answered it, if it had been addressed to him, cannot, I think, be said to be giving an untrue answer. The question is ambiguous, and if a question is ambiguous, and a person bona fide understands it in a particular sense and that sense is a reasonable sense, he cannot be said to be giving an untrue answer if he answers it truly in the sense in which he understands it.'

Where the insurers allege that the insured has been charged with an offence in connection with the driving of any vehicle, it is not sufficient for them to state that they are unable, before discovery, to give particulars of the offence concerned.[18]

(b) Previous Conviction of Usual Driver

A question in a proposal form stating: '[Has] your driver been convicted of any offence in connection with the driving of any motor vehicle?' has been held to be directed to some offence committed in the act of *driving* the car, and not merely to an offence under the Road Traffic Acts.

Thus, in *Revell v London General Insurance Co Ltd*[19] the insured answered 'No' to a question in the above form. Her usual driver had been convicted in 1932 of unlawfully driving a motor car without having a suitable reflecting mirror, and also of using a motor vehicle without having in force an insurance policy in

---

[13] *Taylor v Eagle Star Insurance Co Ltd* (1940) 67 Ll L Rep 136, K B.

[14] (1940) 67 Ll L Rep 136, K B.

[15] Which were offences under the Road Traffic Acts.

[16] (1934) 50 Ll L Rep 114, K B. This case is considered infra.

[17] Ibid, at 139.

[18] *Butcher v Dowlen* [1981] 1 Lloyd's Rep 310, C A, where the insurers could not obtain information about offences from the Drivers and Vehicles Licence Department at Swansea without the insured's consent nor information from the Criminal Records Office via the police without his consent. See the judgment of Stephenson LJ, ibid, at 312: 'I appreciate the difficulty in which insurers and underwriters may find themselves when they have some information to suggest a breach of warranty or an implied term but are not in a position to prove it; and there may be cases in which they have enough material to put particulars of such an allegation in the defence as is here made, to save them from having their defence struck out. All I would say is that these particulars of these allegations given in compliance with the Master's order are, I would not doubt for the moment, the best the defendants can do, but they do not, in my judgment, entitle them to say "the action should go on, we have a defence which we ought to be allowed to put before the Court".'

[19] (1934) 50 Ll L Rep 114, K B. This decision was followed by MacNaghten J in *Taylor v Eagle Star Insurance Co Ltd* (1940) 67 Ll L Rep 136, K B, supra.

respect to third party risks. Both these offences arose under and were created by the Road Traffic Act 1930. MacKinnon J said that the insured had given a truthful answer to the question, and that the insurance company could not avoid liability on that ground, and observed:[20]

> 'I think that a reasonable person reading this question might quite reasonably regard the purpose of the question as being directed to the carefulness of the driver who is likely to be driving cars under this policy. The most expert and careful driver in the world, who has never been convicted of any offence of careless driving, who never for a moment has departed from the most perfect standard of good and careful driving, could still become liable to a conviction of an offence under these two sections for being in a stationary motor car which had not got a reflecting mirror, and for being out on the road in a stationary motor car which did not have in regard to it a third-party insurance policy in existence.
>
> The real offence, taking these two types of offence, is using a car without a reflecting mirror or without an insurance policy. In itself the offence has nothing to do with the careful or skilful manner or the careless or unskilful manner in which the car is being driven on the road, or its danger as a moving object. I think that the ordinary reasonable man in the street, asked this question, not only might quite honestly say: "No, neither I nor my driver has ever been convicted of an offence in connection with driving this motor car," but when the questioner says, "Well, but were not you convicted of not having a mirror?", he might quite reasonably say: "Yes, but I never thought of that. I do not call that an offence in connection with the driving of the car. As a matter of fact the mirror had fallen off, and I had not noticed it and I had not appreciated it, and it happened when the car was stationary at the side of the road." However, I do not know that I need go into illustrations of that sort. I am not satisfied that reading this question as a reasonable person would and ought to have read it that it was untrue or inaccurate to reply "No" and to omit to say "Yes," by reason of these two convictions, one about the reflecting mirror and the other about the insurance policy.'

(c) Previous Conviction of Insured's Chauffeur

The previous convictions of the insured's chauffeur have been held to be material facts which the insured should have disclosed.

Thus, in *Jester-Barnes v Licenses and General Insurance Co Ltd*[1] the insurance company was held to be entitled to avoid liability because the insured had failed to disclose the fact that his chauffeur, who habitually drove the car, had been convicted in March 1925, and in April 1929 of driving in a manner dangerous to the public, and of using an unlicensed car in 1930.

(d) Previous Conviction of Insured's Son

In *Bond v Commercial Union Assurance Co Ltd*[2] when the proposal form was filled in and the policy was granted, the proposer knew that his son was likely to drive the insured car and had motoring convictions. It was held by the Divisional Court of the King's Bench Division[3] that these were material facts which should have been disclosed, and that, since they had not been disclosed, the insurance company was entitled to avoid liability.

---

[20] (1934) 50 Ll L Rep at 117.
[1] (1934) 49 Ll L Rep 231, K B. The insured also failed to disclose his own previous convictions.
[2] (1930) 36 Ll L Rep 107.
[3] Lord Hanworth M R and Greer L J.

5 Details of Car Proposed to be Insured

(a) *Age of car*

The age of a car has been held to be material.

Thus, in *Santer v Poland*[4] the proposer stated in a proposal form that his Napier car was manufactured in 1918, whereas the correct date of manufacture was 1916. Bailhache J held that the underwriters were entitled to avoid liability on the policy because the proposer's statement was untrue.[5]

(b) *'Cost Price' of Car*

Where a proposal form asks the proposer to state the 'cost price' of the vehicle to be insured, and the answer which he gives is the total of the price actually paid to a dealer and also of the allowance for another car which he gives her when he trades it in, this is not an untrue statement entitling the insurance company to repudiate liability on a policy which includes a 'basis' clause.[6]

Thus, in *Brewtnall v Cornhill Insurance Co Ltd*[7] the question in the proposal form stated: 'Cost price to proposer?' The answer which the proposer gave was '£145'. In fact, she had paid £45 to a dealer who had given her an allowance of £100 in respect of another car which she traded in. The car was destroyed, and the insurance company repudiated liability on the ground that the proposer had made an untrue statement, and had concealed a material fact. The Divisional Court of the King's Bench Division[8] held that the defence failed, and that the company was liable.

Charles J said:[9]

> 'It is said that the cost price to the proposer here is not £145 at all, it is £45; so that if the outstanding £100 which was the value of the [traded-in] car was to be taken into consideration, it ought to have been shown by the proposer in full. Now the proposal form does not say: "What is the consideration given for the car?" It says: "What is the cost price to the proposer?"; and, speaking for myself, the answer given—£145—in these circumstances is not untrue. I do not think it conceals a material fact.'

The learned Judge then said that if the insurance company really wished, in asking the question as to the cost price to the proposer, to have all the ingredients of the costs—not only the cash but all the ingredients—set out in the proposal form, it should frame the question in such a way as would show to the proposer what it was that was expected of him, and just what was intended.

---

[4] (1924) 19 Ll L Rep 29, K B.

[5] In fact, the underwriters had offered to pay £160 in settlement of the claim, but this was refused by the insured. Nevertheless, even though judgment had been given in their favour, the underwriters again offered to pay £160. Bailhache J said that he was glad to hear it and that it was very fair. Counsel added: 'Lloyd's underwriters always are fair.'

[6] *Brewtnall v Cornhill Insurance Co Ltd* (1931) 40 Ll L Rep 166.

[7] (1931) 40 Ll L Rep 166.

[8] Swift and Charles JJ.

[9] (1931) 40 Ll L Rep 166 at 167.

(c) 'Actual Price' paid by Owner

In *Allen v Universal Automobile Insurance Co Ltd*[10] the proposer was asked a question in the proposal form which stated: "What was actual price paid by owner?" He answered £285. In fact he had only paid £271. Lord Wright[11] said that the answer was inaccurate, and since the truth of the proposer's statement had been warranted, the insurance company was entitled to repudiate liability in respect of a loss under the policy.

(d) Ownership of Vehicle

Where a person states in proposal form that he is the owner of the vehicle to be insured, and he is not so in fact, that amounts to a material misrepresentation, and the insurance company is entitled to avoid liability on that ground.[12] Further, where other cars are substituted for the original one with the permission of the company, it is implied that he is the owner of the substituted cars.[13]

In *Guardian Assurance Co Ltd v Sutherland*[14] a proposer named Sutherland, in requesting that a policy be issued in respect of a Mercedes registration No BXD 1, stated in answer to a question in the proposal form that he was the owner of it. In fact, it belonged to another man named Sidebotham. Later Sutherland asked for a Lancia to be substituted for BXD 1. A fortnight later a telegram reached the company saying 'Please cover me on Mercedes EYT 114 as well as Lancia', and was signed 'Sutherland'. The insurance company sent him a cover note in respect of EYT 114. In fact, it was the property of Green Park Motors Ltd. While EYT 114 was being driven by Sidebotham with Sutherland's permission, it collided with a motor cycle and a third party was injured. When a claim was made against the company, it repudiated liability on the ground that the policy had been obtained by misrepresentation.

Branson J accepted this contention, and held that the claim failed. He said it had been argued by counsel for Sidebotham that, although the contract of insurance relating to BXD 1 was obtained by misrepresentation because Sutherland was not the owner, when the Lancia was substituted for BXD 1, a new contract arose which was not invalidated by misrepresentation.

On this point the learned Judge said:[15]

'This contention is disposed of by the language of the form [asking for the substitution to be made]. The form shows that they kept the old contract alive. The same applies when EYT 114 was substituted for the Lancia. The existing contract was altered but it was still to be kept alive.'

In any event even if the cover note in respect of EYT 114 was a new contract, it was plainly obtained by a material misrepresentation. The telegram purporting to come from one who was already insured in respect of the Lancia which he had declared to be his own property, clearly represented that EYT

---

10 (1933) 45 Ll L Rep 55, K B.
11 Sitting as an additional Judge.
12 *Guardian Assurance Co Ltd v Sutherland* (1939) 63 Ll L Rep 220, K B.
13 Ibid.
14 (1939) 63 Ll L Rep 220, K B. The case is referred to on another point, viz whether it could be said that Sidebotham was driving with the consent of Sutherland when, in fact, at the time of the accident the car had already been sold by Green Park Motors Ltd, at p 242, post.
15 (1939) 63 Ll L Rep 220 at 223, K B.

114 was Sutherland's property, and that he was asking for cover against his liabilities in respect of it. It could not be successfully argued that it was not material for the company to know that Sutherland had nothing to do with the car.

In *James v British General Insurance Co Ltd*[16] when the insured claimed an indemnity from the insurance company in respect of damages which he had had to pay to a third party as the result of a motor accident, liability was denied on the ground that the insured had stated that he was the owner of the insured car, a Fiat, whereas, in fact, he was not.

Roche J reviewed the evidence on this point,[17] and held that this contention had not been made out, and that the claim succeeded. He observed:[18]

> 'When he came to acquire the Fiat, he had not got all the money. The plaintiff says it was given: whether it was a gift out and out or an advance, it is not necessary for me to determine; but I find that it was put at the disposition of the plaintiff for the purpose of purchasing the Fiat car, with the intention and on the terms that that was to be the plaintiff's own. The point taken against that contention was that the Fiat car was registered in the name of the father and not of the plaintiff. That was so, but there is nothing in the Motor Car Acts or the schedule thereto to say that a motor car is to be registered in the name of the owner. Frequently, or not infrequently, it is not so registered, and I find that I have been told the truth about this matter: that the registration in the father's name was for some family reasons, to make it appear that the father had some interest in this matter and was not giving this son an unfair amount of money as compared with another brother. It may be—I do not know—that it was considered wise that the father, as he had advanced the money, should have some control over the car in regard to the sale of the car; because a person in whose name it is registered has a good deal of control over the disposition of the car. To that extent and to that extent only had the father any interest in the matter. At best and at most, it was the right of a lender of money and not the right of the owner of the car.'

His Lordship said that he accepted the evidence on this point, and found that the car was the insured's own in the sense that he was the legal owner of it. He was the person entitled to the use and possession of the car, and, in the sense in which the words were used in the proposal form and the policy, he was the owner.

(e) *Situation of Garage*

In one case the situation of the garage where the insured vehicle is usually kept was held not to be material.[19]

In *Dawsons Ltd v Bonnin*[20] the proposer wished to insure a lorry against fire and third party risks. A question in the proposal form said: 'State full address at which the vehicle will be usually garaged'. He answered: '46 Cadogan Street, Glasgow'. There was no accommodation for lorries there, and the lorry was, in fact, garaged at the insured's garage at Dovehill Farm, Newlands, on the outskirts of Glasgow. The lorry was destroyed by fire in that garage, and the

---

[16] (1927) 27 Ll L Rep 328, K B. The case is considered on other points, viz (i) whether the insured has given untrue answers as to his state of health; and (ii) whether the insurance was void as being against public policy, at p 195, ante and Ivamy, *General Principles of Insurance Law* (4th edn, 1979), p 283, respectively.

[17] The evidence is set out in (1927) 27 Ll L Rep 328 at 329 and 331.

[18] Ibid, at 331.

[19] *Dawsons Ltd v Bonnin* [1922] 2 A C 413, H L.

[20] [1922] 2 A C 413, H L.

insured claimed an indemnity under the policy. The insurers refused to pay on the ground that there had been a misrepresentation as to a material fact, ie the situation of the garage.

The House of Lords[1] held that the answer, though untrue, was not a material mis-statement.

Viscount Haldane said:[2]

> 'The chief risks covered by the policy were in the main wholly unconnected with fire at the garage, and the percentage of the premium to be allocated to the risks was very small . . . In all probability no importance would have been attached to any answer to the . . . question in the proposal form of the effect that Dovehill was to be the place of garage.'

Viscount Finlay observed:[3]

> 'In the case of an ordinary policy covering a motor against fire risk the question of the garage might be very material. Its structure[4] and locality might affect the chances of fire or the chance of fire being extinguished if it should break out, but as to the present policy the evidence . . . is quite distinct that the risk of fire in the garage is so insignificant in comparison with the other risks insured, which are those of the road, including fire on the road, which might result from self-ignition, that it is ignored in fixing the premium.'

The House of Lords, however, held[5] that the claim against the insurers failed because the policy contained a 'basis' clause[6] whereby the proposer had warranted the truth of his statements, and this warranty had been broken since the answer given to the question in the proposal form was untrue.

(f) Use of Garage by IRA

In *Johnson & Perrott Ltd v Holmes*[7] a motor policy taken out by a garage proprietor in Ireland covered loss by riots and civil commotions. In April 1922 the garage was entered at night by some armed men who removed the insured car. At the time when the insurance was effected the garage had been used by the Irish Republican Army. In an action on the policy the insurer contended that he was entitled to avoid liability because, in failing to disclose the fact that the garage had been so used, the insured had concealed a material fact. Rowlatt J held that there had been no concealment, and that the claim on the policy succeeded. In the course of his judgment he said.[8]

> 'I do not think there was any concealment of any material fact. It is suggested that a material fact concealed was that Messrs Johnson & Perrott had a garage which was used by the IRA, and in it was the car. It was not a car of which it might have been assumed that it was put away in some shed and nobody knew anything about it. A witness was called. He was one Beale,

---

1 Viscount Haldane, Viscount Finlay, Viscount Cave, Lord Dunedin and Lord Wrenbury.
2 [1922] 2 AC 413 at 420.
3 Ibid, at 429. See further the speech of Lord Dunedin, ibid, at 434; and that of Lord Wrenbury, ibid, at 438.
4 No question as to the *structure* (as distinct from the locality) of the garage was asked in the proposal form. See the speech of Lord Wrenbury: ibid, at 438.
5 By a majority—Viscount Haldane, Viscount Cave, and Lord Dunedin; Lord Finlay and Lord Wrenbury dissenting.
6 As to the 'basis' clause, see Ivamy, *General Principles of Insurance Law* (4th edn, 1979), pp 181–183.
7 (1925) 21 Ll L Rep 330, KB. The case is considered on another point, viz whether the loss fell within the terms of an exception, p 270, post.
8 (1925) 21 Ll L Rep 330 at 332.

who was invited to say it was a material fact. He said it was, but he could not say why when I asked him; and I am not certain he understood the question. This is all the help I could get.'

6 Previous Losses and Accidents to Cars Owned by Proposer

(a) Previous Losses of Cars

The fact that the proposer has suffered losses of cars on previous occasions has been held to be material.

In *Farra v Hetherington*[9] the insured had effected an insurance policy in respect of an Arrol-Aster saloon car, which was stolen when he left it in the street. The proposal form which was declared to be the 'basis' of the contract contained the question: 'How many accidents or losses have arisen during the past three years in connection with this or any other motor vehicle owned or driven by you or your driver?' The answer which he gave was: 'See your records under policy on Chrysler.[10] I also held policy during last year with Employers' Mutual[11] on this car and a previous one on which there have been three claims costing £28 13s 9d.' The underwriters repudiated liability on the ground that a Morris previously belonging to him had, during the period of 3 years before the signing of the proposal form, been 'borrowed' on three separate occasions. On the first occasion it was found undamaged the next day. On the second occasion it was found the next day. But on the third occasion it was stolen and never seen again.

Lord Hewart LCJ held that the claim failed. The information about the Morris was material, and should have been disclosed.

One of the expert witnesses[12] in the case expressed the opinion that the fact that a car had been borrowed on three occasions should be disclosed on any proposal for insurance. It might indicate that the owner was careless about his car and left it in tempting positions.

Another expert witness[13] said that the fact that a car had been stolen once and returned after a short time undamaged would not be regarded as a material fact with regard to the acceptance of a risk. But if the car had been stolen three times, he would inquire into the circumstances and make inquiries from other companies.

(b) Previous Accidents to Cars Belonging to Insured

In *Trustee of GH Mundy (a Bankrupt) v Blackmore*[14] a question in a proposal form, which was made the 'basis' of the contract, asked the proposer to state what accidents had been suffered by cars belonging to him. He replied: 'With 8 cars insured at the same time a few minor accidents; also ran off the road in France owing to tyre bursting'. In fact, there had also been an accident to one of the

---

[9] (1931) 40 Ll L Rep 132, K B.
[10] Another car owned by the plaintiff and insured with the defendants.
[11] Ie the Employers' Mutual Insurance Association Ltd.
[12] The joint manager of the Employers' Mutual Insurance Association Ltd.
[13] Who after a great deal of experience with insurance companies was now an assessor and surveyor on his own account.
[14] (1928) 32 Ll L Rep 150, Ch.

insured cars whilst it was being driven for him. It was involved in a head-on crash resulting in the gearbox being thrown out of line and both axles being bent, the cost of repairs amounting to £130. Tomlin J held that this was a material fact which should have been disclosed. Since it had not, the underwriter was entitled to avoid liability.

The learned Judge said that the question had been raised whether the accident was one which could fairly be described as a 'minor' one, and observed.[15]

'It is said that when an insurance company accepts a proposal containing a statement like this without making inquiries as to the character of the accident, they cannot afterwards say, "We do not think this was a minor accident. You ought to have mentioned it specifically, and, therefore, we are entitled to repudiate the policy." No doubt this is true where you are dealing with a state of things upon which there may be a fair division of opinion, but there must be a class of accident which no reasonably fair-minded man would regard as a minor accident, and it seems to me that the insurance company is entitled to say that no reasonably fair-minded man would have included in the phrase "minor accident" such an accident as that in question.

What is a minor or a major accident? I do not know, and I do not propose to define either of them. When I meet with a major accident, I know it. When I meet with a minor accident, I know it.'

In concluding that it was a major accident he added:[16]

'In this particular case, to say that when two cars meet, head on, with the result that one of them has both axles bent, its gear-box thrown out of line, and other damage necessitating the expenditure of £130 or £140, was a minor accident, is in my view incorrect. My view is that it is a major accident, and no reasonably fair-minded man would have any other view, notwithstanding that the original cost of the car was £1,200. I do not think a man who was honest could come to the conclusion that an accident of that sort could fairly be described as a minor accident, and would say that it was not incumbent on him to mention it. The accident ought to have been mentioned, and failure to do so is sufficient to entitle the underwriter to repudiate the policy.'

7 Other Insurers

(a) Names of Previous Insurers

The names of previous insurers have been held to be a material fact and ones which ought to have been disclosed by the proposer.

In *Dent v Blackmore*[17] the proposer in May 1925 in answer to the question in a proposal form: 'Have you previously held a motor insurance policy; if so, please state the name of the insurance company', had stated 'The Sun Insurance Co'. He had been insured from the Spring of 1924 to the Spring of 1925 with that company, but he had also been insured with the Car and General Insurance Corporation from the Spring of 1922 to the Spring of 1923. The truth of the statements in the proposal form was made the 'basis' of the contract. McCardie J held that the answer given was untrue, and the underwriters were entitled to avoid liability.[18] There had also been non-disclosure of a material fact, and they could repudiate on that ground as well.[19]

---

15 (1928) 32 Ll L Rep 150, CR at 152.
16 Ibid, at 152.
17 (1927) 29 Ll L Rep 9, KB.
18 Ibid, at 11.
19 Ibid, at 12.

His Lordship said that he agreed with a submission by counsel that a man was not bound to mention a policy of a generation ago, which could have no bearing at all upon the position at the present time. But the policy effected with the Car and General Insurance Corporation was:[20]

> 'A policy not in remote times, but a policy which Mr Dent held in the immediate past, and a policy which it is important to remember because a significant series of accidents took place during the period that that policy was running. There were no less than 5 accidents at least, possibly 6, while the Car & General Insurance Corporation policy was running, and the total of the claims against the insurance company under that policy was no less than £107. To my mind, the answer of Mr Dent was wholly untrue when he mentioned the Sun Insurance Company. He kept back the fact that in 1922 and 1923 he had been insured with the Car & General Insurance Corporation, and in my opinion he kept back that fact because if he had mentioned the Car & General Insurance Corporation, the Lloyd's gentlemen who underwrote this policy would at once have inquired and most probably have refused to issue a policy at all.'

(b) Refusals by Other Companies to Issue a Policy

The refusal by another company to issue a policy has been held to be a material fact which ought to have been disclosed by the proposer.

In *Trustee of G H Mundy (a Bankrupt) v Blackmore*[1] the proposer was asked the following question in a proposal form, which was made the 'basis' of the contract: 'Has any company at any time in respect of any motor insurance declined your proposal?' He answered 'No'. In fact, his proposal for motor insurance had been declined by two underwriters on separate occasions. This fact was not disclosed to Blackmore, who was one of the underwriters for Red Star Motor Policies at Lloyd's. Tomlin J held that the refusals should have been disclosed, and, since they had not, the underwriter was entitled to avoid liability.

He observed:[2]

> 'It was suggested that there was some practice at Lloyd's by which when one underwriter declines the risk, he has got to disclose his refusal to the next underwriter with whom you want to place it. I am not in a position to express any opinion as to what the practice at Lloyd's may be. It is not an issue that has been directly raised. It is enough for me to say that I am satisfied that in this case there has been a prior refusal of this risk by an underwriter which ought to have been disclosed to the "Red Star" underwriter before he accepted the proposal of the assured. So far as this case is concerned the answer to this question was a false representation, and upon that the underwriter was entitled to repudiate the claim.'

In *Holts Motors Ltd v South East Lancashire Insurance Co Ltd*[3] a proposal form in respect of a lorry contained the question: 'Has any company or underwriter

---

[20] (1927) 29 Ll L Rep 9, K B, at 11. See also a passage in the judgment of Rowlatt J in *Broad & Montague Ltd v South East Lancashire Insurance Co Ltd* (1931) 40 Ll L Rep 328 at 331, K B, where his Lordship referred to the evidence of a witness who said that people often only retained their last policy. The learned Judge added (at 331): 'When you come to think of it, it would grow into a very difficult matter if a clause of this kind came to be too harshly applied, because, in the case of a company which never dies, to a person who lives for some time and successively insures cars with various people over a great number of years it is rather hard if he is to be required when he is making a proposal, perhaps, to recall all the companies with whom he has insured, without any question arising or there being any significance about it, during the last 50 years.'

[1] (1928) 32 Ll L Rep 150, Ch.

[2] Ibid, at 152.

[3] (1930) 37 Ll L Rep 1, C A. This case is considered on another point, p 211, post.

declined to insure?' The proposer answered: 'No'. The proposal form contained a 'basis' clause under which he warranted the truth of his answers. In fact, he had sent through insurance brokers another proposal form to the Bell Assurance Association. But they declined to accept it telling them that 'they would rather not entertain this insurance owing to the information received'. The brokers either for politeness or for some other reason did not tell the proposer of the refusal, but merely said that 'Our arrangement with the 'Bell' does not specifically include commercial cars'. All connection with these brokers had ceased when the proposer applied for the policy with the South East Lancashire Insurance Co Ltd, for he negotiated it through other brokers. When a loss under the policy took place, the company repudiated liability on the ground that the answer given to the question was untrue.

The Court of Appeal[4] accepted this contention by the company, and held that the claim failed.

Greer LJ said:[5]

'The question next to be considered is whether the statement was, in fact, untrue. As regards the "Bell" policy, I do not myself understand how the contrary can be contended. The appellants applied to the "Bell" company through agents who were not their regular agents, but who were their agents for the purpose of making application for an insurance on a Studebaker car. The "Bell" company refused to comply with that application and refused to issue a policy on the car in question; and they did so for reasons which are stated as from "information received." I do not think that it matters very much whether they refused it for one reason or another reason; they, in fact, refused it, and it is untrue to say that a company had not declined to insure one of the appellants' motor vehicles.'

(c) Previous Refusal to Renew Insurance

The fact that another insurance company has refused to renew the insurance policy for the insured has been held to be material.

In *Holts Motors Ltd v South East Lancashire Insurance Co Ltd*[6] a proposal form concerning a lorry contained the question: 'Has any company or underwriter declined to insure?' The proposer said: 'No'. In fact, he had insured it with the Lion Underwriters Association. When the policy which was issued by the 'Lion' had nearly expired, the 'Lion' wrote to the brokers for the insured stating that they could not invite renewal of the policy 'owing to the claims experience'. The brokers passed on the letter to the proposer. This matter was not disclosed to the South East Lancashire Insurance Co Ltd, which repudiated liability on the ground that the answer which the proposer had given to the question was untrue. The policy contained a 'basis' clause under which the proposer warranted the truth of his answers.[7] The Court of Appeal[8] held that the insurance company was not liable.

Scrutton LJ said[9] that there was concealment of a fact which should have been disclosed. The proposer had said that he forgot it or did not think much of

---

4 Scrutton, Greer and Slesser, LJ.
5 (1930) 37 Ll L Rep 1 at 5. See also the judgment of Scrutton LJ, ibid, at 3.
6 (1930) 37 Ll L Rep 1 CA. The case is considered on another point, p 210, ante.
7 As to the 'basis' clause, see generally Ivamy, *General Principles of Insurance Law* (4th edn, 1979), pp 181–185.
8 Scrutton, Greer and Slesser LJJ.
9 (1930) 37 Ll L Rep 1 at 4.

it, but 'owing to the claims experience' as a reason for not renewing it was a very substantial matter.

The learned Lord Justice also alluded to the fact that the answer which had been given was true in words, although untrue in substance. But he applied the rule of construction that the fact that the answer was literally true did not protect the insured where the answer was nevertheless false, when taken in relation to other relevant facts which were not stated.[10]

He added:[11]

> 'A further question arises as to the "Lion" assurance as to whether the question is answered truthfully: "Has any company or underwriter declined to insure?" They have said they did not invite renewal "owing to the claims experience", and [Counsel's] answer on behalf of the plaintiff is: "Well, they were never asked to, and you cannot decline a thing you were never asked to do." That may be so in ordinary life, but I am quite clear, with such knowledge and experience as I have, that in the underwriting world and the insurance world a transaction like that, though expressed in polite terms, would be treated by everybody as a declining to insure; and, if so, the question has been answered wrongly.'

Greer LJ, however, said[12] that he did not desire to say anything in regard to the question whether there was a refusal to insure by the 'Lion'. It was a somewhat difficult question, and for his part it was not necessary that he should indicate what view he had upon it.

In *Broad & Montague Ltd v South East Lancashire Insurance Co Ltd*[13] the proposer in respect of an insurance of a lorry was asked the question: 'Has any company or underwriter declined to insure?' The answer given was 'Yes', and the insurance company was told orally that the Leadenhall Motor Policies Association had refused to renew a previous policy on the ground that they were no longer accepting haulage risks. But, in fact, the Cornhill Insurance Co Ltd had refused to renew the proposer's policies. The proposal form contained a 'basis' clause in which the proposer warranted the truth of the answer. Rowlatt J held that the South East Lancashire Insurance Co Ltd against which the proposer had made a claim in respect of a loss under the policy, was entitled to repudiate liability. He observed:[14]

> 'That being so and the fact being that not only Leadenhall but another company had declined, I think that is a mis-statement. If the truth is that the Leadenhall and the Cornhill had both refused this policy, it is certainly not true to say that the Leadenhall had refused, and stop there. That to my mind is either a mis-statement, omission or suppression, or whatever you like to call it. It is a breach of the obligation to make a true statement in this proposal form. So far as that goes and upon the face of it that is an untrue statement.'

Where the policy is being negotiated through a broker who knows that another insurance company has declined to renew an insurance for his client, he is under a duty to disclose this fact to the company to which the new proposal is addressed. If a policy is issued, that company is entitled to avoid liability on the ground that there has been a non-disclosure of a material fact.[15]

---

[10] As to the rule of construction that the whole truth must be told, see Ivamy, op cit, pp 189–191.
[11] (1930) 37 Ll L Rep 1 at 4.
[12] Ibid, at 5.
[13] (1931) 40 Ll L Rep 328, K B.
[14] Ibid, at 330.
[15] *Cornhill Insurance Co Ltd v L and B Assenheim* (1937) 58 Ll L Rep 27, K B.

In *Cornhill Insurance Co Ltd v L and B Assenheim*[16] the defendants were insured in respect of two Studebaker lorries. They later insured a Chevrolet lorry with the plaintiffs. Subsequently the other insurers wrote to the defendants' brokers informing them that they would not invite renewal of the policy in respect of the Studebaker lorries. The two Studebaker lorries were then insured with the plaintiffs under the same policy as the Chevrolet lorry. The plaintiffs claimed that they were entitled to avoid liability because the fact that the other insurers had not invited renewal of the policy in respect of the Studebakers had not been disclosed by the defendants' brokers. There was a conflict of evidence as to whether or not such disclosure had been made.

MacKinnon J held that, on the evidence[17], the plaintiffs had satisfactorily established that they were not informed of the refusal to renew, and accordingly could avoid liability on the policy.

(d) Requirement by Other Companies of Fulfilment of Special Terms

The requirement by another insurance company of the fulfilment of special terms by the insured as the basis on which an existing policy would be renewed has been held to be a material fact, which the proposer is under a duty to disclose.[18]

In *Dent v Blackmore*[19] the proposer had given the answer 'No' to a question in a proposal form, which was made the 'basis' of the contract, stating: 'Has any company or underwriter at any time in respect of any motor insurance . . . required an increased premium or altered or special terms?' In fact, another company refused to renew the policy in view of the number of claims he had made unless he was willing to bear the first £10 of any future claim.[20] This refusal was not disclosed. McCardie J held that the answer given was untrue, and that on this ground the underwriter could avoid liability.[1] He also held that there had been non-disclosure of a material fact, and for this reason also there could be no liability.[2]

But in *MacKay v London General Insurance Co Ltd*[3] a different conclusion as to the materiality was reached, though the Court held that the insurance company could still avoid liability because the insured had contracted that the proposal and declaration should be the 'basis' of the contract between him and the company, and his answer was untrue in fact.

In this case the question in the proposal form stated: 'Has any office or underwriter . . . required an increased premium or special condition?' The proposer said 'No'. But as a boy of 18 he had desired to insure a motor cycle, and Ocean Accident and Guarantee Corporation Ltd had stipulated that he should pay or take over the first £2 10s 0d of the insurance himself. Swift J held that that was a 'special condition', and the answer given was inaccurate. It was also quite immaterial.

---

16 (1937) 58 Ll L Rep 27, K B.
17 The evidence is set out in detail ibid., at 30–31.
18 *Dent v Blackmore* (1927) 29 Ll L Rep 9, K B.
19 (1927) 29 Ll L Rep 9, K B.
20 The evidence on this point is set out ibid, at 11–12.
1 Ibid, at 12.
2 Ibid, at 12.
3 (1935) 51 Ll L Rep 201, K B.

(e) Cancellation of Other Policies for Non-payment of Premiums

In *Norman v Gresham Fire and Accident Insurance Society Ltd*[4] the proposer failed to disclose that two policies effected with another insurance company had been terminated for non-payment of the premiums due in respect of them. Lewis J held (obiter)[5] that this was a material fact which should have been disclosed. He observed:[6]

> 'I find as a fact . . . that the question as to whether or not a would-be assured or a person who is proposing to seek insurance has had policies cancelled is, in my view, material. It seems to me—and I have heard evidence with regard to it—that it must be material for an insurance company to know whether or not the person whose risk they are accepting is (to put it quite broadly) a person of substance who can not only pay his premiums but also, as was pointed out to me by one of the witnesses, particularly in motor insurance, a person who does not get his policies cancelled for non-payment of premiums, because that shows that they are persons who are, without putting it too high, impecunious, and therefore are not likely to be able to spend money in order to give care and attention to their motor vehicles being insured.'

TIME AT WHICH ANSWER GIVEN MUST BE CORRECT

In *Whitwell v Autocar Fire and Accident Co Ltd*[7] a question in a proposal form stated: 'Has any insurance company or underwriter declined or cancelled your insurance or required an increased premium or refused to renew?' The proposer filled up the proposal form on 30 April giving the answer 'No' to this question. On 1 May the insurance company accepted the proposal. The car which the proposer was insuring was the property of Roadways Transport Development Ltd, and he was acquiring it on hire-purchase terms. On 28 April the secretary of that company was told by the United British Insurance Company that they would not insure the car, but he did not pass on this information to the proposer before the proposal had been accepted. The Autocar Fire and Accident Insurance Co Ltd sought to avoid liability on the policy on the ground that the answer which the proposer had given to the question was incorrect.

Clauson J held that the company was liable. The company had failed to prove that the answer given by the proposer was untrue at the time at which it was made.

WAIVER OF NON-DISCLOSURE

Whether the conduct of the insurer amounts to a waiver of the duty of disclosure is a matter of fact in each case.[8]

---

[4] (1935) 52 Ll L Rep 292.

[5] The case was decided on the ground that the insurance company was not liable because the evidence showed that there was no concluded contract between the parties. See the conclusion of the learned Judge on this point, ibid, at 300.

[6] Ibid, at 301.

[7] (1927) 27 Ll L Rep 418, Ch D.

[8] See as to other branches of insurance, Ivamy, *General Principles of Insurance Law* (4th edn, 1979), p 178.

The fact that an insurance company invokes an arbitration clause in a policy does not mean that it thereby affirms the validity of the policy, and thereby debars itself from relying on the defence of non-disclosure of a material fact by the insured.

In *Jester-Barnes v Licenses and General Insurance Co Ltd*[9] the insurance company pleaded that it was entitled to avoid liability on the policy by reason of the non-disclosure of the previous convictions of the insured[10] and of his chauffeur.[11] The insured, however, contended that, by asking the Court to stay the action on the policy because it contained an arbitration clause, the company had asserted and affirmed the validity and effectiveness of the whole of the policy, and could not plead non-disclosure of a material fact. This argument was rejected by MacKinnon J who said:[12]

> '[Counsel] says that by applying to the Court to stay the action under the arbitration clause, that asserted the validity and effectiveness of the arbitration clause and incidentally asserted and affirmed the validity and effectiveness of the whole of this policy, and having an order of the Court that it is an effective policy, the [company] are estopped from asserting that the policy is not valid and not effective and that they can seek to set it aside. There is no suggested authority about this. [Counsel] said the point was raised, but not decided, by the House of Lords in the case of *Bank of Ireland and Macaura v Northern Assurance Co Ltd*[13] and it is therefore one of first impression of a matter of principle.
>   I think this is quite an impossible contention. If there is an arbitration clause of this type, which has always been called the *Scott v Avery*[14] clause, in a policy, and an assured starts an action, it is a common thing for the insurance company to apply for a stay, and it is inevitable that it should be granted, because not only is it an essential result of the contract he entered into that it should be stayed, but in the assured's own interest it must be stayed, because if it were allowed to go on, the only result would be that the insurance company could plead that he has not got an award, and that, therefore, he cannot possibly recover anything in an action which may be brought. Therefore, at the earliest possible stage an action, brought either by forgetfulness or mistake or something, on a policy which contains that type of arbitration clause, has to be stayed, the parties going to arbitration. The proposition that that having happened, the insurance company are then in the arbitration precluded from asserting any breach of condition in the policy, or any failure to disclose, or anything of that sort, I think, is quite an impossible proposition. The application to stay is made under one clause in the policy and is directed to one purpose only; it is not an affirmation that it is a good policy, or by implication an affirmation that they admit the validity of the policy and that they disclaim any intention to rely, if the facts prove it possible, upon a breach of condition express or implied in the policy.'

THE BURDEN OF PROOF

The burden of proving that the proposer had made a mis-statement in the proposal form lies on the insurance company.[15]

---

9 (1934) 49 Ll L Rep 231.
10 See p 201, ante.
11 See p 203, ante.
12 (1934) 49 Ll L Rep 231 at 238.
13 (1925) 21 Ll L Rep 333.
14 (1856) 5 H L Cas 811.
15 *Adams v London General Insurance Co* (1932) 42 Ll L Rep 56 (Liverpool Assizes). The same rule is applied in other branches of insurance. See Ivamy, *General Principles of Insurance Law* (4th edn, 1979), pp 193–195.

Thus in *Adams v London General Insurance Co*[16] the insured, a Mr Blacklock, was asked the following question in a proposal form: 'How long have you held a driving licence?', and answered 'Four years'. The insurance company alleged that this statement was untrue because he had only held a licence for a few months.

Swift J held that the burden of proving the mis-statement lay on the company, and in reviewing the evidence observed:[17]

> 'That Blacklock is a liar I am quite prepared to believe. Everybody has said that he is. He is not here for himself to say that he is not. Everybody had said that he is a disreputable person who got himself convicted and sent to prison under discreditable circumstances, and I am quite ready to accept that he is a person who does say that which is not true. But my trouble is to know which of these statements which he makes is untrue. When he applies for a licence and says: "This is the first application I have made for a licence," is he speaking the truth or is he not? When he says: "I have been driving a motor car for four years," is he speaking the truth or not? I do not know. I have his two conflicting statements. On 29 or 30 October, I think—it does not matter which it was—he says: "This is my first application for a licence." A little while later he says to the insurance company: "I have been driving for four years." Obviously the two statements cannot be right. One or the other is false—which, I do not know.'

His Lordship concluded that in these circumstances the company had not discharged the burden of proving that the insured had made statements the effect of which was to vitiate the policy.

Again, in *Babatsikos v Car Owners' Mutual Insurance Co Ltd* Pape J, giving judgment in the Supreme Court of Victoria, held[18] that the burden of proving that the insured had made a material misrepresentation in the proposal form, viz that he had wrongly stated '3 years and 4 months' in answer to the question 'How long have you held a driver's licence?', lay on the insurer and that, on the evidence, this burden had not been discharged.[19]

CONTINUING WARRANTIES

Sometimes the statements made by the insured in the proposal form will be construed as warranties that the circumstances stated in it will continue in the future, and do not relate merely to the time at which they were made.[20]

If the statement is construed as a warranty and any alteration in the circumstances takes place, the insurers are entitled to repudiate liability on the ground that the warranty has been broken.

(a) 'Vehicle to be Driven in One Shift per 24 Hours'

In *Farr v Motor Traders' Mutual Insurance Society Ltd*[1] the owner of two taxicabs wished to insure them. In answer to a question in the proposal form he stated that each cab was to be driven in one shift per 24 hours. In August one of them

---

[16] (1932) 42 Ll L Rep 56.
[17] Ibid, at 57.
[18] [1970] 2 Lloyd's Rep 314 at 318.
[19] Ibid, at 326.
[20] See Ivamy, op. cit, p 172.
[1] [1920] 3 K B 669, C A.

was undergoing repair and could not be used, so the other one was driven in two shifts for a short time. From that time the two cabs were driven in one shift only. In November the cab, which had been used in two shifts per twenty-four hours, was damaged in an accident. The insured claimed under the policy. The insurance company declined to pay, contending that the statement by the insured in the proposal form amounted to a warranty, and that since the warranty had been broken, they were not liable.

The Court of Appeal[2] held that the claim succeeded. The statement was not a warranty. It was only descriptive of the risk and meant that the vehicle would not be covered whilst it was being driven in two shifts, but that it would be covered when it was being driven in one shift per 24 hours.

Bankes LJ said:[3]

'The question is whether we are to construe the question and answer, as the defendants contend, as a warranty, the effect of which would be that in August, when the cab was driven in two shifts per day, the policy came to an end; or whether we are to construe them, as Rowlatt J has construed them, as words descriptive of the risk, indicating that whilst the cab is driven in one shift per 24 hours the risk will be covered, but that if in any one day of 24 hours the cab is driven in more than one shift, the risk will no longer be covered and will cease to attach until the owner resumes the practice of driving the cab in one shift only. In my opinion, having regard to the nature of the question, it is impossible to construe the answer thereto as a warranty.'

(b) 'Commercial Purposes Only'

In *Roberts v Anglo Saxon Insurance Association Ltd*[4] a car had been insured under a policy covering specified risks including that of fire. In the proposal form which was made the basis of the contract[5] in answer to the question 'State clearly the purpose for which the vehicle will be used' the proposer had said 'Commercial'. The policy contained a clause which stated 'Warranted used only for commercial purposes'. During the currency of the policy the vehicle was destroyed by fire when it was not being used for commercial purposes. The insured claimed against the insurance company, and an award was made by an arbitrator in favour of the insured, but the Court of Appeal[6] set it aside because his reasoning and interpretation of the words of the policy as stated on the face of the award were erroneous. This was the actual decision of the Court, but Bankes LJ held obiter that the words were not a warranty, but only descriptive of the risk. He observed:[7]

'If this matter had come before me either as an arbitrator or as a Judge of first instance or as a Judge sitting to decide the question on a special case stated for the opinion of the Court, I should have had no hesitation whatever in saying that in my opinion the true construction of this clause is the construction which was put upon the language of the insurance policy in the case of *Farr v Motor Traders' Mutual Insurance Society*,[8] namely, that in this class of policy when

---

2 Bankes, Warrington and Scrutton LJJ.
3 [1920] 3 K B 669 at 674.
4 (1927) 27 Ll L Rep 313, C A.
5 As to the 'basis' clause, see Ivamy, *General Principles of Insurance Law* (4th edn, 1979), pp 181–183.
6 Bankes and Scrutton LJJ, Romer J.
7 (1927) 27 Ll L Rep 313,. See also ibid, at 315. See also the judgment of Scrutton LJ, ibid, at 316, and that of Romer J, ibid, at 317 which were both to the same effect.
8 [1920] 3 K B 669. See p 216, ante.

persons insert clauses, whether described as warranties or whether described as part of the description of the vehicle, indicating that the vehicle is to be used in some restricted way, my opinion in that case, and in this case and in similar cases, is and would be that the parties had used that language as words descriptive of the risk, and that, as a result, when the vehicle is not being used in accordance with the description, it is not covered; but it does not follow at all that because it is used on some one occasion, or on more than one occasion, for other than the described use, the policy is avoided. It does not follow at all. If the proper construction, on its language, is a description of the limitation of the liability, then the effect would be that the vehicle would be off cover during the period during which it was not being used for the warranted purpose, but that it would come again on the cover when the vehicle was again used for the warranted purpose. I am quite clear about that, and I have no difficulty in expressing my opinion in reference to that matter.'

(c) 'Lorry to be Used for Purposes of Delivering Coal'

In *Provincial Insurance Co Ltd v Morgan and Foxon*[9] in the proposal form completed by the proposer he stated that the lorry which was to be insured was to be used for the delivery of coal. The proposal form was made the 'basis' of the contract,[10] and he warranted the truth of the answers which he had given. The lorry was used on the day of the accident hauling timber for the Forestry Commission, but was being used for the delivery of coal at the time of the accident. The insured claimed under the policy, but the insurance company denied liability, and contended that the insured by using the lorry for hauling timber was guilty of a breach of warranty.

It was held by the House of Lords[11] that the statement in the proposal form was not a warranty, but was merely descriptive of the risk insured.

Lord Russell of Killowen said:[12]

'I cannot read the above statements in the proposal form as being more than statements by the proposers of their intentions as to the user of the vehicle and the goods to be carried in it, and so as descriptive of the risk. If it had really been the intention of the insurance company that the carrying of goods other than coal at any time should free them from liability in respect of an accident happening subsequently, it was incumbent on them to make that abundantly clear to the proposers.'

(d) Drivers not under 21 nor with less than Twelve Months' Experience

In *Sweeney v Kennedy*[13] question 9 in a proposal form stated: 'Are any of your drivers under 21 years of age or with less than 12 months' driving experience?' The proposer answered: 'No'. At the date of the signing of the proposal form no driver employed by the proposer was under 21 years of age or had less than 12 months' driving experience. The proposer stated that 'this declaration shall be held to be promissory, and so form the "basis"[14] of the contract between me

---

9 (1932) 44 Ll L Rep 275, H L.
10 As to the 'basis' clause, see Ivamy, *General Principles of Insurance Law* (4th edn, 1979), pp 181–183.
11 Viscount Buckmaster, Lord Blanesburgh, Lord Russell of Killowen, Lord Warrington of Clyffe and Lord Wright.
12 (1932) 44 Ll L Rep 275 at 278.
13 (1948) 82 Ll L Rep 294, Eire Divisional Court. This case is considered on another point, viz, alteration of the risk, at p 277, post.
14 As to the 'basis' clause, see Ivamy, *General Principles of Insurance Law* (4th edn, 1979), pp 181–183.

and the underwriters.' At the time of the accident in which a third party was injured, the insured's son was driving a lorry covered by the policy. He had had over 12 months' driving experience, but was under 21 years of age. When a claim was made against the insurers, liability was denied on the ground that the answer given to the question amounted to a continuing warranty, and that this warranty had been broken because the driver was under 21.

Kingsmill Moore J giving judgment in the Eire Divisional Court, held that the answer had no reference to the future, nor was such an intention to be presumed from the words of the proposer's declaration.

He said that the argument by counsel for the insurers was that the question and answer, taken by themselves, must in all the circumstances of the case be construed as amounting to a warranty that no driver aged under 21 or with less than 12 months' experience would be employed during the currency of the policy. The question and answer, so far as grammar was concerned, dealt only with the point of time when the answer was given. But counsel said that the question was meaningless unless it was construed as referring to the future, and that by necessary intendment it must so refer.

In rejecting this argument his Lordship said:[15]

> 'The value of the underwriters of Q9 was to find out with what sort of person they were dealing. Obviously, if Mr. Sweeney habitually employed young and inexperienced drivers, it was a matter to be taken into consideration. Here, also, if the underwriters intended to refer to the future, it is most unfortunate that a printed document tendered by Lloyd's underwriters to persons desiring to insure with them should not be so expressed. Here, also, had they intended that this question should carry the meaning which they now suggest, nothing would have been easier than to say so. Here, also, if they did not mean it, I am at a loss to see how the point comes to be taken.'

Counsel for the insurers also relied particularly on the sentence 'I agree that this declaration shall be held to be promissory and so form the basis of the contract'. He contended that the word 'promise' and its cognate words must always refer to a future time.

But the learned Judge rejected this contention and said:[16]

---

[15] 82 Ll L Rep at 299. His Lordship referred with approval to the decision in *Woolfall and Rimmer Ltd v Moyle* [1942] 1 K B 66 (employers' liability insurance), where the Court of Appeal held that the answer 'Yes' given in reply to the question 'Are your machinery, plant and ways properly fenced and guarded and otherwise in good order and condition' did not relate to the future. He considered that the words used by Lord Greene M R, in that case in the following passage were entirely applicable to the present case. The Master of the Rolls had there observed ([1942] 1 K B 66 at 70): 'In my opinion, there is not a particle of justification for reading into that perfectly simple question any element of futurity whatsoever. The argument that the Court should read into it such an element was based, as I understood it, on the suggestion that the answer would be valueless from the underwriters' point of view unless that were done. I entirely disagree. The value of the question to the underwriters, as I construe it, is that it enables them to find out with what sort of person they are dealing, that is, whether or not he keeps his machinery, plant and ways properly fenced and guarded and otherwise in good order and condition. Obviously, if he was careless about that, so that at the time the question was answered his machinery, plant and ways were not in good order and condition, the risk would be of a different character. If the underwriters intended to refer to the future, it is most unfortunate that a printed document of this kind, tendered by Lloyd's underwriters to persons desiring to insure with them, should not be so expressed. Had they intended that this question should carry the meaning which they now suggest, nothing would have been easier than to say so. If they did not mean it, I am at a loss to understand how the point comes to be taken'.

[16] (1948) 82 Ll L Rep 294 at 299, Eire Divisional Court.

'In this I think he is in error. The most usual meaning of the word "to promise" is "to undertake to do or abstain from doing something in the future." But there is a well-recognized second usage in which "to promise" means "to assert confidently, to declare." Such an assertion usually refers to a future state of affairs, but it may also refer to the present, as in the phrase, "I promise you that it is so." It is true that the Oxford Dictionary classes this latter usage as colloquial or archaic. But an archaism or two in an insurance policy will not give a lawyer familiar with their verbiage too violent a shock. Certain marine policies seem compounded of little else but archaisms.'

He said that he accepted the argument of counsel for the insured that the words were used in this second meaning, and remarked:[17]

'The interpretation so given by [Counsel for the insured] to the word "promissory" in the proposal form, though unusual, involves no violation of grammar or language. In this interpretation the word can be applied accurately and intelligibly to questions whether they refer to past, present or future. If this question refers to the future, the answer becomes a warranty as to the existence of a state of affairs in the future. When the question is so couched as to refer to the present or the past, then the answer is a warranty that a certain state of affairs exists in the present or existed in the past. [Counsel for the insurers'] interpretation, on the other hand, not merely tortures language but involves a person who has answered an apparently straightforward question as to the present or past, in a concealed warranty as to the future. Such a carefully camouflaged method of extracting a future warranty would hardly commend itself to this Court, and I would be loath to attribute such an intention to the underwriters.'

He concluded by saying that it was difficult to see how any insured could answer the vital ninth question without involving himself in difficulties. In the words of the learned Judge:[18]

'Mr Sweeney's answer of "No" was correct in fact. But according to the contention of the underwriters this answer involved a promise never to employ a driver aged under 21 or without 12 months' driving experience. Was Sweeney to safeguard himself by explaining that in certain circumstances he might be obliged, for a longer or shorter time, to employ a driver aged under 21? How far was he to elaborate the circumstances which had not yet arisen and which might be difficult to foresee? I cannot conceive that an applicant for insurance, who is asked a specific question, is bound to do more than give a truthful answer to such question, or that there is any obligation to provide answers to questions which are not asked.'

(e) 'Driver not under 25'

In *Kirkbride v Donner*[19] question 11 (a) in a proposal form asked: 'Will the car to your knowledge be driven by any person under 25?' The proposer's answer was 'Yes, self'. She signed a declaration at the end of the proposal form stating that the declaration was promissory and was the 'basis' of the contract[20]. Subsequently the car was driven by her brother, who was under 25, and was stolen whilst parked outside a club. When a claim was made under the policy, the insurer repudiated liability on the ground that the answer constituted a continuing warranty and that this had been broken. Deputy Judge Tibber held that the insurer was liable because, when the proposer made the declaration that she would be the only person under 25 who would drive the car, she had not intended that the car would be driven by anyone else (including her brother), and consequently there was no breach of warranty.

---

[17] (1948) 82 Ll L Rep 294 at 300.
[18] Ibid, at 300.
[19] [1974] 1 Lloyd's Rep 549, Mayor's and City of London Ct.
[20] As to the 'basis clause' see Ivamy, *General Principles of Insurance Law* (4th edn, 1979) pp 181–183.

He observed:[1]

'Well now I take the view that what this question 11 means on the face of it is this: "Will the car to your knowledge be driven by any person under 25 years of age in your present state of knowledge, and having regard to your present intentions, will the car be driven by anyone under 25?" and I accept entirely that Miss Kirkbride at that time, in her then state of knowledge and having regard to her future intentions, certainly did not intend that the car would be driven by anybody under the age of 25 including her younger brother. Then I was asked to turn to the declaration and say: Ah well it is made promissory, she must have understood or have been intended to understand by that, that not only was she warranting for the present that was the situation, but that that situation would continue into the future. I cannot find that it does mean that. It might possibly do so, it could do so I suppose, but it seems to me that this document has got to be construed against the insurance company, and I just cannot accept that there was no clearer way in which the insurance company could put this intention. It is perfectly simple to find a form of words to express the construction for which the [insurers] contend. They have not used that and I do not think that it means any more than this: At the time of signing the insurance policy those are my intentions and that is my intention. If that is right, and that is the view, of course, I hold, then there has been no breach of warranty such as to entitle the insurers to decline liability under the policy.'

---

[1] [1974] 1 Lloyd's Rep at 553.

CHAPTER 26

The contents of the policy

The contents of a motor insurance policy vary from insurance company to insurance company. Each insurance company has its own standard form of policy.[1] There is no standard form of policy in use at Lloyd's.

Certain matters are dealt with in the body of the policy, whilst others are set out in the Schedule to the policy.

MATTERS SET OUT IN THE BODY OF POLICY

The matters with which comprehensive policies usually deal are:

1. Third party liability
2. Extension clauses.
3. Accidental damage or loss.
4. Personal accident.
5. Medical expenses.
6. Contents of vehicle.
7. Garage.
8. Transit.
9. Overseas touring.
10. Laying up.
11. Legal defence and technical advice.
12. 'No claim' bonus.
13. Conditions.[2]
14. Exceptions.[3]
15. Cancellation of the policy.

1 Third Party Liability

The insurers undertake to indemnify the insured in respect of all sums which he may become legally liable to pay by way of:

a. compensation for death of or bodily injury to any person (including passengers) caused by or arising out of the use of the vehicle;
b. medical treatment required as a result of bodily injury to any person under the Road Traffic Act 1972, s 155;
c. compensation for damage caused by the vehicle to any property belonging to a third person.

---

[1] Specimen forms of motor policies are set out in Appendix VI, pp 416–441, post.
[2] See pp 271–278 et seq, post.
[3] See pp 247–270 et seq, post.

2 Extension Clauses

The indemnity provided by the policy extends to any person driving the vehicle with the consent of or on the order of the insured provided that such a driver is not entitled to indemnity under any other policy and holds a licence to drive the vehicle.[4]

The policy also covers the insured whilst he is driving another vehicle with the consent of the owner.[5]

At the insured's request the indemnity given by the policy will be extended to any passenger whilst entering into, dismounting from or travelling in the vehicle. Thus, if the passenger opens the car door and causes an accident as a result of doing so, he will be entitled to be indemnified in respect of any damages which he has to pay to a third party.

3 Accidental Damage or Loss

The insurers will indemnify the insured in respect of all damage or loss to the vehicle and its accessories caused by any accidental external and physical means, fire, lightning, explosion, burglary, theft, or any attempt thereat, and the malicious act of any person.

But they are not liable for loss of use, consequential loss, wear and tear, depreciation, mechanical or electrical breakdown or any damage to the tyres caused by the application of the brakes or road punctures.

If the car is damaged, the insurers will indemnify the insured in respect of any sum he has had to pay in getting it moved to the nearest garage.

The insurers will pay for the cost of the repairs, but in no case will be liable for a greater sum than the maximum market value stated in the policy.

Where the insurers pay for a total loss, they also undertake to pay for the unexpired portion of the Road Fund licence if an allowance cannot be obtained from the taxation authorities.

If the vehicle is a total loss, the salvage must be transferred to the insurers, and the insurance is deemed to be at an end without return of premium.

4 Personal Accident

The policy usually provides that a sum of money be paid by the insurers in the event of bodily injury to the insured or to his wife caused by accidental, external, visible means whilst driving or riding in or entering or dismounting from the vehicle. Usually there is a clause stating that the insurers will not be liable unless death or disablement results within a specified time. Nor will they be liable in respect of death or injury to any person over 75 years of age.

5 Medical Expenses

The insurers undertake to pay any medical expenses up to a specified figure to any person suffering injury whilst travelling in the vehicle.

---

[4] See pp 233–243, post.
[5] See pp 243–246, post.

6 Contents of Vehicle

In the event of loss or damage to rugs, coats or luggage, whilst in the vehicle, due to fire, theft or accidental means, as specified, a specified maximum sum will be paid by the insurers.

7 Garage

If the garage, in which the car is normally kept, is destroyed or damaged by fire, the insurers undertake to pay a specified maximum amount, provided that the garage is not covered under any other policy.

8 Transit

The policy usually covers loss or damage to the car whilst in transit by road, rail, waterway, lift, or by recognised short sea routes (though sometimes in this case notice must be given in advance to the insurers).

9 Overseas Touring

The insurers are willing to extend the indemnity provided by the policy to the vehicle whilst it is being used abroad provided that proper notice of the insured's intention to take it abroad is given to them, and other formalities are complied with.

10 Laying Up

Where the vehicle is to be laid up for a period of not less than 30 consecutive days otherwise than as the result of an accident, the insured may be entitled to obtain a rebate of premium provided he gives due notice to the insurers.

11 Legal Defence and Technical Advice

The insurers have the right to, and will, at the request of the insured, provide legal representation at inquests, legal defence of proceedings in the Magistrates' Courts, and legal defence in respect of a charge of manslaughter or of causing death by dangerous driving.

Engineering advice in connection with the vehicle will be given free except where an inspection and report is necessary.

12 'No Claim' Bonus

Where no claim has been made under the policy, the insurers usually allow a reduction from the renewal premium in accordance with a specified scale.

13 Conditions

A number of matters are made 'conditions' of the policy.[6]

---

6 See pp 271–278, post.

14 Exceptions

A number of exceptions are usually set out in the policy.[7]

15 Cancellation of the Policy

Usually the insurers are given a first right by the terms of the policy at any time to cancel it by giving 7 days' notice by registered letter to the insured's last known address.[8] In this event, they become liable to return a pro rata portion of the premium in respect of the unexpired period.

Further, the insured can cancel the policy by previous notice in writing and upon surrender of the certificate of insurance. Provided no claim has arisen and no claim is pending, the insurers must then return the proportion of the premium after charging premium on the basis of the published scale of 'Short Period Insurances' for the time during which the insurance has been in force.

Whether the policy is determined by the insurers or the insured, rights or claims arising prior to the expiration of the notice are not affected.

MATTERS SET OUT IN THE SCHEDULE

The Schedule sets out the name and the address of the insured, the policy number, the registration number of the vehicle, the commencing and expiry dates, the renewal date, and the business or occupation of the insured.

Also specified are the make of car, its cubic capacity, the year of make, the type of body, the maximum market value, the amount of the premium, and the type of policy, eg third party only, or comprehensive. The Schedule also describes the use to which the vehicle may be put, eg 'private purposes'. This term is usually expressly defined in the body of the policy.

---

[7] See pp 247–270, post.
[8] As to cancellation of a policy, see further, Ivamy, *General Principles of Insurance Law* (4th edn, 1979), pp 248–250, 252–253.

CHAPTER 27

Injury to the insured

A clause in a typical motor insurance policy[1] provides that:

'[The Company] will pay

Personal injury to [the Policyholder] or [the Policyholder's] spouse

a) £1,000 if the Policyholder or the Policyholder's spouse suffers accidental injury:
    ● in direct connection with your Motor Car
    ● while travelling in, or getting into or out of, any other private car which does not belong to you
    and within three calendar months the injury is the sole cause of:
    ● death, or
    ● total and permanent loss of all sight in one or both eyes, or
    ● total loss by physical severance or total and permanent loss of use of one or both hands or feet.
    The maximum amount payable for any one person following any one accident is £1,000. Payment will be made direct to the injured person or to their legal personal representatives.
    If [the Policyholder] or [the Policyholder's] spouse have any other motor insurance with [the Company], payment will be made under one policy only.

    Increased benefit if wearing a seat belt

b) If at the time the injured person is wearing a seat belt, the amount payable will be increased to £5,000.

[The company] will not pay

Injuries arising if:
    ● the injured person is younger than 25 or older than 75 years of age at the time of injury
    ● the injury is a result of suicide or attempted suicide
    ● the Policyholder is a corporate body or firm
    ● caused by earthquake
    ● caused by riot or civil commotion other than in Great Britain, the Isle of Man or the Channel Islands
    ● the injury is caused or aggravated by any pre-existing illness or condition.

'Personal Injuries'

The words 'personal injuries' cover a situation where the insured dies as a result of his injuries.

In *Lloyds Bank Ltd v Eagle Star Insurance Co Ltd*[2] the policy stated that:

'If the insured shall sustain any personal injury caused by violent accidental external and visible means . . . whilst riding in any private motor car . . . and if such injury shall be the

---

[1] See eg the clause in the motor car policy issued by the Commercial Union Assurance Co Ltd and set out in Appendix VI, p 425, post.
[2] [1951] 1 Lloyd's Rep 385, K B.

sole direct and immediate cause within 90 days of the occurrence of such injury of . . . the death of the insured, the sum of £1,000 . . . shall be paid to the insured's executors.'

The insured was injured in a motor accident whilst travelling in a motor car. He died the next day. The company disputed liability on the ground that the clause set out above only applied to a case where the insured was injured and not killed. Jones J gave judgment against the company on this point,[3] and observed:[4]

'It is argued by [Counsel], on behalf of Lloyds Bank, the executors of Mr Rush, that the proviso must be confined to cases of personal injury, and must not be extended to the case of death; and he relied particularly, in support of that argument, on the fact that in the latter part of the proviso the distinction is drawn between death, and injury and disablement; and that is a circumstance to which very close regard must be paid. On the other hand, the clause is headed "Personal Accidents," and the effect of the clause is to make the insurance company liable, subject to the proviso, to pay compensation to the executors of the insured person in the event of the insured sustaining personal injury which results either in death (sub-par (a) of Clause 4), or in certain disablements as set out in sub-par. (b), or in the disablements set out in sub-par. (c) of that clause; and it seems to me that the expression "Personal injuries" should be taken to mean personal injury which results in death, or personal injury which results in disablement, and that the true construction of this proviso is that the company is not to be liable to pay compensation in respect of personal injuries which result in death, or personal injuries which do not result in death, in the case of an insured person who is under the age of 16 or over the age of 65.'

'Death as Result Solely of Bodily Injury'

In *Smith v Cornhill Insurance Co Ltd*[5] the policy stated that the sum of £1,000 would be paid to the estate of the insured in the event of death provided that:

'Death occurs within 6 weeks from the date of the accident and as the result solely of bodily injury caused by violent, external and visible means sustained by the insured whilst riding in, mounting into or dismounting from the insured car.'

The car was found on its side in some undergrowth 10 yards off the road, and the insured was discovered dead in a river not far away. Her feet were stuck in some mud. She was in an upright position with the water a few inches over her head. The post-mortem examination showed that she had not been drowned.[6] But she had had a severe head injury resulting in brain damage.

The insured's executrix claimed £1,000 as due under the policy, but the insurance company refused to pay on the ground that there had been two accidents; the first one to the car and the second one when the insured stepped into the water. The company maintained that, because it could not be determined to what extent the injury from the first accident contributed to the second, it could not be said that the insured's death was 'caused solely by bodily injury'.

Atkinson J held that the company was liable on the policy. Death was due to shock on entering the water. But the entry into the water did not amount to a novus actus interveniens breaking the chain of causation starting with the accident and leading up to the death. Accordingly, death resulted solely from bodily injury caused by the accident.

---

3 But he held that the company was not liable because the insured was over the age limits stated in the policy. See p 228, post.
4 [1951] 1 Lloyd's Rep 385 at 386.
5 (1938) 61 Ll L Rep 122, K B.
6 The evidence is set out at ibid, at 124–125.

In the words of the learned Judge:[7]

> 'There was only one cause here, the injury sustained in the accident. There was no independency between anything that followed and that accident; so that the causation of events, each one the result of the preceding event, lead back to the accident and in my opinion that was the sole cause of this death.'

Age of Insured

The policy often contains an exception whereby the liability of the company is excluded in any event where the insured is under or above a specified age.

Thus, in *Lloyds Bank Ltd v Eagle Star Insurance Co Ltd*[8] the relevant clause in the policy ran:

> 'Provided always that under this clause . . . the company shall not be liable to pay compensation in respect of personal injuries sustained by or happening to the insured if under the age of 16 years or over the age of 65 years.'

In the above case the insured was 65 years seven months at the date of his death in a motor accident. The insurance company repudiated liability on the ground that he was over the age of 65. Jones J, giving judgment in the King's Bench Division, held that the company was entitled to do so.

His Lordship said:[9]

> 'I have to look at the proviso and form my view as to what I think is the proper construction of these words, as to whether the proviso applies to the case of a man who has attained his 65th birthday, or whether it only applies to a man who has attained his 66th birthday; in other words, do the words "over the age of 65 years" mean "after the attainment of the 65th birthday," or do they mean "when the 66th birthday had been attained?"
>
> It seems to me that the proper construction of the proviso is to say that the words "Over the age of 65 years" are words which include a person aged 65 years and 7 months. I think that in the proviso there are two limits stated, one of which is the insured's 16th birthday, and the other is the insured's 65th birthday, and that the proper construction is that the proviso applies to anyone who has lived beyond the attainment of his 65th birthday.'

---

7 (1938) 61 Ll L Rep 122 at 130, K B.

8 [1951] 1 Lloyd's Rep 385, K B.

9 Ibid, at 387. The case is criticised in 67 L Q R 289 in the following terms: 'It might be argued, however, with respect, that until a person reaches his sixty-sixth birthday he is not over the age of sixty-five, and that in view of this doubt the policy should be construed against the company. If the company had wished to protect itself on this point, it would have been easy to provide that the insurance policy was not effective after the assured's sixty-fifth birthday. The ordinary man, it is submitted, would say that he was not over sixty-five until he had reached his sixty-sixth birthday. The cases cited to the learned Judge related to the criminal law and were, therefore, of doubtful relevance in a civil case.'

CHAPTER 28

Loss of or damage to the insured vehicle

A motor insurance policy covers the insured in respect of the loss of or damage to the vehicle.

Thus, a typical clause[1] in a policy states:

'[The company] will pay . . .

The cost of repair or replacement for loss or damage to [the Policyholder's] Motor Car and its accessories, spare parts or components, whether on [the Policyholder's] Motor Car or in [the Policyholder's] private garage. The maximum amount payable will be the reasonable market value immediately prior to the loss or damage.'

'The Vehicle'

The term 'vehicle' includes the tyres. Thus, in *Brown v Zurich General Accident and Liability Insurance Co Ltd*,[2] where there was a condition that the insured had to take all reasonable steps to maintain 'the vehicle in an efficient condition', and it was proved that the front tyres were worn smooth,[3] it was contended by the insured that this was not a breach of the condition because the 'vehicle' did not include the tyres, but only meant the mechanical parts of the vehicle. This construction, however, was rejected by Sellers J, who considered that the meaning which one would normally apply was that it meant the vehicle complete with tyres.[4]

Where a vehicle is dismantled into two pieces and one piece is removed for the purpose of repair, this does not prevent it from still being a 'vehicle', and, therefore, covered by the policy.[5]

Thus, in *Seaton v London General Insurance Co Ltd*[6] a lorry was insured and its engine was removed for the purpose of repair in the insured's workshop, which was 150 yards away from the garage where the vehicle was normally kept. Whilst the engine was in the workshop, it was destroyed by fire. The insurance company repudiated liability on the ground that the policy only covered the insured property when it was in a complete condition. Du Parcq J rejected this construction, and held that the insured was entitled to succeed in his claim under the policy. It was impossible to say that the insured was not covered by the policy because he divided the lorry into two, and took the engine to another part of his premises. In the words of his Lordship:[7]

---

[1] See, eg the clause in the motor car policy issued by the Commercial Union Assurance Co Ltd and set out in Appendix VI, p 423, post.

[2] [1954] 2 Lloyd's Rep 243, QB.

[3] As to the Court's decision that this constituted a breach of the condition, see p 272, post.

[4] [1954] 2 Lloyd's Rep 243 at 247.

[5] *Seaton v London General Insurance Co Ltd* (1932) 43 Ll L Rep 398, KB.

[6] (1932) 43 Ll L Rep 398, KB.

[7] Ibid, at 398, 399, KB.

'It is said with some force by [Counsel] that this seems very hard on the company if they are liable for that, and that they did not insure against loss of two vehicles, and that if he is going to be allowed to divide up his vehicle into two or more sections, it seems hard on the company. The answer is that one must look against what risks the company have insured him, and it seems to be almost beyond dispute that the mere fact that he has taken the engine out of the vehicle does not prevent the vehicle as a whole from being insured. I agree that, the moment you take a thing into two pieces, in one sense the risk is increased, but the mere fact that it may be possible for the assured under the policy to do things which mean that at one time the risks undertaken by the company are greater than at another time does not mean that if the assured does any of these things, he ceases to be insured. It may be that under the terms of the policy and with the latitude allowed the company at times would find themselves under a heavier liability at one time than another.'

'Accessories'

Where a taxi-cab and its accessories are insured against loss or damage, the word 'accessories' has been held in *Rowan v Universal Insurance Co Ltd*[8] to include a taximeter.

In this case the relevant clause stated:

'The company will indemnify the insured against loss or damage to any of the insured's motor vehicles . . . including the accessories belonging thereto thereon caused by fire . . . up to the market value of the motor vehicle at the time of such loss or damage but not exceeding . . . £150.'

The taxicab and the taximeter were destroyed by fire. The County Court Judge[9] held that the market value of the cab was £80, and that of the accessories was £25, but that the insured was barred by the terms of the policy from recovering £25 in respect of the damage to the taximeter, and that he could only recover £80. The Court of Appeal held that the insured was entitled to £105.

Scott LJ said:[10]

'The motor vehicle, as described in the proposal, was a taxicab, the proposal being one on the company's own printed form, describing it as a ''Proposal for insurance of taxicabs''. I venture to think that there can be little doubt that a taxicab is a motor vehicle with a taximeter on it, and, that being so, the clause which describes the motor vehicle as one ''including the accessories belonging thereto thereon'' includes the taximeter.'

Clauson LJ observed:[11]

'I find it quite impossible to accept the construction which the learned Judge saw his way to put upon Clause 4 of the policy. I agree that it is awkwardly expressed and could have been better drafted, but it seems to me to be reasonably clear that the company undertakes to indemnify the assured against loss of or damage to the motor vehicle including accessories belonging thereto thereon, but that the limit of liability is measured by the market value of the motor vehicle. ''The motor vehicle'' in that sentence following immediately after the words which explain that for the purpose of this section the motor vehicle includes the accessories, it seems to me to lead plainly to the result that the limit of liability is measured again by the market value of the motor vehicle with the accessories.'

The term 'accessories' does not apply to the engine of a car, for it is an essential part of the vehicle.[12]

---

[8] (1939) 64 Ll L Rep 288.

[9] Judge Drucquer in Brentford County Court.

[10] (1939) 64 Ll L Rep 288, at 289.

[11] Ibid, at 289.

[12] *Seaton v London General Insurance Co Ltd* (1932) 43 Ll L Rep 398 at 400, K B, per Du Parcq J.

Loss of Vehicle

In *Webster v General Accident, Fire and Life Assurance Corpn Ltd*[13] the insured wished to sell his car, and placed it in the hands of a car dealer for the purpose of its being sold at an auction. The reserve price was not reached, and the dealer informed him that he had received a private offer, but this was untrue. The insured allowed him to retain possession of it. The car was subsequently sold at another auction by the dealer, but all the dealer did was to give the insured a number of cheques, all of which were dishonoured. So the insured claimed from his insurance company under a clause in the policy which said that the company would indemnify him against any 'loss of or damage to the vehicle'. Parker J held that the company was liable, observing in the course of his judgment:[14]

> 'Where a chattel is handed over voluntarily by the owner to another, it may make it difficult for him thereafter to prove a loss; it may be also that in such a case what is lost is not the chattel but the proceeds if the chattel was handed over for sale. No one would suggest, I think—to take a concrete example—that if the owner of a chattel handed over the chattel to X for sale, X representing (if you like) and honestly representing that he had a buyer and the chattel being duly sold, but X misappropriating the proceeds and never paying them over, there had been a loss of the chattel. What had been lost there was the proceeds of sale. But equally it seems to me that if a chattel is handed over to an agent, whether as a result or not of a fraudulent misrepresentation, and the agent then proceeds to deal with the chattel in a way which amounts to a conversion of the chattel, there may be a loss.'

But a different conclusion was reached in *Eisinger v General Accident, Fire and Life Assurance Corpn Ltd.*[15] In this case the insured sold his car to a person who persuaded him to allow him to take it away at once in exchange for a cheque for £745. The cheque was not met on presentation. The insured claimed an indemnity from his insurance company on the ground that there had been a 'loss' within the meaning of the policy.

Lord Goddard CJ held that the claim failed because what the insured lost was the proceeds of sale and not the car, and said:[16]

> 'Has there been a loss of the motor car? What the assured did was to sell this motor car to a man who did not pay for it. The man was, no doubt, a rogue and a swindler, getting the goods by false pretences. Having possessed himself of a cheque book, he gave this assured a cheque for £745. . . . Nevertheless, the assured went on with the transaction and sold the car. It is a clear case of obtaining a car by false pretences. But that passed the property in the car. You cannot say that the assured has lost the car; what he has lost is the proceeds of sale. He has lost the price which the man promised to pay him, and did pay him, or purported to pay him, by a worthless cheque.
> I cannot hold that there is a loss within the meaning of the policy.'

In *Webster v General Accident, Fire and Life Assurance Corpn Ltd*[17] the company also pleaded that even if what happened could constitute a loss, there was on the facts of the case no loss proved because the insured had at all times known where the car was, and that if steps had been taken, he could have recovered it, or at any rate, he had not shown that it was irrecoverable.

---

[13] [1953] 1 Lloyd's Rep 123, QB.
[14] Ibid, at 128.
[15] [1955] 2 Lloyd's Rep 95, QB.
[16] Ibid, at 96.
[17] [1953] 1 Lloyd's Rep 123, QB.

In dealing with this point Parker J said that it was important to bear in mind that the policy concerned was a non-marine one, and that no question of constructive total loss applied. According to passages in *Moore v Evans*[18] it was clear that it was never necessary for an insured to prove that in all circumstances the goods were irrecoverable. Every case depended upon its own facts. An insured was not entitled to sit by and do nothing. Equally, he was not bound to launch into legal proceedings or if necessary carry them to the House of Lords. The test was whether he had taken all reasonable steps, and having taken all reasonable steps whether recovery was uncertain.

In the present case after the cheque had finally been returned 'Account Closed', the insured saw the police at three different police stations about his position, and received the advice that it was hopeless for him to try and recover the car. In all the circumstances his Lordship felt that the insured had taken all reasonable steps.

---

[18] [1917] 1 K B 458, where Bankes L J said (at 471): 'Mere temporary deprivation would not under ordinary circumstances constitute a loss. On the other hand, complete deprivation amounting to a certainty that the goods could never be recovered is not necessary to constitute a loss. It is between those two extremes that the difficult cases lie, and no assistance can be derived from putting cases which are clearly on one side or the other of the dividing line between the two. If assistance is to be obtained at all from considering a hypothetical case, it can only be done by taking one which raises somewhat similar considerations to the case which we have to decide.'

CHAPTER 29

Extension clauses

Extension clauses are of two types. The first kind affords cover to any person driving with the consent of the insured, and the second protects the insured whilst he is driving any other car which does not belong to him.

PERSONS DRIVING WITH THE CONSENT OF THE INSURED

A typical clause[1] states that:

'The Company will indemnify the Insured Person against all sums which he shall become legally liable to pay for damages and claimant's costs and expenses and any other costs and expenses incurred with its written consent in respect of bodily injury (fatal or otherwise) or damage to material, property (payment in respect of such damage being limited to £5,000,000 in respect of any one claim or number of claims arising out of one cause) arising as a result of an accident caused by or in connection with the Vehicle, or the loading or unloading of the Vehicle.

"Insured Person" shall mean any one or more of the following on whose behalf payment is claimed:

1   The Policyholder.
2   Any person entitled to drive by the terms of the Certificate.
3   The employer or partner of any person whose business use is permitted by the terms of the Certificate.
4   Any person using (but not driving) the Vehicle with the permission of the Policyholder for social, domestic and pleasure purposes provided that such use is permitted by the terms of the Certificate.
5   At the request of the Policyholder, any person (other than the person driving) in or getting into or getting out of the Vehicle.
6   At the request of the Policyholder, the Owner of the Vehicle.
7   The attendant of the Vehicle.'

Construction of Clause

In *Williams v Baltic Insurance Association of London Ltd*[2] the construction of the extension clause in the policy was one of the matters in issue. The policy stated that the insurance company would indemnify the insured, Mr Williams, in respect of:

'Sums for which the insured or any licensed personal friend or relative of the insured while driving the car with the insured's general knowledge and consent shall become legally liable in compensation for loss of life or accidental bodily injury caused to any person.'

---

[1] See, eg the clause in the motor car policy issued by the Commercial Union Assurance Co Ltd and set out in Appendix VI, p 438, post.
[2] (1924) 19 Ll L Rep 126, K B.

The insured's sister was a licensed driver. Whilst driving the car with his consent, she was involved in an accident, and the passengers were injured. Damages were awarded against her, and when a claim for an indemnity was made against the insurance company, liability was denied on the ground that the only thing covered by the clause was the sum which the insured might become legally liable to pay because a friend or relative drove the car with his knowledge.

Roche J held that this construction of the terms of the policy was wrong, and that the company was liable. He observed[3]:

> 'That would seem to insure Miss Bransby Williams. She was licensed driver. She was a relative of the insured. She was driving his car with his general knowledge and consent. She became legally liable to pay compensation for accidental bodily injury. I hold without the slightest doubt and hesitation on the plain meaning of these words that what happened was the very thing covered by this clause.
>
> The contention of [Counsel] for the insurance company depends on a strained interpretation of the clause and the introduction of a number of words not there. It is to this effect that, since the indemnity was to be to the insured, Mr B Williams, the only thing that was covered by the clause was the sums which the insured, Mr Bransby Williams, might become legally liable to pay where he became legally liable to pay it because the licensed personal friend or relative drove the car with his knowledge or consent. All I can say is that in my judgment the words of the policy are incapable of meaning and do not mean what is suggested.'

Merely because the policy states that the insurance company will indemnify 'any person who is driving the vehicle on the policy-holder's order or with his permission', this does not make the policy assignable and so render the company liable to an assignee of the vehicle when he is driving it.[4]

Thus, in *Peters v General Accident, Fire and Life Assurance Corpn Ltd*[5] the insured, a Mr Coomber, had effected a policy covering himself and any person driving with his consent. In July 1935 he sold the insured car to a Mr Pope, who drove it on 8 September 1935, and was involved in an accident in which personal injuries were suffered by a third party. The insurance company repudiated liability on the ground that the policy issued to Coomber had lapsed on the sale of the car to Pope and was not assignable. This argument was accepted by the Court of Appeal[6], which held that the claim against the company failed.

Sir Wilfrid Greene M R said:[7]

> 'It appears to me to be as plain as anything can be that a contract of that kind is in its very nature not assignable. The effect of the assignment, if it were possible to assign, was stated by [Counsel] to be that from and after the assignment the name of Mr Pope, the assignee, would have taken the place of Mr Coomber in the policy, and the policy would have to be read as though Mr Pope's name was mentioned instead of Mr Coomber's; in other words, the effect of the assignment would be to impose upon the insurance company an obligation to indemnify a new assured or persons ordered or permitted to drive by that new assured. That appears to me to be altering in toto the character of the risk under a policy of this kind. The risk that A B is going to incur liability by driving his motor car, or that persons authorised by A B are going to cause injury by driving his motor car is one thing. The risk that C D will

---

[3] (1924) 19 Ll L Rep 126 at 127, K B.

[4] *Peters v General Accident Fire and Life Assurance Corpn Ltd* (1938) 60 Ll L Rep 311, C A.

[5] (1938) 60 Ll L Rep 311, C A. The question as to whether Pope was driving with Coomber's consent was also in issue in this case. See on this point, p 241, post.

[6] Sir Wilfrid Greene M R, Scott and MacKinnon L J J.

[7] (1938) 60 Ll L Rep 311 at 312.

incur liability by driving a motor car or persons authorised by C D will incur liability through driving a motor car is, or may be, a totally different thing.

The insurance company in this case, as in every case, makes inquiries as to the driving record of the person proposing to take out a policy of insurance with them. The business reasons of that are obvious, because a man with a good record will be received at an ordinary rate of premium and a man with a bad record may not be received at all or may be asked to pay a higher premium. The policy is in a very true sense one in which a personal element is inherent of such a character as to make it in my opinion quite impossible to say that the policy is one assignable at the volition of the assured.'

Not a Wagering Policy

In *Williams v Baltic Insurance Association of London Ltd*[8] it was held by Roche J that the extension clause in the policy giving an indemnity to the insured and any person driving with his consent was not in the nature of gaming and wagering and was not made void by the Life Assurance Act 1774.

His Lordship said that he would be very much surprised if any person, who had a policy such as this and who, knowing that his son or daughter or other member of the family might have occasion to drive his car, took care to have one policy insuring himself and all the other members of the family, thought that he was gaming.

The company had pleaded that it was a gaming and wagering policy prohibited by law. Section 1 of the Act of 1774 said that no insurance should be made by any person on the life of any other person or on any other event wherein the person for whose benefit or on whose account the policy was made should have no interest or by way of gaming or wagering. But s 4 of the Act stated that 'Provided always that nothing herein contained shall extend . . . to insurances bona fide by any person on ships, goods or merchandizes; but every such insurance shall be as valid . . . as if this Act had not been passed'.

Roche J said that a common notion had prevailed that the proviso in the Act excepted only policies of marine insurance. But there was no authority to that effect. The proviso did not except insurances on goods on ships, but insurances on ships, goods or merchandises. This view had been adopted by the Court of Queen's Bench in *Waters v Monarch Fire and Life Insurance Co*,[9] where a warehouseman recovered on an insurance policy for the benefit of third parties to whom he was not liable.

Roche J followed this decision, and observed:[10]

'I am satisfied that this is a policy on goods; that the motor car is the subject-matter of the insurance. The motor car is a chattel and is goods just as those which the warehouseman held.

But it is said that this clause, governing what is called third-party risk, is not an insurance on goods. That in my judgment is an argument based on an altogether too narrow construction of this section of the Act. If that argument were right, as far as I can judge, the collision clauses in the marine policy which are not clauses on the ship or on the goods would be within the mischief of the earlier part of the Act and within its scope. It has long ago been held that the ordinary policy on ships does not carry with it the protection covered by the well-known collision clauses. It is in a different sense cover against third-party and similar risks as much as this clause is. That is my reason for holding that this policy is an insurance

---

8 (1924) 19 Ll L Rep 126, K B.
9 (1856) 5 E & B 870.
10 (1924) 19 Ll L Rep 126 at 128.

upon the car and that incidentally one of the clauses contains provisions against third-party risks.'

His Lordship said[11] that it therefore became immaterial to decide what the position would be if he had held that the Act of 1774 did apply to the policy, ie whether it had to be shown that the insured was interested in his sister's immunity from claims by third parties, and whether the sister could recover under the policy because she had not been named on it as required by s 2 of the Act.[12]

Giving of Permission a Question of Fact

In order to make the insurer liable on the policy it must be shown that, at the time of the accident, the permitted driver and not another person was actually driving the vehicle.

Thus, in *Paget v Poland*[13] Mrs Fraser permitted Miss Macfie to drive the insured's car. Miss Macfie was an experienced driver. The journey commenced with her at the wheel, but later the driving was taken over by a Miss Paget, and an accident occurred. In her action against the insurer it was held that there was no evidence that she was driving with the insured's consent, and that the claim failed.

Lewis J said:[14]

> 'I saw Mrs Fraser in the witness-box and I am quite satisfied that Mrs Fraser, who from the very beginning had said: "I never gave any sanction to Miss Paget to drive the car," is a lady who is telling the truth. Some comment was made that in the first action, when Miss Macfie brought her action against the two young ladies, Mrs Fraser was not called. It is a little difficult to see why. This is the first time Mrs Fraser has given any evidence with regard to this case, but that she has said all along that she never gave her consent to Miss Paget driving the car is undoubted. It is not a question of her saying nothing: she definitely said to her daughter, in effect, that she could have the car to go to Cambridge if she got somebody to drive, but that person was not to be Miss Paget. How it can be suggested in those circumstances that Miss Paget was driving with the consent of Mrs Fraser is doing violation to the language of the policy and to common sense. Something was said to the effect that if some experienced driver was in the car while Miss Paget was driving, Mrs Fraser would not have objected. Mrs Fraser told me, and I accept it, that no suggestion of that sort was made at the time, and when she was pressed by [Counsel] as to what she would have done, she said: "It was never raised at all." She said she was not quite sure; she might or might not. In my view that is not giving a consent at all. Because a person in a different set of circumstances, when the matter has never before been put to them, says: "I might or might not have given that consent," that is a very long way away from giving your consent for a person to drive your car.'

---

11 (1924) 19 Ll L Rep 126 at 128.
12 Section 2 states: 'And . . . it shall not be lawful to make any policy or policies on the life or lives of any person or persons, or other event or events, without inserting in such policy or policies the person or persons name or names interested therein, or for whose use, benefit, or on whose account such policy is so made or underwrote.' On this point Roche J said (1924) 19 Ll L Rep at 128): 'If it were necessary to come to a decision, I should feel myself unable to come to the conclusion that Miss Williams was inserted in this policy within the meaning of section 2 of the Act of 1774'.
13 (1947) 80 Ll L Rep 283, K B.
14 Ibid, at 285.

In *Tattersall v Drysdale*[15] a Mr Gilling was a director of a firm of motor dealers named Gray Bros & Kemp Ltd. A customer traded in his old car in exchange for a new one. The new one could not be delivered at once, so Gilling lent him his own car until delivery could be made. Gilling was anxious that the customer should insure it in his own name. The customer communicated with his own insurance company, but before he had supplied them with sufficient information, he was involved in an accident whilst driving Gilling's car. The question arose as to whether he was driving the car with Gilling's consent because, if he were, he could claim an indemnity under Gilling's policy.

Goddard J held that the claim succeeded, and observed.[16]

'As to the question of permission, I am clearly of opinion that he was driving with Mr Gilling's permission. It was said that Mr Gilling never intended that the plaintiff should drive the car until he had himself insured it. The truth is that no bargain about insurance was ever made. Mr Gilling, on handing over his car after the bargain had been made, wished the plaintiff to insure it and he was willing to do so, but he was allowed to drive it as he wished, and Messrs Gray Bros & Kemp, in whose hands Mr Gilling had left the matter and at whose garage the plaintiff kept the car, knew he had not got it on to his policy. I have no hesitation in holding that there is nothing in that point.'

In *Browning v Phoenix Assurance Co Ltd*[17] the policy provided that the company would indemnify any person who was driving the car 'on the insured's order or with his permission'. The plaintiff, a garage employee, was permitted by the insured to drive the car at his convenience for the sole purpose of warming the oil before it was drained at the garage so that it would run out freely. The employee was involved in an accident while driving the car, and claimed that the insurance company was liable to indemnify him in respect of damages payable to third parties who had been injured. Pilcher J held that the claim failed, for the accident had happened when the employee was driving for his own purpose on the day after the oil had been drained,[18] and the insured had given him no permission to do this. Consequently the car was not at risk at the time.

The learned Judge observed:[19]

'[The insured] said that he had authorised the plaintiff "to drive the car at his convenience to get it thoroughly warm before draining off the oil". He said nothing about authorising the plaintiff to drive it for any other purpose . . . I accordingly determine that the request made or the permission given by [the insured] was a request made or a permission given to drive the car for a longish run at his convenience, taking the family as passengers, for the sole purpose of getting the transmission oil well warmed up before it was drained. It is now clear that the plaintiff was not driving the car for this purpose when he met with the accident and consequently was not driving it "on the insured's order or with his permission", and that the car was, therefore, not at risk under the policy at the time of the accident.'

Permission Given by Insured's Agent

The permission to drive may be given to another driver by the insured himself. But it is sufficient if it is given by his authorised agent, eg as in *Pailor v*

---

15 (1935) 52 Ll L Rep 21, K B. Another aspect of this case, viz whether the customer was insured is considered at p 245, post.

16 (1935), 52 Ll L Rep 21 at 24, K B.

17 [1960] 2 Lloyd's Rep 360, Q B.

18 See ibid at 364.

19 Ibid, at 367.

Co-operative Insurance Society Ltd[20] where the facts showed that the insured had left it to her husband to give consent to the other driver, and Scrutton LJ said:[1] 'That being so, the consent of the agent appears to me to be quite sufficient to bring that matter, as far as that is concerned, within the policy'.

Persons in Policyholder's 'Employment'

In *Burton v Road Transport and General Insurance Co Ltd*[2] the insured was a motor dealer named Cross. He was insured under a Motor Trader's Policy, which contained an extension clause stating that the insurance company would 'treat as though he were the insured any person in the insured's employ . . . who is driving such vehicle on the insured's order or with his permission'. The car concerned was being driven[3] by a Mr Westwood to demonstrate to a prospective purchaser, and was involved in an accident in which a third party was injured. The company denied liability on the ground that Westwood was not in the 'employ' of Cross, and so the loss was not covered by the policy.

Branson J held that the company was liable. Westwood was engaged by Cross in the hope that he would be able to procure a contract for the sale of the car to the prospective purchaser.[4] In driving the car for this purpose, Westwood was Cross's agent. Accordingly, he was a person driving on the insured's order and with his permission for the purpose of the insured's business. He was, therefore, a person in the insured's 'employ'. The word 'employment' did not mean 'employment under a contract of service'.[5]

His Lordship said:[6]

> 'I think it is plain that the true position between these parties was that Cross was using—let me use a neutral word for the moment—Westwood in the hopes that Westwood would be able to procure a contract for the sale of this car to somebody who was being introduced by Westwood, and the way in which Cross was using Westwood was in directing him and permitting him to take the car and to take the proposed purchaser for a demonstration drive. I think that, when so engaged, Westwood was acting as the agent for Cross.
>
> The question then is whether, while so acting, he can fairly be said to have been in the "employment" of Cross within the meaning of those words as used in this policy. [Counsel] argues that "employment" in the policy can only mean employment under a contract of service. It is plain enough that the word "employment" in its ordinary meaning in English may mean employment both under a contract of service and employment in a dozen other ways. I can find nothing in this policy which makes it right or proper to restrict the word "employment" to a meaning which, if that policy had got to express it properly, could only be expressed by writing into the policy after the word "employment" the words "under a

---

[20] (1930) 38 Ll L Rep 237, C A.

[1] Ibid, at 239.

[2] (1939) 63 Ll L Rep 253, K B.

[3] In pursuance of an arrangement which had been in existence for some two or three years. See ibid, at 255.

[4] For the evidence see ibid., pp 255–256.

[5] His Lordship referred to *Morgan v Parr* [1921] 2 K B 379, where it had been held that the use of the word 'employment' did not connote employment under a contract of service. In that case the question was whether an offence had been committed by Parr, a newsvendor, in unlawfully employing a child in street trading contrary to the Employment of Children Act 1903, s 3 (2). The Divisional Court held that the child had been 'employed' by the newsvendor, even though the relation between them was that of principal and agent, and not of master and servant, and, therefore, there was no contract of service.

[6] (1939) 63 Ll L Rep 253 at 256.

contract of service''. It is not necessary to imply those words, nor is it necessary, in order to give business effect to this document, to restrict the meaning of the word ''employment'' to employment under a contract of service.'

'Licence' includes 'Provisional Licence'

The term 'licence' has been held to include a provisional licence for the purpose of an extension clause in a policy whereby the cover given by it is extended to any person who holds a licence to drive a vehicle, and is driving it with the insured's consent.[7]

Thus, in *Rendlesham v Dunne (Pennine Insurance Co Ltd, Third Party)*[8] the insurance company agreed to indemnify all persons driving the insured's car with his consent provided that such person held a licence to drive the insured vehicle. A permitted driver was involved in an accident in which a third party was involved. He held a provisional licence only, and was not accompanied by a qualified driver as required by the Road Traffic Act 1960. When a claim for an indemnity was made against the insurance company, payment was refused on the ground that the driver did not hold a 'full licence' which was the meaning to be given to the word 'licence' in the policy.

Judge Herbert held that this contention failed, and said that it was impossible to restrict the meaning of the word 'licence' to that of a 'full licence'. It was true that the word 'licence' was used in the Road Traffic Act 1960 to include both types of licence. But he could not think that it was possible to say that a person had not got a licence to drive a car on the road because he had failed to comply with a condition upon which he had been granted a licence.

Disqualified Driver

Where a policy is extended to cover a person who is driving with the permission of the insured provided that he is not disqualified from holding a licence, the word 'disqualified' has been held to mean 'disqualified' by an order of the Court, and does not mean prohibited from holding a licence by reason of mental or physical disability.[9]

In *Edwards v Griffiths*[10] the defendant was charged with an offence of using a motor tractor without there being in force a policy against third party risks contrary to the Road Traffic Act 1930, s 35.[11] The policy stated that the vehicle could be driven by any person with the policy holder's permission 'provided that he held a licence to drive the vehicle or had held or was not disqualified for holding or obtaining such a licence'. The defendant was driving the tractor with the permission of the policy holder. At the time of the alleged offence he had no licence, and, being under the care of the local authority under the

---

[7] *Rendlesham v Dunne (Pennine Insurance Co Ltd, Third Party)* [1964] 1 Lloyd's Rep 192 (Westminster County Court).

[8] [1964] 1 Lloyd's Rep 192. This case is considered on another point, viz whether there had been a breach of a condition in the policy requiring the insured 'to safeguard the car from loss or damage', see p 276, post.

[9] *Edwards v Griffiths* [1953] 2 All ER 874, [1953] 1 WLR 1199.

[10] [1953] 2 All ER 874, [1953] 1 WLR 1199.

[11] Now Road Traffic Act 1972, s 143.

Mental Deficiency Acts 1913–1938[12] because of his mental condition, he would not be able to obtain a licence. He could have been prosecuted for driving without a licence, but the police prosecuted him for driving whilst uninsured.

The Divisional Court of the Queen's Bench Division[13] held that the charge failed, for the defendant was insured within the meaning of the terms of the policy since the word 'disqualified' meant 'disqualified' by an order of the Court, and there was no such disqualification of the defendant in the present case.

In the words of Lord Goddard C J:[14]

> 'It is true that, by reference to s 4 (2), it may be argued that under the provisions of the Act relating to physical fitness and age a person may be said to be disqualified for obtaining a licence, but what we have to decide is whether or not as between the assured and the insurers these words "not disqualified for holding or obtaining such a licence" refer merely to the provision of disqualification by order of the court on conviction. Prima facie, the person who is driving with the permission of the policy holder is covered. It is further provided by the certificate that the person who is driving, whether he is the policy holder or a person driving with permission, must hold or must have held a licence to drive. The words "and is not disqualified for holding or obtaining such a licence" following immediately after the words "has held" seem to me to indicate clearly that the insurers are contemplating the case of a man who has held a licence, but has been disqualified for holding it, meaning disqualified for getting a new one or holding his current licence by reason of an order of the court.'

Where Insured Himself is Injured through Negligence of Permitted Driver

Where the permitted driver causes injury to the insured, he is entitled to an indemnity under the policy.

Thus, in *Digby v General Accident, Fire and Life Assurance Corpn Ltd*[15] the insured's[16] chauffeur was driving her when he was involved in an accident for which he was found to be responsible. She was awarded damages against him, and he claimed an indemnity from the insurance company on the ground that he was a 'permitted driver' under a policy, section 2 of which stated that:

> '1   [The company will pay] all sums which the policyholder shall become legally liable to pay in respect of any claim by any person (including passengers in the automobile) for loss of life or accidental bodily injury . . . caused by or through or in connection with such automobile . . .
>
> 3   The insurance under this section shall also extend to indemnify in like manner any person whilst driving . . . on the order or with the permission of the policyholder.'

The insurance company denied liability on the ground that, when the insurance policy was extended under s 2 (3), the words 'any person' in s 2 (1) did not include the policy holder, but were limited to third parties, ie those who were not parties to the policy but were members of the public.

---

[12] Now the Mental Health Act 1983.
[13] Lord Goddard C J, Parker and Donovan J J.
[14] [1953] 2 All E R 874 at 876, D C.
[15] (1942) 73 Ll L Rep 175, H L.
[16] The insured was Miss Merle Oberon, the film star. The accident resulted in the film company discontinuing production of the film 'I, Claudius'.

The House of Lords[17] held that the claim succeeded. In the words of Lord Atkin:[18]

> 'It is necessary, however, to consider the second argument for the insurers, which, as I understand it, is that the indemnity given in s 2 (3) to the person driving "on the order or with the permission of the policyholder," whom I will call the authorised driver, is in terms a promise to indemnify "in like manner". This refers back to s 2 (1), the indemnity to the policyholder; and as that clause does not indemnify the policyholder against a claim by the policyholder, so, it is said, the authorised driver receives no indemnity against a claim by the policyholder.
> S 2 (3) begins anew with a fresh promise of indemnity. "The insurance under this section shall also extend to indemnify in like manner any person whilst driving," etc. The subject of indemnity is to be ascertained by reference. To me it seems clear that on making the necessary reference the words should read "extend to indemnify [an authorised driver] against all sums which he shall become liable to pay in respect of any claim by any person," etc. "Any person" must receive its ordinary meaning: on this occasion the policyholder is plainly "any person"; the authorised driver is excluded because as before he can be under no liability to himself.'

He went on to say that he could not help thinking that the judgments of those who thought otherwise[19] were unconsciously affected by the unusual and perhaps unexpected spectacle of a master suing a chauffeur and recovering heavy damages against him, no doubt with a view to eventual recovery from the insurance company. But this kind of insurance was not limited to the rich owners of 35 hp Buicks. It was given to the poor owner of a small runabout, who might lend his car for a week-end or for days to an equally impoverished friend. If during that period the borrower were to run down and injure the owner, it would be in no way strange that the driver should be indemnified from his liability, and the injured owner should receive the benefit of the indemnity.[20]

Effect of Sale of Insured Car

Once the insured car is sold, an extension clause providing an indemnity for anyone driving on the policyholder's order or with his permission will be ineffective.

Thus, in *Peters v General Accident Fire and Life Assurance Corpn Ltd*[1] the insured, a Mr Coomber, had effected a policy in September 1934 covering himself and any person driving the insured car with his permission. In July 1935 he sold the car to a Mr Pope, who was driving it in September 1935 when he was involved in an accident in which personal injuries were suffered by a third party. The insurance company repudiated liability on the ground that the property in the car had passed to Pope by reason of the sale, and that Pope was driving the car as his own car at the time of the accident, and not by the order or permission of

---

[17] Lord Atkin, Lord Wright and Lord Porter; Viscount Simon L C, and Viscount Maugham, dissenting.

[18] (1942) 73 Ll L Rep 175 at 184.

[19] MacKinnon and Goddard L JJ, in the Court of Appeal (1940) 67 Ll L Rep 205) and Viscount Simon L C, and Viscount Maugham in the House of Lords.

[20] See to the same effect the speech of Lord Wright: (1942) 73 Ll L Rep 175 at 186.

[1] (1938) 60 Ll L Rep 311, C A. The question as to whether the policy was assignable was also in issue in this case. See on this point, p 234, ante.

Coomber. This argument was accepted by the Court of Appeal,[2] which held
that the claim against the company failed.

Sir Wilfrid Greene M R said:[3]

> 'At the date when the accident took place the entire property in this car was vested in Pope.
> He had bought the car. On the sale of the car the property passed to him, and although
> [Counsel] at one stage of the argument appeared to suggest that it had not, when his attention
> was called to the evidence, he felt himself constrained to give up that point. The property,
> therefore, passed to the purchaser long before this accident took place. The circumstance that
> he had not paid the whole of the purchase price is irrelevant for that purpose, because that
> circumstance does not leave in the vendor, Mr Coomber, any interest in the car. There is no
> vendor's lien, or anything of that sort. The car had become the out-and-out property of Pope.
> Now, when Pope was using that car, he was not using it by the permission of Coomber. It is
> an entire misuse of language to say that. He was using it as owner and by virtue of his rights as
> owner and not by virtue of any permission of Coomber.'

Further, in *Guardian Assurance Co Ltd v Sutherland*[4] one of the issues[5] was
whether the person who was driving the vehicle at the time of the accident was
doing so with the insured's permission. In fact, 3 days before the accident the
car had been sold to another person. Branson J held that the extension clause
was inoperative, and that the company was under no liability on the policy, and
observed:[6]

> 'It was proved that [the insured] had no interest whatever in [the car]. He had no right to give
> or to refuse permission to drive it.'

Effect of Death of Insured

Where the policy contains a clause extending cover to any driver who is driving
the vehicle with the permission of the insured, the permission, if not already
withdrawn, may continue even after the death of the insured.

In *Kelly v Cornhill Insurance Co Ltd*:[7]

> A father had insured his car for 12 months from 26 April 1959, and allowed his son to drive it.
> He died on 2 June 1959. The son continued to drive it, and was involved in an accident on 4
> February, 1960.
>
> *Held*, by the House of Lords[8] (by a majority of 3 to 2) that the insurance company was liable
> on the policy, for the permission to the son continued until it was shown to have been
> terminated. The term 'permission' in the context of the policy was not so rigid that it could
> not refer to a period after the insured's death.

Lord Dilhorne L C said:[9]

> 'It was argued that it was inherent in the grant of permission, that the permittor should have
> power during the period covered by the permission to revoke or to cancel it. On this basis, it

---

[2] (1938) 60 Ll L Rep 311 at 313.

[3] Sir Wilfrid Greene M R, Scott and MacKinnon L JJ.

[4] (1939) 63 Ll L Rep 220, K B.

[5] The question whether the policy had been obtained by misrepresentation in that the insured had
stated in the proposal form that he was the owner of the car whereas in fact he was not, is
considered at p 205, ante.

[6] (1939) 63 Ll L Rep 220 at 224.

[7] [1964] 1 All E R 321, H L.

[8] Lord Dilhorne L C, Lord Reid and Lord Morris of Borth-y-Gest; Lord Hodson and Lord
Guest, dissenting.

[9] [1964] 1 All E R 321 at 323. See also the judgment of Lord Reid, ibid, at pp 326–328, and that
of Lord Morris of Borth-y-Gest, ibid, at 332.

was contended that any permission given by the [father] during his lifetime ceased on his death, or alternatively, within a reasonable time thereafter, or in the further alternative when the person to whom permission had been given had notice of the death . . . There is, in my view, nothing in the policy which supports the argument that the word ''permission'' in the policy meant and only meant permission which during its currency the insured had power to revoke. The word ''permission'' by itself cannot be construed as implying that the permission must be one which there is power to revoke, or can endure only so long as the grantor is in a position to revoke it.'

Lord Hodson, however, in a dissenting speech[10], said that he could not agree that, on the construction of the policy, the word 'permission' could be so extended as to cover the son's claim. He considered that the father's permission to the son ceased on the father's death. When the accident occurred, the father was no longer alive to give the permission, and the car was no longer his since he was dead. Permission presupposed a power to withhold or extend the permission, and he could not see how this difficulty could be surmounted. It was true that difficult situations might arise, and it was said to be absurd that a permitted journey could not be completed, if notification of the death was received during its course, without the cover of the insurance being lost, and a criminal offence being committed. The risk of prosecution in such a case would be remote, and the risk of penalty being inflicted even more distant, and he could not accept the argument in terrorem as compelling him to construe the policy in favour of the son. By his death the car became vested in the insured's executor, and there had been a change of ownership which brought the permission to an end as effectively as a sale of the vehicle during his lifetime would have put it out of his power to give such permission.

INSURED DRIVING CARS OTHER THAN THE INSURED VEHICLE

A typical clause in a policy states that:[11]

'[The Company] will pay . . .
The amount of:
. . . damages and claimant's costs and expenses
. . . any other costs and expenses agreed between [the Policyholder and the Company] in writing arising from bodily injury or damage to property for which the Insured person may be liable at law resulting from an accident . . . while an Insured Person is driving another car or motor cycle, but only when this is permitted in the Policyholder's Certificate.'

Other Vehicle only on Approval

Whether the car which the insured is driving actually belongs to him or whether he has only bought it 'on approval' will depend on the circumstances. If he only has it 'on approval', then it cannot be said that it 'belongs' to him.

Thus, in *Bullock v Bellamy*[12] the policy indemnified the insured 'While personally driving any other private car not belonging to or hired to the assured for

---

[10] [1964] 1 All ER 321 at 332–333. See also the dissenting judgment of Lord Guest, ibid, at 335.
[11] See eg the clause in the motor car policy issued by the Commercial Union Assurance Co Ltd and set out in Appendix VI, p 424, post.
[12] (1940) 67 Ll L Rep 392, K B.

pleasure purposes'. The insured wished to buy a car. A dealer showed him one, and allowed him to drive it away so that he could try it out and test its petrol consumption. Whilst the trial run was taking place, the insured, who was driving the car at the time, was involved in an accident in which a third party was injured. Two days later he returned the car to the dealer as unsuitable. The underwriters disputed liability on the ground that the insured had bought the car, and so the extension clause did not apply. Evidence was adduced to show that he had 'adopted' the transaction within the meaning of s 18, r 4, of the Sale of Goods Act 1893,[13] and had therefore become the owner of the vehicle. It was alleged that he had applied to the insurance brokers to have his insurance transferred from his old car to the car in question, and had admitted to a police officer at the time of the accident that he had 'bought' it.

After reviewing the evidence, Cassels J held that the car was only 'on approval', and that the insured had never adopted the transaction so as to make the car his property. Consequently the underwriters were liable on the policy. The insured had only communicated with the brokers to make sure that he was insured in respect of the trial run. It was true that the insured had told the policeman that he had bought the car. But on that occasion his wife, who was with him at the time, had also said 'You have not bought it'. In his Lordship's opinion those words accurately described the position.

Effect of Sale of Insured Car

Where the insured car is sold, the indemnity extended to the insured whilst driving any other car comes to an end.

Thus, in *Rogerson v Scottish Automobile and General Insurance Co Ltd*[14] the policy covered the insured's legal liability in respect of his use 'of any motor car (other than a hired car) provided that such car is at the time of the accident being used instead of "the insured car"'. The car which the insured originally had was a Lancia with a torpedo-shaped body. During the currency of the policy, without informing the insurance company, he exchanged the car for a Lancia with a saloon body. Shortly afterwards while driving the substituted car, he was involved in an accident, and judgment in favour of an injured third party was given against him. When he sued on the policy, the company repudiated liability on the ground that the substituted car was not being used 'instead of' the insured car, for the insured had parted with the property in and possession of the insured car. The company contended that the protection afforded in respect of the use of any motor car other than the insured car was intended to apply to temporary or occasional use only, such as driving a car lent by a friend. Otherwise an owner might insure a small car of low value and claim that the policy covered third party risks arising from the use of a large and expensive car owned at the same time or subsequently bought by him.

The House of Lords[15] accepted this argument, and held that the action failed. In the course of his judgment Lord Buckmaster said:[16]

---

13 Now the Sale of Goods Act 1979, s 18, r 4. As to the passing of property when goods are sold on approval, see generally Chalmers, *Sale of Goods Act 1979* (18th edn, 1981), pp 146, 147-8, 150-1.

14 (1931) 41 Ll L Rep 1, H L.

15 Lords Buckmaster, Warrington of Clyffe, Russell of Killowen and MacMillan.

16 (1931) 41 Ll L Rep 1 at 2.

'The contention for the [insured] is that any car which, during the period of the insurance, is, in fact, taking the place of the insured car, is within the meaning of the phrase, and that an accident caused by its use is an accident the liability in respect of which is covered by the policy. That is not my view of the matter. To me this policy depends upon the hypothesis that there is, in fact, an insured car. When once the car which is the subject of this policy is sold, the owner's rights in respect of it cease and the policy so far as the car is concerned is at an end . . . It is my opinion that that clause assumes that there is "the insured car", the use of which, if an accident arises, would entitle the assured to the benefit of the policy. If, instead of the car that could be so used, another is used in its place, then the car that is used in its place is entitled to the same privilege as the original car. But if it be assumed that the original car be sold and another car taken in its place, the result would be, if the [insured's] contention were correct, that it might be possible to shift the insurance from car to car during the whole period of 12 months for which the policy runs, and that although there is no express limitation on the nature of the car that may be regarded as a substitute.'

A similar decision was given in *Tattersall v Drysdale*.[17] In this case the policy effected by the insured, a director of a firm of motor dealers, stated that it extended to cover anyone driving with the permission of the insured[18] 'provided that such person is not entitled to an indemnity under any other policy'. The insured lent the car to a customer,[19] who had traded in an old car and was awaiting delivery of a new one. The customer was involved in an accident, and claimed that he was entitled to an indemnity under the insured's policy, because his own policy, which contained a similar extension clause, had ceased to cover him because he had traded in his own car. Consequently he alleged that the proviso in the insured's policy did not apply, for he was not 'a person entitled to an indemnity under any other policy'.

Goddard J held that the claim under the insured's policy succeeded because the customer had parted with his own car and was no longer interested under his own policy. He observed:[20]

'I now turn to the question whether the plaintiff's policy was in force at the time of the accident. It is argued that it was not, because he had sold the car referred to in the policy and the company had not yet accepted the Riley which he was then using. The answer to the question mainly depends on whether this case is governed by *Rogerson v Scottish Automobile and General Insurance Co Ltd*[1]. The words of the extension clause in this policy are different from those used in *Rogerson's* case, and [Counsel] argues that the latter case really turned only on the construction placed on the phrase "instead of the insured car", which does not appear in the clause under consideration. But in my judgment that view is too narrow. I think that both in the Court of Appeal and the House of Lords the decisive factor was that the subject-matter of the insurance was the specified car, and that as the assured had parted with it, he no longer was interested in the policy.

The true view, in my judgment, is that the policy insures the assured in respect of the ownership and user of a particular car, the premium being calculated, as was found in *Rogerson's* case, partly on value and partly on horse-power. It gives the assured by the extension clause a privilege or further protection while using another car temporarily, but it is the scheduled car which is always the subject of the insurance. Though the words differ in the two policies, the effect and intention seem to me to be the same, and express provision is made for what is to happen when the assured parts with the car. To construe this policy otherwise would be to hold in effect that two distinct insurances were granted, one in respect of the scheduled car and another wholly irrespective of the ownership of any car. It may be that a

---

17 (1935) 52 Ll L Rep 21 K B.
18 As to 'permitted drivers', see pp 233–243, ante.
19 The Court found, as a fact, that the customer was driving with the insured's permission. This aspect of the case is considered at p 237, ante.
20 (1935) 52 Ll L Rep 21 at 24.
1 (1930) 38 Ll L Rep 142, C A; affd (1931) 41 Ll L Rep 1, H L.

person who does not own a car can get a policy which would insure him against third-party risks whenever he happens to be driving a car belonging to someone else; but the clause I am considering is expressly stated to be an extension clause, that is, extending the benefits of this policy, and accordingly, if the assured ceases to be interested in the subject-matter of the insurance, the extension falls with the rest of the policy.'

Whether 'Van' a 'Motor Car'

In *Laurence v Davies (Norwich Union Fire Insurance Society Ltd, Third Party)*[2] the insured had effected a policy by which the insurers agreed to indemnify him against liability for damages in respect of injury to any person arising out of an accident caused by or in connection with 'the driving by the insured of any motor car . . . not belonging to him and not hired to him under a hire-purchase agreement.'

Whilst the insured was driving a Ford Transit van, it was involved in an accident in which his passenger was injured. Damages were awarded against the insured and he claimed an indemnity from the insurers. The insurers denied liability on the ground that the insured was not covered whilst he was driving a van for it was not a 'motor car' within the meaning of the policy. The insured, however, maintained that the van was a 'motor car', within the meaning of the Road Traffic Act 1960, s 253 (2)[3] and that the policy must be construed *contra proferentem*.[4]

Dunn J held that the action succeeded, for, on the true construction of the policy, the van was a 'motor car', and consequently the insured was covered whilst driving it. He observed:[5]

'I accept that the first principle of construction of a contract is to follow the natural and ordinary meaning of the words but I accept the submissions of [Counsel] that the words must be considered in their context and that these words were used in the context of motor insurance. It is, of course, an offence to drive a vehicle if it is not insured and in the special case of motor insurance I accept [Counsel's] submission that if insurers desire to place some meaning on words like "motor car" or "motor cycle" or "private motor car" or "motor vehicle" other than those contained in the Road Traffic Act, they should make it abundantly clear in the policy, and if they fail to do so, then the words will be deemed to have those meanings.'

---

[2] [1972] 2 Lloyd's Rep 231 (Exeter Crown Court).

[3] Which is now replaced by the Road Traffic Act 1972, s 190(2), which states that 'motor car' means 'a mechanically propelled vehicle, not being a motor cycle or an invalid carriage, which is constructed itself to carry a load or passengers and the weight of which unladen—

(a) If it is constructed solely for the carriage of passengers and their effects, is adapted to carry not more than seven passengers exclusive of the driver, and is fitted with tyres of such type as may be specified in regulations made by the Secretary of State, does not exceed three tons;

(b) if it is constructed or adapted for use for the conveyance of goods or burden of any description, does not exceed three tons, or three tons and a half if the vehicle carries a container or containers for holding for the purpose of its propulsion any fuel which is wholly gaseous at 60° Fahrenheit under a pressure of 30 inches of mercury or plant and materials for producing such fuel;

(c) does not exceed two tons and a half in a case falling within neither of the foregoing paragraphs'.

[4] As to the *contra proferentem* rule, see Ivamy, *General Principles of Insurance Law* (4th edn, 1979), pp 386–392.

[5] [1972] 2 Lloyd's Rep 231 at 233.

CHAPTER 30

The exceptions in the policy

The policy usually provides that the insurers are not to be liable for any loss or damage whilst the vehicle is being used for racing, pace-making or speed trials, or is taking part in motor rallies, being used for any purpose other than one which is authorised by the terms of the policy, drawing a trailer, or carrying a greater number of passengers than it is constructed to carry.[1]

Further, they will not be liable whilst the vehicle is being driven in an unsafe, defective or damaged condition, and they will only be liable if the driver holds a licence to drive or has held and is not disqualified from holding or obtaining such a licence. There is no liability for any loss or damage caused directly or indirectly by war, invasion, hostilities, acts of foreign enemies, civil war, revolution, rebellion, insurrection, military or usurped power or seizure, arrest, confiscation, requisition, destruction of or damage to property by order of any government or public authority; nor is there any liability for any loss or damage consequent on earthquake, nor consequent on riot and/or civil commotion occurring elsewhere than in Great Britain or Northern Ireland or the Channel Islands.

Sometimes special policies are arranged to cover risks normally excepted from the scope of the ordinary type of policy.

SOME USUAL EXCEPTIONS

Decided cases which have concerned the interpretation of words found in various exception clauses in common use relate to:

1   The condition of the vehicle.
2   The condition of the insured.
3   Restriction of driving of the vehicle by named drivers only.
4   The driving qualification of the insured or other driver.
5   The area of operation.
6   The restriction as to the carriage of personal luggage only.
7   The restriction as to the type of use.
8   Loss in the course of warfare, disturbance of the peace, earthquake, etc.

---

[1] As to exception clauses generally, see Ivamy, *General Principles of Insurance Law* (4th edn, 1979), pp 276–281

1 Condition of the Vehicle

'Being Driven in an Unsafe or Unroadworthy Condition'

Sometimes the policy contains an exception stating that the insurance company will not be liable 'whilst the vehicle is being driven in an unsafe or unroadworthy condition'.

In one case it has been held that to bring the loss within an exception in these terms the insurer must prove that the vehicle was not only unroadworthy at the time of the accident but also when it set out on its journey.[2]

Thus, in *Barrett v London General Insurance Co Ltd*[3] the policy contained an exception which excluded liability for loss or damage 'whilst driving the car in an unsafe or unroadworthy condition'. An accident occurred, and a third party was injured. The insured claimed under the policy, but the insurance company contended that the loss fell within the exception. Goddard J said that the onus of proving that the loss fell within the exception lay on the company, and that it had not succeeded in doing so. All that had been proved was that at the moment of the accident the car was unsafe and unroadworthy because the footbrake failed to work. It was necessary for the company to go further, and prove that the car was unsafe or unroadworthy when it set out on its journey. This had not been proved, so the learned Judge held that the insured was entitled to succeed.

Goddard J said that considerable assistance could be obtained from well settled principles in the law of marine insurance, and observed:[4]

> 'It is elementary in marine insurance that the owner of the vessel impliedly warrants that it is seaworthy. So far as I know, it has not yet been decided whether there is the same implied warranty in the case of a motor car, and it seems to me that the object of the exclusion is to put the underwriters of a motor car policy in the same position in this respect as those of a marine policy. It matters not, in the result, whether the protection is given to the insurers by means of a warranty express or implied, or by an express clause exempting them if the vehicle or vessel is not fit for the element, be it land or sea, on which it is to be used. Now, it is settled law that there is an implied warranty that a ship is seaworthy at the time of sailing, but there is no warranty that she shall continue seaworthy throughout the voyage.'

He then went on to say:[5]

> 'In my judgment, this doctrine should apply to the clause I am now considering, and it should be read as meaning that the car must be roadworthy when it sets out on its journey. Were it otherwise, consider what the result would be. I cannot do better than quote the courageous illustration given by [Counsel] in the course of his argument. He said that if a stone, or something of that nature, caused the cable to break during the course of the journey, and an accident to a third party immediately followed because the brake in consequence failed, the underwriters would not be liable. Everyone knows that in a motor car something may give or go wrong in the course of the journey which may, temporarily at any rate, put the car out of control, and that from a variety of causes; and if in such circumstances this exclusion is to relieve the underwriters, it seems to me that the indemnity given by the policy would be exceedingly precarious.'

His Lordship also said[6] that it had been argued that, because the car had an efficient handbrake, it could not be said to be unsafe or unroadworthy, even

---

2 *Barrett v London General Insurance Co Ltd* (1934) 50 Ll L Rep 99, K B.
3 (1934) 50Ll L Rep 99, K B.
4 Ibid, at 101.
5 Ibid, at 102.
6 Ibid, at 103.

though the footbrake was defective. But he himself did not agree with that contention. No doubt the accident might have been avoided if the insured had used his handbrake, but this was not decisive of the case against the insurance company. It would be impossible to hold that a car put on the road with one of its braking systems wholly ineffective was otherwise than in an unsafe condition.

The fact that the insured did not know of the unsafe condition of the vehicle is irrelevant.

Thus, in *Trickett v Queensland Insurance Co Ltd*[7] the wording of the exception clause was in similar terms, viz 'being driven in a damaged or unsafe condition'. Here a collision occurred at night and the insured was killed. It was proved that at the time it occurred the lights of the car were not working, nor had they been working some time before the accident.[8] The Privy Council[9] held that the loss fell within the exception, and that the insurance company was not liable on the policy.

One of the arguments put forward on behalf of the insured was that to escape liability the insurance company had to prove that the insured knew of the defective condition of the lights, but the Court held that this contention was unsound. Lord Alness said:[10]

'Their Lordships cannot find any justification for supplementing the terms of the proviso by adding to it the words "to the knowledge of the driver", as they are invited to do by the [assured], or for reforming the contract into which he entered. It is not immaterial to observe in this connection that, in certain of the other provisos which are adjacent to that with which the Board are concerned, the knowledge of the assured is set out eo nomine, where it is intended that knowledge should form a condition of the contract between the parties.'

He then went on to say that in any event their Lordships, on the evidence, would have great difficulty in holding that the insured was ignorant of the unlit condition of the car.

The Court also rejected the argument that on the analogy of the law of marine insurance the exception only applied where the car was in a damaged condition at the beginning of its journey, or that, in other words, there was no continuing warranty by the driver of the roadworthiness of the car. On this point Lord Alness said:[11]

'The third point argued by [Counsel] for the [insured] is quite independent of the previous two points. His contention depends for its validity on certain dicta of Goddard J in *Barrett v London General Insurance Co*.[12] All that their Lordships find it necessary to say regarding that judgment is that, while not questioning the conclusion reached by the learned Judge on the facts of the case, they find great difficulty in agreeing with the reasons upon which that conclusion was based. They are not able to assimilate, as did the learned Judge, the position of a ship at sea with that of a motor car on land and in rigidly applying the same code of law to both cases. For reasons which are too obvious to be stressed in detail, their Lordships think the analogy imperfect and indeed misleading. They are of opinion that the argument based by the [insured] on the identity of the conditions which govern the seaworthiness of a ship at sea and the roadworthiness of a car on land is unsound.'

---

[7] (1936) 53 Ll L Rep 225, PC.
[8] The evidence is set out, ibid, at 226.
[9] Lord Alness, Lord Roche and Rowlatt J.
[10] (1936) 53 Ll L Rep 225 at 228,
[11] Ibid, at 228.
[12] [1935] 1 K B 238.

But in *Clarke v National Insurance and Guarantee Corpn Ltd*[13] a different view was expressed as to the usefulness of the analogy of cases concerning seaworthiness in marine insurance.

Harman L J said:[14]

'Against that there was the decision in a case in the Privy Council which said it was not a good comparison to make. They were there dealing with a case of Goddard J's, as he then was, of *Barrett v London General Insurance Co Ltd*,[15] where Goddard J took in a motor car case the comparison of the implied warranty of seaworthiness and held that so on the road it only applied at the outset of the voyage. With all respect to that very eminent Judge, he was not considering the clause he had to construe. There again he was construing something about being driven, that is to say during the voyage, and any help he thought he got from a warranty at the start of the voyage does not seem to me to have been in point. It was on that point that Lord Alness in giving the judgment of the Privy Council in *Trickett v Queensland Insurance Co Ltd*[16] said this:[17]

"... They [—that is the Board—] are not able to assimilate, as did the learned judge, the position of a ship at sea with that of a motor car on land, and rigidly apply the same code of law to both cases. For reasons which are too obvious to be stressed in detail, their Lordships think the analogy imperfect and indeed misleading. They are of opinion that the argument based by the [insured] on the identity of the conditions which govern the seaworthiness of a ship at sea and the roadworthiness of a car on land is unsound."

That expresses it, if I may say so, rather broadly and it was not necessary for the decision the Board were making to do more than say that they did not follow Goddard J's decision. Nevertheless, those words it was which caused Davies J, sitting in the Court below, to say that he ought to set aside the seaworthy cases. I agree that you cannot rigidly apply them and they are no more than a help, but nevertheless it does seem to me to be a significant point in a case about roadworthiness that when you are considering seaworthiness, you may consider whether the ship is overloaded or not.'

Again, Havers J observed:[18]

'I have myself found some assistance from the cases dealing with seaworthiness in contracts for carriage by sea and in marine insurance. I bear in mind the observations which were made in the Privy Council in the case of *Trickett v Queensland Insurance Co Ltd*,[19] [by] Lord Alness[20] ... giving full weight to those dicta. I still think that the shipping cases are of some assistance in construing this section.'

Although a car may be mechanically sound when unloaded, it is not roadworthy if, when loaded with passengers, it cannot be driven safely.

In *Clarke v National Insurance and Guarantee Corpn Ltd*[1]

An exception clause in a motor car policy stated that the insurance company was not to be liable for loss or damage while the car was 'being driven in an unsafe or unroadworthy condition.' The car concerned was a Ford Anglia designed to carry 4 people. Whilst driving it with 8 passengers on board, the insured was involved in an accident. It was proved that by reason of the overloading the steering, braking and control of the vehicle were impaired. In a claim under the policy—

Held by the Court of Appeal that the exception applied and the insurance company was not liable.

---

13 [1963] 2 Lloyd's Rep 35, C A.
14 Ibid, at 38.
15 [1934] 1 K B 238.
16 [1936] A C 159.
17 Ibid, at 165.
18 [1963] 2 Lloyd's Rep 35, at 42.
19 [1936] A C 159.
20 Ibid, at 165.
1 [1964] 1 Q B 199, [1963] 3 All E R 375, C A.

In the course of his judgment Harman LJ observed:[2]

'This car was grossly overloaded; that was agreed by everybody. That it *could* be driven safely the experts agreed, but not over 25 miles per hour. Its steering was affected, it was liable to go out round the corners, and so on, and the experts generally agreed that though one could, by keeping to the side of the road driving with very great precautions, perform a journey, and even this trip which the [assured] was on, in safety, yet looked at in the ordinary way for ordinary purposes and going at an ordinary sort of pace, this car was unsafe. There are two views about this matter, and one of them is this. It was not . . . the condition of the car which caused the trouble, but the misuse of the car by [the assured], and that is not a matter which comes within the exception. On the other hand, Counsel for the [insurance company] says that when looking at this car standing at the kerb loaded up with nine persons just before it started, anybody would say that the car in that condition was unroadworthy, unsafe, and that . . . it was being driven in an unroadworthy condition . . . I think that, on the whole, this exception did apply. I think that one must regard the car as it was as it proceeded along the road, not look at it empty before it was loaded up and say: "This was a safe and mechanically sound car".'

In *A P Salmon Contractors Ltd v Monksfield*[3] an exception in the policy concerning a lorry stated:

'*Condition of the Insured Vehicle and Right of Inspection.*—The Insured shall take all reasonable steps to safeguard from loss or damage and maintain [the vehicle] in a substantial and thoroughly safe condition . . . The underwriters shall not be liable if [the] vehicle is driven or used in an unsafe condition.'

Part of a load of plywood tied with wire fell off the lorry, which was owned by the insured and driven by one of their employees, and injured a pedestrian, who was awarded damages of £285. When a claim was brought by the insured for an indemnity under the policy, the underwriter refused to pay on the ground[4] that the loss fell within the exception since the vehicle was not properly loaded and was used in an unsafe condition.

Judge Graham Rogers, giving judgment in the Mayor's and City of London Court, held that the underwriter was liable. He considered[5] that the present case was distinguishable from *Clarke v National Insurance and Guarantee Corpn Ltd*[6] where the overloading was the sole cause of the unsafeness of the vehicle. In the present case the faulty loading had no such effect.

The fact that a towing chain, by which an insured vehicle is towing another lorry, is defective does not mean that the insurers can rely on an exception stating that they are not to be liable for loss or damage 'through the driving of any insured vehicle in an unsafe condition either before or after an accident'.[7]

In *Jenkins v Deane*[8] whilst the insured vehicle, a Ford, was towing another lorry which had broken down, the tow rope broke and an accident occurred. The insurers maintained that they were not liable because the vehicle was being

---

2 [1963] 3 All E R 375 C A at 377. See also the judgment of Pearson LJ, ibid, at 379–380, and that of Havers J, ibid, at 381.
3 [1970] 1 Lloyd's Rep 387.
4 Another issue in the case was whether the underwriter could rely on an exception excluding liability for 'death or bodily injury to any person . . . caused by the spreading of material or substance from the insured vehicle or load carried by such vehicle'. As to this point, see p 253, post.
5 [1970] 1 Lloyd's Rep 387 at 390.
6 Supra.
7 *Jenkins v Deane* (1933) 47 Ll L Rep 342, K B.
8 (1933) 47 Ll L Rep 342, K B.

driven in an unsafe condition, and that therefore the loss fell within the exception. Goddard J held that this defence failed, and said:[9]

> 'It is said that because the tow chain was defective and because it got round the wheels or steering gear of the towed lorry, causing it to get out of control, the damage was caused by an insured vehicle being in an unsafe condition . . . There is no suggestion that the Ford lorry was in an unsafe condition, and the tow chain was no part of the vehicle. If a tug takes a vessel in tow and the tow line is defective and breaks, would anyone say that this proved that the tug itself is unsafe? I think not.'

Vehicle Conveying Excess Load

In *Jenkins v Deane*[10] the policy contained an exception stating that the underwriters would not be liable for loss or damage whilst the insured vehicle was 'conveying any load in excess of that for which it was constructed.' The insured vehicle, a Ford, was towing another lorry which had broken down. An accident occurred when the second lorry got out of control after the towing chain broke. The insurers contended that they were not liable because the exception applied since the Ford was towing the other lorry, and the weight of that lorry and its load had to be added to the load of the Ford, thus exceeding the load limit specified in the policy, viz $2\frac{1}{2}$ tons. This argument was rejected by Goddard J, who remarked:[11]

> 'It is said that as the Ford was towing the other lorry, the weight of that lorry and its load is to be added to the load of the Ford. I do not so read that clause. It has not in my opinion anything to do with towing, but merely with the weight superimposed on the vehicle itself. Giving the ordinary meaning to the words, I am unable to see how it can be said that in giving a tow, a vehicle or a vessel is conveying a load. The words do not appear to me appropriate. Nor does the reason for the insertion of the condition apply to a tow. Weight that can be carried has no relation to weight that can be drawn. No one, I suppose, could carry a garden roller, but most people can draw one.'

Where a private car is carrying more passengers than it is built to carry, the insurance company is not entitled to repudiate liability on the ground that an exception in its policy provides that it is not to be responsible for loss or damage caused or arising whilst the vehicle is 'conveying any load in excess of that for which it was constructed.'[12]

Thus, in *Houghton v Trafalgar Insurance Co Ltd*[13] the policy contained an exception in the above form. The car concerned skidded and was damaged beyond repair. It also damaged property belonging to a third party. At the time of the accident the car had five passengers in it, although it was constructed to carry four only. The insurance company claimed that it was not liable because the vehicle was carrying an excess load. The Court of Appeal[14] held that the insured's claim under the policy succeeded.

Somervell L J said:[15]

---

9 (1933) 47 Ll L Rep 342 at 346, K B.

10 (1933) 47 Ll L Rep 342, K B.

11 Ibid, at 345.

12 *Houghton v Trafalgar Insurance Co Ltd* [1953] 2 Lloyd's Rep 503, C A.

13 [1953] 2 Lloyd's Rep 503, C A.

14 Somervell, Denning and Romer, L JJ.

15 [1953] 2 Lloyd's Rep 503, at 504. Denning L J said (ibid, at 505) that the exception was only

'In my opinion, the words relied on, ''any load in excess of that for which it was constructed,'' only clearly cover cases where there is a weight load specified in respect of the motor vehicle, be it lorry or van. I agree that the earlier words in the clause obviously are applicable to an ordinary private car in respect of which there is no such specified weight load. But there was, of course—and I think it would have been inadmissible anyhow—no evidence as to whether this was a form which was used for lorries as well as ordinary private motor cars. I do not think that matters. We have to construe the words in their ordinary meaning, and I think those words clearly only cover the case which I have put. If that is right, they cannot avail the insurance company in the present case.'

He said that he thought that it would need the plainest possible words if it were desired to exclude the insurance cover by reason of the fact that there was at the back one passenger more than the seating accommodation allowed for. All sorts of obscurities and difficulties might rise. He added that if any insurance company wished to put forward a policy which would be inapplicable when an extra passenger was carried, he hoped that it would print the clause in red so that the insured would have it drawn to his particular attention.

Spreading of Material

Another issue[16] in *A P Salmon Contractors Ltd v Monksfield*[17] was whether the underwriter could repudiate liability on the ground that the injury to the pedestrian[18] fell within an exception in the policy which stated that

'The Underwriters shall not be liable in respect of . . . death of or bodily injury to any person . . . caused by the spreading of material or substance from the insured vehicle or load carried by such vehicle.'

Counsel for the underwriter contended that any escape of part of a load from a vehicle was a 'spreading of material' from the load carried within the terms of the exception, and that accordingly the underwriter was not liable. It was argued that 'spreading' could in this context be either transitive or intransitive, and was not limited to a positive act such as the spreading of grit on to a road, but included an accidental spreading of part of the load. Counsel relied on definitions of 'spread' in the Shorter Oxford English Dictionary, eg 'to send out in various directions', and 'to distribute'.

Judge Graham Rogers, however, held that the exception did not apply, for he considered that in the present context the word 'spreading' was used transitively, ie a deliberate diffusion or dissemination, and that 'spread' was not the word which one would use if one were contemplating excluding from the terms of an insurance policy the accidental fall of part of a load from a lorry.

---

applicable to cases where there was a specified weight which must not be exceeded as in the case of lorries. Romer L J said (ibid, at 505) that any clause which purported to have the effect alleged by the insurance company ought to be clear and unambiguous so that the motorist knew exactly where he stood. The provision was neither clear nor unambiguous. If applied to a private car, he had not the slightest idea what it meant.

16 The other issue was whether the loss fell within an exception stating that the underwriter would not be liable 'if [the] vehicle is driven or used in an unsafe condition'. As to this point, see p 251, ante.

17 [1970] 1 Lloyd's Rep 387, Mayor's and City of London Court.

18 For the facts of the case, see p 251, ante.

Where the Insured Vehicle has a Trailer

A lorry, which is being towed by an insured vehicle, is not a 'trailer' for the purpose of an exception excluding the liability of an insurance company for loss or damage 'whilst the insured vehicle has a trailer attached thereto'.[19]

In *Jenkins v Deane*[20] the insurers repudiated liability on a policy containing such a clause on the ground that, at the time of an accident in which the insured vehicle was involved, it was towing another vehicle, and, therefore, the loss came within the exception. This contention was rejected by Goddard J. In the course of his judgment he observed:[1]

> 'I think the trailer referred to in the clause is a truck or wagon, commonly referred to as a trailer, used for increasing the space available for the conveyance of goods, and that the term cannot be fairly applied to a temporarily broken down motor vehicle which is taken in tow.'

2 Condition of the Insured

The policy in *Louden v British Merchants' Insurance Co Ltd*[2] contained an exception which stated that the insurance company was not to be liable for any injury sustained by the insured 'whilst under the influence of drugs or intoxicating liquor'. The insured was travelling as a passenger in a friend's car, and lost his life in an accident when the vehicle failed to negotiate a bend and ended up in a ditch. There was no doubt that he was drunk.[3] Lawton J held that an action brought by the insured's personal representative claiming the sum of £1,000 payable in the case of death failed on the ground that the loss fell within the exception.

The learned Judge rejected the contention of counsel that the words 'sustained whilst under the influence of intoxicating liquor' were so uncertain as to their meaning that no effect should be given to them. On this point his Lordship observed:[4]

> 'The words used in the exemption clause of the policy before me have probably been used for many years in policies giving assurance against injury. Counsel for the [insurers] referred to *Mair v Railway Passengers Assurance Co Ltd.*[5] The policy in that case provided that the assurance should not extend to any death or injury happening while the assured was under the influence of intoxicating liquor. The case came before Lord Coleridge C J and Denman J, by way of an application for a new trial on the ground that the verdict had been against the weight of evidence. Both learned Judges construed the words, ''while the assured is under the influence of intoxicating liquor,'' although it may not have been necessary for the purposes of their judgment to do so. Neither seems to have thought that the words were so uncertain as to be incapable of construction. Both were of the opinion that these words connoted a disturbance

---

[19] *Jenkins v Deane* (1933) 47 Ll L Rep 342, K B.

[20] (1933) 47 Ll L Rep 342, K B.

[1] Ibid, at 346.

[2] [1961] 1 Lloyd's Rep 154, Q B.

[3] At the time of the accident his blood alcohol was at least 268 milligrammes per 100 millilitres. See ibid, at 158. The learned Judge remarked (ibid, at 158): 'There was a very high degree of probability that the higher centres of his brain had been so affected by the alcohol he had consumed as to cause him to lose control of his faculties, particularly his faculty of judgment and of controlling the finer movements of his limbs and extremities'.

[4] Ibid, at 157.

[5] (1877) 37 L T 356.

of the facilties, Lord Coleridge C J,[6] using the words, "as disturbs the balance of a man's mind," and Denman J[7] the words, "disturbing the quiet, calm, intelligent exercise of the faculties".'

He said that he would therefore adopt the construction in *Mair v Railway Passengers Assurance Co Ltd*[8] even though it had been expressed in mid-19th century idiom. He would add no gloss as to do so might add confusion where none might have existed among insurers and policy holders during the past eighty-four years.

Further, he considered that on its proper construction the exception did not imply a causal connection between the bodily injury and the state of being under the influence of drink. The word 'whilst' had a temporal meaning only.[9]

3 Restriction of Driving by Named Drivers Only

The policy may provide that the insured is only covered whilst he alone is driving the vehicle.

In *Herbert v Railway Passengers Assurance Co*[10] the insured, a Mr Wilkinson, effected a policy which stated:

'The company shall not be liable in respect of any accident incurred while any motor cycle is being driven by any person other than the insured or is for the purpose of being driven by him in charge of any person other than the insured.'

Wilkinson was driving with a friend to a football match. He had a severe cold and was feeling unwell, so he allowed his friend to drive the motor cycle. An accident occurred, and injury was suffered by a third party. When a claim was made against the insurance company, liability was repudiated on the ground that the insured was only covered while the motor cycle was being driven by him and no one else.

Porter J held that this was the true construction of the policy, and that the company was not liable. In considering the argument of counsel for the insured that it was possible to interpret the policy in a different manner, he said:[11]

'[Counsel] suggests, and has put before me with force and ingenuity the suggestion, that one might read it as if the words "driven by," as well as "or is for the purpose of being driven by," were qualified by and form part of the phrase which continues—"in the charge of any person other than the insured." Let me make a little plainer what I mean by that. What is meant by that, as [Counsel] says, is that instead of reading the sub-clause (b): "The company shall not be liable while the vehicle is being driven by any person other than the insured or is for the purpose of being driven by him in the charge of any other person," one ought to read it: "is being driven by any person other than the insured, in the charge of any person other than the insured," or is for the purpose of being driven by him in the charge of any person

---

6 (1877) 37 L T 356, at 358.

7 Ibid, at 359.

8 Supra.

9 [1961] 1 Lloyd's Rep at 158. It is surprising that no mention was made in this case of *Givens v Baloise Marine Insurance Co Ltd* (1959) 17 D L R (2d) 7 (Ontario Court of Appeal) where the facts were precisely similar, though the policy was not a motor insurance policy but one in respect of personal accident. Here, too, it was held by a majority (Laidlaw and McGillivray J J A; Le Bel J A dissenting) that a causative connection between the intoxication and the death need not be shown.

10 (1938) 60 Ll L Rep 143, K B.

11 Ibid, at 145.

other than the insured. Now, if that is true, leaving out immaterial words, one would have to read it in this way: ''The insurer shall not be liable while the motor [cycle] is both being driven by any person other than the insured and in the charge of any other person than the insured.'' That does not seem to me something which is either required or which could be said to meet any object, or to be the natural reading of the words. In my view, neither is that a construction which would be a natural construction of the words, nor am I able to accept that as being the true construction of the policy.'

Again, in *GFP Units Ltd v Monksfield*[12] where the policy restricted the driving of the car to a person who controlled a company and to his wife, and a mechanic drove it on a joy-ride and damaged it, Roskill LJ[13] held that the insurers were not liable.

4 Driving Qualification of Insured or Other Driver

A common exception states that:

'The company shall not be liable . . . unless the person driving holds a licence to drive such vehicle or has held and is not disqualified for holding or obtaining such a licence.'

Where the insured is a limited company, and the policy states that the insurers will not be liable for loss or damage whilst the vehicle is 'being driven by the insured, unless he (i) holds a licence to drive such vehicle or (ii) has held or is not disqualified for holding or obtaining such a licence', the words 'being driven by the insured' mean 'being driven by or on behalf of the insured'. Accordingly, no successful claim can be made under the policy unless the driver employed by the company and driving the vehicle at the time of the accident causing loss had a licence to drive.[14]

Thus, in *Lester Bros (Coal Merchants) Ltd v Avon Insurance Co Ltd*[15] the insurance company was not liable where the licence, which had been applied for by the driver, had not been granted to the driver until three days after the accident, for at that moment he did not hold a licence, and so came within the words of the exception in the policy.

In *Haworth v Dawson*[16] a car hire firm named G & K Hire Ltd were insured under a policy which stated that the insurance company

'will . . . indemnify the insured and any person hiring any of the cars specified in the First Schedule hereto who shall have completed the company's driving proposal form which shall be deemed to be the basis of the contract between such hirer who does not come within the category of excluded hirers.'

As regards the categories of excluded hirers it was stated:

'*Clause* 2—no person shall be a hirer . . . until the insured shall have satisfied himself by an actual driving test that the prospective hirer is a careful and competent driver of motor cars.

Clause 3—no person shall be a hirer . . . until he shall have completed a hirer driving proposal form on the form supplied by the company for that purpose.

---

12 [1972] 2 Lloyd's Rep 79, QB.
13 Sitting as an additional Judge of the Queen's Bench Division.
14 *Lester Bros (Coal Merchants) Ltd v Avon Insurance Co Ltd* (1942) 72 Ll L Rep 109, KB.
15 (1942) 72 Ll L Rep 109, KB.
16 (1946) 80 Ll L Rep 19, KB. This case is considered on another point—viz whether the insurance company had waived compliance with the conditions 2 and 4 set out in the text above—at p 277, post.

Clause 4—no person shall be a hirer . . . unless he holds a current driving licence which must be the continuation without a break of a driving licence issued at least 12 months prior to the date of the hire and be free from any endorsements.'

A man named Dawson hired a car from the insured, and was involved in an accident in which personal injuries were received by a pedal cyclist. The question arose as to whether the insurance company was liable for the loss. The company pleaded that Dawson's licence had been twice endorsed for speeding, that he had not been given a driving test by the insured, that consequently he came within the description of 'excluded hirers,' and that therefore it was not liable.

Lewis J held that Dawson was an 'excluded hirer', and that the company was not liable. He observed:[17]

'The question is whether or not, in view of the fact that this man Dawson, in fact, had two endorsements for speeding, and, in fact, had no test at all, he is covered by this policy, or whether G & K Hire Ltd are covered by this policy. It is quite clear, in the circumstances which I have described, that he came within the category of persons described within the policy as "excluded hirers", and, that being so, I confess I am in very great difficulty in deciding, and, indeed, cannot decide, that this man is covered by the policy.'

The policy in *Spraggon v Dominion Insurance Co Ltd*[18] was in similar terms to that in *Haworth v Dawson*.[19] In this case Warnes, a car hire firm, took no steps to satisfy itself that Tomrley, the prospective hirer, had a driving licence of the required kind, for it had been endorsed. The Court of Appeal[20] held that the hirer was an 'excluded hirer', and that the company was not liable on the policy.

Sir Wilfrid Greene M R said:[1]

'It is perfectly clear upon the face of the documents that Tomrley was not insured. In the original policy issued to Warnes, persons of the description of Tomrley were excluded. The reason why he was excluded from the policy was the fact that he held no proper driving licence. He may also have been a member of an excluded class, but apparently there is no evidence about that. Therefore, it is apparent that under the policy issued to Warnes, Tomrley was not insured at all.'

5 Area of Operation

Sometimes the vehicle is insured only when it is being operated in a specified area. If it is outside the area, there is no liability on the part of the insurer. Whether it is being operated in the area is a question of fact.

Thus, in *A W and E Palmer v Cornhill Insurance Co Ltd*[2] there was no restriction as to the area in which a lorry was to be used when the policy was first issued. The vehicle was involved in an accident at the Welsh Harp on the North Circular Road in London. The insurance company denied liability on the ground that by later oral agreement between the parties the policy had been varied by a term restricting the use of the lorry to the area of Mepal in

---

[17] (1946) 80 Ll L Rep at 23, K B.
[18] (1941) 69 Ll L Rep 1, C A.
[19] Supra.
[20] Sir Wilfrid Greene M R, MacKinnon and Du Parcq L JJ.
[1] (1941) 69 Ll L Rep 1 at 3.
[2] (1935) 52 Ll L Rep 78, K B.

Cambridgeshire. Horridge J accepted the evidence given on behalf of the company,[3] and held that the claim failed.

6 Restriction as to Carriage of Personal Luggage Only

In *Piddington v Co-operative Insurance Society Ltd*[4] the policy contained an exception stating that the insurance company would not be liable for any loss or damage whilst the car was 'conveying goods other than personal luggage'. Two laths of wood had been attached by the insured to his car to be brought to his home to be used for a trellis in his garden. Whilst they were so attached, he was involved in an accident. The insurance company contended that it was not liable because the car was conveying goods other than personal luggage. Lawrence J held that this contention failed, that the goods were 'personal luggage', and that the company was liable. He observed:[5]

> 'Any other construction seems to me to lead to the conclusion that the carriage of a packet of seeds, or a rose bush, or the various other articles which ordinary users of private motor cars habitually carry home for the adornment or use of their families, or homes, or their gardens . . . would be goods "other than personal luggage" within the meaning of this policy.'

7 Restriction as to Type of Use

The use of the vehicle may be restricted by the terms of the policy, eg the insured may be covered only whilst the vehicle is being used:

> 'For the business of the insured and for his social, domestic and pleasure purposes excluding use for the carriage of passengers for hire or reward and use for pace-making or speed testing.'

'Social, Domestic and Pleasure Purposes'

In *Wood v General Accident, Fire and Life Assurance Corpn Ltd*[6] an employee of the insured was driving a car with his consent, and thus was a 'permitted driver'[7] within the meaning of the policy. The policy stated that the insurance company would indemnify a 'permitted driver' in respect of loss or damage whilst the vehicle was being used 'for social, domestic and pleasure purposes'. The policy holder was riding as a passenger in the car, and was injured in a collision. The employee claimed an indemnity from the company in respect of the damages which he had to pay his employer as a result of a judgment given against him in the High Court.

At the time of the accident the insured was riding in his own car because it was more convenient for him to do so rather than travel in a hired car. Further, it was more comfortable, pleasurable and restful. He was the owner of a garage at Tulse Hill, and was travelling to Oxford Street to visit a firm with which he intended to negotiate a contract in connection with his business. The company refused to indemnify the employee on the ground that the car was not being

---

[3] The evidence is set out (1935) 52 Ll L Rep 78 at 79, K B.
[4] (1934) 48 Ll L Rep 235, K B.
[5] Ibid, at 237.
[6] (1948) 82 Ll L Rep 77, K B.
[7] As to 'permitted drivers', see pp 233–243, ante.

used for 'social, domestic and pleasure purposes', and contended that the loss therefore was not covered by the policy.

Morris J accepted this argument, and held that the claim failed, saying:[8]

> 'The words that are used in this policy are well-known and well-used words. It seems to me that, on the facts as found, it would not be reasonable to say that this was a journey that was for "social, domestic and pleasure purposes" . . .
>
> On the facts as found, the situation here was that somebody in the employment of the policy holder, in connection with his work, during time for which he was paid, on the order of his employer, drove the car to Oxford Street. That journey to Oxford Street was undertaken by the employer because, as is found, the employer hoped and intended, at the end of the journey, to negotiate a contract in connection with his garage business with Messrs Francis & Pearse Ltd. It seems to me that it would be to give an unnatural meaning to words if it were to be held that that journey was for either social or domestic or pleasure purposes.'

In *Seddon v Binions (Zurich Insurance Co Ltd, Third Party)*[9], a Mr Binions was issued with a policy, which entitled him to drive cars in addition to his own, provided that they were being used for 'social, domestic and pleasure purposes'. His son carried on business as a carpet layer, and on Sundays the father used to go and help him. One Sunday the son was being assisted by an employee named Hale. Hale had toothache so the father drove him in the son's car to a dentist. The father would have gone home to lunch in any case. In the course of the journey, the father was involved in an accident and Mr Seddons was injured. Mr Seddon's claim was compromised by the son's insurers, who now sought to recover half the damages from the father's insurers.

The Court of Appeal[10] held that the claim failed, for, on the evidence, the father was not driving the son's car for 'social, domestic and pleasure purposes'. Roskill LJ said that the essential character of the journey was the use of the son's car by the father to take Hale to a dentist which was user for a business purpose.[11]

'Business of the Insured'

Where the proposer effects a policy in respect of a car and cover is provided while it is used for the business of the insured, and the business of the insured has been converted into a limited company, the insurer is not under a duty to indemnify him, for the business insured is that of the proposer, and that has ceased to exist when the company is formed.[12]

Thus, in *Levinger v Licenses and General Insurance Co Ltd*[13] the proposer for a motor insurance policy started a millinery business early in 1934. In March 1934 it was turned into a company under the title of the Beech Hat Co Ltd. In the proposal form she stated that the car would be used for 'social, domestic and pleasure purposes' and also for any business or trade purposes of the insured. The proposer was involved in an accident in which a third party was injured,

---

8 (1948) 82 Ll L Rep 77 at 81, K B.
9 [1978] 1 Lloyd's Rep 381, C A.
10 Megaw, Roskill and Browne L JJ.
11 [1978] 1 Lloyd's Rep 381 at 385. See also the judgment of Browne L J, ibid, at 386, and that of Megaw L J, ibid, at 387.
12 *Levinger v Licenses and General Insurance Co Ltd* (1936) 54 Ll L Rep 68, Ch D.
13 (1936) 54 Ll L Rep 68, Ch D.

and had to pay damages to him. When the proposer claimed to be indemnified by the insurance company, the company repudiated liability on the ground that, when the accident took place, the car was engaged in the business of the company and not in that of the proposer, for at that date the business had been turned into a company, and she herself had no business to which the policy could attach.

Eve J said:[14]

> 'I can well imagine that many persons in Mrs Levinger's position would treat the business as hers. But though one must not be too strict in reading this language, one must not disregard language of which the construction is plain; and, after the formation of the company and the transfer of the assets of the business to the company, language which would attach to that the expression "Mrs Levinger's business" would be quite inaccurate. It is an abuse of words. From the moment when the company's title was complete it was the business of the company only.
>
> Unfortunately, not appreciating possibly the dangers which lie in these matters of insurance, the parties have allowed this policy to be issued in terms, or the proposal form to be framed, so as to debar the company from any relief. The company has no interest in this policy. The company is not insured nor is the business which is insured that of the company. The business insured is that of the lady, and that ceased to exist in every respect when the company was formed. It is not, therefore, a policy which gives the company the protection they claim, and in those circumstances, attaching as I must do to the very simple and plain language "the business of the assured" its proper and only reasonable meaning, I must hold that this action is misconceived and must be dismissed, with costs.'

In *Passmore v Vulcan Boiler and General Insurance Co Ltd*[15] the policy contained an exception stating that the company would not be liable for loss or damage whilst the vehicle was 'being used otherwise than in accordance with the "Description of Use" contained in this policy'. The 'Description of Use' stated 'Use for social, domestic and pleasure purposes and use for the business of the insured as stated in the Schedule hereto . . .'. The business of the insured was described in the Schedule as 'carrying or engaged in the business or profession of representative and no other for the purposes of this insurance'.

The insured was a representative of a hosiery firm. She was being driven by a Mrs Cooke, who was also a representative in the same firm, when an accident occurred. The insured had caused it through negligently interfering with Mrs Cooke's driving, and, on being sued by Mrs Cooke, had to pay her damages. She claimed an indemnity from the company. The company denied liability on the ground that the loss fell within the exception because at the time of the accident the car, although being used for the purpose of the business of the insured, was also being used for the business of Mrs Cooke, and so was being used otherwise than in accordance with the 'description of use' in the policy.

Du Parcq J held that this contention would be upheld, and said:[16]

> 'The words of the policy are that the insurers shall not be liable in respect of any accident caused while the insured motor vehicle is being used otherwise than in accordance with the "description of use". Was it being used otherwise than in accordance with the description— "otherwise than for social, domestic and pleasure purposes and use for the business of the insured"? It was not being used for social, domestic or pleasure purposes. Was it being used otherwise than for the business of the insured? I do not think one can answer that question

---

[14] (1936) 54 Ll L Rep 68, at 69, C L D
[15] (1936) 54 Ll L Rep 92, K B. This decision was followed by Pilcher J in *Browning v Phoenix Assurance Co Ltd* [1960] 2 Lloyd's Rep 360, Q B. See p 262, post.
[16] (1936) 54 Ll L Rep 92 at 94, K B.

otherwise than in the affirmative. It was. It was being used for the business of Mrs Cooke. I see no escape from that. It is immaterial to consider whether Mrs Cooke's business is similar to or identical with the business of Miss Passmore. The insurers are entitled to know what the business is for which a car is going to be used, and they are entitled to say that before they cover a risk they must have an opportunity of judging what the risk is. [Counsel] says quite truly that the principle would be the same if Mrs Cooke had been travelling in some quite different goods. There may be cases where the nature of the goods and the district to be covered may be of vital importance. I think, therefore, that I should be doing an injustice to the insurance company in coming to any other conclusion than that there is no escape from the words of the policy.'

The learned Judge, however, indicated that the position might be different if the insured had given a lift to a friend, who happened to be on business of his own. He said that:[17]

'A case might arise where the person insured under the policy would extend a courtesy to a friend or acquaintance, or it might be to a stranger, who was, in fact, carrying on some business and was assisted in carrying on that business by the facilities which were given to him by the insured. In such a case, if the facts found were that the insured, as a matter of kindness, courtesy or charity, gave a lift—to use a colloquial phrase—to someone who happened to be on business of his own, I have no doubt that the proper view to take would be that the car was, for the time being, being used for a social purpose, and it would not the less be used for a social purpose because the person benefiting by the courtesy was on business.

But that is not what happened here. The arbitrator has excluded any considerations of that kind. Miss Passmore did not say to Mrs Cooke, "I shall be pleased to give you a lift as a friend." The car was being used first for the purposes of Miss Passmore's business, and secondly, and in addition, for the purposes of Mrs Cooke's business.'

In *DHR Moody (Chemists) Ltd v Iron Trades Mutual Insurance Co Ltd*[18] a company carrying on business as chemists insured a car under a policy which confined its cover to the use of the vehicle

'for social, domestic and pleasure purposes and use for the business of the Insured including carriage of goods'. [—namely the business of pharmacists and no other—] . . .

One of the insured's employees was the chairman of the Town Twinning Committee of the Clacton UDC. The town was twinned with the French town of Valence, and arrangements were made for a delegation from Valence to visit Clacton. The clerk to the Council asked the insured's employee whether the insured would be willing to lend the Council a car to take the French visitors to London Airport at the end of their visit. The insured agreed to do so, and the clerk accompanied by two other Council officials, whilst driving back from the airport after seeing off the visitors, was involved in an accident, and the car was damaged to the extent of £560. When a claim was made under the policy, the insurers repudiated liability on the ground that at the time of the accident the car was being used otherwise than in accordance with the 'description of use clause' set out above for (i) the activities of the Council in encouraging social contact with Valence could not be regarded as social ones and the car when used for those activities was not being used for a social purpose; and (ii) the car was being used by the clerk to the Council to enable him to carry out his duties ie for a 'business purpose'.

It was held that the claim succeeded. Wrangham J said that the car was being used to bring back from the airport persons who had been seeing off their

---

17 (1936) 54 Ll L Rep 92 at 94, K B.
18 [1971] 1 Lloyd's Rep 386, Q B D.

visitors, and prima facie that would be a social activity.[19] Just as an individual's activities could be divided into business activities, so could those of a local authority, and in the present case the Council's activity in trying to encourage social contact with Valence was a social and not a business one, and a car being used in the course of that activity was being used for a social purpose.[20] Again, the fact that the clerk was fulfilling his duty to his employer by driving it did not of itself prevent the use of the car being for a social purpose.[1] Persons like the insured who made cars available to the Council for a social purpose were extending a courtesy to them and were therefore using them 'for a social purpose'.[2]

'Vehicle Used for Purpose of Motor Trade'

The policy in *Browning v Phoenix Assurance Co Ltd*[3] stated that the insurance company was to be liable if the loss or damage took place whilst the car was being used 'for social, domestic and pleasure purposes', but not when used 'for any purpose in connection with the motor trade'. A 'permitted driver',[4] who was a garage employee, was involved in an accident, and claimed that he had been authorised to take the car out in his own time with his family as passengers, and to give it a general test to see that it had been properly serviced. Pilcher J decided the case on other grounds, viz that at the time of the accident he was not driving on the insured's order and with his permission,[5] and that in any event the company was not liable.

But he went on to say, obiter, that, even if the employee had been authorised (which in his own view he had not), the loss fell within the exception. The user would have been for a permitted and also for a specifically excluded purpose. He considered that in these circumstances the plaintiff would not have been able to recover.

He concluded:[6]

> 'In this connection I was referred to the case of *Passmore v Vulcan Boiler and General Insurance Co Ltd*[7] . . . That case was decided by Du Parcq J, as he then was, on a special case stated by an arbitrator. The case, therefore, has stood for nearly 25 years, and I was informed that during this period it has never been commented upon adversely or, apparently, expressly followed. On the findings of fact of the arbitrator in that case Du Parcq J found, in substance, that the car with which he was concerned was being used for two purposes, one of which was permitted and the other of which was not covered because it was a use "otherwise than for the business of the assured." This being so, he held, on those findings of fact of the arbitrator that the assured was not entitled to recover . . . I am happy to say that had it been necessary for me to determine this point, I should respectfully have agreed with Du Parcq J's decision.'

---

[19] [1971] 1 Lloyd's Rep 386 QBD at 388. His Lordship, however, said that if the visitors were merchants who had come to see their customers, seeing them off would be a business activity because it would all be part of the attempted negotiation of business: ibid, at 388.
[20] [1971] I Lloyd's Rep 386 at 388, QBD.
[1] Ibid, at 388.
[2] Ibid, at 389.
[3] [1960] 2 Lloyd's Rep 360, QB.
[4] As to 'permitted drivers' see pp 233–243, ante.
[5] On this point, see p 237, ante.
[6] [1960] 2 Lloyd's Rep 360 at 367.
[7] (1936) 54 Ll L Rep 92, KB.

In *Gray v Blackmore*[8] the insured was a garage proprietor, and was issued with a policy which stated that it did not cover any loss or damage or liability whilst the car was being used 'otherwise than for private purposes'. 'Private purposes' were defined as meaning 'social, domestic and pleasure purposes and use by the assured in connection with his business or profession. The term "private purposes" does not include . . . use for any purpose in connection with the motor trade.'

A car broke down in London, and the insured was requested by the owner's son to repair it on the road or, if he could not do so, he was to remove it. The insured found that it was impossible to repair it on the spot. He therefore used the insured car to tow it to his garage. The tow rope was fixed up, and after the cars had moved about two yards, a pedestrian tripped over the rope and was injured. When a claim for an indemnity was made against the insurer, liability was denied on the ground that the accident had taken place when the car was being used for a purpose connected with the motor trade.

Branson J held that the car was being so used, and dismissed the action. As to the interpretation of the clause set out above, he said:[9]

'An attempt has been made to say that the two branches of that clause are mutually inconsistent, and that the policy having been issued in pursuance of the proposal signed by a man who said he was a garage proprietor, it must be read as though the second sentence of the clause was deleted, as allowing the assured to use the car in connection with his business. I cannot so treat the clause. In order to ascertain what is the definition of "private purposes" it is necessary to read the whole definition. The definition contains two branches, one of which includes something which prima facie would not come under the heading of "private purposes," and the rest of which excludes something which the first branch has brought in, and it is impossible to say they are mutually inconsistent. What one has to do is to read the whole thing together and to come to a conclusion upon it. If that is done, there is no difficulty at all. If the assured is a person whose business is the motor trade, well, then, the second part of it prevents the first part of it from allowing him to use the car for the purposes of his business.

In my opinion, therefore, it is quite clear that, upon the policy as it stands, if this car was being used for any purpose in connection with the motor trade, the policy did not cover it.'

His Lordship then reviewed the facts[10] and concluded:[11]

'Now, upon those facts it seems to me to be quite plain that the plaintiff went to the scene of this accident in pursuance of an order given to him as a garage proprietor to go and see what was the matter with the car, to repair it on the spot if possible, and to arrange for its removal if it was not possible to repair it on the spot. In other words, he was in charge of the car as the person who was commissioned to repair it and to remove it from the road. I think that when he went there, he went in order to do this work, which was work in connection with the motor trade. I think that while he was there he was doing work in connection with his business, which was a business in connection with the motor trade, and that the attempt which was made in argument, and to some extent by the evidence of Mr Gray, to suggest that, having gone there in the one capacity, he suddenly switches over to another capacity in order to do the towing, is a hopeless attempt to get out of what is the real fact in the case.'

'Carriage of Goods in connection with any trade'

In *Jones v Welsh Insurance Corpn Ltd*[12] the policy contained an exception which stated that the company would not be liable in respect of a claim if the vehicle

---

[8] (1933) 47 Ll L Rep 69, K B.
[9] Ibid, at 72.
[10] The facts are set out ibid, at 72–73.
[11] Ibid, at 73.
[12] (1937) 59 Ll L Rep 13, K B.

were being used otherwise than in accordance with the 'Description of Use' clause contained in the policy. This clause stated that the vehicle was covered whilst it was being used for social, domestic and pleasure purposes by the insured in connection with his business 'but excluding always use for the carriage of goods . . . in connection with any trade or business'. The insured carried on business as a motor engineer. But he kept a few sheep, as was almost a universal habit of the hill district in Wales where he lived. With his permission his brother was driving the car (as was allowed under the policy),[13] and carried two sheep and two lambs from a field, which the insured rented, to his father's house. An accident occurred in which a third party was injured. The insured claimed an indemnity under the policy, but the company refused to pay on the ground that the car was being used otherwise than in accordance with the 'Description of Use' because it was being used 'in connection with a trade'.

The insured contended that he was only keeping the sheep as a hobby, but Goddard J held that he was carrying on a business. So the loss fell outside the terms of the policy, and the claim failed.

He observed:[14]

> 'Now, though Thomas says he kept sheep as a hobby, and in one sense that is no doubt true, it is equally clear that he kept them with the intention of selling the lambs, and possibly the sheep also, to butchers or farmers when opportunity offered. He hoped to make some profit by so doing. I am asked to hold that he was only keeping the sheep for pleasure, for something to occupy his spare time, and because amusement was hard to come by in so remote a district. People no doubt do breed sheep as a hobby; pedigree animals are often bred for the interest that they give to the owner and the hope of winning prizes at shows. But sheep-breeding is hardly a pastime in the proper sense of the word, and though I have no doubt that Thomas felt as much interest in his little flock as a breeder would in a pedigree flock, I cannot avoid the conclusion that the real object in view was the making of a little extra money to supplement his wages as a mechanic. A mechanic earning £2 14s a week cannot afford the luxury of stock-breeding solely for pleasure and enjoyment; nor does Thomas pretend that he was breeding lambs for the purpose of killing them for food for himself and his family. The truth is that he was a sheep-farmer, though on a very small scale, and I think I am bound to hold that he was carrying on that business as a sideline, so to speak, but none the less it was a business. The car at the time of the accident was accordingly being used, not by the insured in person in connection with his business of a motor mechanic, but was being used for the carriage of goods in connection with the business of sheep farming.'

'Use for Hiring'

(i) The General Position.   In *Wyatt v Guildhall Insurance Co Ltd*[15] the policy covered 'use for social, domestic and pleasure purposes and use by the insured in person in connection with his business . . . excluding use for hiring'. The insured had met a Mr Hartman, who was a friend of his, and the plaintiff, and said that he was going to London and that he would take both of them there for 25/- each. The insured's purpose in going to London was to give evidence for a friend of his, who had been charged with a criminal offence. The plaintiff and Hartman each paid the money to the insured. On the way to London the car collided with a lorry and the plaintiff was injured. The insured could not satisfy

---

[13] As to 'permitted drivers', see pp 233–243, ante.

[14] (1937) 59 Ll L Rep 13 at 15.

[15] (1937) 57 Ll L Rep 90, K B.

the judgment given against him, so the plaintiff sued the insurance company. The company pleaded that it was not liable because at the time of the accident the car was 'being used for hiring'.

Branson J accepted this contention, and held that the claim failed. He observed:[16]

> 'Whether one treats it as a case in which the use of the car for the purpose of taking two people to London for a consideration takes the user out of the words "use for social, domestic and pleasure purposes," or whether one takes the view, seeing that the proposal form is a proposal for an insurance under Class 1, which means paying a lesser fee than would be required if the car was used for business or trade purposes and which would be smaller still than the premium under Class 3 which does not exclude hiring, that "hiring" is intended to include use for a money payment, I think the same result follows. I read the "description of use" as a whole, and I have formed the opinion that it does not cover the case of a car which is being used to convey people for payment from one place to another, even though the owner of the car might have been intending to take the same journey by himself, and having the opportunity of making a little money by carrying somebody else he took it.'

In *McCarthy v British Oak Insurance Co Ltd*[17] the insured was covered whilst the car was being used for social, domestic and pleasure purposes. But the policy excluded use for hiring. He permitted[18] a man named Roskam to borrow it (as was allowed under the policy), so that he could take some friends with him on a pleasure trip to see the illuminations at Southend. An arrangement was made whereby the friends said that they would pay for the petrol and oil. Whilst Roskam was driving, he collided with the plaintiff, who was injured. Roskam could not pay the damages awarded against him, so the plaintiff sued[19] the insurance company. The company contended that the vehicle was being 'used for hiring', and so there was no liability.

Atkinson J held that the claim succeeded. The car was being used for social, domestic and pleasure purposes. He said that what was intended to be hit or excluded by the policy was something which was a genuine business contract for hiring—something which was a real hiring, doing something for a stipulated reward, a stipulated quid pro quo. He did not think that there was any hiring here. All the circumstances had to be looked at.

His Lordship's attention was referred to *Wyatt v Guildhall Insurance Co Ltd.*[20] But he said that in that case there was no question of pleasure or social purposes. It was a genuine business of hiring. In the present case there was no such business arrangement at all. It was a joint pleasure party, and there was no hiring of the car. Roskam did not make a penny out of it. He was to do the borrowing of the car for his friends, and they were to pay the cost of the petrol and oil.

The learned Judge then said:[1]

> 'If [Counsel] is right about this, it seems to me a great many users of cars almost every day of their lives must be stepping out of the cover of their insurance policies. Supposing I wanted to

---

[16] (1937) 59 Ll L Rep 90, K B at 93.
[17] (1938) 61 Ll L Rep 194.
[18] As to 'permitted drivers', see pp 233–243, ante.
[19] Under the Road Traffic Act 1934, s 10, which is now re-enacted by the Road Traffic Act 1972, s 149. As to the rights of third parties to claim against the insurers under that Act, see pp 450–451, post.
[20] Supra.
[1] (1938) 61 Ll L Rep 194 at 196.

go to a certain place and I say to my son, who has his car conveniently at hand, ''Will you let us use your car; will you drive me and your mother to so-and-so, and I will pay the petrol, we are going on a picnic?'' The mere fact that I agree to pay for the petrol, if [Counsel] is right, is to take that drive out of the cover of the policy, and the insurance company can say: ''Oh, you, the insured''—that is my son—''were using this for hiring because you drove your father and mother, they paying for the petrol'.'

In *Bonham v Zurich General Accident and Liability Insurance Co Ltd*[2] the policy covered the vehicle when used for social, domestic and pleasure purposes and use by the insured in person in connection with his business. But it excluded 'use for hiring'. The insured carried three passengers every day from Northampton to his place of work at Market Harborough. His passengers all worked there too. Two of them regularly and habitually paid him in return for their carriage at the rate of 1s 2d per return journey, the rate being based on the cost of the railway fare between the two towns. He never asked them for payment. The third passenger paid nothing. The insured would have carried the passengers even if they had not paid him at all. One of the passengers was killed when the car was being driven by the insured. The insured was held liable to the executor of the deceased's estate, and claimed an indemnity under the policy. The insurance company refused to pay on the ground that at the time of the accident the vehicle was being 'used for hiring'.

The Court of Appeal[3] held that this defence succeeded,[4] but by a majority[5] decided the case on another ground,[6] and held that the claim failed.

In *Orr v Trafalgar Insurance Co Ltd*[7] the policy granted an indemnity to the insured whilst the insured vehicle was being used solely for the purposes stated in the Schedule to the policy. The Schedule stated that the use of the vehicle was limited to private purposes only, and a note printed on the policy stated that 'private purposes' meant 'social, domestic and pleasure purposes and use by the insured in person travelling to and from his permanent place of business.' There was also an exception in the policy stating that the company was not to be liable 'whilst any such car is being used for private or public hire.'

The insured, Prescott, was on a visit to the premises of a garage and car-hire business. The owner, named Gallagher, received a telephone call from a customer named Moore, asking him to take him to the railway station. His own car would not start, so he asked Prescott, who was a friend of his, to pick up Moore in the insured car instead, since it was waiting outside and time would be saved. Gallagher told Moore to expect the car in about ten minutes. After Moore had been waiting for twenty minutes he saw a car coming towards him. He beckoned to it with a view to hitch-hiking to the railway station. Prescott was driving the car and Moore got into it. On the way to the station the car knocked down the Orr. Prescott telephoned Gallagher and told him what had happened. Gallagher subsequently picked up Moore and took him to the

---

2 (1945) 78 Ll L Rep 245, C A.
3 MacKinnon and Du Parcq LJJ, and Uthwatt J.
4 See the judgment of MacKinnon LJ (1945) 78 Ll L Rep 245 at 247: 'It was said on the facts found . . . [the insured] was not using it only for his own business, for going to his work, but that he was using it for hiring. I think it is sufficient to say that upon those facts I am quite satisfied that the car was not on this occasion being hired by him. I think we are all agreed upon that'.
5 Du Parcq LJ and Uthwatt J: MacKinnon LJ, dissenting.
6 Viz that there had been a breach of a condition of the policy.
7 (1948) 82 Ll L Rep 1, C A.

station, but he was late and the train had gone. Moore asked him what the charge would be, and Gallagher said that it would be nothing.

Prescott could not pay the damages awarded to Orr, so Orr sued[8] the insurance company, which repudiated liability on the ground that the insured at the time of the accident was using the vehicle for private hire.

The Court of Appeal[9] held that the action failed because the loss fell within the exception. Although there was no express mention of any payment for hire, it was implied from the conduct of the parties that Moore would pay either Prescott or Gallagher for the journey to the station.

Tucker LJ said:[10]

'It is clear that when the question arises as to whether or not a motor car is being used for the purpose of private hire, that necessarily involves a decision as to whether or not there was at the material time an obligation, express or implied, to make payment for the journey in question. In the present circumstances I think that if Prescott had completed the journey to Lime Street Station without mishap and had, at the conclusion of the journey, asked Mr Moore for some reasonable remuneration for that journey, and Moore had refused to pay, either Prescott or Gallagher—and it matters not which—could have recovered.'

Asquith LJ delivered judgment to the same effect, and observed:[11]

'I am satisfied that Moore would not have expected to obtain Prescott's car and services for nothing, any more than Gallagher's car and services for nothing. It is quite true that no express mention seems to have been made of payment between Prescott and Moore while they were together, but there might well have been such a mention but for the accident. Having regard to the accident, it was quite natural that payment should not be demanded. It does not follow from its not being demanded that there was not initially an implied contract constituted by conduct to make payment—a contractual obligation waived in consequence of the accident itself. If there was such an obligation on Moore to pay, it does not seem to me to matter whether that obligation was owed to Gallagher or to Prescott; in either case Prescott's car was being used for hire.'

(ii) Undertaking by Insurers.   In 1975 motor insurers issued the following undertaking: 'The receipt of contributions as part of a car-sharing arrangement for social or other similar purposes in respect of the carriage of passengers on a journey in a vehicle insured under a private car policy will not be regarded as constituting the carriage of persons for hire or reward (or the use of the vehicle for hiring) provided that: (a) the vehicle is not constructed or adapted to carry more than 7 passengers excluding the driver); (b) the passengers are not being carried in the business of carrying passengers; (c) the total contributions received for the journey concerned do not involve an element of profit.'[12]

8 Loss in the course of Warfare, Disturbance of the Peace, Earthquake, etc.

A typical exception in a policy states that:

---

8 Under the Road Traffic Act 1934, s 10, which is now re-enacted by the Road Traffic Act 1972, s 149.
9 Tucker, Asquith and Singleton LJJ.
10 (1948) 82 Ll L Rep 1 at 6.
11 Ibid, at p 6.
12 See Department of Transport circular 9/78, Annex 4.

'The company shall not be liable in respect of . . . any consequence of war, invasion, act of foreign enemy, hostilities (whether war be declared or not) civil war, rebellion, revolution, insurrection or military or usurped power except so far as is necessary to meet the requirements of the Road Traffic Acts . . . and accident, injury, loss or damage . . . arising during . . . or in consequence of (a) earthquake or (b) riot or civil commotion occurring elsewhere than in Great Britain, the Isle of Man or the Channel Islands.'

The above words are common exceptions in almost all branches of insurance law, and are treated together in another place in this work.[13]

As regards motor insurance the only exception of this type which is considered in the decided cases has concerned 'civil commotion'.

'Civil Commotion'[14]

In *Cooper v General Accident, Fire and Life Assurance Corpn*[15] the policy contained an exception which excluded liability for:

'Loss or damage occasioned through riot or civil commotion occurring within the land limits of Ireland.'

The insured effected an insurance policy in respect of his car on May 7, 1920. The garage was close to his house at Ballinrea in the district of Douglas, County Cork. On 28 October 1920, he put it in there as usual. Later he heard a noise in the yard near the garage and opened the back door of the house. A voice said 'shut that door'. This happened three times. All he saw was an arm, which held what might have been a revolver or a stick. Shortly afterwards he saw the car moving off. He claimed for a loss under the policy, but the company pleaded the exception clause on the ground that the loss was occasioned through 'civil commotion'.

The House of Lords held[16] that the claim failed. It was common knowledge that there was a state of guerilla warfare in parts of Cork County and in the City of Cork, and that the combatants largely availed themselves of cars in their attacks on the police and the military forces. For warfare of this kind the possession of cars was of great service. In order to come within the terms of the exception it did not have to be proved that there was a commotion at the time and place where the loss occurred.[17] If the loss was occasioned through, ie if it took place as a consequence of civil commotion, the case fell within the exception, and the company was not liable.[18] In concluding that the car was lost as a result of a 'civil commotion', and not as a result of the action of an ordinary thief, Viscount Finlay said:[19]

'It appears to me to be inconsistent with any probability that that was the action of any ordinary motor thief. The manner in which, instead of endeavouring to carry out the abstraction quietly, he said in a tone apparently of command three times "Shut that door," when the owner, who was in the house, ventured to take some interest in what was happening in his

---

[13] See Ivamy, *General Principles of Insurance Law* (4th edn, 1979), pp 276–281.

[14] As to the exception of 'civil commotion', see generally Ivamy, *General Principles of Insurance Law* (4th edn, 1979), pp 278–279.

[15] (1922) 13 Ll L Rep 219, H L.

[16] Viscount Cave L C, Viscount Finlay, Lord Dunedin, Lord Atkinson and Lord Sumner.

[17] See the judgment of Viscount Cave L C (1922) 13 Ll L Rep 219 at 220, and that of Viscount Finlay, ibid, at 221.

[18] See the judgment of Viscount Cave L C, ibid at 220.

[19] Ibid, at 221.

own garage to his own property—all these circumstances go to show that those who were engaged in this abstraction must have been acting with some force behind them which made them feel they were masters of the situation, and it appears to me to be quite inconsistent with the idea that it was any ordinary motor thief who was guilty of the removal of this car.'

This case was applied by the House of Lords in *Thomas Boggan v Motor Union Insurance Co.*[20] Here the policy contained an exception which excluded the liability of the insurance company in respect of:

'Loss or damage arising during (unless it is proved by the insured that the loss or damage was not occasioned thereby) or in consequence of earthquake, war, invasion, civil commotion, military or usurped power.'

On 7 November, 1920, during the currency of the policy the insured's chauffeur was driving at a good speed on the road at Watescross, which was some miles from Wexford. Three or four men appeared in the road, each armed with a revolver. One of them told him to get out of the car, and he was taken to an outhouse, kept there for $3\frac{1}{2}$ to 4 hours and then released. The car was driven away, and the insured claimed under the policy. The House of Lords[1] dismissed the action on the ground that the loss fell within the exception, for it had taken place as result of a 'civil commotion' and also of a 'riot'.

The Earl of Birkenhead said that the circumstances were not those of a normal theft. They differed in almost every important incident from what one would expect in the case of an ordinary theft, in which the thieves might be expected to remove themselves from the scene. He considered that the present case was similar to that in *Cooper v General Accident, Fire and Life Assurance Corpn*,[2] and quoted with approval the words of Viscount Finlay set out above. The manner in which the situation in the present case was handled by the armed men who took the car made it perfectly plain that, in their judgment, they had little to fear from the police or any other authority, and that they were, in Viscount Finlay's words 'masters of the situation'.[3]

After reviewing the evidence he said:[4]

'I can only draw one inference, that this was a case in which the car was taken by men who were working and that they purported to work in the interests of those who were carrying out disorder and engaged in violent courses in Ireland of which the motive was not the motive of private gain. We are not concerned closely to inquire whether we are to see in the act which was done a case of civil commotion or whether one is to see a case of riot there. If I were myself bound to reach a conclusion on this point, I should say it was both civil commotion and riot. That it was civil commotion is in my judgment evident from the parts of the evidence to which I have directed attention.'

SPECIAL POLICIES COVERING RISKS USUALLY EXCEPTED

Special policies are issued to cover risks normally excepted from the scope of the usual form of policy, eg 'loss by riot' may be expressly insured against.

---

[20] (1923) 16 Ll L Rep 64, H L.
[1] Earl of Birkenhead, Lord Atkinson, Lord Shaw, Lord Wrenbury and Lord Carson.
[2] (1922) 13 Ll L Rep 219, H L. See p 268, ante.
[3] (1923) 16 Ll L Rep 64 at 66. The evidence was also reviewed by Lord Wrenbury ibid, at 66–67.
[4] Ibid, at 66.

Damage Caused by Riot

In *Crozier v Thompson*[5] the insured had taken out a policy of insurance in respect of a car to cover damage directly caused by war, riot and civil commotion. During the troubles in Ireland the vehicle was damaged by running into a trench, which had been dug by Sinn Feiners.[6] Lush J held that the damage had been directly caused by 'riot' and 'civil commotion' and that the insurance company was liable. He said:[7]

> 'It is agreed that the Sinn Feiners did dig this trench in the road and the motor car ran into it. What more immediate cause of the damage to the motor car can you find than that? It is true that if, owing to the trench being cut, the assured had gone by another road to escape the danger of the trench and had met with an accident while on another route, although the accident would not have happened but for the cutting of the trench, the cutting of the trench would not in that case have been the real cause of the accident. But here nothing of that kind occurred; there was an immediate connection between the cutting of the trench and the damage because the motor car ran into the trench, and thus met with the injury. I think, therefore, the policy did cover the loss.'

'Damage under Military or Police Authority'

The policy in *Johnson & Perrott Ltd v Holmes*[8] covered loss by riots and civil commotions, and included damage caused by the military and/or police unless acting under military and/or police authority. The insured car was lost during the Irish disturbances in 1922. It was never seen again after the garage in which it was kept was entered at night by a party of armed men. In an action on the policy the insurer contended that the car had been stolen under military authority, but Rowlatt J held that the insured's claim succeeded, because the insurer had failed to prove that the loss fell within the exception. The men who came to the garage were lawless looters. It had not been shown that they were members of the Irish Republican Army.

In the words of the learned Judge:[9]

> 'I am asked to say that the men were authorised members of the I R A, but how is Mr Perrott to know that? He had nothing to show; he could not say what brigade or division it was. All he could say was: "People came and took my car." More than that he could not say. Afterwards he puts an entry in his book[10] so that if anything can be recovered, it might be got from the I R A. That I think makes it clear to me that my judgment . . . must be in favour of the [insured].'

---

[5] (1922) 12 Ll L Rep 291, K B.
[6] An Irish political movement formed in 1905 to further Irish economic and cultural self-determination. See *Chambers' Encyclopaedia* (1955), Vol XII, p 572.
[7] (1922) 12 Ll L Rep 291 at 292.
[8] (1925) 21 Ll L Rep 330, K B. The case is considered on another point, viz the alleged non-disclosure of a material fact, at p 207, ante.
[9] (1925) 21 Ll L Rep at 332.
[10] As to this point see ibid at 332 where Rowlatt J said: 'Then there were curious operations in the books, because long after all this had happened there were operations in the books which purport to debit the I R A with this car. Apparently they wanted to debit somebody, and when the underwriters objected to the claim, they put it in their books as against the I R A. I do not believe there was ever in the minds of Messrs Johnson & Perrott the slightest idea of debiting the I R A. They did not know and had not the materials for debiting them.'

CHAPTER 31

The conditions of the policy

The policy usually contains a number of conditions[1] which are expressly stated to be conditions precedent to the liability of the insurers.[2] Further, if any such condition is broken, the insured and any other person claiming an indemnity under the policy is to be jointly and severally liable to repay the insurers any sum which may have been applied to the satisfaction or settlement of claims.

Thus, there is generally a condition that the insured must take all reasonable and proper care and precautions to prevent accidents. He must exercise reasonable care in the selection of competent and sober drivers only. He must comply with all statutory enactments and local regulations. He must maintain and keep the car in good order and repair. He must take all reasonable steps to safeguard the car from loss or damage, and must allow the insurers or their representatives at all times to examine it.

The insured must give notice to the insurers of any loss under the policy,[3] and must not make any claim knowing it to be false or fraudulent.[4]

He must make no admission of liability or offer or promise of payment without the written consent of the insurers.

For convenience the conditions relating to giving notice of a loss to the insurers are treated elsewhere in this book.[5]

Decided cases concerning other conditions may be grouped under the following heads:

1 Maintaining the vehicle in an efficient condition.
2 Keeping the vehicle in a good state of repair.
3 The use of care to avoid accidents.
4 Acting to the detriment of the insurer's interest.
5 Safeguarding the vehicle from loss or damage.
6 Transporting the insured's own goods.
7 The duty to see that the driver had passed a driving test.
8 The employment of 'under age' drivers.

---

[1] As to conditions generally, see Ivamy, *General Principles of Insurance Law* (4th edn 1979), pp 288–318.

[2] See, eg the conditions of the motor car policy issued by the Commerical Union Assurance Co Ltd and set out in Appendix VI, p 417et seq, post.

[3] See pp 279–281, post.

[4] As to fraudulent claims generally, see Ivamy, *General Principles of Insurance Law* (4th edn, 1979), pp 433–438.

[5] See pp 279–281, post.

1 'Maintaining Vehicle in an Efficient Condition'

In *Jones v Provincial Insurance Co Ltd*[6] the policy provided that 'The insured shall take all reasonable steps to maintain [the] vehicle in an efficient condition'.

When a car was being driven down a hill, it overturned on a bend. It was not proved how the accident happened. The handbrake was efficient, but there was no footbrake at all. On a claim being made under the policy, the insurance company contended that the insured was guilty of a breach of condition. Roche J held that this contention would be upheld, and that the company could repudiate liability, saying:[7]

> 'It cannot be denied for one moment that there is here a term, condition and provision that the insured shall take all reasonable steps to maintain the vehicle in an efficient condition, and it is perfectly plain that the due and faithful observance of that is a condition precedent; and it is found to be broken.'

The identical words were used in the relevant condition of the policy in *Brown v Zurich General Accident and Liability Insurance Co Ltd*[8] In this case a van was damaged as a result of a skid on an icy surface. A claim was made under the policy, but the insurance company repudiated liability on the ground that the insured had failed to maintain the vehicle in an efficient condition. It was proved that, at the time of the accident, those parts of both front tyres which adhered to the road were smooth, being completely devoid of any trace of tread, though not worn down to the canvas at any point. The insured knew of these defects before the accident. Sellers J held that the insured had failed to take all reasonable steps to maintain the vehicle in an efficient condition, and that therefore the company was not liable.

As to the meaning of the term 'efficient condition' his Lordship said:[9]

> 'It seems to me that speaking quite generally . . . "efficient condition" of a vehicle really involves the taking of reasonable steps to make the vehicle or keep the vehicle roadworthy— that is in an efficient condition for the purpose for which it was going to be used, namely, to run upon the roads.'

When this definition was drawn to the attention of Sheriff-Substitute Middleton in the Scots case of *McInnes v National Motor and Accident Insurance Union Ltd*[10], he said that he did not agree with it, for if what was meant was 'to keep the vehicle roadworthy', he was surprised that those were not the words which were used. In his view no such limitation of the words was justified. 'Efficient' was a word in common usage both in contracts and statutes. It could have no precise meaning applicable to all situations any more than the word 'reasonable'. Its application would vary almost infinitely with the circumstances. He himself felt that:[11]

---

6 (1929) 35 Ll L Rep 135, K B.
7 Ibid, at 136.
8 [1954] 2 Lloyd's Rep 243, QB.
9 Ibid, at 246. See further the examiner's report of the state of a lorry in *New India Assurance Co Ltd v Yeo Beng Chow* [1972] 2 All E R 293 at 295, P C, the issue in the case being whether the condition in the policy applied to the whole policy or only to one section of it. See the speech of Viscount Dilhorne, ibid, at 296.
10 [1963] 2 Lloyd's Rep 415 (Sheriff Court of Lanark).
11 Ibid, at 417.

' "Efficient condition" means capable of doing what is normally and reasonably required of it. In the case of a motor vehicle it should not be difficult to decide whether the use wherein it failed was one within the reasonable contemplation of the parties to a policy of insurance.'

In *Conn v Westminster Motor Insurance Association Ltd*[12] a condition in a policy in respect of a taxi-cab stated that the insured was 'to take all reasonable steps to maintain the vehicle in an efficient condition'. An accident occurred, and the insurance company repudiated liability on the ground that the insured had broken the condition because the brakes were inefficient and the tyres were worn.

The Court of Appeal[13] held that the brakes were effective, and that their state could be ascertained only by dismantling them.[14] The company had failed to show that the insured had failed to take all reasonable steps to maintain the brakes in an efficient condition.

Salmon LJ said:[15]

'They relied not only upon what they contended was the inefficient condition of the tyres, but also on the inefficient condition of the brakes. They took the view, not without reason, that the inefficient condition of the brakes might well (and probably did) have something to do with this accident. The plaintiff, however, was able to produce evidence which the learned Lord Justice[16] accepted (as he was fully entitled to do) that some nine days before the accident the plaintiff had had the brakes checked, recentralised and adjusted for 5s 9d. Moreover, the Lord Justice further accepted the plaintiff's evidence that, although it may be that as a rule the sort of defects from which these brakes suffered would have been all too apparent to anyone driving the car, this plaintiff, in fact, did not appreciate that the cab was suffering from any such defects and had no reason to do so. It, therefore, followed on those findings that, although the brakes were inefficient, it could not be said that the plaintiff had failed to take reasonable steps to maintain them. He had sent the vehicle in for examination nine days before the accident. He had no reason to suppose that the garage had not done its work properly for 5s 9d, and the brakes appeared to be all right during the intervening period.'

But the Court held that the claim for an indemnity made by the insured against the company failed because he had broken the condition set out above, for the tyres were worn. Willmer LJ said that the vehicle was equipped with two front tyres which, on the evidence called on behalf of the insured, were described as 'unroadworthy' and 'dangerous'. The insured knew that at any rate one of the tyres had absolutely no tread on it at all.

Davies LJ said:

'That being so, did the plaintiff take reasonable steps to maintain the vehicle in an efficient condition? He took no steps at all; that is admitted. Admittedly he knew that the near-side tyre had no tread. He says that he did not knew that the off-side tyre had no tread and was down to the canvas. But it seems to me quite impossible to imagine that, with knowledge of the condition of the near-side tyre, he would not look at and observe the condition of the off-side tyre. Did he know, or ought he to have known, the condition of those two tyres? Again, it appears that the answer to that is inevitably "Yes." It was staring him in the face. He must have known the condition of both tyres. He must have known, as any car driver and particularly someone who has been driving a taxi-cab for very many years would know, that front tyres in that condition are unroadworthy and, indeed, unsafe.'

---

12 [1966] 1 Lloyd's Rep 407, CA.
13 Willmer, Davies and Salmon LJJ.
14 The evidence is set out in [1966] 1 Lloyd's Rep 407 at 410–411.
15 Ibid, at 414.
16 Sellers LJ, in the Court below.

2 'Keeping Vehicle in Good State of Repair'

In *Liverpool Corpn v J H and R Roberts and Marsh (Garthwaite, Third Party)*[17] the owners of a motor coach insured it under a policy which contained a condition stating:

> 'The insured shall take all due and reasonable precaution to safeguard the property insured, and to keep it in a good state of repair. The underwriters shall not be liable for damage or injury caused through driving the motor vehicle in an unsafe condition either before or after the accident.'

The insured failed to obtain an indemnity from the insurance company when it was shown that owing to the inadequate system of maintenance the brakes had become defective. The front brake linings were excessively worn and thin, automatic adjusters had been allowed to get into such a state that they were barely working, and the servo system was ineffective as a result of some clogging of the passages which had to remain reasonably open in order that the vacuum system might exercise force upon the brake shoes.[18] The retarding effect of the handbrake was far less than was requisite.

Cumming-Bruce J held that the insured were in breach of condition in that they had failed personally to keep the vehicle in a good state of repair. The Court considered that the condition stating that 'the insured shall take all due and reasonable precaution to keep it in a good state of repair' imposed a personal obligation on the insured, but that it did not impose on them any vicarious liability for the casual negligence of their employees.[19] The failure to keep the coach in a proper state of repair was due to a partner in the firm not exercising any adequate system to procure the periodical inspection, maintenance and testing of the footbrake.

It was contended by counsel for the third party, who had been injured in an accident caused by the defective brakes of the coach, that the second sentence of the condition had the effect of imposing an absolute liability to keep the vehicle in a safe state, so that there would be a breach of the condition if the vehicle was objectively in an unsafe state, irrespective of the knowledge of want of reasonable precautions on the part of the insured.

This argument did not commend itself to his Lordship, who considered that the words used merely expressed the consequences in terms of contractual liability of a failure on the part of the insured to exercise the duty imposed by the first sentence of the condition. They did not impose a separate and absolute obligation independent of the obligation in the first sentence.[20]

---

17 [1964] 2 Lloyd's Rep 219 (Liverpool Assizes).
18 See the review of the evidence, ibid, at 222–223.
19 Ibid, at 224. On this point the learned Judge applied *Woolfall and Rimmer Ltd v Moyle* [1942] 1 K B 66, C A (employer's liability insurance), where it was held that the insured had complied with a condition requiring him 'to take reasonable precautions to prevent accidents, and to comply with all statutory regulations', for he had entrusted to a competent foreman the task of providing suitable and safe materials for scaffolding.
20 [1964] 2 Lloyd's Rep at 224.

3 'Use of Care to Avoid Accidents'

In *National Farmers Union Mutual Insurance Society Ltd v Dawson*[1] the policy contained a condition which stated:

> 'The insured shall keep every motor car insured by this policy in an efficient state of repair and shall use all care and diligence to avoid accidents and to prevent loss and to employ only steady and sober drivers.'

When driving his car at night under the influence of alcohol so that he was incapable of controlling the vehicle, the insured collided with a motor cyclist, who was injured. The insurance company settled the claim of the injured motor cyclist, and then sought to recover from the insured the sums paid on the ground that he was guilty of a breach of condition.

Lord Caldecote C J, held that the company was entitled to do so. Counsel for the insured contended that the words of the condition were repugnant to the main purpose and object of the policy, which was an insurance against liability to pay damages to third persons for the negligence of the insured, but his Lordship concluded that there was no such repugnance, and that there had been a clear breach of condition. He observed:[2]

> 'First of all, take the part of Condition 3, as it is called, which is an obligation or undertaking to use all care and diligence to employ only steady and sober drivers. If the assured chose to employ a number of drunken drivers, or one drunken driver, why should he not be held to have broken his contract, and if damage results from the employment of the drunken driver, why should he not be liable to pay the damages which ensue as a result of that, for a breach of his undertaking? So, if the assured does not use all care and diligence to avoid accidents, because he sends the car out with no brakes or no horn or no lamps, or utterly unfit in some way or other for use upon the road, I think he has broken his contract, and this case provides, perhaps, a better example than any I have given. It would seem astonishing to say that he has used all care and diligence to avoid accidents if he, when in a drunken state, or, at any rate, in a state of having consumed so much alcoholic liquor as to be unfit to have proper control over a vehicle on the road, goes upon the road. I think he has not used all care and diligence to avoid accidents if that is what he does. I think it is an unsafe guide to a proper interpretation of this clause to look solely, or indeed to look at all, at the marginal note upon which [Counsel] strongly insisted. It quite obviously deals with something more than the employment of steady drivers; indeed, the marginal note itself says "Selection of Drivers and Cars," and I can see no reason why, in the language of the section, the assured should be excused from using care and diligence to avoid accidents, quite apart from anything he may do in the course of driving the car. There is no repugnance, I think, to the first part of the policy. The assured might use all care and diligence in accordance with the condition, and yet be guilty of an act of negligence, or he might fail to use all care and diligence without being found guilty of negligence on the road and so liable to pay damages.'

4 Acting to Detriment of Insurer's Interest

In *Dickinson v Del Solar (Mobile and General Insurance Co Ltd, Third Parties)*[3] the insured, Del Solar, was a member of the staff of the Peruvian Legation in London. He took out a policy of motor insurance containing a condition which stated that 'the assured . . . shall not in any way act to the detriment or prejudice of the [insurance company's] interests'. The car knocked down a third party, and, in the action which followed, the Peruvian Minister directed him

---

[1] (1941) 70 Ll L Rep 167, K B.
[2] Ibid, at 170.
[3] (1929) 34 Ll L Rep 445 K B. The case is considered on another point at p 289, post.

not to plead diplomatic privilege.[4] The third party was awarded damages, but the insurance company refused to indemnify the insured on the ground that the waiver of his immunity was an 'act to the detriment or prejudice' of its interests. Lord Hewart CJ held that this contention failed, and that the company was bound to indemnify the insured. There had been no breach of condition, for the insured was bound to obey the direction of his Minister in the matter.

5 'Safeguarding Vehicle from Loss or Damage'

Where the policy provides that the car must be 'safeguarded from loss or damage', this relates to the physical state of the car, and not to damage caused by a person driving in contravention of the terms of his driving licence.[5]

In *Rendlesham v Dunne (Pennine Insurance Co Ltd, Third Party)*[6] a condition in the policy stated that 'the insured should take all reasonable steps to safeguard the motor car from loss and damage.' A learner driver was driving the insured vehicle with the permission of the insured, and was responsible for an accident in which a third party was injured. At the time of the accident he was not accompanied by a qualified driver as required by the terms of his provisional driving licence. When a claim for an indemnity was made against the insurance company, liability was denied on the ground that there had been a breach of the condition set out above in that the insured, by permitting the learner driver to drive unaccompanied, had failed to safeguard the car from loss or damage.

Judge Herbert held that there had been no breach of condition, and said that the clause was concerned with the physical condition of the car, and did not refer to damage caused, eg by the negligent driving of the insured or of somebody in contravention of the terms of his licence. Moreover, there was no evidence in the present case that there was any loss or damage to the insured's car at all.

6 Transporting the Insured's Own Goods

One of the contentions raised in *Provincial Insurance Co Ltd v Morgan and Foxon*[7] was that the insured had broken condition 6 of the policy which stated:

> 'It is a condition precedent to any liability on the part of the company under this policy (i) that the terms, provisions, conditions and indorsements hereof, so far as they relate to anything to be done or complied with by the insured, are duly and faithfully observed . . .'

In this case the lorry insured under the policy had been used for hauling timber for the Forestry Commission, whereas the insured's business was that of

---

4 As to this point see ibid, at 447. The Minister had forbidden the insured to plead diplomatic immunity inasmuch as the collision had taken place when the car was being used not for official but for private purposes.

5 *Rendlesham v Dunne (Pennine Insurance Co Ltd Third Party)* [1964] 1 Lloyd's Rep 192 (Westminster County Court).

6 [1964] 1 Lloyd's Rep 192. The case is considered on another point, viz whether a full or only a provisional licence was required in order for a 'permitted driver' to come within the terms of an extension clause of the policy—at p 239, ante.

7 (1932) 44 Ll L Rep 275, H L. The case is referred to on another point, viz whether the statements in the proposal form as to the intended use of the vehicle were merely descriptive of the risk insured—see p 218, ante.

a coal merchant. One of the indorsements on the policy was under the heading of 'Indorsements and use clauses', and stated 'Transportation of own goods in connection with the insured's business within stated'. The House of Lords[8] held that the condition had not been broken. Lord Russell of Killowen said:[9]

> 'A further point was raised, viz that Condition 6 freed the insurance company from liability by reason of the presence in the policy immediately after the schedule of the following words: "Indorsements and use clauses. Transportation of own goods in connection with the insured's business within stated." It was said that this was an indorsement by which the insured contracted that only their "own goods" in connection with their coal business should be carried in the vehicle, and that the carriage of the timber was (within Condition 6) a failure duly and faithfully to observe that indorsement, meaning no doubt a failure to comply with some obligation imposed by the indorsement.
>
> I have read the policy with this in view, but I have been unable to discover how or where any obligation is imposed on the insured by this indorsement. It may be that we have here some form of commercial shorthand which an expert could transcribe into a contractual obligation. I am unequal to the task.'

7 Duty to see that Driver had Passed Driving Test

In *Haworth v Dawson*[10] a car hire firm had effected a policy in which both they and anyone hiring a car from them were covered, provided that they were satisfied by an actual driving test that he was a careful and competent driver of motor cars. Further, he had to have a current licence free from any endorsements.

In fact, the hirer had two endorsements for speeding, and no test had been carried out to see whether he was a competent driver. The insurance company claimed that it was not liable under the policy, but the insured contended that compliance with the conditions set out above had been waived, and that it could not therefore dispute liability.

Lewis J held that the plea of waiver failed. The insurance company had never been informed[11] that the hirer's licence had been endorsed, nor that the insured had not actually tested him. Consequently the question of waiver did not arise.

8 Employment of 'Under Age' Drivers

In *Sweeney v Kennedy*[12] the proposer in answer to a question stating 'Are any of your drivers under twenty-one years of age or with less than twelve months' experience?' replied 'No'. One of the lorries covered by the policy was involved in an accident whilst it was being unloaded, and a third party was fatally injured. At the time of the accident it was being driven by the insured's son, who had twelve months' driving experience but was under twenty-one. When a claim for an indemnity was made against the insurance company, payment was

---

8 Viscount Buckmaster, Lord Blanesburgh, Lord Russell of Killowen, Lord Warrington of Clyffe and Lord Wright.
9 (1932) 44 Ll L Rep 275 at 279.
10 (1946) 80 Ll L Rep 19, K B. The case is considered on another point—viz whether the hirer came within the category of an 'excluded hirer' and so was not covered by the policy—at p 256, ante.
11 The evidence is set out (1946) 80 Ll L Rep at 21–22.
12 (1948) 82 Ll L Rep 294, Eire Divisional Court. Another issue in the case—viz whether the answer given to the question was a warranty as to the future—is considered at p 218, ante.

refused on the ground that the employment of a driver under twenty-one years of age amounted to such an alteration in the character of the risk as would avoid the policy.

Kingsmill Moore J giving judgment in the Eire Divisional Court, rejected this argument and held that the company was liable. He said that whether a change of risk was so great as to avoid an insurance must always be a question of degree and a question of the opinion of the Court in the circumstances of the case. He could see a vast difference between the risks involved in insuring a merchantman and a privateer;[13] a smaller but still very substantial difference between the risks involved in insuring an explosive and non-explosive demolition;[14] and a very exiguous difference between the risks of insuring when a driver was under or over twenty-one.

He then observed:[15]

> 'The law provides that licences to drive motor vehicles may be given to persons of specified ages, the ages varying with the class of the vehicle; and when a person is driving a vehicle of the category which by his age he is entitled to drive, there is, I think, some presumption that, as far as age reflects on competency, he is competent to drive it. Certainly this would be an honest and reasonable view for an insured person to take in a case where he had not been expressly limited by the terms of the policy to the employment of drivers over 21. Certain categories of vehicle may not, by law, be driven by persons under 21, and as the framework of the proposal form was apt to cover an application for insurance of such vehicles, he might reasonably consider that Q 9 was designed to call attention to this fact. If insurers take a different view as to the proper age of drivers from the view of the law, it is open to them—indeed, I would say incumbent upon them—to make this clear by the insertion of specific provisions in the policy, and not to attempt to secure their ends by a side wind. I hold that there was no such alteration in the subject-matter of the insurance as would or could avoid the policy.'

---

[13] As in *Denison v Modigliani* (1794) 5 Term Rep 580 (marine insurance), where a vessel insured for a trading voyage sailed with a general letter of marque and the Court of King's Bench held that there had been an alteration of the risk and that the insurer was discharged from liability. Lord Kenyon CJ said (ibid, at 581): 'This is such an alteration of circumstances from the condition of the vessel at the time of the insurance, as ought to discharge the underwriters, unless it were done with their consent'. Grose J observed (ibid, at 582): 'This, therefore, was a direct departure from the nature of the contract, as understood between the parties'.

[14] As in *Beauchamp v National Mutual Indemnity Insurance Co Ltd* (1937) 57 Ll L Rep 272 (workmen's compensation insurance), where the insured had warranted that no explosives would be used in the work of demolishing a mill. They were used, in fact, and the mill collapsed injuring the insured's workmen. Finlay J held that there had been an alteration of the risk, and that the insurance company was not liable.

[15] (1948) 82 Ll L Rep 294 at 297.

CHAPTER 32

The claim

The principal matters arising in respect of a claim[1] under the policy which require special consideration are the following:
1   Special duties of the insured after the accident.
2   Particulars of claim.
3   The amount recoverable.
4   Conduct of proceedings.
5   Disclaimer of liability.

1 SPECIAL DUTIES OF THE INSURED AFTER THE ACCIDENT

General Nature of Duties

The policy usually imposes on the insured the following duties:
1   To give the insurers notice of any accident causing personal injury or damage to property as soon as the accident comes to his knowledge.
2   To obtain the names and addresses of any witnesses of the accident.
3   To give the insurers notice of any claim made against him in respect of the accident, forwarding to the insurers the originals of any letters or other documents received from any claimant, within a specified time.
4   To give the insurers any information or assistance which they may require for the purpose of resisting or settling any claim.
5   Not to settle or make any payment in respect of any claim, or admit liability or make any other admission with respect to the accident or any claim arising therefrom, without the written consent of the insurers.

Notice of Loss

A usual condition provides that notice of loss must be given within a specified time, otherwise the insurance company will not be liable.

In *The Administratrix of Mary Madge Verelst v Motor Union Insurance Co Ltd*[2] the policy contained a condition stating that:

'In case of any accident, injury, damage or loss covered under this policy, the insured or the insured's personal representative for the time being shall give notice together with the fullest

---

[1] As to the making of claims generally in all branches of insurance, see Ivamy, *General Principles of Insurance Law* (4th edn 1979), pp 420–438.
[2] (1925) 21 Ll L Rep 227, K B.

information . . . in writing to the head office of the company of such loss as soon as possible after it has come to the knowledge of the insured or the insured's representative for the time being.'

During the currency of the policy on 14 January 1923, the insured, who was visiting India, was killed in a motor accident whilst being driven by her brother. The administratrix of her estate did not know the name of the insurance company with which the insured had effected a policy. But in January 1924 she came across the policy amongst some old papers belonging to the insured. She immediately gave notice to the insurance company of a claim under the policy. The company repudiated liability on the ground of breach of the condition set out above.

Roche J upholding the award of an arbitrator, held that the company was liable. There had been no breach of the condition, for notice had, on the facts, been given 'as soon as possible after it had come to the knowledge of the administratrix'.

His Lordship said:[3]

'There are two grounds upon which the submission has been put as to the error of the arbitrator. It is said that "as soon as possible" is a matter of construction in this case and means "as soon as anybody could give notice." Reliance is placed on certain expressions in the case of the *Hydraulic Engineering Co v McHaffie*.[4] The words which most aptly summarise the view of the Court and illustrate the contention of the company are the words in the judgment of Cotton LJ,[5] where he says that by the words "as soon as possible" the defendants must be taken to have meant that they would make the gun as quickly as it could be made in the largest establishment with the best appliances.

The other view suggested on the other side as to what this clause means is that it means as soon as possible to the legal representative under the existing circumstances which prevailed and applied. In support or in illustration of that view of the meaning of the condition the case of *Hick v Raymond and Reid*,[6] was cited in support of this contention that Condition 1 had no reference to the case of death. [Counsel] referred me to *Clyde Accident Co v Kenrich*.[7] The arbitrator obviously from his decision adopted the construction of the clause which the claimant has contended for; and I am quite unable to hold that he was wrong. On the contrary, I think and hold that he was right putting that construction on the clause.'

In *Baltic Insurance Association of London Ltd v Cambrian Coaching and Goods Transport Ltd*[8] a condition provided that:

'Notice shall be given in writing to the Association immediately on the occurrence of any accident or loss'.

A bus belonging to the insured was involved in an accident on 29 November. On 17 December the insured wrote a letter to the insurance company stating 'We enclose driver's report and correspondence which has passed with regard to this matter. We regret delay in this matter but you will see the reason for it'. The correspondence referred to was from another insurance company acting on behalf of a third party, who had been injured in the accident. The insured also sent in a claim form at the same time as the letter. The insurance company

---

3 (1925) 21 Ll L Rep 229, K B.
4 (1878) 4 Q B D 670.
5 Ibid, at 676.
6 [1893] A C 22.
7 54 American State Rep 486.
8 (1926) 25 Ll L Rep 195, K B.

contended that there had been a breach of condition because the notice had not been given 'immediately on the occurrence of any accident or loss.'

Mackinnon J held that there had been no breach of condition, and that the company was liable. It had been contended by the company that on 29 or 30 November the bus driver told a man named Watson, who was employed by the insured, about the accident, and that Watson's knowledge was that of the insured, who, therefore, knew about it on 30 November or 1 December. On this point his Lordship said:[9]

'The question is whether the plaintiffs, on whom I think the onus is, have established that there has been a breach by the defendants of this undertaking that notice shall be given in writing to the Association immediately upon the occurrence of any accident or loss. I do not gather that [Counsel] says that the fact that the driver knew on 29 November would be sufficient knowledge of the defendants to involve them in liability of handing on his knowledge, and even if it were so, it cannot avail the plaintiffs in this case, because it is apparent from the information sent in the letter of 17 December and accepted and received as being within a reasonable time, that it must have been to the knowledge of the driver on 29 November that an accident had happened. Does it make any difference that not only the driver knew but that he told another man in the defendants' employ—a man named Watson—and that Watson did not for some days hand it on to the responsible person? . . .

I am quite satisfied on the evidence that the defendants' claims manager did not know anything about this matter. He did not receive any report from Watson or the driver until after the receipt of the letter of 1 December from the Phœnix Insurance Co. If the driver's knowledge would not be sufficient knowledge of the defendants so as to make it necessary immediately to inform the plaintiffs, I do not see why Watson's should. Watson was the man whose duty it was to collect any reports of the drivers and bring them round to the responsible officer. I will assume that the driver did say something to Watson on 29 or 30 November, though I have no doubt the driver was telling us what he believes is accurate and honest, but I very much doubt after this lapse of time that he can be certain of it. But even assuming he did say something to Watson on 29 or 30 November, I am not satisfied that thereupon there came upon the assured a duty under this condition of communicating that information to the insurance company, when the responsible officials of the assured, the people properly concerned with claims and with forwarding information under the insurance policy, knew nothing about it whatever. I do not see any difference between the knowledge of Watson or of the driver, and that the driver had knowledge of the accident about 29 November must have been apparent to the plaintiffs when they received the information contained in the letter of 17 December and accepted that as sufficient.'

Accordingly, the insurance company had failed to show that there had been any breach of condition.

Waiver of Giving of Notice of Claim

In *Webster v General Accident, Fire and Life Assurance Corpn Ltd*[10] the insurance company pleaded that it was not liable on the ground that the insured had not complied with a condition of the policy stating that:

'The policy holder or his legal personal representative shall give notice in writing to the head office or any branch office of the Corporation as soon as possible after the occurrence of any accident and/or loss and/or damage with full particulars thereof.'

The loss of the insured car took place on 26 February 1952. On May 19 the insured's solicitor went to see the company's metropolitan claims manager,

---

9 (1926) 25 Ll L Rep 195 at 197, K B.
10 [1953] 1 Q B 520, [1953] 1 All E R 663.

and told him the whole story as known at that time, and made it clear that he was making a claim that there had been a loss within the meaning of the policy. The claims manager said that he would report to his head office. On 28 July a formal claim was made in writing, and on the back under the heading 'Description of Occurrence' the words 'Fully explained (a) to London General Manager; (b) to company's solicitor . . .' were inserted. Parker J held that the facts proved constituted a waiver, for the company had led the insured, however unintentionally, to think that it was unnecessary formally to comply with the condition set out above.

In *Brook v Trafalgar Insurance Co Ltd*[11] the policy contained a condition which stated:

> 'Notice of any accident or loss must be given in writing to the company at its head office immediately upon the occurrence of such accident or loss . . . In the event of failure to comply with the terms of this condition and, in particular, if within seven days the company has not been notified as above set forth, then all benefit under this policy shall be forfeited.'

The insured vehicle was destroyed by fire on 17 December 1943. The loss was reported on 18 December by the insured to the provincial agent of the company, who had effected the policy on his behalf. The agent supplied him with a claim form, which was completed by the insured and dated 3 January 1944. The form was then sent on by the agent to the head office of the insurance company in London. The company denied liability on the ground that the notification of the loss was out of time. The Court of Appeal[12] held that this plea succeeded, and that the insured had lost all benefit under the policy. No plea of waiver[13] had been made by the insured in reply to the company's denial of liability under the conditions of the policy, nor had an application been made in the trial Court to introduce such an issue, and the Judge[14] should not have considered such an issue at all. In any event there was no evidence to show that the agent had any authority to waive the express condition of notice having to be sent to the head office of the company. Further, even if he had had such authority, there was no evidence to show that he had, in fact, waived compliance with the condition.

Tucker LJ said:[15]

> 'First of all, in my view, there was no evidence at all that Mr Nelson was an agent having authority to waive the written conditions of the policy. The only evidence that he was an agent at all was contained in the schedule to the policy where he is put in as "Agent: J Nelson." That clearly indicates he was an agent of some kind, but, especially in connection with insurance matters, there are all kinds and various degrees of agency. The mere fact that a man is described in a policy as an agent is not in itself sufficient to show that he has authority conferred upon him to waive the express conditions of the policy, one of which incidentally it is to be observed, viz No 9, provides that "Any alteration in the terms of this policy is only binding upon the company when made at the head office under the hand of a managing director or secretary." '

11　(1946) 79 Ll L Rep 365, C A.

12　Scott, Tucker and Bucknill LJJ.

13　As to the need for a plea of waiver to be expressly made, see Ivamy, *General Principles of Insurance Law* (4th edn 1979), p 316.

14　Stable J.

15　(1946) 79 Ll L Rep 365 at 368. See also the judgment of Scott LJ, ibid, at 367–368.

Making of Admissions of Liability

A condition often states that the insured must not make an admission of liability.

Thus, a condition of a typical policy states:[16]

'The payment of claims is dependent on . . . not admitting liability or making an offer or promise of payment without [the Company's] written consent . . .'

In *Terry v Trafalgar Insurance Co Ltd*[17] the policy provided that:

'No liability shall be admitted or legal expenses be incurred nor any offer, promise or payment made to Third Parties without the Company's written consent . . .'

The insured collided with a car driven by a third party. He apologised to the third party, and verbally accepted responsibility for the accident. Later the same day he wrote a letter to him stating:

'It appears that my insurance company covers me over and above a £50 claim. It, therefore, seems that as damage to your vehicle was not severe, I will pay for the making good. Technically the blame for the accident falls on me, and as I do not wish to bring to my insurance [company's] notice the accident, the best course for me is as above.'

The third party discovered that the damage to his car was estimated to be considerably in excess of £50, so he informed both the insured and the insured's insurance company of this. The insured sought to be indemnified by the company, but liability was repudiated on the ground that there had been a breach of the condition set out above. The insured contended (inter alia) that (i) the condition was contrary to public policy; and (ii) the condition was subject to the implication that no liability should be admitted if it was to the prejudice of the company.

Judge Graham Rogers giving judgment in the Mayor's and City of London Court held that the claim failed. He considered that the condition was not contrary to public policy, and observed on this point:[18]

'[Counsel] contended that that condition was an agreement prejudicial to the administration of justice, tending to cause the insured person to lie about what had happened, or at least conceal the truth. In my view this is a fanciful argument; the condition does not require the insured to lie, but to refrain from admissions of liability. There is a world of difference between giving a factual account of what happened, without giving any expression of opinion as to blame, and an admission of liability. This is and has been for many years a standard condition of motor insurance policies, and in my view it is clearly a necessary and proper one for the protection of insurance companies.'

As to the insured's second contention the learned Judge said[19] that he had no hesitation in holding that the company was prejudiced, for by his letter written within hours of the accident the company was shut out from any negotiations and deprived of a possible chance of a favourable settlement.

---

16 See condition 2 (f) in the motor car policy issued by the Commercial Union Assurance Co Ltd and set out in Appendix VI, p 418, post.

17 [1970] 1 Lloyd's Rep 524.

18 Ibid, at 526.

19 Ibid, at 526.

2 PARTICULARS OF CLAIM

Usual Contents of Claim Form

The insured, in making his claim under the policy, is usually required to fill in a claim form. The details which he is asked to give usually include the following:

(a) *The description of the vehicle involved in the accident*

For example, the make of the vehicle, its c.c., registration number, year of make, for what purposes it was being used.

(b) *The details of the accident*

These include eg the date and time of the accident, the place of the accident, the speed immediately before the accident and on impact, the state of the weather and of the road, whether the vehicle's lights were being used, whether a police officer took particulars. A sketch map, showing the scene of the accident and the position of the vehicle and of any other vehicles or persons involved in the accident, is usually required.

(c) *The cause of the accident*

The insured is required to explain as fully as possible how the accident happened, and to state what steps were taken to avoid it.

(d) *The consequences of the accident*

The insured is required to state the nature of any injury or damage caused by the accident, including the names and addresses of the persons who were injured or whose property was damaged, together with the name and address of the insurers, if known.

(e) *The character of the driver*

The insured is required to give the name and address of the person driving the vehicle at the time of the accident, and to state his age, and, if he is an employee, the time during which he has been in the service of the insured. The insured is further required to state whether he has been concerned in any previous accidents, and to give particulars of any motoring offences and endorsements on his licence (if any). The details of the licence held by the driver of the vehicle must be given, eg the number, its date of issue, whether it is a full or a provisional one. The length of time for which the driver has held a licence may also have to be given. Where he has been licensed to drive since April 1934, he may have to give the date on which the driving test was passed by him.

(f) The witnesses of the accident

The insured is required to give the names and addresses of any independent witnesses or of passengers travelling in the vehicle at the time of the accident.

(g) Number of vehicles in use

In the case of insurances on commercial vehicles, the insured is usually required to state the number of vehicles in use or drivers actually at work on the day of the accident.

Delivery of Particulars of Loss[20]

In *Yorkshire Insurance Co Ltd v Thomas Craine*[1] a car dealer insured the cars on his premises against fire. Condition No 11 of the policy stated:

'On the happening of any loss or damage the insured must forthwith give notice in writing thereof to the company, and must within 15 days after the loss or damage or such further time as the company may in writing allow on that behalf, deliver to the company a claim for the loss and damage, containing in particular an account as is reasonably practicable of all the articles or items of property destroyed or damaged.'

A fire took place on 30 September 1917, and the claim should have been delivered on or before 15 October. An application in writing was made on that day to extend for a week the time to lodge formal claims. The insurance company by a letter extended the time to 4 pm on 22 October. A further extension was then granted up to 12 noon on 26 October. The claim was not lodged within that time.
Condition No 12 stated:

'On the happening of any loss or damage the company may, so long as the claim is not adjusted, without thereby incurring any liability; (a) enter, and take, and keep possession of the building or premises where the loss or damage has happened.'

Acting under powers given by this condition the company entered into possession of the insured's premises and remained in possession for 4 months. When the insured sued on the policy, the company pleaded that there had been a breach of condition No 11 in that the claim had not been delivered in time. The Privy Council[2] held that the plea failed, and that the insured was entitled to an indemnity in respect of the loss.
Lord Atkinson said that the opening words of condition No 12 suggested that adjustment was all that remained to be done to the claim. They presupposed that a valid claim against the company had been made and all that remained to be done was to adjust the amount of it. If no claim had been made, or a claim was so defective that it gave no right to obtain any money under the policy, it would be ridiculous to refer to the adjustment of it. Until the company accepted

---

[20] As to delivery of particulars of loss, see generally Ivamy, *General Principles of Insurance Law* (4th edn 1979) pp 426–430.
[1] (1922) 11 Ll L Rep 1, 67; 12 Ll L Rep 399, PC.
[2] Lord Buckmaster, Lord Atkinson, Lord Sumner, Lord Parmoor and Lord Wrenbury.

the claim of the insured as valid, imposing on them a liability, there would be nothing to adjust.

He went on to say that by going into possession of the premises the company had waived the breach of condition No 11, and observed:[3]

> 'These two conditions are interdependent, the one upon the other; and the powers conferred by the second are only authorised to be used when the requirements of the first as to claims, at least, have been fulfilled. If that be so, then, in their Lordships' view, it is not competent for either of the companies, if they have gone into or continued in the possession of the premises of the assured after they have received and accepted the assured's claims to contend that those claims fail to comply with the terms of condition 11. They are estopped by their conduct from doing so, since they cannot insist that their own action was unauthorised and illegal. It could only be legal if claims valid or accepted as valid had been made by the insured upon and delivered to them. Many authorities on the subject of estoppel by conduct might be cited; for instance, in *Wing v Harvey*[4] it was held in the Court of Appeal that the acceptance of premiums, with the knowledge of circumstances entitling the insurer to avoid the policy, estopped him from averring that by reason of those circumstances the policy was not valid. Again, a man, who acting as a director of a company takes part in the allotment of shares to himself, cannot in any action for calls be permitted to say that his appointment as director or the allotment to him of the shares was irregular and ultra vires. So the companies here, if by the act of their authorised agent they go into possession and retained possession of the premises of the assured, expel him from there and only allow him to enter into them by their permission, they cannot be permitted to say that the circumstances legalising their action did not, in fact, exist.'

In *Cox v Orion Insurance Co Ltd*,[5] the company issued a policy to the insured containing (inter alia) the following conditions:-

> 2 The insured or the insured's legal personal representatives shall give notice in writing to the head or any branch office of the company as soon as possible after any accident, loss or damage and shall deliver within 7 days or such further time as the company may allow after notice received, detailed particulars in writing in such form and accompanied by such proofs as the company may require.
> 8 The due observance of the terms, conditions and indorsements so far as they relate to anything to be done or complied with by the insured . . . shall be conditions precedent to any liability of the company to make any payments under this policy.'

On 24 December 1977, the insured was driving his car when it collided with a stationary vehicle. He was under the influence of drink at the time. On 12 January 1978 he made a claim on the insurance company in which he said that a Mr Martin was driving the car without his permission when the accident occurred. He said that he had picked up Mr Martin to drop him home and left him sitting in the car whilst he himself went into his own house. Mr Martin took the ignition key. After some time, the insured returned but the car was gone. He decided to walk to the police to report the matter, but then saw Mr Martin driving the car when it collided with the stationary one. He declared that the particulars which he had given were true and correct. The insurance company repudiated liability, so he issued a writ claiming an indemnity under the policy.

The Court of Appeal[6] held that there would be judgment for the insurance company because the insured was in breach of condition 2 of the policy. He had

---

[3] (1922) 12 Ll L Rep 399 at 400.
[4] (1854) 5 De G M & G 265.
[5] [1982] R T R 1, C A.
[6] Waller, Donaldson and O'Connor L JJ.

not given detailed particulars of the accident, but had given particulars of an entirely different one. It was an accident involving his car but was an accident involving his car being driven by another man, who, he was saying, had stolen it. The implications of describing the accident in that way would lead the insurance company in an entirely different direction.

Waiver of Notice of Intended Prosecution

In *Lickiss v Milestone Motor Policies at Lloyd's*[7] a motor cyclist claimed from the insurers an indemnity in respect of the damages which he had been required to pay to a third party as the result of an accident for which he himself was responsible. The policy contained a condition stating that:

> 'The insured shall give full particulars in writing to Milestone Motor Policies, London House. . . . as soon as possible after the occurence of any accident, loss or damage and shall forward immediately any letter, notice of intended prosecution, writ, summons or process relating thereto.'

The accident happened on 17 May 1964. The insured received a notice of intended prosecution, but did not tell the insurers about it. The insurers, however, were informed by a letter from the police written on 18 June that proceedings against him were pending. On 23 June they wrote a letter to him saying that 'We understand that proceedings are being taken against you on 2 July . . . It would be appreciated if you would let us know why you have not notified us of these proceedings since we will wish to arrange your defence'. Later the insurers denied liability on the ground that there had been a breach of condition in that the insured had not sent them a notice of the intended prosection.

The Court of Appeal[8] held that the insured was entitled to an indemnity because the insurers' letter of 23 June was a waiver of the breach of condition
Lord Denning M R said:[9]

> 'The letter of 23 June 1964, was a waiver of the condition. The principle of waiver is simply this: that if one party by his conduct leads another to believe that the strict rights arising under the contract will not be insisted on, intending that the other should act on that belief, and he does act on it, then the first party will not afterwards be allowed to insist on the strict rights when it would be inequitable for him so to do (see *Plasticmoda Societa per Azioni v Davidsons (Manchester) Ltd*).[10] When the insurers got the letter from the police on 18 June they could have asked for the notice of prosecution and the summons if they had wanted them. Instead of doing so, they merely wrote to the motor cyclist on 23 June saying: "It would be appreciated if you would let us know why you have not notified us of these proceedings." By not asking for the documents, they as good as said that they did not want them. So he did not send them. I do not think that they should be allowed now to complain of not receiving them. I think that they waived the condition.'

Salmon LJ said[11] that any reasonable person receiving the insurers' letter would have concluded that, having learnt all about the intended prosecution,

---

7 [1966] 2 All E R 972, C A. The case is considered on another point: viz choice of solicitor by insured, at p 297, post.
8 Lord Denning M R, Danckwerts and Salmon LJJ.
9 [1966] 2 All E R 972, at 975.
10 [1952] 1 Lloyd's Rep 527.
11]1966] 2 All E R 972 at 976.

they no longer required him to notify them of it or send them the summons. All that they wanted was to be told why he had not done so already.

3 THE AMOUNT RECOVERABLE

In the absence of any limitation in the policy, the insured is entitled to recover the whole amount for which he is legally liable to the person injured.

The amount for which the insurers are to be liable, may, however, be limited by the terms of the policy,[12] in which case the insurers may reserve the right to pay the insured the maximum amount payable under the policy, and thus relieve themselves from any further liability. The extent to which they are relieved from further liability depends on the language of the policy.

Unless the policy fixes the maximum amount payable during the currency of the policy, the limitation applies only to a particular accident, and does not prevent the insured from claiming further indemnities, subject to the limitation in each case, in respect of any number of accidents arising during the currency of the policy.[13]

There is often an excess clause whereby the insured is required to pay the first £25 of any claim himself.[14]

Sometimes there is a special clause relating to inexperienced drivers. Thus, a clause in a typical policy[15] states:

> '[The Company] will not pay for:-
> An Excess of £50 for each loss or damage to [the Policyholder's] Motor Car (other than when [the Policyholder's] Motor Car is in the hands of a member of the motor trade for servicing or repair) while it is being driven by any person who:-
> —is under 25 years of age, or
> —holds a provisional driving licence, or
> —has held for less than 12 months a full licence to drive a vehicle of the same class as [the Policyholder's] Motor Car.
> This in addition to any Excess shown in the schedule.'

The policy sometimes provides that if any loss or damage or liability covered by it is also covered in whole or in part by any other policy, the insurers are not to be liable to pay more than their rateable proportion.[16]

A usual provision in the policy is that if the insured makes any claim knowing it to be false or fraudulent as regards amount or otherwise, the policy is to become null and void and all claims under it shall be forfeited.[17]

'Legally Liable to Pay'

Where an insured, who might have claimed diplomatic immunity, submits to the jurisdiction of the Court and is held responsible for injuries caused to a third

---

[12] As to limitations on the amount recoverable, see Ivamy, *General Principles of Insurance Law* (4th edn 1979), pp 458–462.

[13] As to successive losses, see Ivamy, ibid, 457–458.

[14] As to excess clauses, see Ivamy, ibid, 461–462.

[15] See the exception in the motor car policy issued by the Commercial Union Assurance Co Ltd and set out in Appendix VI, p 423, post.

[16] As to contribution clauses, see Ivamy, op cit, pp 458–460.

[17] As to fraudulent claims, see Ivamy, op cit, pp 433–438.

party, he is 'legally liable' to that third party, and the insurance company must indemnify him accordingly.

In *Dickinson v Del Solar (Mobile and General Insurance Co Ltd, Third Parties)*[18] the policy contained a term to the effect that the insurance company would indemnify the insured 'against any legal liability to members of the public in respect of any accidental personal injury sustained or caused through the driving or management of the insured vehicle.' The insured was an employee of the Peruvian Legation in London. The car which he was driving was involved in an accident, and a third party was injured. The company refused to indemnify the insured on the ground that he was under no legal liability to the third party, and was immune from civil process. Lord Hewart CJ held that the contention failed. A diplomatic agent was not immune from legal liability for any wrongful acts, but was not liable to be sued in the English Courts unless he submitted to the jurisdiction. Diplomatic privilege had been waived[19] in the present case, and the insured had submitted to the jurisdiction of the Court. The insured was, therefore, legally liable to the third party, for the accident had been caused by his negligent driving. The loss fell within the policy, and the company must indemnify the insured.

The Lord Chief Justice said:[20]

> 'In my opinion, diplomatic agents are not, in virtue of their privileges as such, immune from legal liability for any wrongful acts. The accurate statement is, I think, that they are not liable to be sued in the English Courts unless they submit to the jurisdiction. Diplomatic privilege does not import immunity from legal liability, but only exemption from local jurisdiction. The privilege is the privilege of the sovereign by whom the diplomatic agent is accredited, and it may be waived with the sanction of the sovereign or of the official superior to the agent. (*Taylor v Best;*[1] *Re Suarez, Suarez v Suarez.*[2])
>
> In the present case the privilege was waived and jurisdiction was submitted to by the entry of appearance (*Re Suarez, Suarez v Suarez;*[3] *Duff Development Co v Kelantan Government*[4]) and, inasmuch as the [insured] had so submitted to the jurisdiction, it was no longer open to him to set up privilege. If privilege had been pleaded as a defence, the defence could, in the circumstances, have been struck out. The [insured], I think, was bound to obey the direction of his Minister in the matter.
>
> In these circumstances it does not appear to me that there has been, on the part of the [insured], any breach of the conditions of the policy, and the judgment clearly creates a legal liability against which the insurance company have agreed to indemnify him.'

Excess Clause

In *Beacon Insurance Co Ltd v Langdale*[5] a condition in the policy stated that 'the company . . . shall be entitled if it so desires to take over and conduct in the name of the insured the defence or settlement of any claim or to prosecute in the name of the insured for its own benefit any claim for indemnity or damages or otherwise'. Another condition stated that the insured was 'liable to pay the

---

[18] (1929) 34 Ll L Rep 445, K B.
[19] See on this point, p 275, ante.
[20] (1929) 34 Ll L Rep 445 at 448.
[1] (1854) 14 C B 487.
[2] [1918] 1 Ch 176.
[3] Ibid, at 193.
[4] [1924] A C 797.
[5] (1939) 65 Ll L Rep 57, C A.

first £5, or any less amount for which the claim may be settled, of each claim arising under this policy'. The insured was involved in an accident with a pedal cyclist. The company entered into a settlement with the cyclist to avoid litigation, paid him £45, and claimed £5 from the insured. The Court of Appeal[6] held that the settlement was within the powers of the company, that it had acted bona fide,[7] and that the insured was liable.

In the words of Slesser LJ:[8]

'Once it is conceded, or once it is found, that the insurance company have the power to settle the claim, then the event which is contemplated in this provision has arisen. There has been a settlement, and thereupon the assured has agreed, it is declared, that he is liable to pay the first £5 for which the claim may be settled. That seems to me to conclude the matter. There are three ways in which he may become liable to pay the £5: first, if the whole claim or settlement is less than £5, he himself bears it; secondly, if the case is settled in the discretion as provided in the contract, he has to bear £5; and thirdly, "it is further agreed that if the company shall make any payment in full of any such claim the insured will reimburse the company up to the aforementioned sum of £5". That is not the present case; the present case is one in which the claim has been settled, and competently settled, by the insurance company, and thereupon arises the necessary condition of liability on the insured to pay the first £5.

This appeal therefore fails and must be dismissed with costs.'

Recovery of 'First £25' and Amount of 'No Claim' Bonus from Third Party

Where an insured has to pay the amount of an excess clause, eg the first £25, and also loses his 'no claim' bonus[9] he may include these items as part of any damages which he claims from a third party who is at fault.

In *Ironfield v Eastern Gas Board*[10] the plaintiff was driving a car with the permission of the insured. He ran into the back of an unlit lorry belonging to the Gas Board. He was in no way to blame. The car was badly damaged and he suffered personal injuries. The insured claimed against the insurance company, but because of an excess clause had to pay the first £10 himself. He also lost his no claim bonus, which amounted to £15 10s 7d. In his claim for damages against the Gas Board the plaintiff included a claim for special damage for these two items.

Streatfeild J held that he was entitled to succeed, for, though strictly speaking the damage to the car had been suffered by the insured, there seemed to be no reason to increase legal costs by insisting that the insured should be joined as a co-plaintiff to the action. It seemed to be the sensible thing for the sums claimed to be recovered in the present action, and for the plaintiff to pay them back to the insured. The damage not being the fault of the insured, it seemed to be very hard that he should be required not only to pay the first £10 of the loss but also

---

6 Slesser and Luxmoore LJJ, Atkinson J.

7 Slesser LJ in (1939) 65 Ll L Rep 57 at 58, quoted with approval the words of Sir Wilfrid Greene MR, in *Groom v Crocker* [1939] 1 KB 194 at 203: 'The effect of the provisions in question is, I think, to give to the insurers the right to decide upon the proper tactics to pursue in the conduct of the action, provided that they do so in what they bona fide consider to be the common interest of themselves and their assured'.

8 (1939) 65 Ll L Rep 57 at 58.

9 As to 'no claim' bonus, see p 224, ante.

10 [1964] 1 All ER 544n (Bury St Edmunds Assizes).

that he should lose his 'no claim' bonus. The items were part of the damage which had resulted from the accident, and the insured should be put into the same position as though he had not made any claim. Accordingly, judgment was given in respect of these two items on the plaintiff's undertaking to hand the money to the insured.

Where both Policies have Rateable Proportion Clauses

In *Gale v Motor Union Insurance Co Ltd; Loyst v General Accident, Fire and Life Assurance Corpn Ltd*[11] a Mr Gale had an ABC car and insured it with the Motor Union Insurance Co Ltd. The policy contained an extension clause—condition 6—giving an indemnity 'to any relation or friend driving with the insured's consent and not being insured under any other policy'. It also stated in condition 10 that:

'If at the time of the happening of any accident, injury, damage or loss covered by this policy, there shall be subsisting any other insurance or indemnity of any nature whatsoever covering the same whether effected by the insured or by any other person . . . then the company shall not be liable to pay or contribute towards any such damage or loss more than a rateable proportion of any sum or sums payable in respect thereof for compensation.'

A Mr Loyst was both a relative and friend of Gale. He was driving the ABC car when he collided with and injured a motor cyclist. The motor cyclist was awarded damages against Loyst.

Loyst owned a Morris car, which he had insured with the General Accident, Fire and Life Assurance Corporation. The policy included in its scope an indemnity in favour of the insured

'whilst personally driving a car not belonging to him provided the insured's own car is not in use at the same time, and provided that there is no other insurance in respect of such car whereby the insured may be indemnified'.

The policy also stated in condition 5:

'If at the time of the occurrence of any accident, loss or damage there shall be any other indemnity or insurance subsisting whether effected by the insured or by any other person, the Corporation shall not be liable to pay or contribute more than a rateable proportion of any sums payable in respect of such accident, loss or damage'.

Gale and Loyst united in making a claim against both insurance companies, and each company said that it was not liable. Roche J held that each company was liable rateably,[12] and said:[13]

'If one looks at the material conditions of the Motor Union Insurance Co policy, those two conditions must in my judgment be read together as relating to, explaining and qualifying one another. Condition 5 of the General Assurance Corporation policy, though not precisely in the same terms, is substantially in my opinion to the same effect as Condition 10 of the Motor Union Insurance Co policy. [Counsel] concedes that in construing Condition 6 "not being insured under any other policy" must be construed to mean "not being covered against the risk in question under any other policy"; and the real effect of his argument was not that the Motor Union Insurance Co was not liable at all, but that the liability was a rateable liability to be shared with the General Assurance Corporation. His argument went on in this

---

[11] (1926) 26 Ll L Rep 65, KB.
[12] Counsel agreed that 'rateably' meant that each company paid half: ibid, at 67.
[13] Ibid, at 67.

way, that the proper construction of s 2 (2) of the General Assurance Corporation policy was that it meant very much or exactly the same as Condition 6 of the Motor Union Insurance Co policy; that it limited the indemnity which was granted to Loyst while he was personally driving some other car to such cases as those where he had not any indemnity from anybody else. It is said by [Counsel] on behalf of the General Assurance Corporation that the words "whereby the assured may be indemnified" substantially add nothing except that they make more forcible the conclusion which ought to be drawn from the rest of s 2 (2), namely, that it is a provision that Loyst will be indemnified if he is driving an uninsured car. In my judgment there is nothing in the subsection which justifies that conclusion. The words "whereby the assured may be indemnified" do not allude to a possible or contingent indemnity. They mean this, "provided there is no other insurance in respect of such other car under which the assured might secure an indemnity in the existing circumstances, if, of course, he complied with the terms of such other insurance."

He then went on to observe:[14]

'Each of the policies in existence provides for indemnity in circumstances of a general nature such as happened, and each of them provided that if there is another operative insurance, it—the policy in question—was not to be used to give any indemnity, but each of them on the other hand provided that, if there were two policies which were operative, there was to be rateable contribution or payment. Now the proper construction of these clauses is not to deprive the assured of the indemnity altogether, which would be the effect of the policies if Condition 10 of the Motor Union Insurance Co policy and Condition 5 of the General Assurance Corporation policy stood alone. The effect of the second conditions is to qualify or alter the result which would flow from the unaided operation of the earlier clauses. In my opinion the proper award in this case is that the claimants should be paid rateably in respect of this accident by the Motor Union Insurance Co and the General Assurance Corporation.'

Hiring of Another Car pending settlement of Dispute

In *Player v Anglo-Saxon Insurance Association Ltd*[15] the insured sent a cheque to the insurance company in respect of the premium. The company received it and paid it into their bank account. The same day his car came into collision with a cow and was badly damaged. He claimed under the policy, but the company said that he was not insured under the policy, and returned his premium by their own cheque. Because the use of the car was necessary for his business, he gave the company 12 days in which to repair it, at the end of which he hired a car in its place. By a condition in the policy he could not repair his own car to the extent of more than £10, because if he did so, he would lose all his rights under the policy.

Later the company admitted liability, and paid for the damage to the car. But the insured claimed a further payment in respect of the expense he had incurred in hiring another car pending the dispute. He could not make a claim for such payment under the policy because it did not provide an indemnity in respect of consequential loss.[16]

The County Court Judge[17] held that the insured was entitled to be paid from the lapse of a reasonable time (ie the 12 days the insured had given the company in which to repair the vehicle) in which the repairs could have been effected up to a point at which proceedings for enforcing the policy could reasonably have

14 (1926) 26 Ll L Rep at 67, K B.
15 (1930) 38 Ll L Rep 62.
16 See (1930) 38 Ll L Rep 62.
17 Judge Parsons, sitting in Bristol County Court.

been commenced, ie up to 6 days before the action was in fact begun. Damages were accordingly fixed on this basis at £40.

The decision was affirmed by the Divisional Court of the King's Bench Division[18] where Swift J said:[19]

> 'Mr Player was entitled to receive that amount. To my mind there can be no question about it. This is not a claim by Mr Player under the policy in the sense that he is claiming moneys due under the policy, but what he is saying is: "Here is a policy under which I am prohibited from repairing my car, and the company must do it, and instead of repairing my car they say that the policy is non-existent." Then he says: "Pending such time that I can have the policy enforced by the Courts, I am bound to starve or hire another car in its place to do my business; I prefer to do the latter, and you must repay me for it." It seems to me that the learned County Court Judge was right in coming to the conclusion he did.'

Right to Sue other Party Unaffected

Even where there is a 'knock for knock' agreement between two insurers[20], and the insured is indemnified by one of them in respect of his loss less the amount of an excess clause, he is still entitled to sue the other party to a collision for the full amount of the loss.[1]

In *Morley v Moore*[2] there was a 'knock for knock' agreement between two insurance companies, which had insured the plaintiff and the defendant respectively. A collision occurred between the plaintiff's car and the defendant's car due to the negligent driving of the defendant. The cost of the repairs came to £33 2s 8d. There was a £5 excess clause in the plaintiff's policy, so his insurance company paid him £28 2s 8d.

The company indicated to him that they did not want him to make any claim against the defendant in respect of the £28 2s 8d. which they had paid by way of indemnity. Nevertheless the plaintiff did sue the defendant for the whole amount viz £33 2s 8d. The defendant pleaded that the claim as to the amount of £28 2s 8d. was made by the plaintiff as trustee for the insurers, and that since as *cestuis que trustent* they had waived the claim, the amount ceased to be recoverable as a matter of law.

The Court of Appeal[3] held that the plaintiff was entitled to the whole amount £33 2s 8d.

In the course of his judgment Sir Boyd Merriman P said:[4]

---

18 Swift and Acton, JJ.

19 (1930) 38 Ll L Rep 62 at 63.

20 See *Hobbs v Marlowe* [1978] A C 16, [1977] 2 All E R 241, H L, where the relevant clause in the 'knock for knock' agreement stated: 'IN THE EVENT OF (1) Damage being caused to any of the vehicles in connection with which indemnity is granted against Damage and/or Third Party Risks by the parties hereto resulting from a collision . . . each party shall bear its own loss (if any) in respect of such damage irrespective of legal liability and proviso (E). The absence of a claim or of notice of accident by a Policyholder or other person indemnified by such Policy shall not prevent the operation of this Agreement between the parties hereto. Where this Agreement provides that the loss or part thereof shall be borne by a party hereto, and the loss is paid by the other party hereto, the purposes of this Agreement shall be effected by reimbursement between such parties subject to the limits of the Policies issued by such parties.'

1 *Morley v Moore* (1936) 55 Ll L Rep 10, C A.

2 (1936) 55 Ll L Rep 10, C A.

3 Sir Boyd Merriman P, Scott L J, and Eve J.

4 (1936) 55 Ll L Rep 10 at 13.

'What is said has occurred in this case as a result of the direction by the insurance company (which for my part I cannot see that they had the slightest right to give, namely, the direction of the insurance company that the assured was not to sue the wrongdoer) is that if nevertheless he does sue the wrongdoer and recovers the £28, he recovers it on what is called a resulting trust in favour of the wrongdoer and has to hand it back to him. That is a conception which seems to me to be very like nonsense. It is true that if called upon to do so, the assured is obliged to sue or to allow the insurance company to sue in respect of a particular loss that they have paid, and if the assured recovers it, he is obliged to hand that sum over to them because it is impressed with a trust on their behalf; but putting that trust at its highest, I am unable to understand how it can be said that the *cestui que trust*, that is the insurance company, by taking a particular course which is not warranted by any independent contract, and by disclaiming their own right as a *cestui que trust*, can impose upon the assured another *cestui que trust* from whom at Common Law he is entitled to recover as damages what is said to be the subject of the trust. I do not think there is any such thing as a *cestui que trust* imposing against the will of the trustee some other *cestui que trust* so as to be a substitute, and I am quite sure there is no such thing as a *cestui que trust* not merely being able to substitute somebody else against the will of the trustee, but being able to substitute such person on the terms of a different trust. The thing seems to me to be fantastic.'

The learned President said that there was no need for this elaborate conception. If the insurance company insisted on their rights, these were perfectly plain. They could have the £28 which had been recovered, and the plaintiff had never attempted to say that they might not have it. They alone were the people who had said that they did not want to have it, and that the plaintiff was not entitled to recover it for them. But they had never bound themselves by any obligation not to take the money if and when the plaintiff offered it to them. The fact that they chose to forgo their legal right to receive this sum from the insured did not impose any obligation upon him. They might choose to make to the insured a present of the £28, but that did not affect his legal right to recover damages from the wrongdoer.[5]

He said that he hoped that the result of this judgment would be that plaintiffs would realise that they still had whatever might be their full rights accompanied by whatever duties resulted from the exercise of those rights, notwithstanding arrangements made behind the scenes between the insurance companies.

Scott LJ agreeing, said:[6]

'Even although the plaintiff's insurers may have told him that they did not want to be handed over any part of his recovery from the defendant to the extent of the £28 which they were interested in, although they may have told him not to sue for it, and although there was a "knock for knock" agreement between them and the defendant's insurers, in my view none of those facts gives rise to any defence known to the law or the principles of equity, so far as I know them. My view is that there is no right whatever in an insurer to indicate to his assured as to whether he shall or shall not abstain from enforcing his remedies against a third party which go in diminution of the loss against which the policy is issued; they have an absolute right to require him to enforce his remedies, but, in my opinion, they have no right to prevent

---

[5] The question whether the insurers had a right under the doctrine of subrogation to prevent the insured from prosecuting his remedies against a third party for losses for which they had already indemnified him did not arise in *Hobbs v Marlowe* [1977] 2 All ER 241, HL. Lord Diplock, however, said (ibid, at 254) that all standard forms of motor insurance policies contained express provisions giving to the insurers the right to institute, conduct and settle legal proceedings in the name of the insured; so the rights of the insurers were unlikely to depend on the application of the doctrine of subrogation alone but to involve consideration of express clauses in insurance policies.

[6] (1936) 55 Ll L Rep 10 at 14.

him enforcing them. Their right is a right purely consequential on the nature of the contract of indemnity, and it arises because of it being a contract of indemnity, and nothing more, namely, if the assured obtains payment, whether by enforcing an action at law or by obtaining an ex gratia payment, the underwriters or the insurers are entitled to be paid the amount paid by them to him by way of strict indemnity, and no more. To my mind that is the remedy of the insurers, and that is the only remedy they have in respect of the assured's rights of recovery at Common Law.'

Eve J also concurred.

Morley v Moore[7] was subsequently approved by the House of Lords[8] in *Hobbs v Marlowe*[9].

Position where one Policy is Invalid

Where a company has entered into a 'knock for knock' agreement with another company, and one of the vehicles involved in a collision is not covered at all by a policy issued by one of the companies, the agreement does not apply.

Thus, in *Bell Assurance Association v Licenses and General Insurance Corpn and Guarantee Fund Ltd.*[10] two insurance companies had entered into a 'knock for knock' agreement, which provided:

'On the occurrence of a collision between a vehicle insured with one of the above mentioned companies and insured with the other above mentioned company, each company shall bear the cost of making good the damage (if any) actually caused by such collision to the vehicle insured with itself.'

A man named Smith was the owner of a car, and was insured with the plaintiff insurance company. A collision took place between Smith's car and one belonging to a Mr Seaman. Seaman was not insured at all, but the car had been included in a policy which had been taken out with the defendant insurance company by a Mr Cowell. At the time of the collision Cowell had no insurable interest in Seaman's car.

When a claim was made by Seaman against the defendant insurance company to recover the amount of the damage done to his car, the company denied liability on the ground that he was not insured with them at all. So he brought an action against Smith, who was defended by the plaintiff insurance company, and eventually the company had to pay him £257. The plaintiff company then sued the defendant company for this sum, claiming that the particular case came within the terms of the 'knock for knock' agreement set out above.

The Court of Appeal[11] held that the claim failed because, at the time of the collision, there was no enforceable policy in respect of Seaman's vehicle, and the vehicle did not come within the language of the agreement.

Bankes LJ said that counsel for the plaintiff insurance company contended that if at the material time, ie at the moment of the collision, either vehicle was, in fact, mentioned in a policy in respect of which a premium had been paid and which had not lapsed by effluxion of time, it was within the meaning of this

---

[7] (1936) 55 Ll L Rep 10 C A.
[8] Lord Elwyn-Jones L C, Viscount Dilhorne, Lord Diplock, Lord Simon of Glaisdale and Lord Salmon.
[9] [1978] A C 16; [1977] 2 All E R 241, H L.
[10] (1923) 17 Ll L Rep 100, C A.
[11] Bankes, Scrutton and Atkin LJJ.

agreement an 'insured vehicle', whether the policy was enforceable or whether it was not.

But the learned Lord Justice said that he could not take that view at all, and observed:[12]

> 'I think it makes no difference whether the parties, for short, spoke of "insured vehicle," or whether they had written it out at length and had spoken of "the person whose interest in the vehicle is insured." In each case what the agreement is referring to is a policy which is enforceable at the material time, that is, the moment of collision. That that is so I think follows from what must have been the intention of the parties, namely, that each should bear its own loss, not that one should bear its real actual loss and the other should be treated as though it were bearing a loss although it bore no loss at all. The words in the first paragraph of the agreement bear that out because they provide that in the event of a collision taking place each company shall bear the cost of making good the damage (if any) actually caused to the vehicle insured with itself. That must, of course, refer to actual liability. It does not create a liability which does not exist under the policy. It refers to an actual liability created and existing under the policy.'

Scrutton and Atkin LJJ delivered concurring judgments.

Whether 'Knock for Knock' Agreement against Public Policy

In *Morley v Moore*[13] Sir Boyd Merriman P also referred to the question whether a 'knock for knock' agreement was against public policy if used to prejudice insured persons when insisting upon the exercise of the whole of their legal rights, but his remarks were only obiter. He observed:[14]

> 'If, contrary to the opinion that I have been expressing, the combined effect of arrangements whereby the assured is regarded as his own insurer for a certain proportion of the loss and this agreement colloquially known as a "knock for knock" agreement is used seriously to prejudice insured persons when insisting upon the whole of their legal rights, I should wish to consider whether the agreement were contrary to public policy. It is unnecessary to say more for the moment, but if I were to consider that, I should want to know a great deal more exactly than I do know at present precisely what are the terms of that agreement, and I should wish to hear some further argument upon the subject.'

4 THE CONDUCT OF THE PROCEEDINGS

The policy usually provides that the insurers are entitled to take absolute control of all negotiations and proceedings, and are entitled to use the name of the insured to settle any claims and to abandon it at any time if they think fit.

Thus, a condition of a typical policy[15] states:

> '[Policyholder's] recognition of [Company's] right . . .
> —to take over and deal with in [the Policyholder's] name the defence or settlement of any claim . . .
> —to take proceedings in [the Policyholder's] name, but at [the Company's] expense, to recover compensation for any payment made under this policy for [the Company's] benefit.'

---

[12] (1923) 17 Ll L Rep 100, at 101.
[13] (1936), 55 Ll L Rep 10, C A.
[14] Ibid, at 14.
[15] See the condition in the motor car policy (comprehensive) issued by the Commercial Union Assurance Co Ltd and set out in Appendix VI, p 418, post.

In *Lickiss v Milestone Motor Policies at Lloyd's*[16] a motor cyclist was involved in an accident in which a third party was injured. Proceedings were taken against him. He pleaded guilty at the magistrates' court, and was fined £5. He claimed an indemnity in respect of the damages, which he had had to pay to the third party, but the insurers repudiated liability on the ground that their position had been prejudiced by his plea of guilty, and that he was in breach of a condition in the policy which stated:

'The underwriters will pay all legal charges and expenses incurred with their written consent in defending any claim . . . and will at the insured's request (or may at their option) arrange for and pay the fee of a solicitor to represent the insured at any coroner's inquest . . . or for defending in any court of summary jurisdiction any proceedings.'

The County Court Judge,[17] before whom the case was first tried, held that there had been no breach of the condition. His decision was not contested when the case went to the Court of Appeal[18] on another issue.[19]

But Lord Denning M R said:[20]

'They said that they were entitled to insist on conducting the defence of the motor cyclist at the magistrates' court by their own solicitor. They were entitled to represent him. It was in "their option" under s 1 (b). The judge rejected that contention. He said it was contrary to public policy. A man who is accused is entitled to have a solicitor of his own choice or to defend himself if he likes. The insurers cannot compel him to have their own solicitor. I think that that is clearly right. Before us Counsel for the insurers did not dispute the validity of the Judge's ruling. He further doubted whether the clause, on its true construction, would have given them the right which they claimed to represent him.'

5 DISCLAIMER OF LIABILITY

A condition may impose a time limit for the institution of legal proceedings against the insurers if they have disclaimed liability.

Thus, in *Walker v Pennine Insurance Co Ltd*,[1] a condition in the policy stated:

'If the company shall disclaim liability to the insured for any claim hereunder and if within 12 calendar months from the date of such disclaimer legal proceedings have not been instituted in . . . Great Britain . . . in respect thereof by the insured or the insured's duly authorised representatives then the claim shall for all purposes be deemed to have been abandoned and shall not thereafter be recoverable hereunder.'

On 5 August 1970, the insured was driving a car, in which Miss Walters was a passenger, when it collided with another car and she was injured. Her solicitors wrote to the insured claiming that he was negligent, and suggesting that he pass their letter to the insurers. Subsequently, on 30 December 1970, the solicitors wrote direct to the insurers. On 3 February 1971, the insured's brokers passed to the insured a letter from the insurers stating that they disclaimed liability because the car was not in a roadworthy state at the time of the

---

16 [1966] 2 All E R 972, [1966] 1 W L R 1334, C A.
17 Judge Ingress Bell, at Blackpool County Court.
18 Lord Denning M R, Danckwerts and Salmon L JJ.
19 Viz whether a breach of another condition relating to the giving of notice to the insurers of intended prosecution had been waived. See p 287, ante.
20 [1966] 2 All E R 972 at 975.
1 [1980] 2 Lloyd's Rep 156, C A.

accident as there were 8 persons in the car. On 27 March 1971, the insurers sent a letter to the insured's solicitors stating that they were not prepared to reconsider their decision. On 25 October 1972, Miss Walters issued a writ against the insured claiming damages, and in March 1973 obtained judgment in default of appearance. In 1975, the damages were to be assessed, and on 7 July 1975, the insured's solicitors reopened correspondence with the insurers. On 25 November 1976, judgment was entered for £6,065. The insured then sought a declaration that the insurers must indemnify him.

The Court of Appeal[2] refused to grant the declaration on the ground that the proceedings were deemed to be abandoned under the condition set out above because they had not been taken within 12 months of the insurers' disclaimer of liability. Roskill LJ said[3] that it seemed strange, in the absence of explanation, that although he was being advised at the time, nobody had seemed to have thought about, or drawn attention to the condition set out above, or to have appreciated that once the insurers had repudiated liability under the policy in the letters concerned, the insured was at risk of losing his claim for indemnity in its entirety, whatever its merits, unless he brought proceedings for a declaration of liability against the insurers within 12 months from the date of the repudiation of that liability.

---

[2] Roskill and Brightman LJJ, and Sir David Cairns.
[3] [1980] 2 Lloyd's Rep at 160.

CHAPTER 33

Compulsory motor insurance

Certain persons are required by law to effect a motor insurance policy[1] where they use a motor vehicle on a road or permit others to do so. The insurance policy must be in force and must fulfil certain requirements. A certificate of insurance must be issued. There are special regulations concerning International Motor Insurance Cards. An action lies for breach of statutory duty.

PERSONS REQUIRED TO INSURE

The General Rule

It is not lawful for a person[2] to use or to cause or permit any other person to use motor vehicle on a road unless there is in force in relation to the use of the vehicle by that person or that other person, as the case may be, such a policy of insurance or such a security in respect of third party risks as complies with the requirements of Part VI of the Road Traffic Act 1972.[3]

If a person acts in contravention of this provision, he is liable on summary conviction to a fine not exceeding level 3 on the standard scale or to imprisonment for a term not exceeding 3 months, or to both such fine and imprisonment.[4]

A person charged with using a motor vehicle in contravention of this provision is not to be convicted if he proves that:

i   the vehicle did not belong to him and was not in his possession under a contract of hiring or of loan;

ii   he was using the vehicle in the course of his employment; and

iii   he neither knew nor had reason to believe that there was not in force in relation to the vehicle such a policy or security.[5]

---

1   The policy is required to provide cover for an unlimited amount. For a case in British Honduras (now Belize) where a policy was not required to cover 'liability in respect of any sum in excess of 4,000 dollars arising out of any one claim by any one person', see *Harker v Caledonian Insurance Co* [1980] 1 Lloyd's Rep 556, H L.

2   The words 'a person' do not merely mean any owner: *Williamson v O'Keefe* [1947] 1 All E R 307, K B D. See the judgment of Lord Goddard L C J, ibid, at p 308.

3   Road Traffic Act 1972, s 143 (1). Part VI of the Act does not apply to invalid carriages: ibid., s 143 (3) 'Invalid carriage' means 'a mechanically propelled vehicle the weight of which unladen does not exceed 5cwt and which is specially designed and constructed, and not merely adapted, for the use of a person suffering from some physical defect or disability and is used solely by such a person': ibid., s 190 (5). As to the requirements of the policy, see pp 315–318, post. Part VI of the Act is set out in Appendix VIII, p 445, post.

4   Ibid, s 143 (1) and Sch 4, Pt I, as amended by the Criminal Justice Act 1982, s 38 (1).

5   Ibid, s 143 (2).

Exceptions to the General Rule

The general rule does not apply to a vehicle:[6]

1   owned by a person who has deposited and keeps deposited with the Accountant General of the Supreme Court the sum of £15,000, at a time when the vehicle is being driven under the owner's control;[7]

2   owned by a local authority, at a time when the vehicle is being driven under the owner's control;

3   owned by a police authority or the Receiver for the Metropolitan Police District at a time when it is being driven under the owner's control;

4   at a time when it is being driven for police purposes by or under the direction of a police constable or by a person employed by a police authority, or employed by the Receiver;

5   at a time when it is being driven on a journey to or from any place undertaken for salvage[8] purposes pursuant to Pt IX of the Merchant Shipping Act 1894;

6   used for the purpose of its being furnished in pursuance of a direction under the Army Act 1955, s 166 (2) (b) or under the Air Force Act 1955, s. 166 (2) (b).[9]

7   owned by the London Transport Executive or by its wholly owned subsidiary while the vehicle is being driven under the owner's control.

8   made available by the Secretary of State to any person, body or local authority in pursuance of s 11 or s 13 of the National Health Reorganization Act 1973 at a time when it is being used in accordance with the terms on which it is so made available.

But it is an offence for a person to use a vehicle which is mentioned above and registered in Great Britain or any trailer, whether or not coupled, in the territory other than Great Britain or Gibraltar of the member States of the Communities unless a policy of insurance is in force in relation to the person using the vehicle which insures him in respect of any liability which may be incurred by him in respect of the use of the vehicle in such territory according to the law of compulsory insurance against civil liability in respect of the use of vehicles of the State where the liability may be incurred.[10]

'USE'

A person is not guilty of an offence under s 143 (1) of the Act of 1972 unless the vehicle is being 'used' on a road.

---

[6] Road Traffic Act 1972, s 144 (1) (2), as amended.

[7] 'Under the owner's control' means, in relation to a vehicle, that it is being driven by the owner or by a servant of the owner in the course of his employment or is otherwise subject to the control of the owner: ibid., s 158 (1).

[8] 'Salvage' means the preservation of a vessel which is wrecked, stranded or in distress, or the lives of persons belonging to, or the cargo or apparel of, such a vessel: ibid, s 158 (1).

[9] These sections relate to the requisitioning of vehicles by the Army and by the Royal Air Force respectively.

[10] Motor Vehicles (Compulsory Insurance) (No 2) Regulations 1973 (SI 1973 2143) reg 5. The Regulations are set out in Appendix IX, p 457, post.

The word 'use' means "have the use of" a motor vehicle.

Thus, in *Elliott v Grey*[11] the defendant was the owner of a car parked in the road outside his house. It had broken down and could not be driven and had remained there since 20 December 1958. He jacked up the car so that its wheels were off the ground and removed the battery. He decided not to drive the car until it had been repaired and on 7 February 1959 terminated his insurance cover. On that very day he cleaned the car, oiled its locks, sent the battery to be recharged and replaced the old carburettor with a new one. He unjacked the car, but it could not be mechanically propelled because the engine would not work. The Divisional Court of the Queen's Bench Division[12] held that the defendant was rightly convicted of using the car on a road whilst uninsured contrary to s. 35 (1) of the Road Traffic Act 1930.[13]

Lord Parker LCJ observed:[14]

'It seems to me that the word "use" . . . . is . . . really equivalent to "have the use of a motor vehicle on a road". Indeed the definition which Counsel for the [defendant] suggested, and which, I think was that "use" means to have the advantage of a vehicle as a means of transport including for any period or time between journeys, itself suggests availability. In other words, it is really equivalent to what Counsel for the [prosecutor] suggests by the expression "have the use of". In the present case, although this car could not be driven, there is nothing to suggest that it could not be moved. As I pointed out in argument, for all we know it was on the top of a hill and a little boy could release the brake and the car could go careering down the hill. In the absence, at any rate, of a finding that it was immovable as, for instance, that the wheels were removed or something of that sort, I cannot think that this car was not fairly and squarely within the words which I have used "have the use of a motor vehicle on the road." '[15]

The word 'use' is not co-terminous with 'drive' or 'to be in charge of.'[16]

Again, it is clear that there may be more than one person who is 'using' a vehicle at any given time.[17]

A person does not 'use' a vehicle unless there is present, in the person alleged to be the user, an element of controlling, managing or operating the vehicle at the relevant time.

Thus, in *Brown v Roberts*[18] the second defendant, who was the owner of a van, was held not to have committed an offence under s 35 (1) of the Road Traffic Act 1930[19] in that he had not insured against liability incurred by the first defendant, who was a passenger, towards the plaintiff, a pedestrian, who was injured when he negligently opened the door of the van in which he was travelling.

Megaw J said:[20]

---

11 [1960] 1 QB 367, [1959] 3 All ER 733.

12 Lord Parker LCJ, Cassels and Edmund Davies JJ.

13 Now s 143 (1) of the Road Traffic Act 1972.

14 [1959] 3 All ER 733 at 736.

15 Counsel for the prosecutor further contended that, even if the car was completely immobilised, an offence would be committed. Lord Parker LCJ, however, said that for his part he found it unnecessary in the present case to go so far: ibid, at 736.

16 *Brown v Roberts* [1963] 2 All ER 263 at 267, QBD (per Megaw J). See also *Elliott v Grey* [1959] 3 All ER 733 at 736

17 *Brown v Roberts*, supra, at 267 (per Megaw J).

18 Supra.

19 Now s 143 (1) of the Road Traffic Act 1972.

20 [1963] 2 All ER 263 at 269. Counsel for the second defendant pointed out that if the second defendant were held to be liable for 'using' the vehicle, it would mean that very many people,

'Precisely what the extent of [the] element [of control] may be, it is unnecessary to seek to define. There was no such element present in the relationship between the first defendant and the second defendant's van. I do not accept that the control of management or operation of a door of a vehicle by the passenger entering or alighting amounts to the necessary control or management or operating of the vehicle.'

In *Leathley v Tatton*,[1] the accused went with 2 friends to look at a car with a view to buying it. Its owner did not turn up. One of the friends had a key which fitted the car. The car would not start, so one of the friends got into the driving seat and pushed the car. When it started, he jumped into the passenger seat.

The Divisional Court of the Queen's Bench Division[2] held that the accused was 'using' the vehicle within the meaning of the Road Traffic Act 1972, s 143. Ackner J[3] said that there was a clear situation in which the accused and his friend were acting in concert, a joint enterprise, the purpose of which was to set the car going and for the purpose of the accused seeing how it functioned. The accused was 'using' the car directly for his own purposes.

In *Bennett v Richardson*,[4] the accused, a blind man, was sitting in the back of an ice cream van. He helped to drive the vehicle and keep it clean, and served the ice cream whilst his partner drove.

The Divisional Court of the Queen's Bench Division[5] held that the accused was not 'using' the vehicle. Lord Widgery LCJ said[6] that the relationship of the accused and the driver was not that of employer and employee, and it was only in that case that the accused could be convicted of 'using' the vehicle.

In *B (a Minor) v Knight*,[7] a Mr O'Nion took a van without the owner's consent. The accused was in no way concerned with the taking. O'Nion drove the van to a place where he picked up the accused, who got into the van as a passenger, and O'Nion drove off. The accused did not then know that the van had been taken without the owner's consent. But he did learn of this, and remained on board. He did not ask to get out because he did not fancy the idea of walking home.

The Divisional Court of the Queen's Bench Division[8] held that the accused was not 'using' the van. Donaldson LJ, said[9] that he was quite unable to detect any element of joint enterprise. The vehicle was being 'used' by O'Nion and was not being 'used' by the accused. He was simply getting a lift from O'Nion in the course of O'Nion's use.

---

probably millions, since 1930, had been committing a criminal offence every time they had entered a bus or taxi unless it turned out that there was in force an insurance policy covering the possible liability to these parties for negligence whilst the passengers were travelling in, or getting out of, the bus or taxi. See the judgment of Megaw J, ibid, at 267.

[1] [1980] R T R 21, DC.
[2] Geoffrey Lane LJ, and Ackner, J.
[3] [1980] R T R at 22.
[4] [1980] R T R 358, DC.
[5] Lord Widgery LCJ, and Stocker J.
[6] [1980] R T R 358 at 360.
[7] [1981] R T R 136, DC.
[8] Donaldson LJ, and Comyn J.
[9] [1981] R T R 136 at 138.

'CAUSE OR PERMIT'

The Meaning of the Words

In defining the words 'cause or permit' Lord Wright in *McLeod (or Houston) v Buchanan*[10] observed:[11]

'To "cause" the user involves some express or positive mandate from the person "causing" to the other person, or some authority from the former to the latter, arising in the circumstances of the case. To "permit" is a looser and vaguer term. It may denote an express permission, general or particular, as distinguished from a mandate. The other person is not told to use the vehicle in the particular way, but he is told that he may do so if he desires. However, the word also includes cases in which permission is merely inferred. If the other person is given control of the vehicle, permission may be inferred if the vehicle is left to the other person's disposal in such circumstances as to carry with it a reasonable implication of a discretion or liberty to use it in the manner in which it was used. In order to prove permission it is not necessary to show knowledge of similar user in the past, or actual notice that the vehicle might be, or was likely to be, so used, or that the accused was guilty of a reckless disregard of the probabilities of the case, or a wilful closing of his eyes. He may not have thought at all of his duties under the section.'

His Lordship, however, went on to say[12] that it was unnecessary in the present case to consider whether the section covered cases where the custodian had used the vehicle in a manner outside what any reasonable person could have contemplated. To impose that unqualified obligation on a person, who parted with the control of a vehicle without any definite arrangement as to its use, might promote the general policy of securing that all vehicles should be insured, but he himself questioned whether the parting with control without definite express restriction gave a permission within the meaning of the section for unrestricted use. A definite arrangement could be shown, without express words, by an implication from the circumstances.

In interpreting the words 'cause or permit' MacKinnon LJ said in *Goodbarne v Buck*:[13]

'The offence is "to cause or permit any other person to use". There are two different verbs. The second one "permit", I think, is much easier to construe and to interpret, than the first one, "cause". In order to make a person liable for permitting another person to use a motor vehicle, it is obvious that he must be in a position to forbid the other person to use the motor vehicle. As at present advised, I can see no ground on which any person can be in a position to use a motor vehicle except in a case where the person charged is the owner of the car. If one is the owner of a car or of a van, one can forbid or one can permit another to use it.'

In *Lloyd v Singleton*,[14] however, Lord Goddard CJ, pointed out[15] that these reservations by MacKinnon LJ, were clearly per incuriam, and he had no thought of all the various permutations which could arise. Thus, the situation could arise in which the car was entrusted by the owner to a driver authorised by him who had the care, management and control of the car, and that person was entitled to permit certain people to drive but not others. Again, suppose a man, owning a car and employing a chauffeur, left the car in the care of the

---

10 [1940] 2 All E R 179 H L.
11 Ibid, at 187.
12 [1940] 2 All E R 179, H L.
13 [1940] 1 All E R 613 at 616, C A.
14 [1953] 1 Q B 357, [1953] 1 All E R 291, Q B D.
15 Ibid, at 293.

chauffuer. If, when his employer was not in the car, the chauffeur allowed someone else to drive it, the chauffeur was permitting the use of it. The employer was not permitting the use of it because he did not know it was being used. He had given no authority to the chauffeur to allow other people to drive. In the ordinary way he would forbid the chauffeur to allow other people to drive, but, whether the chauffeur was actually forbidden or not, he was the person who permitted the driving, and that case was not in the mind of MacKinnon LJ when he made the observation.

Examples

Whether a person has 'caused or permitted' another person to drive is a matter of fact in each case.

In *Watkins v O'Shaughnessy*[16] a purchaser of a car at an auction had employed a driver to collect it from the auction premises at which it had been sold to her. The Court of Appeal[17] held that, on the evidence,[18] the auctioneers had not 'caused or permitted' him to drive the vehicle, for once the sale was completed they had no control over him, and the acts of their servants in lending him trade plates for the purpose of driving it away, and in supplying him with a slip originally issued to one of the auctioneers' drivers, but altered so that it showed his name instead, were quite unauthorised. Scott LJ said:[19]

> 'I can conceive no legal ground at all for assuming that auctioneers, who had nothing to do with the delivery of cars bought at their auction mart, had given servants at the auction mart any authority whatever for the taking away of cars from the auction mart. There is, therefore, no ground for submitting . . . that there was a general authority of these servants which would make the actual authority to do the particular act a question that did not affect the legal liability of their principals. In my view, what they did was wholly outside the scope of their general authority. No evidence was given that their act was in any way expressly authorised by the auctioneers.'

In *Goodbarne v Buck*[20] a person had helped his brother obtain an insurance policy in respect of a car.

The insurance company later disclaimed liability on the ground that the proposal form for it contained a mis-statement. The Court of Appeal[1] held that, on the evidence,[2] he had not 'caused or permitted' his brother to drive the vehicle. MacKinnon LJ observed:[3]

> 'All that can be said, however, is that [he] assisted his brother in getting a worthless piece of paper in place of an effective insurance policy. Yet even if he did that, and it was proved that he did that, I do not see that he can be prosecuted successfully upon an allegation that he had caused [his brother] to use the vehicle on the road without an effective policy.'

In *McLeod (or Houston) v Buchanan*[4] a solicitor owned an isolated farm, and appointed his brother as a manager of it. He bought a Humber car for him and

---

16 [1939] 1 All ER 385.
17 Scott, Clauson and Finlay L.JJ.
18 For the evidence, see [1939] 1 All ER 385 at 386–387.
19 Ibid, at 389. See also the judgment of Clauson LJ, ibid, at 390.
20 [1940] 1 All ER 613. C A.
1 MacKinnon and Clauson L.JJ, and Charles J.
2 For the evidence, see [1940] 1 All ER 613 at 616–618.
3 Ibid, at 618.
4 [1940] 2 All ER 179, HL.

for the use of the farm. A policy was effected giving cover to the brother both for private purposes and the farm business. The Humber was not reliable, so the solicitor authorised the brother to buy a Ford van, but the policy which was issued covered the use of the vehicle 'in connection with the policy holder's business only'. The brother used the car for private purposes, and the question arose as the whether the solicitor had 'caused or permitted' the brother to drive whilst uninsured. The House of Lords[5] held that, on the evidence,[6] it had been established that he had given permission. Lord Wright observed:[7]

'In my opinion, the evidence shows that the control of the vehicle was handed over to [the brother] for the same user as the Humber car had been handed over to him . . . namely, for the purposes of the commercial business of the farm, and for such reasonable personal use as was natural and usual where the farm was as remote and solitary as the farm in question . . . [The brother] was never informed that the terms of the insurance had been altered, or that he was not to use the van for private purposes . . . The van was perfectly suitable for [the brother] to drive by himself, or even to take his wife and friends . . . In my opinion, the necessary permission is established.'

In *Lyons v May*[8] a garage proprietor drove a lorry, which he was repairing, back to the owner's premises on being requested to to so. There was no policy effected by the owner, and none effected by the garage proprietor except in respect of himself and any authorised employee, though this fact was unknown to the owner. The Divisional Court of the King's Bench Division[9] held that the owner had caused or permitted the garage proprietor to drive the vehicle. Lord Goddard C J said:[10]

'The cases which have been cited to us show that *scienter* is not necessary, that is to say, a person who is ignorant of the fact that there is no policy of insurance covering a vehicle, may, nevertheless, be held to commit an offence if he permits the use of the vehicle. It is difficult to say that the [owner] did not permit the garage proprietor to drive the lorry, because he asked him to do so and the garage proprietor agreed. The [owner] did not ask the garage proprietor whether he had a policy which would cover his driving of the lorry, and the [owner's] policy clearly covered only the [owner]. Therefore, this Court feels that an offence has been committed.'

In *Lloyd v Singleton*[11] the defendant was charged with permitting his brother to use a vehicle without a policy of insurance being in effect in relation to that user. The car belonged to Axfords Ltd, and had been insured by a Mr Rubin, who was the managing director. The defendant was the assistant manager. He was allowed to drive the car on the company's business. He had full discretion as to permitting the use of the car and who was to drive it so long as it was being used for the business of the company or another company, of which Rubin was also the managing director. So long as the car was being used by persons in the employment of the company on the company's business, it was lawful use for which the defendant was entitled to permit, and one which would be covered by the insurance policy. The defendant was taken ill and asked his brother, who

---

5 Viscount Caldecote LC, Lord Thankerton, Lord Russell of Killowen, Lord Wright and Lord Romer.
6 For the evidence, see [1940] 2 All E R 179 at 181–183.
7 Ibid, at 188. See also the judgment of Viscount Caldecott LC, ibid, at 183 and that of Lord Russell of Killowen, ibid, at 185.
8 [1948] 2 All E R 1062, DC.
9 Lord Goddard C J, Hilbery and Birkett JJ.
10 [1948] 2 All E R 1062 at 1063.
11 [1953] 1 QB 357, [1953] 1 All E R 291, DC.

has nothing to do with the companies, to drive the car home. The brother had no policy of insurance. The justices dismissed the charge in view of the dictum of MacKinnon LJ in *Goodbarne v Buck*[12] to the effect that only an owner could give 'permission'. The Divisional Court of the Queen's Bench Division[13] held that this dictum was given per incuriam,[14] and that the justices had not come to a correct determination in point of law. The case was accordingly remitted to them to consider the policy and to come to a conclusion whether or not the car was insured.

In *Thompson v Lodwick*[15] a Mr Lodwick was asked by a Mr Sunderland, who was the owner of a car and was the holder of a provisional licence, to supervise his driving of the vehicle. Mr Lodwick agreed and sat in the front passenger seat. He made no inquiries about Mr Sunderland's insurance cover.

The Divisional Court of the Queen's Bench[16] held that Mr Lodwick had not 'permitted' Mr Sunderland to drive the vehicle. Stephen Brown J said[17] that the accused was not in a position to forbid the use of the vehicle by the man who was its owner.

'MOTOR VEHICLE'

Section 190 (1) of the Road Traffic Act 1972 states:

'In this Act "motor vehicle" means a mechanically propelled vehicle intended or adapted for use on roads . . .'

'Mechanically Propelled'

Whether a vehicle can be a mechanically propelled vehicle will depend on the circumstances.

Thus, in *Smart v Allan*[18] the defendant was convicted by the justices of using a Rover car without there being a policy of insurance to it in force contrary to s 201 of the Road Traffic Act 1960.[19] Evidence was given that he had bought the vehicle for £2 as scrap, he had towed it on two wheels from place to place and ultimately left it in the road, the engine did not work, the tyres were flat, one tyre was missing, the engine was in a rusty condition, it did not have a gearbox or a battery, the engine was not complete and it certainly could not move of its own accord. The defendant appealed, and his conviction was quashed by the Divisional Court of the Queen's Bench Division.[20] Lord Parker LCJ observed:[1]

---

[12] [1940] 1 All E R 613 at 616.
[13] Lord Goddard C J, Croom-Johnson and Pearson JJ.
[14] As to this point, see p 303, ante.
[15] [1983] R T R 76.
[16] May LJ, and Stephen Brown J.
[17] [1983] R T R at 80.
[18] [1963] 1 Q B 291, [1962] 3 All E R 893.
[19] Now s 143 (1) of the Road Traffic Act 1972.
[20] Lord Parker LCJ, Gorman and Salmon JJ.
[1] [1962] 3 All E R 893 at 896.

'Where, as in the present case, there is no reasonable prospect of the vehicle ever being made mobile again, it seems to me that, at any rate at that stage, a vehicle has ceased to be a mechanically propelled vehicle. If that is the correct approach, as I think it is, it follows that there was no evidence in the present case on which the justices, properly directing themselves as to the law, could have said that this vehicle was a mechanically propelled vehicle. All the evidence in this case was the other way.'

On the other hand, in *Newberry v Simmonds*[2] the justices found the defendant not guilty of using a mechanically propelled vehicle without a Road Fund licence contrary to s 15 of the Vehicles (Excise) Act 1949.[3] He had given evidence that the car had been stolen by a person unknown, and contended that the car was not a mechanically propelled vehicle. There was no other evidence that the car had, in fact, an engine, and it was not clear whether the justices had accepted the evidence that the car had been stolen. The prosecution appealed, and the appeal was allowed by the Divisional Court of the Queen's Bench Division[4], and the case was remitted to the justices with a direction to convict. Widgery J delivering the judgment of the Court, observed:[5]

'We are, however, satisfied that a motor car does not cease to be a mechanically propelled vehicle on the mere removal of the engine if the evidence admits the possibility that the engine may be replaced and the motive power restored. In the present case, therefore, the fact that the [prosecution] had not proved that there was an engine in the car was of no significance because the absence of an engine would not be conclusive. Further, even if the justices accepted the evidence of the [defendant], that evidence was not in itself sufficient to take a vehicle, which was in other respects an "ordinary motor car", out of the classification of a mechanically propelled vehicle. On the totality of the evidence the justices had no alternative but to find the charge proved.'

Again, in *Law v Thomas*[6] the justices were ordered to convict the defendant of using a car on the road whilst uninsured. The car was not in working order because it had a blown core plug. It was held that the vehicle was a 'mechanically propelled vehicle' for the purposes of s 201 of the Road Traffic Act 1960, for the engine worked as soon as the plug was replaced.

In *Lawrence v Howlett*[7] the Divisional Court of the Queen's Bench Division held that the defendant was not guilty of using a bicycle, which was fitted with an auxiliary engine, without an insurance policy relating to it being in force, because, on the evidence, the auxiliary engine was not in working order since its cylinder, piston and connecting rod had been removed, and accordingly it was no longer a 'mechanically propelled vehicle'.

On the other hand, in *Floyd v Bush*[8] the Divisional Court of the Queen's Bench Division held that where the defendant used a bicycle, which was fitted with an auxiliary motor, but only pedalled it without operating the motor, it was a 'mechanically propelled vehicle', and the defendant had to be insured in respect to it.

---

2 [1961] 2 Q B 345, [1961] 2 All E R 318.
3 This Act contained no definition of a 'mechanically propelled vehicle', but the Court accepted that the words had the same meaning as in s. 1 of the Road Traffic Act 1930 (now s 190 (1)) of the Road Traffic Act 1972). See the judgment of Widgery J:[1961] 2 All E R 318 at 320.
4 Lord Parker L C J, Winn and Widgery J J.
5 [1961] 2 All E R 318 at 320.
6 (1964) 108 Sol Jo 158.
7 [1952] 2 All E R 74.
8 [1953] 1 All E R 265, [1953] 1 WLR 242.

Burden of Proof

Whether the burden of proving that the vehicle is a 'mechanically propelled vehicle' lies on the prosecution or on the defendant is not yet settled. In *Newberry v Simmonds*[9] Widgery J observed:[10]

> 'It is not necessary to decide, where in a state of facts as these justices partially investigated, the onus of proof would rest. It may perhaps arise some time for consideration, whether because the owner of a vehicle would normally have peculiarly within his own knowledge all the relevant facts, the onus of proof should be regarded as shifting to him, once his vehicle has been shown to be by appearance a motor car, to establish that it was at the material time no longer a "mechanically propelled vehicle".'

'Intended or Adapted for Use on Roads'

In *Burns v Currell*[11] Lord Parker LCJ said[12] that the word 'intended' did not mean 'intended by the user of the vehicle either at the moment of the alleged offence or for the future', nor did it mean the intention of the manufacturer or the wholesaler or the retailer, and it might be that it was not referring to the intention as such of any particular purpose. He himself preferred to make the test: 'Whether a reasonable person looking at the vehicle would say that one of its users would be a road user'. In deciding that question the reasonable man would not have to envisage what some man losing his senses would do with a vehicle; nor an isolated user nor a user in an emergency. The real question was: 'Is some general use on the roads contemplated as one of the users?'

'Go Kart'

In *Burns v Currell*[13] the justices convicted the accused of driving a 'go kart' on a road without an insurance policy relating to it being in force contrary to s 201 of the Road Traffic Act 1960.[14] The vehicle had an engine at the rear. It had a tubular frame mounted on four small wheels, and was equipped with a single seat, steering-wheel and steering column. It had no horn, springs, parking-brake, driving mirror or wings, but was equipped with an efficient silencer. It had brakes which operated on the rear wheels only. Its maximum speed was 40 mph. This was the first time in which it had been used on a road. The accused appealed.

The Divisional Court of the Queen's Bench Division[15] held that the appeal would be allowed. Lord Parker LCJ observed:[16]

> 'The real question is: Is some general use on the roads contemplated as one of the users? Approaching the matter in that way at the end of the case, the justices would have to ask themselves: Has it been proved beyond a reasonable doubt that any reasonable person looking at the "go kart" would say that one of it uses would be use on the road? For my part, I

---

9 [1961] 2 All E R 318.
10 Ibid, at 320.
11 [1963] 2 All E R 297.
12 Ibid, at 300.
13 Supra.
14 Now s 143 (1) of the Road Traffic Act 1972.
15 Lord Paker LCJ, Ashworth and Winn JJ.
16 [1963] 2 All E R 297 at 300.

have come to the conclusion that there really was no such evidence before them as to satisfy them on that point according to the ordinary standard of proof. The evidence was that the [accused] had used this vehicle on this day alone and that he had never used it before. There was no evidence that other people used these vehicles on the road, nor is it suggested by the justices that they came to their conclusion, as they would be entitled to up to a point, on their own experience and knowledge. As I have said, all that they had before them was that a ''go-kart'' had been used on a road to which the public had access on this one occasion. Looked at in that way, so far as this matter of ''intended'' is concerned, I do not think that the justices had any material on which they could feel sure so as to be able to convict.'

His Lordship went on to say[17] (obiter) that 'adapted', when used disjunctively with 'intended' and not with the word 'constructed', was used in its adjectival sense ie it meant 'apt' or 'fit', and in the present case it had not been proved that the 'go kart' was fit or apt. It was undoubtedly capable of being used on the road, but 'adapted' adjectivally meant considerably more than that. If, however, 'adapted' meant 'altered', there was no question of the 'go kart' having been altered.

He pointed out,[18] however, that, on proof of a general user, not this sole use but a general user, of 'go karts' on roads, a bench of magistrates would be fully entitled to hold that they were 'motor vehicles' within s 253 (1) of the Road Traffic Act 1960.[19]

Farm Tractor

In *Woodward v James Young (Contractors) Ltd*,[20] an ordinary farm tractor was held to be a vehicle 'intended or adapted for use' on the road.

Dumper

In *Daley v. Hargreaves*[1] a dumper ie a four-wheeled mechanically propelled vehicle with pneumatic tyres and reversible seats to enable it to be driven backwards or forwards had mechanically operated scoops to collect material, but had no windscreen, or lights, or speedometer or driving mirror. The Divisional Court of the Queen's Bench Division[2] held that the dumper was not 'intended or adapted for use on roads'. Lord Parker LCJ said[3] that he would like to emphasize that it must not be taken as the result of the decision that dumpers of the type used in the present case were not motor vehicles 'intended or adapted for use on roads', and that it might well be that in another case, on fuller evidence, the Court would be able to say that similar dumpers were clearly such vehicles.

In *Macdonald v Carmichael, Orr v Carmichael*[4] the Court of Justiciary also held that a similar type of dumper was not a motor vehicle 'intended or adapted for

---

17 [1963] 2 All E R 297 at 300. See also *Woodward v James Young (Contractors) Ltd* 1958 J C 28 at 33 (per Lord Thomson).
18 [1963] 2 All E R 297 at 301.
19 Now s 190 (1) of the Road Traffic Act 1972.
20 1958 S C (J) 28.
1 [1961] 1 All E R 552.
2 Lord Parker LC J, Salmon and Winn JJ.
3 [1961] 1 All E R 552 at 556. See also the judgment of Salmon J, ibid at 556.
4 1941 S C (J) 27.

use on roads'. Again, in *Chalgray Ltd v Apsley*[5] the Divisional Court of the Queen's Bench Division held that a 15 cwt dumper carrying building materials on a road for about 100 yards to a building site was not such a vehicle for, on the evidence, it was only occasionally used as part of the construction plant.

Racing Car

On the evidence given in *Brown v Abbott*[6], where a car had been modified for racing by the installation of a different engine, the removal of the passenger seats and perspex instead of glass being fitted in the windscreen, the Divisional Court of the Queen's Bench Division upheld the justices' decision that no insurance policy was required for it whilst it was being towed along a road for it was not a vehicle 'intended or adapted for use on roads'.

'ROAD'

The word 'road' is defined by s 196 of the Road Traffic Act 1972 as:

> 'any highway and any other road to which the public has access and includes bridges over which a road passes.'

Whether any particular road is a 'road' within this definition will depend on the circumstances.

Car Park

In *Griffin v Squires*[7] the defendant was charged with driving a car on a road whilst uninsured. The car had been parked in a car park, and she drove it for 10 yards until it went through a hedge and came to rest on a lawn adjoining the car park. The car park was open to all members of the public without payment. At one corner there was an opening of about 15 feet abutting a private footpath leading to a bowling club. The footpath was used by the club members who had to cross the car park to reach the footpath. But the footpath was not habitually used by the public. The justices dismissed the charge on the ground that the car park itself nor the car park as part of the private footpath was a 'road', and their decision was upheld by the Divisional Court of the Queen's Bench Division.[8]

Dock Roads

Dock roads except those vested in the Port of London Authority[9] are not roads for the purpose of s. 196 of the Act of 1972.[10]

---

[5] (1965) 109 Sol Jo 394.

[6] (1965) 109 Sol Jo 437, DC.

[7] [1958] 3 All E R 468.

[8] Lord Parker CJ, Streatfeild and Diplock JJ. See the judgment of Lord Parker CJ, ibid at 470 and that of Streatfeild J, ibid at 471.

[9] Port of London Act 1968, s 199.

[10] *Buchanan v Motor Insurers' Bureau* [1955] 1 All E R 607, [1955]]1 WLR 488.

POLICY IN FORCE

Meaning of 'In Force'

Section 143 (1) of the Road Traffic Act 1972 does not require that there should be in force a policy of insurance which covers the personal liability of the driver. It is sufficient that there should be a policy in force covering the then use of the car in respect of third party risks.

Thus, in *John T Ellis Ltd v Hinds*[11] Humphreys J observed:[12]

'It is not any particular person who uses the vehicle who is required by s 35[13] to be insured. What is required is that the user on the road by the person or persons, in fact, using the road should be covered by insurance in respect of third party risks. In the present case the [accused], as the owners [of the vehicle], had a policy which indemnified them against any liability which might be incurred by claim in respect of death or bodily injury to any person arising out of the use on the road of the vehicle. The policy was, therefore, one which complied with s 36 (1)[14] of the Act. The contention of Counsel for the [prosecutor] is that something further is required by s 35, namely, an insurance indemnifying the driver . . . I find nothing in the section to support that contention. I think the true view of the section is that what must be covered by insurance in respect of third party risks is the use on the road of the vehicle by the driver.'[15]

A policy is 'in force' for the purpose of s 143 (1) even if it is voidable by the insurers eg on the ground that it has been obtained by misrepresentation, provided that it has not been avoided, in fact, by the time proceedings are brought under s 143 (1) against the defendant. Thus, in *Durrant v Maclaren*[16] Ormerod J said:[17]

'[Counsel's] argument is that, if by any means an insurance policy may be avoided or may be void ab initio, then it cannot be a 'policy in force'. Quite clearly when s 35 [of the Road Traffic Act 1930] was passed, that might have been the position, but s 10 of the [Road Traffic Act 1934][18] does provide that the policy is in force and remains in force once a certificate of insurance has been given, and the insurance company must pay if judgment is obtained, in respect of an accident unless proceedings are taken under s 10 (2). No proceedings of that kind have been taken in this case, and, therefore, until such proceedings are taken, the insurance company remain liable to pay any damages providing a judgment is obtained in spite of the fact that the proposed insured has made clearly false statements in his proposal.'[19]

Where a policy in respect of a motor tractor contained an indorsement enabling it to be used with two trailers, and the insured used the tractor to draw two laden trailers which was illegal, the policy was held by the Divisional Court of the Queen's Bench Division[20] to be 'in force' because it insured him not

---

11 [1947] K B 475, [1947] 1 All E R 337, D C.
12 Ibid, at 341.
13 Ie of the Road Traffic Act 1930, which is now replaced by s 143 of the Road Traffic Act 1972.
14 Ie of the Road Traffic Act 1930. This section is now replaced by s 143 of the Road Traffic Act 1972.
15 See also the judgment of Lord Goddard C J: [1947] 1 All E R 337 at 339; *Marsh v Moores* [1949] 2 K B 208, [1949] 2 All E R 27; *Lister v Romford Ice and Cold Storage Co Ltd* [1957] 1 All E R 125 at 136, H L (per Lord Morton of Henryton) and at 143 (per Lord Tucker).
16 [1956] 2 Lloyd's Rep 70, D C.
17 Ibid, at 73.
18 Now s 149 (3) of the Road Traffic Act 1972.
19 See also the judgment of Donovan J: [1956] 2 Lloyd's Rep 70 at 73; *Goodbarne v Buck* [1939] 4 All E R 107, affd [1940] 1 KB 771, [1940] 1 All E R 613.
20 Lord Goddard C J, Hilbery and Bryne JJ.

against the consequences of the illegal user of the tractor, but against the consequences of its being negligently driven.[1] Lord Goddard C J observed:[2]

> 'It is an offence against the Road Traffic Act 1930, s 18 (1)[3] for a tractor to draw two laden trailers. When this vehicle was being driven on the road and was stopped by the police, it was drawing two trailers and they were both laden. The policy says nothing about laden trailers. It simply allows the vehicle to be used with two trailers, and, whatever else this policy does, it certainly does not insure the [accused] against the consequences of using the tractor in that manner. If the policy had insured him against using the tractor illegally, to that extent it would have been ineffective, but I am far from saying that such a term would have vitiated the whole policy. There may be more than one insurance contained in a policy, and if it were possible to imagine an insurance company insuring a person against the consequences of a breach of the Road Traffic Acts—which has nothing to do with injury to third persons—I daresay that that part of the policy would be void. This, however, is an insurance against the consequences that may arise owing to the negligent driving of the vehicle, because a third party can only claim if there has been negligent driving. If there had been negligent driving, it matters not whether there were two trailers behind the tractor or whether there were no trailers behind it. If a tractor is driven negligently, an injured person has a right to compensation, and under this policy the insurance company promise to indemnify the [accused]. This is nothing more than a policy which insures the [accused] against the consequences of negligent driving. There is nothing illegal in that.'

But where a policy contains an exception stating that no indemnity will be granted where the vehicle is drawing a greater number of trailers than is permitted by law and the vehicle is used, in fact, to draw more than this number, no policy is 'in force'.[4]

Statements by Insurers

Where as a matter of construction of the words of the policy itself it is doubtful whether the policy is 'in force' or not, the Court may accept a statement by the insurance company that it would regard itself as being 'on risk'.[5]

Thus, in *Carnill v Rowland*[6] the insurance company had issued a policy in respect of a motor cycle combination. The policy contained an exception stating that the insurance company was under no liability unless the sidecar were permanently attached. The insured removed the sidecar body but left the chassis and the third wheel attached to the motor cycle. Evidence was given by the insurance company that it would have regarded itself as being 'on risk' in these circumstances. The Divisional Court of the Queen's Bench Division[7] accepted this statement, and held that the justices had rightly dismissed the

---

[1] *Leggate v Brown* [1950] 2 All E R 564.

[2] Ibid, at 565.

[3] Now replaced by the Road Traffic Act 1972, s 65.

[4] *Kerridge v Rush* [1952] 2 Lloyd's Rep 305, See the judgment of Lord Goddard C J, ibid, at 307. See also *Robb v McKechnie* 1936 S C (J) 25.

[5] In 1951, with the sanction of the Home Office, it was arranged that police authorities who were in doubt whether a particular policy covered a particular driver at a particular time might consult the committee of underwriters at Lloyd's to find out whether in the particular circumstances they would regard themselves at risk. See the judgment of Lord Goddard C J, in *Edwards v Griffiths* [1953] 2 All E R 874 at 875, where, however, this course was not taken by the police authorities.

[6] [1953] 1 All E R 486, [1953] 1 WLR 380.

[7] Lord Goddard C J, Lynskey and Pearson J J.

charge against the insured for driving it whilst uninsured, since in view of the statement by the insurance company, the policy was 'in force'. Lynskey J said:[8]

> 'If you have a clause which is open to two constructions, it is for the Court to construe that condition in the policy contra proferentem, that is, against the insurance company. The question here was whether or not this motor cycle was fitted with a sidecar. What is the meaning of "a sidecar permanently attached" may be a question of doubt. According to the evidence before the justices, the insurance company read the policy as putting them on risk when the cycle was in the condition in which it was found at the time when this offence was alleged to have been committed, namely, fitted with a chassis and a third wheel, but with the body of the sidecar temporarily absent. If that was a construction of the meaning of a sidecar which was impossible on the wording of the policy, one would be able to say that the justices had no right to find as they did, but it seems to me that the meaning of "sidecar permanently attached" is open to two constructions. The insurance company took one and the justices accepted that and also that the insurance company were on risk and the [accused] was covered.'

But if a condition in a policy is so broad that it has only one meaning, and that meaning is to exclude the insurance company from liability when the vehicle is used either for certain purposes or under certain conditions, the Court is bound by that clause and must act on it.[9]

Production of Insurance Policy

In *Edwards v Griffiths*[10] Lord Goddard CJ,[11] said that if an employer held a policy of insurance, an employee who drove on his instructions was covered, provided that the policy was not confined to the holder of the policy. He himself felt that it would be better in all these cases, and he desired police authorities to take notice, always to take the precaution of having the policy before the Court. That could be done by issuing a subpoena requiring the insured to produce the policy to the Court.

Examples of whether Policy Gave Cover

(a) Criminal Cases

In *Carnill v Rowland*[12] the policy, which provided cover only if a sidecar were attached to a motor cycle combination, was held to satisfy the statutory requirements even though the sidecar body had been removed from the chassis.

In *Leggate v Brown*[13] a policy in respect of a tractor providing cover when drawing two trailers was effective even though it was illegal to draw them laden. On the other hand, in *Kerridge v Rush*[14] the policy in respect of a tractor was not effective because a condition stating that no more trailers than were

---

[8] [1953] 1 All E R 486 at 488. See also the judgment of Lord Goddard CJ, ibid, at 487 and that of Pearson J, ibid, at 488.
[9] [1953] 1 All E R 486 at 488 (per Lynskey J).
[10] [1953] 2 All E R 874.
[11] Ibid, at 875.
[12] [1953] 1 All E R 486, [1953] 1 WLR 380.
[13] [1950] 2 All E R 564.
[14] [1952] 2 Lloyd's Rep. 305.

allowed by law to be drawn by it could be drawn was found to have been broken.

In *Bryan v Forrow*[15] a cover note stated that the owner of a lorry was insured in relation to the user of it provided it was being driven by him 'or his paid driver'. He was unable to drive one day and agreed with a customer for whom he was carrying some goods that the lorry should be driven by a driver employed by and paid by the customer. He said that he would reimburse the customer in respect of the driver's wages. The Divisional Court of the King's Bench Division[16] held that the cover note was 'in force', for the words 'or his paid driver' meant a driver who was driving for the insured and who was paid as a driver. It was not necessary for the driver to be paid by or in the general employment of the owner, who accordingly was not guilty of permitting the lorry to be on the road whilst uninsured. Lord Goddard C J said:[17]

> 'When one considers the whole of that portion of the cover note, one sees that the contrast is between the professional driver and the non-professional driver—the paid driver and the paid employee. The paid employee must not drive the vehicle. It must be a paid driver, and the words "paid driver" are capable of two constructions. They can either mean "the above-named proposer and the driver paid by him," or they can mean "the above-named proposer and a driver driving for him who is a paid driver." In my view, Quarter Sessions[18] were justified in holding that the latter construction was right, and on this document I think, the insurance company would have been liable if there had been an accident while Norton[19] was driving, because he was a paid driver and was driving for the proposer on that day.'

In *Baugh v Crago*[20] the defendant allowed a Mr Logue to use a van in the honest belief that he was the holder of a driving licence. In fact, Logue had no licence and the insurance policy was ineffective. The defendant was charged with permitting him to drive when there was no effective policy. The charge was dismissed by the justices on the ground of the defendant's honest belief. The prosecutor appealed. The Divisional Court of the Queen's Bench Division[1] allowed the appeal and remitted the case to the justices with a direction to convict. Lord Widgery L C J said that the defendant's honet belief was not enough to excuse him. The defendant, unlike the accused in an earlier case[2], had not imposed a condition on the use of the vehicle that permission would not be granted unless and until the driver was covered by insurance.[3]

(b) Civil Cases

The policy may limit the use of the vehicle to certain specified purposes. If the vehicle is used for other purposes, the insurers are not liable for any loss which may be suffered by the insured.[4]

If the policy does not cover the insured by reason of a limitation as to use, he can, of course, be charged with using the vehicle whilst uninsured, and

---

[15] [1950] 1 All E R 294.
[16] Lord Goddard, Bryne and Morris, JJ.
[17] [1950] 1 All E R 294 at 295.
[18] Ie Essex Quarter Sessions, who stated a Case for the High Court.
[19] Ie the driver paid by the customer.
[20] [1976] 1 Lloyd's Rep 563.
[1] Lord Widgery L C J, O'Connor and Lawson JJ.
[2] *Newbury v Davis* [1974] R T R 367.
[3] [1976] 1 Lloyd's Rep at 564.
[4] See pp 258-267, ante.

prosecutions could have been brought against drivers in a number of civil cases where they were found to have used or permitted the use of their vehicles otherwise than in accordance with the use specified in the policy.

Thus, the policy may state that it applies only where the vehicle is being driven by the insured alone,[5] or by someone with his permission.[6] It may cover the insured for social, domestic and pleasure purposes only,[7] for purposes of his business,[8] for use otherwise than for hiring,[9] for use otherwise than for the purpose of the motor trade,[10] a specified area of operation,[11] and may limit its use to the carriage of personal luggage only.[12]

There may also be a clause in the policy to the effect that it does not apply if the vehicle is being driven in an unsafe or unroadworthy condition,[13] or if it is carrying an excess load,[14] or if the insured is under the influence of intoxicating liquor,[15] or the insured or another person driving with his consent is disqualified from holding or obtaining a driving licence.[16] In these cases, too, the insured could be prosecuted for driving or permitting another person to drive whilst uninsured.

It is to be noticed, however, that although the exceptions are valid as between the insured and the insurer, the exceptions specified in s 148 of the Road Traffic Act 1972 are of no effect as regards third parties.[17]

REQUIREMENTS IN RESPECT OF POLICIES

In order to comply with Part VI of the Road Traffic Act 1972 the policy must:[18]

---

5 *Herbert v Railway Passengers Assurance Co* [1938] 1 All E R 650, K B (see p 255, ante).

6 *Williams v Baltic Insurance Association of London Ltd* [1924] 2 K B 282, K B (see p 235, ante); *Peters v General Accident Fire and Life Assurance Corpn Ltd* [1938] 2 All E R 267, C A (see p 241 ante); *Paget v Poland* (1947) 80 Ll L Rep 283, K B (see p 236, ante); *Tattersall v Drysdale* [1935] 2 K B 174, K B. (see p 237, ante; *Pailor v Co-operative Insurance Society Ltd* (1930) 38 Ll L Rep 237, C A (see p 237, ante) *Burton v Road Transport and General Insurance Co Ltd* (1939) 63 Ll L Rep 253, K B (see p 238, ante); *Rendlesham v Dunne Pennine Insurance Co Ltd, Third Party* [1964] 1 Lloyd's Rep 192 (Westminster County Court) (see p 239, ante); *Kelly v Cornhill Insurance Co Ltd* [1964] 1 All E R 321, H L (see p 242, ante).

7 *Wood v General Accident, Fire and Life Assurance Corpn Ltd* (1948) 82 Ll L Rep 77, K B. See p 258, ante.

8 *Levinger v Licenses and General Insurance Co Ltd* (1936) 54 Ll L Rep 68, ChD (see p 259, ante); *Passmore v Vulcan Boiler and General Insurance Co Ltd* (1936) 154 L T 258, K B (see p 260, ante).

9 *Wyatt v Guildhall Insurance Co Ltd* [1937] 1 K B 653, [1937] 1 All E R 792, K B (see p 264, ante); *McCarthy v British Oak Insurance Co Ltd* [1938] 3 All E R 1 (see p 265, ante); *Bonham v Zurich General Accident and Liability Insurance Co Ltd* [1945] K B 292, [1945] 1 All E R 427, C A (see p 266, ante); *Orr v Trafalgar Insurance Co Ltd* (1948) 82 Ll L Rep 1, C A (see p 226, ante).

10 *Browning v Phoenix Assurance Co Ltd* [1960] 2 Lloyd's Rep 360, Q B (see p 262, ante); *Gray v Blackmore* [1933] 1 K B 95, K B (see p 263, ante).

11 *A W and E Palmer v Cornhill Insurance Co Ltd* (1935) 52 Ll L Rep 78, K B (see p 257, ante).

12 *Piddington v Co-operative Insurance Society Ltd* [1934] 2 K B 236, K B (see p 258, ante).

13 *Trickett v Queensland Insurance Co Ltd* [1936] A C 159, P C (see p 249, ante); *Clarke v National Insurance and Guarantee Corpn Ltd* [1964] 1 Q B 199, [1963] 3 All E R 375, C A (see p 250, ante).

14 *Jenkins v Deane* (1933) 47 Ll L Rep 342, K B (see p 252, ante); *Houghton v Trafalgar Insurance Co Ltd* [1954] 1 Q B 247, [1953] 2 All E R 1409, C A (see p 252, ante).

15 *Louden v British Merchants' Insurance Co Ltd* [1961] 1 All E R 705, Q B (see p 254, ante).

16 *Lester Bros (Coal Merchants) Ltd v Avon Insurance Co Ltd* (1942) 72 Ll L Rep 109, K B (see p 256, ante); *Haworth v Dawson* (1946) 80 Ll L Rep 19, K B (see p 256, ante); *Spraggon v Dominion Insurance Co Ltd* (1941) 69 Ll L Rep 1, C A (see p 257, ante).

17 See pp 448-450, post.

18 Road Traffic Act 1972, s 145, as amended.

1   be issued by an authorised insurer; and
2   insure the person[19] specified in the policy in respect of any liability which may be incurred by him in respect of the death or bodily injury to any person caused by or arising out of the use of the vehicle on the road; and
3   insure him in respect of any liability which may be incurred in respect of the use of the vehicle, whether or not coupled, in the territory other than Great Britain and Gibraltar of each of the member States of the European Economic Communities according to the law of compulsory insurance against civil liability in respect of the use of vehicles of the State where the liability may be incurred; and
4   insure him in respect of any liability which may be incurred by him relating to payment for emergency treatment.

Authorised Insurer

This term means 'a person or body of persons carrying on insurance business within Group 2 in Part II of Sch 2 to the Insurance Companies Act 1982 and being a member of the Motor Insurers' Bureau'.[20]

Liability in Respect of Third Persons

(a) The General Rule

It is important to notice that insurance is not compulsory in respect of liability concerning damage to the *property* of a third party.

The effect of the Road Traffic Act 1972, s 145, is that, with certain exceptions stated below, insurance cover is required in respect of any liability in respect of the death or bodily injury to any person including a passenger caused by, or arising out of, the use of the vehicle on a road.

Any antecedent agreement[1] or understanding between the user of the vehicle and a passenger[2] is of no effect so far as it purports or might be held

a   to negative or restrict any liability of the user of the vehicle to cover risk to the passenger; or
b   to impose any conditions with respect to the enforcement of any such liability of the user.[3]

The fact that the passenger has willingly accepted as his the risk of negligence on the part of the user is not to be treated as negativing any such liability of the user.[4]

(b) Exceptions

The policy of insurance, however, is not required to cover

i   liability in respect of the death, arising out of and in the course of his employment, of a person in the employment of a person insured by the policy or bodily injury sustained by such a person arising out of and in the course of his employment;[5] or
ii   any contractual liability.[6]

---

[19] Or persons or classes of persons specified in the policy.
[20] Road Traffic Act 1972 s 145 (2), as amended. As to the Motor Insurers' Bureau, see pp 446-447, post.
[1] Ie an agreement made at any time before the liability arose: Road Traffic Act 1972, s 148 (3).
[2] Or a person entering or getting on to, or alighting from, the vehicle: ibid, s 148 (3).
[3] Ibid, s 148 (3).
[4] Ibid, s 148 (3).
[5] Road Traffic Act 1972, s 145 (4) (a).
[6] Ibid, s 145 (4) (b).

Effect of Payment of Fares by Passengers

To the extent that a policy

(a) restricts the insurance of the persons insured by the policy to the use of the vehicle for specified purposes (eg social, domestic and pleasure purposes[7]) of a non-commercial character; or

(b) excludes from that policy
  (i) the use of the vehicle for hire or reward[8]; or
  (ii) business or commercial use of the vehicle; or
  (iii) use of the vehicle for specified purposes of a business or commercial character[9],

then, the use of a vehicle on a journey in the course of which one or more passengers are carried at separate fares is to be treated as falling within that restriction or as not falling within that exclusion, as the case may be, if certain conditions are satisfied.[10]

These conditions are

(a) the vehicle is not adapted to carry more than 8 passengers and is not a motor cycle;

(b) the fare or aggregate of the fares paid in respect of the journey does not exceed the amount of the running costs of the vehicle;[11] and

(c) the arrangements for the payment of fares by the passenger or passengers carried at separate fares were made before the journey began[12].

Payment for Emergency Treatment

Where medical or surgical treatment or examination is immediately required as a result of bodily injury (including fatal injury) to a person caused by or arising out of a motor vehicle on a road, and the treatment or examination so required[13] is effected by a legally qualified medical practitioner, the person who was using the vehicle at the time of the event out of which the bodily injury arose must on a claim being made pay to the practitioner the following fees:

i a fee of £10.90 in respect of each person in whose case the emergency treatment is effected by him; and

ii a sum, in respect of any distance in excess of two miles which he must cover in order to proceed from the place whence he is summoned to the place where the emergency treatment is carried out by him and to return to the place whence he is summoned, equal to 21p for every complete mile and additional part of a mile of that distance.[14]

---

7 See pp 258-259, ante.

8 See pp 264-267, ante.

9 See pp 259-262, ante.

10 Road Traffic Act 1972, s 148 (5). This subsection applies however the restrictions or exclusions are framed or worded: ibid, s 148 (7).

11 'Running costs' are to be taken to include an appropriate amount in respect of depreciation and general wear': ibid, s 148 (6) (b).

12 Ibid, s 148 (6). This subsection applies however the restrictions or exclusions are framed or worded: ibid, s 148 (7).

13 This treatment is referred to in Pt VI of the Road Traffic Act 1972 as 'emergency treatment': ibid, s 155 (1).

14 Ibid, s 155 (1).

Where emergency treatment is effected by more than one practitioner, the fee of £10.90 and the payment in respect of the mileage covered must be paid to the practitioner by whom it is first effected.[15]

Where emergency treatment is first effected in a hospital, the fee of £10.90 must be paid to the hospital.[16]

Liability in respect of emergency treatment incurred by the person using the vehicle is, where the event out of which it arose was caused by the wrongful act of another person, treated for the purposes of any claim to recover damage by reason of that wrongful act as damage sustained by the person using the vehicle.[17]

A claim for payment may be made at the time when the emergency teatment is effected, by oral request to the person who was using the vehicle, and if not so made, must be made in writing served on him within seven days from the day on which the emergency treatment was effected.[18]

REQUIREMENTS IN RESPECT OF SECURITIES

The security must be given either by an authorised insurer or by some body of persons which carries on in the United Kingdom the business of giving securities of a like kind and has deposited and keeps deposited with the Accountant General of the Supreme Court the sum of £15,000 in respect of that business.[19]

The security must consist of an undertaking by the giver of the security to make good, subject to any conditions specified therein, any failure by the owner of the vehicle or such other person or persons as may be specified in the security duly to discharge any liability which may be incurred by him or them, being a liability required to be covered by a policy of insurance.[20] But in the case of liabilities arising out of the use of a motor vehicle on a road in Great Britain the amount secured need not exceed

   (a) in the case of an undertaking relating to the use of a public service vehicle (within the meaning of Part III of the Road Traffic Act 1960), £25,000;

   (b) in any other case, £5,000.[1]

Effect of Payment of Fares by Passengers

The effect of the payment of fares by passengers is the same as in the case of the requirements in respect of policies.[2]

---

15 Road Traffic Act 1972, s 155 (1).
16 Ibid, s 155 (2).
17 Ibid, s 155 (3).
18 Ibid, s 156 (2).
19 Ibid, s 146 (2).
20 Ibid, s 146 (3).
 1 Ibid.
 2 Ibid, s 148 (5), (6).

REQUIREMENTS IN RESPECT OF DEPOSITS

An alternative to a policy or a security is the deposit of £15,000 with the Accountant General of the Supreme Court.[3]

Any person wishing to deposit this sum may apply to the Secretary of State for a warrant which shall be a sufficient authority for the Accountant General to issue a direction for the payment into the Bank of England to the credit of his account by the depositor.[4] In lieu, wholly or in part, of the deposit of money the depositor may deposit an equivalent amount of securities in which cash under the control or subject to the order of the Court may for the time being be invested.[5]

The Court may, on the application of the depositor, make an order for dealing with any money which has been deposited in Court by its placement to a short-term or long-term investment account[6] or by its investment in any securities in which cash under the control or subject to the order of the Court may for the time being be invested.[7]

Any interest, dividend or income accruing due on money or securities deposited with the Court must, subject to any order of the Court, be paid to the depositor at his request.[8]

In any case where it is just and equitable to do so, and in particular in any of the following cases:

a where a depositor complies or satisfies the Court that he intends to comply with Part VI of the Road Traffic Act 1972 by effecting a policy of insurance[9] or obtaining a security[10]

b where
   i a depositor ceases to own, or to control the use of, a motor vehicle, or
   ii a depositor has ceased altogether to carry on in the United Kingdom the business of giving securities under Part VI of the Act
   and in either case all liabilities in respect of which money or securities were deposited in Court have been satisfied or otherwise provided for,

the Court may, on the application of the depositor, order any money or securities to be paid or transferred out of Court to him or otherwise as the Court may direct.[11]

The issue of any warrant or any error in it does not make the Secretary of State or any person signing on his behalf in any manner liable for or in respect of any money or security deposited in Court or any securities for the time being representing them, or the interest, dividends or income accruing due on them.[12]

---

[3] Road Traffic Act 1972, s 144 (1). See p 300, ante.
[4] Motor Vehicles (Third-Party Risks Deposits) Regulations 1967 (SI 1967/1326), reg 4. The Regulations are set out in Appendix X, p 461, post.
[5] Motor Vehicles (Third-Party Risks Deposits) Regulations 1967 (SI 1967/1326), reg 4.
[6] The words 'short-term investment account' and 'long-term investment account' have the same meanings as in the Administration of Justice Act 1965, s 6 (1) (a): ibid, reg 3 (1).
[7] Ibid, reg 5 (1).
[8] Ibid, reg 6 (2).
[9] See pp 315-318, ante.
[10] See p 318, ante.
[11] Motor Vehicles (Third-Party Risks Deposits) Regulations 1967 (SI 1967/1326), reg 6.
[12] Ibid, reg 7.

CERTIFICATE OF INSURANCE OR SECURITY

Need for Certificate

Section 147 (1) of the Road Traffic Act 1972 states:

> 'A policy of insurance shall be of no effect for the purposes of this Part[13] of this Act unless and until there is delivered by the insurer to the person by whom the policy is effected a certificate (in this Part of this Act referred to as a "certificate of insurance") in the prescribed form and containing such particulars of any conditions subject to which the policy is issued and of any other matters as may be prescribed.'

It is provided by s 147 (2) that:

> 'A security shall be of no effect for the purposes of this Part[14] of this Act unless and until there is delivered by the person giving the security to the person to whom it is given a certificate (in this Part of this Act referred to as a "certificate of security") in the prescribed form and containing such particulars of any conditions subject to which the security is issued and of any other matters as may be prescribed.'

Form of Certificate

Section 147 (3) states that:

> 'Different forms and different particulars may be prescribed for the purposes of subsection (1) or (2) of this section in relation to different cases or circumstances.'

The forms for the certificate of insurance are prescribed by the Motor Vehicles (Third Party Risks) Regulations 1972.[15] One form relates to one or more specified vehicles and states that the certificate must contain:[16]

i   the registration mark of the vehicle
ii   the name of the policy holder
iii the effective date of the commencement of the insurance for the purpose of the relevant law
iv   the date of expiry of the insurance
v   the persons or classes of persons entitled to drive
vi   limitations as to use.

Another form relates to vehicles other than specified vehicles and sets out similar requirements.[17]

Every policy[18] in the form of a covering note issued by a company must have printed on its back a certificate in a specified form.[19]

There is a specified form[20] for the certificate of security. This must contain:

i   the name of the holder
ii   the effective date of the commencement of security for the purposes of the relevant law
iii the date of expiry of the security
iv   the conditions to which the security is subject.

---

13 Ie Pt VI.
14 Ie Pt VI.
15 SI 1972/1217, as amended. The Regulations are set out in Appendix X, p 461, post.
16 Ibid, Sch, Pt I, Form A. See Appendix X, p 467, post.
17 Ibid, Sch, Pt II, Form B. See Appendix X, p 467, post.
18 Ibid, r 4 (3).
19 Ibid, Sch, Pt I, Form C. See Appendix X, p 467, post.
20 Ibid, Sch, Pt I, Form D. See Appendix X, p 468, post.

Every certificate must be printed and completed in black on white paper or similar material.[1] It must not contain any advertising matter either on its face or its back.[2] The whole of each form prescribed by the Regulations must appear on the face of the form, the items being in the order so set out, and the certification by the authorised insurers being set out at the end of the form.[3]

Issue of Certificate

Every certificate of insurance or certificate of security must be issued not later than 4 days after the date on which the policy or security to which it relates is issued or renewed.[4]

Keeping of Records by Companies

Every company by whom a policy or a security is issued must keep a record of the following particulars and of any certificates issued:[5]

  i   the full name and address of the person to whom the policy, security or certificate is issued
  ii   in the case of a policy relating to one or more specified motor vehicles the registration mark of each such vehicle
  iii the date on which the policy or security comes into force and the date on which it expires
  iv   in the case of a policy the conditions subject to which the person or classes of persons specified in the policy will be indemnified
  v   in the case of a security the conditions subject to which the undertaking given by the company under the security will be implemented.

Issue of Fresh Certificate

Where any company, by whom a certificate of insurance or a certificate of security has been issued, is satisfied that the certificate has become defaced or has been lost or destroyed, it must, if requested to do so by the person to whom the certificate was issued, issue to him a fresh certificate.[6] In the case of a defaced certificate the company must not issue a fresh certificate unless the defaced certificate is returned to the company.[7]

---

[1] Ibid, Sch, Pt II, para 1. This provision does not prevent the reproduction of a seal or monogram or similar device referred to in para 2 below or the presence of a background pattern (of whatever form and whether coloured or not) on the face of the form which does not materially affect the legibility of the certificate: ibid.

[2] Ibid, Sch, Pt II, para 2. But the name and address of the company by whom the certificate is issued, or a reproduction of the seal of the company or any monogram or similar device of the company, or the name and address of an insurance broker, is not deemed to be advertising matter for the purposes of this paragraph if it is printed or stamped at the foot or on the back of such certificate, or if it forms, or forms part of any such background pattern as is referred to in para 1 above: ibid.

[3] Ibid, Sch, Pt II, para 3.

[4] Ibid, r 6.

[5] Ibid, r 10 (1). There are similar provisions as regards local authorities which own motor vehicles: r 10 (2). Any person who has deposited and keeps deposited £15,000 with the Accountant General of the Supreme Court in accordance with the provisions of s 146 (2) of the Road Traffic Act 1972 (see p 318, ante) must also keep the appropriate records: r 10 (3).

[6] Ibid, r 13.

[7] Ibid, r 13.

Delivery of Certificate

It is essential for the certificate to be delivered to the person by whom the policy is effected. Where a vehicle is subject to a hire-purchase agreement, delivery to the finance company which has let out the vehicle to the insured is insufficient.[8]

Effect of Certificate

No estoppel is created by the issue of a certificate which will prevent the insurer from relying on the terms in policy that will avoid the policy and prevent him from relying on the contention that the policy was obtained by fraud and therefore is not binding on him.

The effect of the certificate is that it enables the insured to say: 'Here is my certificate of insurance, and I am not liable as long as I have got an insurance.'[9]

The certificate is only issued for the purpose of enabling him to produce the document when he is on the road. It is not intended to be a representation that the policy will in any event become a policy on which he will be entitled to recover if an accident happens and damages result.[10]

Surrender of Certificate

Section 147 (4) of the Road Traffic Act 1972 states:

> 'Where a certificate has been delivered under this section and the policy or security to which it relates is cancelled[11] by mutual consent or by virtue of any provision in the policy or security, the person to whom the certificate was delivered shall, within seven days of the taking effect of the cancellation, surrender the certificate to the person by whom the policy was issued or the security was given or, if the certificate has been lost or destroyed, make a statutory declaration to that effect.'

If a person fails to comply with this subsection, he is liable on summary conviction to a fine not exceeding level 3 on the standard scale.[12]

INTERNATIONAL MOTOR INSURANCE CARDS

The Secretary of State for the Environment has power under s 157 of the Road Traffic Act 1972 to make regulations for providing that any provisions of Part VI of the Act (ie the Part dealing with compulsory motor insurance) shall, in relation to vehicles brought into Great Britain by persons making only a temporary stay here, have effect subject to such modifications and adaptations as may be prescribed. The Regulations which have been made are the Motor Vehicles (International Motor Insurance Card) Regulations 1971.[13]

---

[8] *Starkey v Hall* [1936] 2 All E R 18.

[9] *McCormick v National Motor and Accident Insurance Union Ltd* (1934) 40 Com Cas 76, C A at 90 (per Greer L J), See also the judgment of Slesser L J, ibid, at 94 and that of Scrutton L J, ibid, at 85.

[10] Ibid (per Greer, L J).

[11] As to cancellation of the policy, see p 225, ante.

[12] Road Traffic Act 1972, s 147 (4) and Sch 4, Pt I, as amended by the Criminal Justice Act 1982, s 38 (1).

[13] S I 1971 792, as amended. The Regulations, as amended, are set out in Appendix XII, p 473, post.

Validity of Card

By these Regulations an international motor insurance card is valid only if:

a   the vehicle specified in the card is brought into the United Kingdom during the period of validity so specified;

b   the application of the card in Great Britain is indicated thereon;

c   all relevant information provided for in the card has been inscribed therein;

d   the card has been duly signed by the visitor, by the insurer named in the card, and, in the case of a hired vehicle, by every hiring visitor who is named in the card as the insured or user thereof.[14]

Third Party Risks

As respects the use on a road of a vehicle specified in a valid insurance card, being use by the visitor to whom the card was issued, or by any hiring visitor named therein, or by any other person on the order or with the permission of the visitor or hiring visitor, s 143 of the Act of 1972 shall have effect as though the card were a policy of insurance complying with the requirements and having effect for the purposes of Part VI of the Act in relation to such use.[15]

Where the vehicle remains in the United Kingdom after the expiry of the period of validity specified in the card, then, as respects any period whilst it so remains during which the vehicle is in Great Britain, the card is not to be regarded as having ceased to be in force for the purposes of s 143 by reason only of effluxion of the period of validity specified in the card.[16]

Form of Card

The card must be green and must contain the particulars set out in Schedule 1 to the Regulations.[17]

In the Schedule the particulars to be specified include:

1   the name of the foreign Bureau[18] or the British Bureau, as the case may be, under whose authority the card was issued

2   the period of validity

3   the registration number, chassis or engine number of vehicle

4   the make of vehicle

5   the countries to which applicable

6   the name and address of the insured

7   the signature of the insurer.

---

[14] Ibid r 4 (1).

[15] Ibid r 5 (1).

[16] Ibid r 5 (1).

[17] Ibid r 3 (1).

[18] This term means 'a central organisation set up by motor insurers in any country outside the United Kingdom, the Isle of Man and the Channel Islands for the purpose of giving effect to international arrangements for the insurance of motorists against third party risks when entering countries where insurance against such risks is compulsory, and with which organisation the British Bureau [ie the Motor Insurers' Bureau] has entered into such an arrangement: r 3 (1).

BREACH OF STATUTORY DUTY

If a person permits his car to be used by an uninsured driver, he may be sued for breach of statutory duty by a third party, provided that the third party suffers injury or damage as a result of the breach of duty.[19]

Thus, Greer LJ said in *Monk v Warbey:*[20]

'How could Parliament make provision for the protection of third parties against such risks if it did not enable an injured third person to recover for a breach of s 35 of the Road Traffic Act 1930?[1] That section is to be found in Pt II of the Act, which is headed "Provision against third party risks arising out of the use of motor vehicles." It would be a very poor protection of the person injured by the negligence of an uninsured person to whom a car had been lent by an insured person if the person injured had no civil remedy of a breach of the section. The Act provides that every person who owns a car shall take out an insurance of that car in respect of third party risks, and shall provide himself with a certificate of insurance containing particulars of the terms of insurance. If a person be damaged by the breach of a statute, he has a right to recover damages from the person who has broken the provisions of the statute, unless it can be established by looking at the whole of the Act that it was not intended that he should have such a right. I think that so far from it being established in the present case from the whole purpose of the Road Traffic Act 1930 that it was not intended that a person in the position of the plaintiff should have such a right, it is, on the contrary, established that it was intended that he should have this right, because it is clear that the statute was intended for his protection. The power to prosecute for a penalty is no protection whatever to the injured person except in the sense that it affords a strong incentive for people not to break the provisions of the statute. But the power to prosecute is a poor consolation to the man who has been damaged by reason of a breach of the provisions of s 35.'

Maugham LJ stated:[2]

'On the whole, though, as I have already said, I think the question is an arguable one, but not very difficult. I have come to the conclusion, like my brethren, that this case is one where there is nothing in the Act to show that a personal action is precluded by reason of the special remedy, and, further, that upon the true construction of the Act there is sufficient ground for coming to the conclusion that the section was passed for the purpose of giving a remedy to those third party users of the road who might otherwise suffer injury by the negligence of drivers without having any pecuniary remedy which was of any avail. It is true to say that it is only if there is negligence in the driving of a car that the third party user of the road who has been injured has any right of relief; but I cannot help thinking that when the Road Traffic Act 1930 was passed, it was within the knowledge of the Legislature that negligence in the driving of cars was so common an occurrence, and likely to happen to so many people with the result of injury to others, that it was necessary in the public interest to provide a way whereby those third parties might recover damages for the injuries they sustained, although the driver of the car might be a person of no means.'

Roche LJ observed:[3]

'I am not uninfluenced by the existence of sub-s (4) of s 35 of this statute.[4] That, among other things, seems to me to point clearly to the conclusion that it was within the purview of this statute to render effective civil remedies for the mischief dealt with in the statute, and that the last thing that was within the purview of the statute was to limit in any way those civil remedies, and to protect one who suffered damage by reason of a breach of the statute, merely because penalties were provided for in the statute of a criminal nature.'

---

[19] *Monk v Warbey* [1934] All ER Rep 373, CA.
[20] Ibid, at 375.
[1] Now replaced by s 143 of the Road Traffic Act 1972.
[2] [1934] All ER Rep 373 at 379.
[3] Ibid, at 380.
[4] Which stated that a person who had deposited the sum of £15,000 under certain circumstances was no longer bound to enter into any policy of insurance which would protect third parties.

In view of the Agreement between the Secretary of State for the Environment and the Motor Insurers' Bureau as to compensation for the victims of uninsured drivers,[5] the action for breach of statutory duty has lost its importance. But a third party is still at liberty to bring such an action even in spite of the existence of the Agreement,[6] though, of course, he will not be entitled to retain both the compensation paid to him by the Bureau and the amount of damages recovered from the owner of the vehicle.[7]

---

[5] See pp 347-352, post.
[6] *Corfield v Groves* [1950] 1 All ER 488, KB.
[7] Ibid, at 490 (per Hilbery J).

CHAPTER 34

The rights of third parties against the insurers

Where a third party is injured in an accident for which the insured is responsible, he may bring an action against the insured, and if he is successful, the damages will in effect be payable by the insurers, assuming, of course, that the insured has a policy which gives him adequate cover.

Sometimes, however, the insured is unable to pay and goes bankrupt, and the question arises as to whether the third party has any rights against the insurers in these circumstances.

Sometimes the insurers repudiated liability towards a third party on the ground that the insured was guilty, eg of a breach of condition. At one time the third party was left without a remedy in this event. But the position has now to some extent been altered by statute.

If the driver responsible for an accident involving a third party was uninsured or cannot be traced, the third party has no claim against any insurers, but he may make a claim on the Motor Insurers' Bureau.

The liability of insurers towards third parties can perhaps best be considered under the following heads:

A   The Third Parties (Rights Against Insurers) Act 1930.
B   The Road Traffic Act 1972.
C   The Motor Insurers' Bureau.

A THE THIRD PARTIES (RIGHTS AGAINST INSURERS) ACT 1930[1]

In order to understand the need for the Act of 1930, it is necessary to consider the position before it was passed.

1 Position before the Act

Before the Third Parties (Rights against Insurers) Act 1930 was passed, considerable hardship might be caused to a third party if the insured went bankrupt, or, if the insured were a company, it went into liquidation.

This matter is alluded to in *Re Harrington Motor Co Ltd ex p Chaplin.*[2] In this case a third party was knocked down by a motor car belonging to the Harrington Motor Co Ltd. He was awarded damages against the company.

---

[1] The text of the Act is set out in Appendix VII, p 442, post.
[2] [1928] Ch 105, C A.

The company claimed an indemnity from the Universal Automobile Insurance Co Ltd, with which it was insured. The insurance company paid over £420 to the company, but the company went into liquidation. The third party then claimed from the liquidator of the company the proceeds of the insurance policy, but the liquidator refused to pay them on the ground that the money received formed part of the assets of the company which must be divided amongst the creditors as a whole.

The Court of Appeal[3] held that the claim failed. The third party had no right either against the insurance company or the liquidator to require that the money should be handed to him.

Atkin LJ said:[4]

'But the position in law seems to me clearly to be that a third party in a case like the present has no claim in law or in equity of any sort against the insurance company, or against the money paid by the insurance company, nor has he any claim against the person who injures him, the assured, to direct the assured to pay over the sum of money received under the insurance policy to him. The amount that the assured, in fact, received is part of his general assets. As a general rule the expediency of that, I think, cannot be disputed. It obviously would disturb the whole practice of insurance if the claimant against the assured who caused the risk had a direct right of recourse against the insurance company, and we know that in actual practice the assured receives the money—the parties being solvent—and does not pay over necessarily that sum of money to the third party who is injured, but, of course, pays his claim out of his own assets and uses the insurance money, so far as it goes, because it does not always completely meet his liability. [Counsel], in his interesting and able argument, admitted that, apart from insolvency, the third party has no sort of right in equity against the insurance company under the policy. If that is so, that really seems to me to dispose of the case, because I find it impossible to see how a special right, arising out of circumstances which ordinarily occur in cases of solvency, could come into existence merely because the assured happened to be in difficulties or financial weakness, or to become bankrupt or, if a company, to have a winding-up order made against it.'

This decision was followed by the Court of Appeal[5] in *Hood's Trustees v Southern Union General Insurance Co of Australasia*,[6] where the insured went bankrupt, and it was held that the benefit of the indemnity received from the insurance company vested in the trustee in bankruptcy as part of the bankrupt's estate.

The reason for the passing of the Act was also alluded to by Scrutton LJ in *McCormick v National Motor and Accident Insurance Union Ltd*[7] where he said:[8]

'I think there is no doubt as to why the first statute of 1930 was passed. There had been a series of cases dealing partly with collision insurance and partly with other forms of insurance, in which this had happened: a person had claimed indemnity against another person who was insured. He had got a judgment entitling him to £1000, let us say. The defendant then went bankrupt, and the plaintiff who had got that judgment for £1000 wrote to the trustees in bankruptcy and said: "Pay me the £1000." "No", said the trustees in bankruptcy, "this £1000 is the property of the bankruptcy; it is a question for the general body of creditors and not for you. You can prove in respect of the debt for £1000 and you may get £500, or £100, or

---

[3] Lord Hanworth MR, Atkin and Lawrence LJJ.
[4] [1928] Ch 105 at 118. See further the judgment of Lord Hanworth MR at 111–112, 116, and of Lawrence LJ at 124–125.
[5] Lord Hanworth MR, Lawrence and Russell LJJ.
[6] [1928] Ch 793, CA. See the judgment of Lord Hanworth MR at 803.
[7] (1934), 49 Ll L Rep 361, CA.
[8] Ibid, at 363. See further, *Jones v Birch Bros Ltd* (Licenses and General Insurance Co Ltd, Third Parties) [1933] 2 KB 597, CA, per Greer LJ at 611 and *Croxford v Universal Insurance Co Ltd* [1936] 2 KB 253 per Slesser LJ at 266.

nothing, or you may get the £1000, according to the number of other people who prove against the property of the bankrupt.''

There are several cases in regard to that. Of course, that proposition looked wrong, that a man should have got a judgment against a bankrupt for £1000 before the bankruptcy and that the judgment should give him no right over the property of the bankrupt except merely as one of the general body of creditors of the bankrupt. So I think that this Act of 1930 was passed to deal with the difficulty, and it gave a third party who was injured by a motor car certain rights against the defendant against whom he got a judgment if he went bankrupt but not otherwise.'

2 Position after the Act

(a) *Provisions of the Act*

The provisions of the Act relate to:

    i the rights of third parties against insurers on the bankruptcy, etc. of the insured;
   ii the duty to give necessary information to third parties;
  iii settlements between the insurers and the insured.

(i) Rights of Third Parties against Insurers.   The situation mentioned in the cases set out above has been remedied by section 1 of the Act of 1930.

It states that where the insured is insured against third party risks, then in the event of his being made bankrupt or making a composition with his creditors, his rights against the insurer, notwithstanding anything in any Act or rule of law to the contrary, are transferred and vest in the third party to whom liability has been incurred.[9]

The same result will follow if the insured is a company and:

1   a winding up order has been made; or
2   a resolution for a voluntary winding up[10] has been passed; or
3   a receiver or manager of the company's business or undertaking has been duly appointed; or
4   possession has been taken by or on behalf of the holders of any debentures secured by a floating charge, of any property comprised in or subject to the charge.[11]

Section 1 (2) deals with the position where the insured dies insolvent. It enacts that where an order is made[12] for the administration of the estate of a deceased debtor according to the law of bankruptcy, then, if any debt payable in bankruptcy is owing by the deceased in respect of a liability towards a third party, the debtor's rights against the insurer are transferred and vest in the third party.[13]

---

[9] Third Parties (Rights Against Insurers) Act 1930, s 1 (1). Whether the liability to the third party occurs before or after the bankruptcy takes place is immaterial: ibid.
[10] The Act does not apply where the company is wound up voluntarily merely for the purposes of reconstruction or of amalgamation with another company: ibid, s 1 (6).
[11] Ibid, s 1 (1).
[12] Under the Bankruptcy Act 1914, s 130.
[13] Notwithstanding anything in the Bankruptcy Act 1914: Third Parties (Rights Against Insurers) Act 1930, s 1 (2).

If any contract of insurance in respect of third party risks purports, whether directly or indirectly, to avoid the contract or to alter the rights of the parties upon the happening to the insured of any of the events specified above (eg bankruptcy, winding up etc) or the making of an order for the administration of his estate according to the law of bankruptcy, the contract shall be of no effect.[14]

Where the rights of the insured are transferred to the third party in accordance with the provisions of the Act set out above, the insurer is under the same liability to the third party as he would have been under to the insured.[15]

But if the liability of the insurer to the insured exceeds the liability of the insured to the third party, nothing in the Act affects the rights of the insured against the insurer in respect of the excess.[16]

Further, if the liability of the insurer to the insured is less than the liability of the insured to the third party, nothing in the Act affects the rights of the third party against the insured in respect of the balance.[17]

(ii) Duty to Give Necessary Information to Third Parties.   In the event of the insured becoming bankrupt the bankrupt and his trustee in bankruptcy must, at the request of the third party, give him such information as may be reasonably required by him for the purpose of ascertaining whether any rights have been transferred to and vested in him by the Act, and for the purpose of enforcing such rights.[18]

If the insured is a company, the company and the liquidator are under a similar duty.[19]

Any contract of insurance, in so far as it purports, whether directly or indirectly, to avoid the contract or to alter the rights of the parties thereunder upon the giving of the required information or otherwise to prohibit or prevent the giving of the information, is of no effect.[20]

If the information given to any person in pursuance of the above provisions discloses reasonable ground for supposing that there have or may have been transferred to him under the Act rights against any particular insurer, that insurer is under the same duty to supply the required information.[1]

The duty to give information includes a duty to allow all contracts of insurance, receipts for premiums and other relevant documents in the possession or power of the person on whom the duty is imposed, to be inspected and copies of them to be taken.[2]

(iii) Settlement between Insurers and Insured Persons.   Where the insured has become bankrupt, no agreement made between the insurer and the

---

[14] Notwithstanding anything in the Bankruptcy Act 1914: Third Parties (Rights Against Insurers) Act 1930, s 1 (3).

[15] Ibid, s 1 (4).

[16] Ibid.

[17] Ibid.

[18] Ibid, s 2 (1).

[19] Ibid. There are corresponding provisions where, eg, a receiver or manager of the company's business or undertaking is appointed, or an order is made under the Bankruptcy Act 1914, s 130 for the administration of the estate of a deceased debtor according to the law of bankruptcy. See generally Third Parties (Rights against Insurers) Act 1930, s 2 (2).

[20] Ibid, s 2 (1).

[1] Ibid, s 2 (2).

[2] Ibid, s 2 (3).

insured after liability has been incurred to a third party, and after the commencement of the bankruptcy, is effective to defeat the rights transferred to the third party under the Act.[3] Nor is any waiver, assignment, or other disposition made by or payment made to the insured after the commencement of the bankruptcy effective to defeat or affect the third party's rights.[4]

The rights remain the same as if no such agreement, waiver, assignment, disposition or payment had been made.[5]

The Act makes similar provisions where the insured is a company and a winding up order has been made or a resolution for a voluntary winding up has been passed.[6]

(b) Effect of the Act upon the Terms of the Policy

The Act only confers rights on the third party against the insurer if the insured becomes insolvent.

But the terms of the policy between the insurer and the insured are in no way enlarged or modified by the Act, so the insurer may still be entitled to avoid liability to the third party.

Thus, in *McCormick v National Motor and Accident Insurance Union Ltd*[7] a third party had been killed in an accident caused by the insured's negligent driving of a car. The third party's widow was awarded damages against the insured, but he went bankrupt. When she claimed from the insurance company under the Third Parties (Rights Against Insurers) Act 1930, the company repudiated liability on the ground that they were entitled to avoid the policy on the ground that the insured had not disclosed a material fact—viz, that he had been previously convicted of dangerous driving, and that therefore, since the company had a defence to the action if they had been sued by the insured, the action must fail even if brought by the third party.

The Court of Appeal[8] held that this contention succeeded, and that the defences as well as the rights were transferred by the Act of 1930.

Scrutton LJ said:[9]

> 'But the position of the plaintiffs who were suing was this. They could not have sued at all except for the Act of 1930 conferring upon third parties rights against insurers of third party risks in the event of the insured becoming insolvent. That is the only statute that gives them any right to sue, and the statute says that if the defendant becomes bankrupt, the rights of the defendant against the insurer under the contract in respect of any liability shall be transferred to and vest in the third party to whom the liability was so incurred. Now, what is transferred? The rights under the contract. You cannot take the rights under the contract separate from defences under the contract. You cannot say: "I claim indemnity from you and I do not care what conditions there are in the contract which relieve you from having to indemnify." What are transferred are whatever rights there are between the two parties, insurer and insured, under the contract. Consequently the rights which the statute has given to a person who is injured, on the defendant becoming bankrupt, are the rights between the two parties; and if at that time—the time of the judgment—the insurer had a defence to the claim under the policy,

---

[3] Third Parties (Rights Against Insurers) Act 1930, s 3.
[4] Ibid.
[5] Ibid, s 3.
[6] Ibid.
[7] (1934) 49 Ll L Rep 361, CA.
[8] Scrutton, Greer and Slesser LJJ.
[9] (1934) 49 Ll L Rep 361 at 365.

namely: "I am not bound by the policy because you have made material misrepresentations, because you concealed material facts from me when the policy was issued," then that defence is entitled to be used by the insurance company.'

Again, in *Freshwater v Western Australian Insurance Co Ltd*[10] a third party received injuries in a motor accident. The insured went bankrupt, and the third party instituted proceedings against the insurance company under the Act of 1930. The policy contained an arbitration clause, which stated that an award by an arbitrator was to be a condition precedent to any action against them. The company applied to the Court to stay the action brought by the third party until arbitration proceedings had been taken.

The Court of Appeal[11] held that the company was entitled to insist upon arbitration, and that the action should be stayed.

Further, in *Smith v Pearl Assurance Co Ltd*[12] a third party sustained personal injuries while travelling as a passenger in a car being driven by the insured, a Mr Blackmore. He was awarded damages against the insured in an action brought under the Poor Persons' Rules. The insured went bankrupt, so the third party sued the insurance company under the Act of 1930. The company applied for the action to be stayed on the ground that there was an arbitration clause in the policy. The third party pleaded that, if the dispute went to arbitration, he would be hampered by reason of his poverty in establishing his case. But if the matter went to a Court of law, he would have the benefit of the Poor Persons' Rules.

The Court of Appeal[13] refused to stay the action, and held that the personal disability of the third party, whose only title arose through the insured, could not affect the contractual right of the company to claim arbitration under the policy.

Slesser LJ said:[14]

'The position of the present plaintiff, and that of Mr Blackmore, is made clear under the Act of 1930. Whatever his rights were, they are transferred to, and vested in, the plaintiff, and the result may be that, by reason of his poverty, the plaintiff who could have proceeded under the Poor Persons' Rules may have difficulty in finding the money to proceed under the Arbitration Act. These facts cannot, in the circumstances, be any ground for saying that effect should not be given to the contract between Mr Blackmore and the insurance company when its rights and conditions are vested in the plaintiff. If the contention of the appellant's Counsel is right, it seems to me that every person in a state of poverty—certainly such a state of poverty as to entitle him to have recourse the the Poor Persons' Rules—can argue that he is not bound by the arbitration clause. I can find no authority for that, and, if it be a question which is open at all, I do not think that we should exercise our discretion to interfere with the rights of the insurance company merely because of the poverty of the other party to the arbitration clause, or a person deriving title from him.'

(c) Suggested Modification of the Act

In *Smith v Pearl Assurance Co Ltd*[15] Clauson LJ said that perhaps an amendment to the Act of 1930 might be considered desirable so that the third party would

---

[10] (1932) 44 Ll L Rep 282, C A.
[11] Lord Hanworth M R and Romer L J.
[12] [1939] 1 All E R 95, C A.
[13] Slesser, Clauson and Du Parcq L J J. See further the judgment of Clauson L J, [1939] 1 All E R 95 at 97–98.
[14] Ibid, at 97.
[15] [1939] 1 All E R 95 C A.

no longer be bound by an arbitration clause in the policy. In the words of the learned Judge:[16]

> 'I only wish to add that, should it become necessary in the future to deal further legislatively with the matter which was dealt with in the Third Parties (Rights Against Insurers) Act 1930, I trust that those who deal with the matter will carefully consider whether there are not weighty reasons why persons who have the advantage of some such legislative provision should not be freed from the restriction, which might otherwise fall upon them, of being driven to arbitration. That, however, is a matter of policy, upon which I should not be justified in expressing any view. Nevertheless, I do think, having regard to such experience as I have had in these matters, that I am justified in drawing attention to the desirability of that question being very carefully considered, should the occasion arise.'

B THE ROAD TRAFFIC ACT 1972[17]

The Third Parties (Rights Against Insurers) Act 1930[18] gave third parties a right to sue the insurance company, but the company might still be able to avoid liability on the ground that the loss fell within an exception clause in the policy, eg that it had occurred whilst the car was being driven in an unroadworthy state, or that the insured had broken a condition in the policy. This caused considerable hardship to third parties, and further legislation was required. The relevant enactment was s 10 of the Road Traffic Act 1934, which is now replaced by the Road Traffic Act 1972, s 148.

Referring to the unsatisfactory situation before the Act of 1934 was passed, Goddard LJ said in *Zurich General Accident and Liability Insurance Co Ltd v Morrison:*[19]

> 'Part II of the Road Traffic Act 1934 was passed to remedy a state of affairs that became apparent soon after the principle of compulsory insurance against third-party risks had been established by the Road Traffic Act of 1930. That Act and the Third Parties (Rights Against Insurers) Act, passed in the same year, would naturally have led the public, at least those who were neither lawyers nor connected with the business of insurance, to believe that if thereafter they were, through no fault of their own, injured or killed by a motor car, they or their dependants would be certain of recovering damages, even though the wrongdoer was an impecunious person. How wrong they were quickly appeared. Insurance was left in the hands of companies and underwriters who could impose what terms and conditions they chose. Nor was there any standard form of policy, and any company, who could fulfil the not very onerous financial requirements that were necessary for acceptance as an approved insurer, could hedge the policies with so many warranties and conditions that no one advising an injured person could say with any certainty whether, if damages were recovered against the driver of the car, there was a prospect of recovering against the insurers . . . In the case of motor car insurance it was the third parties who needed the warning, and unfortunately they had no voice as to the warranties or conditions that were inserted in policies, though it was only because they held a policy that careless drivers were enabled to drive and put other persons in peril. It is not surprising, therefore, that by 1934 Parliament interfered, and by s 10 of the Act of that year they took steps towards remedying a position which to a great extent nullified the protection that compulsory insurance was intended to afford. Generally speaking, s 10 was designed to prevent conditions in policies from defeating the rights of third parties.'

The Road Traffic Act 1972 provides that:

---

[16] [1939] 1 All ER 95 at 98.
[17] The text of the relevant sections of the Act is set out in Appendix VIII, p 445, post.
[18] See pp 326-332, ante.
[19] (1942) 72 Ll L Rep 167, CA at 174.

1   Certain exceptions and conditions in the policy are ineffective against third parties.
2   The insurers are under a duty to satisfy judgments against insured persons provided that various requirements are complied with.
3   The insurers are entitled to recover from the insured any sum which they have paid to the third party.
4   The bankruptcy of the insured does not affect claims made by third parties.
5   The insured is required to give certain information to the third party.

1 Avoidance of Certain Exceptions and Conditions

Where a certificate of insurance has been delivered to the person by whom a policy has been effected, certain exception clauses[20] and conditions[1] in the policy are of no effect in relation to claims by third parties.[2]

These exceptions are those concerning:[3]

a   the age or physical or mental condition of persons driving the vehicle;
b   the condition of the vehicle;
c   the number of persons the vehicle carries;
d   the weight or physical characteristics of the goods that the vehicle carries;
e   the times at which or the areas within which the vehicle is used;
f   the horsepower or cylinder capacity or value of the vehicle;
g   the carrying on the vehicle of any particular apparatus;
h   the carrying on the vehicle of any particular means of identification other than any means of identification required to be carried by the Vehicles (Excise) Act 1971.

Again, a condition in a policy providing that no liability shall arise under it, or that any liability so arising shall cease in the event of some specified thing being done or omitted to be done after the event giving rise to a claim arising under the policy, is of no effect as against a third party.[4]

'Physical or Mental Condition of Person Driving'

A term in the policy requiring the insured to 'use all care and diligence to avoid accidents and to prevent loss' is not 'one relating to the physical or mental condition of the person driving', and is not, therefore, void as respects liability to a third party.

Thus, in *National Farmers' Union Mutual Insurance Society Ltd v Dawson*,[5] Lord Caldecote C J, said:[6]

---

[20] As to exception clauses, see generally pp 247-270, ante.
[1] As to conditions, see generally pp 271-278, ante.
[2] Road Traffic Act 1972, s 148 (1).
[3] Ibid, s 148 (1).
[4] Ibid, s 148 (2).
[5] (1941) 70 Ll L Rep 167, K B.
[6] Ibid, at 169.

'The argument is that the [assured's] physical condition was the result of failure to use due care and diligence, and that, as the policy contains a condition that the assured shall use all care and diligence to avoid accidents, that is a restriction on the insurance of the assured by reference to his physical condition. One of the restrictions, which has to be omitted from any policy in which it is contained, according to s 12 is a restriction by reference to, inter alia, "the age or physical or mental condition of persons driving the vehicle."

Now, I think that is an ingenious contention, but it is unsound. The policy does not purport to restrict the insurance by reference to the physical condition of persons driving the vehicle. At most it purports to restrict the insurance from applying to cases where the assured has not used all care and diligence, and that is something quite different, in my estimation, from a restriction which refers to the age or physical or mental condition of persons driving the vehicle.'

'Weight or Physical Characteristics of the Goods'

A condition in a policy restricting the use of a vehicle for certain purposes is not a restriction relating to the 'physical characteristics of the goods'. It will therefore be valid as against a third party.

In *Jones v Welsh Insurance Corpn Ltd*[7] the policy covered the use of the insured car for use 'for social, domestic and pleasure purposes' and for use 'in connection with his business or profession'. At the time of the accident the car was being used to carry some sheep which the insured farmed in his spare time. The principal point[8] decided in the case was that the vehicle was being used in the insured's business of a sheep farmer, and not that of a motor mechanic which was his business as stated in the policy. Consequently the insured was not covered by the policy, and the third party failed in his claim against the insurance company.

Counsel contended that the restriction in the policy was void as against the third party because it related to the 'physical characteristics of the goods'. But Goddard J rejected this argument and said:[9]

'The question here is not as to the actual nature of the goods carried or their physical characteristics, but whether the use of the car was for domestic or business purposes, or whether the goods carried, whatever their nature, were in connection with business.'

Freedom to Insert Other Exceptions and Conditions

Except in the above cases any clause in the policy will be valid as against third parties, and the insurer will be able to escape liability.

Thus, Branson J observed in *Gray v Blackmore:*[10]

'It would be an entirely different matter for the legislature to go back to a time before the accident had happened and to say that if anyone chooses to underwrite a policy in connection with a motor car, no limitations as to the time during which, or as the persons by whom, or as to the manner in which, that vehicle can be used can have any avail to save the underwriter from liability. If that were the state of the law, it would mean that there could be no such

---

[7] (1937) 59 Ll L Rep 13, K B.

[8] This issue is considered, at p 263, ante.

[9] (1937) 59 Ll L Rep 13 at 15.

[10] (1933) 47 Ll L Rep 69, K B at 75. This case was principally concerned with the question whether the car was being used at the time of the accident 'for any purpose in connection with the motor trade', see p 263, ante.

policies as are issued at present—policies for example, where a man insures two or three cars, warranting that only one of them shall be in use at a time, and thereby gets a reduction of premium. No underwriter would underwrite such a policy if it could be said that, ex post facto, that condition although broken could not be relied upon, and that he might be liable for the damage done by three cars out at one time, although he had only insured one; and similarly one might imagine any number of ridiculous positions which would arise. I see nothing in the statute which prevents an underwriter and an assured from agreeing to a policy with any conditions that they choose; but if the assured takes the car upon the road in breach of those conditions, it cannot thereby throw a greater obligation upon the underwriter.'

Accordingly an exception, which states that the company is under no liability 'whilst any motor cycle in respect of which indemnity is granted under this policy is carrying a passenger unless a sidecar is attached', is valid.[11]

So, too, is an exception which exempts the company from liability if the vehicle 'is being used for any purpose in connection with the motor trade',[12] or if it is being used otherwise than 'for social, domestic and pleasure purposes and in connection with the insured's business or profession.'[13]

Similarly, an exception stating that the insurance company should not be liable while any car was being driven by the policy holder unless he held a licence to drive such a car, was also held valid as against a third party.[14]

An arbitration clause in the policy will be enforceable against a third party.

Thus, in *Jones v. Birch Bros Ltd (Licenses and General Insurance Co Ltd, Third Parties)*[15] the insured had effected a policy containing a clause stating:

'In the event of any difference arising between the company and the insured under this policy, the same shall be referred to the arbitration of one or two persons in accordance with the statutory provisions for the time being in force applicable thereto, and the obtaining of an award shall be a condition precedent to the liability of the company under this policy.'

The insured was involved in an accident in which a Mr Jones was injured. Jones claimed damages from the insured, who sought to join the insurance company as a third party. The company applied for the proceedings to be stayed on the ground that the policy contained the arbitration clause. Jones, however, contended that the proceedings should not be stayed because the arbitration clause was overridden by the Road Traffic Act 1930, s 38.[16]

The Court of Appeal[17] held that the proceedings should be stayed. The arbitration clause without the *Scott v Avery*[18] addition (ie that part of the clause making the obtaining of an award a condition precedent to the liability of the company) was not overridden by s 38, for the clause stated only that the continuing liability under the policy should be determined in a particular way according to the agreement of the parties. But the Court was not agreed as to the effect of the statute on the *Scott v Avery* addition.

Thus, Scrutton L J said:[19]

11 *Bright v Ashfold* [1932] 2 K B 153.
12 *Gray v Blackmore* [1934] 1 K B 95.
13 *Jones v Welsh Insurance Corpn Ltd* (1937) 59 Ll L Rep 13, K B.
14 *General Accident Fire and Life Assurance Corpn Ltd v Shuttleworth* (1938) 60 Ll L Rep 301, K B.
15 (1933) 46 Ll L Rep 277, C A.
16 Now replaced by the Road Traffic Act 1972, s 148 (2).
17 Scrutton, Greer and Romer, L JJ.
18 (1856) 5 H L Cas 811. As to the *Scott v Avery* clause, see generally Russell, *Law of Arbitration* (20th edn, 1982), pp 66, 199-202.
19 (1933) 46 Ll L Rep 277 at 280.

'I am unable to see how the ordinary arbitration clause without the *Scott v Avery* addition is affected by s 38 of the Road Traffic Act. It does not, in my opinion, provide that any liability under the policy shall cease in the event of a specified thing being omitted to be done, but only that the continuing liability under the policy shall be determined in a particular way according to the agreement of the parties, unless the Court otherwise orders. Nor, in my opinion, does the *Scott v Avery* part of the condition, which, in my opinion, is severable from the other part of the condition, make the matter worse. It is an agreed additional way of enforcing the agreement of the parties.

I do not think it is necessary to determine finally what is the effect of the proviso to s 38. I have an impression that the draftsman did not quite understand what he meant to do, and has not unnaturally left it doubtful what he has done. I find it difficult to think that on the original claim between insured and insurer, at a time when the injured plaintiff has no rights, Parliament intended to alter the contract between insured and insurer in the claim, but to allow the insurer to counterclaim against the insured as if the conditions of the policy were not altered.'

But Greer LJ, said:[20]

'I find some difficulty in reading that section without making it apply to a *Scott v Avery* clause, because a *Scott v Avery* clause is something after the happening of the event giving rise to the claim, namely, the act which causes the damages; and I am inclined to think, though it is unnecessary to decide it, that the effect of that section is that the *Scott v Avery* part of the clause is rendered inoperative for the time being, though subject to the proviso; but I think it is unnecessary to decide that because, even if it is doubtful whether that result would follow, I think it is right to say that there should be a stay of the third party proceedings because they might have the result of rendering the policy inoperative if the action were allowed to proceed; whereas if the arbitration proceeds, the policy would not become inoperative by reason of the *Scott v Avery* clause.'

Again, Romer LJ, said:[1]

'I have felt inclined to decide that the section has no operation upon that addition for reasons that I ventured to indicate to [Counsel]. Since, however, this argument closed, I was informed by Mr Valentine Holmes as *amicus curiae* that there were some observations in some decision in the House of Lords,[2] the authors of which I have not been able to identify, but that was a case indeed in which I was not able to take a note, and it was not inconsistent with the reasons that I was suggesting. I have not had an opportunity of considering that case, and, therefore, I think it better not to express any opinion as to what effect, if any, s 38 has upon the *Scott v Avery* addition to the arbitration clause. I will assume that it renders it void.

That being so, we have an ordinary arbitration clause unaffected by the *Scott v Avery* addition, the addition being, in my opinion, clearly severable from the rest of the clause. That being so, I can see no reason why in the exercise of the Court's discretion the appellant should not be compelled by reason of arbitration to carry out the contract that he deliberately entered into.'

Thus, the insurance company will be liable to a third party even though it might be able to avoid liability as against the insured because, for example:

i   He has admitted liability for an accident and by doing so has been in breach of a condition in the policy.

ii He has failed to comply with a condition requiring him to give notice of a claim within a specified period, thus forfeiting all his rights under the policy.

---

[20] (1933) 46 Ll L Rep 277 at 281.

[1] Ibid, at 292.

[2] His Lordship was probably referring to *Cayzer, Irvine & Co Ltd v Board of Trade* (1927) 28 Ll L Rep 113.

2 Duty of Insurers to Satisfy Judgments against Insured Persons

If after a certificate of insurance[3] has been delivered to the person by whom a policy has been effected, judgment in respect of any liability required to be covered under s 145[4] of the Road Traffic Act 1972, is obtained against any person who is insured by the policy, the insurer must pay to the persons entitled to the benefit of the judgment any sum payable thereunder in respect of the liability.[5]

This duty is placed on the insurer even though the insurer may be entitled to avoid or cancel the policy, or may, in fact, have avoided or cancelled it.[6]

In addition to the sum which must be paid by the insurer to the persons entitled to the judgment in respect of liability, the insurer must also pay the costs and interest on the judgment debt where awarded by the Court.[7]

Circumstances in which the Insurers will not be Liable

In certain circumstances the insurer will not be liable even where the third party has been awarded judgment against the insured.

This situation arises where:

a The insurer had no notice of the bringing of the proceedings by the third party against the insured.

b The execution of the judgment, which has been obtained by the third party, has been stayed.

c The policy has been cancelled.

d The insurer has obtained a declaration of the Court that he is entitled to avoid the policy on the ground that it was obtained by non-disclosure or misrepresentation of a material fact.

---

[3] A policy of insurance is of no effect for the purposes of Pt VI of the Road Traffic Act 1972 unless there is delivered to the person by whom the policy is effected a certificate of insurance in the prescribed form and containing such particulars of any conditions subject to which the policy is issued and of any other matters as may be prescribed: Road Traffic Act 1972, s 147 (1). See p 320, ante. The prescribed form and particulars are set out in the Motor Vehicles (Third Party Risks) Regulations 1972: S I 1972/1217. See Appendix X, p 461, post.

[4] The general rule laid down by s 145 (3) is that 'the policy:

   (a)   must insure such person, persons or classes of persons specified in the policy in respect of any liability which may be incurred by him or them in respect of the death or in respect of the death of or bodily injury to any person caused by, or arising out of the use of the vehicle on the road; and

  (aa) must insure him or them in respect of any liability which may be incurred by him or them in respect of the use of the vehicle and of any trailer, whether or not coupled, in the territory other than Great Britain and Gibraltar of each of the member States of the Communities according to the law on compulsory insurance against civil liability in respect of the use of vehicles of the State where the liability may be incurred; and

   (b)   must also insure him or them in respect of any liability which may be incurred by him or them under the provisions of . . . Part [VI] of [the Act of 1972] relating to payment for emergency treatment.'

But by s 145 (4) 'the policy is not required to cover:

   (a)   liability in respect of the death, arising out of and in the course of his employment of a person in the employment of a person insured by the policy or of bodily injury sustained by such a person arising out of and in the course of his employment; or

   (b)   any contractual liability.'

[5] Road Traffic Act 1972, s 149 (1).

[6] Ibid, s 149 (1).

[7] Ibid, s 149 (1).

a No Notice of Proceedings

No sum is payable by the insurer in respect of any judgment, unless before or within 7 days after the commencement of the proceeding s in which judgment was given, the insurer had notice of the bringing of the proceedings.[8]

Meaning of 'proceedings'   In *McGoona v Motor Insurers' Bureau and Marsh*[9] Lawton J, held (obiter) that the word 'proceedings' meant 'legal proceedings', and that the mere notification of the making of a claim was not sufficient. He observed:[10]

> 'Notification that a claim may be made is not notification of the commencement of proceedings and there is obviously good reason why the commencement of proceedings is the material time. Insurers may have repudiated liability as against their assured but they may have their own reasons for taking over control of any litigation there may be. In may well be that if the facts are gone into, for example, a plaintiff may have no grounds of claim at all and unless the insurers have notice of the commencement of the proceedings, they are not in a position to intervene. It is important from the insurers' point of view, too, that they have notice not later than seven days after the commencement of proceedings because of the danger of judgment in default of appearance being given against a defendant assured. All these considerations leave me in no doubt that "proceedings" mean legal proceedings.'

Kind of notice required   As to what kind of notice is required, this has not been judicially determined.[11]

Notice to Agent. The notice where given to an insurers's agent should be a formal notice. A notice merely given in the course of a casual conversation is not sufficient.

Thus, in *Herbert v Railway Passengers Assurance Co*[12] a third party was injured in a road accident, and judgment was obtained against the insured, a Mr Wilkinson. Wilkinson referred the matter to the insurance company. But they repudiated liability on the ground that they had had no notice of the proceedings by the third party either before or within 7 days of the commencement of such proceedings.[13] It was contended by the third party that notice had been indirectly given by Wilkinson to the company through an agent, a Mr Ackery, who effected the insurance.

After reviewing the evidence on this point, Porter J, held that proper notice had not been given to the company, and that they could avoid liability.

He observed:[14]

> 'The other question which I have to determine is the question whether the plaintiff in the present case is precluded by the fact that no notice was given to the insurance company, the defendants in the present case. So far as that is concerned, of course, no direct notice was given, but it is said that notice was given to the gentleman who was the agent for the insurance company for effecting the insurance—Mr Ackery. I am not going to determine what the exact

---

8   Road Traffic Act 1972, s 149 (2).

9   [1969] 2 Lloyd's Rep 34, Q B D.

10   Ibid, at 46.

11   In *McGoona v Motor Insurers' Bureau and Marsh* [1969] 2 Lloyd's Rep 34, Q B D Lawton J, said (ibid at 47) that he found it unnecessary to decide the point because it was quite clear on the facts of the case in regard to the notice of the claim that no notice of any kind of the commencement of proceedings was in fact given within seven days.

12   (1938) 60 Ll L Rep 143 K B.

13   The relevant statute at the date of this case was the Road Traffic Act 1934, s 10 (2) (a), which has now been replaced by the Road Traffic Act 1972, s 149 (2).

14   (1938) 60 Ll L Rep 143 at 146.

position of Mr Ackery was. I am not saying anything about that position except this, and it is rather that insurance companies may know the attitude which perhaps one thinks they ought to take, rather than the attitude which is a legal one. Again, let me qualify it with this: in saying that, I am not giving a considered opinion; it may be that there are other grounds which may want consideration, but if an agent is an agent to effect a policy, and conducts the negotiations for effecting the policy, and if afterwards to that person clear notice were given, I should think that an insurance company, whatever their legal liabilities, might well recognise that as being a notice, given under the section, that proceedings had been begun. But even if that is right, I think that for that purpose it must really be a notice in the sense that it is given formally as a notice; it must not be some mere piece of casual conversation. Here, I can see no reason why Mr Ackery should regard Mr Wilkinson's statement as a matter which he ought to pass on to the insurance company, or as a matter which he should remember at all. In the course of casual conversation, Mr Wilkinson, who had come up to see his former companions, mentioned than an action had been brought against him—in a friendly casual conversation. To my mind, that can in no sense be regarded as being a notice as required by the Act. It must be something much more formal than that, something which would indicate to the company's agent, if agent he was for that purpose, that a notice was being given.'

His Lordship went on to say[15] that his general view was that even where a company repudiated their liability, their repudiation was not sufficient to acquit the person claiming from showing that notice had been given to them. Where an Act of Parliament stipulated that recovery should not take place except in certain events, those events must take place before the plaintiff could recover. This was not the ordinary case of the waiver[16] by the insurers of an obligation which they themselves had imposed.

Absence of Notice. If the insurer wishes to rely on absence of notice, this should be expressly pleaded.

Thus, in *Baker v Provident Accident and White Cross Insurance Co Ltd*[17] in which the principal question was whether an injured passenger was carried in the vehicle 'by reason of or in pursuance of a contract of employment', Cassels J held that the action brought against the insurance company[18] failed because the passenger was not at the moment of the accident riding as a passenger with the permission of the insured. But his Lordship then observed, in relation to the question whether the company had notice of the proceedings, which the passenger had brought against the insured:[19]

'There was one other matter perhaps, with which I ought to have dealt, and that was the question of notice. My view is that that should have been pleaded, and, if the matter had reached such a stage that that point had become of importance, I should have granted an adjournment at the cost of the [insurance company] in order that the lack of notice might be pleaded. However, the matter, in view of my judgment, ceases to be of importance.'

Commencement of the Proceedings. The question arose in *Cross v British Oak Insurance Co Ltd*[20] as to whether proceedings were commenced when a third party notice[1] was given to the insurance company or when the third party counterclaimed against the insured.

---

15 (1938) 60 Ll L Rep 143 at 146.
16 As to what constitutes a waiver of a breach of a condition, see generally Ivamy, *General Principles of Insurance Law* (4th Edn, 1979), pp 310-317.
17 [1939] 2 All E R 690, K B.
18 Under the Road Traffic Act 1934, s 10, which is now replaced by the Road Traffic Act 1972, s 149.
19 [1939] 2 All E R 690 at 697.
20 (1938) 60 Ll L Rep 46, K B.
1 As to third party proceedings, see R S C Order 16, and *The Supreme Court Practice* 1982, Vol 1, pp 259-279.

In this case the insurance company had insured a Mr Fowler against third party risks. An accident occurred in which a Mr Cross and a Mr Baker were injured. Baker commenced an action against Fowler, and Cross was brought in as a third party because Fowler maintained that the accident was caused by Cross's negligence. On 24 March the insurance company was informed that leave had been given by the Court to bring in Cross as a third party. Subsequently Cross counterclaimed for damages against Fowler, and judgment was entered for Cross, but was never satisfied. No notice of the counterclaim was ever given to the insurance company.

Cross claimed a declaration that the company was liable to him. The company repudiated liability on the ground that the 'proceedings commenced' when the counterclaim was made by Cross, and since no notice of the counter-claim had been given, they were under no liability. Cross, however, contended that the 'proceedings commenced' when the third party notice had been given to the company.

It was held by Du Parcq J that the company's contention would be upheld and that, since no notice of the counterclaim had been given, the company was under no liability.

In reviewing the arguments of counsel[2] the learned Judge said:[3]

> 'Now, when were the proceedings commenced? One might say: "Well, the proceedings in which the judgment was given were commenced when Baker began his action in the County Court. That was the commencement of the proceedings. Ultimately, the third party is brought in; a judgment is given in his favour in those proceedings which Baker began when he issued a plaint"; or one may say that that cannot be what the Act means, but that the proceedings in which the judgment was given began when Cross was brought in as a third party, because when he was brought in as a third party, it was for the first time possible for any judgment to be given which would affect his rights. When once he was brought in as a third party, it was, at any rate, possible that he would counterclaim, and anyone receiving notice that Cross is a third party and studying, as he should, the procedure of the County Court, would know that there might be a counterclaim by Cross. Thirdly, it might be said, and has been said here, that that is not when the proceedings in which judgment was given began. Judgment is given on the claim brought by Cross against Fowler, and it is when Cross first makes the claim against Fowler that the proceedings commenced in which that judgment is given.'

He then said that it would have been impossible for Cross to take any step with a view to giving notice of his claim within 7 days after the commencement of the proceedings if by the word 'proceedings' was meant the action instituted

---

[2] In the course of his judgment his Lordship alluded to the difficulty of construing the section and said, (1938) 60 Ll L Rep 46 at 47: 'One may regret, although perhaps it is useless to do so, that the Act of Parliament is not a little clearer, and when one reads the other sub-section to which I shall have to refer, sub-s. (3), it is difficult to resist the conclusion, although I blame nobody for the fact, that the result of the way in which the Act has been drafted orginally, and for all I know, subsequently amended—whether as a result, it may be, of prolonged debate and much compromise, I know not—is that the Act does not appear to deal by any means with all the contingencies which may arise. Perhaps I should say that the Act seems to have been drafted, or at any rate finally passed, in a form which would lead one to suppose that those responsible for it had not envisaged some of the events which were not likely but were certain to happen, and were legislating either in ignorance or forgetfulness of the procedure in the Courts of the country. That is unfortunate; it makes the position of insurance companies difficult as well as the position of the insured, and it does not make the task of the Judge particularly easy.'

[3] Ibid, at 48.

by Baker. The real question, therefore, was whether the second or the third of the meanings stated above should be given to the words.

He said that, if the subsection[4] stood alone, he should certainly be disposed to think that the view put forward by counsel for the third party was the right one because it might well be said that the proceedings in which this judgment was given were taken when Cross was made a third party. From that moment he had the right to counterclaim. Although, no doubt, there was ample authority for the proposition that a counterclaim was to be regarded as a cross-action and a separate proceeding in that sense, still he would have thought that it was enough if notice were given of the commencement of the third party proceedings. But the difficulty which faced the Court was that of trying to put such a construction on subsection (2) when one also had to consider the effect of subsection (3)[5], which stated that the insurer was not

'entitled to the benefit of this subsection as respects any judgment obtained in proceedings commenced before the commencement of that action [that is to say, the action for a declaration], unless before or within seven days after the commencement of that action he has given notice thereof to the person who is the plaintiff in the said proceedings specifying the non-disclosure or false representation on which he proposes to rely, and any person to whom notice of such an action is so given [this is the proviso to sub-s (3)] shall be entitled, if he thinks fit, to be made a party thereto.'

The proviso that within seven days after the commencement of an action notice should be given to the person who was the plaintiff in the proceedings, construed literally, was absurd because that would mean that the insurer who was proposing to repudiate the policy when his insured issued a writ, must at once inform him that he was entitled to repudiate the policy which, of course, the plaintiff would know perfectly well already. It must mean 'the defendant who counterclaims'. The defendant who counterclaimed must be covered by those words 'the plaintiff in the said proceedings'. He could not be covered by those words 'the plaintiff' or become plaintiff in any sense until he had counterclaimed.

In concluding that the proceedings were commenced when the third party counterclaimed, his Lordship said:[6]

'That view, to which one is forced, seems to me to lend great colour to the argument that the proceedings are taken to be commenced by the counterclaim, because the Legislature seems to have thought of the person who makes the claim as commencing the proceedings so much so that they actually call him the plaintiff, although technically he may not be the plaintiff at all, but a defendant counterclaiming.

It seems to me, therefore, that sub-s (3) gives that strongest indication that "the proceedings in which the judgment was given" means "the proceedings begun by a person who may for this purpose be regarded as the plaintiff, which results in the judgment upon which reliance is placed as against the insurers." If that is right, the plaintiff here cannot succeed.'

Obtaining Declaration. Where an insurance company sues for a declaration, the Court is entitled to make a declaratory order in the absence of the defendant.[7]

---

[4] Viz Road Traffic Act 1934, s 10 (2), which is now replaced by Road Traffic Act 1972, s 149 (2).

[5] Viz s 10 (3) of the Road Traffic Act 1934, which is now replaced by the Road Traffic Act 1972, s 149 (3).

[6] (1938) 60 Ll L Rep 46, K B at 49.

[7] *Guardian Assurance Co Ltd v Sutherland* [1939] 2 All E R 246, K B where the company sued for a declaration under the Road Traffic Act 1934, s 10, which has now been replaced by the Road Traffic Act 1972, s 149.

b Execution of Judgment Stayed

No sum is payable by the insurer in respect of any judgment so long as execution thereon is stayed pending an appeal.[8]

c Policy Cancelled

No sum is payable by the insurer in respect of any liability if, before the happening of the event which was the cause of the death or bodily injury giving rise to the liability, the policy was cancelled by mutual consent or by virtue of any provision contained in it.[9]

But to enable the insurer to escape liability it must also be shown that[10] either:

    (i) before the happening of the event, the certificate of insurance was surrendered to the insurers, or the person to whom the certificate was delivered made a statutory declaration stating that the certificate had been lost or destroyed; or

    (ii) after the happening of the event, but before the expiration of a period of 14 days from the taking effect of the cancellation of the policy, the certificate was surrendered to the insurer, or the person to whom it was delivered made a statutory declaration stating that the certificate had been lost or destroyed; or

    (iii) either before or after the happening of the event but within the period of 14 days from the taking effect of the cancellation of the policy, the insurer had commenced proceedings in respect of the failure to surrender the certificate.[11]

d Policy obtained by Non-Disclosure or Misrepresentation of Material Fact

No sum is payable by an insurer if in an action commenced before, or within 3 months after, the commencement of the proceedings in which the judgment was given, he has obtained a declaration that, apart from any provision contained in the policy, he is entitled to avoid it on the ground that it was obtained by the non-disclosure of a material fact, or by a representation of a fact which was false in some material particular, or, if he has avoided the policy on that ground, that he was entitled to do so apart from any provision contained in it.[12]

---

[8] Road Traffic Act 1972, s 149 (2) (b).

[9] Ibid s 149 (2) (c)

[10] Ibid s 149 (2) (c)

[11] Under the Road Traffic Act 1972, s 147. Section 205 (4) states that 'where a certificate has been delivered . . . and the policy . . . to which it relates is cancelled by mutual consent or by virtue of any provision in the policy . . . , the person to whom the certificate was delivered shall, within seven days from the taking effect of the cancellation, surrender the certificate to the person by whom the policy was issued . . . or, if the certificate has been lost or destroyed, make a statutory declaration to that effect.'

[12] Road Traffic Act 1972, s 149 (3).

The reason why it is fair that the insurer can escape liability on the ground of non-disclosure or misrepresentation by the insured was explained by Scott LJ, in *Merchants' and Manufacturers' Insurance Co Ltd v Hunt*[13] where he said:[14]

'From the extreme hardship that might otherwise result from sub-s (1), sub-s (3) gives the insurer a conditional means of escape. If he discovers that he was induced to make the contract of insurance by some material non-disclosure or misrepresentation which, by ordinary insurance law, and not merely by reason of some special stipulation which he has put in his form of policy, entitles him to avoid the contract, he may obtain a declaration to that effect from the Court, and will then be free of statutory liability to the injured third party. This legislation was obviously intended, inter alia, to effect a fair compromise between the two desirable but conflicting objects—one the one hand, of protecting the public from the danger of impecunious totfeasors on the roads, and, on the other hand, of avoiding the injustice of putting on a wholly innocent and misled insurer the whole pecuniary burden of a policy which, neither in law, nor in equity, is his policy. But it would have been unfair to confer this relief unconditionally. There was an obvious danger of the injured party being deprived of the pecuniary safeguard which was the subject of sub-s (1), through the possibility of the policy being avoided in proceedings under the first part of sub-s (3) without his knowledge, and even by collusion between the insurer and the insured. It was essential that he should have notice of any such action by the insurer, and also to be given the right to appear in it and there defend his rights. Both the requisites are met by the proviso to sub-s (3), which in effect creates two conditions precedent to the existence of the insurer's right to get his declaration under the first part of sub-s (3). The third party gets full notice of the ground of the insurer's claim, and is given an unqualified right to become a party in the insurer's action; and it is particularly to be noted that he is given all the rights of a party to an action without any qualification upon them.'

'*Obtained.*' It must be shown that the policy was *obtained* by non-disclosure or misrepresentation of a material fact, ie that the mind of the particular insurer concerned was affected in deciding whether to accept the risk or in fixing the premium.

Thus MacKinnon LJ, said in *Zurich General Accident and Liability Insurance Co Ltd v Morrison:*[15]

'Under the general law of insurance an insurer can avoid a policy if he proves that there has been misrepresentation or concealment of a material fact by the assured. What is material that which would influence the mind of a prudent insurer in deciding whether to accept the risk, or in fixing the premium. And if this be proved, it is not necessary further to prove that the mind of the actual insurer was so affected. In other words, the assured could not rebut the claim to avoid the policy because of a material representation by a plea that the particular insurer concerned was so stupid, ignorant, or reckless, that he could not exercise the judgment of a prudent insurer and was, in fact, unaffected by anything the assured had represented or concealed.

But under the provisions of this Act of 1934 I think this general rule of insurance law is modified. The section requires the insurer to establish that the policy was "obtained" by non-disclosure or misrepresentation. In such a case as this, therefore, I think the plaintiffs must establish two propositions: (1) that the matter relied on was "material" in the sense that the mind of a prudent insurer would be affected by it, and (2) that in fact their underwriter's mind was so affected and the policy was thereby obtained.'

'*Material.*' The word 'material' means of such a nature as to influence the judgment of a prudent insurer in determining whether he will take the risk and, if so, at what premium and on what conditions.[16]

---

[13] (1941) 68 Ll L Rep 117, C A.
[14] Ibid, at 120.
[15] (1942) 72 Ll L Rep 167, at 172, C A.
[16] Road Traffic Act 1972, s 149 (5) (b). Cf Marine Insurance Act 1906, s 18, which relates to the

Notice to Third Party.   Even if the insurer has obtained such a declaration in an action, he will still be liable to satisfy the judgment obtained in proceedings commenced before the commencement of that action unless before or within 7 days after the commencement of that action he has given notice thereof to the plaintiff in the proceedings specifying the non-disclosure or false representation on which he proposes to rely.[17]

The reason why notice must to given to the third party is that if it were not known by him that the insurance company intended to repudiate liability on the ground of non-disclosure or misrepresentation by the insured, he himself might be involved in useless expense in suing the insured who, in any event, might be unable to pay the damages awarded against him.

This matter is referred to by Goddard LJ in *Zurich General Accident and Liability Insurance Co Ltd v Morrison*[18] where he said:[19]

> 'But insurers are still allowed to repudiate policies obtained by misrepresentation or non-disclosure of material facts. This right, however, was made subject to certain conditions ans restrictions contained in sub-s (3) of s 10. It seems to me that what the Legislature had in mind was that, if an insurer was intending to repudiate a policy, it was only fair that the injured third party should know the grounds on which repudiation was sought before he went to the expense of endeavouring to establish his claim against the assured, who, if not entitled to indemnity, might be unable to satisfy a judgment. It was to prevent an injured party incurring further useless expense. Hence the necessity of the notice prescribed by the proviso to the sub-section.'

Contents of Notice.   Except as against the insured the insurer is not entitled to rely on any matter not specified in the notice.

Thus, in *Zurich General Accident and Liability Insurance Co Ltd v Morrison*[20] a notice was served on a third party containing particulars of misrepresentation and non-disclosure of material facts by the insured. The insurance company sought to rely upon further particulars of non-disclosure contained in an amendment to their statement of claim made more than 7 days after the commencement of the action.

The Court of Appeal[1] held that the further particulars, not being included in the notice served on the third party, could not be relied on by the company as against him. The company's claim to avoid the policy was limited to the particulars contained in the unamended statement of claim.

Goddard LJ said:[2]

> 'The defendants in this case contend that, if they once serve a notice specifying grounds on which at the time they serve it they intend to rely, they are at liberty to set up any further

---

duty of an assured to disclose material circumstances to the insurer. Subsection (2) of this section states: 'Every circumstance is material which would influence the judgment of a prudent insurer in fixing the premium or determining whether he will take the risk'. Section 20 concerns the duty of the assured not to make material misrepresentations to the insurer. Subsection 2 of that section states: 'A representation is material which would influence the judgment of a prudent insurer in fixing the premium or determining whether he will take the risk'. See further, Ivamy, *Marine Insurance* (3rd edn, 1979), pp 41-42, 72.

[17] Road Traffic Act 1972, s 149 (3), proviso.

[18] (1942) 72 Ll L Rep 167, C A.

[19] Ibid, at 174.

[20] (1942) 72 Ll L Rep 167, C A.

[1] Lord Greene M R, MacKinnon and Goddard L J J.

[2] (1942) 82 Ll L Rep 166 at 174. See also the judgments of Lord Greene M R, ibid, at 171, and of MacKinnon L J, ibid, at 172.

grounds of repudiation that they may think will help them and which they subsequently discover if they can get leave to amend their pleading, although the statutory period within which the notice must be served has expired.

Now, be it observed that, as against the assured who must be a party to the action, there is no limitation as to the grounds on which the policy can be disputed, so if something is discovered that was not known when the original pleading was delivered, there may be good reason why an amendment should be granted. But there is every reason why it should not prejudice the third party. If by amending the defence the insurer can in effect add to the notice he has given to the third party, the protection which, in my opinion, the proviso is designed to give to the latter is rendered nugatory. I have no hesitation in holding that, although the proviso does not contain words expressly precluding the insurer from setting up any grounds not mentioned in his notice, that is its effect. This construction was evidently that which appealed to this Court in *Contingency Insurance Co v Lyons*[3]—although, as there is no indication in any report that the case was ever tried, it was evident that the plaintiff realised that it was hopeless to proceed with the action.'

Third Party's Rights to be made Co-defendant. A person to whom notice of such an action is so given is entitled, if he thinks fit, to be made a party thereto.[4]

In construing the meaning of this provision, Scott LJ said in *Merchants' and Manufacturers' Insurance Co Ltd v Hunt*[5] that, in his opinion, the necessary implication of the word 'party' was that he was entitled to be made a party under RSC Ord 16, and that he then acquired all the rights of a defendant.

In this case the insurance company sought a declaration that they were entitled to avoid a policy of insurance issued to the insured, a Mr Hunt, on the ground that it was obtained by non-disclosure of material facts or by a representation of fact that was false in a material particular. A third party named Thorn was injured in an accident, and in the action for the declaration he elected to be made a co-defendant. In answer to a question in the proposal form stating 'Have you or any person who to your knowledge will drive the car been convicted of an offence in connection with a motor vehicle or motor cycle or is any prosecution pending?' Hunt had replied 'No'. His son was driving at the time of the accident, and in a written statement to the insurance company's solicitors admitted that he had previously been convicted of exceeding the speed limit with a motor cycle and of a traffic light offence. The insured concurred with the statement. In the action for the declaration the insurance company maintained that the written statement was admissible in evidence against the third party.

The Court of Appeal[6] rejected this contention, and held that the third party was entitled to strict proof of the facts on which the company's right to a declaration could be founded.[7] Since the company's case had not been so proved, no declaration could be made.

3 Recovery from the Insured of Sum Paid

If the amount, which an insurer becomes liable under s 149 to pay in respect of a liability of the insured, exceeds the amount for which he would, apart from

---

[3] (1939) 65 Ll L Rep 53.

[4] Road Traffic Act 1972, s 149 (3).

[5] (1941) 68 Ll L Rep 117 at 123, CA.

[6] Scott, Luxmoore and Dur Parcq LJJ.

[7] See the judgment of Scott LJ (1941) 68 Ll L Rep 117, ibid, at 123. See also the judgment of Luxmoore LJ, ibid, at 126, and that of Du Parcq LJ, ibid, at 128.

the provisions of the section, be liable under the policy, he is entitled to recover the excess from the insured.[8]

Thus, suppose that the insurer is held liable to pay, eg £10,000 to the third party, and there is a 'basis' clause[9] in the policy whereby the insured warrants the truth of all statements he has made, and the statement is false. In this event the insurer would be entitled to avoid liability on the policy, and nothing would be due to the insured. Accordingly, the insurer would be able to recover the whole of the £10,000 from the insured.

4 Effect of Bankruptcy of the Insured

The bankruptcy of the insured does not affect claims made by third parties.

The Road Traffic Act 1972, s 150 (1) states that where a certificate of insurance has been delivered to the person by whom the policy has been effected, and any of the following events happen, viz:

(i)   the person by whom the policy was effected becomes bankrupt or makes a composition or arrangement with his creditors;

(ii) he dies, and an order is made under the Bankruptcy Act 1914, s 130 for the administration of his estate according to the law of bankruptcy;

(iii) if the person by whom the policy was effected is a company, a winding-up order is made with respect to the company or a resolution for a voluntary winding up is passed with respect thereto, or a receiver or manager of the company's business or undertaking is duly appointed or possession is taken, by or on behalf of the holders of any debentures secured by a floating charge, of any property comprised in or subject to the charge,

the happening of that event does not affect any liability to third parties.[10]

5 Duty of Insured to Give Informtion

A person against whom a claim is made in respect of third party liability, must, on demand of the person making the claim, state whether or not in respect of the liability he was insured by a policy, or would have been so insured if the insurer had not avoided or cancelled the policy.[11]

If he was, or would have been so insured, he must give such particulars with respect to that policy as were specified in the certificate of insurance delivered in respect of the policy.[12]

If without reasonable excuse a person fails to comply with these requirements, or wilfully makes a false statement in reply to any such demand, he is liable on summary conviction to a fine not exceeding level 3 on the standard scale.[13]

---

[8] Road Traffic Act 1972, s 149 (4).

[9] As to the 'basis' clause, see Ivamy, *General Principles of Insurance Law* (4th Edn, 1979), pp 181-183.

[10] Notwithstanding anything in the Third Parties (Rights Against Insurers) Act 1930; Road Traffic Act 1972, s 150 (1). For the provisions of the Act of 1930, see pp 326-332, ante.

[11] Road Traffic Act 1972, s 151 (1).

[12] Ibid, s 151 (1).

[13] Ibid, s 151 (2) and Sch 4, Pt I, as amended by the Criminal Justice Act 1982, s 38 (1).

C THE MOTOR INSURERS' BUREAU

I THE AGREEMENTS OF 1972

In 1972 the Secretary of State for the Environment and the Motor Insurers' Bureau[14] entered into Agreements to secure compensation to victims of road accidents in cases where, notwithstanding the provisions of the Road Traffic Act 1972, they were deprived of compensation through the drivers of the vehicles being uninsured or untraced.[15]

a The Agreement for Compensation of Victims of Uninsured Drivers[16]

The Agreement is divided into

1   the Agreement itself;
2   the notes relating to it.

(1) The Agreement itself

(i) Satisfaction of Claims by Bureau. The principal provision of the agreement is that if judgment in respect of any liability, which is required to be covered by a policy of insurance under Pt VI of the Road Traffic Act 1972, is obtained against any person or persons in any Court in Great Britain, whether or not such person or persons be covered by a contract of insurance, and any such judgment is not satisfied in full within 7 days from the date upon which the person or persons in whose favour the judgment was given became entitled to enforce it, the Bureau will pay or satisfy or cause to be paid or satisfied to or to the satisfaction of the person or persons in whose favour the judgment was given any sum payable or remaining payable thereunder including any sum awarded by the Court in respect of interest on that sum and any taxed costs or any costs awarded by the Court without taxation[17], whatever may be the cause of the failure of the judgment debtor to satisfy the judgment.[18]

In *Cooper v Motor Insurers' Bureau*[19], a Mr Killacky asked Mr Cooper to road test his motorcycle. During the course of the test, Mr Cooper collided with a car and was seriously injured. He claimed damages from Mr Killacky and obtained judgment for £214,207. Mr Killacky was unable to satisfy the judgment, so Mr Cooper brought an action against the Motor Insurers' Bureau. The Bureau contended that it was under no duty to satisfy the judgment which had been obtained by Mr Cooper because it did not arise out of a liability which was required to be covered by a policy of insurance under Pt VI of the Road Traffic Act 1972.

---

14 The Bureau is incorporated under the Companies Act 1929. Its address is Aldermary House, Queen Street, London EC4N 1TR.
15 The Agreements replace two earlier Agreements made in 1971. See the second edition of this book at p 336.
16 For the full text of the Agreement see Appendix XIII, p 479, post.
17 Or such proportion thereof as is attributable to the liability in respect of which a policy of insurance must insure a person in order to comply with Part VI of the Road Traffic Act 1972: cl 1.
18 Ibid.
19 [1983] 1 All E R 353.

Mr Barry Chedlow QC[20] held that Mr Cooper's claim failed, for the Bureau were under no obligation to satisfy the judgment. It did not arise out of a liability which fell to be covered under Pt VI of the Road Traffic Act 1972. The only liability which had to be covered under ss 143[1] and 145 (3) (a)[2] was Mr Cooper's liability to others. Mr Killacky's liability to Mr Cooper was not one which had to be insured against under the Act.[3]

(ii) Conditions Precedent to Bureau's Liability.   There are four conditions[4] precedent to the Bureau's liability:

a *Notice of proceedings*
   Notice of the bringing of the proceedings must be given before or within 7 days after the commencement of the proceedings
   i *to the Bureau* in the case of proceedings in respect of a liability which is either not covered by a contract of insurance or covered by a contract of insurance with an insurer whose identity cannot be ascertained, or
   ii *to the insurer* in the case of proceedings in respect of a liability which is covered by a contract of insurance with an insurer whose identity can be ascertained.
   The condition as to the time limit of 7 days may be waived by the Bureau.[5]
b *Supply of information*
   Such information relating to the proceedings as the Bureau may reasonably require is supplied to the Bureau by the person bringing the proceedings.
c *Judgment against all tortfeasors*
   If so required by the Bureau and subject to full indemnity by it as to costs, the person bringing the proceedings must take all reasonable steps to obtain judgment against all the persons liable in respect of the injury or death of the third party, and in the event of such a person being a servant or agent, against his principal.
d *Assignment of judgment*
   The judgment (whether or not it includes an amount in respect of a liability other than a liability in respect of which a policy of insurance must insure a person in order to comply with Pt VI of the Road Traffic Act 1972) and any order for costs must be assigned to the Bureau or its nominee.

In the event of any dispute as to the reasonableness of a requirement by the Bureau for the supply of information or that any particular step should be taken to obtain judgment against other persons, it may be referred to the Secretary of State whose decision is final.[6]

Where a judgment which includes an amount in respect of a liability other than a liability in respect of which a policy of insurance must insure a person to comply with Pt VI of the Road Traffic Act 1972 has been assigned to the

---

[20] Sitting as a Deputy Judge.
[1] See p 299, ante.
[2] See p 337, ante, note 4, ante.
[3] [1983] 1 All ER at 357.
[4] Clause 5 (1).
[5] See eg *Cooper v Motor Insurers' Bureau* [1983] 1 All ER 353, where it was held (obiter) that there was no waiver and that the Bureau was not precluded from relying on the defence of the absence of the notice. (See the judgment of Mr Barry Chedlow QC, ibid, at 357.)
[6] Clause 5 (2).

Bureau or its nominee, the Bureau must apportion any monies received in pursuance of the judgment according to the proportion which the damages in respect of the liabilities bear to each other, and must account to the person in whose favour the judgment was given in respect of such monies properly apportionable to the other liabilities. Where an order for costs in respect of such a judgment has been so assigned, monies received pursuant to the order must be dealt with in the same manner.[7]

(iii) Period of Agreement. The Agreement is determinable by the Secretary of State at any time or by the Bureau on 12 months' notice without prejudice to the continued operation of the Agreement in respect of accidents occurring before the date of termination.[8]

(iv) Recoveries. Nothing in the Agreement prevents insurers from providing by conditions in their contracts of insurance that all sums paid by them or by the Bureau by virtue of the Agreement made on 31 December 1945 or the present Agreement in or towards the discharge of the liability of their insured shall be recoverable by them or by the Bureau from the insured or from any other person.[9]

(v) Exemptions. The Bureau incurs no liability where
1 the claim arises out of the use of a vehicle owned by or in the possession of the Crown,[10] except where any other person has undertaken responsibility for the existence of a contract of insurance under Part VI of the Road Traffic Act 1972[11] or where the liability is in fact covered by a contract of insurance;
2 the claim arises out of the use of a vehicle which is not required to be covered by a contract of insurance by virtue of the Road Traffic Act 1972, s 144;[12]
3 at the time of the accident the person suffering death or bodily injury in respect of which the claim is made was allowing himself to be carried in a vehicle[13] and

    i knew or had reason to believe that the vehicle had been taken without the consent of the owner or other lawful authority except in a case where
      (a) he believed or had reason to believe that he had lawful authority to be carried or that he would have had the owner's consent if the owner had known of his being carried and the circumstances of his carriage; or

---

[7] Clause 5 (3).
[8] Clause 3.
[9] Clause 4.
[10] A vehicle which has been unlawfully removed from the possession of the Crown is to be taken to continue in that possession whilst it is kept so removed: clause 6 (3) (a).
[11] Whether or not the person or persons liable be in fact covered by a contract of insurance: clause 6 (1) (a).
[12] See p 299, ante.
[13] References to a person being carried in a vehicle include references to his being carried in or upon or entering or getting on to or alighting from the vehicle: clause 6 (3) (b).

(b) he had learned of the circumstances of the taking of the vehicle since the commencement of the journey and it would be unreasonable to expect him to have alighted from the vehicle; or

ii being the owner[14] of or being a person using the vehicle, he was using or causing or permitting the vehicle to be used without there being in force in relation to such use a contract of insurance as would comply with Pt VI of the Act, knowing or having reason to believe that no such contract was in force.[15]

The words 'had reason to believe' refer to a rational process of thought, and are quite different from the words 'having a reasonable belief'.[16]

Thus, in *Porter v Motor Insurers' Bureau*[17], Mrs Porter, while on holiday in Holland, bought a car intending to ship it to Nigeria. She was unable to afford to do so, so she brought it back to England. She was told by the Customs authorities at Harwich that she must not drive it away as she was not insured, and that if she wanted to get it to London, she should arrange for an insured driver to drive it for her. She left the car at Harwich and returned to London. Subsequently, she recounted the whole story to a Mr Addo, who drove a car which she knew belonged to him or his employers. He then volunteered to drive her car back from Harwich to London. They went to Harwich, and on the way back, an accident occurred and Mrs Porter was injured. She claimed damages for negligence from Mr Addo and obtained judgment against him. The judgment was not satisfied, so Mrs Porter applied for a declaration that the Motor Insurers' Bureau were liable to indemnify her. The Bureau denied liability under clause 6 of the Agreement set out above as she was permitting the vehicle to be used without there being in force a contract of insurance complying with Pt VI of the Road Traffic Act 1972 'knowing or having reason to believe that no such contract was in force'.

Forbes J ruled that a declaration would be granted, for, on the evidence, Mrs Porter had made it clear that she needed an insured driver. She was entitled to rely on the assumption that he was such a driver. There was nothing which should have caused her to have reason to believe that no contract of insurance was in force. The words in clause 6 did not say 'having a reasonable belief that no such contract was in force'. 'Having reason to believe' was a reference to a rational process of thought, and that was quite a different thing from 'having a reasonable belief'.

His Lordship observed[18]:—

'The first is that it does not say "having reasonable belief that no such contract was in force." The words are "having reason to believe." It seems to me that those two expressions are

---

14 'Owner' in relation to a vehicle, which is the subject of a hiring agreement or a hire-purchase agreement, means the person in possession of the vehicle under that agreement: clause 6 (3) (c).

15 Clause 6 (1). The exemption specified in sub-para (1) (c) of this clause applies only in a case where the judgment in respect of which the claim against the Bureau was made was obtained in respect of a liability which is required to be covered by a policy of insurance under Pt VI of the Road Traffic Act 1972 incurred by the owner or a person using the vehicle in which the person who suffered death or bodily injury was being carried: clause 6 (2).

16 *Porter v Motor Insurers' Bureau* [1978] 2 Lloyd's Rep 463, at 469 (per Forbes J).

17 [1978] 2 Lloyd's Rep 463.

18 Ibid, at 469.

wholly dissimilar. "Having reason to believe" is a reference to a rational process of thought. "Having a reasonable belief" is a reference to the man on the Clapham omnibus. The other thing which it does not say is "having no reason to believe that such contract was in force" There is the biggest distinction in the world it seems to me between words saying "having reason to believe no such contract was in force" and "having no reason to believe that such a contract was". The onus is thrown wholly differently in those two circumstances. And be it said that if the Motor Insurers' Bureau and the Government in drawing up this agreement had intended that this document should say or should cover the circumstances envisaged by such words as "having no reasonable belief that such a contract was in force" or indeed "having no reason to believe that such a contract was in force", it would have been the simplest thing in the world to write those words into this contract. The fact that they were not so written seems to me to indicate quite clearly that one has to construe the words as they are, "having reason to believe that no such contract was in force." What reason is advanced? What reason could Mrs Porter have, in the circumstances I have outlined, to believe that no such contract was in force? Really there is none, and [Counsel] is driven back strictly to the argument that those words do not mean what they say. They either mean "having no reason to believe that such a contract was in force", or alternatively they mean "not having a reasonable belief that such a contract was in force". I reject both those arguments. It seems to me that the words must be construed exactly as they lie. In this case in the circumstances I have outlined, Mrs Porter having made clear to Mr Addo that the car was not insured, that she required an insured driver, and he in those circumstances having volunteered to drive, she was perfectly entitled to rely on the assumption that he was an insured driver. That is going much further than she needs to, because I cannot see anywhere here anything which should have caused Mrs Porter to have reason to believe that no such contract was in force. And, of course, some such reason there would have to be in order to defeat her claim on the agreement against the Motor Insurers' Bureau.'

(vi) Employment of Agents.   Nothing in the Agreement prevents the Bureau from performing its obligations under it by agents.[19]

(2) The Notes to the Agreement

The notes are set out for the guidance of those who may have a claim on the Bureau. They are advised to make a careful study of the Agreement itself.

The principal note[20] repeats what is already stated in cl 1 of the Agreement. It says that if damages are awarded by a Court in respect of death or personal injury arising out of the use of a motor vehicle on a road in circumstances where the liability is required to be covered by insurance under Pt VI of the Road Traffic Act 1972, and such damages or any part of them, remain unpaid 7 days after the judgment becomes enforceable the Bureau will pay the unrecovered amount (including any interest awarded by the Court and costs) to the person in whose favour the judgment has been given against an assignment of the judgment debt. This applies whether the judgment debtor is a British resident or a foreign visitor.

Nothing in the Agreement affects the position at law of the parties to an action for damages arising out of the driving of a motor vehicle. The Bureau's liability under the Agreement can only arise when the plaintiff has successfully established his case against the person or persons liable in the usual manner and judgment has been given in his favour. There is nothing to exclude the acceptance of compensation by the plaintiff under a settlement negotiated between the plaintiff and the alleged person liable or the Bureau.[1]

---

19 Clause 7.
20 Note 2.
1 Note 3.

In cases where it is ascertained that there is an existence a policy issued in compliance with the Road Traffic Act 1972, the insurer concerned will normally act as the agent of the Bureau, and subject to notice of the bringing of proceedings being given before or within 7 days of their commencement, will handle claims within .the terms of the Agreement, even if the use of the vehicle at the time of the accident was outside the terms of the policy or the insurer is entitled to repudiate liability under the policy for any other reason.[2] This arrangement is without prejudice to any rights which insurers may have against their policy holders, and there is nothing in the Agreement affecting any obligations imposed on a policy holder by his policy.[3]

In cases where there is no policy, or for any reason the existence of a policy is in doubt or where there is a policy but the identity of the insurer cannot be ascertained, the victim or those acting on his behalf must notify the Bureau of the claim. It is a condition of the Bureau's liability that it should receive notification before or within 7 days after the commencement of proceedings against the alleged person liable. In practice, however, it is preferable to notify the Bureau in all cases where the name of the insurer is not speedily forthcoming.[4]

Claims arising out of the use of uninsured vehicles owned by or in possession of the Crown will in the majority of cases be outside the scope of the Bureau's liability. In such cases the approach should be made to the responsible authority in the usual way. The same benefits in respect of compensation will be afforded by the Crown to the victim in such cases as they would receive were the accident caused by a private vehicle, except where the victim is a serviceman or servicewoman whose death or injury gives rise to an entitlement to a pension or other compensation from public funds.[5]

The Bureau has no liability under this Agreement to pay compensation in respect of any person who may suffer personal injuries or death resulting from the use on a road of a vehicle, the owner or driver of which cannot be traced.[6]

b The Agreement for Compensation of Victims of Untraced Drivers[7]

The Agreement is divided into

1   the Agreement itself;
2   the notes relating to it.

(1) The Agreement itself

Duration.   The Agreement may be determined at any time by the Secretary of State for the Environment or by the Bureau by either of them giving to the other not less than 12 months' previous notice in writing.[8]

---

[2] Note 4. In the latter connection victims and those acting on their behalf are reminded of the requirements as to the giving of notice to the insurer if the protection afforded to third parties by s 149 of the Road Traffic Act 1972 is sought: ibid.
[3] Ibid.
[4] Note 4.
[5] Note 5.
[6] Note 6.
[7] The full text of the Agreement and the Notes is set out in Appendix XIII, p 484, post.
[8] Clause 24.

Scope of Agreement.   In general, the Agreement applies to any case in which an application is made to the Bureau for a payment in respect of the death of or bodily injury to any person caused by or arising out of the use of a motor vehicle on a road in Great Britain and the case is one in which the following conditions are fulfilled:

a   the applicant for the payment either

  i   is unable to trace any person rsponsible for the death or injury; or
  ii   where the death or injury was caused partly by the untraced person and partly either by an identified person or persons or by some other untraced person or persons whose master or principal can be identified, is unable to trace one of those persons;

b   the death or injury was caused in such circumstances that on the balance of probabilities the untraced person would be liable to pay damages to the applicant in respect of the death or injury[9];

c   the liability of the untraced person to pay damages to the applicant is one which was required to be covered by insurance under Pt VI of the Road Traffic Act 1972;[10]

d   the death or injury was not caused by the use of the vehicle by the untraced person as a weapon ie in a deliberate attempt to run down the deceased or injured person; and

e   the application is made in writing within 3 years from the date of the event giving rise to the death or injury.[11]

The Agreement does not apply to a case in which

1   the death or bodily injury was caused by or arose out of the use of a motor vehicle which was owned by or in the possession of the Crown[12] unless the case is one in which some other person has undertaken the responsibility for the existence of a contract of insurance under Pt VI of the Road Traffic Act 1972;

2   at the time of the accident the person suffering death or bodily injury was allowing himself to be carried in a vehicle[13] and

  i   knew or had reason to believe that the vehicle had been taken without the consent of the owner or other lawful authority, except in a case where

---

9   In *Elizabeth v Motor Insurers' Bureau* [1981] R T R 405, a van suddenly braked and a motorcyclist, who was following behind, collided with it and suffered personal injuries. The driver of the van was untraced so the motorcyclist claimed against the Bureau. The claim was referred to an arbitrator, who held that the motorcyclist had not proved on a balance of probabilities that the driver had been negligent. The motor-cyclist appealed. The Court of Appeal (Lord Denning M R, Shaw and Oliver L JJ) allowed the appeal on the ground that the arbitrator had not applied the burden of proof correctly, for the sudden braking of the van was prima facie evidence of negligence. The case was referred to another arbitrator for decision.

10   It is assumed for this purpose, in the absence of evidence to the contrary, that the vehicle was being used in circumstances in which the user was required by Pt VI of the Act to be insured or secured against third party risks: clause 1 (1).

11   Ibid.

12   A vehicle which has been unlawfully removed from that possession of the Crown is to be taken to continue in that possession whilst it is kept so removed: clause 1 (4) (a).

13   References to a person being carried in a vehicle include references to his being carried in or upon, or entering or getting on to or alighting from the vehicle: clause 1 (4) (b).

(a) he believed or had reason to believe that he had lawful authority to be carried or that he would have had the owner's consent if the owner had known of his being carried and the circumstances of his carriage; or

(b) he had learned of the circumstances of the taking of the vehicle since the commencement of the journey and it would be unreasonable to expect him to have alighted from the vehicle; or

ii being the owner[14] of or being a person using the vehicle he was using or causing the vehicle to be used without there being in force in relation to such use a policy of insurance or such security as would comply with Pt VI of the Act, knowing or having reason to believe that no such policy or security was in force.[15]

Persons entitled to apply.   An application to the Bureau for a payment in respect of the death of or bodily injury to any person may be made by

i the 'applicant' ie the person for whose benefit the payment is to be made; or

ii any solicitor acting for him; or

iii any other person whom the Bureau may be prepared to accept as acting for him.[16]

Any decision, award or payment given or made or other thing done in accordance with the Agreement to or by a person acting on behalf of the applicant or in relation to an application made by such a person must, whatever may be the age, or the circumstances affecting the capacity, of the applicant, be treated as having the same effect as if it had been done to or by, or in relation to an application made by, an applicant of full age and capacity.[17]

Assessing amount of award.   *i The General Rules.* On any application made to it in a case to which the Agreement applies the Bureau must award to the applicant a payment of an amount which is assessed in the same manner as a Court would assess the damages which the applicant would have been entitled to recover from the untraced person in respect of the death or injury if proceedings to enforce a claim for damages were successfully brought by the applicant against the untraced person.[18]

In the assessment of the amount to which the applicant is entitled in respect of loss of earnings if he has received his wages or salary in full or in part from his employer, whether or not upon an undertaking given by the applicant to reimburse his employer if he recovers damages, he is not to the extent of the amount so received to be regarded as having sustained a loss of earnings.[19]

ii Where death or injury only partly caused by untraced person. Where the death or

---

[14] 'Owner' in relation to a vehicle which is the subject of a hiring agreement or a hire-purchase agreement means the person in possession of the vehicle under that agreement: clause 1 (4) (b).

[15] Clause 1 (2). The exemption specified in sub-para 2 (b) of this clause, applies only in a case where the application is made to the Bureau in respect of a liability arising out of the use of the vehicle in which the person who suffered death or bodily injury was being carried: clause 1 (3).

[16] Clause 2 (1).

[17] Clause 2 (2).

[18] Clause 3.

[19] Clause 4. (b).

bodily injury in respect of which an application has been made to the Bureau under the Agreement was caused partly by the untraced person and partly either by an identified person, or by identified persons, or by some other untraced person or persons whose master or principal can be identified and was so caused in circumstances making the identified person or persons or any such master or principal liable to the applicant in respect of the death or injury and

a the applicant has obtained a judgment in respect of the death or injury against the identified person or against one or more of the identified persons or against any person liable as their master or principal or the master or principal of any other person which has not been satisfied in full within 3 months from the date on which the applicant became entitled to enforce it; or

b the applicant

   i has not obtained and has not been required by the Bureau to obtain a judgment in respect of the death or injury against the identified person or persons or against any person liable as the master or principal of such identified person or persons or as the master or principal of any other person; and

  ii has not received any payment by way of compensation from any such person or persons

then there are special rules for the calculation of the amount to be awarded.[20]

If the judgment mentioned above is wholly unsatisfied within the period of 3 months from the date on which the applicant became entitled to enforce it, the amount to be awarded shall be an amount equal to the untraced person's contribution to a full award.[1]

If the judgment mentioned above is satisfied in part only within the specified period of 3 months, the amount to be awarded

   i if the unsatisfied part of the judgment is less than the untraced person's contribution to a full award, shall be an amount equal to the unsatisfied part; *or*

  ii if the unsatisfied part of the judgment is equal to or greater than the amount of the untraced person's contribution to a full award, shall be an amount equal to the untraced person's contribution.[2]

If the applicant has not obtained judgment or been required by the Bureau to obtain judgment against an identified person or persons liable as the master or principal of such person, or the master or principal of any other person, and has not received any payment by way of compensation from any such person or persons, the amount to be awarded shall be an amount equal to the untraced person's contribution to a full award.[3]

---

[20] Clause 5 (1), (2), (3).
[1] Clause 5 (4) (a). 'Full award' means the amount which would have fallen to be awarded to the applicant if the untraced person had been wholly responsible for the death or injury: clause 6 (a). 'Untraced person's contribution' means the proportion of a full award which on the balance of probabilities would have been apportioned by a Court as the share to be borne by the untraced person in the responsibility for the event giving rise to the death or injury if proceedings to recover damages had been brought by the applicant against the untraced person and all other persons having a share in that responsibility: clause 6 (b).
[2] Clause 5 (4) (b).
[3] Clause 5 (4) (c).

There are detailed provisions as to the position where there is an appeal from the judgment or where proceedings are taken to set it aside.[4]

Conditions precedent to Bureau's liability.   There are three conditions precedent to the Bureau's liability:[5]

    i *Assistance.*—The applicant must give all such assistance as may reasonably be required by or on behalf of the Bureau to enable any investigation to be carried out under the Agreement, including the furnishing of statements and information either in writing, or, if so required, orally at any interview between the applicant and the person acting on behalf of the Bureau.

    ii *Steps to obtain judgment.*—If so required by the Bureau at any time before it has communicated its decision upon the application to the applicant, he must take all such steps as in the circumstances it is reasonable to require him to take to obtain judgment against any person or persons in respect of their liability to him as having caused or contributed to the death or injury or as being the master or principal of any person who has caused or contributed to that injury.

    iii *Assignment of judgment.*—If so required by the Bureau the applicant must assign to it or to its nominee any judgment obtained by him in respect of the death or injury to which his application to the Bureau relates upon such terms as will secure that the Bureau or its nominee shall be accountable to the applicant for any amount by which the aggregate of all sums received by the Bureau or its nominee under the judgment (after deducting all reasonable expenses incurred in effecting such recovery) exceeds the amount payable by the Bureau to the applicant under the Agreement.

If the Bureau requires the applicant to bring proceedings against any specified person or persons, the Bureau must indemnify him against all costs reasonably incurred by him in complying with the requirement unless the result of the proceedings materially contributes to establish that the untraced person did not cause or contribute to the death or injury.[6] Further, the applicant must, if so required by the Bureau and at its expense, furnish the Bureau with a transcript of any official shorthand note taken in the proceedings of any evidence given or judgment delivered therein.[7]

In the event of a dispute between the applicant and the Bureau as to the reasonableness of any requirement by it or whether costs were reasonably incurred, the dispute must be referred to the Secretary of State for the Environment whose decision is final.[8] But if the dispute concerns the question whether the Bureau is required to indemnify the applicant in respect of such costs, the dispute shall, in so far as it depends on the question whether the result of any proceedings which the Bureau has required him to bring against any

---

[4] Clause 5 (5).
[5] Clause 6 (1).
[6] Clause 6 (2) (a).
[7] Clause 6 (2) (b).
[8] Clause 6 (3).

specified person or persons have or have not materially contributed to establish that the untraced person did not cause or contribute to the death or injury, be referred to an arbitrator, whose decision on that question shall be final.[9]

Investigation of application. The Bureau must cause any application made to it for payment to be investigated.[10] Unless the Bureau decides that the application should be rejected because a preliminary investigation has disclosed that the case is not one to which the Agreement applies, it must cause a report to be made on the application.[11] On the basis of the report the Bureau must decide whether to make an award. If it does decide to make an award, the amount of the award must be calculated in accordance with the provisions set out above.[12]

Before coming to a decision on any application made to it under the Agreement, the Bureau is entitled to request the applicant to furnish it with a statutory declaration to be made by him setting out to the best of his knowledge, information and belief the facts and circumstances upon which the claim to an award is based, or such of those facts and circumstances as may be specified by the Bureau.[13]

Notification of decision. The Bureau must notify the decision to the applicant, and must:

a if the application is rejected because a preliminary investigation has disclosed that it is not one made in a case to which the Agreement applies, give the reasons for the rejection; or

b if the application has been fully investigated, furnish him with a statement setting out

  i the circumstances in which the death or injury occurred and the evidence bearing thereon,

  ii the circumstances relevant to the assessment of the amount to be awarded and the evidence bearing thereon, and

  iii if it refuses to make an award, the reasons for its refusal; and

c specify the way in which the amount of the award has been computed.[14]

Where the Bureau has decided that it will not indemnify the applicant against the costs of any proceedings which they have required him to bring against any specified person or persons on the ground that those proceedings have materially contributed to establish that the untraced person did not cause or contribute to the death or injury, it must give notice of that decision to the applicant.[15] The Bureau must give the reasons for the decision and must furnish the applicant with any copy of any such transcript of any evidence given or judgment delivered in those proceedings which it regards as relevant to that decision.[16]

---

9 Clause 6 (3).
10 Clause 7.
11 Ibid.
12 Ibid.
13 Clause 8.
14 Clause 9 (1).
15 Clause 9 (2).
16 Ibid.

Payment of award. On being notified by the applicant that the Bureau's award is accepted or after the expiration of the time allowed for lodging an appeal, the Bureau must pay him the amount of the award.[17] Such payment discharges the Bureau from all liability under the Agreement.[18]

Appeal. The applicant has a right of appeal against the Bureau's decision. Appeal lies to an arbitrator selected by the Secretary of State for the Environment from a panel of Queen's Counsel appointed by the Lord Chancellor.[19]

Appeal lies on the following grounds:

a that the case is one to which the Agreement applies and that his application should be fully investigated by the Bureau with a view to its deciding whether to make an award to him, and, if so, the amount of that award; or

b where the application has been fully investigated,

i that the Bureau was wrong in refusing to make an award; or

ii that the amount awarded is insufficient; or

iii in a case where a decision not to indemnify him against the costs of any proceedings which it has required him to bring has been notified, that that decision was wrong.[20]

The applicant is allowed a period of 6 weeks from the date when notice of the decision was given to him in which to give the Bureau notice that he wishes to appeal.[1] He cannot appeal where he has previously notified the Bureau that he accepts its decision.[2]

The notice of appeal must state the grounds of the appeal, and must be accompanied by an undertaking to be given by the applicant or by the person acting on his behalf that

a the applicant will accept the arbitrator's decision; and

b the arbitrator's fee will be paid to the Bureau by the applicant or by the person giving the undertaking in any case where the Bureau is entitled to reimbursement of that fee.[3]

The applicant may, when giving notice of his appeal or at any time before doing so, make comments to the Bureau on its decision, and may supply it with such particulars as he may think fit of any other evidence not contained in the written statement supplied by him to the Bureau which he considers is relevant to the application.[4]

---

[17] Clause 10.

[18] Ibid.

[19] Clause 18. Where a person is injured by a vehicle driven by an untraced driver, and the Bureau decides that the untraced driver would not be liable to pay damages to him, the injured person is not entitled to bring an action against the Bureau to have the validity of his claim decided by the Court: *Persson v London Country Buses* [1974] 1 All ER 1251, CA. (See the judgment of James LJ, ibid, at 1255).

[20] Clause 11.

[1] Ibid.

[2] Ibid.

[3] Clause 12. For the circumstances in which the Bureau is entitled to reimbursement, see clause 22, p 360, post.

[4] Clause 13.

The Bureau may, before submitting the applicant's appeal to the arbitrator, cause an investigation to be made into this further evidence, and must report to him the result of that investigation and of any change in its decision which may result from it. The applicant may, with in 6 weeks from the date on which this report was sent to him, unless he withdraws his appeal, make such comments on it as he desires to have submitted to the arbitrator.[5]

Where the Bureau receives from the applicant a notice of appeal in which the only ground of appeal is that the amount awarded is insufficient, it may, before submitting the appeal to the arbitrator, give notice to the applicant that if the appeal proceeds, it will request the arbitrator to decide whether the case is one in which the Bureau should make an award at all. If the Bureau does give such a notice, it must at the same time furnish the applicant with a statement setting out such comments as it may consider relevant to the decision which the arbitrator should come to on that question.[6]

Where the Bureau gives such a notice to the applicant, he may within 6 weeks from the date on which the notice is given make such comments to the Bureau, and supply it with such particulars of other evidence not contained in any written statement furnished by him to the Bureau as he may consider relevant to the question which the arbitrator is by the notice requested to decide.[7]

Where the Bureau receives notice of an appeal, it must, unless the appeal has been previously withdrawn, submit the appeal to an arbitrator for decision. It must send to him:

a the application made by the applicant;
b a copy of its decision as notified to the applicant; and
c a copy of all statements, declarations, notices, undertakings, comments, transcripts, particulars or reports furnished, given or sent by the applicant or any person acting for him to the Bureau or by the Bureau to the applicant or a person acting for him.[8]

If the appeal is against a decision by the Bureau rejecting an application because a preliminary investigation has disclosed that the case is not one to which the Agreement applies, the arbitrator must decide whether it does or does not apply. If he decides that it is such a case, he must remit the application to the Bureau for full investigation and for a decision by the Bureau in accordance with the provisions of the Agreement.[9]

---

[5] Clause 13.
[6] Clause 14 (1).
[7] Clause 14 (2).
[8] Clause 15. In a case where the Bureau causes an investigation to be made into further evidence submitted by the applicant, the appeal must not be sent until the expiration of six weeks from the date on which it sends him a report as to the result of that investigation: ibid. Where the only ground of appeal is that the amount awarded is insufficient, and the Bureau gives notice that if the appeal proceeds, it will request the arbitrator to decide whether the case is one in which the Bureau should make an award at all, the Bureau must not submit the appeal until the expiration of six weeks from the date on which it gave notice: ibid. If the Bureau has caused an investigation to be made into any evidence supplied by the applicant in a case where the only ground of appeal is that the amount awarded is insufficient, the appeal must not be submitted until the expiration of six weeks from the date on which the Bureau sent the applicant a report as to the result of that investigation: ibid.
[9] Clause 16 (a).

If the appeal is against a decision by the Bureau given after an application has been fully investigated by the Bureau (whether before the appeal or in consequence of its being remitted), the arbitrator must decide whether the Bureau should make an award to the applicant, and, if so, the amount which should be awarded.[10]

If the appeal relates to a dispute which has arisen between the applicant and the Bureau as to whether the Bureau is required to indemnify him in connection with proceedings to be brought by him against any specified person or persons, the arbitrator must also give his decision on that dispute.[11]

The arbitrator must decide the appeal on the documents submitted to him and no further evidence must be produced to him. But the arbitrator is entitled to ask the Bureau to make any further investigation which he considers desirable, and to submit a written report of its findings to him for his consideration. The Bureau must send a copy of any such report to the applicant. The applicant is entitled to submit written comments on it to the Bureau within 4 weeks of the date on which the copy was sent to him. The Bureau must transmit those comments to the arbitrator for his consideration.[12]

The arbitrator must notify the Bureau of his decision on any appeal, and the Bureau must forthwith send the applicant a copy of the decision.[13]

The Bureau must pay the applicant any amount which the arbitrator has decided shall be awarded. Such payment discharges the Bureau from all liability under the Agreement.[14]

Each party to the appeal must bear his own costs.[15]

The Bureau must pay to the arbitrator a fee approved by the Lord Chancellor after consultation with it. But the arbitrator may in his discretion, in any case where it appears to him that there were no reasonable grounds for the appeal, decide that his fee ought to be paid by the applicant. If the arbitrator so decides, the person giving the undertaking required above is liable to reimburse the Bureau the amount of the fee paid by it to the arbitrator except in so far as that amount is deducted by the Bureau from any amount which it is liable to pay the applicant in consequence of the arbitrator's decision.[16]

Establishment of Trust.   If in any case it appears to the Bureau that by reason of the applicant being under the age of majority or of any other circumstances affecting his capacity to manage his affairs it would be in his interest that all or some part of the amount which would otherwise be payable to him under an award made under the Agreement should be administered for him by the Family Welfare Association or by some other body or person under a trust, the Bureau may establish for that purpose a trust of the whole or part of the amount to take effect for such period and subject to such provisions as may appear to the Bureau appropriate in the circumstances of the case.[17]

---

[10] Clause 16 (b).
[11] Clause 16 (c).
[12] Clause 17.
[13] Clause 19.
[14] Clause 20.
[15] Clause 21.
[16] Clause 22.
[17] Clause 23.

(2) The Notes to the Agreement

The notes are set out for the guidance of those who may have a claim on the Bureau. They are advised to make a careful study of the Agreement itself.

II LIABILITY IN RESPECT OF INTENTIONAL CRIMINAL ACT

The Motor Insurers' Bureau will be liable to a third party injured by an uninsured driver even though that driver intentionally causes the injury.

In *Hardy v Motor Insurers' Bureau*[18] a security officer at a factory stopped a a van driven by a person employed there because it had on its windscreen a stolen Road Fund licence. The driver, who was uninsured, suddenly drove off whilst the officer had his hand on the door and his head and shoulders inside the van, and dragged him along the ground intentionally causing him serious injury. The Court of Appeal held that the Bureau was liable to indemnify the officer, even though the driver himself, if he had been insured, would not have been able to recover on the policy of insurance, because it would have been against public policy to allow him to do so. In the words of Lord Denning M R[19]:

> 'If the motorist is guilty of a crime involving a wicked and deliberate intent, and he is made to pay damages to an injured person, he is not entitled to recover on the policy. But if he does not pay the damages, then the injured third party can recover against the insurers under s 207 of the Road Traffic Act 1960[20]; for it is a liability which the motorist under the statute was required to cover. The injured third party is not affected by the disability which attached to the motorist himself. So here, the liability of [the driver] to the [officer] was a liability which [he] was required to cover by a policy of insurance, even though it arose out of his wilful and culpable criminal act. If [he] had been insured, he himself would be disabled from recovering from the insurers. But the injured third party would not be disabled from recovering from them. Seeing that he was not insured, the [Bureau] must treat the case as if he were. [It] must pay the injured third party, even though [the driver] was guilty of felony'.

III ACCIDENTS OCCURRING ONLY PARTLY ON 'ROAD'

As has been pointed out above, the Bureau is under a duty to indemnify the third party only if the injuries arise out of the use of a vehicle on a road,[1] the word 'road' being defined under s 196 of the Road Traffic Act 1972 as 'any highway and any other road to which the public has access'.[2]

The Bureau will be liable even if only part of the vehicle causing the injury is on a 'road' at the time of the accident.

Thus, in *Randall v Motor Insurers' Bureau*[3] the plaintiff, a school caretaker, had been told by his employers to stop the unauthorised tipping of rubbish at a site which had been cleared at the rear of the school. He tried to stop the driver of a lorry from doing so, but the driver drove straight at him, and he was injured when the lorry's wheel ran over his leg. This happened when part of the lorry was on private ground and the greater part of it was on a public road. The plaintiff sued the driver for damages and was awarded £1,316. The judgment was not satisfied, and the driver's insurance company repudiated liability on

---

[18] [1964] 2 All E R 742, C A.

[19] Ibid, at 746. See also the judgments of Pearson L J, ibid, at 749–750, and of Diplock L J, ibid, at 752.

[20] Now replaced by the Road Traffic Act 1972, s 149 (3)

[1] See p 299, ante.

[2] See p 310, ante.

[3] [1969] 1 All E R 21, Q B D.

the ground of non-disclosure of a material fact. So the plaintiff claimed from the Bureau. Megaw J held that the action succeeded. The fact that the rear part of the lorry, including the wheel which ran over the plaintiff's leg, was still on private property did not affect the conclusion that the lorry was then using the road. It was the use of the lorry on the road which caused the injury.

His Lordship observed:[4]

> 'It is not suggested on behalf of the plaintiff that the driveway in the school's property was a road. It is not suggested on behalf of the defendants that Hillsborough Road, including the pedestrian pavement, was not a road. There is no dispute that Mr Scott[5] incurred liability to the plaintiff in respect of bodily injury. The one and only question in dispute is: Was it bodily injury caused by, or arising out of, the use of the Dodge lorry on a road? In my judgment, the answer to that question on the facts of this case is "Yes". I have no doubt that in common sense and in the ordinary use of language the lorry was being used on a road—Hillsborough Road—at the time when the plaintiff sustained the serious injury of which he complains. If anything turns on the precise time of the incident, which, again as a matter of common sense, cannot be divided into a series of separate incidents, the determining factor is the time when the wheel of the lorry ran over the plaintiff's leg. At that time the greater part of the lorry was on the road, and the lorry as a whole was using the road. The fact that the rear part of the lorry including the wheel which ran over the plaintiff's leg, was still, just, on private property does not, in my view, affect the conclusion that the lorry was then using the road. It was the use of the lorry on the road—the fact that it was being driven further on to the road in order to drive away along the road—which caused the injury. Certainly the injury arose out of the use of the lorry on that road. The fact that the plaintiff, when he was injured, was still—though only just—on private property and that the wheel which caused the injury was still, just, on private property does not, to my mind, affect the conclusion. The plaintiff therefore succeeds in his claim.'

IV CAN BUREAU BE ADDED AS DEFENDANT?
Whether the Bureau is entitled under R SC Ord 15, r 6 (2) (b)[6] to be added as a defendant in an action brought by the third party depends on whether the third party is a victim of

a   an uninsured driver; or
b   an untraced driver.

(a) Victim of uninsured driver

Where the third party is injured by an uninsured driver, the Bureau is entitled to be added as a party to the action brought by the third party against the driver, for the Bureau has no power under the Agreement of 22 November, 1972[7] made between the Motor Insurers' Bureau and the Secretary of State for the Environment, to control the steps taken in the litigation by the third party, and otherwise would be bound to stand idly by watching him get judgment against the defendant without saying a word, whilst in the end it was the Bureau which had to foot the bill.

---

[4] [1969] 1 All E R 21 at 24, Q B D.

[5] Ie the driver of the lorry.

[6] Which states that: 'At any stage of the proceedings in any cause or matter the Court may on such terms as it thinks just and either of its own motion or on application . . . (b) order any person who ought to have been joined as a party or whose presence before the Court is necessary to ensure that all matters in dispute in the cause or matter may be effectually and completely determined and adjudicated upon be added as a party'.

[7] See pp 347-352, ante, and Appendix XIII, pp 481-484, post.

Thus, in *Gurtner v Circuit*[8]—a case decided at the time when the earlier Agreement of 17 June, 1946[9] was in force[10]—a pedestrian was knocked down by a motorist, and suffered personal injuries. He brought an action against the motorist who had gone to Canada in the meanwhile and all efforts to trace him had failed. The motorist's insurers were not known.

The Court of Appeal[11] granted the Bureau's application to be added as a defendant. Lord Denning M R stated:[12]

'It seems to me that, when two parties are in dispute in an action at law and the determination of that dispute will directly affect a third person in his legal rights or in his pocket, in that he will be bound to foot the bill, then the Court in its discretion may allow him to be added as a party on such terms as it thinks fit. By so doing the Court achieves the object of the rule. It enables all matters in dispute "to be effectually and completely determined and adjudicated upon" between all those directly concerned in the outcome. I would apply this proposition to the present case. If the Motor Insurers' Bureau are not allowed to come in as a defendant, what will happen? The order for substituted service will go unchallenged. The service on the defendant will be good, even though he knows nothing of the proceedings. He will not enter an appearance. The plaintiff will sign judgment in default of appearance. The judgment will be for damages to be assessed. The Master will assess the damages with no-one to oppose. The judgment will be completed for the ascertained sum. The defendant will not pay it. Then the plaintiff will be able to come down on the Motor Insurers' Bureau and call on them to pay because they have made a solemn agreement that they will pay . . . It is thus apparent that the Motor Insurers' Bureau are vitally concerned in the outcome of the action. They are directly affected, not only in their legal rights, but also in their pocket. They ought to be allowed to come in as defendants. It would be most unjust if they were bound to stand idly by watching the plaintiff get judgment against the defendant without saying a word when they are the people who have to foot the bill.'

(b) Victim of untraced driver

Where the third party is injured by an untraced driver and the Motor Insurers' Bureau acting under Clause 6 (1) (b)[13] of the Agreement[14] made with the Secretary of State for the Environment on 22 November, 1972, requests him to take proceedings against an identified person, the Bureau is not entitled under R S C Ord 15, r 6 (2) (b) to be added as a party for such an addition is not 'necessary' to ensure that all matters in dispute in the action may be effectually and completely determined and adjudicated upon.[15]

---

8 [1968] 2 QB 587, [1968] 1 All E R 328, C A, disapproving *Fire Auto and Marine Insurance Co Ltd v Greene* [1964] 2 QB 687, [1964] 2 All E R 761, QB, where John Stephenson J refused to allow the Bureau to be added as a defendant in a case where an insurance company sought to avoid liability under the Road Traffic Act 1960, s 207 (3) on the ground that the insured had failed to disclose a material fact. The learned Judge considered that all the matters in dispute in the action between the parties could be effectually and completely determined and adjudicated upon without the addition of the Bureau as a defendant. He suggested, however (ibid, at 768), that the law should be changed so that the Bureau would be given a right in every action under s 207 (3) to be added as a defendant.

9 See p 000, ante.

10 No substantial change in the relevant part of the Agreement of 1946 has been made in the Agreement of 22 November, 1972 which has now replaced it.

11 Lord Denning M R, Diplock and Salmon L JJ.

12 [1968] 1 All E R 328 at 332.

13 See p 356, ante, and Appendix XIII, p 489, post.

14 See pp 352-361, ante, and Appendix XIII, pp 484-496, post.

15 *White v London Transport Executive and Motor Insurers' Bureau* [1971] 2 QB 721, [1971] 3 All E R 1, C A.

Thus, in *White v London Transport Executive and Motor Insurers' Bureau*[16] the plaintiff was travelling in a bus owned by the first defendant. It braked violently when a van cut in front of it and she was injured. The van driver was never traced. The first defendant contended that the van driver was solely to blame. Acting under clause 6 (1) (b) of the Agreement of 21 April 1969[17] the Motor Insurers' Bureau required the plaintiff to take all reasonable steps to obtain judgment against the first defendant and requested her to bring an action. In the action which she brought against the first defendant, the Bureau wanted to allege that the plaintiff's claim for damages was excessive, and that she was guilty of contributory negligence. The Bureau now applied to be added as a defendant under RSC Ord 15, r 6 (2) (b). The Court of Appeal[18] refused to grant the application for the adding of the Bureau as a defendant was not necessary to ensure that all matters in dispute in the cause might be effectually and completely determined. The Bureau was sufficiently protected in that under clause 6 (1) (b) of the Agreement it had requested the plaintiff to take all such steps as were necessary to get judgment against an identified person. All matters would then be properly and fully investigated.

Lord Denning M R, observed:[19]

> 'It seems to me that if the Bureau were allowed to come into the action, it would be open to their Counsel on the one hand to cross-examine Mrs White about contributory negligence and damages: and then, on the other hand, to cross-examine London Transport Executive's witnesses to show that they were wholly or in part to blame. Such an exceptional course might be permissible if it were *necessary* to ensure that all the matters in dispute could be effectually determined. But I do not see that it is necessary in the least. In my judgment, seeing that Mrs White is bringing the action on the discretion of the Bureau, she will be bound to pursue the action with vigilance and skill against London Transport Executive, doing all she can to make them liable in part or whole. So far as London Transport Executive is concerned, they will do their best to defend the action by disputing negligence, by alleging contributory negligence, and questioning the damages. So all the matters will be properly and fully investigated without the necessity of joining the Bureau. Accordingly I doubt whether this joinder is "necessary" within the opening words of RSC Ord 15, r 6 (2) (b).'

Edmund Davies L J, emphasised[20] the fact that under the Agreement of 1946[1] no powers of control over the steps taken in litigation by the third party were conferred on the Bureau, whereas the Agreement of 1969 contained quite different terms and conferred on the Bureau considerable powers of control; eg it could insist upon the applicant giving full information regarding the basis of his claim against the proposed defendant,[2] and could call on him to furnish a statutory declaration for that purpose.[3]

---

16 [1971] 2 Lloyd's Rep 256, C A.
17 See now clause 6 (1) (b) of the Agreement of 22 November 1972.
18 Lord Denning M R, Edmund Davies and Stamp L J J.
19 [1971] 2 Lloyd's Rep 256 at 259. See also the judgment of Edmund Davies L J, ibid at 259, and that of Stamp L J, ibid, at 260.
1 See p 347, ante. The Agreement of 1946 is now superseded by that of 1972. See p 347, ante.
2 See clause 6 of the Agreement of 1969, which is now clause 6 of the Agreement of 1972. See p 356, ante, and Appendix XIII, p 489, post.
3 See clause 8 of the Agreement of 1969, which is now clause 8 of the Agreement of 1972. See p 357, ante, and Appendix XIII, p 490, post.

Lord Denning M R,[4] and Stamp L J,[5] also held that even if the adding of the Bureau as a party was 'necessary', the Court would not have exercised its discretion to make such an order. Edmund Davies L J expressed no opinion on this point.

V PRIVITY OF CONTRACT

The Agreements of 1972 are on the face of them contracts between the Secretary of State for the Environment and the Motor Insurers' Bureau, and are not enforceable by a third party. When an action has been brought against it, the Bureau has not taken the point that the third party was not privy to the Agreements,[6] and has said that it will never do so.[7] In one case Lord Denning M R said that he hoped that the point never would be taken.[8] The Court has not raised any objection independently.[9]

---

[4] [1971] 2 Lloyd's Rep 256 at 259.

[5] Ibid, at 260.

[6] Eg *Lees v Motor Insurer's Bureau* [1952] 2 All E R 511; *Buchanan v Motor Insurers' Bureau* [1955] 1 All ER 607, [1955] 1 WLR 488; *Coward v Motor Insurers' Bureau* [1963] 1 QB 259, [1962] 1 All ER 531; *Hardy v Motor Insurers' Bureau* [1964] 2 QB 745, [1964] 2 All ER 742, CA; *Randall v Motor Insurers' Bureau* [1969] 1 All ER 21, [1968] 1 WLR 1900; *Albert v Motor Insurers' Bureau* [1971] 2 All ER 1345, HL; *Motor Insurers' Bureau v Meanen* [1971] 2 All ER 1372, HL.

[7] *Albert v Motor Insurers' Bureau,* supra, at 1354 (per Viscount Dilhorne).

[8] *Hardy v Motor Insurers' Bureau,* supra, at 757, and 744.

[9] See *Coward v Motor Insurers' Bureau,* supra at 265, and 533.

APPENDICES

PART I—FIRE INSURANCE

Appendix I

SPECIMEN PROPOSAL FORMS IN RESPECT OF FIRE
INSURANCE ISSUED BY INSURANCE COMPANIES

The detailed contents of proposal forms in respect of fire insurance vary from
company to company.

With the kind permission of the Sun Alliance & London Insurance Group
some of the proposal forms in current use issued by that company are reproduced in this Appendix.

These are:

    A Fire Insurance.[1]
    B Motor Trade (Internal Risks) Insurance.[2]
    C Consequential Loss Insurance.[3]

---

[1] See p 370.
[2] See p 371, post.
[3] See p 373, post.

A FIRE INSURANCE

Proposal for Fire Insurance

All insurances are underwritten for the Group by Sun Alliance and London Insurance Limited (incorporated in England)

Proposer
Full name
(Block letters, please)   Tel. No.

Address
(Block letters, please)   Postcode

Occupation

Property to be insured
Situation:

Occupation:

	Predominant construction		Sums to be insured (Please see note overleaf)		
	Walls	Roof	Buildings (see Note 1)	Business Fixtures, Fittings, Plant and Machinery (see Note 2)	Stock and Materials in Trade (see Note 3)
			Subject to Average	Subject to Average	Subject to Average
a) Main building or range			£	£	£
b) Other buildings – please list:			£	£	£
			£	£	£
			£	£	£
			£	£	£

c) Rent (years)   £

d) Other items – please specify – Subject to Average: £

Total sum to be insured   £

Notes:
1 The insurance on buildings includes landlord's fixtures and fittings, fences, walls and gates. The sum insured should be sufficient to include Architects' and Surveyors' fees, the cost of removal of debris and any additional costs which arise in complying with the requirements of Public or Local Authorities.
2 Business Fixtures etc. includes utensils in trade but excludes landlord's fixtures and fittings.
3 The sum insured on Stock etc. should include the value of goods in trust or on commission for which you are responsible.
4 Unless specifically mentioned, the following are not insured – money, securities, stamps, documents, manuscripts, business books, computer systems records, patterns, moulds, models, plans, designs or explosives.

1 Extensions of cover ·
a) Is the policy to be extended to include the following perils?
(Please tick if required)

Aircraft ☐	Earthquake ☐
Explosion ☐	Storm and flood ☐
Riot ☐	Burst water apparatus ☐
Malicious damage ☐	Impact ☐

b) If so, are the premises specially
exposed to any of these additional perils?

2 In respect of the perils to which this proposal relates, at this
or any other address at which you have or had an interest
a) have you suffered loss or damage within the last 10 years, whether insured or not?

b) have you been insured previously? If so,
state the name of all the Insurers concerned.

c) has any Company or Underwriter at any time declined
a proposal from you or refused to renew your policy
or asked you to place your insurance elsewhere?

d) has any Company or Underwriter at any time
imposed amended terms for renewal of your policy?

N.B. If the answer to
any of these questions
is 'Yes', please give
details on a separate
sheet.

3 May we send you information regarding Loss of Profits insurance?

Signature   Date

(Signing this form does not bind you to complete the insurance)

Sun Alliance Insurance Group

Sun Alliance and London Insurance Limited is registered in England No. 638918. Registered Office: 1 Bartholomew Lane London EC2N 2AB
311001F (5-80)

B MOTOR TRADE (INTERNAL RISKS) INSURANCE

Proposal for Motor Trade (Internal Risks) Insurance

Please reply to:
66 Cheapside London EC2V 6BH
Telephone 01-236 2366

Before completing this proposal please note specially that failure to disclose all material information i.e. information which is likely to influence the acceptance of the risk and the terms applied could invalidate the insurance. If you are in any doubt as to whether any information is material, it should be disclosed.

Use **block capitals** throughout unless the question requires a box to be ticked.

1 Full name

Date of birth

Tel. No.

2 Address

Date of construction of premises

Number and Street

Town

County

Postcode

3 Address of your premises
(if not as in 2 above or more than one premises to be insured).

Date of construction of premises

Number and Street

Town

County

Postcode

4 In which of the following vehicle activities are you engaged?

i) Sale of vehicles ☐

ii) Sale of vehicle parts, accessories, etc ☐

iii) Repairs, servicing and maintenance ☐

iv) Vehicle testing ☐

v) Do-It-Yourself facilities ☐

vi) Car washing facilities ☐

vii) Sales of high performance/sports/prestige cars ☐

viii) Vehicle body building ☐

ix) Heavy commercial vehicle repairs ☐

x) Public service vehicle repairs ☐

xi) Exhaust or tyre replacement services ☐

xii) Preparation of vehicles for rallies or competitions ☐

xiii) Any other activities (give details) ☐

Note If your activities include any of items vii) to xiii) inclusive please indicate any from which you derive more than 20% of your annual turnover and state percentage

5 Do you have any machinery or plant (other than compressors, welders, fuel pumps and car hoists not exceeding 6 ft (1.8 metres) lift)? Yes ☐ No ☐

If 'Yes' give details.

6 State the maximum number of persons (including partners, directors, employees and self-employed sub-contractors) who will be engaged in the business during the coming year

Of the above number state how many have had less than 2 years experience in the trade (persons engaged solely in clerical or petrol filling duties should not be counted for this purpose).

7 Have any accidents, losses or claims (whether covered by insurance or not) occurred during the past 4 years in connection with any of the risks described in the prospectus (including any optional extensions of cover which you wish to effect)? Yes ☐ No ☐

If 'Yes' give details.

8 i) Has any Insurer during the past four years refused you insurance at normal rates and terms for any of the risks described in the prospectus (including optional extensions)? Yes ☐ No ☐

If 'Yes' give details.

ii) Indicate name of present Insurer and the number of years No Claim Discount to which you are entitled.

Years

(Enclose the renewal notice from your present Insurer as evidence of your No Claim Discount)

9 Do you require quotations for any of the following optional extensions described in the prospectus?
If 'Yes' answer the questions appearing against those selected

i)   Fire and Explosion (Vehicles)   Yes☐ No☐   a) Do you wish to include your own vehicles
(including stock vehicles)?   Yes☐ No☐

b) State maximum total value of all vehicles to be
insured (Sum Insured)   £

---

ii) a) Liability for repair, servicing or maintenance
or sale of parts   Yes☐ No☐

b) Liability for sale or supply of vehicles   Yes☐ No☐   State estimated total number of vehicles to be sold
in the coming year

c) Liability for sale or supply of other goods   Yes☐ No☐   Describe the nature of the goods and state percentage
of annual turnover derived from this aspect of your
business

---

iii) Defective title   Yes☐ No☐   a) Will you keep accurate records of all purchase/
part exchange transactions for secondhand vehicles?   Yes☐ No☐

b) Will you always refer to HP Information Ltd, before
acquiring a secondhand vehicle?   Yes☐ No☐

c) Will you always pay for secondhand vehicles by
cheque?   Yes☐ No☐

d) State estimated total number of secondhand
vehicles to be acquired in the coming year

---

iv) Vehicles held under 'Sale or Return' Agreement   Yes☐ No☐   a) Will the vehicles be kept in a locked building when
the premises are closed for business?   Yes☐ No☐

b) State estimated maximum number of vehicles to be
held at any one time

---

v) Loss of use – customers' vehicles   Yes☐ No☐   If 'Yes', tick box for limit required

£10☐   £15☐   £20☐   £25☐   per day

---

vi) Customers' property   Yes☐ No☐   If 'Yes', tick box for limit required

£100☐   £200☐   £300☐

---

vii) Theft and malicious damage   Yes☐ No☐   State maximum number of vehicles which may be
a) left in the open

b) kept in a locked building

when the premises are closed for business

---

10 If our quotation is acceptable, when is the insurance to commence?

Declaration

I/We declare that to the best of my/our knowledge and belief the statements made by me/us or on my/our behalf are true and complete and that
I/we have not withheld any information material to this proposal. I/We accept full responsibility for statements made on my/our behalf.

I/We agree that this proposal and declaration shall be the basis of the contract between me/us and Sun Alliance and London Insurance Limited and
I/we agree to be bound by the terms of the Policy.

Signature :   Date :

If you did not complete the answers to the above questions **yourself** please also sign the following declaration

I have read the above questions and answers and accept full responsibility therefor

Signature :   Date :

A specimen policy form is available on request

Sun Alliance Insurance Group

116501 (1-79)   Sun Alliance and London Insurance Limited is registered in England No. 638918. Registered Office: 1 Bartholomew Lane London EC2N 2AB

C CONSEQUENTIAL LOSS INSURANCE

Proposal for Consequential Loss Insurance

Maximum indemnity period _____ months

Gross Profit computed as follows:—

Annual turnover (less discounts allowed and bad debts)		£
Closing stock		£
		£

Less:—

Opening stock	£	
Stock purchased (less discounts received)	£	
Payroll/Wages (if insured by a separate 'dual basis' item – see below) £		
List any other items which vary directly with turnover		
	£	
	£	£
Annual Gross Profit	£	
Margin for expansion and inflation	£	
	£	
Proportionate increase if Maximum Indemnity Period exceeds 12 months	£	
Sum Insured	£	

Employees' remuneration (including National Insurance contributions, bonuses, overtime, holiday pay and all other payments pertaining to remuneration)

  a) Full payroll: Annual payroll £ _____ included in Gross Profit above

  b) 'Dual Basis' Payroll/Wages (delete as appropriate):

Initial period of full cover _____ weeks and percentage thereafter _____ per cent. required

Annual payroll/wage roll	£
Margin for expansion and inflation	£
	£
Proportionate increase if Maximum Indemnity Period exceeds 12 months	£
Sum Insured	£

1 Full name(s)
(Block letters, please) _____ Tel. No. _____

2 Full address
(Block letters, please) _____ Postal Code _____

3 Nature of business _____

4 Situation of premises _____

5 Please refer to **Additional perils** and delete any of the following perils **not** required

Explosion	Earthquake	Riot	Storm and flood	Impact
Aircraft	Sprinkler leakage	Malicious damage	Burst pipes	

6 Do you wish to discuss an extension of the cover to include collapse, explosion or overheating of steam plant?

7 The insurance does not include losses sustained through failure to collect outstanding debts due to inability to trace them following destruction of your business records. A Book Debts policy is available to cover this contingency. Do you require a quotation?   Yes/No

continued over

8 Which **extensions** would you like to discuss?
Please mark those which interest you   ☐ a   ☐ b   ☐ c   ☐ d   ☐ e   ☐ f   ☐ g

9 When does your financial year end?

10 Name and address
of your professional accountants

11 Are your boilers and economisers
insured against explosion?

12 Give Policy number and name of Insurers
covering the premises against fire

13 Are there any other insurances on the same
property for Consequential Loss?

If so, give details

14 Do you occupy any business premises
not included in this proposal?

15 In respect of any of the perils to which this proposal relates, have you previously
a) submitted a proposal to any Company or Underwriter?

b) suffered any loss or damage at these or other premises or made any
claim in respect of property in which you had an interest?

If so, give details

16 Has any Company or Underwriter at any time in respect of any of your insurances at these
or other premises declined to renew a policy or imposed amended terms for renewal?

If so, give details

Signature   Date

(Signing this form does not bind you to complete the insurance)

Sun Alliance Insurance Group

Sun Alliance and London Insurance Limited is registered in England No. 638918. Registered Office: 1 Bartholomew Lane London EC2N 2AB

312008C (2-81)

Appendix II

SPECIMEN FIRE INSURANCE POLICIES ISSUED BY
INSURANCE COMPANIES

The detailed contents of fire insurance policies vary from company to company.

With the kind permission of the Guardian Royal Exchange Assurance Group some of the policies in current use issued by that company are reproduced in this Appendix

These are:

A   Fire policy.
B   Collective fire policy.
C   Sprinkler Leakage policy.

A FIRE POLICY

**Guardian
Royal Exchange
Assurance**

FIRE INSURANCE POLICY

IN CONSIDERATION of the Insured named in the Schedule hereto paying to the Guardian Royal Exchange Assurance Limited (hereinafter called the Company) the First Premium mentioned in the said Schedule.

The Company agrees (subject to the Conditions contained herein or endorsed or otherwise expressed hereon which Conditions shall so far as the nature of them respectively will permit be deemed to be conditions precedent to the right of the Insured to recover hereunder) that if after payment of the premium the Property insured described in the said Schedule, or any part of such property, be destroyed or damaged by

(1)   Fire (whether resulting from explosion or otherwise) not occasioned by or happening through
- *(a)*   its own spontaneous fermentation or heating or its undergoing any process involving the application of heat,
- *(b)*   earthquake, subterranean fire, riot, civil commotion, war, invasion, act of foreign enemy, hostilities (whether war be declared or not), civil war, rebellion, revolution, insurrection or military or usurped power;

(2)   Lightning;

(3)   Explosion, not occasioned by or happening through any of the perils specified in 1 *(b)* above,
- *(a)*   of boilers used for domestic purposes only,
- *(b)*   in a building not being part of any gas works, of gas used for domestic purposes or used for lighting or heating the building;

at any time before 4 o'clock in the afternoon of the last day of the period of insurance named in the said Schedule or of any subsequent period in respect of which the Insured shall have paid and the Company shall have accepted the premium required for the renewal of this Policy, the Company will pay to the Insured the value of the property at the time of the happening of its destruction or the amount of such damage or at its option reinstate or replace such property or any part thereof.

Provided that the liability of the Company shall in no case exceed in respect of each item the sum expressed in the said Schedule to be insured thereon or in the whole the total sum insured hereby or such other sum or sums as may be substituted therefor by memorandum hereon or attached hereto signed by or on behalf of the Company.

On behalf of the Company

General Manager

ZF4 (3/80)

CONDITIONS

1 Misdescription

This Policy shall be voidable in the event of misrepresentation, misdescription or non-disclosure in any material particular.

2 Alteration

This Policy shall be avoided with respect to any item thereof in regard to which there be any alteration after the commencement of this insurance
(1) by removal
or (2) whereby the risk of destruction or damage is increased
or (3) whereby the Insured's interest ceases except by Will or operation of law,
unless such alteration be admitted by memorandum signed by or on behalf of the Company.

3 Exclusions

This Policy does not cover
(a) Destruction or damage by explosion (whether the explosion be occasioned by fire or otherwise), except as stated on the face of this Policy.
(b) Loss or destruction of or damage to any property whatsoever or any loss or expense whatsoever resulting or arising therefrom or any consequential loss directly or indirectly caused by or contributed to by or arising from
(i) ionising radiations or contamination by radioactivity from any nuclear fuel or from any nuclear waste from the combustion of nuclear fuel
(ii) the radioactive, toxic, explosive or other hazardous properties of any explosive nuclear assembly or nuclear component thereof.
(c) Goods held in trust or on commission, money, securities, stamps, documents, manuscripts, computer systems records, business books, patterns, models, moulds, plans, designs, explosives, unless specially mentioned as insured by this Policy.
(d) Destruction of or damage to property which, at the time of the happening of such destruction or damage, is insured by, or would, but for the existence of this Policy, be insured by any Marine Policy or Policies, except in respect of any excess beyond the amount which would have been payable under the Marine Policy or Policies had this Insurance not been effected.
(e) loss or destruction of or damage to any property in NORTHERN IRELAND or loss resulting therefrom caused by or happening through or in consequence of—
(i) civil commotion
(ii) any unlawful, wanton or malicious act committed maliciously by a person or persons acting on behalf of or in connection with any unlawful association.
For the purpose of this condition:—
"Unlawful Association" means any organisation which is engaged in terrorism and includes an organisation which at any relevant time is a proscribed organisation within the meaning of the Northern Ireland (Emergency Provisions) Act, 1973. "Terrorism" means the use of violence for political ends and includes any use of violence for the purpose of putting the public or any section of the public in fear.
In any action, suit or other proceedings where the Company alleges that by reason of the provisions of this condition any loss, destruction or damage is not covered by this policy the burden of proving that such loss, destruction or damage is covered shall be upon the Insured.

4 Claims

On the happening of any destruction or damage the Insured shall forthwith give notice thereof in writing to the Company and shall within 30 days after such destruction or damage, or such further time as the Company may in writing allow, at his own expense deliver to the Company a claim in writing containing as particular an account as may be reasonably practicable of the several articles or portions of property destroyed or damaged and of the amount of destruction or damage thereto respectively having regard to their value at the time of the destruction or damage together with details of any other Insurances on any property hereby insured. The Insured shall also give to the Company all such proofs and information with respect to the claim as may reasonably be required together with (if demanded) a statutory declaration of the truth of the claim and of any matters connected therewith. No claim under this Policy shall be payable unless the terms of this condition have been complied with.'

5 Fraud

If the claim be in any respect fraudulent or if any fraudulent means or devices be used by the Insured or anyone acting on his behalf to obtain any benefit under this Policy or if any destruction or damage be occasioned by the wilful act or with the connivance of the Insured all benefit under this Policy shall be forfeited.

6 Reinstatement

If the Company elects or becomes bound to reinstate or replace any property the Insured shall at his own expense produce and give to the Company all such plans, documents, books and information as the Company may reasonably require. The Company shall not be bound to reinstate exactly or completely, but only as circumstances permit and in reasonably sufficient manner and shall not in any case be bound to expend in respect of any one of the items insured more than the sum insured thereon.

7 Company's rights after a fire

On the happening of any destruction or damage in respect of which a claim is or may be made under this Policy the Company and every person authorised by the Company may, without thereby incurring any liability, and without diminishing the right of the Company to rely upon any conditions of this Policy, enter, take or keep possession of the building or premises where the destruction or damage has happened, and may take possession of or require to be delivered to them any of the property hereby insured and may keep possession of and deal with such property for all reasonable purposes and in any reasonable manner. This Condition shall be evidence of the leave and licence of the Insured to the Company so to do. If the Insured or anyone acting on his behalf shall not comply with the requirements of the Company or shall hinder or obstruct the Company in doing any of the above-mentioned acts, then all benefit under this Policy shall be forfeited. The Insured shall not in any case be entitled to abandon any property to the Company whether taken possession of by the Company or not.

8 Contribution and average

If at the time of any destruction of or damage to any property hereby insured there be any other Insurance effected by or on behalf of the Insured covering any of the property destroyed or damaged, the liability of the Company hereunder shall be limited to its rateable proportion of such destruction or damage.
If any such other Insurance shall be subject to any Condition of Average this Policy, if not already subject to any Condition of Average, shall be subject to Average in like manner.
If any other Insurance effected by or on behalf of the Insured is expressed to cover any of the property hereby insured, but is subject to any provision whereby it is excluded from ranking concurrently with this Policy either in whole or in part or from contributing ratably to the destruction or damage, the liability of the Company hereunder shall be limited to such proportion of the destruction or damage as the sum hereby insured bears to the value of the property.

9 Subrogation

Any claimant under this Policy shall at the request and at the expense of the Company do and concur in doing and permit to be done all such acts and things as may be necessary or reasonably required by the Company for the purpose of enforcing any rights and remedies, or of obtaining relief or indemnity from other parties to which the Company shall be or would become entitled or subrogated upon its paying for or making good any destruction or damage under this Policy, whether such acts and things shall be or become necessary or required before or after his indemnification by the Company.

10 Warranties

Every Warranty to which the property insured or any item thereof is, or may be, made subject, shall from the time the Warranty attaches apply and continue to be in force during the whole currency of this Policy, and non-compliance with any such Warranty, whether it increases the risk or not shall be a bar to any claim in respect of such property or item; provided that whenever this Policy is renewed a claim in respect of destruction or damage occurring during the renewal period shall not be barred by reason of a Warranty not having been complied with at any time before the commencement of such period.

11 Arbitration

If any difference shall arise as to the amount to be paid under this Policy (liability being otherwise admitted) such difference shall be referred to an Arbitrator to be appointed by the parties in accordance with the Statutory Provisions in that behalf for the time being in force. Where any difference is by this Condition to be referred to arbitration the making of an Award shall be a condition precedent to any right of action against the Company.

SCHEDULE

Branch   Policy No.

Agent   No.

THE INSURED	
ADDRESS	

THE PERIOD OF INSURANCE	
From •	to at four o'clock in the afternoon

Cancelled Policy No. (if any)	Renewal Date
FIRST PREMIUM £	ANNUAL PREMIUM £

Policy pages attached

The Property Insured	Sum Insured thereon

The sum insured by each item of this policy covering property is declared to be separately but similarly subject to Average.

PRO RATA CONDITION OF AVERAGE

Whenever a sum insured is declared to be subject to Average, if the property covered thereby shall at the breaking out of any fire or at the commencement of any destruction of or damage to such property by any other peril hereby insured against be collectively of greater value than such sum insured, then the Insured shall be considered as being his own insurer for the difference and shall bear a ratable share of the loss accordingly.

Total Sum Insured

Examined ....

Authorised ....

ZF5 (UK & X) (4/76)

B COLLECTIVE FIRE POLICY

POLICY OF INSURANCE

This policy should be read carefully and its terms noted

IN CONSIDERATION of the Insured named in the schedule hereto paying the premium mentioned in the said schedule to the Insurers named herein or to Insurers whose names are, with the consent of the Insured, substituted therefor by memorandum hereon or attached hereto signed by or on behalf of all the Insurers concerned (such Insurers or substituted Insurers, as the case may be, being hereinafter called "the Insurers")

THE INSURERS SEVERALLY AGREE each for the proportion set against its name (subject to the conditions contained herein or endorsed or otherwise expressed hereon which conditions shall so far as the nature of them respectively will permit be deemed to be conditions precedent to the right of the Insured to recover hereunder) that if after payment of the premium the property insured described in the said schedule or any part of such property be destroyed or damaged by

(1)   Fire (whether resulting from explosion or otherwise) not occasioned by or happening through

     (a)   its own spontaneous fermentation or heating or its undergoing any process involving the application of heat,

     (b)   earthquake, subterranean fire, riot, civil commotion, war, invasion, act of foreign enemy, hostilities (whether war be declared or not), civil war, rebellion, revolution, insurrection or military or usurped power;

(2)   Lightning;

(3)   Explosion, not occasioned by or happening through any of the perils specified in 1 (b) above,

     (i)   of boilers used for domestic purposes only,

     (ii)   in a building not being part of any gas works, of gas used for domestic purposes or used for lighting or heating the building;

at any time before 4 o'clock in the afternoon of the last day of the period of insurance named in the said schedule or of any subsequent period in respect of which the Insured shall have paid and the Insurers shall have accepted the premium required for the renewal of this policy, the Insurers will pay to the Insured the value of the property at the time of the happening of its destruction or the amount of such damage or the Insurers at their option will reinstate or replace such property or any part thereof

PROVIDED THAT—

(1)   The liability of the Insurers shall in no case exceed in respect of each item the sum expressed in the said schedule to be insured thereon or in the whole the total sum insured hereby, or such other sum or sums as may be substituted therefor by memorandum hereon or attached hereto signed by or on behalf of the Insurers

(2)   The liability of each of the Insurers individually in respect of such destruction or damage shall be limited to the proportion set against its name or such other proportion as may be substituted therefor by memorandum hereon or attached hereto signed by or on behalf of the Insurers.

IN WITNESS WHEREOF I being a representative of the Leading Office which is duly authorised by the Insurers have hereunto subscribed my name on their behalf

The Insurers	Proportion of the Specification	Reference Numbers
(Leading Office)		

Policy No.

THE SCHEDULE

THE INSURED

THE PROPERTY INSURED   As detailed in the specification attached hereto which is
                              declared to be incorporated in and to form part of this policy.

TOTAL SPECIFICATION SUM INSURED £

THE SUM INSURED HEREBY   £

                              being   % of the total specification sum insured

PERIOD OF INSURANCE   from
                                to

                              at four o'clock in the afternoon

RENEWAL DATE

FIRST PREMIUM   £

ANNUAL PREMIUM   £

CONDITIONS

1.   This policy shall be voidable in the event of misrepresentation, misdescription or non-disclosure in any material particular.

2.   This policy shall be avoided with respect to any item thereof in regard to which there be any alteration after the commencement of this insurance
      (1)   by removal
or   (2)   whereby the risk of destruction or damage is increased
or   (3)   whereby the Insured's interest ceases except by will or operation of law
      unless such alteration be admitted by memorandum signed by or on behalf of the Insurers.

3.   This policy does not cover:—
      (a)   Destruction or damage by explosion (whether the explosion be occasioned by fire or otherwise) } except as stated on the face of this policy
      (b)   Loss or destruction of or damage to any property whatsoever or any loss or expense whatsoever resulting or arising therefrom or any consequential loss directly or indirectly caused by or contributed to by or arising from—
             (i)   ionising radiations or contamination by radioactivity from any nuclear fuel or from any nuclear waste from the combustion of nuclear fuel
             (ii)   the radioactive, toxic, explosive or other hazardous properties of any explosive nuclear assembly or nuclear component thereof.
      (c)   Goods held in trust or on commission, money, securities, stamps, documents, manuscripts, business books, computer systems records, patterns, models, moulds, plans, designs, explosives } unless specially mentioned as insured by this policy.
      (d)   Destruction of or damage to property which, at the time of the happening of such destruction or damage, is insured by, or would, but for the existence of this policy, be insured by any marine policy or policies, except in respect of any excess beyond the amount which would have been payable under the marine policy or policies had this insurance not been effected.
      (e)   loss or destruction of or damage to any property in NORTHERN IRELAND or loss resulting therefrom caused by or happening through or in consequence of—
             (i)   civil commotion
             (ii)   any unlawful, wanton or malicious act committed maliciously by a person or persons acting on behalf of or in connection with any unlawful association.
             For the purpose of this condition:—
             "Unlawful Association" means any organisation which is engaged in terrorism and includes an organisation which at any relevant time is a proscribed organisation within the meaning of the Northern Ireland (Emergency Provisions) Act, 1973.
             "Terrorism" means the use of violence for political ends and includes any use of violence for the purpose of putting the public or any section of the public in fear.
             In any action, suit or other proceedings where the Insurers allege that by reason of the provisions of this condition any loss, destruction or damage is not covered by this policy the burden of proving that such loss, destruction or damage is covered shall be upon the Insured.

4.   On the happening of any destruction or damage the Insured shall forthwith give notice thereof in writing to the first named of the Insurers and shall within 30 days after such destruction or damage, or such further time as the Insurers may in writing allow, at his own expense deliver to the Insurers a claim in writing containing as particular an account as may be reasonably practicable of the several articles or portions of property destroyed or damaged and of the amount of destruction or damage thereto respectively having regard to their value at the time of the destruction or damage together with details of any other insurances on any property hereby insured. The Insured shall also give to the Insurers all such proofs and information with respect to the claim as may reasonably be required together with (if demanded) a statutory declaration of the truth of the claim and of any matters connected therewith. No claim under this policy shall be payable unless the terms of this condition have been complied with.

5.   If the claim be in any respect fraudulent or if any fraudulent means or devices be used by the Insured or anyone acting on his behalf to obtain any benefit under this policy or if any destruction or damage be occasioned by the wilful act or with the connivance of the Insured all benefit under this policy shall be forfeited.

6.   If the Insurers elect or become bound to reinstate or replace any property the Insured shall at his own expense produce and give to the Insurers all such plans, documents, books, and information as the Insurers may reasonably require. The Insurers shall not be bound to reinstate exactly or completely, but only as circumstances permit and in reasonably sufficient manner and shall not in any case be bound to expend in respect of any one of the items insured more than the sum insured thereon.

7.   On the happening of any destruction or damage in respect of which a claim is or may be made under this policy the Insurers and every person authorised by the Insurers may, without thereby incurring any liability, and without diminishing the right of the Insurers to rely upon any conditions of this policy, enter, take or keep possession of the building or premises where the destruction or damage has happened and may take possession of or require to be delivered to them any of the property hereby insured and may keep possession of and deal with such property for all reasonable purposes and in any reasonable manner. This condition shall be evidence of the leave and licence of the Insured to the Insurers so to do. If the Insured or anyone acting on his behalf shall not comply with the requirements of the Insurers or shall hinder or obstruct the Insurers in doing any of the above-mentioned acts, then all benefit under this policy shall be forfeited. The Insured shall not in any case be entitled to abandon any property to the Insurers whether taken possession of by the Insurers or not.

8.   If at the time of any destruction of or damage to any property hereby insured there be any other insurance effected by or on behalf of the Insured covering any of the property destroyed or damaged the liability of each of the Insurers hereunder shall be limited to its rateable proportion of such destruction or damage.
      If any such other insurance shall be subject to any condition of average, this policy, if not already subject to any condition of average, shall be subject to average in like manner.
      If any other insurance effected by or on behalf of the Insured is expressed to cover any of the property hereby insured, but is subject to any provision whereby it is excluded from ranking concurrently with this policy either in whole or in part or from contributing rateably to the destruction or damage the liability of the Insurers hereunder shall be limited to such proportion of the destruction or damage as the sum hereby insured bears to the value of the property.

9.   Any claimant under this policy shall at the request and at the expense of the Insurers do and concur in doing and permit to be done all such acts and things as may be necessary or reasonably required by the Insurers for the purpose of enforcing any rights and remedies, or of obtaining relief or indemnity from other parties to which the Insurers shall be or would become entitled or subrogated upon their paying for or making good any destruction or damage under this policy, whether such acts and things shall be or become necessary or required before or after his indemnification by the Insurers.

10.   Every warranty to which the property insured or any item thereof is or may be, made subject shall from the time the warranty attaches apply and continue to be in force during the whole currency of this policy and non-compliance with any such warranty, whether it increases the risk or not, shall be a bar to any claim in respect of such property or item: provided that whenever this policy is renewed a claim in respect of destruction or damage occurring during the renewal period shall not be barred by reason of a warranty not having been complied with at any time before the commencement of such period.

11.   All differences arising out of this policy shall be referred to the decision of an arbitrator to be appointed in writing by the parties in difference or if they cannot agree upon a single arbitrator to the decision of two arbitrators, one to be appointed in writing by each of the parties within one calendar month after having been required in writing so to do by either of the parties or, in case the arbitrators do not agree, of an umpire appointed in writing by the arbitrators before entering upon the reference. The umpire shall sit with the arbitrators and preside at their meetings, and the making of an award shall be a condition precedent to any right of action against the Insurers. After the expiration of one year after any destruction or damage the Insurers shall not be liable in respect of any claim thereof unless such claim shall in the meantime have been referred to arbitration.

COL. (FIRE) (EIRE) (10/79)

SCHEDULE

Branch   Policy No.

Agent   No.

THE INSURED	
ADDRESS	

THE PERIOD OF INSURANCE	
From	to at four o'clock in the afternoon

Cancelled Policy No. (if any)	Renewal Date
FIRST PREMIUM £	ANNUAL PREMIUM £

Policy pages attached

The Property Insured	Sum Insured thereon

The sum insured by each item of this policy covering property is declared to be separately but similarly subject to Average.

PRO RATA CONDITION OF AVERAGE

Whenever a sum insured is declared to be subject to Average, if the property covered thereby shall at the breaking out of any fire or at the commencement of any destruction of or damage to such property by any other peril hereby insured against be collectively of greater value than such sum insured, then the Insured shall be considered as being his own insurer for the difference and shall bear a ratable share of the loss accordingly.

Total Sum Insured

Examined ....

Authorised ....

ZF5 (UK & X) (4/76)

C SPRINKLER LEAKAGE POLICY

Guardian Royal Exchange Assurance

SPRINKLER LEAKAGE INSURANCE POLICY

IN CONSIDERATION of the Insured named in the Schedule hereto paying to the Guardian Royal Exchange Assurance plc (hereinafter called the Company) the First Premium mentioned in the said Schedule.

The Company agrees (subject to the Conditions contained herein or endorsed or otherwise expressed hereon which Conditions shall so far as the nature of them respectively will permit be deemed to be conditions precedent to the right of the Insured to recover hereunder) that if after payment of the premium the Property insured described in the said Schedule, or any part of such property, be destroyed or damaged by

> Water discharged or leaking from the Automatic Sprinkler Installation(s) in the premises provided that such discharge or leakage of water be accidental and shall not be occasioned by or happen through –

> (a)   freezing whilst the premises in the Insured's ownership and/or tenancy are empty or disused,

> (b)   heat caused by fire,

> (c)   explosion (including the blowing up of buildings or blasting), earthquake, subterranean fire, riot, civil commotion, war, invasion, act of foreign enemy, hostilities (whether war be declared or not), civil war, rebellion, revolution, insurrection or military or usurped power;

at any time before 4 o'clock in the afternoon of the last day of the period of insurance named in the said Schedule or of any subsequent period in respect of which the Insured shall have paid and the Company shall have accepted the premium required for the renewal of this Policy, the Company will pay to the Insured the value of the property at the time of the happening of its destruction or the amount of such damage or at its option reinstate or replace such property or any part thereof

Provided that the liability of the Company shall in no case exceed in respect of each item the sum expressed in the said Schedule to be insured thereon or in the whole the total sum insured hereby or such other sum or sums as may be substituted therefor by memorandum hereon or attached hereto signed by or on behalf of the Company.

On behalf of the Company

CONDITIONS

1 MISDESCRIPTION   This Policy shall be voidable in the event of misrepresentation, misdescription or non-disclosure in any material particular.

2 ALTERATION   This Policy shall be avoided with respect to any item thereof in regard to which there be any alteration after the commencement of this insurance

    (1)   by removal

or   (2)   whereby the risk of destruction or damage is increased

or   (3)   whereby the Insured's interest ceases except by Will or operation of law

unless such alteration be admitted by memorandum signed by or on behalf of the Company.

3 EXCLUSIONS   This Policy does not cover

(a)   Damage to the Automatic Sprinkler Installation(s) other than that caused by water accidentally discharged or leaking from the Installation(s).

(b)   Loss or destruction of or damage to any property whatsoever or any loss or expense whatsoever resulting or arising therefrom or any consequential loss directly or indirectly caused by or contributed to by or arising from

(i)   ionising radiations or contamination by radioactivity from any nuclear fuel or from any nuclear waste from the combustion of nuclear fuel

(ii)   the radioactive, toxic, explosive or other hazardous properties of any explosive nuclear assembly or nuclear component thereof.

(c)   Goods held in trust or on commission, money,) unless specially
securities, stamps, documents, manuscripts,) mentioned as insured
computer systems records, business books,) by this Policy.
patterns, models, moulds, plans, designs,)
explosives,

(d)   Destruction of or damage to property which, at the time of the happening of such destruction or damage, is insured by, or would, but for the existence of this Policy, be insured by any Marine Policy or Policies, except in respect of any excess beyond the amount which would have been payable under the Marine Policy or Policies had this Insurance not been effected.

(e)   Loss or destruction of or damage to any property in NORTHERN IRELAND or loss resulting therefrom caused by or happening through or in consequence of:

(i)   civil commotion

(ii)   any unlawful wanton or malicious act committed maliciously by a person or persons acting on behalf of or in connection with any unlawful association.

For the purpose of this Condition -

"Unlawful association" means any organisation which is engaged in terrorism and includes an organisation which at any relevant time is a proscribed organisation within the meaning of the Northern Ireland (Emergency Provisions) Act, 1973.

"Terrorism" means the use of violence for political ends and includes any use of violence for the purpose of putting the public or any section of the public in fear.

In any action, suit or other proceedings where the Company alleges that by reason of the provisions of this Condition any loss, destruction or damage is not covered by this Policy, the burden of proving that such loss, destruction or damage is covered shall be upon the Insured.

4 MAINTENANCE

The Insured shall take all reasonable steps to prevent Frost and other damage to the Automatic Sprinkler Installation(s) and, so far as his responsibility extends, to maintain the Installation(s) including the Automatic External Alarm Signal in efficient condition.

In the event of any discharge or leakage from the said Installation(s) the Insured shall do and permit to be done all things practicable, whether by removal or otherwise, to save and protect the property insured.

5 CHANGES OR REPAIRS

When any changes, repairs or alterations to the Automatic Sprinkler Installation(s) are proposed written notice thereof is to be given to the Company and their agreement obtained in writing.

6 COMPANY'S RIGHTS OF INSPECTION

The Company shall have access to the premises at all reasonable times for purposes of inspection and if the Company notify the Insured of defects in the construction or condition of the Automatic Sprinkler Installation(s) requiring alteration or repairs the Company may also at their option by notice in writing suspend this insurance until such alterations or repairs be made and approved by the Company.

7 CLAIMS

On the happening of any destruction or damage the Insured shall forthwith give notice thereof in writing to the Company and shall within 30 days after such destruction or damage, or such further time as the Company may in writing allow, at his own expense deliver to the Company a claim in writing containing as particular an account as may be reasonably practicable of the several articles or portions of property destroyed or damaged and of the amount of destruction or damage thereto respectively having regard to their value at the time of the destruction or damage together with details of any other insurances on any property hereby insured. The Insured shall also give to the Company all such proofs and information with respect to the claim as may reasonably be required together with (if demanded) a statutory declaration of the truth of the claim and of any matters connected therewith. No claim under this Policy shall be payable unless the terms of this condition have been complied with.

8 FRAUD

If the claim be in any respect fraudulent or if any fraudulent means or devices be used by the Insured or anyone acting on his behalf to obtain any benefit under this Policy or if any destruction or damage be occasioned by the wilful act or with the connivance of the Insured all benefit under this Policy shall be forfeited.

9 REINSTATEMENT

If the Company elects or becomes bound to reinstate or replace any property the Insured shall at his own expense produce and give to the Company all such plans, documents, books and information as the Company may reasonably require. The Company shall not be bound to reinstate exactly or completely, but only as circumstances permit and in reasonably sufficient manner and shall not in any case be bound to expend in respect of any one of the items insured more than the sum insured thereon.

10 COMPANY'S RIGHTS AFTER A CLAIM

On the happening of any destruction or damage in respect of which a claim is or may be made under this Policy the Company and every person authorised by the Company may, without thereby incurring any liability, and without diminishing the right of the Company to rely upon any conditions of this Policy, enter, take or keep possession of the building or premises where the destruction or damage has happened, and may take possession of or require to be delivered to them any of the property hereby insured and may keep possession of and deal with such property for all reasonable purposes and in any reasonable manner. This Condition shall be evidence of the leave and licence of the Insured to the Company so to do. If the Insured or anyone acting on his behalf shall not comply with the requirements of the Company or shall hinder or obstruct the Company in doing any of the above-mentioned acts, then all benefit under this Policy shall be forfeited. The Insured shall not in any case be entitled to abandon any property to the Company whether taken possession of by the Company or not.

11 CONTRIBUTION AND AVERAGE

If at the time of any destruction of or damage to any property hereby insured there be any other Insurance effected by or on behalf of the Insured covering any of the property destroyed or damaged, the liability of the Company hereunder shall be limited to its ratable proportion of such destruction or damage.
If any such other Insurance shall be subject to any Condition of Average this Policy, if not already subject to any Condition of Average, shall be subject to Average in like manner.

If any other Insurance effected by or on behalf of the Insured is expressed to cover any of the property hereby insured, but is subject to any provision whereby it is excluded from ranking concurrently with this Policy either in whole or in part or from contributing ratably to the destruction or damage, the liability of the Company hereunder shall be limited to such proportion of the destruction or damage as the sum hereby insured bears to the value of the property.

12 SUBROGATION

Any claimant under this Policy shall at the request and at the expense of the Company do and concur in doing and permit to be done all such acts and things as may be necessary or reasonably required by the Company for the purpose of enforcing any rights and remedies, or of obtaining relief or indemnity from other parties to which the Company shall be or would become entitled or subrogated upon its paying for or making good any destruction or damage under this Policy, whether such acts and things shall be or become necessary or required before or after his indemnification by the Company.

13 WARRANTIES

Every Warranty to which the property insured or any item thereof is, or may be, made subject, shall from the time the Warranty attaches apply and continue to be in force during the whole currency of this Policy, and non-compliance with any such Warranty, whether it increases the risk or not shall be a bar to any claim in respect of such property or item: provided that whenever this Policy is renewed a claim in respect of destruction or damage occurring during the renewal period shall not be barred by reason of a Warranty not having been complied with at any time before the commencement of such period.

14 ARBITRATION

If any difference shall arise as to the amount to be paid under this Policy (liability being otherwise admitted) such difference shall be referred to an Arbitrator to be appointed by the parties in accordance with the Statutory Provisions in that behalf for the time being in force. Where any difference is by this Condition to be referred to arbitration the making of an Award shall be a condition precedent to any right of action against the Company.

SCHEDULE

Branch   Policy No.

Agent   No.

THE INSURED	
ADDRESS	

THE PERIOD OF INSURANCE
From

to
at four o'clock in the afternoon

Cancelled Policy No (if any)	Renewal Date
FIRST PREMIUM £	ANNUAL PREMIUM £

Policy pages attached

The Property Insured	Sum Insured thereon

The sum insured by each item of this policy covering property is declared to be separately but similarly subject to Average.

PRO RATA CONDITION OF AVERAGE

Whenever a sum insured is declared to be subject to Average, if the property covered thereby shall at the breaking out of any fire or at the commencement of any destruction of or damage to such property by any other peril hereby insured against be collectively of greater value than such sum insured, then the Insured shall be considered as being his own insurer for the difference and shall bear a ratable share of the loss accordingly.

Total Sum Insured

Examined ....

Authorised ....

ZF5 (UK & X) (4/76)

Appendix III

LLOYD'S FORMS OF POLICIES AND PROPOSAL FORMS

The following forms are reproduced with the permission of Lloyd's Under-writers' Fire and Non-Marine Association:

    A   Lloyd's Fire Policy (C Form).
    B   Lloyd's Fire Policy (Consequential Loss Insurance) (Form M (J)).
    C   Lloyd's Profit Insurance Proposal Form.

A LLOYD'S FIRE POLICY (C FORM)

C

Form approved by Lloyd's
Underwriters' Non Marine
Association.

Any person not an Underwriting
Member of Lloyd's subscribing this Policy,
or any person uttering the same if so
subscribed, will be liable to be proceeded
against under Lloyd's Acts.

Printed at Lloyd's, London, England

33

No Policy or other Contract dated on or after 1st Jan., 1924, will be recognised by the Committee of Lloyd's as entitling the holder to the benefit of the Funds and/or Guarantees lodged by the Underwriters of the Policy or Contract as security for their liabilities unless it bears at foot the Seal of Lloyd's Policy Signing Office.

LLOYD'S FIRE POLICY

(Subscribed only by Underwriting Members of Lloyd's all of whom have complied with the requirements of the Insurance Companies Act, 1958, as to security and otherwise.)

Whereas the Assured named in the Schedule herein have paid the premium specified in the Schedule to the Underwriting Members of Lloyd's who have hereunto subscribed their Names (hereinafter called " the Underwriters "),

NOW WE THE UNDERWRITERS hereby agree, to the extent and in the manner hereinafter provided, to insure the property specified in the Schedule against loss or damage sustained during the period specified in the Schedule from the perils specified in the Schedule.

EXCLUSIONS

This Policy does NOT cover

(a) damage to any dynamo, transformer, motor, wiring, main or other electrical appliance directly caused by short-circuiting, overrunning, excessive pressure or leakage of electricity but this Exclusion does not apply to damage thereto by fire resulting from such causes and originating outside the appliance;

(b) loss or damage directly or indirectly caused by or contributed to by or arising from ionising radiations or contamination by radioactivity from any nuclear fuel or from any nuclear waste from the combustion of nuclear fuel;

(c) loss or damage directly or indirectly occasioned by, happening through or in consequence of war, invasion, acts of foreign enemies, hostilities (whether war be declared or not), civil war, rebellion, revolution, insurrection, military or usurped power, riots, civil commotions or confiscation or nationalisation or requisition or destruction of or damage to property by or under the order of any government or public or local authority.

(d) loss of or damage to Computer Systems' Records.

CONDITIONS

1. This Policy is subject to the Condition of Average, that is to say, if the property covered by this Insurance shall at the time of any loss be of greater value than the sum insured hereby, the Assured shall only be entitled to recover hereunder such proportion of the said loss as the sum insured by this Policy bears to the total value of the said property.

2. If the Assured shall make any claim knowing the same to be false or fraudulent, as regards amount or otherwise, this Policy shall become void and all claim hereunder shall be forfeited.

Now know Ye that We the Underwriters, Members of the Syndicates whose definitive numbers in the after-mentioned List of Underwriting Members of Lloyd's are set out in the attached Table, hereby bind ourselves each for his own part and not one for another, our Heirs, Executors and Administrators, and in respect of his due proportion only, to pay or make good to the Assured or to the Assured's Executors or Administrators all such Loss and/or Damage as aforesaid not exceeding the total sum insured specified in the Schedule, such payment to be made after such Loss and/or Damage is proved, and the due proportion for which each of us, the Underwriters, is liable shall be ascertained by reference to his share, as shown in the said List, of the Amount, Percentage or Proportion of the total sum insured hereunder which is in the Table set opposite the definitive number of the Syndicate of which such Underwriter is a Member AND FURTHER THAT the List of Underwriting Members of Lloyd's referred to above shows their respective Syndicates and Shares therein, is deemed to be incorporated in and to form part of this Policy, bears the number specified in the attached Table and is available for inspection at Lloyd's Policy Signing Office by the Assured or his or their representatives and a true copy of the material parts of the said List certified by the General Manager of Lloyd's Policy Signing Office will be furnished to the Assured on application.

In Witness whereof the General Manager of Lloyd's Policy Signing Office has subscribed his name on behalf of each of us.

LLOYD'S POLICY SIGNING OFFICE,

Form C (22-1-70)
N.M.A. 1751

GENERAL MANAGER.

Page issued September 1973

34

SCHEDULE

Policy No. /	
The name and address of the Assured	
The property insured	
Situated	
The total sum insured hereunder	

The perils   1. Fire and/or Lightning
 	
          2.(a) Fire consequent upon Explosion wherever the explosion occurs.
 	
            (b) Explosion consequent upon Fire on the premises insured.
 	
            (c) Explosion of domestic boilers and/or of gas used for domestic purposes or for heating and/or lighting.	

Premium	
The period of insurance from to and for such further period or periods as may be mutually agreed upon.	

Dated in London, the

(Note: The equivalent Certificate is N.M.A. 1752.)

Page issued September 1973

B LLOYD'S FIRE POLICY (CONSEQUENTIAL LOSS INSURANCE) (FORM M (J)) WITH ATTACHMENTS

57

M (J)

Form approved by Lloyd's
Underwriters' Non-Marine
Association.

Any person not an Underwriting Member
of Lloyd's subscribing this Policy, or any
person uttering the same if so subscribed,
will be liable to be proceeded against
under Lloyd's Acts.

Printed at Lloyd's, London, England.

No Policy or other Contract dated on or after 1st Jan., 1924, will be recognised by the Committee of Lloyd's as entitling the holder to the benefit of the Funds and/or Guarantees lodged by the Underwriters of the Policy or Contract as security for their liabilities unless it bears at foot the Seal of Lloyd's Policy Signing Office.

LLOYD'S FIRE POLICY

(Consequential Loss Insurance)

(Subscribed only by Underwriting Members of Lloyd's all of whom have complied with the requirements of the Insurance Companies Act, 1958, as to security and otherwise.)

Whereas the Assured named in the Schedule herein carrying on the business specified in the said Schedule (hereinafter referred to as "the Business") in the Premises specified in the said Schedule (hereinafter referred to as "the Premises") has paid the premium specified in the said Schedule to the Underwriting Members of Lloyd's who have hereunto subscribed their Names (hereinafter referred to as "the Underwriters"), the Underwriters hereby agree with the Assured that, if during the Period of Insurance specified in the said Schedule any Building or other property or any part thereof used by the Assured at the Premises for the purpose of the Business be destroyed or damaged by

1. Fire, Lightning or Explosion as are covered under the Assured's Material Damage Fire Policies,
2. Boiler and Economiser Explosion occurring within the Premises, or
3. Such Additional Perils stated in Section 11 of the Schedule as the Material Damage Policy has been extended to cover or have been separately insured against

(all such destruction or damage so caused being hereinafter termed "Damage") and the Business carried on by the Assured at the Premises be in consequence thereof interrupted or interfered with,

We the Underwriters, to the extent and in the manner hereinafter provided, will pay to the Assured in respect of each item in the Schedule hereto the amount of loss resulting from such interruption or interference,

Provided always that at the time of the happening of the Damage there shall be in force an insurance covering the interest of the Assured in the property at the Premises against such Damage and that payment shall have been made or liability admitted therefor under such insurance.

CONDITIONS

1. The Assured shall use due diligence and do and concur in doing all things reasonably practicable to minimise any interruption of or interference with the Business and to avoid or diminish the loss whether by taking other premises or by any other means.

2. If at the time of any loss there shall be any other subsisting insurance covering such loss, or any part thereof, the Underwriters shall not be liable to pay more than their rateable proportion of the loss.

3. This Policy does not cover loss resulting from Damage
   (a) directly or indirectly occasioned by, happening through or in consequence of war, invasion, acts of foreign enemies, hostilities (whether war be declared or not), civil war, rebellion, revolution, insurrection, military or usurped power, riots or civil commotions, or confiscation or nationalisation or requisition or damage to property by or under the order of any government or public or local authority, or
   (b) directly or indirectly caused by or contributed to by or arising from ionising radiations or contamination by radioactivity from any nuclear fuel or from any nuclear waste from the combustion of nuclear fuel.

4. If the Assured shall make any claim knowing the same to be false or fraudulent, as regards amount or otherwise, this Policy shall become void and all claim hereunder shall be forfeited.

Now know Ye that We, the Underwriters, members of the Syndicate(s) whose definitive Number(s) in the attached list are set out in the Table overleaf, or attached overleaf, hereby bind Ourselves, each for his own part and not one for another, our Heirs, Executors and Administrators, and in respect of his due proportion only, to pay to the Assured or to the Assured's Executors or Administrators all such Loss as aforesaid, not exceeding the Sum(s) Insured specified in the aforesaid Schedule, such payment to be made within Seven Days after such Loss is proved, and so that the due proportion for which each of Us the Underwriters is liable shall be ascertained by reference to his proportion as ascertained according to the said list of the Amount, Percentage or Proportion of the Total Sum Insured which is in the said Table set opposite the definitive Number of the Syndicate of which such Underwriter is a member.

In Witness whereof the Manager of Lloyd's Policy Signing Office has subscribed his Name on behalf of each of Us.

LLOYD'S POLICY SIGNING OFFICE,

MANAGER.

Form M (J)   (13.4.67)
N.M.A. 1688

58

SCHEDULE

1. The Policy No.	/
2. The Assured	
of	
3. The Business	
4. The Premises	
5. The Period of Insurance	
commencing	
and ending	**and for such further period or periods as may be mutually agreed upon**
6. The period referred to in the Definition of **Indemnity Period** in the Specification	months

7. Items (to which the attached Specification(s) and/or Clause(s) refer)

Specification(s) and/or Clause(s) to be attached

1. **Gross Profit**		£	M(J)A or M(J)B
2. **Wages**			
(a) Dual Basis	Initial Period : weeks / Succeeding Percentage : % / Consolidated Period : weeks	£	M(J)C
OR			
(b) Limited Period Basis	Limited Period : weeks	£	M(J)D
3. **Auditor's Charges**		£	NMA 1538
	Total Sum Insured	£	

8. **The Premium** £

9. To be completed if the **Insurance** is on the "Net Profit and Standing Charges" basis and Specification M(J)A is attached to this Policy.

Insured Standing Charges

10. To be completed if the Insurance is on the "Difference" basis and Specification M(J)B is attached to this Policy.

Specified Working Expenses

11. **Additional Perils**

12. List of Specifications and Clauses which are declared to be incorporated in and to form an integral part of this Policy.

Specification(s)

Clause(s)

Dated in London, the

(Note: The equivalent Certificate is N.M.A. 1591.)

59

M(J) A   **NET PROFIT AND STANDING CHARGES BASIS SPECIFICATION**
(For Attachment to Form M(J))

(Approved by Lloyd's Underwriters' Non-Marine Association.)

GROSS PROFIT

The insurance under Item 1 of Section 7 of the Schedule is limited to loss of Gross Profit due to
(a) REDUCTION IN TURNOVER and (b) INCREASE IN COST OF WORKING and the amount payable as
indemnity thereunder shall be:—
(a) **In Respect of Reduction in Turnover:** the sum produced by applying the Rate of Gross Profit to
the amount by which the Turnover during the Indemnity Period shall, in consequence of the
Damage, fall short of the Standard Turnover,
(b) **In Respect of Increase in Cost of Working:** the additional expenditure (subject to the provisions
of Memo. 2) necessarily and reasonably incurred for the sole purpose of avoiding or diminishing
the reduction in Turnover which but for that expenditure would have taken place during the
Indemnity Period in consequence of the Damage, but not exceeding the sum produced by applying
the Rate of Gross Profit to the amount of the reduction thereby avoided,

less any sum saved during the Indemnity Period in respect of such of the Insured Standing Charges as may cease or be
reduced in consequence of the Damage,

PROVIDED THAT, if the sum insured by this Item be less than the sum produced by applying the Rate of Gross Profit
to the Annual Turnover (or if the period specified in Section 6 of the Schedule is greater than 12 months to that
proportion of the Annual Turnover which such period bears to 12 months), the amount payable shall be proportionately
reduced.

DEFINITIONS

Gross Profit—The sum produced by adding to the Net Profit the amount of the Insured Standing Charges, or if
there be no Net Profit the amount of the Insured Standing Charges less such a proportion of any net trading loss as
the amount of the Insured Standing Charges bears to all the Standing Charges of the Business.

Net Profit—The net trading profit (exclusive of all capital receipts and accretions and all outlay properly chargeable
to capital) resulting from the Business of the Assured at the Premises after due provision has been made for all Standing
and other charges including depreciation, but before the deduction of any taxation chargeable on profits.

Insured Standing Charges (which the Assured elects to insure as part of Gross Profit)—as listed in Section 9 of the
Schedule.

Turnover—The money paid or payable to the Assured for goods sold and delivered and for services rendered in
course of the Business at the Premises.

Indemnity Period—The period, beginning with the occurrence of the Damage and ending not later than the last day
of the period specified in Section 6 of the Schedule, during which the results of the Business shall be affected in
consequence of the Damage.

Rate of Gross Profit—The rate of Gross Profit earned
on the Turnover during the financial year immediately
before the date of the Damage

Annual Turnover—The Turnover during the twelve
months immediately before the date of the Damage

Standard Turnover—The Turnover during that period
in the twelve months immediately before the date of the
Damage which corresponds with the Indemnity Period

to which such adjustments shall be made as may be
necessary to provide for the trend of the Business and for
variations in or special circumstances affecting the Business
either before or after the Damage or which would have
affected the Business had the Damage not occurred, so that
the figures thus adjusted shall represent as nearly as may
be reasonably practicable the results which but for the
Damage would have been obtained during the relative
period after the Damage.

ADJUSTMENT OF PREMIUM

In the event of the Gross Profit earned (or if the period specified in Section 6 of the Schedule is greater than 12
months, that proportion of the Gross Profit earned which such period bears to 12 months) as certified by the Assured's
Auditors, for the financial year most nearly concurrent with the period of insurance being less than the sum insured
thereon, a pro rata return of premium not exceeding 50% of the premium paid on such sum insured for such period of
insurance will be made in respect of the difference. If any Damage shall have occurred giving rise to a claim under
this Policy, such return shall be made in respect only of so much of the difference as is not due to such Damage.

MEMORANDA

1. If during the Indemnity Period goods shall be sold or services rendered elsewhere than at the Premises for the
benefit of the Business either by the Assured or by others on their behalf the money paid or payable in respect of such
sales or services shall be brought into account in arriving at the Turnover during the Indemnity Period.

2. If any standing charges of the Business be not insured by this Policy then in computing the amount recoverable
hereunder as Increase in Cost of Working that proportion only of the additional expenditure shall be brought into
account which the sum of the Net Profit and Insured Standing Charges bears to the sum of the Net Profit and all the
standing charges.

3. If the Business be conducted in Departments, the independent trading results of which are ascertainable, the
provisions of clauses (a) and (b) of this Specification relating to Item 1 of Section 7 of the Schedule shall apply
separately to each Department affected by the Damage except that if the Sum Insured by the said Item be less than the
aggregate of the sums produced by applying the Rate of Gross Profit for each Department of the Business (whether
affected by the Damage or not) to the relative Annual Turnover thereof (or if the period specified in Section 6 of the
Schedule is greater than 12 months to that proportion of the relative Annual Turnover thereof which such period bears
to 12 months), the amount payable shall be proportionately reduced.

(30.3.67)
N.M.A. 1534.

60

M(J) B

DIFFERENCE BASIS SPECIFICATION
(For Attachment to Form M(J))

(Approved by Lloyd's Underwriters' Non-Marine Association.)

GROSS PROFIT

The insurance under Item 1 of Section 7 of the Schedule is limited to loss of Gross Profit due to
(a) REDUCTION IN TURNOVER and (b) INCREASE IN COST OF WORKING and the amount payable as indemnity thereunder shall be:—

> (a) **In Respect of Reduction in Turnover:** the sum produced by applying the Rate of Gross Profit to the amount by which the Turnover during the Indemnity Period shall, in consequence of the Damage, fall short of the Standard Turnover,
>
> (b) **In Respect of Increase in Cost of Working:** the additional expenditure (subject to the provisions of Memo. 2) necessarily and reasonably incurred for the sole purpose of avoiding or diminishing the reduction in Turnover which but for that expenditure would have taken place during the Indemnity Period in consequence of the Damage, but not exceeding the sum produced by applying the Rate of Gross Profit to the amount of the reduction thereby avoided,

less any sum saved during the Indemnity Period in respect of such of the charges and expenses of the Business payable out of Gross Profit as may cease or be reduced in consequence of the Damage,

PROVIDED THAT if the sum insured by this Item be less than the sum produced by applying the Rate of Gross Profit to the Annual Turnover (or if the period specified in Section 6 of the Schedule is greater than 12 months to that proportion of the Annual Turnover which such period bears to 12 months), the amount payable shall be proportionately reduced.

DEFINITIONS

Gross Profit—The amount by which
(i) the sum of
> (a) the Turnover (less any Discounts allowed) and
> (b) the amount of the Closing Stock and Closing Work in Progress

shall exceed
(ii) the sum of the amounts of
> (a) the Opening Stock and Opening Work in Progress,
> (b) Purchases of Stock, Raw Materials and Components (less any Discounts received) and
> (c) the Specified Working Expenses.

The amounts of the Opening and Closing Stocks and Work in Progress shall be arrived at in accordance with the Assured's normal accountancy methods, due provision being made for depreciation.

Specified Working Expenses (which the Assured elects not to insure as part of Gross Profit)—as listed in Section 10 of the Schedule—The words and expressions used in this definition shall have the meaning usually attached to them in the books and accounts of the Assured.

Turnover—The money paid or payable to the Assured for goods sold and delivered and for services rendered in course of the Business at the Premises.

Indemnity Period—The period, beginning with the occurrence of the Damage and ending not later than the last day of the period specified in Section 6 of the Schedule, during which the results of the Business shall be affected in consequence of the Damage.

Rate of Gross Profit—The rate of Gross Profit earned on the Turnover during the financial year immediately before the date of the Damage	to which such adjustments shall be made as may be necessary to provide for the trend of the Business and for variations in or special circumstances affecting the Business either before or after the Damage or which would have affected the Business had the Damage not occurred, so that the figures thus adjusted shall represent as nearly as may be reasonably practicable the results which but for the Damage would have been obtained during the relative period after the Damage.
Annual Turnover—The Turnover during the twelve months immediately before the date of the Damage	
Standard Turnover—The Turnover during that period in the twelve months immediately before the date of the Damage which corresponds with the Indemnity Period	

ADJUSTMENT OF PREMIUM

In the event of the Gross Profit earned (or if the period specified in Section 6 of the Schedule is greater than 12 months, that proportion of the Gross Profit earned which such period bears to 12 months) as certified by the Assured's Auditors, for the financial year most nearly concurrent with the period of insurance being less than the sum insured thereon, a pro rata return of premium not exceeding 50% of the premium paid on such sum insured for such period of insurance will be made in respect of the difference. If any Damage shall have occurred giving rise to a claim under this Policy, such return shall be made in respect only of so much of the difference as is not due to such Damage.

MEMORANDA

1. If during the Indemnity Period goods shall be sold or services rendered elsewhere than at the Premises for the benefit of the Business either by the Assured or by others on their behalf the money paid or payable in respect of such sales or services shall be brought into account in arriving at the Turnover during the Indemnity Period.

2. If any standing charges of the Business be not insured by this Policy (having been deducted in arriving at the Gross Profit as defined herein) then in computing the amount recoverable hereunder as Increase in Cost of Working that proportion only of the additional expenditure shall be brought into account which the Gross Profit bears to the Sum of the Gross Profit and the uninsured standing charges.

3. If the Business be conducted in Departments, the independent trading results of which are ascertainable, the provisions of clauses (a) and (b) of this Specification relating to Item 1 of Section 7 of the Schedule shall apply separately to each Department affected by the Damage except that if the Sum Insured by the said Item be less than the aggregate of the sums produced by applying the Rate of Gross Profit for each Department of the Business (whether affected by the Damage or not) to the relative Annual Turnover thereof (or if the period specified in Section 6 of the Schedule is greater than 12 months to that proportion of the relative Annual Turnover thereof which such period bears to 12 months), the amount payable shall be proportionately reduced.

(30 3 67)
N M A 1534

61

M(J) C   WAGES SPECIFICATION: DUAL BASIS WORDING

(For Attachment to Form M(J))

(Approved by Lloyd's Underwriters' Non-Marine Association.)

The Insurance under Item 2(a) of Section 7 of the Schedule is limited to loss of Wages and the amount payable as indemnity thereunder shall be:—

(a) **In Respect of Reduction in Turnover**

(i) during the portion of the Indemnity Period beginning with the occurrence of the Damage and ending not later than the number of weeks thereafter described in the Schedule as the Initial Period
the sum produced by applying the Rate of Wages to the Shortage in Turnover during the said portion of the Indemnity Period,

less any saving during the said portion of the Indemnity Period through reduction in consequence of the Damage in the amount of Wages paid,

(ii) during the remaining portion of the Indemnity Period
the sum produced by applying the Rate of Wages to the Shortage in Turnover during the said remaining portion of the Indemnity Period,

less any saving during the said remaining portion of the Indemnity Period through reduction in consequence of the Damage in the amount of Wages paid,

but not exceeding the sum produced by applying that percentage (described in the Schedule as the Succeeding Percentage) of the Rate of Wages to the Shortage in Turnover during the said remaining portion of the Indemnity Period, increased by such amount as is deducted for savings under the terms of Clause (a) (i) above,

Note: At the option of the Assured the number of weeks referred to in Clause (a) (i) above may be increased to the number of weeks described in the Schedule as the Consolidated Period but in this event the amount arrived at under the provisions of Clause (a) (ii) above shall not exceed such amount as is deducted under Clause (a) (i) above for savings effected during the said increased number of weeks.

(b) **In Respect of Increase In Cost of Working**

so much of the additional expenditure as exceeds the amount paid under Gross Profit Insurance necessarily, and reasonably incurred for the sole purpose of avoiding or diminishing the reduction in Turnover which but for that expenditure would have taken place during the Indemnity Period in consequence of the Damage, but not more than the additional amount which would have been payable in respect of reduction in Turnover under the provisions of Clauses (a) (i) and (ii) of this Item had such expenditure not been incurred,

PROVIDED THAT if the sum insured by this Item be less than the sum produced by applying the Rate of Wages to the Annual Turnover (or if the period specified in Section 6 of the Schedule is greater than 12 months to that proportion of the Annual Turnover which such period bears to 12 months), the amount payable shall be proportionately reduced.

DEFINITIONS

Wages—The remuneration (including National Insurance Contributions, Payments pertaining to Wages, Bonuses, Holiday Pay and the like) of all employees other than those whose remuneration is treated as Salaries in the Assured's books of account.

Indemnity Period—The period, beginning with the occurrence of the Damage and ending not later than the last day of the period specified in Section 6 of the Schedule, during which the results of the Business shall be affected in consequence of the Damage.

Turnover—The money paid or payable to the Assured for goods sold and delivered and for services rendered in course of the Business at the Premises.

Shortage in Turnover—The amount by which the Turnover during a period shall in consequence of the Damage fall short of the part of the Standard Turnover which relates to that period.

Rate of Wages—The rate of Wages to Turnover during the financial year immediately before the date of the Damage

Annual Turnover—The Turnover during the twelve months immediately before the date of the Damage

Standard Turnover—The Turnover during that period in the twelve months immediately before the date of the Damage which corresponds with the Indemnity Period

to which such adjustments shall be made as may be necessary to provide for the trend of the Business and for variations in or special circumstances affecting the Business either before or after the Damage or which would have affected the Business had the Damage not occurred, so that the figures thus adjusted shall represent as nearly as may be reasonably practicable the results which but for the Damage would have been obtained during the relative period after the Damage.

ADJUSTMENT OF PREMIUM

In the event of the Wages paid (or if the period specified in Section 6 of the Schedule is greater than 12 months, that proportion of the Wages paid which such period bears to 12 months) as certified by the Assured's Auditors, for the financial year most nearly concurrent with the period of insurance being less than the sum insured thereon, a pro rata return of premium not exceeding 50% of the premium paid on such sum insured for such period of insurance will be made in respect of the difference. If any Damage shall have occurred giving rise to a claim under this Policy, such return shall be made in respect only of so much of the difference as is not due to such Damage.

MEMORANDA

1. If during the Indemnity Period goods shall be sold or services rendered elsewhere than at the Premises for the benefit of the Business either by the Assured or by others on their behalf the money paid or payable in respect of such sales or services shall be brought into account in arriving at the Turnover during the Indemnity Period.

2. If the Business be conducted in Departments, the independent trading results of which are ascertainable, the provisions of clauses (a) and (b) of this Specification relating to Item 2 (a) of Section 7 of the Schedule shall apply separately to each Department affected by the Damage except that if the Sum Insured by the said Item be less than the aggregate of the sums produced by applying the Rate of Wages for each Department of the Business (whether affected by the Damage or not) to the relative Annual Turnover thereof (or if the period specified in Section 6 of the Schedule is greater than 12 months to that proportion of the relative Annual Turnover thereof which such period bears to 12 months), the amount payable shall be proportionately reduced.

30.3.67)
N.M.A. 1536

62

M(J)D

WAGES SPECIFICATION : LIMITED PERIOD WORDING
(For Attachment to Form M(J))

(Approved by Lloyd's Underwriters' Non-Marine Association.)

The Insurance under Item 2 (b) of Section 7 of the Schedule is limited to the loss incurred by the Assured by the payment of Wages for a period beginning with the occurrence of the Damage and ending not later than the number of weeks thereafter described in the Schedule as the Limited Period.

The amount payable as indemnity under this Item shall be the actual amount which the Assured shall pay as Wages for such period to employees whose services cannot in consequence of the Damage be utilised by the Assured at all and an equitable part of the Wages paid for such period to employees whose services cannot in consequence of the Damage be utilised by the Assured to the full,

PROVIDED THAT, if the sum insured by this Item shall be less than the aggregate amount of the Wages that would have been paid during the number of weeks described in the Schedule as the Limited Period immediately following the Damage had the Damage not occurred, the amount payable shall be proportionately reduced.

For the purpose of this Item the term Wages shall mean the remuneration (including National Insurance Contributions, Payments pertaining to Wages, Bonuses, Holiday Pay and the like) of all employees other than those whose remuneration is insured as part of Gross Profit under Item 1 of Section 7 of the Schedule.

ADJUSTMENT OF PREMIUM
In the event of the sum insured under this Item being greater than the amount arrived at by taking that proportion of the Wages paid by the Assured during the accounting period most nearly concurrent with any period of insurance which the Limited Period specified in the Schedule bears to 52 weeks, a pro rata return of premium not exceeding 50 per cent. of the premium paid on such sum insured for such period of insurance will be made in respect of the difference,

PROVIDED THAT, if any Damage shall have occurred giving rise to a claim under this Item, no such return of premium shall be made.

(30.3.67)
N.M.A. 1537

C. LLOYD'S PROFIT INSURANCE PROPOSAL FORM

1. Sums Insured:

Profits Insurance is designed to indemnify against loss of profits and wages during the chosen *Indemnity Period following damage*, and this damage can occur on the last day of a period of insurance for which the Sums Insured are fixed, as readily as on the first.

The Policy contains provisions which will reduce the amount of indemnity if the Sums Insured prove to be inadequate. On the other hand, allowance is made for the difficulty in accurately forecasting upward trends, by providing for a proportionate rebate of up to 50% of the premium paid on Gross Profit and Wages, if the actual results prove to be less than the Sums Insured.

Whilst therefore the last available Trading and Profit and Loss Accounts will provide a basic guide to the Sums Insured, it is important to adjust these figures to take into account not only known expansion and increased figures, but also future trends of the business, planned developments and all other factors tending to increase the cover eventually required, projecting these right through any Indemnity Period *commencing at any time during the period of insurance.*

2. Insured Standing Charges:

In electing which charges *to insure*, all charges should be reviewed to establish:—

    (a) whether they would vary in all circumstances in direct proportion to Turnover, in which case insurance is unnecessary: Raw Materials, Packaging, Freight, may come in this category;

    (b) whether they would not vary in all circumstances in direct proportion to Turnover, in which case they should be included for insurance: Rent, Rates, Advertising, etc. may fall under this heading;

3. Specified Working Expenses:

In electing which expenses *not to insure*, all expenses should be similarly reviewed to establish:—

    (a) whether they would vary in all circumstances in direct proportion to Turnover, in which case they can be specified to be deducted in arriving at the sum to be insured—examples as at 2(a) above;

    (b) whether they would not vary in all circumstances in direct proportion to Turnover, in which case they should not be deducted in arriving at the sum to be insured—examples as at 2(b) above;

4. Wages:

Method A. Dual Wages Basis.

(See Part III A of Proposal Form, *infra*)

This method provides cover for a selected period, and a proportion of cover for the remainder of the Indemnity Period.

Method B. Limited Period Cover.

(See Part III B of Proposal Form, *infra*)

(Where wages covered will discontinue after selected time).

This method provides cover only for the period selected.

If Gross Profit is to be insured on the Net Profit and Standing Charges basis, any wages *not insured* under Methods A. or B. must be specified and defined in the Insured Standing Charges.

If Gross Profit is to be insured on the Difference Basis, Wages *insured* under Methods A. or B. should be specified and defined in the Specified Working Expenses.

PART I

Name of Proposer

      Head Office

Description of Trade/Business

Address/es of Premises to be insured

Policy to commence: Expire:

Indemnity Period: Months

Sums Insured   (as arrived at in Parts II & III hereof)

1. On Gross Profit : £

2. On Wages   : £   (100% for ...... weeks and ....% for remainder of indemnity period.)

or: ...... weeks wages : £

3. On Auditors Charges : £   for producing and certifying any details required in connection with a claim.

Perils (It is necessary that there is in force a policy covering the material loss due to such Perils.)

    (a) Fire, Lightning or Explosion as covered under the Material Damage Fire policies and Boiler or Economiser Explosion occurring within the premises.

    (b) The following additional perils may be covered (Please delete those not required).

        1. Explosion (other than covered in (a) above) excluding explosion of vessels, machines or apparatus in which internal pressure is due to steam only and belonging to or under the control of the Assured.

        2. Aircraft and other aerial devices or articles dropped therefrom.

        3. Riots and Civil Commotion (a) without or (b) with Malicious Damage. (Indicate which).

        4. Earthquake. 5. Storm and Tempest. 6. Flood. 7. Burst Pipes.

        8. Impact by road vehicles not belonging to or under the control of the Assured.

        Other perils can be considered by Underwriters.

Extension to insure the effect on the Assured's business of *damage as covered hereon to premises which are not owned or occupied by the Assured.*

(a) *Suppliers, Sub-Contractors or storage at other premises.*

Name	*Goods or services concerned*	*Address of Premises*	*Limit Required % of Sums Insured*
....			
....			,,
....			,,

(b) *Customers*

Name	Goods or services concerned	Address of Premises	Percentage of Turnover
....			%
....			%
....			%

(c) *Other extensions*

(Such as failure of electricity, gas or water supplies due to the perils insured hereunder. This section can usually be extended to cover Accidental Damage which can arise prior to intake point).

Please state requirements

PART II: GROSS PROFIT

Select Basis: either A. Net Profit plus Standing Charges

B. Difference between Turnover and Specified Working Expenses and complete either A or B below.

A. *Net Profit and Standing Charges Basis.*

(Standing Charges are charges which the Assured elects to insure as part of Gross Profit—see Notes at beginning of Proposal Form).

Standing Charges

Total of Net Profit and Standing Charges for last financial year   £

Add allowance for possible increases over last financial year (see Notes)   £
                                                                                   £

Increase proportionately where Indemnity Period is more than 12 months   £
                                                                                   £

Salaries are normally included as a Standing Charge; Wages unless to be insured in full should be dealt with in Part III.

B. *Difference Basis*

Gross Profit being: *Last Financial Year*

(1) Turnover (less any Discounts allowed)   £

add (2) Closing Stock and Closing Work in Progress.   £
                                                                        £

deduct (1) Opening Stock and Opening Work in Progress.   £

(2) Purchases of Stock, Raw Materials and
     Components (less any discounts
     received)   £

(3) Specified Working Expenses   £

SPECIFIED WORKING EXPENSES having
reduced the sum insured are expenses which the
Assured elects not to insure (see Note).

                                     Gross Profit £

add allowance for possible increase over last
Financial Year (see Note).   £

                                   £

increase proportionately where indemnity
period is more than 12 months.   £

                                   £

Wages, as opposed to Salaries (unless to be insured in full) should be included as a
Specified Working Expense. For further information see Part III.

PART III: WAGES

Select *either* A. Dual Wages Basis
     or   B. Limited Period Basis
     and complete either A or B below.

A. *Dual Basis*

This basis enables all employees to be retained
for a limited period and a proportion to be
retained for the remainder of the Indemnity
Period. Flexibility is provided to retain all or
a greater proportion for a lesser period and to
re-engage employees prior to resumption.

Total Annual Wage Roll (including National
Insurance Contributions, Payments pertaining
to Wages, Bonuses and Holiday Pay and the
like)   £

add allowance for possible increases over last
Financial Year (see Notes on Page 1)   £

                                   £

Increase proportionately where Indemnity
Period is more than 12 months.   £

                                   £

Coverage required: 100% for .... weeks
(minimum 4)

.... % for remainder of
Indemnity Period (minimum 10%)

The premium will vary according to the coverage selected (see Notes)

B. *Limited Period Basis*

.... Weeks wages   £ _____

This basis enables employees whose wages are insured under this item to be retained for the selected period.

The Sum Insured is the normal wages for the selected period (including National Insurance etc.) paid to the employees concerned allowing for possible wage increase.

The premium is fixed according to the period selected.

PART IV: GENERAL QUESTIONS

(1) Are you insured against Fire and other perils to be insured?
Please give name of Insurers, amount and expiry date.

(2) Are you at present insured against Loss of Profits?
Please give particulars as above.

(3) Please give details of any past losses.

Date	Cause	Material Damage Amount	Profits Amount

(4) Have you ever been declined Insurance for the Perils proposed? If so please give details.

(5) Please state date at which your financial year ends.

(6) Age of present business.

(7) Name and address of Auditors.

Signing this Form does not bind the Proposer to complete the Insurance but it is agreed that this Form shall be the basis of the contract should a Policy be issued.

I/We hereby declare that the above statements and particulars are true and that I/We have not suppressed or mis-stated any material facts.

Signature of Proposer...   Date   ....

Appendix IV

REPORTS OF CASES ARISING OUT OF THE JAMAICA EARTHQUAKE 1907

In January 1907 a disastrous earthquake occurred in Jamaica. Considerable litigation ensued. Several cases concerning insurance law were decided, and these are not readily available since they were not reported in the law reports.

Accordingly, for easy reference they are set out in this Appendix.

The cases are:

    A   *Tootal, Broadhurst, Lee Co Ltd v London and Lancashire Fire Insurance Co.*[1]
    B   *Pawsey & Co v Scottish Union and National Insurance Co.*[2]
    C   *Kingston General Comrs v Sun Insurance Office.*[3]

A Tootal, Broadhurst, Lee Co Ltd v London and Lancashire Fire Insurance Co

Tried before Bigham J and a special jury on 7 April 1908, and the following days.

This was one of the actions against fire insurance companies—the only one tried in England—which arose out of the conflagration in Kingston, Jamaica, on 14 January 1907, the day of the great earthquake.

The plaintiffs in the action were the owners of certain buildings in Kingston, Jamaica, where they kept a large stock of goods of various kinds. The policies sued on were four in number and covered, inter alia, dry goods and general merchandise whilst in premises occupied as a warehouse at No 46, Port Royal Street, Kingston, and in a detached bonded store at the rear of this building.

By the conditions of three of the policies in question which were in the same form, it was provided, inter alia, as follows:

2. If a building or any part thereof shall fall except as a result of fire, all insurance by this company on it or its contents shall immediately cease and determine.
3. This policy does not cover . . . loss or damage by fire occasioned . . . by or through . . . any earthquake.

By the conditions of the remaining policy it was provided, inter alia:

4. The insurance does not under any circumstances cover . . . loss or damage occasioned by or happening through . . . the fall of any building or part thereof except as the result of fire.

---

[1] See infra.
[2] See p 406, post.
[3] See p 411, post.

5. The insurance does not cover loss or damage by fire during (unless it be proved by the insured that the loss or damage was not occasioned thereby) or in consequence of . . . earthquake.

The plaintiffs by their points of claim alleged that the whole of the property covered by the policies in question was destroyed by fire, and they claimed a declaration that the defendants were liable to indemnify them in an amount to be subsequently ascertained by agreement or arbitration.

The defendants by their points of defence, so far as material, relied on the clauses above set out, and alleged (paragraph 6) that the plaintiffs' buildings or part of them fell otherwise than as the result of fire and/or that the alleged loss or damage was occasioned by or happened through such fall and (paragraph 7) that the fire occurred during and/or was occasioned by and, or through and, or in consequence of earthquake.

It was admitted at the trial that the fire which damaged the plaintiffs' goods originated in a building occupied by one Curphey, situated at No 87, King Street, Kingston, some 500 yards distant from the plaintiffs' premises, at about 3.30 pm, and that the plaintiffs' premises were destroyed at about 11 pm on the same day.

The defendants' evidence was directed to show (1) that the fire at No 87, King Street, was occasioned by or through or in consequence of the earthquake which occurred at about 3.30 pm on 14 January 1907, and spread by natural causes to the building containing the property insured and they therefore contended that the loss of the plaintiffs' goods was covered by the words of the exceptions; and (2) that the buildings in which the goods were stored had 'fallen' within the meaning of the condition before the fire reached them.

The plaintiffs' case, on the other hand, was (1) that the fire at No 87, King Street, began before the earthquake, and therefore that the provisions in the policies exempting the defendants from liability for loss or damage by fire occasioned by, through or in consequence of earthquake did not apply; (2) that, even supposing the fire at No 87, King Street, had been occasioned by, through or in consequence of the earthquake, the fire on the plaintiffs' premises did not fall within the exception in the policies, and could not be said to be proximately caused by earthquake, having regard to the interval of distance of time, and the changes of the wind, or, in other words, that the fire, when it reached the plaintiffs' premises, had been disconnected from the earthquake. With regard to the fall of the buildings, they contended that the clause in the policies meant such a fall as involved the complete destruction of the buildings, and that there was no such fall of the buildings containing the property insured before the fire.

During the argument a discussion took place as to the application of the doctrine of proximate cause, and Bigham J said that the contention put forward on behalf of the plaintiffs that, by reason of a change of wind, the chain of causation between the earthquake and the fire was broken, could not be correct, since wind did not cause, though it might carry, fire. After stating that the rule as to proximate cause was the same in fire insurance as in marine insurance, the learned Judge continued:

'The plaintiffs are entitled to recover because the proximate cause of the loss of their goods was fire. There is no doubt about that. But then the exception raises quite different considerations. The interpretation of the exception depends upon the language used in the exception.

The rule of insurance law as to proximate cause may not apply where there is a special contract. Earthquake cannot, as I understand, proximately cause fire. If the jerking caused by the earthquake occasioned burning coals to be thrown out of a grate on to some material, I doubt whether in that case, according to the rule, the proximate cause is the earthquake at all. The proximate cause is the burning coal falling on to the material. The remote cause is the earthquake, which causes the burning coal to jump out of the grate on to the material.

I shall tell the jury that if they find that the fire at Curphey's was set in operation by the earthquake, and then spread by natural causes to the plaintiffs' goods, their verdict must be for the defendants.

If somebody took a burning fire-brand out of Curphey's, which had been lit by the conflagration in Curphey's and then walked into the plaintiffs' place and threw the fire-brand into the plaintiffs' place, that could not be an earthquake fire.'

In the course of his summing up, Bigham J said:

'The action, as you know, is brought by Tootal, Broadhurst, Lee Co Ltd, who are a large company engaged as merchants in exporting Manchester goods. They have, and had at the time of the earthquake, a branch of their business established in Kingston, Jamaica, under the superintendence of Mr King, their agent. You know, and this is the cardinal point in the case, that on 14 January 1907, their goods contained in two buildings, one which has been called the main building, where their offices were, and the other which has been called the bonded store, where their goods were upon which duty had not yet been paid, were destroyed by fire. They had two policies issued to them by the defendant company, who are a large fire insurance company, to cover a risk of fire in respect of those goods; and it is upon those policies that this action is brought.

There is no doubt that the goods were destroyed by fire, and that they were, therefore, destroyed by the risk against which the defendant company had undertaken to indemnify the plaintiffs. So that the only question is whether the defendants have been able to make out to your satisfaction that they are, by the terms of the policy, for some reason or other—one of two reasons—entitled to refuse to pay.

The excuses for refusing to pay are to be found endorsed upon the policies, and they are as much part of the contract as that which is expressed on the front of the policy, by which they undertake to pay in the event of fire. The only difference is this, and it is an important difference and one that you must bear in mind, that, whereas it is for the plaintiffs to show that their goods have been burnt, it is for the defendants to show to your satisfaction that the circumstances which constitute an excuse for non-payment of the claim have, in fact, arisen. To use common legal language, the onus of proof so far as the excuse goes, is an onus which rests upon the defendant company.

Now, the excuses are two. The first is that the loss was caused by or through an earthquake; that is to say, the fire was occasioned by an earthquake. I will read to you the very words of the policy in a moment. The second excuse is that the buildings in which the goods were stored had fallen before they were devoured by fire, and that by the terms of the contract the insurance company from that moment, and, therefore, before the fire devoured the goods, became absolved from their liability to make good any loss by fire.

These are the two clauses. I am reading only one policy, because it appears to me that there is no distinction, and if Counsel suggests that there is, they must now interrupt me and tell me so. I am reading only one policy, because to my mind the policies are both couched in the same, though not identical, language: "If the building or any part thereof shall fall, this insurance shall immediately cease and determine." The other clause is this: "This policy does not cover loss or damage by fire occasioned by or through an earthquake." Now, remember that what you have to decide in this case is whether the evidence taken as a whole establishes one or other of those answers to the undoubted claim of the plaintiffs.

It is common ground—I am speaking about the earthquake clause—that the fire which devoured the plaintiffs' goods originated in Curphey's place—in what particular part of Curphey's place is a most important question—but it is common ground that the fire origi-nated in Curphey's place. And it is also common ground—and this you must bear in mind—that, having originated in Curphey's place, it spread down to the premises of the plaintiffs and burnt their goods, and I tell you, as a matter of law, and you must accept this from me and act upon it, that if the fire in Curphey's place was what may be called, within the terms of this contract, an earthquake fire, and if it spread, as admittedly it did, to Tootal, Broadhurst's premises which were at some distance, without the intervention of any other cause except natural causes, the defendants are entitled to your verdict. I may have to return to that point before I finish, but I want to point out to you what you have to keep your minds upon during the time that I shall have to address you. If you find that the fire at Curphey's was set in operation by the earthquake, and then spread by natural causes without the intervention of any other cause, that is, spread by wind or by one thing catching fire from another, and soon—that is what I call natural causes—and then spread without the intervention of any other cause to the plaintiffs' goods, then your verdict must be for the defendants.

The plaintiffs have done in the conduct of this case that which they were entitled to do. They have taken upon themselves to anticipate the defendants' case by calling witnesses to rebut it. I do not know whether you follow what I mean. They might have said, as apparently persons who were the plaintiffs in Jamaica did say: "We prove that our goods have been burnt—that is all; and now it is for you to prove that you come within the excuse." But they have not taken that course here. They have taken another course, which they are quite entitled to take, and they have said: "We will call our evidence to show that the theory which we know you are going to set up, that the fire, for instance, took place in Ayton's premises, is not true. Therefore they have begun with their witnesses." '

The learned Judge then dealt in detail with the evidence and, continuing, said:—

'If you think that the fall of either the main buildings or the bonded store was of such a substantial and important part of the building as to impair its usefulness as a building and to leave the remaining part of the building subject to an increased risk of fire, if you think that either of the two buildings had fallen to that extent, then you are entitled to find on that part of the case either in respect to the one building or the other in favour of the defendants.

And, finally, you must remember that this is what is called an exception in the policy, and it is for the defendants to satisfy you that the exception has arisen which excuses them. They must not leave your minds in any reasonable doubt about it, because if they do that, they have not discharged the burden which is upon them. They promise by their policy to pay if the loss is by fire; but there is this exception: "If we can prove that the fire was"—what I call an earthquake fire—"then we are not to pay; but we are to pay unless we can prove that." Therefore I say to you that you must be satisfied by the defendants that this was an earthquake fire in the sense in which I have explained to you. If you are not satisfied, then you ought to find for the plaintiffs; if you are satisfied that it was an earthquake fire, then you must find for the defendants."

The jury found a verdict for the defendants, and judgment was given accordingly.

B Pawsey & Co *v* Scottish Union and National Insurance Co

Tried before Lumb J and a special jury, at Mandeville, Jamaica, on 28, October 1907, and the following days.

This was an action arising out of the conflagration in Kingston, Jamaica, on 14 January 1907, the day on which the disastrous earthquake occurred in that island.

The action was brought to recover £8,000 under four policies of insurance against loss by fire on stock-in-trade in the plaintiffs' stores at No 104, Harbour Street, and No 19, Port Royal Street, Kingston. The defendants relied, inter alia, on the earthquake clauses in the policies sued on, three of which contained a condition providing that such policies did not cover 'loss or damage by fire occasioned by or happening through . . . earthquake', and the fourth a condition providing that such policy did not cover 'loss or damage by fire during (unless it be proved by the insured that the loss or damage was not occasioned thereby) or in consequence of . . . earthquake . . . or other convulsion of nature,' and pleaded that the loss or damage by fire was occasioned by or happened through earthquake, and alternatively that such loss or damage by fire occurred during or in consequence of earthquake or other convulsion of nature.

The plaintiffs having proved the destruction of their stock by fire, the defendants opened their case and called their evidence, which was directed to show that within a few minutes after the earthquake shock at 3.30 pm on 14 January 1907, fires broke out in different parts of Kingston; that one of these fires originated at No 87, King Street, and spread thence in a southerly direction; that another fire originated at Nos 94 and 92, Harbour Street; that both of such fires were occasioned by, or happened through or in consequence of earthquake; and that the fire at the plaintiffs' premises was caused by the spreading from one or other of these fires. They further adduced scientific evidence as to the duration of the earthquake with a view to proving that the fire at the plaintiffs' premises occurred during the earthquake. The plaintiffs' case, on the other hand, was that the fire at No 87, King Street, had its origin before the time of the great shock and therefore was not an earthquake fire; that the fire at Nos 94 and 92, Harbour Street, was caused by sparks from the fire at No 87, King Street; and even if this were not proved, that the defendants' evidence as to the origin of that fire was not sufficient to satisfy their onus of proof as to the fire at Nos 94 and 92, Harbour Street, being an earthquake fire, and was equally consistent with its having been caused by human agency, such as the striking of matches by persons entombed in the ruins.

Lumb J in the course of his summing up to the jury, said:

> 'The exemption clause frees the defendants from liability for loss by fire if occasioned by, happening through, during or in consequence of earthquake. The meaning of that exemption is that the fire must originate through an earthquake as the cause. It is not necessary that the fire which destroyed the plaintiffs' goods should have originated in his own building. If the fire originated by earthquake in any other building, and that fire was transmitted through several other buildings to the plaintiffs', the defendants would not be liable, because that fire would be a fire caused by earthquake. The burden of proof is on the defendants; that is to say, they have to prove that the fire which destroyed the plaintiffs' goods was caused by earthquake . . . the defendants must prove to your satisfaction that the fire was within the exemption clause, that is, that it was an earthquake-caused fire. If you are unable to find from the evidence how the fire which destroyed the plaintiffs' goods originated, you must say so in your answers to the questions that I am going to put to you . . .
>
> In dealing with these questions the question of what has been described as "the proximate cause" has been raised. "Proximate cause" means the active, efficient cause that sets in motion a train of events which brings about a result, without the intervention of any force started and working actively from a new and independent source . . .'

His Honour proceeded to deal with the evidence and left the following questions to the jury: (1) Was the fire which destroyed the plaintiffs' goods occasioned by or did it happen through earthquake? (2) Did the fire which destroyed the plaintiffs' goods occur during or in consequence of earthquake? (3) Was there any intervening force sufficient of itself to cause the fire which destroyed the plaintiffs' goods?

The jury unanimously found a negative answer to the first two questions, and judgment was accordingly given for the plaintiffs.

The defendants appealed to the Supreme Court of Jamaica on the ground that the verdict was against the weight of evidence and also on the ground of the learned Judge's misdirection and failure to direct the jury.

The appeal was heard before Fielding Clarke C J, and Lumb and Vickers JJ, on 16 December 1907, and the following days, and judgment dismissing the appeal was delivered on 1 February 1908.

In the course of his judgment Fielding Clarke C J said:—

> It was submitted for the defendants that Mr. Justice Lumb in putting the question as to the loss or damage by fire "during" the earthquake, should have told the jury that it was immaterial whether such fire was occasioned by, or happened through, or occurred in consequence of earthquake. Scientific evidence was given for the defendants with a view to proving that the earthquake was still going on while the plaintiffs' store was being burnt. This evidence, whether of any practical value or not, is obviously immaterial unless the exception in the policy of loss or damage by fire during earthquake related to any fire however caused. I cannot gather from this policy that such was the meaning. Taking the words in brackets, "unless etc", and reading into them the word "earthquake", the condition runs thus: "The insurance does not cover loss or damage by fire during (earthquake) unless it be proved by the insured that the loss or damage was not occasioned by (earthquake)." The meaning clearly is that if the insured proves that loss or damage by fire during earthquake was not occasioned by earthquake, the insurer is to indemnify. Apart, therefore, from the condition as to proof by the insured, the insurer is protected by the condition only when the loss or damage by fire was occasioned by earthquake; and it follows that, in my opinion, there was no misdirection in the instruction to the jury, that to exempt the defendants from indemnifying the plaintiffs in respect of a fire during earthquake "the fire must originate through the earthquake as the cause."
>
> It was submitted for the defendants in the next place that in his direction as to burden of proof the Judge should not have included loss or damage by fire during earthquake, because the exception clause in the policy in question expressly provides that in such case the insured must prove that the loss or damage was occasioned by earthquake. I think the proof referred to in the condition is merely preliminary proof to satisfy the insurer, and has no connection with evidence in an action. The proof referred to might have been required before action, but, as it was waived, the condition cannot be set up in any way. For the above reasons I think the motion fails so far as it is based on misdirection. . . '

The defendants afterwards appealed to the Privy Council on the same grounds, and the hearing took place on 22 July 1908, and the following days, before Lords Macnaghten, Atkinson, and Collins, and Sir Arthur Wilson.

The judgment of the Privy Council dismissing the appeal was delivered by Sir Arthur Wilson on 16 October 1908, and was as follows:

> 'At the close of the arguments in this case, on 4 August last, their Lordships intimated that they would humbly advise His Majesty that the appeal should be dismissed with costs. It remains to state somewhat more fully than could then be done, the reasons which led their Lordships to tender that advice.
>
> The action out of which the appeal arises was brought in the Supreme Court of Jamaica by the respondents against the appellants, upon four policies of fire insurance, issued by the appellants in favour of the respondents, the subject-matter insured being the stock-in-trade in the premises No 104, Harbour Street, Kingston, and adjoining premises. Each of the first three policies contained a clause to the effect that the policy did not cover "loss or damage by fire occasioned by or happening through . . . earthquakes". The fourth policy contained a clause to the effect that the policy did not cover "loss or damage by fire during (unless it be proved by the insured that the loss or damage was not occasioned thereby) or in consequence of . . . earthquake". The appellants denied liability.
>
> The action was tried at Mandeville (the venue having been changed from Kingston on the application of the appellants) before Lumb J and a special jury.
>
> At the trial it was not disputed that the property insured was destroyed by fire on 14 January 1907. The principal question, stated in its broadest form, was whether the fire that did the damage was occasioned by earthquake, so as to fall within the clauses of the policies protecting the appellants from liability for damage caused by such fires.
>
> Upon this question the learned Judge placed upon the appellants the burden of establishing the affirmative, and that ruling seems to have been accepted at the trial. Nor was it disputed on the argument of this appeal so far as the first three policies are concerned. As to them, therefore, there is no question before their Lordships of the burden of proof. Objection was

taken on the argument of this appeal to the ruling as applied in the fourth policy. And it may be convenient to deal with this point at once.

The learned Judge at the trial, in dealing with the burden of proof, treated all the four policies alike, placing the burden upon the appellants. It was contended that in this there was misdirection as to the fourth policy; that as to it the proper direction was that, if the loss by fire occurred during the earthquake, the burden lay upon the respondents to show that the earthquake was not the cause.

Their Lordships are of opinion that the contention of the appellants on this point is correct, and that the proper ruling would have been that suggested. But the difference between the one ruling and the other is material only if the loss by fire occurred during the earthquake, and whether it did so or not was a question for the jury. That question was left to the jury, and left with a proper direction, and answered in the negative. The misdirection complained of thus became inoperative.

The trial lasted for sixteen days, and much evidence was called on both sides. At the close of the trial the questions left by the learned Judge to the jury and the answers of the jury thereto were as follows:

1. Was the fire which destroyed the respondents's property occasioned by or did it happen through an earthquake? No.
2. Did the fire which destroyed the respondents' property occur during or in consequence of an earthquake? No.
3. Was there any intervening force sufficient to cause the fire to destroy the respondents' property? The jury did not answer this question.

Upon these findings judgment was entered for the respondents.

The appellants moved to the Supreme Court to set aside the verdict and judgment, and to order a new trial or to enter judgment for the appellants. The motion was heard before the learned Chief Justice and Lumb and Vickers JJ; and after argument the motion was dismissed. Against that judgment the present appeal has been brought, in which the appellants ask that a new trial should be ordered.

Certain facts not in dispute must be kept in mind to order to appreciate the matters which are the subject of controversy.

Harbour Street, on the south side of which the respondents' premises were situated, is a broad street nearly fifty feet wide, running east and west. It is crossed at right angles by King Street at a point some distance to the west, and by Church Street at a point a short distance to the east of the respondents' premises, both King Street and Church Street being streets of about the same width as Harbour Street.

On the day on which the respondents' property was burned, 14 January 1907, a violent shock of earthquake occurred causing widespread destruction in Kingston. The hour is accepted by both sides as 3.30 pm and the duration of the shock is stated by witnesses as about half a minute. During the night and day that followed minor shocks seem to have been perceived, but the substantial mischief was done by the first shock, and it is the only one with which the present appeal is directly concerned.

In the afternoon of 14 January near the time of the great earthquake shock, three fires broke out in Kingston. One was in Princess Street, a considerable distance to the west of the respondents' premises. Nothing turns upon this fire for the purposes of the present appeal. Another fire broke out in No 87, King Street, a house on the west side of that street near its northern end. This lay to the north and a little to the west of the respondents' premises, at a distance (according to evidence which does not appear to have been disputed) of about a quarter of a mile. A third fire broke out in the premises of No 92, Harbour Street, known as the Army and Navy Stores, lying six numbers to the east of the respondents' premises, but separated therefrom (between Nos 100 and 102) by the width of Church Street, which crosses at that point.

These last-mentioned two fires and the questions arising as to the origins of each and the connection of either or both with the destruction of the respondents' premises formed the subject of inquiry at the trial, and are the matter for consideration upon this appeal.

The verdict of the jury was in favour of the respondents, and the substantial ground of appeal is that that verdict was wrong. The rule acted upon by this Board, as well as by other appellate tribunals, in cases where the verdict of a jury is thus impugned, is clear and well settled. It is not enough to show that adverse criticism may justly be applied to the verdict or to the evidence upon which it was based. It is not enough to show that a contrary verdict might well have been found. It is not enough that those sitting in appeal should consider that such a contrary verdict would have been preferable to that actually returned. It is for the jury to decide questions of fact, and their decision upon such questions cannot be interfered with by an appellate tribunal unless it be shown that that decision was one which could not reasonably have been arrived at upon the evidence before the jury. That is the test to be applied in the present case; and this was clearly recognized by the learned Counsel for the appellants.

On behalf of the appellants it was contended, first, that the fire which destroyed the respondents' property was due to the extension of the Harbour Street conflagration which broke out in No 92 of that street. It was contended, secondly, that the Harbour Street fire arose independently of any other fire, and that it was caused by earthquake. It was contended, thirdly, that, even if the first contention failed, and if it could be supposed that the fire, which destroyed the property insured, came from the extension of the King Street fire, still that fire was a fire caused by earthquake.

The respondents denied each of the allegations of the appellants. They further contended affirmatively that the fire which destroyed the property insured either was or might have been caused by an extension of the King Street fire, and that that fire was not an earthquake fire, but had broken out before the shock occurred.

Three questions thus arose—first, where did the fire come from which destroyed the property insured? Secondly, what was the origin of the Harbour Street fire? Thirdly, what was the origin of the King Street fire?

As to the first of these questions, three answers have been suggested, and each has credible evidence to support it. The view primarily contended for by the appellants was that the Harbour Street fire, originating in the Army and Navy Stores, travelled westward along the south side of Harbour Street, crossing Church Street on its way and so reached the respondents' premises in a direct line. That this was what happened is mainly supported by the evidence of Robert Jones, but other witnesses go far to corroborate him. The letters written immediately afterwards by the resident member of the respondents' firm, to his partners in England, express the same view. But this is of the less importance, because the writer was not speaking of matters within his own personal knowledge. If the jury accepted this view (whether they did so or not it is impossible to say), they certainly acted not unreasonably.

The second answer to the question under consideration is that the Harbour Street fire was checked in its direct progress westward by the width of Church Street and by the overflow, by earthquake, of the house on the west of that street; that the fire found its way to a building known as the Beehive at the corner on the north of Harbour Street and east of Church Street; and that from the Beehive the fire spread obliquely to the insured property. This account of the matter is supported mainly by the evidence of the witness John MacDonald. If the jury accepted this account, it could not be said they acted unreasonably. But this is of the less importance, because the result is the same, whether this view or the first should be accepted. The matter is, however, of weight as showing the obscurity which surrounds the most elementary facts of the case.

A third answer to the question is that the fire which destroyed the insured property was not, or may not have been, due to the spread from the east of that Harbour Street fire which began in the Army and Navy Stores, but was or may have been due to the spread from the north of the King Street fire. The King Street fire was in full blaze half an hour to three-quarters of an hour (the witnesses vary) before that in the Army and Navy Stores was first seen. There was evidence from which the jury might have considered that the King Street fire spread rapidly towards the south; that it did so spread sooner or later seems clear. And there was the positive evidence of Herbert Mackenzie that the fire from the north had reached De Sousa's premises in Water Lane, and that there were in a blaze by the time when the respondents' premises took fire. De Sousa's premises appear to have been within sixty yards to the due north of the respondents, the intermediate buildings, according to MacDonald's evidence, having fallen in the earthquake. Mackenzie's evidence on this subject receives substantial corroboration from that of other witnesses. And their Lordships cannot say that the jury may not have been justified in accepting it. And, if so, it follows, in their Lordships' opinion, that the jury were not unreasonable in concluding, if they did so conclude, that the destruction of the insured property was due, or might well have been due, to the spread of the King Street fire, or to it and the Harbour Street fire conjointly.

The second question relates to the origin of the Harbour Street fire, whether it was a fire occasioned by the earthquake. The earthquake shock is admitted on both sides to have occurred at 3.30. The outbreak of the Harbour Street fire is put by various witnesses at an interval of half to three-quarters of an hour after the shock. It cannot, therefore, in their Lordships' opinion, be said that the fire followed the earthquake shock so quickly as to lead to any very strong presumption that the one event was the cause of the other.

Apart from any such presumption the case of the appellants on this point rests entirely upon the theory that the fire in the Army and Navy Stores began with the ignition of certain boxes of matches in those Stores. The Stores were overthrown by the earthquake; and the evidence is that there were standing upon a shelf in the stores, near where the fire was first perceived, ten or twelve parcels each containing a gross of boxes of safety matches. It was contended that some of the matches must be presumed to have come in contact with some of the prepared surface, in consequence of the fall of the shelf when the premises were wrecked. This, however, is necessarily a somewhat speculative view. Their Lordships think it impossible to say that the jury were bound to accept it as conclusively correct. They might well have been of opinion that that view was insufficiently supported, and that the origin of the fire was not accounted for.

The third question for consideration is whether the jury were bound to find that the King Street fire was occasioned by the earthquake, a question which has to be dealt with in case the jury may have been of opinion that the damage to the property insured resulted from the spread of that fire.

Their Lordships are of opinion that the jury might reasonably have formed the opinion that the King Street fire had broken out before the earthquake shock, or, at least, that it was not conclusively shown to have resulted from that shock. The difference in time between the accounts given of that fire by different witnesses is only a few minutes, for there is no doubt that within a very few minutes after the shock, if not a few minutes before it, the premises No 87, King Street, were in full blaze. There was direct evidence, especially that of Mrs Calnek, that the fire was seen before the earthquake. It was said for the appellants that her evidence was so inherently improbable that it ought to have been rejected altogether; but it did not stand alone. The evidence of Duperley is not open to the same criticism; the evidence of the witnesses from a distance, who say that they saw smoke rising before the earthquake shock, demanded the most serious consideration of the jury; and more than one of the other witnesses tended to confirm the view that the fire preceded the earthquake.

The evidence relied upon on behalf of the appellants to show that the fire followed the earthquake, was very important, and if the jury accepted it, it would be impossible to say that their doing so was unreasonable. But it was not in all points evidence of a wholly satisfactory character, and their Lordships are of opinion that on the whole of the evidence the jury might reasonably have found that the fire was not shown to have resulted from the earthquake.

The result is that, in their Lordships' opinion, the jury might reasonably have considered that the fire which destroyed the respondents' property was due to the spread of the Harbour Street fire, or that it was due to the spread of the King Street fire, or that it was uncertain to which it was due, or whether to both.

Their Lordships are further of opinion that the jury might reasonably have thought that the Harbour Street fire was not shown to have resulted from the earthquake.

They also think that, on the materials before them, the jury might reasonably have held that the King Street fire broke out before the earthquake.'

C Kingston General Commissioners v Sun Insurance Office

Tried before Cargill J and a special jury at Montego Bay, Jamaica, on 2 November 1907, and the following days, and heard on appeal before the Supreme Court of Jamaica (Fielding Clarke C J, Lumb and Vickers JJ.) on 20 December 1907, and the following days.

The action was brought to recover the sum of £1,100 on two policies of insurance covering the building known as No 24, Church Street, Kingston, and certain scientific instruments contained therein. The building and the instruments were destroyed in the conflagration referred to in the preceding cases, and the issues raised were substantially the same. It was admitted that the fire which burned the plaintiffs' premises originated at No 87, King Street, and therefore the only question which arose was when and how such fire originated.

The only question left to the jury was: 'Have the plaintiffs proved to your satisfaction that the fire which originated at No 87, King Street, started before the commencement of the earthquake on 14 January 1907?' The question was answered in the affirmative, and judgment was accordingly given for the plaintiffs.

The defendants appealed to the Supreme Court of Jamaica on the ground that the verdict was against the weight of evidence. The Court (Fielding Clarke C J dissenting) dismissed the appeal on 1 February 1908, on the ground that it was impossible to say that the jury were so wrong that their verdict ought to be set aside.

Fielding Clarke C J:

'In considering the excepted peril of fire caused by earthquake, a wrong application of the distinction between proximate and remote cause must be guarded against. Earthquake is always a remote rather than a proximate cause of fire, and to apply the maxim ie *causa proxima non remota spectatur*) reasonably would be to strike the exception out of the contract. If earthquake is to be treated as a direct or proximate cause of fire at the place where it starts the fire, I think that, in this sense, it must continue to be the cause of fire as long as the fire spreads from conditions resulting from earthquake merely by the ordinary agencies of atmosphere and breeze, and I am unable to draw any distinction in such a case between the extension of the fire to an adjoining house and its extension through several houses or streets to a distant building. If there were evidence of some new force or incident of an unusual nature, unconnected with the earthquake, which had the independent effect of extending the conflagration to the insured premises, there might, I think, perhaps be a question of fact for the jury whether a cause of loss more proximate than the earthquake had intervened, even if such new force or incident should be in itself incapable of producing ignition. However this may be, the intervention of such new force or incident cannot, in my judgment, be presumed as a matter of law from the mere spread of the fire.'

The rest of the Court expressed no opinion on this point.

The defendants afterwards appealed to the Privy Council, but abandoned their appeal after the decision of the Privy Council in the preceding case.

PART II—MOTOR INSURANCE

Appendix V

SPECIMEN PROPOSAL FORM IN RESPECT OF
MOTOR INSURANCE

With the kind permission of the Commercial Union Assurance Co Ltd a
proposal form in respect of a private motor car is reproduced on the following
page.

Commercial Union Assurance
Motor Car Insurance
Proposal Form

ASSURANCE

Please answer all questions carefully and correctly, as it is an offence under the Road Traffic Act to make any false statement or withhold any material information for the purpose of obtaining a Certificate of Motor Insurance.

PLEASE USE BLOCK CAPITALS

Surname (Mr./Mrs./Miss)

First name(s)

Address

Postcode

Telephone No.

Occupation(s) (If more than one, state all)

Address at which your car is kept (if not as above)

Insurance required (please tick appropriate box)

Comprehensive ☐

Own damage excess (if required)   £50 ☐   or £75 ☐

Third Party, Fire and Theft ☐

Third Party ☐

Please indicate Class of Use required.

Class C (Pleasure) ☐ Use by anyone for social, domestic and pleasure (including travel to and from usual place of work). Use for hiring or any business purpose is excluded.

Class A (Pleasure and *personal* business) ☐ Use by anyone for social, domestic and pleasure and by you in person for your business. Use for hiring, motor trade purposes and commercial travelling is excluded.

Class B (Pleasure and business) ☐ Use by anyone for social, domestic and pleasure and by any person for your or your employer's or partner's business. The carriage of passengers for hire or reward is excluded.

Note: All classes exclude use for racing, competitions, rallies or trials.

Will your car be used for any purpose not provided for in the class of use indicated? [YES/NO] (if YES please give details)

What date do you require insurance to commence?

No insurance will be in force until you receive an official cover note. Commercial Union Assurance reserve the right to decline any proposal.

FOR OFFICE USE

Policy Number MP _____ Premium _____ Points total _____

Agent's name _____ Branch and Agent No. ⌞_⌞_⌞_⌞_⌞_⌞_⌞_⌞_⌟

Period of insurance From _____ to _____ Renewal date _____

Your car(s)

Make and Model including whether L, GL, S etc.	Type of Body e.g. Saloon, Hatchback, Coupé etc	Year of Make	Cubic Capacity	Seating Capacity	Value	Registration Number

	YES/NO	If YES, please give details
a) Has the car been converted, adapted or modified in any way?		
b) Is the car (i) owned by a person other than yourself? or (ii) registered in the name of a person other than yourself?	(i) (ii)	
c) Are you the owner of any other motor vehicles?		

Drivers

When completing 1 and 2 below, please give details for yourself and your spouse (whether likely to drive or not) and all other persons who to your knowledge may drive your car.

1a) Full Name	Occupation(s)	Date of Birth	Type of licence currently held (e.g. Full, Provisional or International)	Date driving test passed
(Myself)				
(My spouse)				

b) Do you wish driving to be restricted to:

yourself [YES/NO] or yourself and spouse [YES/NO] If NO who will be the main driver? [_____]

When completing Question 2 below you are not required to include convictions regarded as 'spent' by virtue of the Rehabilitation of Offenders Act, 1974.

	YES/NO	If YES, please give details
2. Has any person mentioned above:		
a) been involved in any motor accident or loss within the last 3 years		
b) been convicted of any motoring offence within the last 5 years, or is any prosecution pending		
c) been disqualified from driving		
d) defective vision or hearing, or suffered at any time from diabetes, fits or any heart complaint or any other disease or infirmity		
e) been refused motor insurance, renewal or had any special terms or conditions imposed by any insurer?		

3. a) Have you held or do you now hold a car insurance policy?	Name of Company	Expiry Date
b) Are you entitled to a no claim discount? You need to send proof of no claim discount (e.g. your last renewal notice).	No. of Years	

Any other facts known to you which are likely to affect acceptance or assessment of the risks proposed for insurance must be disclosed. Should you have any doubt about what you should disclose, do not hesitate to tell us or your insurance adviser. This is for your own protection, as failure to disclose may mean that your policy will not provide you with the cover you require, or may perhaps invalidate the policy altogether.

Declaration

I declare that the statements and particulars given in this proposal are, to the best of my knowledge and belief, true and complete, and that this proposal shall form the basis of my contract with Commercial Union Assurance Company plc.

I agree that the insurance will not be in force until the proposal has been accepted by the Company, except to the extent of any official cover note which may be issued.

Signed _____ Date _____

Appendix VI

SPECIMEN MOTOR INSURANCE POLICIES

With the kind permission of the Commercial Union Assurance Co. Ltd. various types of motor insurance policies are reproduced below.

The policies are:

A   Motor Car Policy.
B   Motor Cycle Policy.
C   Commercial Motor Vehicle Policy.

A MOTOR CAR POLICY

Here is your new insurance policy. Please examine it together with the schedule and Certificate of Motor Insurance, to make sure you have the protection you need. It is important that these and any amendments are read together to avoid misunderstanding.

Almost certainly your needs will change. If they do, please let us know – your policy is designed for easy amendment or extension.

How your Insurance operates

Your Motor Car policy is a contract between us the Company and you our Policyholder. The policy, current schedule and Certificate of Motor Insurance combine to show the extent of your insurance. The proposal form and declaration which you signed is the basis of this contract.

We agree to pay for any damage, loss or liability as set out in this policy, which occurs during any period of insurance for which you have paid a premium.

Our Promise of Service

We wish to provide you with a high standard of service and to meet any claims covered by this policy honestly, fairly and promptly. Should you have any reason to believe that we have not done so, and you wish to make a complaint, please contact your broker or agent. If you do not have a professional adviser please contact your CU branch manager who has wide authority. He will be ready to help you with your problems.

In the unlikely event that you are still not satisfied, contact our Consumer Relations Executive at St. Helen's, 1 Undershaft, London EC3P 3DQ or telephone 01-283 7500. If you the Policyholder are a private individual, you also have the right to make an appeal to the Insurance Ombudsman as we are members of the Insurance Ombudsman Bureau. We must abide by his decision, but if you are still unsatisfied you have the right to take the matter further.

By authority of the Board

General Conditions

We will act in good faith in all our dealings with you.

Claims Procedure

1 If damage to your **Motor Car** is covered by this policy, you may authorise its repair without telling us first. You must however send to us as soon as reasonably possible a detailed estimate of the cost and we reserve the right to seek alternative estimates.

2 The payment of claims is dependent on:
Your own observance of the following:

a) taking reasonable steps to safeguard against accident, injury, loss or damage and maintaining your **Motor Car** in a safe and roadworthy condition.

b) your **Motor Car** (or any borrowed vehicle) only being driven or used as permitted by the **Certificate**. Regardless of this, when your **Motor Car** is in the hands of a member of the motor trade for servicing or repair, the insurance continues to operate to protect you the **Policyholder.**

c) reporting in writing to us as soon as reasonably possible full details of any incident which may result in a claim under this policy.

d) forwarding to us every writ, summons, legal process or other communication in connection with the claim immediately upon receipt.

e) giving us all necessary information and assistance that we may require.

f) not admitting liability or making an offer or promise of payment without our written consent.

g) notifying the police as soon as reasonably possible of loss or damage caused by theft. You also have an obligation to notify the police in certain circumstances if you are involved in a road accident.

Your recognition of our right:

h) to take over and deal with in your name the defence or settlement of any claim.

i) to take proceedings in your name, but at our expense, to recover compensation for any payment made under this policy for our benefit.

j) to make to the legal owner or to the hire purchase company any payment for loss or damage, if we know the **Motor Car** is owned by someone other than the **Policyholder** or is the subject of a hiring or hire purchase agreement.

k) if a claim is not covered by this policy — to recover from the **Insured Person** any payment made solely because of the compulsory insurance law of a country to which this policy applies.

l) to settle your claim on a proportionate basis if you have other insurance covering the same loss, damage or liability.

General Exceptions

1 This policy does not insure any destruction of, or damage to any property or any consequential loss or any legal liability directly or indirectly caused by, or contributed to, or arising from:

Radioactive contamination
- ionising radiations or contamination by radioactivity from any nuclear fuel or from any nuclear waste from the combustion of nuclear fuel
- the radioactive, toxic, explosive or other hazardous properties of any explosive nuclear assembly or component.

War risks
- war, invasion, act of foreign enemy, hostilities (whether war be declared or not), civil war, rebellion, revolution or military or usurped power.

Sonic bangs
- pressure waves caused by aircraft and other aerial devices.

Additional liabilities
2 If you enter into any agreement which could mean you incur additional liabilities, this policy will not operate for those additional liabilities.

General Conditions (continued)

m) where we have accepted a claim but the amount to be paid is in dispute — to refer the matter to an independent arbitrator acceptable to the parties involved. This does not affect the right to refer also to the Insurance Ombudsman.

Any other person entitled to claim the benefit of this policy must also observe its terms and conditions.

Change of (or additional) car
3 You must tell us immediately of any additional or replacement car you wish to have insured. If you do not tell us and an accident happens with the car concerned then this policy does not operate. You may have to pay an additional premium for either an additional or replacement car and equally you may be entitled to a refund of premium for a sold or replacement car. The amount of additional or refund of premium will depend on the period remaining to renewal from the effective date of the change.

Cancellation
4 You may cancel this policy at any time by letter. We may cancel this policy by sending seven days notice by recorded delivery letter or registered letter to your last known address. Any return of premium due will depend on when the policy was taken out, how long it had been in force, and whether any claims have been made. The Certificate must be returned to us and any refund will be calculated from the date it is received.

Definition of words

Policyholder
The person shown as the policyholder in the schedule.

If there is more than one person named in the schedule as the policyholder, this policy applies both jointly and individually.

Certificate
Your current valid Certificate of Motor Insurance which has the same number as this policy.

The **Certificate**, not the policy, is the document which you may be required to produce to the police as evidence of insurance. The **Certificate** also sets out who may drive the car, who may use it and for what purpose.

Motor Car
Any vehicle described in the "Description of Vehicles" in your **Certificate.**

Insured Person
The term Insured Person in paragraph 2 headed Liability means:

- the **Policyholder**
- other persons who are permitted by your **Certificate** to drive or use the vehicle
- the employer or partner of any person whose business use is permitted by your **Certificate**
- at your request
  a) any person getting into or out of or travelling in your **Motor Car**
  b) the owner of the **Motor Car** if someone other than yourself.

Excess
The amount you pay towards the agreed cost of any claim for loss or damage to your **Motor Car.**

Excesses do not apply when:

- the loss or damage is caused by fire, self-ignition, lightning, explosion, theft or attempted theft
- the only damage is breakage of the windscreen or windows and any scratching of the bodywork incidental to the breakage.

Interpretation

Car Sharing

Should you carry passengers for social or other similar purposes and receive a contribution to your costs, we will not regard this as constituting the carriage of passengers for hire or reward (or the use of the vehicle for hiring) provided that:

a) the vehicle is not constructed or adapted to carry more than 8 passengers (excluding the driver)

b) the passengers are not being carried in the course of a business of carrying passengers

c) the total contributions received for the journey concerned do not involve an element of profit.

Note:
If in any doubt whether a car sharing arrangement is covered by your motor insurance you should immediately seek confirmation from us.

6

Insurance Provided

The insurance provided is shown in your current schedule and this determines which paragraphs of this policy apply.

Insurance Provided	Paragraphs which apply
● Comprehensive	All
● Third Party Fire and Theft	All except 3, 4 & 6, but paragraph 1 applies only to losses resulting from: – fire – self-ignition – lightning – explosion – theft or attempted theft
● Third Party	All except 1, 3, 4 & 6

The insurance provided will operate throughout the British Isles including transit by sea between its ports. You also have insurance for any vehicle to which this policy applies for the minimum insurance required to comply with the laws relating to compulsory insurance of vehicles in the following countries:

● **EEC** — Belgium, Denmark, France, Germany (West), Greece, Holland, Italy, Luxembourg

● **Other European Countries** — Austria, Czechoslovakia, Finland, Germany (East), Hungary, Norway, Sweden, Switzerland

● any other country for which the Commission of the EEC is satisfied that arrangements have been made to meet the requirements of EEC Directives on insurance.

Motor Car Policy (continued)

We will pay:

Damage

Loss or damage to your Motor Car

1 a) The cost of repair or replacement for loss or damage to your **Motor Car** and its accessories, spare parts or components, whether on your **Motor Car** or in your private garage. The maximum amount payable will be the reasonable market value immediately prior to the loss or damage.

New car replacement

b) The cost of replacing your **Motor Car** at your request (subject to the consent of any other interested party) with a new one of the same make and model (if available in the United Kingdom) if within 12 months from its date of first registration as new, your **Motor Car** is:

- stolen and not recovered, or

- damaged in any single accident and the cost of repair or replacement exceeds 50% of the United Kingdom list price (including taxes) when your **Motor Car** was new.

Towing and delivery charges

c) ● The reasonable costs of protection and removal to the nearest repairers if, as a result of any loss or damage which is insured by this paragraph, your **Motor Car** is disabled.

● The reasonable cost of delivery to the **Policyholder** in the British Isles after repair.

We will not pay for:

1 ● The total amount of any **Excess** shown in the schedule for loss or damage to your **Motor Car**

● An **Excess** of £50 for each loss or damage to your **Motor Car** (other than when your **Motor Car** is in the hands of a member of the motor trade for servicing or repair) while it is being driven by any person who:

- is under 25 years of age, or

- holds a provisional driving licence, or

- has held for less than 12 months a full licence to drive a vehicle of the same class as your **Motor Car**

This is in addition to any **Excess** shown in the schedule

● Wear and tear, depreciation, mechanical or electrical breakdown

● Damage to tyres by the application of brakes or by road punctures, cuts or bursts

● Loss of use

● Loss or damage due to:

- earthquake

- riot or civil commotion other than in Great Britain, the Isle of Man or the Channel Islands.

Motor Car Policy (continued)

We will pay:

Liability

Liability to other people and their property

2 a) The amount of:
- damages and claimant's costs and expenses
- any other costs and expenses agreed between us in writing

arising from bodily injury or damage to property for which the **Insured Person** may be liable at law resulting from an accident involving your **Motor Car.**

Legal representation

b) At your request:
- the solicitor's fee for:
  - representation at any coroner's inquest or fatal enquiry
  - defending in any Court of Summary Jurisdiction any proceedings
- the reasonable costs agreed by us for:
  - legal services for defence in the event of proceedings being taken for manslaughter or reckless driving causing death

arising from an accident which may result in a claim.

Driving borrowed vehicles

c) For liability to other people and their property, as shown in paragraphs 2a) & b), while an **Insured Person** is driving another car or motor cycle, but only when this is permitted by your **Certificate.**

We will not pay for:

2 Losses under the whole of this paragraph for:
- damage caused by an **Insured Person** to his own property or property which is in his custody or control
- damage to your **Motor Car** or any borrowed vehicle
- bodily injury to any person arising out of and in the course of their employment by an **Insured Person.**

9

Motor Car Policy (continued)

We will pay:

Personal injury to you or your spouse

3 a) £1,000 if the **Policyholder** or the **Policyholder's** spouse suffers accidental injury:

- in direct connection with your **Motor Car**
- while travelling in, or getting into or out of, any other private car which does not belong to you

and within three calendar months the injury is the sole cause of:

- death, or
- total and permanent loss of all sight in one or both eyes, or
- total loss by physical severance or total and permanent loss of use of one or both hands or feet.

The maximum amount payable for any one person following any one accident is £1,000.

Payment will be made direct to the injured person or to their legal personal representatives.

If you or your spouse have any other motor insurance with us, payment will be made under one policy only.

Increased benefit if wearing a seat belt

b) If at the time the injured person is wearing a seat belt, the amount payable will be increased to £5,000.

We will not pay for:

3 Injuries arising if:

- the injured person is younger than 25 or older than 75 years of age at the time of injury
- the injury is a result of suicide or attempted suicide
- the **Policyholder** is a corporate body or firm
- caused by earthquake
- caused by riot or civil commotion other than in Great Britain, the Isle of Man or the Channel Islands
- the injury is caused or aggravated by any pre-existing illness or condition.

10

Motor Car Policy (continued)

We will pay:

Medical expenses

4 Up to £100 for each person for medical expenses incurred from injuries suffered in an accident while in your **Motor Car.**

Emergency treatment

5 The cost of emergency treatment incurred under the Road Traffic Acts and arising from the use of a vehicle covered under this policy.

Personal belongings

6 Up to £100 in total for accidental loss of or damage to any personal belongings while in or on your **Motor Car.**

We will not pay for:

6 • Money, stamps, documents and securities
   • Goods or samples carried in connection with any trade.

11

No Claim Discount

Scale

If **no** claim is made or arises under this policy in a period of insurance, we will reduce your renewal premium as follows:

Claim free Period of Insurance	No Claim Discount premium reduction
1 year	30%
2 years	40%
3 years	50%
4 years or more	60%

If only **one** claim is made or arises in any year of insurance, the premium reduction at next renewal will be:

No Claim Discount at last renewal	No Claim Discount premium reduction at next renewal
30%	Nil
40%	Nil
50%	30%
60%	40%

If **more than one** claim is made or arises in any year of insurance, there will be no No Claim Discount reduction from the next renewal premium.

If this policy applies to more than one car, your No Claim Discount will apply as if a separate policy had been issued for each car.

No Claim Discount is not transferable from one person to another.

Protected no claim discount

Your no claim discount will not be lost if:

Policyholders aged 50 or over

● the **Policyholder** has attained his 50th birthday and is entitled to a 60% No Claim Discount premium reduction.

Windscreen breakage

● the only claim is for the breakage of the windscreen or windows of the **Motor Car** and incidental scratching of the bodywork.

Car being serviced or repaired

● a claim involving your **Motor Car** occurs while it is in the hands of a member of the motor trade for servicing or repair.

Emergency treatment

● the only payment is for emergency treatment as required by the Road Traffic Acts.

12

B MOTOR CYCLE POLICY

YP26A
6/83

CU Motor Cycle Policy

Here is your new insurance policy. Please examine it together with the schedule and Certificate of Motor Insurance, to make sure you have the protection you need. It is important that these and any amendments are read together to avoid misunderstanding.

Almost certainly your needs will change. If they do, please let us know – your policy is designed for easy amendment or extension.

How your Insurance operates

Your Motor Cycle policy is a contract between us the Company and you our Policyholder. The policy, current schedule and Certificate of Motor Insurance combine to show the extent of your insurance. The proposal form and declaration which you signed is the basis of this contract.

We agree to pay for any damage, loss or liability as set out in this policy, which occurs during any period of insurance for which you have paid a premium.

Our Promise of Service

We wish to provide you with a high standard of service and to meet any claims covered by this policy honestly, fairly and promptly. Should you have any reason to believe that we have not done so, and you wish to make a complaint, please contact your broker or agent. If you do not have a professional adviser please contact your CU branch manager who has wide authority. He will be ready to help you with your problems.

In the unlikely event that you are still not satisfied, contact our Consumer Relations Executive at St. Helen's, 1 Undershaft, London EC3P 3DQ or telephone 01-283 7500. If you the Policyholder are a private individual, you also have the right to make an appeal to the Insurance Ombudsman as we are members of the Insurance Ombudsman Bureau. We must abide by his decision, but if you are still unsatisfied you have the right to take the matter further.

By authority of the Board

General Conditions

We will act in good faith in all our dealings with you.

Claims Procedure

1   If damage to your **Motor Cycle** is covered by this policy, you may authorise its repair without telling us first. You must however send to us as soon as reasonably possible a detailed estimate of the cost and we reserve the right to seek alternative estimates.

2   The payment of claims is dependent on:

Your own observance of the following:

a) taking reasonable steps to safeguard against accident, injury, loss or damage and maintaining your **Motor Cycle** in a safe and roadworthy condition.

b) your **Motor Cycle** (or any borrowed motor cycle) only being driven or used as permitted by the **Certificate**. Regardless of this, when your **Motor Cycle** is in the hands of a member of the motor trade for servicing or repair, the insurance continues to operate to protect you the **Policyholder.**

c) reporting in writing to us as soon as reasonably possible full details of any incident which may result in a claim under this policy.

d) forwarding to us every writ, summons, legal process or other communication in connection with the claim immediately upon receipt.

e) giving us all necessary information and assistance that we may require.

f) not admitting liability or making an offer or promise of payment without our written consent.

g) notifying the police as soon as reasonably possible of loss or damage caused by theft. You also have an obligation to notify the police in certain circumstances if you are involved in a road accident.

Your recognition of our right:

h) to take over and deal with in your name the defence or settlement of any claim.

i) to take proceedings in your name, but at our expense, to recover compensation for any payment made under this policy for our benefit.

j) to make to the legal owner or to the hire purchase company any payment for loss or damage, if we know the **Motor Cycle** is owned by someone other than the **Policyholder** or is the subject of a hiring or hire purchase agreement.

k) if a claim is not covered by this policy — to recover from the **Insured Person** any payment made solely because of the compulsory insurance law of a country to which this policy applies.

l) to settle your claim on a proportionate basis if you have other insurance covering the same loss, damage or liability.

3

General Exceptions

1 This policy does not insure any destruction of, or damage to any property or any consequential loss or any legal liability directly or indirectly caused by, or contributed to, or arising from:

Radioactive contamination

- ionising radiations or contamination by radioactivity from any nuclear fuel or from any nuclear waste from the combustion of nuclear fuel
- the radioactive, toxic, explosive or other hazardous properties of any explosive nuclear assembly or component.

War risks

- war, invasion, act of foreign enemy, hostilities (whether war be declared or not), civil war, rebellion, revolution or military or usurped power.

Sonic bangs

- pressure waves caused by aircraft and other aerial devices.

Additional liabilities

2 If you enter into any agreement which could mean you incur additional liabilities, this policy will not operate for those additional liabilities.

General Conditions (continued)

m) where we have accepted a claim but the amount to be paid is in dispute — to refer the matter to an independent arbitrator acceptable to the parties involved. This does not affect the right to refer also to the Insurance Ombudsman.

Any other person entitled to claim the benefit of this policy must also observe its terms and conditions.

Cancellation

3 We may cancel this policy by sending seven days notice by recorded delivery letter or registered letter to your last known address. The **Certificate** must be returned to us and any refund will be calculated from the date it is received.

Definition of words

Policyholder
The person shown as the policyholder in the schedule.
If there is more than one person named in the schedule as the policyholder, this policy applies both jointly and individually.

Certificate
Your current valid Certificate of Motor Insurance which has the same number as this policy.
The **Certificate**, not the policy, is the document which you may be required to produce to the police as evidence of insurance. The **Certificate** also sets out who may drive the motor cycle, who may use it and for what purpose.

Motor Cycle
Any vehicle described in the "Description of Vehicles" in your **Certificate.**

Insured Person
The term Insured Person in paragraph 2 headed Liability means:

- the **Policyholder**
- other persons who are permitted by your **Certificate** to drive or use the motor cycle
- the employer or partner of any person whose business use is permitted by your **Certificate**
- at your request
  a) any person getting on or off or travelling on your **Motor Cycle**
  b) the owner of the **Motor Cycle** if someone other than yourself.

Excess
The amount you pay towards the agreed cost of any claim for loss or damage to your **Motor Cycle.**

Excesses do not apply when the loss or damage is caused by fire, self-ignition, lightning, explosion, theft or attempted theft.

Insurance Provided

The insurance provided is shown in your current schedule and this determines which paragraphs of this policy apply.

Insurance Provided	Paragraphs which apply
● Comprehensive	All
● Third Party Fire and Theft	All — but paragraph 1 applies only to losses resulting from: – fire – self-ignition – lightning – explosion – theft or attempted theft
● Third Party	All except 1

The insurance provided will operate throughout the British Isles including transit by sea between its ports. You also have insurance for any motor cycle to which this policy applies for the minimum insurance required to comply with the laws relating to compulsory insurance of vehicles in the following countries:

● **EEC** — Belgium, Denmark, France, Germany (West), Greece, Holland, Italy, Luxembourg

● **Other European Countries** — Austria, Czechoslovakia, Finland, Germany (East), Hungary, Norway, Sweden, Switzerland

● any other country for which the Commission of the EEC is satisfied that arrangements have been made to meet the requirements of EEC Directives on insurance.

Motor Cycle Policy (continued)

We will pay:

Damage

Loss or damage to your Motor Cycle

1 ● The cost of repair or replacement for loss or damage to your **Motor Cycle** and its accessories, spare parts or components while on your **Motor Cycle**.
The maximum amount payable will be the reasonable market value immediately prior to the loss or damage.

● The reasonable costs of protection and removal to the nearest repairers if, as a result of any loss or damage which is insured by this paragraph, your **Motor Cycle** is disabled.

● The reasonable cost of delivery to the **Policyholder** in the British Isles after repair.

We will not pay for:

1 ● An **Excess** of £25 for each loss or damage to your **Motor Cycle** (other than when your **Motor Cycle** is in the hands of a member of the motor trade for servicing or repair); this amount is increased to £40 while it is being driven by any person who is under 25 years of age.
This is in addition to any **Excess** shown in the schedule

● Wear and tear, depreciation, mechanical or electrical breakdown

● Damage to tyres by the application of brakes or by road punctures, cuts or bursts

● Loss or damage to accessories, spare parts or components by theft or attempted theft, unless the **Motor Cycle** is stolen at the same time

● Loss of use

● Loss or damage due to:
  – earthquake
  – riot or civil commotion other than in Great Britain, the Isle of Man or the Channel Islands.

Motor Cycle Policy (continued)

We will pay:

Liability

Liability to other people and their property

2 a) The amount of:

- damages and claimant's costs and expenses
- any other costs and expenses agreed between us in writing

arising from bodily injury or damage to property for which the **Insured Person** may be liable at law resulting from an accident involving your **Motor Cycle.**

Legal representation

b) At your request the solicitor's fee for:

- representation at any coroner's inquest or fatal enquiry
- defending in any Court of Summary Jurisdiction any proceedings

arising from an accident which may result in a claim.

Driving borrowed motor cycles

c) For liability to other people and their property, as shown in paragraphs 2a) & b), while an **Insured Person** is driving another motor cycle, but only when this is permitted by your **Certificate.**

Emergency treatment

3 The cost of emergency treatment incurred under the Road Traffic Acts and arising from the use of a motor cycle covered under this policy.

We will not pay for:

2 Losses under the whole of this paragraph for:

- damage caused by an **Insured Person** to his own property or property which is in his custody or control
- damage to your **Motor Cycle** or any borrowed motor cycle
- bodily injury to any person arising out of and in the course of their employment by an **Insured Person.**

No Claim Discount

Scale

If no claim is made or arises under this policy in a period of insurance, we will reduce your renewal premium as follows:

Claim free Period of Insurance	No Claim Discount premium reduction
the preceding year	10%

If this policy applies to more than one **Motor Cycle** your No Claim Discount will apply as if a separate policy had been issued for each motor cycle.

No Claim Discount is not transferrable from one person to another.

Protected no claim discount

Your no claim discount will not be lost if:

Motor cycle being serviced or repaired

● a claim involving your **Motor Cycle** occurs while it is in the hands of a member of the motor trade for servicing or repair.

Emergency treatment

● the only payment is for emergency treatment as required by the Road Traffic Acts.

C COMMERCIAL MOTOR VEHICLE POLICY

Commercial Union Motor Vehicle Policy

Commercial Union Assurance Company Limited ('the Company') will provide insurance as expressed in this Policy during any Period of Insurance in respect of which the Policyholder has paid, or agreed to pay, the premium: if more than one person is named as the Policyholder the insurance granted by this Policy applies jointly and individually to all such persons.

Insurance Provided

Where the Insurance Provided is:

1   "Comprehensive", all Sections of this Policy apply.
2   "Third Party Fire and Theft", Section VII does not apply and Section I applies only in respect of loss or damage caused directly by fire, self-ignition, lightning, explosion or by theft or attempted theft.
3   "Third Party", Section I and VII and Condition 8 of this Policy do not apply.

Territorial Limits

Section III applies

Definition of the Vehicle

"Vehicle" means:

1   Any Vehicle mentioned by Description or by Registration Mark in the Certificate of Motor Insurance (referred to in this Policy as "the Certificate") bearing the number of this Policy as the Certificate Number which has been delivered to the Policyholder and remains effective.
2   Any trailer details of which have been notified to the Company.

Section I

Loss of or Damage to the Vehicle Authority to Repair the Vehicle

The Company will pay for loss of or damage to the Vehicle including the accessories and spare parts or components whilst on the Vehicle and the reasonable cost of protection removal and redelivery to the Policyholder after repair of such loss or damage. Payment may be made at the Company's option either for the cost of repair, reinstatement or replacement or by cash for the amount of the loss or damage agreed between the Company and the Policyholder, but not in any event exceeding the reasonable market value at the time of the loss or damage. The Company will also pay the reasonable cost of protection and removal to the nearest repairers if, as a result of any insured loss or damage, the Vehicle is disabled.

The Policyholder may authorise the repair of the Vehicle provided that a detailed estimate of the cost is sent to the Company immediately. The Company reserves the right to seek alternative estimates.

Exceptions to Section I

The Company shall not be liable in respect of

1   depreciation, wear and tear, mechanical or electrical breakdown, or damage to tyres by application of brakes or by road punctures, cuts or bursts.
2   loss of use.
3   the first £25 of the amount payable for each loss or damage to the Vehicle (other than by fire, self-ignition, lightning, explosion or by theft or attempted theft) which occurs while the Vehicle is being driven by any person who

a   is under 22 years of age, or
b   holds a Provisional licence, or
c   has not held a licence (other than a Provisional licence) for a period of

i   one year in the case of a licence issued within the United Kingdom, the Isle of Man or the Channel Islands,
    or
ii two years in the case of a licence issued elsewhere to drive a vehicle of the same class as the Vehicle.

Section II

Liability to Third Parties

The Company will indemnify the Insured Person against all sums which he shall become legally liable to pay for damages and claimant's costs and expenses and any other costs and expenses incurred with its written consent in respect of bodily injury (fatal or otherwise) or damage to material, property (payment in respect of such damage being limited to £5,000,000 in respect of any one claim or number of claims arising out of one cause) arising as a result of an accident caused by or in connection with the Vehicle, or the loading or unloading of the Vehicle.

Legal Representation

Manslaughter

In addition the Company will pay

1   The Solicitor's fee for
   i   representation at any coroner's inquest or fatal enquiry and/or
   ii defending in any Court of Summary Jurisdiction any proceedings

relating to any event which may be the subject of payment under this Section.

2   The reasonable costs for legal services for defence in the event of proceedings being taken for manslaughter or reckless driving causing death where the death in either case may be the subject of payment under this Section.

Insured Person

"Insured Person" shall mean any one or more of the following on whose behalf payment is claimed.

1   The Policyholder.

2   Any person entitled to drive by the terms of the Certificate.

3   The employer or partner of any person whose business use is permitted by the terms of the Certificate.

4   Any person using (but not driving) the Vehicle with the permission of the Policyholder for social, domestic and pleasure purposes provided that such use is permitted by the terms of the Certificate.

5   At the request of the Policyholder, any person (other than the person driving) in or getting into or getting out of the Vehicle.

6   At the request of the Policyholder, the Owner of the Vehicle.

7   The attendant of the Vehicle.

Attached Trailer

The "Vehicle" shall include any trailer or any one disabled mechanically propelled vehicle which is attached to the Vehicle.

Unlicensed Drivers

Any requirements of the Certificate that the person driving must hold, or have held, a licence to drive shall be inoperative when a licence is not required by law, provided that the terms of the Certificate are otherwise observed and that the person driving is of an age to hold a licence to drive the Vehicle.

Application of Policy Limits

In the event of any accident involving payment on behalf of more than one Insured Person any limitation by the terms of this Policy (or of any endorsement thereon) of the amount of any payment shall apply to the aggregate amount of such payment on behalf of all such Insured Persons and such payment shall apply in priority to the Policyholder.

Exceptions to Section II

The Company shall not be liable in respect of

1   bodily injury or damage to material property caused or arising beyond the limits of any carriageway or thoroughfare in connection with
   a   the bringing of the load to the Vehicle for loading on the Vehicle
   b   the taking away of the load from the Vehicle after unloading from the Vehicle
   by any person other than the driver or attendant of the Vehicle.

2   loss of or damage to
   a   material property belonging to or held in trust by or in the custody or control of the Policyholder or the Insured Person.
   b   the Vehicle.
   c   property being conveyed by the Vehicle.

3   bodily injury to any person arising out of and in the course of such person's employment by the Insured Person.

4   any claim if the Insured Person (other than the Policyholder) is entitled to claim payment or indemnity under any other policy.

5   liability arising in connection with the operation as a tool of the Vehicle, where the Vehicle is designed to operate primarily as a tool, or plant forming part of the Vehicle or attached thereto except so far as is necessary to meet the requirements of the Road Traffic Acts.

Section III

Territorial Limits

The Policy will apply in respect of

1   bodily injury, loss of or damage to material property occurring in the British Isles, or in the course of transit by sea between any ports therein including processes of loading and unloading.

2   the minimum indemnity required to comply with the laws relating to compulsory insurance of vehicles in any country which is a member of the European Economic Community and any other country in respect of which the Commission of the European Economic Community is satisfied that arrangements have been made to meet the requirements of Article 7 (2) of the E.E.C. Directive on insurance of civil liabilities arising from the use of vehicles (No. 72/166/CEE).

3   any Vehicle for which an International Motor Insurance Card (Green Card) has been issued and remains effective

   a   while it is in any country to which such Green Card applies.

   b   in direct connection with the transit (including processes of loading and unloading) of the Vehicle between any ports in countries to which the Green Card applies provided always that such transit shall be by any recognised sea passage of not longer duration under normal conditions than 65 hours.

   The Company will also indemnify the Policyholder against liability incurred by him for the enforced payment of Customs Duty on the Vehicle after temporary importation thereof into any country to which the Green Card applies provided that such liability arises as the direct result of any loss of or damage to the Vehicle which loss or damage is the subject of indemnity under this Policy.

Section IV

Contingency Cover for Employees Vehicles

The Company will indemnify the Policyholder in the terms of Section II of this Policy while any motor vehicle owned by a person in the Policyholder's employ is being used in connection with the Policyholder's business by any person in the Policyholder's employ but not in respect of loss of or damage to such motor vehicle nor if there is any other existing insurance covering the same liability.

Section V

Emergency Treatment

The Company will pay the cost of emergency treatment of injuries caused by or arising out of the use of any motor vehicle for which cover is provided under this Policy where liability for such treatment arises under the Road Traffic Acts.

A payment by reason of this Section shall not be regarded as a claim under this Policy for the purpose of Section VIII.

Section VI

Vehicle in the Custody of a Motor Trader

So far as payment to, and the liability of, the Policyholder is concerned General Exception 1 shall not apply whilst the Vehicle is in the custody or control of a member of the Motor Trade for the purposes of its overhaul, upkeep or repair and any payment made shall not be

   a   regarded as a claim under this Policy for the purpose of Section VIII nor

   b   subject to any deduction by reason of Exception 3 to Section I.

Section VII

Windscreen Breakage

Where the only damage which the Vehicle sustains is breakage of the windscreen or any other window and incidental scratching of bodywork, the Company will not regard as a claim for the purposes of Section VIII any payment which may be made for the cost of replacing the broken glass or making good the damaged bodywork. Furthermore, any stipulation in this Policy that the Company will not pay for the first portion of any claim shall not apply to payments made under this Section.

Section VIII

No Claim Discount

The Company will reduce the renewal premium in accordance with the following scale if no claim is made or arises under this Policy in the undernoted period of insurance preceding the renewal date.

Period of Insurance	Reduction
the preceding year	15%
the preceding two consecutive years	30%

No Claim Discount is not transferable from one person to another. If this Policy applies to more than one Vehicle the No Claim Discount shall be applied as if a separate Policy had been issued in respect of each such Vehicle.

General Exceptions

The Company will not pay for

1   any claim if to the knowledge of the Insured Person the Vehicle is at the time of the accident being driven, or used, other than in accordance with the terms of the Certificate.

2   liability assumed by the Policyholder by agreement and which would not have attached in the absence of such agreement unless the conduct and control of claims is vested in the Company and will not in any event pay for liability in respect of liquidated damages or under any penalty clause.

3   a   loss or destruction of or damage to any property whatsoever or any loss or expense whatsoever resulting or arising therefrom or any consequential loss.

   b   any legal liability of whatsoever nature, directly or indirectly caused by or contributed to by or arising from

   i   ionising radiations or contamination by radioactivity from any irradiated nuclear fuel or from any nuclear waste from the combustion of nuclear fuel.

   ii   the radioactive toxic, explosive or other hazardous properties of any explosive nuclear assembly or nuclear component thereof.

4   any consequence of war, invasion, act of foreign enemy hostilities (whether war be declared or not), civil war, rebellion, revolution, insurrection or military or usurped power, except so far as is necessary to meet the requirements of the Road Traffic Acts.

5   any bodily injury, loss of or damage to material property (except under Section II) arising during or in consequence of riot or civil commotion occurring elsewhere than in Great Britain, the Isle of Man or the Channel Islands.

6   loss, destruction or damage (except under Section II) directly occasioned by pressure waves caused by aircraft and other aerial devices travelling at sonic or supersonic speeds.

Conditions

Identification

1   This Policy, any endorsement thereon, the Motor Insurance Policy Schedule and the Certificate(s) are to be read together, and any word(s) or expression(s) to which a specific meaning has been attached in any of them shall bear the same meaning wherever it/they may appear.

   For the purposes of this Policy the word

   i   "Insured" appearing on any endorsement hereon shall have the same meaning as the word "Policyholder".

   ii   "Clause" appearing on any endorsement hereon shall have the same meaning as the word "Section".

Claims Procedure

2   Any bodily injury, loss of or damage to material property involving the Vehicle must be reported to the Company in writing with full details as soon as possible.

   Every Communication relating to such occurrence must be sent to the Company immediately and the Policyholder, or any other person on whose behalf payment is claimed, shall give all such assistance as the Company may require.

   No admission of liability or offer or promise of payment, whether expressed or implied, shall be made without the written consent of the Company which shall be entitled at its own discretion to take over and conduct in the name of the Policyholder (or any other person entitled to indemnity or payment under this Policy) the defence or settlement of any claim, or to prosecute in the name of the Policyholder (or such other person) for its own benefit any claim for indemnity or damages or otherwise.

Claims Control

3   In connection with any one claim or number of claims arising out of one cause for payment against liability in respect of loss of or damage to material property the Company may at any time pay to the Policyholder the amount of the indemnity provided by this Policy (after deduction, of any sum or sums already paid as compensation) or any less amount for which such claim or claims can be settled. Upon such payment being made the Company shall relinquish the conduct and control of, and be under no further liability, in connection with such claim or claims except for the payment of costs and expenses of litigation recoverable or incurred in respect of matters prior to the date of such payment.

Other Insurances

4 If at the time any claim arises under this Policy there is any other existing insurance covering the same accident, injury, loss or damage the Company shall not be liable to pay or contribute more than its rateable proportion of any loss, damage, compensation, costs or expenses. Nothing however in this Condition shall impose on the Company any obligation to make any payment under this Policy from which it would have been relieved under Exception 4 to Section II or Section IV of this Policy but for the terms of this Condition.

Vehicle Maintenance Safeguarding from Loss

5 The Policyholder shall take all reasonable steps to safeguard against bodily injury, loss of or damage to material property and shall maintain the Vehicle in efficient condition: at all times the Company shall have free access to examine the Vehicle.

Policy Cancellation Procedure

6 This Policy may be cancelled by the Company sending seven days' notice by registered letter to the last known address of the Policyholder (and in the case of Northern Ireland to the Ministry of Home Affairs, Northern Ireland) who shall then be entitled to a proportionate return of premium.

Hiring Agreement

7 If to the knowledge of the Company the Vehicle is owned by any person other than the Policyholder or is the subject of a hiring or hire purchase agreement, any payment for loss or damage for which the Company is liable shall be made to the Owner or the Hire Purchase Company whose signed receipt shall then be an adequate discharge to the Company.

Arbitration

8 If any difference shall arise as to the amount to be paid under this Policy (liability being otherwise admitted) such difference shall be referred to an Arbitrator to be appointed by the parties in accordance with the Statutory provisions in that behalf for the time being in force. Where any difference is by this Condition to be referred to arbitration, the making of an Award shall be a condition precedent to any right of action against the Company.

Avoidance of Certain Terms

Right of Recovery

9 Nothing in this Policy or any endorsement thereon shall affect the right of any person insured by this Policy (or of any other person) to recover an amount under or by virtue of the provisions of the law of any territory in which this Policy operates relating to the insurance of liability to Third Parties.

But the Policyholder shall repay to the Company all sums paid by the Company which the Company would not have been liable to pay but for the provisions of such law.

Change of or Additional Vehicle

10 The Policyholder shall notify to the Company details of any additional or replacement Motor Vehicle immediately on acquisition. In the absence of such notification the insurance granted by this Policy shall not operate in respect of such Motor Vehicle and the Company will not pay for any accident, injury, loss or damage arising as a result of an accident caused by or in connection with such Motor Vehicle.

The Policyholder shall

i pay to the Company any additional premium which may be due as a result of the acquisition of the Motor Vehicle and

ii notify the Company of the disposal of the Motor Vehicle in order to qualify for any refund of premium which may be allowable.

Signed on behalf of the Company.

By authority of the Board.

Agency

Branch & Agent No.

Policy No.
MV

The Policyholder
Name
Address

Postcode
carrying on or engaged in the business of

Period of Insurance

(a) from the

to the

} both dates inclusive

(b) any subsequent period for which the Policyholder shall pay and the Company shall agree to accept the premium required.

Net Premium   £

Insurance Provided

1. **Comprehensive**
2. **Third Party Fire and Theft**
3. **Third Party**

}

Refer to the effective Certificate for details of permitted driver(s) and use(s)

. . . .

Excess
In respect of each and every occurrence the Company shall not be liable under Section I for the first £. . . . .
of any amount otherwise payable in respect of loss of or damage to the Motor Vehicle other than by fire self-ignition lightning explosion or by theft or attempted theft.
The sum specified shall be in addition to any other amount for which the Company is not liable under this Policy (See Exception 3 to Section 1)

MOTOR VEHICLE/FLEET POLICY X26/Y29 SCHEDULE.

Appendix VII

THIRD PARTIES (RIGHTS AGAINST INSURERS) ACT 1930

(20 & 21 Geo 5 c 25)

An Act to confer on third parties rights against insurers of third-party risks in the event of the insured becoming insolvent, and in certain other events. [10 July 1930]

Be it enacted by the King's most Excellent Majesty, by and with the advice and consent of the Lords Spiritual and Temporal, and Commons, in this present Parliament assembled, and by the authority of the same, as follows:

1. Rights of third parties against insurers on bankruptcy etc of the insured.

(1) Where under any contract of insurance a person (hereinafter referred to as the insured) is insured against liabilities to third parties which he may incur, then—

  (a) in the event of the insured becoming bankrupt or making a composition or arrangement with his creditors; or

  (b) in the case of the insured being a company, in the event of a winding-up order being made, or a resolution for a voluntary winding-up being passed, with respect to the company, or of a receiver or manager of the company's business or undertaking being duly appointed, or of possession being taken, by or on behalf of the holders of any debentures secured by a floating charge, of any property comprised in or subject to the charge;

if, either before or after that event, any such liability as aforesaid is incurred by the insured, his rights against the insurer under the contract in respect of the liability shall, notwithstanding anything in any Act or rule of law to the contrary, be transferred to and vest in the third party to whom the liability was so incurred.

(2) Where an order is made under section one hundred and thirty of the Bankruptcy Act 1914, for the administration of the estate of a deceased debtor according to the law of bankruptcy, then, if any debt provable in bankruptcy is owing by the deceased in respect of a liability against which he was insured under a contract of insurance as being a liability to a third party, the deceased debtor's rights against the insurer under the contract in respect of that liability shall, notwithstanding anything in the said Act, be transferred to and vest in the person to whom the debt is owing.

(3) In so far as any contract of insurance made after the commencement of this Act in respect of any liability of the insured to third parties purports, whether directly or indirectly, to avoid the contract or to alter the rights of the parties thereunder upon the happening to the insured of any of the events specified in paragraph (a) or paragraph (b) of subsection (1) of this section or upon the making of an order under section one hundred and thirty of the Bankruptcy Act

1914, in respect of his estate, the contract shall be of no effect.

(4) Upon a transfer under subsection (1) or subsection (2) of this section, the insurer shall, subject to the provisions of section three of this Act, be under the same liability to the third party as he would have been under to the insured, but—

> (a) if the liability of the insurer to the insured exceeds the liability of the insured to the third party, nothing in this Act shall affect the rights of the insured against the insurer in respect of the excess; and
>
> (b) if the liability of the insurer to the insured is less than the liability of the insured to the third party, nothing in this Act shall affect the rights of the third party against the insured in respect of the balance.

(5) For the purposes of this Act, the expression 'liabilities to third parties', in relation to a person insured under any contract of insurance, shall not include any liability of that person in the capacity of insurer under some other contract of insurance.

(6) This Act shall not apply—

> (a) where a company is wound up voluntarily merely for the purposes of reconstruction or of amalgamation with another company; or
>
> (b) [*Repealed*].

2. Duty to give necessary information to third parties.

(1) In the event of any person becoming bankrupt or making a composition or arrangement with his creditors, or in the event of an order being made under section one hundred and thirty of the Bankruptcy Act 1914, in respect of the estate of any person, or in the event of a winding-up order being made, or a resolution for a voluntary winding-up being passed, with respect to any company or of a receiver or manager of the company's business or undertaking being duly appointed or of possession being taken by or on behalf of the holders of any debentures secured by a floating charge of any property comprised in or subject to the charge it shall be the duty of the bankrupt, debtor, personal representative of the deceased debtor or company, and, as the case may be, of the trustee in bankruptcy, trustee, liquidator, receiver, or manager, or person in possession of the property to give at the request of any person claiming that the bankrupt, debtor, deceased debtor, or company is under a liability to him such information as may reasonably be required by him for the purpose of ascertaining whether any rights have been transferred to and vested in him by this Act and for the purpose of enforcing such rights, if any, and any contract of insurance, in so far as it purports, whether directly or indirectly, to avoid the contract or to alter the rights of the parties thereunder upon the giving of any such information in the events aforesaid or otherwise to prohibit or prevent the giving thereof in the said events shall be of no effect.

(2) If the information given to any person in pursuance of subsection (1) of this section discloses reasonable ground for supposing that there have or may have been transferred to him under this Act rights against any particular insurer, that insurer shall be subject to the same duty as is imposed by the said subsection on the persons therein mentioned.

(3) The duty to give information imposed by this section shall include a duty to allow all contracts of insurance, receipts for premiums, and other relevant

documents in the possession or power of the person on whom the duty is so imposed to be inspected and copies thereof to be taken.

3. Settlement between insurers and insured persons.

Where the insured has become bankrupt or where in the case of the insured being a company, a winding-up order has been made or a resolution for a voluntary winding-up has been passed, with respect to the company, no agreement made between the insurer and the insured after liability has been incurred to a third party and after the commencement of the bankruptcy or winding-up, as the case may be, nor any waiver, assignment, or other disposition made by, or payment made to the insured after the commencement aforesaid shall be effective to defeat or affect the rights transferred to the third party under this Act, but those rights shall be the same as if no such agreement, waiver, assignment, disposition or payment had been made.

[4. This section applies to Scotland only.]

5. Short title.

This Act may be cited as the Third Parties (Rights Against Insurers) Act 1930.

Appendix VIII

ROAD TRAFFIC ACT 1972[1]

(1972 c 20)

PART VI

THIRD-PARTY LIABILITIES
Compulsory insurance or security against third-party risks.

143. Users of motor vehicles to be insured or secured against third party risks.
(1) Subject to the provisions of this Part of this Act, it shall not be lawful for a person to use, or to cause or permit any other person to use, a motor vehicle on a road unless there is in force in relation to the use of the vehicle by that person or that other person, as the case may be, such a policy of insurance or such a security in respect of third-party risks as complies with the requirements of this Part of this Act; and if a person acts in contravention of this section he shall be guilty of an offence.
(2) A person charged with using a motor vehicle in contravention of this section shall not be convicted if he proves that the vehicle did not belong to him and was not in his possession under a contract of hiring or of loan, that he was using the vehicle in the course of his employment and that he neither knew nor had reason to believe that there was not in force in relation to the vehicle such a policy of insurance or security as is mentioned in subsection (1) above.
(3) This Part of this Act shall not apply to invalid carriages.

144. Exceptions from requirement of third party insurance or security.
(1) Section 143 or this Act shall not apply to a vehicle owned by a person who has deposited and keeps deposited with the Accountant General of the Supreme Court the sum of £15,000, at a time when the vehicle is being driven under the owner's control.
(2) The said section 143 shall not apply—
    (a) to a vehicle owned by the council of a county, . . . or county district in England or Wales, the Common Council of the City of London, the council of a London borough, the Greater London Council, a county, town or district council in Scotland, or by a joint board or joint committee in England or Wales, or joint committee in Scotland, which is so constituted as to include among its members representatives of any such council, at a time when the vehicle is being driven under the owner's control;

---

[1] The Act is printed as amended.

(b) to a vehicle owned by a police authority or the Receiver for the Metropolitan Police District, at a time when it is being driven under the
owner's control, or to a vehicle at a time when it is being driven for
police purposes by or under the direction of a constable, or by a person
employed by a police authority, or employed by the said Receiver; or

(c) to a vehicle at a time when it is being driven on a journey to or from
any place undertaken for salvage purposes pursuant to Part IX of the
Merchant Shipping Act 1894;

(d) to the use of a vehicle for the purpose of its being furnished in pursuance of a direction under paragraph (b) of section 166(2) of the Army
Act 1955 or under the corresponding provision of the Air Force Act
1955;

(e) to a vehicle owned by the London Transport Executive or by a body
which is within the meaning of the Transport (London) Act 1969 (but
disregarding section 51 (5) of the Transport Act 1968) a wholly-owned
subsidiary of that Executive, at a time when the vehicle is being driven
under the owner's control;

(f) to a vehicle which is made available by the Secretary of State to any
person, body or local authority in pursuance of section 11 or section 13
of the National Health Service Reorganisation Act 1973 at a time
when it is being used in accordance with the terms on which it is so
made available.

145. Requirements in respect of policies of insurance.
(1) In order to comply with the requirements of this Part of this Act, a policy of
insurance must satisfy the following conditions.
(2) The policy must be issued by an authorised insurer, that is to say, a person
or body of persons carrying on insurance business within Group 2 in Part II of
Schedule 2 to the Insurance Companies Act 1982 and being a member of the
Motor Insurers' Bureau, a company limited by guarantee and incorporated
under the Companies Act 1929 on 14th June 1946.
(3) Subject to subsection (4) below, the policy—

(a) must insure such person, persons or classes of persons as may be
specified in the policy in respect of any liability which may be incurred
by him or them in respect of the death of or bodily injury to any person
caused by, or arising out of, the use of the vehicle on a road in Great
Britain; and

(aa) must insure him or them in respect of any liability which may be
incurred by him or them in respect of the use of the vehicle and of any
trailer, whether or not coupled, in the territory other than Great
Britain and Gibraltar of each of the member states of the Communities
according to the law on compulsory insurance against civil liability in
respect of the use of vehicles of the state where the liability may be
incurred; and

(b) must also insure him or them in respect of any liability which may be
incurred by him or them under the provisions of this Part of this Act
relating to payment for emergency treatment.

(4) The policy shall not, by virtue of subsection (3) (a) above, be required to
cover—

(a) liability in respect of the death, arising out of and in the course of his employment, of a person in the employment of a person insured by the policy or of bodily injury sustained by such a person arising out of and in the course of his employment; or
(b) any contractual liability.

146. Requirements in respect of securities.
(1) In order to comply with the requirements of this Part of this Act, a security must satisfy the following conditions.
(2) The security must be given either by an authorised insurer or by some body of persons which carries on in the United Kingdom the business of giving securities of a like kind and has deposited and keeps deposited with the Accountant General of the Supreme Court the sum of £15,000 in respect of that business.
(3) The security must consist of an undertaking by the giver of the security to make good, subject to any conditions specified therein . . . any failure by the owner of the vehicle or such other persons or classes of persons as may be specified in the security duly to discharge any liability which may be incurred by him or them, being a liability required under section 145 of this Act to be covered by a policy of insurance:

Provided that in the case of liabilites arising out of the use of a motor vehicle on a road in Great Britain the amount secured need not exceed—

(a) in the case of an undertaking relating to the use of public service vehicles (within the meaning of Part III of the Road Traffic Act 1960), £25,000;
(b) in any other case, £5,000.

147. Issue and surrender of certificates of insurance and of security.
(1) A policy of insurance shall be of no effect for the purposes of this Part of this Act unless and until there is delivered by the insurer to the person by whom the policy is effected a certificate (in this Part of this Act referred to as a 'certificate of insurance') in the prescribed form and containing such particulars of any conditions subject to which the policy is issued and of any other matters as may be prescribed.
(2) A security shall be of no effect for the purposes of this Part of this Act unless and until there is delivered by the person giving the security to the person to whom it is given a certificate (in this Part of this Act referred to as a 'certificate of security') in the prescribed form and containing such particulars of any conditions subject to which the security is issued and of any other matters as may be prescribed.
(3) Different forms and different particulars may be prescribed for the purposes of subsection (1) or (2) above in relation to different cases or circumstances.
(4) Where a certificate has been delivered under this section and the policy or security to which it relates is cancelled by mutual consent or by virtue of any provision in the policy or security, the person to whom the certificate was delivered shall, within seven days from the taking effect of the cancellation, surrender the certificate to the person by whom the policy was issued or the security was given or, if the certificate has been lost or destroyed, make a

statutory declaration to that effect; and a person who fails to comply with this subsection shall be guilty of an offence.

148. Avoidance of certain exceptions to policies or securities and of certain agreements etc as to risks required to be covered thereby.
(1) Where a certificate of insurance or certificate of security has been delivered under section 147 of this Act to the person by whom a policy has been effected or to whom a security has been given, so much of the policy or security as purports to restrict, as the case may be, the insurance of the persons insured by the policy or the operation of the security by reference to any of the following matters, that is to say

(a) the age or physical or mental condition of persons driving the vehicle, or
(b) the condition of the vehicle, or
(c) the number of persons that the vehicle carries, or
(d) the weight or physical characteristics of the goods that the vehicle carries, or
(e) the times at which or the areas within which the vehicle is used, or
(f) the horsepower or cylinder capacity or value of the vehicle, or
(g) the carrying on the vehicle of any particular apparatus, or
(h) the carrying on the vehicle of any particular means of identification other than any means of identification required to be carried by or under the Vehicles (Excise) Act 1971

shall, as respect such liabilites as are required to be covered by a policy under section 145 of this Act, be of no effect:
Provided that nothing in this subsection shall require an insurer or the giver of a security to pay any sum in respect of the liability of any person otherwise than in or towards the discharge of that liability, and any sum paid by an insurer or the giver of a security in or towards the discharge of any liability of any person which is covered by the policy or security by virtue only of this subsection shall be recoverable by the insurer or giver of the security from that person.
(2) A condition in a policy or security issued or given for the purposes of this Part of this Act providing that no liability shall arise under the policy or security, or that any liability so arising shall cease, in the event of some specified thing being done or omitted to be done after the happening of the event giving rise to a claim under the policy or security, shall be of no effect in connection with such liabilities as are required to be covered by a policy under section 145 of this Act:
Provided that nothing in this subsection shall be taken to render void any provision in a policy or security requiring the person insured or secured to pay to the insurer or the giver of the security any sums which the latter may have become liable to pay under the policy or security and which have been applied to the satisfaction of the claims of third parties.
(3) Where a person uses a motor vehicle in circumstances such that under section 143 of this Act there is required to be in force in relation to his use of it such a policy of insurance or security as is mentioned in subsection (1) of that section, then, if any other person is carried in or upon the vehicle while the user is so using it, any antecedent agreement or understanding between them

(whether intended to be legally binding or not) shall be of no effect so far as it purports or might be held

(a) to negative or restrict any such liability of the user in respect of persons carried in or upon the vehicle as is required by section 145 of this Act to be covered by a policy of insurance; or

(b) to impose any conditions with respect to the enforcement of any such liability of the user;

and the fact that a person so carried has willingly accepted as his the risk of negligence on the part of the user shall not be treated as negativing any such liability of the user.

For the purposes of this subsection references to a person being carried in or upon a vehicle include references to a person entering or getting on to, or alighting from, the vehicle, and the reference to an antecedent agreement is to one made at any time before the liability arose.

(4) Notwithstanding anything in any enactment, a person issuing a policy of insurance under section 145 of this Act shall be liable to indemnify the persons or classes of persons specified in the policy in respect of any liability which the policy purports to cover in the case of those persons or classes of persons.

(5) To the extent that a policy or security issued or given for the purposes of this Part of this Act—

(a) restricts, as the case may be, the insurance of the persons insured by the policy or the operation of the security to use of the vehicle for specified purposes (for example, social, domestic and pleasure purposes) of a non-commercial character; or

(b) excludes from, as the case may be, that insurance or the operation of the security—

(i) use of the vehicle for hire or reward; or

(ii) business or commercial use of the vehicle; or

(iii) use of the vehicle for specified purposes of a business or commercial character,

then, for the purposes of that policy or security so far as it relates to such liabilities as are required to be covered by a policy under section 145 of this Act, the use of a vehicle on a journey in the course of which one or more passengers are carried at separate fares shall, if the conditions specified in subsection (6) below are satisfied, be treated as falling within that restriction or as not falling within that exclusion, as the case may be.

(6) The conditions referred to in subsection (5) above are—

(a) the vehicle is not adapted to carry more than eight passengers and is not a motor cycle;

(b) the fare or aggregate of the fares paid in respect of the journey does not exceed the amount of the running costs of the vehicle for the journey (which for the purposes of this paragraph shall be taken to include an appropriate amount in respect of depreciation and general wear); and

(c) the arrangements for the payment of fares by the passenger or passengers carried at separate fares were made before the journey began.

(7) Subsections (5) and (6) above apply however the restrictions or exclusions

described in subsection (5) are framed or worded; and in those subsections 'fare' and 'separate fares' have the same meaning as in section 2(4) of the Transport Act 1980.

149. Duty of insurers or persons giving security to satisfy judgment against persons insured or secured against third party risks.
(1) If, after a certificate of insurance or certificate of security has been delivered under section 147 of this Act to the person by whom a policy has been effected or to whom a security has been given, judgment in respect of any such liability as is required to be covered by a policy of insurance under section 145 of this Act (being a liability covered by the terms of the policy or security to which the certificate relates) is obtained against any person who is insured by the policy or whose liability is covered by the security, as the case may be, then, notwithstanding that the insurer may be entitled to avoid or cancel, or may have avoided or cancelled, the policy or security, he shall, subject to the provisions of this section, pay to the persons entitled to the benefit of the judgment any sum payable thereunder in respect of the liability, including any amount payable in respect of costs and any sum payable in respect of interest on that sum by virtue of any enactment relating to interest on judgments.
(2) No sum shall be payable by an insurer under the foregoing provisions of this section

(a) in respect of any judgment, unless before or within seven days after the commencement of the proceedings in which the judgment was given, the insurer had notice of the bringing of the proceedings; or
(b) in respect of any judgment, so long as execution thereof is stayed pending an appeal; or
(c) in connection with any liability, if before the happening of the event which was the cause of the death or bodily injury giving rise to the liability, the policy or security was cancelled by mutual consent or by virtue of any provision contained therein, and either
  (i) before the happening of the said event the certificate was surrendered to the insurer, or the person to whom the certificate was delivered made a statutory declaration stating that the certificate had been lost or destroyed, or
  (ii) after the happening of the said event, but before the expiration of a period of fourteen days from the taking effect of the cancellation of the policy or security, the certificate was surrendered to the insurer, or the person to whom it was delivered made such a statutory declaration as aforesaid; or
  (iii) either before or after the happening of the said event, but within the said period of fourteen days, the insurer has commenced proceedings under this Act in respect of the failure to surrender the certificate.

(3) No sum shall be payable by an insurer under the foregoing provisions of this section if, in an action commenced before, or within three months after, the commencement of the proceedings in which the judgment was given, he has obtained a declaration that, apart from any provision contained in the policy or security, he is entitled to avoid it on the ground that it was obtained by the non-disclosure of a material fact, or by a representation of fact which was false

in some material particular, or, if he has avoided the policy or security on that ground, that he was entitled so to do apart from any provision contained in it:

Provided that an insurer who has obtained such a declaration as aforesaid in an action shall not thereby become entitled to the benefit of this subsection as respects any judgment obtained in proceedings commenced before the commencement of that action unless before, or within seven days after, the commencement of that action he has given notice thereof to the person who is the plaintiff in the said proceedings specifying the non-disclosure or false representation on which he proposes to rely; and a person to whom notice of such an action is so given shall be entitled, if he thinks fit, to be made a party thereto.

(4) If the amount which an insurer becomes liable under this section to pay in respect of a liability of a person who is insured by a policy or whose liability is covered by a security exceeds the amount for which he would, apart from the provisions of this section, be liable under the policy or security in respect of that liability, he shall be entitled to recover the excess from that person.

(5) In this section

(a) 'insurer' includes a person giving a security;

(b) 'material' means of such a nature as to influence the judgment of a prudent insurer in determining whether he will take the risk and, if so, at what premium and on what conditions; and

(c) 'liability covered by the terms of the policy or security' means a liability which is covered by the policy or security or which would be so covered but for the fact that the insurer is entitled to avoid or cancel, or has avoided or cancelled, the policy or security.

(6) In the application of this section to Scotland, the words 'by virtue of any enactment relating to interest on judgments' in subsection (1) shall be omitted and for the reference in the proviso to subsection (3) to a plaintiff there shall be substituted a reference to a pursuer.

150. Bankruptcy etc of insured or secured persons not to affect claims by third parties.

(1) Where, after a certificate of insurance or certificate of security has been delivered under section 147 of this Act to the person by whom a policy has been effected or to whom a security has been given, any of the following events happens, that is to say

(a) the person by whom the policy was effected or to whom the security was given becomes bankrupt or makes a composition or arrangement with his creditors,

(b) the said person dies, and an order is made under section 130 of the Bankruptcy Act 1914 for the administration of his estate according to the law of bankruptcy,

(c) if the said person is a company, a winding-up order is made with respect to the company or a resolution for a voluntary winding up is passed with respect thereto, or a receiver or manager of the company's business or undertaking is duly appointed or possession is taken, by or on behalf of the holders of any debentures secured by a floating charge, of any property comprised in or subject to the charge, the happening of that event shall, notwithstanding anything in the Third Parties (Rights Against Insurers) Act 1930, not affect any such liability of the said person as is required to be covered by a policy of insurance under section 145 of this Act, but nothing in this subsection shall affect any rights conferred by that Act on the person to whom the liability was incurred, being rights so conferred against the person by whom the policy was issued or the security was given.

(2) In the application of this section to Scotland 'company' includes a limited partnership, and the reference to an order's being made under section 130 of the Bankruptcy Act 1914 for the administration of a person's estate according to the law of bankruptcy shall be deemed to include a reference to an award's being made of sequestration of his estate and a reference to an appointment's being made under section 163 of the Bankruptcy (Scotland) Act 1913 of a judicial factor to administer his estate.

151. Duty to give information as to insurance or security where claim made.

(1) A person against whom a claim is made in respect of any such liability as is required to be covered by a policy of insurance under section 145 of this Act shall, on demand by or on behalf of the person making the claim

(a) state whether or not, in respect of that liability, he was insured by a policy having effect for the purposes of this Part of this Act or had in force a security having effect for those purposes, or would have been so insured or would have had in force such a security if the insurer or, as the case may be, the giver of the security had not avoided or cancelled the policy or security, and

(b) if he was or would have been so insured, or had or would have had in force such a security, give such particulars with respect to that policy or security as were specified in any certificate of insurance or security delivered in respect of that policy or security, as the case may be, under section 147 of this Act, or where no such certificate was delivered under the said section the following particulars, that is to say, the registration mark or other identifying particulars of the vehicle concerned, the number or other identifying particulars of the insurance policy issued in respect of the vehicle, the name of the insurer and the period of the insurance cover.

(2) If without reasonable excuse, a person fails to comply with the provisions of subsection (1) above, or wilfully makes a false statement in reply to any such demand as aforesaid, he shall be guilty of an offence.

152. Deposits.

(1) Where a person has deposited a sum with the Accountant General of the Supreme Court under section 144 or 146 of this Act, then so long as any liabilites incurred by him, being such liabilites as are required to be covered by a policy of insurance under section 145 of this Act, have not been discharged or otherwise provided for no part of that sum shall be applicable in discharge of any other liabilites incurred by him.

(2) Any regulations made, or having effect as if made, by the Secretary of State or the Board of Trade under section 20 of the Insurance Companies Act 1958

which apply to deposits made by insurers carrying on motor vehicle insurance business shall, with such necessary modifications and adaptations as, after consultation with the Lord Chancellor, may be prescribed, apply to deposits made with the said Accountant General under section 144 or 146 of this Act; and there may, after such consultation as aforesaid, be made by regulations with respect to the said deposits such provisions as might be made by the Secretary of Sate or the Board of Trade under section 20 of the said Act of 1958 with respect to deposits under that Act.

153. Power to require evidence of insurance or security on application for vehicle excise licence.

Provision may be made by regulations under section 37 of the Vehicles (Excise) Act 1971 for requiring a person applying for a licence under that Act in respect of a motor vehicle to produce such evidence as may be prescribed that either

(a) on the date when the licence comes into operation there will be in force the necessary policy of insurance or the necessary security in relation to the use of the vehicle by the applicant or by other persons on his order or with his permission; or

(b) the vehicle is a vehicle to which section 143 of this Act does not apply at a time when it is being driven under the owner's control.

Payments for treatment of traffic casualties

154. Payment for hospital treatment of traffic casualties.

(1) Where a payment, other than a payment under section 155 of this Act, is made (whether or not with an admission of liability)

(a) by an authorised insurer, the payment being made under or in consequence of a policy issued under section 145 of this Act, or

(b) by the owner of a vehicle in relation to the use of which a security under this Part of this Act is in force, or

(c) by the owner of a vehicle who has made a deposit under this Part of this Act,

in respect of the death of, or bodily injury to, any person arising out of the use of a motor vehicle on a road or in a place to which the public have a right of access, and the person who has so died or been bodily injured has to the knowlege of the insurer or owner, as the case may be, received treatment at a hospital, whether as an in-patient or as an out-patient, in respect of the injury so arising, the insurer or owner shall pay the expenses reasonably incurred by the hospital in affording the treatment, after deducting from the expenses any moneys actually received in payment of a specific charge for the treatment, not being moneys received under any contributory scheme:

Provided that the amount to be paid shall not exceed £1525 for each person treated as an in-patient or £152.50 for each person treated as an out-patient.

(2) For the purposes of this section 'expenses reasonably incurred' means

(a) in relation to a person who receives treatment at a hospital as an in-patient, an amount for each day he is maintained in the hospital representing the average daily cost, for each in-patient, of the maintenance of the hospital and the staff thereof and the maintenance and treatment of the in-patients therein; and

(b) in relation to a person who receives treatment at a hospital as an out-patient, reasonable expenses actually incurred.

155. Payment for emergency treatment of traffic casualities.

(1) Where medical or surgical treatment or examination is immediately required as a result of bodily injury (including fatal injury) to a person caused by, or arising out of, the use of a motor vehicle on a road, and the treatment or examination so required (in this Part of this Act referred to as 'emergency treatment') is effected by a legally qualified medical practitioner, the person who was using the vehicle at the time of the event out of which the bodily injury arose shall, on a claim's being made in accordance with the provisions of section 156 of this Act, pay to the practitioner, or, where emergency treatment is effected by more than one practitioner, to the practitioner by whom it is first effected

(a) a fee of £10.90 in respect of each person in whose case the emergency treatment is effected by him; and

(b) a sum, in respect of any distance in excess of two miles which he must cover in order to proceed from the place whence he is summoned to the place where the emergency treatment is carried out by him and to return to the first-mentioned place, equal to 18 new pence for every complete mile and additional part of a mile of that distance.

(2) Where emergency treatment is first effected in a hospital, the provisions of subsection (1) above with respect to payment of a fee shall, so far as applicable, but subject (as regards the recipient of a payment) to the provisions of section 156 of this Act, have effect with the substitution of references to the hospital for references to a legally qualified medical practitioner.

(3) Liability incurred under this section by the person using a vehicle shall, where the event out of which it arose was caused by the wrongful act of another person, be treated for the purposes of any claim to recover damage by reason of that wrongful act as damage sustained by the person using the vehicle.

156. Supplementary provisions as to payments for treatment.

(1) A payment falling to be made under section 154 or 155 of this Act in respect of treatment in a hospital shall be made

(a) in the case of a hospital vested in the Secretary of State for the purposes of the National Health Service Act 1977 to the Area Health Authority, District Health Authority or special health authority responsible for the administration of the hospital or to the Secretary of State if no such authority is so responsible,

(b) [*repealed*]

(c) [*repealed*]

(d) in the case of any other hospital, to the hospital.

(2) A claim for a payment under section 155 of this Act may be made at the time when the emergency treatment is effected, by oral request to the person who was using the vehicle, and if not so made must be made by request in writing served on him within seven days from the day on which the emergency treatment was effected; and any such request in writing

(a) must be signed by the claimant or in the case of a hospital, by an executive officer of the Authority or hospital claiming the payment or by an officer of the Secretary of State, must state the name and address of the claimant, the circumstances in which the emergency treatment was effected, and that it was first effected by the claimant or, in the case of a hospital, in the hospital,

(b) may be served by delivering it to the person who was using the vehicle or by sending it in a prepaid registered letter, or the recorded delivery service, addressed to him at his usual or last-known address.

(3) A sum payable under the said section 155 shall be recoverable as if it were a simple contract debt due from the person who was using the vehicle to the practitioner, Authority or hospital, or the Secretary of State.

(4) A payment made under the said section 155 shall operate as a discharge, to the extent of the amount paid, of any liability of the person who was using the vehicle, or of any other person, to pay any sum in respect of the expenses or remuneration of the practitioner or hospital concerned of or for effecting the emergency treatment.

(5) A chief officer of police shall, if so requested by a person who alleges that he is entitled to claim a payment under the said section 155, furnish to that person any information at the disposal of the chief officer as to the identification marks of any motor vehicle which that person alleges to be a vehicle out of the use of which the bodily injury arose and as to the identity and address of the person who was using the vehicle at the time of the event out of which it arose.

Supplementary

157. Regulations for purposes of Part VI.

The Secretary of State may make regulations for any purpose for which regulations may be made under this Part of this Act and for prescribing anything which may be prescribed under this Part of this Act and generally for the purpose of carrying this Part of this Act into effect, and in particular, but without prejudice to the generality of the foregoing provisions, may make regulations

(a) as to the forms to be used for the purposes of this Part of this Act;

(b) as to applications for and the issue of certificates of insurance and certificates of security and any other documents which may be prescribed, and as to the keeping of records of documents and the furnishing of particulars thereof or the giving of information with respect thereto to the Secretary of State or a chief officer of police;

(c) as to the issue of copies of any such certificates or other documents which are lost or destroyed;

(d) as to the custody, production, cancellation and surrender of any such certificates or other documents;

(e) for providing that any provisions of this Part of this Act shall, in relation to vehicles brought into Great Britain by persons making only a temporary stay therein, have effect subject to such modifications and adaptations as may be prescribed.

158. Interpretation of Part VI.

(1) In this Part of this Act, except where the context otherwise requires, the following expressions have the meanings hereby assigned to them respectively, that is to say

'authorised insurer' has the meaning assigned to it by section 145 (2) of this Act;

'hospital' means an institution, not being an institution carried on for profit, which provides medical or surgical treatment for in-patients;

'policy of insurance' includes a covering note;

'prescribed' means prescribed by regulations;

'regulations' means regulations made under section 157 of this Act;

'salvage' means the preservation of a vessel which is wrecked, stranded or in distress, or the lives of persons belonging to, or the cargo or apparel of, such a vessel;

'under the owner's control' means, in relation to a vehicle, that it is being driven by the owner or by a servant of the owner in the course of his employment or is otherwise subject to the control of the owner.

(2) In any provision of this Part of this Act relating to the surrender, or the loss or destruction, of a certificate of insurance or certificate of security, references to such a certificate shall, in relation to policies or securites under which more than one certificate is issued, be construed as references to all certificates and shall, where any copy has been issued of any certificate, be construed as including a reference to that copy.

Appendix IX

THE MOTOR VEHICLES (COMPULSORY INSURANCE) (NO 2) REGULATIONS 1973

(S I 1973/2143)

The Secretary of State for the Environment, being a Minister designated for the purposes of section 2(2) of the European Communities Act 1972 in relation to compulsory insurance in respect of, and other means of providing for, civil liability in relation to motor vehicles and trailers, in the exercise of powers conferred by that section, hereby makes the following Regulations:—

1. (1) These Regulations shall come into operation on 1 January 1974 and may be cited as the Motor Vehicles (Compulsory Insurance) (No 2) Regulations 1973.

(2) The Motor Vehicles (Compulsory Insurance) Regulations 1973 are hereby revoked.

2. (1) In these Regulations 'vehicle' means any motor vehicle intended for travel on land and propelled by mechanical power, but not running on rails, and any trailer, whether or not coupled, and references to a relevant foreign state are references to Austria, Czechoslovakia, Finland, the German Democratic Republic, Hungary, Norway, Sweden or Switzerland.

(2) For the purposes of these Regulations the territory in which a vehicle is normally based is—

(a) the territory of the state in which the vehicle is registered, or

(b) in cases where no registration is required for the type of vehicle, but the vehicle bears an insurance plate or distinguishing sign analogous to a registration plate, the territory of the state in which the insurance plate or the sign is issued, or

(c) in cases where neither registration plate nor insurance plate nor distinguishing sign is required for the type of vehicle, the territory of the state in which the keeper of the vehicle is permanently resident.

(3) The Interpretation Act 1889 shall apply for the interpretation of these Regulations as it applies for the interpretation of an Act of Parliament.

3. *(amends the Road Traffic Act 1972, s 145 (3)).*

4. *(amends the Road Traffic Act 1972, s 146 (3)).*

5. (1) It shall be an offence for a person to use a specified motor vehicle registered in Great Britain, or any trailer kept by a person permanently resident in Great Britain, whether or not coupled, in the territory other than Great Britain and Gibraltar of any of the member states of the Communities, unless a policy of insurance is in force in relation to the person using that vehicle which insures him in respect of any liability which may be incurred by him in respect of the use of the vehicle in such territory according to the law on compulsory insurance against civil liability in respect of the use of vehicles of the state where the liability may be incurred.

(2) In this Regulation 'specified motor vehicle' means a motor vehicle which is exempted from the provisions of section 143 of the Road Traffic Act 1972 (users of motor vehicles to be insured or secured against third-party risks) by virtue of section 144 of that Act.

(3) A person guilty of an offence under this Regulation shall be liable on summary conviction to a fine not exceeding £50 or to imprisonment for a term not exceeding three months, or to both such fine and such imprisonment.

(4) Proceedings for an offence under this Regulation may be taken, and the offence may for all incidental purposes be treated as having been committed in any place in Great Britain.

(5) Sections 180 (time within which summary proceedings for certain offences must be commenced) and 181 (evidence by certificate) of the Road Traffic Act 1972 shall apply for the purposes of an offence under this Regulation as if such an offence were an offence under that Act to which those sections had been applied by column 7 of Part I of Schedule 4 to that Act.

6. (1) Any person appointed by the Secretary of State for the purpose (in this Regulation referred to as an 'appointed person') may require a person having custody of any vehicle, being a vehicle which is normally based in the territory of a state (other than a relevant foreign state) which is not a member of the Communities or in the non-European territory of a member state or in Gibraltar, when entering Great Britain to produce evidence that any loss or injury which may be caused by such a vehicle is covered throughout the territory in which the treaty establishing the European Economic Community is in force, in accordance with the requirements of the laws of the various member states on compulsory insurance against civil liability in respect of the use of vehicles.

(2) An appointed person may, if no such evidence is produced or if he is not satisfied by such evidence, prohibit the use of the vehicle in Great Britain.

(3) Where an appointed person prohibits the use of a vehicle under this Regulation, he may also direct the driver to remove the vehicle to such place and subject to such conditions as are specified in the direction; and the prohibition shall not apply to the removal of the vehicle in accordance with the direction.

(4) Any person who—

(a) uses a vehicle or causes or permits a vehicle to be used in contravention of a prohibition imposed under paragraph (2) of this Regulation, or

(b) refuses, neglects or otherwise fails to comply in a reasonable time with a direction given under paragraph (3) of this Regulation,

shall be guilty of an offence and shall be liable on summary conviction to a fine not exceeding £50.

(5) Section 181 of the Road Traffic Act 1972 shall apply for the purposes of an offence under this Regulation as if such an offence were an offence under that Act to which that section had been applied by column 7 of Part 1 of Schedule 4 to that Act.

(6) A prohibition under paragraph (2) of this Regulation may be removed by an appointed person if he is satisfied that appropriate action has been taken to remove or remedy the circumstances in consequence of which the prohibition was imposed.

7. (1) Where a constable in uniform has reasonable cause to suspect the driver of a vehicle of having committed an offence under the preceding Regulation, the constable may detain the vehicle, and for that purpose may give a direction, specifying an appropriate person and directing the vehicle to be removed by that person to such place and subject to such conditions as are specified in the direction; and the prohibition shall not apply to the removal of the vehicle in accordance with that direction.

(2) Where under paragraph (1) of this Regulation a constable—

   (a) detains a motor vehicle drawing a trailer, or
   (b) detains a trailer drawn by a motor vehicle,

then, for the purpose of securing the removal of the trailer, he may also (in a case falling within sub-paragraph (a) above) detain the trailer or (in a case falling within sub-paragraph (b) above) detain the motor vehicle; and a direction under paragraph (1) of this Regulation may require both the motor vehicle and the trailer to be removed to the place specified in the direction.

(3) A vehicle which, in accordance with a direction given under paragraph (1) of this Regulation, is removed to a place specified in the direction shall be detained in that place, or in any other place to which it is removed in accordance with a further direction given under that paragraph, until a constable (or, if that place is in the occupation of the Secretary of State, the Secretary of State) authorises the vehicle to be released on being satisfied—

   (a) that the prohibition (if any) imposed in respect of the vehicle under the preceding Regulation has been removed, or that no such prohibition was imposed, or
   (b) that appropriate arrangements have been made for removing or remedying the circumstances in consequence of which any such prohibition was imposed, or
   (c) that the vehicle will be taken forthwith to a place from which it will be taken out of Great Britain to a place not in the European territory other than Gibraltar of a member state of the Communities, and not in the territory of a relevant foreign state.

(4) Any person who—

   (a) drives a vehicle in accordance with a direction given under this Regulation, or
   (b) is in charge of a place at which a vehicle is detained under this Regulation,

shall not be liable for any damage to, or loss in respect of, the vehicle or its load unless it is shown that he did not take reasonable care of the vehicle while driving it or, as the case may be, did not, while the vehicle was detained in that place, take reasonable care of the vehicle or (if the vehicle was detained there with its load) did not take reasonable care of its load.

(5) In this Regulation 'appropriate person'—

   (a) in relation to a direction to remove a motor vehicle, other than a motor vehicle drawing a trailer, means a person licensed to drive vehicles of the class to which the vehicle belongs, and

    (b) in relation to a direction to remove a trailer, or to remove a motor vehicle drawing a trailer, means a person licensed to drive vehicles of a class which, when the direction is complied with, will include the motor vehicle drawing the trailer in accordance with that direction.

8. Nothing in section 145 (2) (policies to be issued by authorised insurers) and section 147 (1) (policies to be of no effect unless certificates issued) of the Road Traffic Act 1972 shall apply in the case of an insurance policy which is issued elsewhere than in the United Kingdom in respect of a vehicle normally based in the territory other than the United Kingdom and Gibraltar of a member State of the Communities or of a relevant foreign state.

9. *(amends the Road Traffic Act 1972, ss 151 (1), 169 (2)).*

Signed by authority of the Secretary of State.

John Peyton,
Minister for Transport Industries,
18 December 1973.   Department of the Environment.

Appendix X

THE MOTOR VEHICLES (THIRD PARTY RISKS) REGULATIONS 1972

(S I 1972/1217)[1]

The Secretary of State for the Environment, in exercise of his powers under sections 147, 157 and 162 of the Road Traffic Act 1972, and under section 37 of the Vehicles (Excise) Act 1971, as extended by section 153 of the Road Traffic Act 1972, and of all other enabling powers, and after consultation with representative organisations in accordance with the provisions of section 199 (2) of the Road Traffic Act 1972, hereby makes the following Regulations:—

Commencement and citation

1. These Regulations shall come into operation on 1st November 1972, and may be cited as the Motor Vehicles (Third Party Risks) Regulations 1972.

2. The Motor Vehicles (Third Party Risks) Regulations 1961[2] and the Motor Vehicles (Third Party Risks) (Amendment) Regulations 1969[3] are hereby revoked.

Temporary use of existing forms

3. Nothing in these Regulations shall affect the validity of any certificate which has been issued before these Regulations came into force in a form prescribed by the Motor Vehicles (Third Party Risks) Regulations 1961, as amended by the Motor Vehicles (Third Party Risks) (Amendment) Regulations 1969, as in force immediately before the coming into operation of these Regulations, and any certificate in such a form may continue to be issued until the expiration of three years from the coming into force of these Regulations.

Interpretation

4. (1) In these Regulations, unless the context otherwise requires, the following expressions have the meanings hereby respectively assigned to them:

'the Act' means the Road Traffic Act 1972;
'company' means an authorised insurer within the meaning of Part VI of the Act or a body of persons by whom a security may be given in pursuance of the said Part VI;

---

[1] The Regulations are printed as amended.
[2] S I 1961/1465.
[3] S I 1969/1733.

'motor vehicle' has the meaning assigned to it by sections 190, 192 and 193 of the Act, but excludes any invalid carriage, tramcar or trolley vehicle to which Part VI of the Act does not apply;

'policy' means a policy of insurance in respect of third party risks arising out of the use of motor vehicles which complies with the requirements of Part VI of the Act and includes a covering note;

'security' means a security in respect of third party risks arising out of the use of motor vehicles which complies with the requirements of Part VI of the Act;

'specified body' means—

(a)   any of the local authorities referred to in paragraph (a) of section 144 (2) of the Act; or

(b)   a Passenger Transport Executive established under an order made under section 9 of the Transport Act 1968, or a subsidiary of that Executive, being an Executive or subsidiary or a wholly-owned subsidiary to whose vehicles section 144 (2) (a) of the Act has been applied; or

(c)   the London Transport Executive or a wholly-owned subsidiary of that Executive referred to in paragraph (e) of section 144 (2) of the Act.

(2) Any reference in these Regulations to a certificate in Form A, B, C, D, E, or F shall be construed as a reference to a certificate in the form so headed and set out in Part I of the Schedule to these Regulations which has been duly made and completed subject to and in accordance with the provisions set out in Part 2 of the said Schedule.

(3) Any reference in these Regulations to any enactment shall be construed as a reference to that enactment as amended by any subsequent enactment.

(4) The Interpretation Act 1889, shall apply for the interpretation of these Regulations as it applies for the interpretation of an Act of Parliament, and as if for the purposes of section 38 of that Act these Regulations were an Act of Parliament and the Regulations revoked by Regulation 2 of these Regulations were Acts of Parliament thereby repealed.

Issue of certificates of insurance or security

5. (1) A company shall issue to every holder of a security or of a policy other than a covering note issued by the company:

(a)   in the case of a policy or security relating to one or more specified vehicles a certificate of insurance in Form A or a certificate of security in Form D in respect of each such vehicle;

(b)   in the case of a policy or security relating to vehicles other than specified vehicles such number of certificates in Form B or Form D as may be necessary for the purpose of complying with requirements of section 162 (1) of the Act of these Regulations as to the production of evidence that a motor vehicle is not being driven in contravention of section 143 of the Act:

Provided that where a security is intended to cover the use of more than ten motor vehicles at one time the company by whom it was issued may, subject to the consent of the Secretary of State, issue one certificate only, and where such consent has been given the holder of

the security may issue duplicate copies of such certificate duly authenticated by him up to such number and subject to such conditions as the
Secretary of State may determine.

(2) Notwithstanding the foregoing provisions of this Regulation, where as
respects third party risks a policy or security relating to a specified vehicle
extends also to the driving by the holder of other motor vehicles, not being
specified vehicles, the certificate may be in Form A or Form D, as the case may
be, containing a statement in either case that the policy or security extends to
such driving of other motor vehicles. Where such a certificate is issued by a
company they may, and shall in accordance with a demand made to them by
the holder, issue to him a further such certificate or a certificate in Form B.

(3) Every policy in the form of a covering note issued by a company
shall have printed thereon or on the back thereof a certificate of insurance in
Form C.

6. Every certificate of insurance or certificate of security shall be issued not
later than four days after the date on which the policy or security to which it
relates is issued or renewed.

Production of evidence as alternatives to certificates

7. The following evidence that a motor vehicle is not or was not being driven in
contravention of section 143 of the Act may be produced in pursuance of
section 162 of the Act as an alternative to the production of a certificate of
insurance or a certificate of security:

(1) a duplicate copy of a certificate of security issued in accordance with
the proviso to sub-paragraph (b) of paragraph (1) of Regulation 5 of
these Regulations;

(2) in the case of a motor vehicle of which the owner has for the time being
deposited with the Accountant-General of the Supreme Court the sum
of fifteen thousand pounds in accordance with the provisions of section
144 (1) of the Act, a certificate in Form E signed by the owner of the
motor vehicle or by some person authorised by him in that behalf that
such sum is on deposit;

(3) in the case of a motor vehicle owned by a specified body, a police
authority or Receiver for the metropolitan police district, a certificate
in Form F signed by some person authorised in that behalf by such
specified body, police authority or Receiver as the case may be that the
said motor vehicle is owned by the said specified body, police authority or Receiver.

(4) in the case of a vehicle normally based in the territory other than the
United Kingdom and Gibraltar of a member state of the Communities
or of Austria, Czechoslavakia, Finland, the German Democratic
Republic, Hungary, Norway, Sweden or Switzerland, a document
issued by the insurer of the vehicle which indicates the name of the
insurer, the number or other identifying particulars of the insurance
policy issued in respect of the vehicle and the period of the insurance
cover. In this paragraph the territory of the state in which a vehicle is
normally based is

(a) the territory of the state in which the vehicle is registered, or

(b) in cases where no registration is required for the type of vehicle, but the vehicle bears an insurance plate or distinguishing sign analogous to a registration plate, the territory of the state in which the insurance plate or the sign is issued, or

(c) in cases where neither registration plate nor insurance plate nor distinguishing sign is required for the type of vehicle, the territory of the state in which the keeper of the vehicle is permanently resident.

8. Any certificate issued in accordance with paragraph (2) or (3) of the preceding Regulation shall be destroyed by the owner of the vehicle to which it relates before the motor vehicle is sold or otherwise disposed of.

Production of evidence of insurance or security on application for excise licences

9. (1) Any person applying for a vehicle licence under the Vehicles (Excise) Act 1971, shall, except as hereinafter provided and subject to the provisions of Regulation 8 of the Motor Vehicles (International Motor Insurance Card) Regulations 1971[4], produce to the Secretary of State either:

(a) a certificate of insurance, certificate of security or duplicate copy of a certificate of security issued in accordance with these Regulations indicating that on the date when the licence comes into operation there will be in force the necessary policy or the necessary security in relation to the user of the motor vehicle by the applicant or by other persons on his order or with his permission and such further evidence as may be necessary to establish that the certificate relates to such user; or

(b) in the case where the motor vehicle is one of more than ten motor vehicles owned by the same person in respect of which a policy or policies of insurance have been obtained by him from the same authorised insurer, a statement duly authenticated by the authorised insurer to the effect that on the date when the licence becomes operative an insurance policy which complies with Part VI of the Act will be in force in relation to the use of the motor vehicle; or

(c) evidence that section 143 of the Act does not apply to the motor vehicle at a time when it is being driven under the owner's control, in accordance with the following provisions:

(i) in the case of a motor vehicle of which the owner has for the time being deposited with the Accountant-General of the Supreme Court the sum of fifteen thousand pounds in accordance with the provisions of section 144(1) of the Act, a certificate in Form E signed by the owner of the motor vehicle or by some person authorised by him in that behalf that such sum is on deposit;

(ii) in the case of a motor vehicle owned by a specified body, a police authority or by the Receiver for the metropolitan police district, a certificate in Form F signed by some person authorised in that

---

4 SI 1971/792. See p 473, post.

behalf by such specified body, police authority or Receiver as the case may be that the vehicle in respect of which the application for a licence is made is owned by the said specified body, police authority or Receiver.

(2) A person engaged in the business of letting motor vehicles on hire shall not, when applying for a licence under the Vehicles (Excise) Act 1971, be required to comply with the provisions of paragraph (1) of this Regulation if the motor vehicle in respect of which the licence is applied for is intended to be used solely for the purpose of being let on hire and driven by the person by whom the motor vehicle is hired or by persons under his control.

Keeping of records by companies

10. (1) Every company by whom a policy or a security is issued shall keep a record of the following particulars relative thereto and of any certificates issued in connection therewith:

    (a) the full name and address of the person to whom the policy, security or certificate is issued;

    (b) in the case of a policy relating to one or more specified motor vehicles the registration mark of each such motor vehicle;

    (c) the date on which the policy or security comes into force and the date on which it expires;

    (d) in the case of a policy the conditions subject to which the persons or classes of persons specified in the policy will be indemnified;

    (d) in the case of a security the conditions subject to which the undertaking given by the company under the security will be implemented;

and every such record shall be preserved for one year from the date of expiry of the policy or security.

(2) Every specified body shall keep a record of the motor vehicles owned by them in respect of which a policy or a security has not been obtained, and of any certificates issued by them under these Regulations in respect of such motor vehicles, and of the withdrawal or destruction of any such certificates.

(3) Any person who has deposited and keeps deposited with the Accountant-General of the Supreme Court the sum of fifteen thousand pounds in accordance with the provisions of section 144(1) of the Act shall keep a record of the motor vehicles owned by him and of any certificates issued by him or on his behalf under these Regulations in respect of such motor vehicles and of the withdrawal or destruction of any such certificates.

(4) Any company, specified body or other person by whom records of documents are required by these Regulations to be kept shall without charge furnish to the Secretary of State or to any chief officer of police on request any particulars thereof.

Notification to the Secretary of State of ineffective policies or securities

11. Where to the knowledge of a company a policy or security issued by them ceases to be effective without the consent of the person to whom it was issued, otherwise than by effluxion of time or by reason of his death, the company shall forthwith notify the Secretary of State of the date on which the policy or security ceased to be effective:

Provided that such notification need not be made if the certificate relating to the policy or security has been received by the company from the person to whom the certificate was issued on or before the date on which the policy or security ceases to be effective.

Return of certificates to issuing company

12. (1) The following provisions shall apply in relation to the transfer of a policy or security with the consent of the holder to any other person;

(a) the holder shall, before the policy or security is transferred, return any relative certificates issued for the purposes of these Regulations to the company by whom they were issued; and

(b) the policy or security shall not be transferred to any other person unless and until the certificates have been so returned or the company are satisfied that the certificates have been lost or destroyed.

(2) In any case where with the consent of the person to whom it was issued a policy or security is suspended or ceases to be effective, otherwise than by effluxion of time, in circumstances in which the provisions of section 147 (4) of the Act (relating to the surrender of certificates) do not apply, the holder of the policy or security shall within seven days from the date when it is suspended or ceases to be effective return any relative certificates issued for the purposes of these Regulations to the company by whom they were issued and the company shall not issue a new policy or security to the said holder in respect of the motor vehicles or vehicles to which the said first mentioned policy or security related unless and until the certificates have been returned to the company or the company are satisfied that they have been lost or destroyed.

(3) Where a policy or security is cancelled by mutual consent or by virtue of any provision in the policy or security, any statutory declaration that a certificate has been lost or destroyed made in pursuance of section 147 (4) (which requires any such declaration to be made within a period of seven days from the taking effect of the cancellation) shall be delivered forthwith after it has been made to the company by whom the policy was issued or the security given.

(4) The provisions of the last preceding paragraph shall be without prejudice to the provisions of paragraph (c) of sub-section (2) of section 149 of the Act as to the effect for the purposes of that sub-section of the making of a statutory declaration within the periods therein stated.

Issue of Fresh Certificates

13. Where any company by whom a certificate of insurance or a certificate of security has been issued are satisfied that the certificate has become defaced or has been lost or destroyed they shall, if they are requested to do so by the person to whom the certificate was issued, issue to him a fresh certificate. In the case of a defaced certificate the company shall not issue a fresh certificate unless the defaced certificate is returned to the company.

THE SCHEDULE

PART 1

Forms of Certificates

FORM A

Certificate of Motor Insurance

Certificate No. .... Policy No. .... (Optional)

1. Registration mark of vehicle.
2. Name of policy holder.
3. Effective date of the commencement of insurance for the purposes of the relevant law.
4. Date of expiry of insurance.
5. Persons or classes of persons entitled to drive.
6. Limitations as to use.

I/We hereby certify that the policy to which this certificate relates satisfies the requirements of the relevant law applicable in Great Britain.

....
Authorised Insurers.

Note: For full details of the insurance cover reference should be made to the policy.

FORM B

Certificate of Motor Insurance

Certificate No. .... Policy No. .... (Optional)

1. Description of vehicles.
2. Name of policy holder.
3. Effective date of the commencement of insurance for the purposes of the relevant law.
4. Date of expiry of insurance.
5. Persons or classes of persons entitled to drive.
6. Limitations as to use.

I/We hereby certify that the policy to which this certificate relates satisfies the requirements of the relevant law applicable in Great Britain.

....
Authorised Insurers.

Note: For full details of the insurance cover reference should be made to the policy.

FORM C

Certificate of Motor Insurance

I/We hereby certify that this covering note satisfies the requirements of the relevant law applicable in Great Britain.

....
Authorised Insurers

FORM D

Certificate of Security

Certificate No. ....   Security No. .... (Optional)

1. Name of holder of security.
2. Effective date of the commencement of security for the purposes of the relevant law.
3. Date of expiry of security.
4. Conditions to which security is subject.

I/We hereby certify that the security to which this certificate relates satisfies the requirements of the relevant law applicable in Great Britain.

....
Persons giving security.

Note: For full details of the cover reference should be made to the security.

FORM E

Certificate of Deposit

I/We hereby certify that I am/we are the owner(s) of the vehicle of which the registration mark is .... and that in pursuance of the relevant law applicable in Great Britain, I/we have on deposit with the Accountant-General of the Supreme Court the sum of fifteen thousand pounds.

Signed...
on behalf of.........................

FORM F

Certificate of Ownership

We hereby certify that the vehicle of which the registration mark is.......................................
.... is owned by ....

Signed ....
On behalf of ....

PART 2
Provisions relating to the forms and completion of certificates

1. Every certificate shall be printed and completed in black on white paper or similar material. This provision shall not prevent the reproduction of a seal or monogram or similar device referred to in paragraph 2 of this Part of this Schedule or the presence of a background pattern (of whatever form and whether coloured or not) on the face of the form which does not materially affect the legibility of the certificate.

2. No certificate shall contain any advertising matter, either on the face or on the back thereof:

Provided that the name and address of the company by whom the certificate is issued, or a reproduction of the seal of the company or any monogram or similar device of the company, or the name and address of an insurance broker, shall not be deemed to be advertising matter for the purposes of this paragraph if it is printed or stamped at the foot or on the back of such certificate, or if it forms, or forms part of, any such background pattern as is referred to in the foregoing paragraph.

3. The whole of each form as set out in Part 1 of this Schedule shall in each case appear on the face of the form, the items being in the order so set out and the certification being set out at the end of the form.

4. The particulars to be inserted on the said forms shall so far as possible appear on the face of the form, but where in the case of any of the numbered headings in Forms A, B or D, this cannot conveniently be done, any part of such particulars may be inserted on the back of the form, provided that their presence on the back is clearly indicated under the relevant heading.

5. The particulars inserted on any of the said forms shall not include particulars relating to any exceptions purporting to restrict the insurance under the relevant policy or the operation of the relevant security which are by sub-section (1) of section 148 of the Act rendered of no effect as respects the third party liabilities required by sections 145 and 146 of the Act to be covered by a policy or security.

6. (1) In any case where it is intended that a certificate of insurance, certificate of security or a covering note shall be effective not only in Great Britain, but also in any of the following territories, that is to say, Northern Ireland, the Isle of Man, the Island of Guernsey, the Island of Jersey or the Island of Alderney, Forms A, B, C and D may be modified by the addition thereto, where necessary, of a reference to the relevant legal provisions of such of those territories as may be appropriate.

(2) A certificate of insurance or a certificate of security may contain either on the face or on the back of the certificate a statement as to whether or not the policy of security to which it relates satisfies the requirements of the relevant law in any of the territories referred to in this paragraph.

7. Every certificate of insurance or certificate of security shall be duly authenticated by or on behalf of the company by whom it is issued.

8. A certificate in Form F issued by a subsidiary of a Passenger Transport Executive or by a wholly-owned subsidiary of the London Transport Executive shall indicate under the signature that the issuing body is such a subsidiary of an Executive, which shall there be specified.

Appendix XI

THE MOTOR VEHICLES (THIRD-PARTY RISKS DEPOSITS) REGULATIONS 1967

(S I 1967/1326)

The Minister of Transport, in exercise of the powers conferred upon her by sections 210 (2) and 215 of the Road Traffic Act 1960, section 20 (1) of the Insurance Companies Act 1958, as amended by section 17 of and Schedule 1 to the Administration of Justice Act 1965, and section 14 (3) of the Administration of Justice Act 1965, and of all other enabling powers, and after consultation with the Lord Chancellor and, in accordance with the provisions of section 260 (2) of the Road Traffic Act 1960, with representative organisations, hereby makes the following Regulations:—

Commencement and citation

1. These Regulations may be cited as the Motor Vehicles (Third-Party Risks Deposits) Regulations 1967, and shall come into operation on the 2nd October 1967.

Revocation

2. The Motor Vehicles (Third-Party Risks Deposits) Rules 1952[1] are hereby revoked.

Interpretation

3. (1) In these Regulations, except where the context otherwise requires, the following expressions have the meanings hereby respectively assigned to them:—

'the Act' means the Road Traffic Act 1960;
'the Accountant General' means the Accountant General of the Supreme Court;
'the court' means the High Court;
'the depositor' has the meaning assigned thereto in Regulation 4 of these Regulations;
'long-term investment account' and 'short-term investment account' have

---

[1] S I 1952/1616.

the same meanings as in section 6 (1) (a) of the Administration of Justice Act 1965;

'the Minister' means the Minister of Transport.

(2) The Interpretation Act 1889 shall apply for the interpretation of these Regulations as it applies for the interpretation of an Act of Parliament, and as if for the purposes of section 38 of that Act these Regulations were an Act of Parliament and the Rules revoked by Regulation 2 of these Regulations were an Act of Parliament thereby repealed.

Deposits

4. Any person wishing to deposit with the Accountant General the sum of £15,000 in pursuance of section 202 or section 204 of the Act may apply to the Minister for a warrant which shall be a sufficient authority for the Accountant General to issue a direction for the payment into the Bank of England to the credit of his account by the person named in the warrant (hereinafter referred to as 'the depositor') of the said sum of £15,000 which shall be credited in the books of the Accountant General to an account entitled ex parte the depositor, in respect of the Act:

Provided that in lieu, wholly or in part, of the deposit of money the depositor may deposit an equivalent amount of securities in which cash under the control of or subject to the order of the court may for the time being be invested (the value thereof being taken at a price as near as may be to, but not exceeding, the current market price) and in that case the Minister shall vary her warrant accordingly.

Investment

5. (1) The court may, on the application of the depositor, make an order for dealing with any money which has been deposited in court under the last preceding Regulation by its placement to a short-term or long-term investment acccount or by its investment in any securities in which cash under the control of or subject to the order of the court may for the time being be invested, or for the variation of any existing investment by way of sale and reinvestment, or otherwise, and for the payment of the interest, dividends or income accruing due on such investment.

(2) Any interest, dividend or income accruing due on money or securities deposited with the court under the last preceding Regulation shall, subject to any order of the Court, be paid to the depositor at his request.

(3) Any money which has been deposited with the court under the last preceding Regulation may be placed to a short-term investment account at the request of the depositor.

(4) This Regulation shall apply to any deposit made, or having effect as if made, in pursuance of section 202 or section 204 of the Act, whether under these, or any preceding, Rules or Regulations.

Withdrawal of deposits

6. In any case where it may be just and equitable so to do, and in particular in any of the following cases, that is to say—

(a) where a person who has made a deposit in pursuance of section 202 (1) of the Act, or having effect as if made in pursuance of that section, complies, or satisfies the court that he intends to comply, in some other manner, whether by way of insurance or otherwise with the provisions of Part VI of the Act,

(b) where—

    (i) a person who has made such a deposit as aforesaid ceases to own, or to control the use of, a motor vehicle, or

    (ii) a person who has made a deposit in pursuance of section 204 of the Act, or having effect as if made in pursuance of that section, has ceased altogether to carry on in the United Kingdom the business of giving securities under Part VI of the Act,

and in either case all liabilities in respect of which money or securities were deposited in court have been satisfied or otherwise provided for, the court may, on the application of any such person (of which application notice shall be served on the Minister) order any money or securities deposited in court to be paid or transferred out of court to such person as aforesaid or otherwise as the court may direct.

Warrants

7. The issue of any warrant under Regulation 4 of these Regulations or any error in any such warrant, or in relation thereto, shall not render the Minister or the person signing the warrant on her behalf, in any manner liable for or in respect of any money or security deposited in court, or any securities for the time being representing the same, or the interest, dividends or income accruing due thereon.

Application of Supreme Court Funds Rules

8. Subject to the foregoing Regulations, the relevant provisions of the Rules for the time being in force under section 7 of the Administration of Justice Act 1965 (Rules as to funds in Supreme Court) shall apply to deposits made, or having effect as if made, in pursuance of section 202 or section 204 of the Act, whether under these or any preceding Rules or Regulations.

Given under the Official Seal of the Minister of Transport 6 September 1967.

(L S)

Barbara Castle,
The Minister of Transport.

Appendix XII

MOTOR VEHICLES (INTERNATIONAL MOTOR INSURANCE CARD) REGULATIONS 1971

(S I 1971/792)[1]

The Secretary of State for the Environment in exercise of his powers under sections 211 and 215 of the Road Traffic Act 1960, and section 37(1) of the Vehicles (Excise) Act 1971, and of all other enabling powers and after consultation with representative organisations in accordance with the provisions of section 260(2) of the Road Traffic Act 1960, hereby makes the following Regulations:

Title and commencement

1. These Regulations may be cited as the Motor Vehicles (International Motor Insurance Card) Regulations 1971 and shall come into operation on 10 June 1971.

Revocation

2. The Motor Vehicles (International Motor Insurance Card) Regulations 1969[2] are hereby revoked.

Interpretation

3. (1) In these Regulations:

'the Act' means the Road Traffic Act 1960;
'authorised insurer' has the same meaning as in Part VI of the Act;
'British Bureau' means the Motor Insurers' Bureau incorporated under the Companies Act 1929, and having its registered office at Aldermary House, Queen Street, London, E C 4;
'Foreign Bureau' means a central organisation set up by motor insurers in any country outside the United Kingdom, the Isle of Man and the Channel Islands for the purpose of giving effect to international arrangements for the insurance of motorists against third-party risks when entering countries where insurance against such risks is compulsory, and with which organisation the British Bureau has entered into such an arrangement;

---

[1] The Regulations are printed as amended.
[2] S I 1968/668.

'hired motor vehicle' means a motor vehicle which is:

(a) designed for private use and with seats for not more than eight persons excluding the driver, and

(b) specified in an insurance card, and

(c) last brought into Great Britain by a person making only a temporary stay therein, and

(d) owned and let for hire by a person whose business includes the letting of vehicles for hire and whose principal place of business is outside the United Kingdom;

'hiring visitor' means a person to whom a hired motor vehicle is let on hire, who is making only a temporary stay in Great Britain and is named as the insured or user of that vehicle in the insurance card in which that vehicle is specified;

'insurance card' means an international motor insurance card issued under the authority of a Foreign Bureau or of the British Bureau which is green in colour and

(a) is either in English or a foreign language containing the particulars specified in, and set out in two pages as shown in, Schedule 1 to these Regulations; . . . .

'the Secretary of State' means the Secretary of State for the Environment;

'trade licence' has the same meaning as in the Vehicles (Excise) Act 1971';

'visitor' means a person bringing a motor vehicle into Great Britain, making only a temporary stay therein and named in an insurance card as the insured or user of the vehicle, and includes a hiring visitor who brings a hired motor vehicle into Great Britain, but no other hiring visitor.

(2) Any reference in these Regulations to any provision in an Act of Parliament or in subordinate legislation shall be construed as a reference to that provision as amended by any other such provision.

(3) The Interpretation Act 1889 shall apply for the interpretation of these Regulations as it applies for the interpretation of an Act of Parliament and as if for the purposes of section 38 of that Act these Regulations were an Act of Parliament and the Regulations revoked by Regulation 2 of these Regulations were an Act of Parliament thereby repealed.

Validity of insurance card

4. (1) An insurance card shall be valid for the purposes of these Regulations only if

(a) the motor vehicle specified in the card is brought into the United Kingdom during the period of validity so specified;

(b) the application of the card in Great Britain is indicated thereon;

(c) all relevant information provided for in the card has been inscribed therein;

(d) the card has been duly signed by the visitor, by the insurer named in the card and, in the case of a hired motor vehicle, by every hiring visitor who is named in the card as the insured or user thereof; and

. . . .

(2) The information required to be inscribed in paragraphs 2, 7 and 8 in the page of the card shown in Schedule 1 to these Regulations and marked 'original' . . . . :

(a) in the said paragraph 2, the name of the Foreign Bureau or the British Bureau, as the case may be, under whose authority the card was issued; and

(b) in the said paragraph . . . 7, the name and address of the insured visitor and of every person who is, as respects a hired motor vehicle, a hiring visitor; and

(c) in the said paragraph 8, the name and address of the insurer authorised to issue the card by the Foreign Bureau or the British Bureau, as the case may be, and by whom the card was issued.

Third-party risks arising out of the use of motor vehicles by visitors

5. (1) As respects the use on a road of a motor vehicle specified in a valid insurance card, being use by the visitor to whom the card was issued, or by any hiring visitor named therein, or by any other person on the order or with the permission of the said visitor or of any such hiring visitor, section 201 of the Act shall have effect as though the said card were a policy of insurance complying with the requirements of and having effect for the purposes of Part VI of the Act in relation to such use:

Provided that where the said motor vehicle remains in the United Kingdom after the expiry of the period of validity specified in the card, then as respects any period whilst it so remains during which the vehicle is in Great Britain the said card shall not be regarded as having ceased to be in force for the purposes of the said section 201 by reason only of effluxion of the period of validity specified in the card.

For the purposes of this paragraph a motor vehicle shall be deemed not to have left the United Kingdom whilst it is only in transit between different parts of the United Kingdom.

(2) Any reference in this Regulation and in the next following Regulation to the use on a road of a motor vehicle shall not include any use of the vehicle for the purpose of delivering it to or for the visitor at some place other than the place of entry of the vehicle into Great Britain, which is authorised under a trade licence.

6. (1) For the purposes of sections 226, 230 and 231 of the Act, a valid insurance card shall have effect as though it were a certificate of insurance issued by an authorised insurer and in relation to any claim in respect of any such liability as is required to be covered by a policy of insurance under section 203 of the Act and arising out of the use on a road of a motor vehicle specified in such a card by the visitor to whom it was issued, by any hiring visitor named therein, or by any other person on the order or with the permission of the said visitor or of any such hiring visitor, the person against whom the claim is made shall in lieu of making the statement and giving the particulars referred to in section 209(1) of the Act, give to the person making the claim, on his demand, the serial letter or letters (if any) and serial number shown in the card, the name of the Bureau under whose authority it was issued and the name and address of the person specified therein as the insured.

(2) Any person making or intending to make any such claim as is mentioned in the preceding paragraph of this Regulation shall give notice of the claim in writing to the British Bureau as soon as practicable after the happening of the event out of which the claim arose specifying the nature of the claim and against whom it is made or intended to be made.

(3) [*Repealed*]

7. [*Repealed*]

Production of insurance card on application for excise licence

8. Any visitor or hiring visitor applying for a licence under the Vehicles (Excise) Act 1971 for a motor vehicle specified in a valid insurance card in which he is named as the insured may, during the period of validity specified in the card, in lieu of producing to the licensing authority such evidence as is required by Regulation 9 of the Motor Vehicles (Third Party Risks) Regulations 1961[3], as amended, produce such a card to the licensing authority.

9.[*Repealed*]

Special provision for motor vehicles from Northern Ireland.

10. In the case of a motor vehicle brought from Northern Ireland into Great Britain by a person making only a temporary stay in Great Britain, a policy of insurance or a security which complies with the Road Traffic Act (Northern Ireland) 1970 and which covers the driving of the motor vehicle in Great Britain and any certificate of insurance or certificate of security issued in pursuance of that Act and the Regulations made thereunder in respect of such policy or security shall have effect as a policy of insurance or a security or a certificate of insurance or certificate of security respectively for the purposes of Part VI of the Act, and of the Motor Vehicles (Third Party Risks) Regulations 1961, as amended.

Signed by authority of the Secretary of State 10 May 1971.

---

[3] These regulations have now been replaced by the Motor Vehicles (Third Party Risks) Regulations 1972 (SI 1972/1217) as amended, which are set out in Appendix X, p 461, ante.

SCHEDULE 1

(See Regulation 3)

PARTICULARS TO BE SHOWN IN PAGES OF INSURANCE CARD

ORIGINAL

1. INTERNATIONAL MOTOR INSURANCE CARD

2. ISSUED UNDER THE AUTHORITY OF (NATIONAL INSURERS' BUREAU)

3. VALID	4. Serial and Policy Numbers

VALID

FROM			TO		
Day	Month	Year	Day	Month	Year

(Both Dates Inclusive)

5. Registration Number (or if none) Chassis or engine number.	6. Category and make of Vehicle*

(Cancel Country inapplicable)

A	B	L	NL	CH	CS	D	DK	N	S	SF	E	F	GB
GR	H	I	IL	IRL	IS	MA	P	PL	R	TN	TR	YU	

7. Name and Address of Insured (or User of the vehicle).

8. This Card has been Issued by: (Name and address of Insurer)	9. Signature of Insurer.

*For details of Letter-Code for Category of Vehicle, see next page.

PARTICULARS TO BE SHOWN IN PAGES OF INSURANCE CARD

INTERNATIONAL MOTOR INSURANCE CARD

CARTE INTERNATIONALE D'ASSURANCE AUTOMOBILE

(1) In each country visited, the Bureau of that country assumes, in respect of the use of the vehicle referred to herein, the liability of an Insurer in accordance with the laws relating to compulsory insurance in that country.

(2) After the date of expiry of this Card, liability is assumed by the Bureau of the country visited, if so required by the law of such country or by any agreement with its Government. In such case, the within-mentioned insured undertakes to pay the premium due for the duration of the stay after the date for which the Insurance Card is valid has passed.

(3) I, the within-mentioned insured, hereby authorise the Motor Insurers' Bureau and the Bureaux of any mentioned countries, to which it may delegate such powers, to accept service of legal proceedings, to handle and eventually settle, on my behalf, any claim for damages in respect of liability to third parties required to be covered under the compulsory insurance laws of the country or countries specified herein, which may arise from the use of the vehicle in that country (those countries).

(4) Signature of the Insured

(5) For visitors to Great Britain and Northern Ireland only.
Signature of any other persons who may use the vehicle.

....
(This Insurance Card is only valid when signed by the Insured).

Cards applicable to the following countries must contain detachable copies of the form on the preceding page:

Switzerland

---

*CATEGORY OF VEHICLE (CODE)

A. CAR   C. LORRY OR TRACTOR   E. BUS

B. MOTORCYCLE   D. CYCLE FITTED WITH   F. TRAILER.
                               AUXILIARY ENGINE

SCHEDULE 2
[*Expired*]

Appendix XIII

MOTOR INSURERS' BUREAU

(A) Compensation of Victims of Uninsured Drivers[1]

Text of an Agreement dated 22 November 1972, between the Secretary of State for the Environment and the Motor Insurers' Bureau together with some notes on its scope and purpose.

In accordance with the Agreement made on 31 December 1945 between the Minister of War Transport and insurers transacting compulsory motor vehicle insurance business in Great Britain (published by the Stationery Office under the title 'Motor Vehicle Insurance Fund') a corporation called the 'Motor Insurers' Bureau' entered into an agreement on 17 June 1946 with the Minister of Transport to give effect from 1 July 1946 to the principle recommended in July 1937 by the Departmental Committee under Sir Felix Cassel, (Cmd 5528), to secure compensation to third party victims of road accidents in cases where, notwithstanding the provisions of the Road Traffic Acts relating to compulsory insurance, the victim is deprived of compensation by the absence of insurance, or of effective insurance. That Agreement was replaced by an Agreement which operated in respect of accidents occurring on or after 1 March 1971. The Agreement of 1971 has now been replaced by a new Agreement which operates in respect of accidents occurring on or after 1 December 1972.
The text of the new Agreement is as follows—

MEMORANDUM OF AGREEMENT made the 22nd day of November 1972 between the Secretary of State for the Environment and the Motor Insurers' Bureau, whose registered office is at Aldermary House, Queen Street, London, EC4N 1TR (hereinafter referred to as 'MIB') SUPPLEMENTAL to an Agreement (hereinafter called 'the Principal Agreement') made the 31st Day of December 1945 between the Minister of War Transport and the insurers transacting compulsory motor vehicle insurance business in Great Britain by or on behalf of whom the said Agreement was signed in pursuance of paragraph 1 of which MIB was incorporated.

IT IS HEREBY AGREED AS FOLLOWS:

DEFINITIONS
1. In this Agreement:
   'contract of insurance' means a policy of insurance or a security;
   'insurer' includes the giver of a security'

---

[1] This document is reproduced by kind permission of the Department of the Environment.

'relevant liability' means a liability in respect of which a policy of insurance must insure a person in order to comply with Part VI of the Road Traffic Act 1972.

SATISFACTION OF CLAIMS BY MIB

2. If judgment in respect of any relevant liability is obtained against any person or persons in any Court in Great Britain whether or not such a person or persons be in fact covered by a contract of insurance and any such judgment is not satisfied in full within seven days from the date upon which the person or persons in whose favour the judgment was given became entitled to enforce it then MIB will, subject to the provisions of Clauses 4, 5 and 6 hereof, pay or satisfy or cause to be paid or satisfied to or to the satisfaction of the person or persons in whose favour the judgment was given any sum payable or remaining payable thereunder in respect of the relevant liability including any sum awarded by the Court in respect of interest on that sum and any taxed costs or any costs awarded by the Court without taxation (or such proportion thereof as is attributable to the relevant liability) whatever may be the cause of the failure of the judgment debtor to satisfy the judgment.

PERIOD OF AGREEMENT

3. This Agreement shall be determinable by the Secretary of State at any time or by MIB on twelve months' notice without prejudice to the continued operation of the Agreement in respect of accidents occuring before the date of termination.

RECOVERIES

4. Nothing in this Agreement shall prevent insurers from providing by conditions in their contracts of insurance that all sums paid by them or by MIB by virtue of the Principal Agreement or this Agreement in or towards the discharge of the liability of their assured shall be recoverable by them or by MIB from the assured or from any other person.

CONDITIONS PRECEDENT TO MIB's LIABILITY

5.(1) MIB shall not incur any liability under Clause 2 of this Agreement unless—

    (a) notice of the bringing of the proceedings is given before or within seven days after the commencement of the proceedings—
        (i) to MIB in the case of proceedings in respect of a relevant liability which is either not covered by a contract of insurance or covered by a contract of insurance with an insurer whose identity cannnot be ascertained, or
        (ii) to the insurer in the case of proceedings in respect of a relevant liability which is covered by a contract of insurance with an insurer whose identity can be ascertained;
    (b) such information relating to the proceedings as MIB may reasonably require is supplied to MIB by the person bringing the proceedings;
    (c) if so required by MIB and subject to full indemnity from MIB as to costs the person bringing the proceedings has taken all reasonable steps to obtain judgment against all the persons liable in respect of the

injury or death of the third party and, in the event of such a person being a servant or agent, against his principal;

(d) the judgment referred to in Clause 2 of this Agreement and any judgment referred to in paragraph (c) of this Clause which has been obtained (whether or not either judgment includes an amount in respect of a liability other than a relevant liability) and any order for costs are assigned to MIB or their nominee.

(2) In the event of any dispute as to the reasonableness of a requirement by MIB for the supply of information or that any particular step should be taken to obtain judgment against other persons it may be referred to the Secretary of State whose decision shall be final.

(3) Where a judgment which includes an amount in respect of a liability other than a relevant liability has been assigned to MIB or their nominee in pursuance of paragraph (1)(d) of this Clause MIB shall apportion any monies received in pursuance of the judgment according to the proportion which the damages in respect of the relevant liability bear to the damages in respect of other liabilities and shall account to the person in whose favour the judgment was given in respect of such monies received properly apportionable to the other liabilities. Where an order for costs in respect of such a judgment has been so assigned monies received pursuant to the order shall be dealt with in the same manner.

EXEMPTIONS

6.(1) MIB shall not incur any liability under Clause 2 of this Agreement in a case where:

(a) the claim arises out of the use of a vehicle owned by or in the possession of the Crown, except where any other person has undertaken responsibility for the existence of a contract of insurance under Part VI of the Road Traffic Act 1972 (whether or not the person or persons liable be in fact covered by a contract of insurance) or where the liability is in fact covered by a contract of insurance;

(b) the claim arises out of the use of a vehicle the use of which is not required to be covered by a contract of insurance by virtue of section 144 of the Road Traffic Act 1972, unless the use is in fact covered by such a contract;

(c) at the time of the accident the person suffering death or bodily injury in respect of which the claim is made was allowing himself to be carried in a vehicle and—

(i) knew or had reason to believe that the vehicle had been taken without the consent of the owner or other lawful authority except in a case where—

(A) he believed or had reason to believe that he had lawful authority to be carried or that he would have had the owner's consent if the owner had known of his being carried and the circumstances of his carriage; or

(B) he had learned of the circumstances of the taking of the vehicle since the commencement of the journey and it would be unreasonable to expect him to have alighted from the vehicle; or

(ii) being the owner of or being a person using the vehicle, he was using or causing or permitting the vehicle to be used without there being in force in relation to such use a contract of insurance as would comply with Part VI of the Road Traffic Act 1972, knowing or having reason to believe that no such contract was in force.

(2) The exemption specified in sub-paragraph (1)(c) of this Clause shall apply only in a case where the judgment in respect of which the claim against MIB is made was obtained in respect of a relevant liability incurred by the owner or a person using the vehicle in which the person who suffered death or bodily injury was being carried.

(3) For the purposes of these exemptions:

(a) a vehicle which has been unlawfully removed from the possession of the Crown shall be taken to continue in that possession whilst it is kept so removed;

(b) references to a person being carried in a vehicle include references to his being carried in or upon or entering or getting on to or alighting from the vehicle;

(c) 'owner' in relation to a vehicle which is the subject of a hiring agreement or a hire-purchase agreement, means the person in possession of the vehicle under that agreement.

AGENTS
7. Nothing in this Agreement shall prevent MIB performing their obligations under this Agreement by Agents.

OPERATION
8. This Agreement shall come into operation on the first day of December 1972 in relation to accidents occurring on or after that date. The Agreement made on 1 February 1971 between the Secretary of State and MIB shall cease and determine except in relation to claims arising out of accidents occurring before the first day of December 1972.

IN WITNESS whereof the Secretary of State has caused his Corporate Seal to be hereto affixed and the Motor Insurers' Bureau have caused their Common Seal to be hereto affixed the day and year first above written.

(L S)   THE CORPORATE SEAL of the Secretary of State was hereunto affixed in the presence of P A Waller.

An Assistant Secretary in the Department of the Environment, duly authorised in that behalf.

(L S)   THE COMMON SEAL of the Motor Insurers' Bureau was hereunto affixed in the presence of

R M Livett   } Members of
O Stephen Masefield   } the Council

P F Morgan   Secretary

NOTES

The following notes are for the guidance of those who may have a claim on the Motor Insurers' Bureau under the Agreement, and of their legal advisers, but they must not be taken as rendering unnecessary a careful study of the Agreement itself. Communications on any matter connected with the Agreement should be addressed to the Motor Insurers' Bureau whose address is Aldermary House, Queen Street, London, EC4N 1TR.

1. The Agreement, which operates from 1 December 1972, supersedes earlier Agreements made on 17 June 1946 (which was operative from 1 July 1946) and on 1 February 1971 (which was operative from 1 March 1971) in relation to claims arising out of accidents occurring on or after 1 December 1972.

2. If damages are awarded by a Court in respect of death or personal injury arising out of the use of a motor vehicle on a road in circumstances where the liability is one which was, at the time the accident occurred, required to be covered by insurance and such damages, or any part of them, remain unpaid seven days after the judgment becomes enforceable, the Bureau will, subject to the exceptions in Clause 6 of the Agreement, pay the unrecovered amount (including any interest awarded by the Court and costs) to the person in whose favour the judgment has been given against an assignment of the judgment debt. This applies whether the judgment debtor is a British resident or a foreign visitor.

3. Nothing in the Agreement affects the position at law of the parties to an action for damages arising out of the driving of a motor vehicle. The Bureau's liability under the Agreement can only arise when the plaintiff has successfully established his case against the person or persons liable in the usual manner and judgment has been given in his favour. There is, of course, nothing to exclude the acceptance of compensation by the plaintiff under a settlement negotiated between the plaintiff and the alleged person liable or the Bureau.

4. WHERE THERE IS A POLICY. In cases where it is ascertained that there is in existence a policy issued in compliance with the Road Traffic Act 1972, the insurer concerned will normally act as the agent of the Bureau and, subject to notice being given as provided for in Clause 5(1)(a)(ii), will handle claims within the terms of the Agreement. This will apply even if the use of the vehicle at the time of the accident was outside the terms of the policy or the insurer is entitled to repudiate liability under the policy for any other reason. (In the latter connection, victims and those acting on their behalf are reminded of the requirements as to the giving of notice to the insurer if the protection afforded to third parties by section 149 of the Road Traffic Act is sought.) This arrangement is, of course, without prejudice to any rights insurers may have against their policy holders and, to avoid any possible misapprehension, it is emphasised that there is nothing in this Agreement affecting any obligations imposed on a policy holder by his policy. Policy holders are not released from their contractual obligations to their insurers, although the scheme protects THIRD PARTY VICTIMS from the consequences of failure to observe them. For example, the failure of a policy holder to notify claims to his insurers as required by his policy, although not affecting a victim's right to benefit under the scheme, may leave the policy holder liable to his insurers.

WHERE THERE IS NO POLICY OR THE IDENTITY OF THE INSURER CANNOT BE ASCERTAINED. In cases where there is no policy, or for any reason the existence of a policy is in doubt or where there is a policy but the identity of the insurer cannot be ascertained, the victim or those acting on his behalf must notify the Bureau of the claim. It is a condition of the Bureau's liability that they should receive notification before or within 7 days after the commencement of proceedings against the alleged person liable. In practice, however, it will be preferable to notify the Bureau in all cases where the name of the insurer is not speedily forthcoming.

5. Claims arising out of the use of uninsured vehicles owned by or in the possession of the Crown will in the majority of cases be outside the scope of the Bureau's liability (see Clause 6 of the Agreement). In such cases the approach should be made to the responsible authority in the usual way. The same benefits in respect of compensation will normally be afforded by the Crown to the victims in such cases as they would receive were the accident caused by a private vehicle, except where the victim is a serviceman or servicewoman whose death or injury gives rise to an entitlement to a pension or other compensation from public funds.

6. The Bureau have no liability UNDER THIS AGREEMENT to pay compensation in respect of any person who may suffer personal injuries or death resulting from the use on a road of a vehicle, the owner or driver of which cannot be traced. However, in relation to accidents occurring ON OR AFTER 1 May 1969 and before 1 December 1972, an Agreement dated 21 April 1969 between the Minister of Transport (now the Secretary of State for the Environment) and the Bureau for the Compensation of Victims of Untraced Drivers applies. In relation to accidents occurring on or after 1 December 1972, an Agreement dated 22 November 1972 between the Secretary of State and the Bureau applies.[2] (Copies of these Agreements may be obtained through Her Majesty's Stationery Office, or any bookseller, price 9p and 13p respectively.)

(B) Compensation of Victims of Untraced Drivers[3]

Text of an Agreement dated 22 November 1972 between the Secretary of State for the Environment and the Motor Insurers' Bureau together with some notes on its scope and purpose.

On 21 April 1969 the Minister of Transport and the Motor Insurers' Bureau entered into an Agreement to secure compensation for third party victims of road accidents when the driver responsible for the accident could not be traced. That Agreement has now been replaced by a new Agreement which operates in respect of accidents occurring on or after 1 December 1972. The text of the new Agreement is as follows—

AN AGREEMENT made the 22nd day of November 1972 between the Secretary of State for the Environment and the Motor Insurers' Bureau, whose registered office is at Aldermary House, Queen Street, London, EC4N 1TR (hereinafter referred to as ' MIB')

IT IS HEREBY AGREED as follows:

1. (1) Subject to paragraph (2) of this Clause, this Agreement applies to any case in which an application is made to MIB for a payment in respect of the death of or bodily injury to any person caused by or arising out of the use of a

---

[2] See infra.

[3] This document is reproduced by kind permission of the Department of the Environment.

motor vehicle on a road in Great Britain and the case is one in which the following conditions are fulfilled, that is to say,—

(a) the event giving rise to the death or injury occurred on or after the 1st December 1972;

(b) the applicant for the payment either—

(i) is unable to trace any person responsible for the death or injury, or

(ii) in a case to which Clause 5 hereof applies where more than one person was so responsible, is unable to trace one of those persons.

(Any person so untraced is hereinafter referred to as 'the untraced person');

(c) the death or injury was caused in such circumstances that on the balance of probabilities the untraced person would be liable to pay damages to the applicant in respect of the death or injury;

(d) the liability of the untraced person to pay damages to the applicant is one which is required to be covered by insurance or security under Part VI of the Road Traffic Act 1972, it being assumed for this purpose, in the absence of evidence to the contrary, that the vehicle was being used in circumstances in which the user was required by the said Part VI to be insured or secured against third party risks;

(e) the death or injury was not caused by the use of the vehicle by the untraced person as a weapon, that is to say, in a deliberate attempt to run the deceased or injured person down;

(f) the application is made in writing within three years from the date of the event giving rise to the death or injury.

(2) This Agreement does not apply to a case in which—

(a) the death or bodily injury in respect of which any such application is made was caused by or arose out of the use of a motor vehicle which at the time of the event giving rise to the death or bodily injury was owned by or in the possession of the Crown, unless the case is one in which some other person has undertaken responsibility for the existence of a contract of insurance under Part VI of the Road Traffic Act 1972;

(b) at the time of the accident the person suffering death or bodily injury in respect of which the application is made was allowing himself to be carried in a vehicle and—

(i) knew or had reason to believe that the vehicle had been taken without the consent of the owner or other lawful authority, except in a case where—

(A) he believed or had reason to believe that he had lawful authority to be carried or that he would have had the owner's consent if the owner had known of his being carried and the circumstances of his carriage; or

(B) he had learned of the circumstances of the taking of the vehicle since the commencement of the journey and it would be unreasonable to expect him to have alighted from the vehicle; or

(ii) being the owner of or being a person using the vehicle he was using or causing or permitting the vehicle to be used without there being in force in relation to such use a policy of insurance or such security as would comply with Part VI of the Road Traffic Act 1972, knowing or having reason to believe that no such policy or security was in force.

(3) The exemption from the application of this Agreement specified in sub-paragraph (2) (b) of this Clause shall apply only in a case where the application is made to MIB in respect of a liability arising out of the use of the vehicle in which the person who suffered death or bodily injury was being carried.

(4) For the purpose of paragraph (2) of this Clause:

(a) a vehicle which has been unlawfully removed from the possession of the Crown shall be taken to continue in that possession whilst it is kept so removed;

(b) references to a person being carried in a vehicle include references to his being carried in or upon, or entering or getting on to or alighting from the vehicle;

(c) 'owner' in relation to a vehicle which is the subject of a hiring agreement or a hire-purchase agreement means the person in possession of the vehicle under that agreement.

2. (1) An application to MIB for a payment in respect of the death of or bodily injury to any person may be made either by the person for whose benefit that payment is to be made (hereinafter called 'the applicant') or by any solicitor acting for the applicant or by any other person whom MIB may be prepared to accept as acting for the applicant.

(2) Any decision, award or payment given or made or other thing done in accordance with this Agreement to or by a person acting as aforesaid on behalf of the applicant, or in relation to an application made by such a person, shall, whatever may be the age, or the circumstances affecting the capacity, of the applicant, be treated as having the same effect as if it had been done to or by, or in relation to an application made by, an applicant of full age and capacity.

3. Subject to the following provisions of this Agreement, MIB shall, on any application made to them in a case to which this Agreement applies, award to the applicant in respect of the death or injury in respect of which the application is made a payment of an amount which shall be assessed in like manner as a court, applying English law in a case where the event giving rise to the death or injury occurred in England or Wales or applying the law of Scotland in a case where that event occurred in Scotland, would assess the damages which the applicant would have been entitled to recover from the untraced person in respect of that death or injury if proceedings to enforce a claim for damages in respect thereof were successfully brought by the applicant against the untraced person.

4. In making an award in accordance with Clause 3 hereof:

(a) MIB shall not be required to include in the payment awarded any amount in respect of any damages for loss of expectation of life or for pain or suffering which the applicant might have had a right to claim under the Law Reform (Miscellaneous Provisions) Act 1934, or, as the case may be, under any corresponding rule of law in force in Scotland nor, in a case where the application is made in respect of a death, shall MIB be required to include in the payment awarded any amount in respect of solatium for the grief of any relative of the deceased which the applicant might have had a right to claim under any enactment or rule of law in force in Scotland; and

(b) in assessing the amount to which the applicant is entitled in respect of loss of earnings if the applicant has received his wages or salary in full or in part from his employer, whether or not upon an undertaking given by the applicant to reimburse his employer if he recovers damages, he shall not to the extent of the amount so received be regarded as having sustained a loss of earnings.

5. (1) The Clause applies to any case to which this Agreement applies where the death or bodily injury in respect of which an application has been made to MIB under this Agreement (hereinafter in this Clause referred to as 'the relevant death or injury') was caused partly by the untraced person and partly either by an identified person, or by identified persons, or by some other untraced person or persons whose master or principal can be identified and was so caused in circumstances making the identified person or persons or any such master or principal as aforesaid liable to the applicant in respect of the relevant death or injury.

(2) If in a case to which this Clause applies one or other of the conditions specified in the next following paragraph is satisfied, the amount to be awarded by MIB to the applicant in respect of the relevant death or injury shall be determined in accordance with the provisions of paragraph (4) of this Clause and their liability to the applicant shall be subject also to the provisions of paragraph (7) of this Clause and to Clause 6 hereof.

(3) The conditions referred to in the last foregoing paragraph are:

(a) that the applicant has obtained a judgment in respect of the relevant death or injury against the identified person or against one or more of the identified persons or against any person liable as their master or principal or the master or principal of any other person which has not been satisfied in full within three months from the date on which the applicant became entitled to enforce it; or

(b) that the applicant—

(i) has not obtained and has not been required by MIB to obtain a judgment in respect of the relevant death or injury against the identified person or persons or against any person liable as the master or principal of any such identified person or persons or as the master or principal of any other person, and

(ii) has not received any payment by way of compensation from any such person or persons.

(4) The amount to be awarded by MIB to the applicant in a case to which this Clause applies shall be determined as follows:

(a) if the condition specified in paragraph (3) (a) of this Clause is satisfied and the judgment mentioned in that paragraph is wholly unsatisfied within the period of three months therein referred to, the amount to be awarded shall be an amount equal to the untraced person's contribution to a full award;

(b) if the condition specified in paragraph (3) (a) of this Clause is satisfied but the judgment mentioned in that paragraph is satisfied in part only within the period of three months therein referred to, the amount to be awarded—

   (i) if the unsatisfied part of the said judgment is less than the untraced person's contribution to a full award, shall be an amount equal to that unsatisfied part, or

   (ii) if the unsatisfied part of the said judgment is equal to or greater than the amount of the untraced person's contribution to a full award, shall be an amount equal to the untraced person's said contribution;

(c) if the condition specified in paragraph (3) (b) of this Clause is satisfied, the amount to be awarded shall be an amount equal to the untraced person's contribution to a full award.

(5) The following provisions of this paragraph shall have effect in any case in which an appeal from or any proceeding to set aside any such judgment as is specified in paragraph (3) (a) of this Clause (hereinafter in this Clause referred to as 'the original judgment') is commenced within a period of three months beginning on the date on which the applicant became entitled to enforce the original judgment:

(a) until the said appeal or proceeding is disposed of the foregoing provisions of this Clause shall have effect as if for the period of three months referred to in the said paragraph (3) (a) there were substituted a period expiring on the date when the said appeal or proceeding is disposed of;

(b) if as a result of the said appeal or proceeding the applicant ceases to be entitled to receive any payment in respect of the relevant death or injury from any person or persons against whom he has obtained any such judgment as is specified in the said paragraph (3) (a), the foregoing provisions of this Clause shall have effect as if he had neither obtained nor been required by MIB to obtain a judgment against any person or persons;

(c) if as a result of the said appeal or proceeding, the applicant becomes entitled to recover an amount which differs from that which he was entitled to recover under the original judgment, the foregoing provisions of this Clause shall have effect as if for the reference in the said paragraph (3) (a) to the original judgment there were substituted a reference to the judgment under which the applicant became entitled to the said different amount;

(d) if as a result of the said appeal or proceeding the applicant remains entitled to enforce the original judgment the foregoing provisions of this Clause shall have effect as if for the period of three months referred to in the said paragraph (3) (a) there were substituted a period of three months beginning on the date on which the appeal or other proceeding was disposed of.

The foregoing provisions of this paragraph shall apply also in any case where any judgment given upon any such appeal or proceeding is itself the subject of a further appeal or similar proceeding and shall apply in such a case in relation to that further appeal or proceeding in the same manner as they apply in relation to the first mentioned appeal or proceeding.

(6) In this Clause:

(a) 'full award' means the amount which would have fallen to be awarded to the applicant under Clause 3 hereof in respect of the relevant death or injury if the untraced person had been wholly responsible for that death or injury; and

(b) 'untraced person's contribution' means that proportion of a full award which on the balance of probabilities would have been apportioned by a court as the share to be borne by the untraced person in the responsibility for the event giving rise to the relevant death or injury if proceedings to recover damages in respect of that death or injury had been brought by the applicant against the untraced person and all other persons having a share in that responsibility.

(7) MIB shall not be under any liability in respect of the relevant death or injury if the applicant is entitled to receive compensation from MIB in respect of that death or injury under the Agreement providing for the compensation of victims of uninsured drivers entered into between the Secretary of State and MIB on 22 November 1972.

6. (1) The following shall be conditions precedent to any liability falling upon MIB upon an application made to them under this Agreement in respect of any death or injury, that is to say:

(a) the applicant shall give all such assistance as may reasonably be required by or on behalf of MIB to enable any investigation to be carried out under this Agreement, including, in particular, the furnishing of statements and information either in writing, or, if so required, orally at an interview or interviews between the applicant and any person acting on behalf of MIB;

(b) if so required by MIB at any time before MIB have communicated their decision upon the application to the applicant, the applicant shall, subject to the following provisions of this Clause, take all such steps as in the circumstances it is reasonable to require the applicant to take to obtain judgment against any person or persons in respect of their liability to the applicant in respect of the death or injury as having caused or contributed to that death or injury or as being the master or principal of any person who has caused or contributed to that injury; and

(c) if so required by MIB the applicant shall assign to MIB or to their nominee any judgment obtained by him (whether or not obtained in pursuance of a requirement under subparagraph (b) of this paragraph) in respect of the death or injury to which his application to MIB relates upon such terms as will secure that MIB or their nominee shall be accountable to the applicant for any amount by which the aggregate of all sums recovered by MIB or their nominee under the said judgment (after deducting all reasonable expenses incurred in effecting such recovery) exceeds the amount payable by MIB to the applicant under this Agreement in respect of that death or injury.

(2) If MIB require the applicant to bring proceedings against any specified person or persons:

  (a) MIB shall indemnify the applicant against all costs reasonably incurred by the applicant in complying with that requirement unless the result of those proceedings materially contributes to establish that the untraced person did not cause or contribute to the relevant death or injury; and

  (b) the applicant shall, if so required by MIB and at their expense, furnish MIB with a transcript of any official shorthand note taken in those proceedings of any evidence given or judgment delivered therein.

(3) In the event of a dispute arising between the applicant and MIB as to the reasonableness of any requirement by MIB under paragraph (1) (b) of this Clause, or as to whether any such costs as are referred to in paragraph (2) (a) of this Clause were reasonably incurred, that dispute shall be referred to the Secretary of State whose decision thereon shall be final:

Provided that any dispute arising between the applicant and MIB as to whether MIB are required to indemnify the applicant under paragraph (2) (a) of this Clause shall, in so far as it depends on the question whether the result of any proceedings which MIB have required the applicant to bring against any specified person or persons have or have not materially contributed to establish that the untraced person did not cause or contribute to the relevant death or injury, be referred to the arbitrator in accordance with the following provisions of this Agreement, whose decision on that question shall be final.

7. MIB shall cause any application made to them for a payment under this Agreement to be investigated and, unless MIB decide that the application should be rejected because a preliminary investigation has disclosed that the case is not one to which this Agreement applies, they shall cause a report to be made on the application and on the basis of that report MIB shall decide whether to make an award and, if so, the amount of the award which shall be calculated in accordance with the foregoing provisions of this Agreement.

8. MIB may before coming to a decision on any application made to them under this Agreement request the applicant to furnish them with a statutory declaration to be made by the applicant, setting out to the best of his knowledge, information and belief the facts and circumstances upon which his claim to an award under this Agreement is based, or such of those facts and circumstances as may be specified by MIB.

9. (1) MIB shall notify their decision to the applicant and when so doing shall—

  (a) if the application is rejected because a preliminary investigation has disclosed that it is not one made in a case to which this Agreement applies, give their reasons for the rejection; or

  (b) if the application has been fully investigated furnish him with a statement setting out—

      (i) the circumstances in which the death or injury occurred and the evidence bearing thereon,

      (ii) the circumstances relevant to the assessment of the amount to be awarded to the applicant under this Agreement and the evidence bearing thereon, and

(iii) if they refuse to make an award, their reasons for that refusal; and

(c) in a case to which Clause 5 of this Agreement applies specify the way in which the amount of that award has been computed and its relation to those provisions of Clause 5 which are relevant to its computation.

(2) Where MIB have decided that they will not indemnify the applicant against the costs of any proceedings which they have under Clause 6 (1) (b) hereof required the applicant to bring against any specified person or persons on the ground that those proceedings have materially contributed to establish that the untraced person did not cause or contribute to the relevant death or injury, they shall give notice to the applicant of that decision and when doing so they shall give their reasons for it and furnish the applicant with a copy of any such transcript of any evidence given or judgment delivered in those proceedings as is mentioned in Clause 6 (2) (b) hereof which they regard as relevant to that decision.

10. Subject to the provisions of this Agreement, MIB shall:

(a) on being notified by the applicant that MIB's award is accepted; or

(b) if at the expiration of the period during which the applicant may give notice of an appeal under Clause 11 hereof there has not been given to MIB either any such notification as aforesaid of the acceptance of MIB's award or a notice of an appeal under the said Clause 11,

pay the applicant the amount of that award, and such payment shall discharge MIB from all liability under this Agreement in respect of the death or injury in respect of which that award has been made.

11. The applicant shall have a right of appeal to an arbitrator against any decision notified to him under Clause 9 hereof on any of the following grounds, that is to say,—

(a) that the case is one to which this Agreement applies and that his application should be fully investigated by MIB with a view to their deciding whether to make an award to the applicant and, if so, the amount of that award; or

(b) where the application has been fully investigated—

(i) that MIB were wrong in refusing to make an award, or

(ii) that the amount they have awarded to the applicant is insufficient; or

(c) in a case where a decision not to indemnify the applicant against the costs of any proceedings has been notified under Clause 9 (2) hereof, that that decision was wrong,

if, within six weeks from the date when notice of the decision against which he wishes to appeal was given to him, the applicant, not having previously notified MIB that their decision is accepted, gives notice to MIB that he wishes to appeal against their decision.

12. A notice of appeal under Clause 11 hereof shall state the grounds of the appeal and shall be accompanied by an undertaking to be given by the applicant or by the person acting on his behalf as provided in Clause 2 hereof, that—

(a) the applicant will accept the decision of the arbitrator; and

(b) the arbitrator's fee shall be paid to MIB by the applicant or by the person giving the said undertaking in any case where MIB are entitled to reimbursement of that fee under the provisions of Clause 22 hereof.

13. The applicant may, when giving notice of his appeal or at any time before doing so, make comments to MIB on their decision and may supply them with such particulars as the applicant may think fit of any other evidence not contained in the written statement supplied to the applicant by MIB which he considers is relevant to the application and MIB may, before submitting the applicant's appeal to the arbitrator, cause an investigation to be made into this further evidence and shall report to the applicant the result of that investigation and of any change in their decision which may result from it. The applicant may, within six weeks from the date on which this report was sent to him, unless he withdraws his appeal, make such comments thereon as he may desire to have submitted to the arbitrator.

14. (1) In a case where MIB receive from the applicant a notice of appeal in which the only ground of appeal which is stated is that the amount awarded to the applicant is insufficient MIB may before submitting that appeal to the arbitrator give notice to the applicant that if the appeal proceeds they will request the arbitrator to decide whether the case is one in which MIB should make an award at all and if they do so they shall at the same time furnish the applicant with a statement setting out such comments as they may consider relevant to the decision which the arbitrator should come to on that question.

(2) Where MIB give a notice under paragraph (1) of this Clause, the applicant may within six weeks from the date on which that notice is given make such comments to MIB and supply them with such particulars of other evidence not contained in any written statement furnished to him by MIB as he may consider relevant to the question which the arbitrator is by that notice requested to decide, and Clause 13 hereof shall apply in relation to any comments made or particulars supplied by the applicant under this paragraph as it applies in relation to any comments made or particulars supplied under the said Clause 13.

15. MIB shall, where they receive notice of an appeal from the applicant under the foregoing provisions of this Agreement, unless the appeal is previously withdrawn, submit that appeal (but in a case where they cause such an investigation to be made as is mentioned in Clause 13 hereof, not until the expiration of six weeks from the date on which they sent the applicant a report as to the result of that investigation and, in a case where they gave such a notice to the applicant as is mentioned in Clause 14 (1) hereof, not until the expiration of six weeks from the date on which they gave that notice and, if they have caused an investigation to be made into any evidence supplied under Clause 14 (2) hereof, not until the expiration of six weeks from the date on which they sent the applicant a report as to the result of that investigation) to an arbitrator for a decision, sending to the arbitrator for that purpose the application made by the applicant, a copy of their decision thereon as notified to the applicant and of all statements, declarations, notices, undertakings, comments, transcripts, particulars or reports furnished, given or sent under this Agreement either by the applicant or any person acting for him to MIB or by MIB to the applicant or a person so acting.

16. On any such appeal,

(a) if the appeal is against a decision by MIB rejecting an application because a preliminary investigation has disclosed that the case is not one to which this Agreement applies, the arbitrator shall decide whether the case is or is not one to which this Agreement applies and, if he decides that it is such a case, shall remit the application to MIB for full investigation and for a decision by MIB in accordance with the foregoing provisions of this Agreement;

(b) if the appeal is against a decision by MIB given after an application has been fully investigated by MIB (whether before the appeal or in consequence of its being remitted for such investigation under paragraph (a) of this Clause), the arbitrator shall decide, as may be appropriate, having regards to the grounds stated in the notice of appeal and to any notice given by MIB to the applicant under Clause 14 hereof, whether MIB should make and award under this Agreement to the applicant and, if so, the amount which MIB should award to the applicant under the foregoing provisions of this Agreement;

(c) if the appeal relates to a dispute which has arisen between the applicant and MIB which is required by the proviso to Clause 6 (3) hereof to be referred to the arbitrator, the arbitrator shall also give his decision on that dispute.

17. The arbitrator shall decide the appeal on the documents submitted to him as set out in Clause 15 hereof and no further evidence shall be produced to him: Provided that:

(a) the arbitrator shall be entitled to ask MIB to make any further investigation which he considers desirable and to submit a written report of their findings to him for his consideration; and

(b) MIB shall send a copy of any such report to the applicant who shall be entitled to submit written comments on it to MIB within four weeks of the date on which that copy is sent to him; and

(c) MIB shall transmit those comments to the arbitrator for his consideration.

18. The arbitrator by whom any such appeal as aforesaid shall be decided shall be an arbitrator to be selected by the Secretary of State from two panels of Queen's Counsel appointed respectively by the Lord Chancellor and the Lord Advocate for the purpose of determining appeals under this Agreement, the arbitrator to be selected from the panel appointed by the Lord Chancellor in cases where the event giving rise to the death or injury occurred in England or Wales and from the panel appointed by the Lord Advocate where that event occurred in Scotland.

19. The arbitrator shall notify his decision on any appeal under this Agreement to MIB and MIB shall forthwith send a copy of the arbitrator's decision to the applicant.

20. Subject to the provisions of this Agreement, MIB shall pay the applicant any amount which the arbitrator has decided shall be awarded to the applicant, and such payment shall discharge MIB from all liability under this Agreement in respect of the death or injury in respect of which that decision has been given.

21. Each party to the appeal will bear his own costs.

22. MIB shall pay the arbitrator a fee approved by the Lord Chancellor or the Lord Advocate, as the case may be, after consultation with MIB:

Provided that the arbitrator may in his discretion, in any case where it appears to him that there were no reasonable grounds for the appeal, decide that his fee ought to be paid by the applicant and, where the arbitrator so decides, the person giving the undertaking required by Clause 12 hereof shall be liable to reimburse MIB the amount of the fee paid by them to the arbitrator except in so far as that amount is deducted by MIB from any amount which they are liable to pay to the applicant in consequence of the decision of the arbitrator.

23. If in any case it appears to MIB that by reason of the applicant being under the age of majority or of any other circumstances affecting his capacity to manage his affairs it would be in the interest of the applicant that all or some part of the amount which would otherwise be payable to him under an award made under this Agreement should be administered for him by the Family Welfare Association or by some other body or person under a trust MIB may establish for that purpose a trust of the whole or part of the said amount to take effect for such period and subject to such provisions as may appear to MIB appropriate in the circumstances of the case.

24. This Agreement may be determined at any time by the Secretary of State or by MIB by either of them giving to the other not less than twelve months' previous notice in writing.

Provided that this Agreement shall continue to have effect in respect of any case where the event giving rise to the death or injury occurred before the date on which this Agreement terminates in accordance with any notice so given.

25. This Agreement shall come into operation on 1 December 1972 in relation to accidents occurring on or after that date, and the Agreement made on 21 April 1969 between the Secretary of State and MIB shall cease and determine except in relation to applications arising out of accidents which occurred on or after 1 May 1969 and before the said 1 December 1972.

IN WITNESS whereof the Secretary of State has caused his Corporate Seal to be hereto affixed and the Motor Insurers' Bureau have caused their Common Seal to be hereto affixed the day and year first above written.

(L S)

THE CORPORATE SEAL of the Secretary of State was hereunto affixed in the presence of
P A Waller

An Assistant Secretary in the Department of the Environment, duly authorised in that behalf.

(L S)

The COMMON SEAL of the Motor Insurers' Bureau was hereunto affixed in the presence of

R M Livett   Members of the
O Stephen Masefield   Council

P F Morgan   Secretary

NOTES

The following Notes are for the guidance of those who may wish to make application to the Motor Insurers' Bureau for payment under the Agreement, and for the guidance of their legal advisers, but they must not be taken as rendering unnecessary a careful study of the Agreement itself. Communications connected with the Agreement should be addressed to the Motor Insurers' Bureau, whose address is Aldermary House, Queen Street, London, EC4N 1TR.

1. This Agreement replaces a previous one dated 21 April 1969 which put on a formal basis the arrangements which have existed since 1946 under which the Bureau have made ex gratia payments in respect of death or personal injuries resulting from the use on a road of a motor vehicle the owner or driver of which cannot be traced. Provision is made for an appeal against the Bureau's decision in such cases.

2. The Agreement dated 21 April 1969 applies to a death or bodily injury arising out of an accident occurring on a road in Great Britain on or after 1 May 1969, and before 1 December 1972. This Agreement applies in relation to accidents occurring on or after 1 December 1972.

3. Subject to the terms of the Agreement, the Bureau will accept applications for a payment in respect of the death of, or bodily injury to, any person resulting from the use of a motor vehicle on a road in Great Britain in any case in which:

(a) the applicant for the payment cannot trace any person responsible for the death or injury (or, in certain circumstances, a person partly responsible) (Clause 1 (1) (b)); and

(b) the death or injury was caused in such circumstances that the untraced person would be liable to pay damages to the applicant in respect of the death or injury (Clause 1(1)(c)); and

(c) the untraced person's liability to the applicant is one which at the time the accident occurred, was required to be covered by insurance or security (Clause 1 (1) (d)).

The Bureau will not, however, deal with deliberate 'running down' cases (Clause 1 (1) (e)) nor with certain other cases relating to Crown vehicles and certain categories of 'voluntary' passenger (Clause 1 (2)-(4)).

4. Applications for a payment under the Agreement must be made in writing to the Bureau within 3 years of the date of the accident giving rise to the death or injury (Clause 1 (1) (f)).

5. Under Clause 3, the amount which the Bureau will award will (except for the exclusion of those elements of damages mentioned in Clause 4) be assessed in the same way as a Court would have assessed the amount of damages payable by the untraced person had the applicant been able to bring a successful claim for damages against him.

6. Clause 5 relates to cases where an untraced person and an identified person are each partly responsible for a death or injury, and defines the conditions under which the Bureau will in such cases make a contribution in respect of the responsibility of the untraced person.

7. Under Clause 6 (1) (b), the Bureau may require the applicant to bring proceedings against any identified person who may be responsible for the death

or injury, subject to indemnifying the applicant as to his costs as provided in Clause 6 (2) and (3).

8. On receipt of an application, the Bureau will, if satisfied that the application comes within the terms of the Agreement, investigate the circumstances and, when this has been done, decide whether to make a payment and, if so, how much (Clause 7).

9. The Bureau may request the applicant to make a statutory declaration setting out all, or some, of the facts on which his application is based (Clause 8).

10. The Bureau will notify the applicant of their decision, setting out the circumstances of the case and the evidence on which they base their decision and, if they refuse to make a payment, the reasons for that refusal (Clause 9).

11. If the applicant does not exercise his right to appeal against the Bureau's decision, the Bureau's decision will be final and the applicant will be entitled to be paid the amount awarded by the Bureau (Clause 10).

12. If the applicant wishes to appeal against the decision on the grounds specified in Clause 11, he must notify the Bureau within six weeks of being notified of the decision, and give the undertakings set out in Clause 12.

13. The Bureau may, as a result of comments made by the applicant on their decision, investigate the application further, and if so they will communicate with the applicant again. In such a case, the applicant will have six weeks from the date of that further communication in which to decide whether or not to go on with his appeal (Clause 13).

14. Where the applicant appeals only on the grounds that the amount awarded to him is too low, the Bureau may give him notice that if the matter proceeds to appeal, they will ask the arbitrator to decide also the issue of the Bureau's liability to make any payment. The applicant will have six weeks from the date of any such notice in which to comment to the Bureau on this intention (Clause 14).

15. Appeals will be decided by an arbitrator who will be a Queen's Counsel selected by the Secretary of State for the Environment from one of two panels to be appointed by the Lord Chancellor and the Lord Advocate respectively (Clause 18).

16. All appeals will be decided by the arbitrator on the basis of the relevant documents (as set out in Clause 15) which will be sent to him by the Bureau. If the arbitrator asks the Bureau to make a further investigation, the applicant will have an opportunity to comment on the result of that investigation (Clause 17).

17. The arbitrator may, at his discretion, award the cost of his fee against the applicant if he considers the appeal unreasonable; otherwise, each party to the appeal will bear their own costs, the Bureau paying the arbitrator's fee (Clauses 21 and 22).

18. In certain circumstances, the Bureau may establish a trust for the benefit of an applicant of the whole or part of any award (Clause 23).

INDEX

PART I—FIRE INSURANCE

PART II—MOTOR INSURANCE